MAN HAS CAUSED THE MOST SIGNIFICANT CATASTROPHE IN HUMAN HISTORY, RESULTING NOT IN A GRADUAL DECLINE OF SURVIVING CIVILIZATIONS, BUT A SUDDEN REGRESSION.

TECHNOLOGY HAS BEEN TRADED FOR ANTIQUITY, SCIENCE FOR SUPERSTITION, AND CIVILITY FOR BARBARITY.

COMBAT IS THE KEY TO SURVIVAL IN THIS NEW WORLD – THE MARTIAL WORLD. HERE, THE CORPSES PILE HIGH AS KUNG FU IS FOUND IN ITS MOST LETHAL FORM...

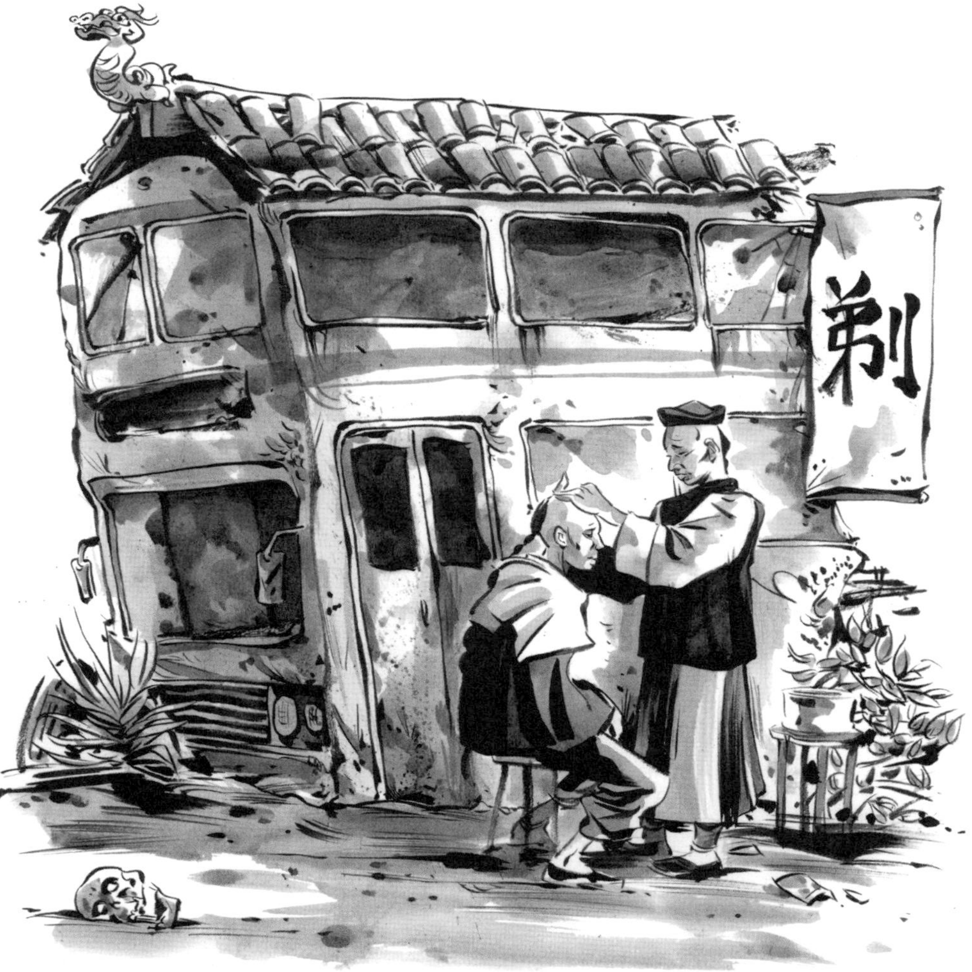
剃

Infinite Kung Fu © 2011 Kagan M<sup>c</sup>Leod
Published by Top Shelf Productions,
PO Box 1282, Marietta GA 30061-1282, USA

Story and art by Kagan M<sup>c</sup>Leod
Publishers: Brett Warnock and Chris Staros

Editing: Leigh Walton, Rob Venditti
Layout: Geneviéve Biloski, Kate Noyes,
Chris Ross, Kagan M<sup>c</sup>Leod
Translation: Harvey Chan, King Wei Chu,
Cong Lu and Mia Sin

First printing, 2011
Printed in Singapore

infinitekungfu.com
topshelfcomix.com
kaganmcleod.com

ISBN: 978-1-891830-83-9

KAGAN McLEOD's

# INFINITE KUNG FU

## Contents

# INTRODUCTION

## BY GORDON LIU

The heavy interest in kung fu was triggered on an international scale through film over 40 years ago. New action heroes such as Bruce Lee, Jet Li, Jackie Chan, my Shaw Brothers co-stars and others were born. Their cinematic performances conveyed the essence of kung fu to the entire world. This ignited people's interest in the study of martial arts. The only constant in kung fu cinema is its ability to keep up with the ever evolving audience's sophisticated tastes. Today CGI and 3D effects play a new role in evolving Chinese kung fu cinema, while preserving its Chinese character. Every culture maintains its distinct character through tradition. However, combining traditional and contemporary aspects will simply enhance a culture. The best book, comic, film or performance will always function most effectively when it has a seamless mixture of these pivotal ingredients.

I wish to express my sincere thanks for the continued support of my films over the years and, hopefully, for many more years to come. Congratulations to Kagan McLeod, a brilliant writer and artist, for successfully creating his unique and much welcome addition to the extended kung fu family. Kung fu cinema doesn't belong to the Chinese, but to the world. Kung fu 'til Infinity!

May Buddha bless you all!

Gordon Liu has appeared in more than eighty films since the early 1970s. His breakthrough role in *The 36th Chamber of Shaolin* cemented his place as a star in the martial arts genre. Other films he has starred in (and which have provided inspiration for this work) include *Shaolin Challenges Ninja, Shaolin and Wu Tang, Clan of the White Lotus* and *Eight Diagram Pole Fighter.*
He is also known for his roles as Johnny Mo and Pai Mei, the white-browed priest in Quentin Tarantino's *Kill Bill* series.

## BY COLIN GEDDES

One of the best jobs I have ever had was being the manager at Suspect Video & Culture, a hole-in-the-wall video store located in a corner of the Toronto city block that houses the mammoth discount store and landmark, Honest Ed's. Suspect was a repository of everything related to deviant film culture and had a staff that, although surly, were deep wells of knowledge on all areas of film culture, high and low, just waiting to be tapped.

The store was jammed full of comics, magazines, toys and dusty shelves of VHS tapes of rare films ranging from horror, sci-fi, biker, anime, conspiracy docs, blaxploitation and, of course, kung fu.

One afternoon I got a call from a woman who had very prim and proper phone manners, who proceeded to ask me if we did special orders. Of course we did, I told her, expecting to get a request for some BBC TV series. But she proceeded to blow my mind with a request for some uber-rare kung fu titles like *Mystery of Chess Boxing, Eight Diagram Pole Fighter*, and others. Clearly these titles were not for her, but for her son's birthday, and I was glad to source those VHS tapes to make the day of a kung fu fan out in the burbs.

A few months later I got to meet the young grasshopper, Kagan McLeod, who turned out to be a lanky and enthusiastic, but shy young adult when he came by the store for a visit. Suspect was often like a cool speakeasy where people hung out and gabbed about their favourite films and swapped trivia. We'd trade facts about our fave martial arts actors and their bouts, like Sammo Hung monkey boxing in *Knockabout* or Lar Kar Yan's smackdowns in *Legend of a Fighter*. Then came the loaded question from Kagan: "I saw that you guys sell zines and comics on consignment. Can I bring in my comic for you to sell?"

Oh no! The worst! That was almost as bad as being pressured to go see a new acquaintance's band perform and then having to say complimentary things about the show. I was anticipating a Xeroxed pamphlet with anime-inspired, big-eyed characters kicking and punching through a hackneyed plot. This was just after *The Matrix*, when so much pop culture was inspired by Hong Kong cinema, but ultimately missing the point about the originality that made that stuff so great. I feared that this earnestly created assortment of stapled papers would gather dust and join the other homemade comics and zines that had failed to find an audience.

When Kagan brought in the goods, I was pummelled by the masterful strokes and penmanship in that first issue of *Infinite Kung Fu*. Not only did it have a story firmly rooted in the elements of kung fu cinema, but it was also peppered with unique stylings and pop-cult crossovers (a P-Funk/Issac Hayes inspired grandmaster?!). The only drawback (no pun intended) to the first issue, was an over reliance on using the computer to clean up and create some of the line-work.

However, in subsequent issues, Kagan abandoned the pixels for a more natural and fluid look, integrating the bold line-work with free and loose sketches that conveyed the martial arts abilities of his story's heroes and villains.

Now that life finds me working for international film festivals and traveling to the east on a regular basis, I have been able to spread the word of Kagan's art and hand deliver issues of *Infinite Kung Fu* to many players in the world of cinema that inspired him, including *Ong Bak* director Prachya Pinkaew, the master kung fu actor and director Sammo Hung and director Wilson Yip (*Ip Man 1* and *2*).

Over the years, Kagan's art and skill has moved beyond the pages of the comic book, and he has become a respected editorial and magazine illustrator. I was proud to open the pages of *Entertainment Weekly* on an airplane one day to find caricatures by Kagan spread throughout the issue.

With this wider reach for his work, Kagan remains true to his roots and dedication to kung fu cinema and b-film culture, and this collection of *Infinite Kung Fu* is a testament to that love.

Now do some finger stretches and prepare yourself for masterful Shaolin scratchings and brushstrokes, all guided by Buddha in this graphic manual of phantasmagorical pugilistic skills!

Colin Geddes is an international programmer for the Toronto International Film Festival® since 1997 and has been responsible for introducing audiences to directors including Takashi Miike (*Ichi The Killer*), Eli Roth (*Cabin Fever*), Alex Aja (*Haute Tension*), Prachya Pinkaew (*Ong Bak*) and Wilson Yip *(SPL a.k.a. Killzone*). Geddes also curated the popular "Kung Fu Fridays" screening series which ran for over a decade, showcasing martial arts and cult cinema from Asia to Toronto audiences. Over the past fifteen years, Geddes has rescued abandoned 35mm prints from Toronto's closed Chinatown cinemas and garbage heaps, and in March 2010, he donated 200 feature films originating from Hong Kong and Taiwan to the University of Toronto. In addition, Geddes has one of North America's largest collections of Hong Kong cinema promotional materials, posters, and lobby cards.

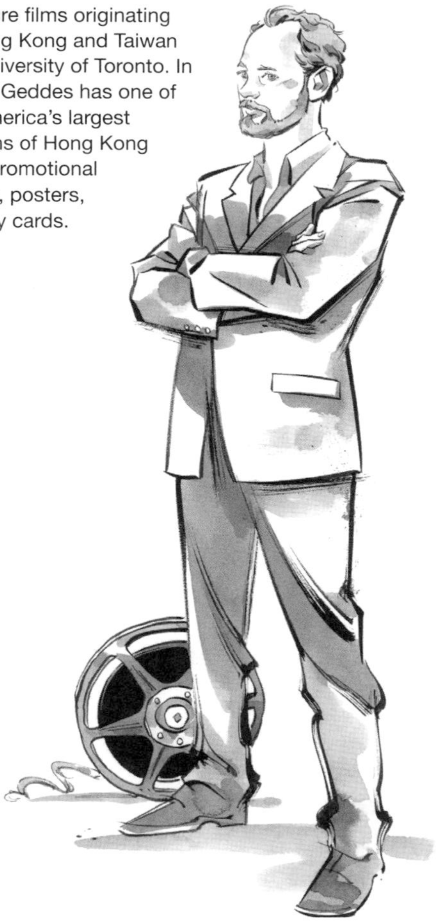

# THE EIGHT IMMORTALS

*A group of legendary beings in Chinese mythology, the Eight Immortals are said to have attained immortality through the study of nature's secrets. As a reference, they are described as follows:*

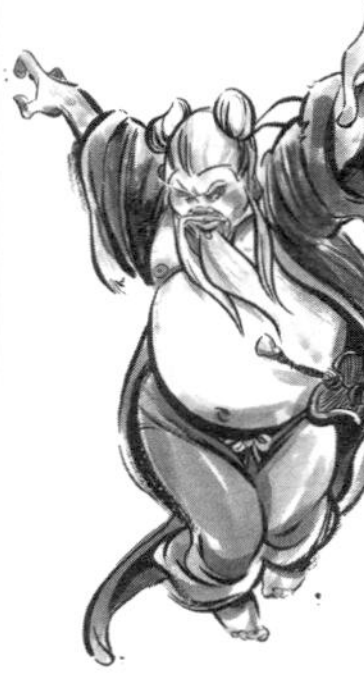

### CHUNG LI CH'UAN
STUDENT:
YANG LEI KUNG

The fat and bare-bellied chief of the Eight Immortals and a master of transmutation. While mixing a potion, he is said to have mistakenly discovered the elixir of life, granting him immortality. His fan, which is his emblem, can revive the souls of the dead.

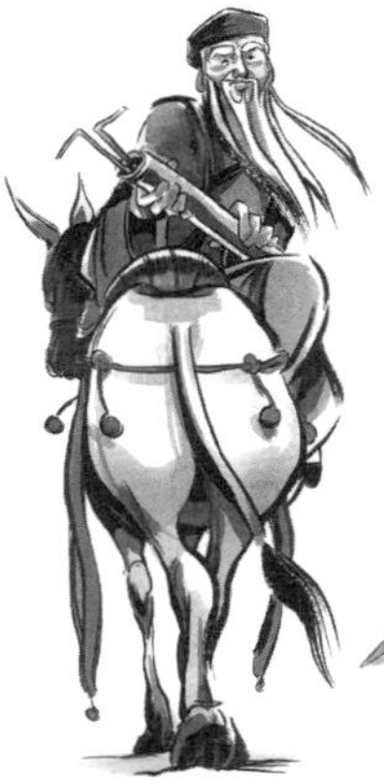

### CHANG KUO LAO
STUDENT:
MOOG JOOGULAR

A recluse with extraordinary supernatural powers, Chang Kuo Lao was over 200 years old when he became immortal. He is frequently accompanied by a white mule, which he rides backwards, that can be folded up and put away in his wallet. His emblem is the Yu Ku, a bamboo drum with two rods to beat it.

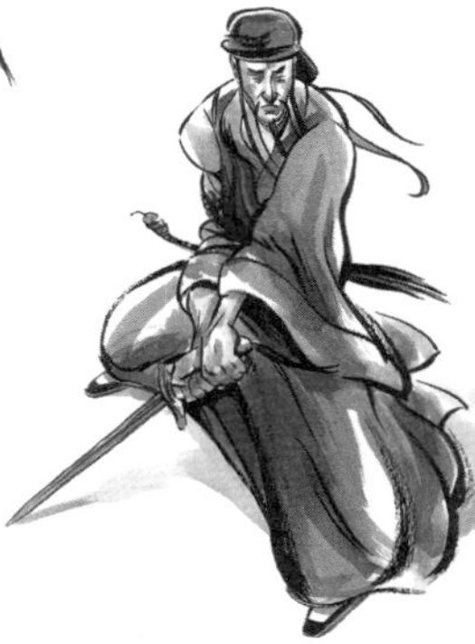

### LU TUNG PIN
STUDENT:
LI ZHAO

A scholar and recluse who learned the secrets of nature from Chung Li Ch'uan. He carries a fly-brush, symbolizing his power of flight, and a magic sword, his emblem. Traveling the martial world with these items, he has slain demons and destroyed evil for centuries.

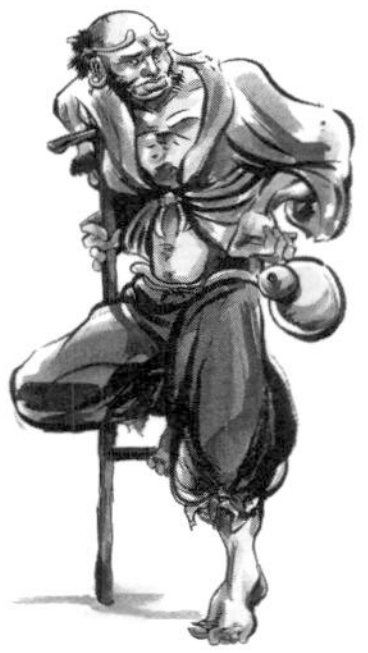

### IRON CRUTCH LI
STUDENT:
BAO CHONG ZI

After returning from the celestial regions one day to find his human body burned by his disciple, Li hastily sought the corpse of somebody recently dead to inhabit. After entering the body of a lame beggar in a nearby wood, he became known as Iron Crutch Li. His emblem is the pilgrim's gourd.

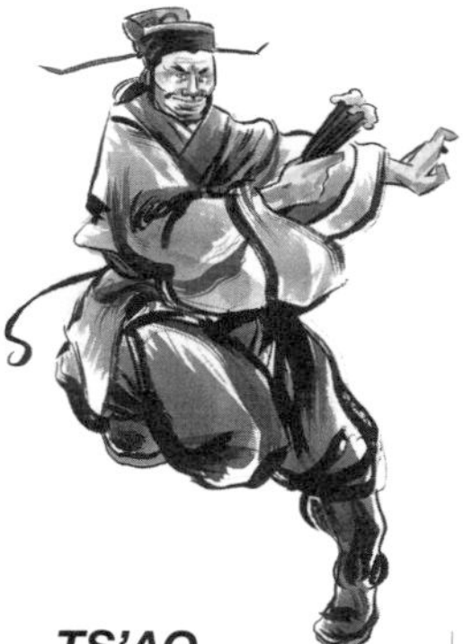

***TS'AO KUO CHIU***

STUDENT:
BUNZO 12

The son of a military commander and brother of a murderer. For fear of being mistaken for his sibling, he left for the mountains and studied the Tao. Upon meeting Chung Li Ch'uan and Lu Tung Pin, he joined them as an immortal. His emblem is a pair of castanets, which authorize his access to the Emperor's palace.

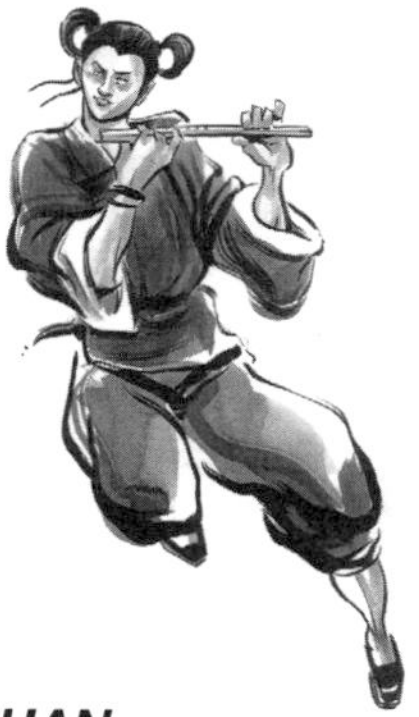

***HAN HSIANG TZU***

STUDENT:
BALD BO

A student of Lu Tung Pin who became Immortal when he fell from a sacred peach tree. His emblem is the flute, which can make flowers bloom and can attract birds and beasts alike with its sounds. He does not know the meaning of money, and upon receiving any, he scatters it about on the ground.

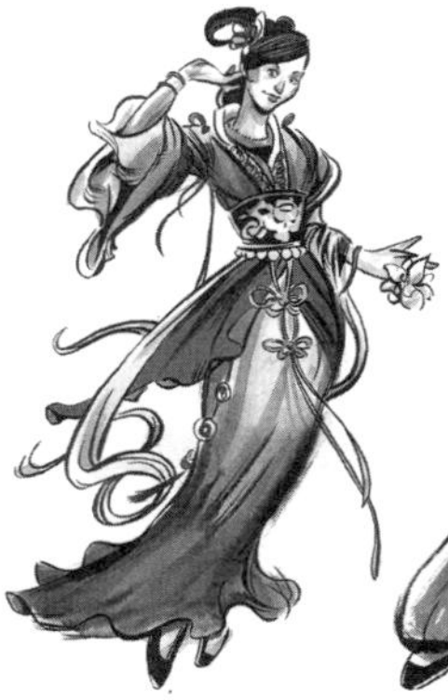

***HO HSIEN KU***

STUDENT:
WINDY

The only female Immortal, she became such by eating a supernatural peach. Her ability to fly over mountains aided her in finding the other Immortals. Once lost in the woods, she was saved from a demon by Lu Tung Pin and his magic sword. Her emblem is the Lotus, which she carries in her hand.

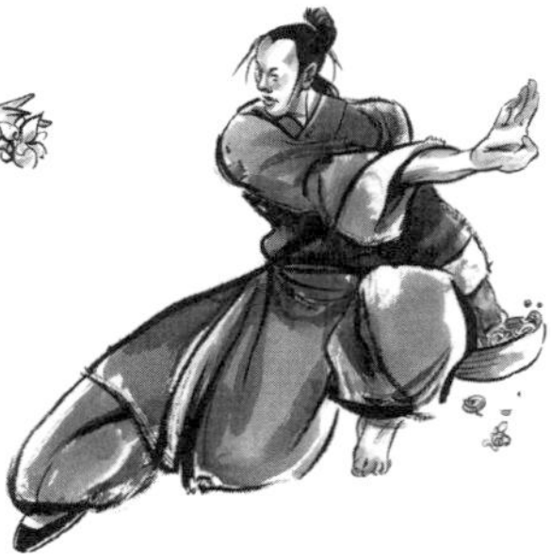

***LAN TS'AI HO***

STUDENT:
GOLDY

Dressed in blue rags and wearing one shoe, Lan Ts'ai Ho wandered the streets singing songs denouncing the brevity of life and its false pleasures. His manners were maniacal and he was particularly effeminate. His emblem is the flower basket.

# INFINITE KUNG FU

功夫無限

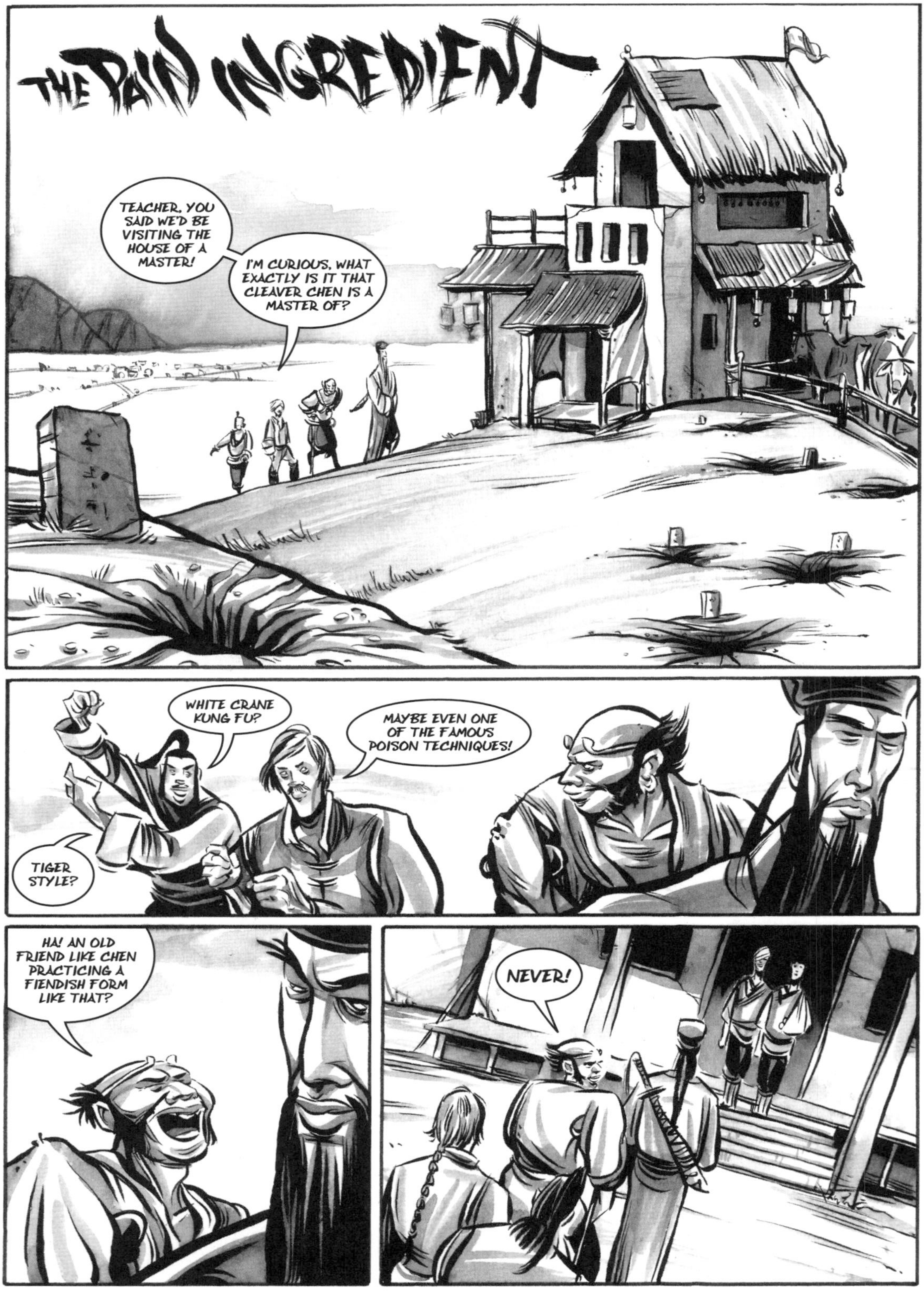
THE PAIN INGREDIENT
TEACHER, YOU SAID WE'D BE VISITING THE HOUSE OF A MASTER!
I'M CURIOUS, WHAT EXACTLY IS IT THAT CLEAVER CHEN IS A MASTER OF?
WHITE CRANE KUNG FU?
TIGER STYLE?
MAYBE EVEN ONE OF THE FAMOUS POISON TECHNIQUES!
HA! AN OLD FRIEND LIKE CHEN PRACTICING A FIENDISH FORM LIKE THAT?
NEVER!

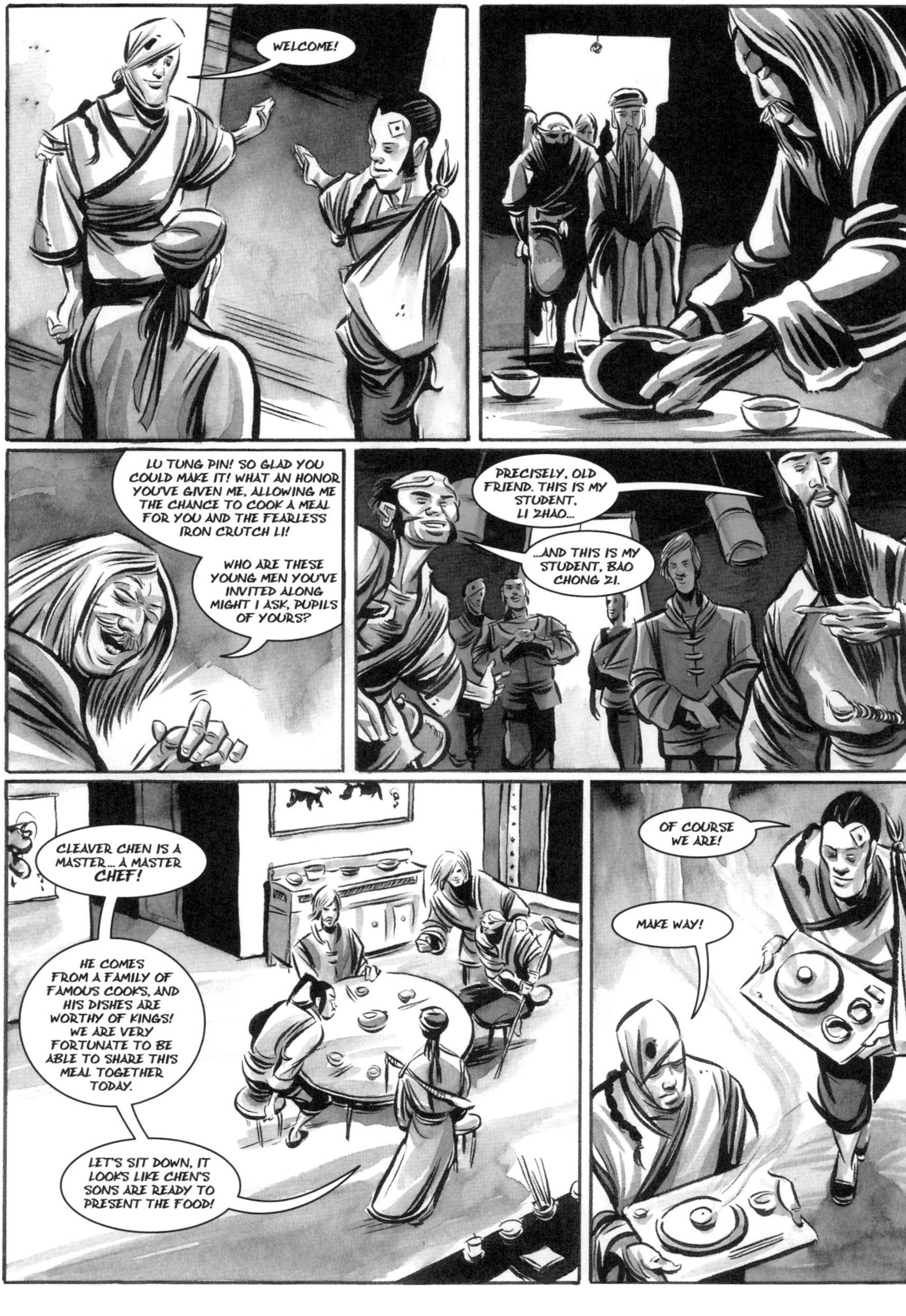
WELCOME!
LU TUNG PIN! SO GLAD YOU COULD MAKE IT! WHAT AN HONOR YOU'VE GIVEN ME, ALLOWING ME THE CHANCE TO COOK A MEAL FOR YOU AND THE FEARLESS IRON CRUTCH LI!
WHO ARE THESE YOUNG MEN YOU'VE INVITED ALONG MIGHT I ASK, PUPILS OF YOURS?
PRECISELY, OLD FRIEND. THIS IS MY STUDENT, LI ZHAO...
...AND THIS IS MY STUDENT, BAO CHONG ZI.
CLEAVER CHEN IS A MASTER... A MASTER CHEF!
HE COMES FROM A FAMILY OF FAMOUS COOKS, AND HIS DISHES ARE WORTHY OF KINGS! WE ARE VERY FORTUNATE TO BE ABLE TO SHARE THIS MEAL TOGETHER TODAY.
LET'S SIT DOWN, IT LOOKS LIKE CHEN'S SONS ARE READY TO PRESENT THE FOOD!
OF COURSE WE ARE!
MAKE WAY!

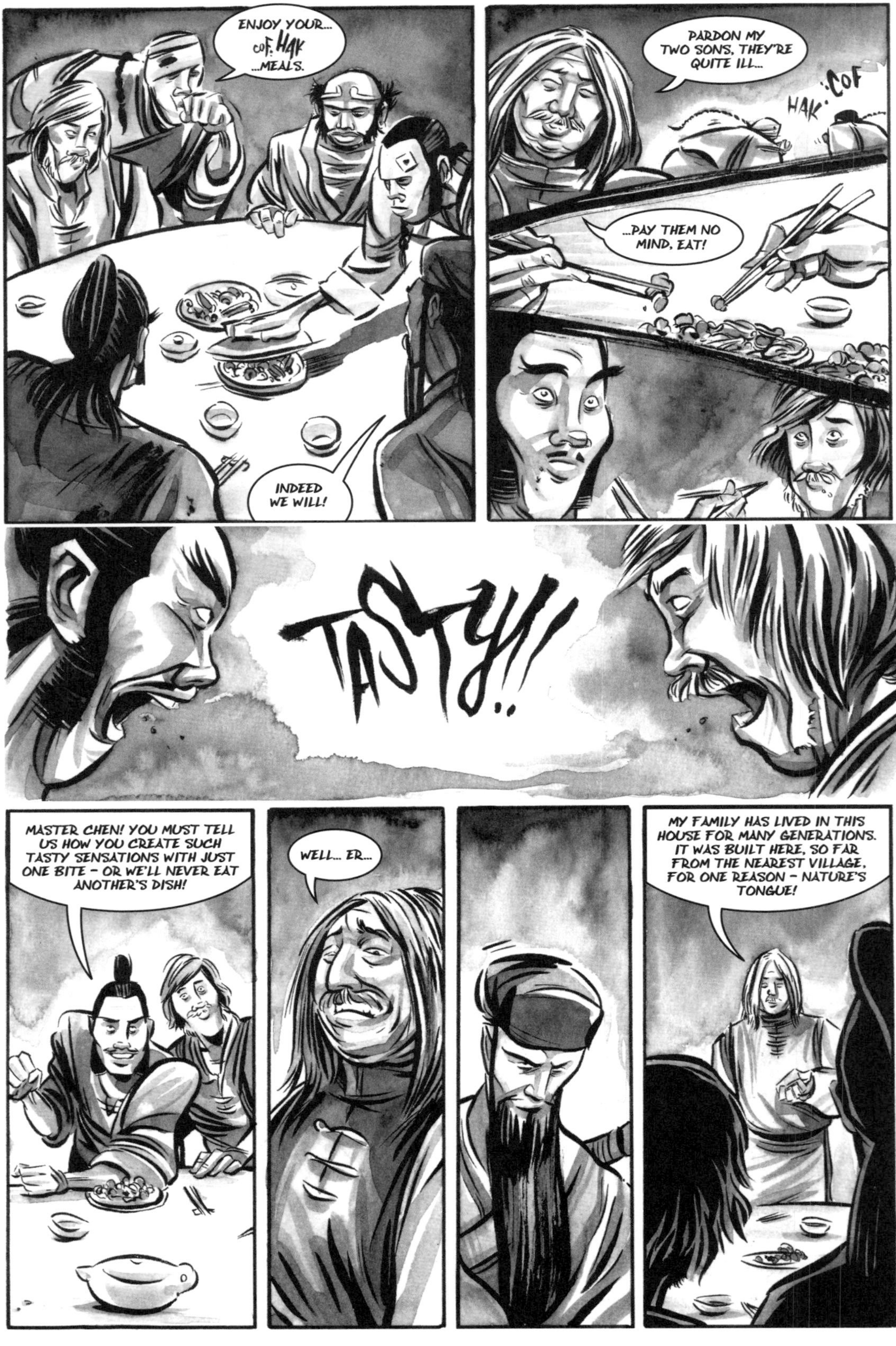

ENJOY YOUR... COF! HAK ...MEALS.
INDEED WE WILL!
PARDON MY TWO SONS, THEY'RE QUITE ILL...
HAK COF
...PAY THEM NO MIND, EAT!
TASTY!!
MASTER CHEN! YOU MUST TELL US HOW YOU CREATE SUCH TASTY SENSATIONS WITH JUST ONE BITE – OR WE'LL NEVER EAT ANOTHER'S DISH!
WELL... ER...
MY FAMILY HAS LIVED IN THIS HOUSE FOR MANY GENERATIONS. IT WAS BUILT HERE, SO FAR FROM THE NEAREST VILLAGE, FOR ONE REASON – NATURE'S TONGUE!

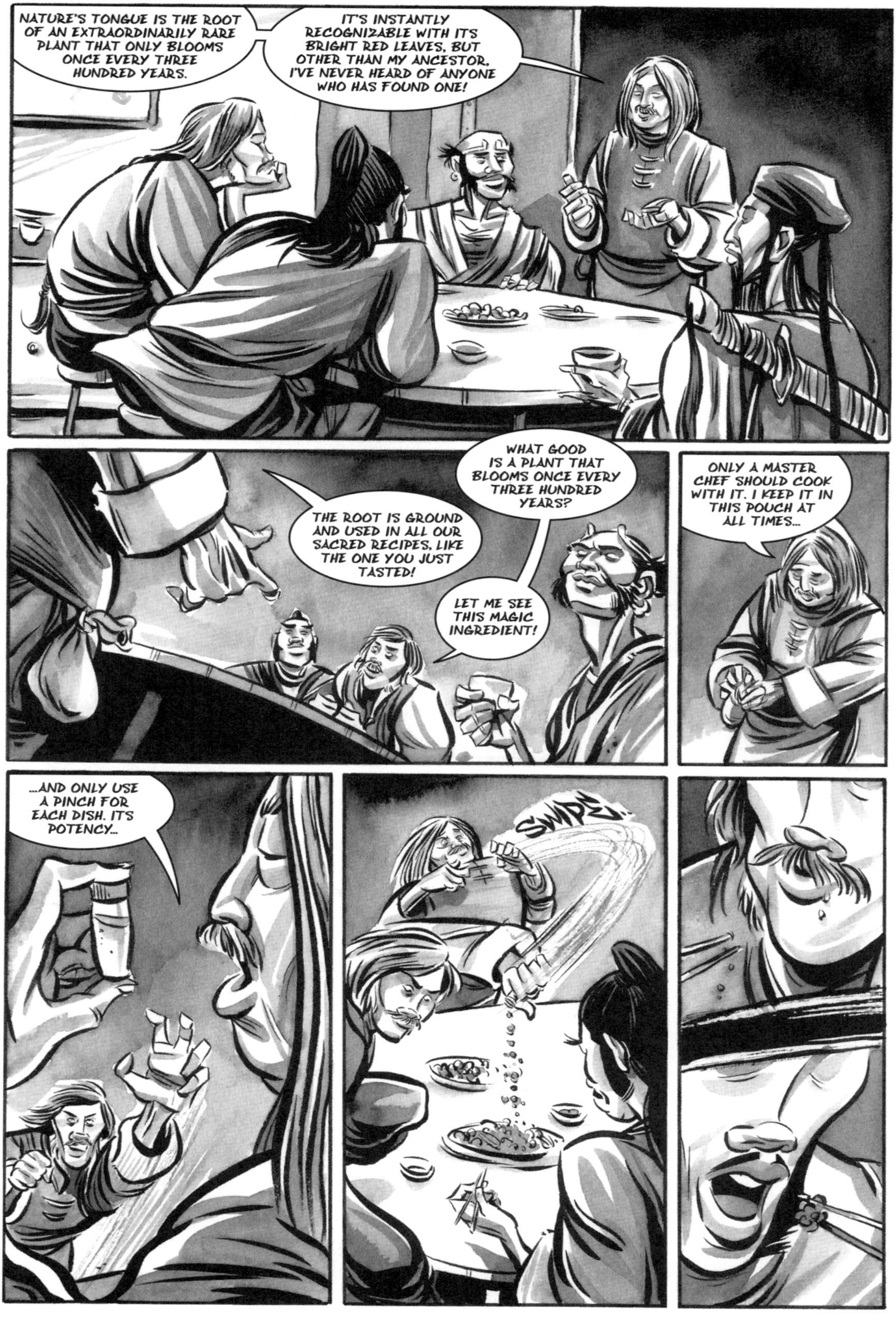
NATURE'S TONGUE IS THE ROOT OF AN EXTRAORDINARILY RARE PLANT THAT ONLY BLOOMS ONCE EVERY THREE HUNDRED YEARS.
IT'S INSTANTLY RECOGNIZABLE WITH ITS BRIGHT RED LEAVES, BUT OTHER THAN MY ANCESTOR, I'VE NEVER HEARD OF ANYONE WHO HAS FOUND ONE!
WHAT GOOD IS A PLANT THAT BLOOMS ONCE EVERY THREE HUNDRED YEARS?
THE ROOT IS GROUND AND USED IN ALL OUR SACRED RECIPES, LIKE THE ONE YOU JUST TASTED!
LET ME SEE THIS MAGIC INGREDIENT!
ONLY A MASTER CHEF SHOULD COOK WITH IT. I KEEP IT IN THIS POUCH AT ALL TIMES...
...AND ONLY USE A PINCH FOR EACH DISH. ITS POTENCY...
SWIPE!

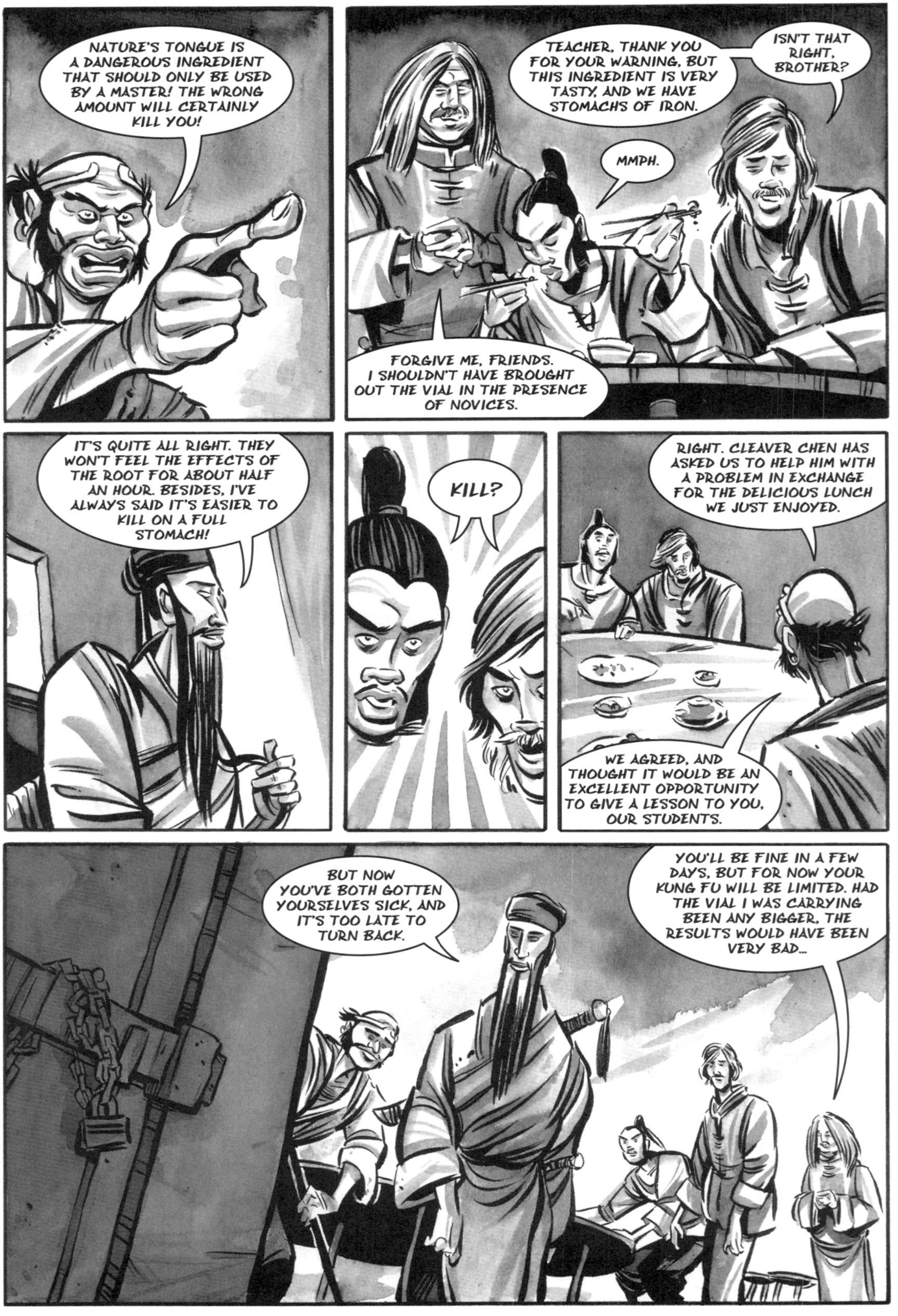
NATURE'S TONGUE IS A DANGEROUS INGREDIENT THAT SHOULD ONLY BE USED BY A MASTER! THE WRONG AMOUNT WILL CERTAINLY KILL YOU!
TEACHER, THANK YOU FOR YOUR WARNING, BUT THIS INGREDIENT IS VERY TASTY, AND WE HAVE STOMACHS OF IRON.
ISN'T THAT RIGHT, BROTHER?
MMPH.
FORGIVE ME, FRIENDS. I SHOULDN'T HAVE BROUGHT OUT THE VIAL IN THE PRESENCE OF NOVICES.
IT'S QUITE ALL RIGHT. THEY WON'T FEEL THE EFFECTS OF THE ROOT FOR ABOUT HALF AN HOUR. BESIDES, I'VE ALWAYS SAID IT'S EASIER TO KILL ON A FULL STOMACH!
KILL?
RIGHT. CLEAVER CHEN HAS ASKED US TO HELP HIM WITH A PROBLEM IN EXCHANGE FOR THE DELICIOUS LUNCH WE JUST ENJOYED.
WE AGREED, AND THOUGHT IT WOULD BE AN EXCELLENT OPPORTUNITY TO GIVE A LESSON TO YOU, OUR STUDENTS.
BUT NOW YOU'VE BOTH GOTTEN YOURSELVES SICK, AND IT'S TOO LATE TO TURN BACK.
YOU'LL BE FINE IN A FEW DAYS, BUT FOR NOW YOUR KUNG FU WILL BE LIMITED. HAD THE VIAL I WAS CARRYING BEEN ANY BIGGER, THE RESULTS WOULD HAVE BEEN VERY BAD...

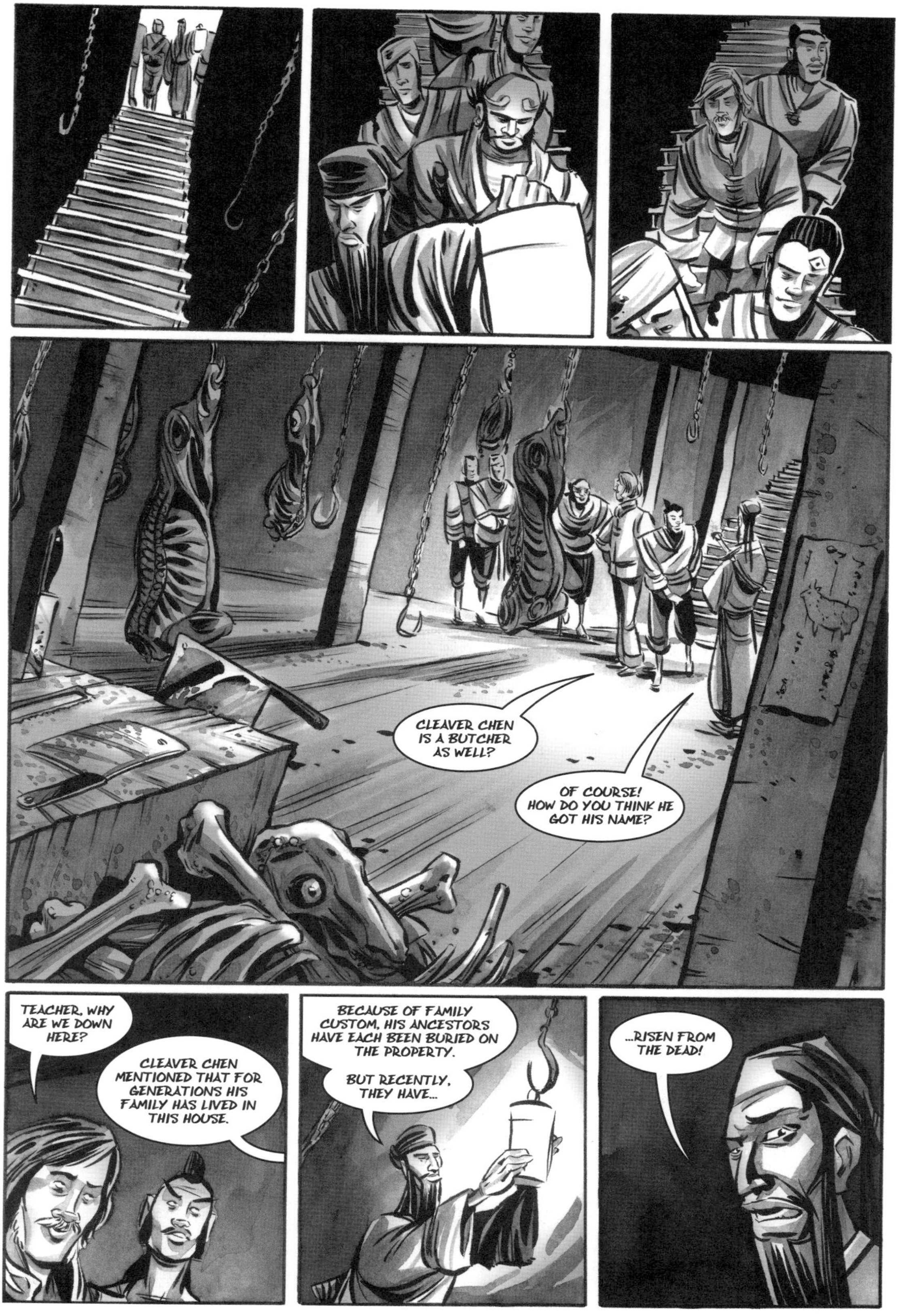
CLEAVER CHEN IS A BUTCHER AS WELL?
OF COURSE! HOW DO YOU THINK HE GOT HIS NAME?
TEACHER, WHY ARE WE DOWN HERE?
CLEAVER CHEN MENTIONED THAT FOR GENERATIONS HIS FAMILY HAS LIVED IN THIS HOUSE.
BECAUSE OF FAMILY CUSTOM, HIS ANCESTORS HAVE EACH BEEN BURIED ON THE PROPERTY.
BUT RECENTLY, THEY HAVE...
...RISEN FROM THE DEAD!

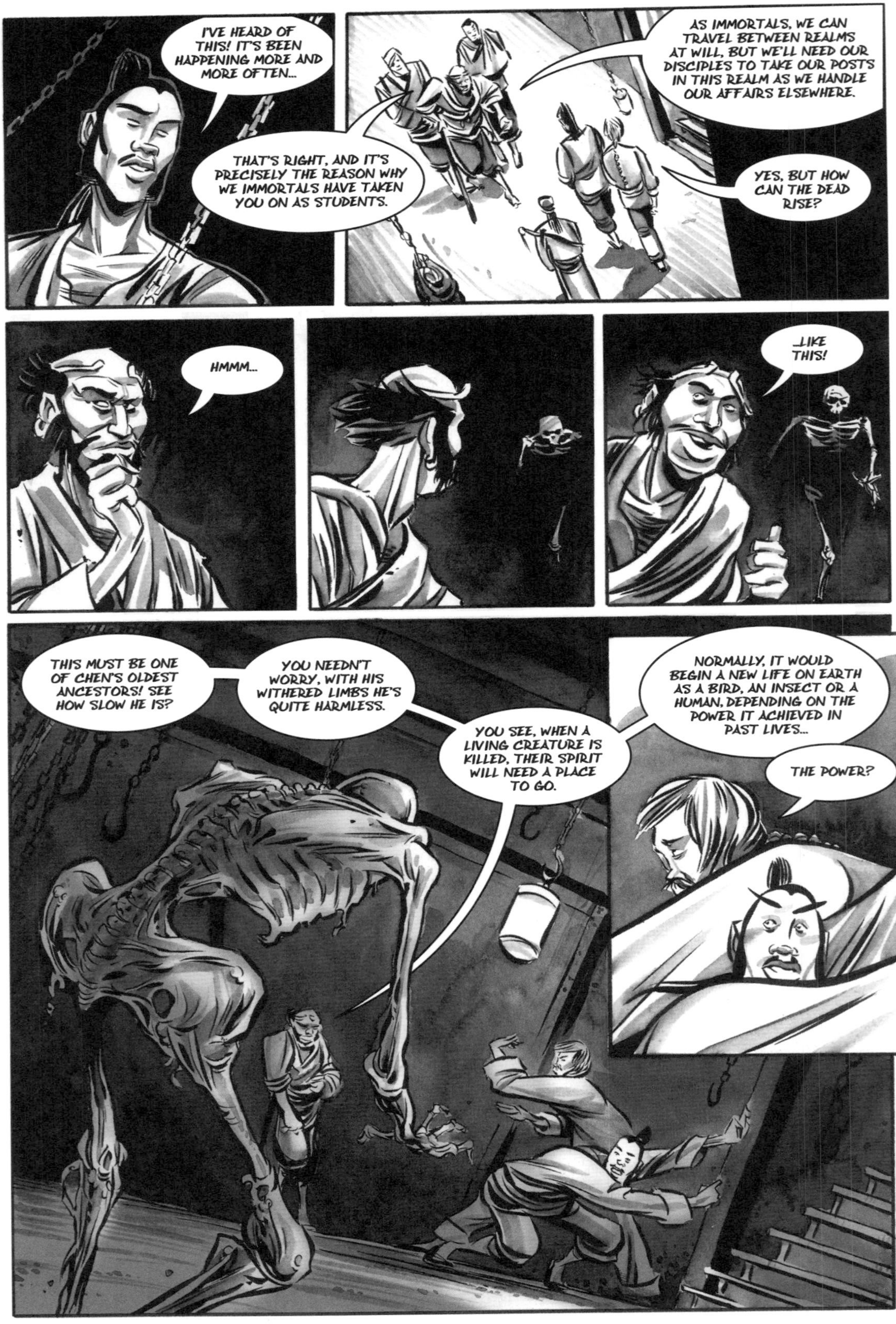
I'VE HEARD OF THIS! IT'S BEEN HAPPENING MORE AND MORE OFTEN...
THAT'S RIGHT, AND IT'S PRECISELY THE REASON WHY WE IMMORTALS HAVE TAKEN YOU ON AS STUDENTS.
AS IMMORTALS, WE CAN TRAVEL BETWEEN REALMS AT WILL, BUT WE'LL NEED OUR DISCIPLES TO TAKE OUR POSTS IN THIS REALM AS WE HANDLE OUR AFFAIRS ELSEWHERE.
YES, BUT HOW CAN THE DEAD RISE?
HMMM...
...LIKE THIS!
THIS MUST BE ONE OF CHEN'S OLDEST ANCESTORS! SEE HOW SLOW HE IS?
YOU NEEDN'T WORRY, WITH HIS WITHERED LIMBS HE'S QUITE HARMLESS.
YOU SEE, WHEN A LIVING CREATURE IS KILLED, THEIR SPIRIT WILL NEED A PLACE TO GO.
NORMALLY, IT WOULD BEGIN A NEW LIFE ON EARTH AS A BIRD, AN INSECT OR A HUMAN, DEPENDING ON THE POWER IT ACHIEVED IN PAST LIVES...
THE POWER?

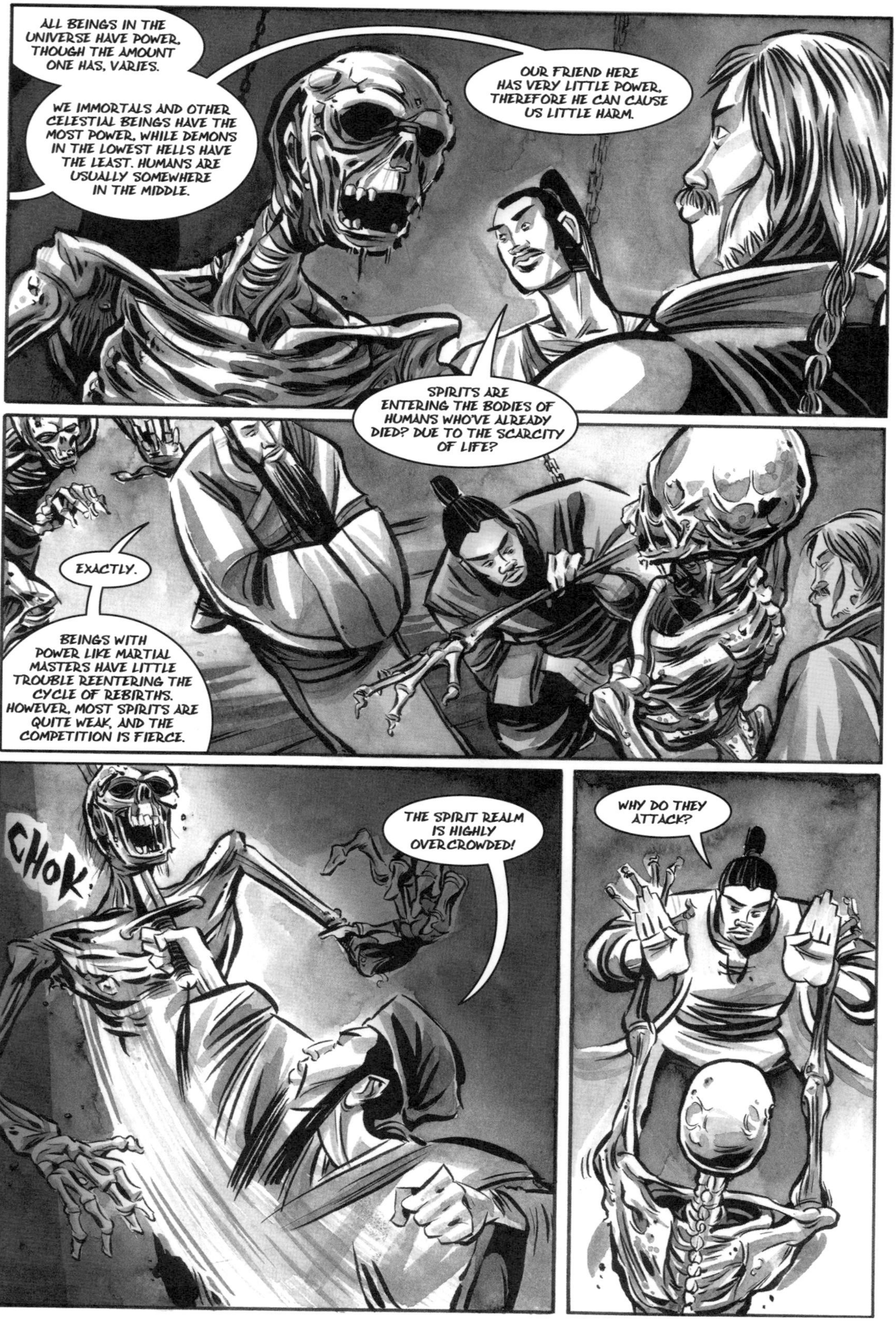
ALL BEINGS IN THE UNIVERSE HAVE POWER, THOUGH THE AMOUNT ONE HAS, VARIES.
WE IMMORTALS AND OTHER CELESTIAL BEINGS HAVE THE MOST POWER, WHILE DEMONS IN THE LOWEST HELLS HAVE THE LEAST. HUMANS ARE USUALLY SOMEWHERE IN THE MIDDLE.
OUR FRIEND HERE HAS VERY LITTLE POWER, THEREFORE HE CAN CAUSE US LITTLE HARM.
SPIRITS ARE ENTERING THE BODIES OF HUMANS WHO'VE ALREADY DIED? DUE TO THE SCARCITY OF LIFE?
EXACTLY.
BEINGS WITH POWER LIKE MARTIAL MASTERS HAVE LITTLE TROUBLE REENTERING THE CYCLE OF REBIRTHS. HOWEVER, MOST SPIRITS ARE QUITE WEAK, AND THE COMPETITION IS FIERCE.
CHOK
THE SPIRIT REALM IS HIGHLY OVERCROWDED!
WHY DO THEY ATTACK?

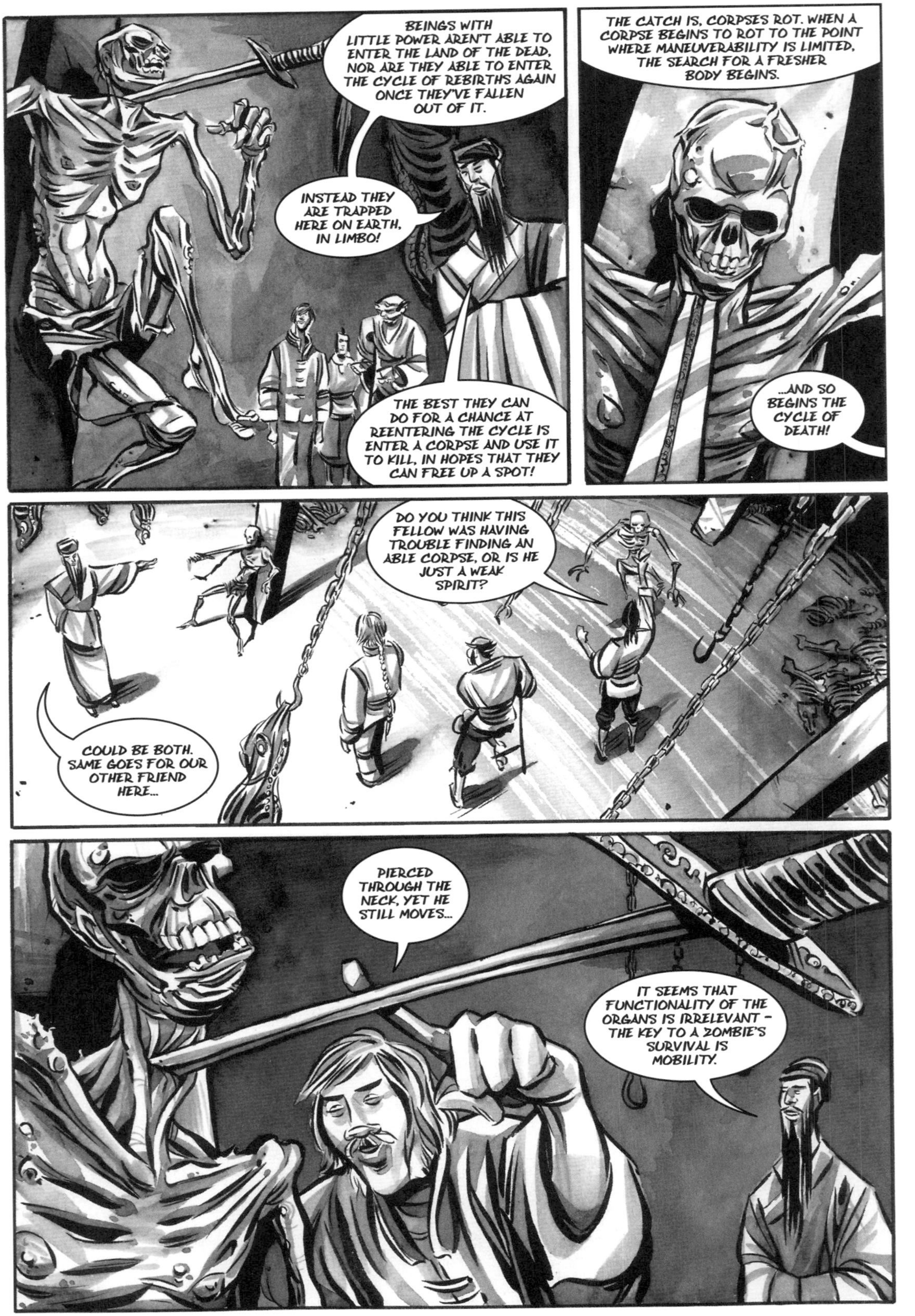
BEINGS WITH LITTLE POWER AREN'T ABLE TO ENTER THE LAND OF THE DEAD, NOR ARE THEY ABLE TO ENTER THE CYCLE OF REBIRTHS AGAIN ONCE THEY'VE FALLEN OUT OF IT.
INSTEAD THEY ARE TRAPPED HERE ON EARTH, IN LIMBO!
THE BEST THEY CAN DO FOR A CHANCE AT REENTERING THE CYCLE IS ENTER A CORPSE AND USE IT TO KILL, IN HOPES THAT THEY CAN FREE UP A SPOT!
THE CATCH IS, CORPSES ROT. WHEN A CORPSE BEGINS TO ROT TO THE POINT WHERE MANEUVERABILITY IS LIMITED, THE SEARCH FOR A FRESHER BODY BEGINS.
...AND SO BEGINS THE CYCLE OF DEATH!
DO YOU THINK THIS FELLOW WAS HAVING TROUBLE FINDING AN ABLE CORPSE, OR IS HE JUST A WEAK SPIRIT?
COULD BE BOTH. SAME GOES FOR OUR OTHER FRIEND HERE...
PIERCED THROUGH THE NECK, YET HE STILL MOVES...
IT SEEMS THAT FUNCTIONALITY OF THE ORGANS IS IRRELEVANT – THE KEY TO A ZOMBIE'S SURVIVAL IS MOBILITY.

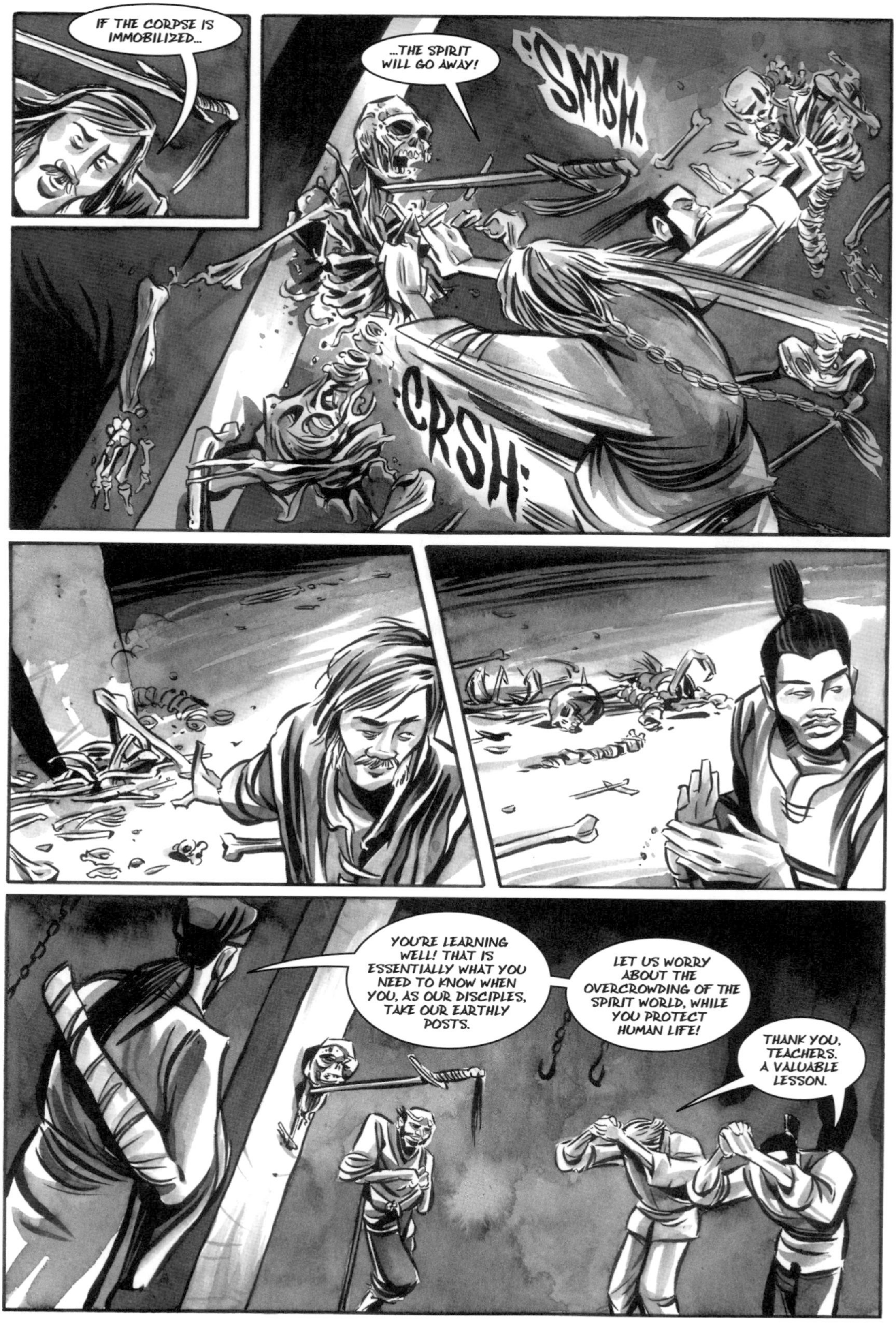

IF THE CORPSE IS IMMOBILIZED...
...THE SPIRIT WILL GO AWAY!
SMSH.
CRSH.
YOU'RE LEARNING WELL! THAT IS ESSENTIALLY WHAT YOU NEED TO KNOW WHEN YOU, AS OUR DISCIPLES, TAKE OUR EARTHLY POSTS.
LET US WORRY ABOUT THE OVERCROWDING OF THE SPIRIT WORLD, WHILE YOU PROTECT HUMAN LIFE!
THANK YOU, TEACHERS. A VALUABLE LESSON.

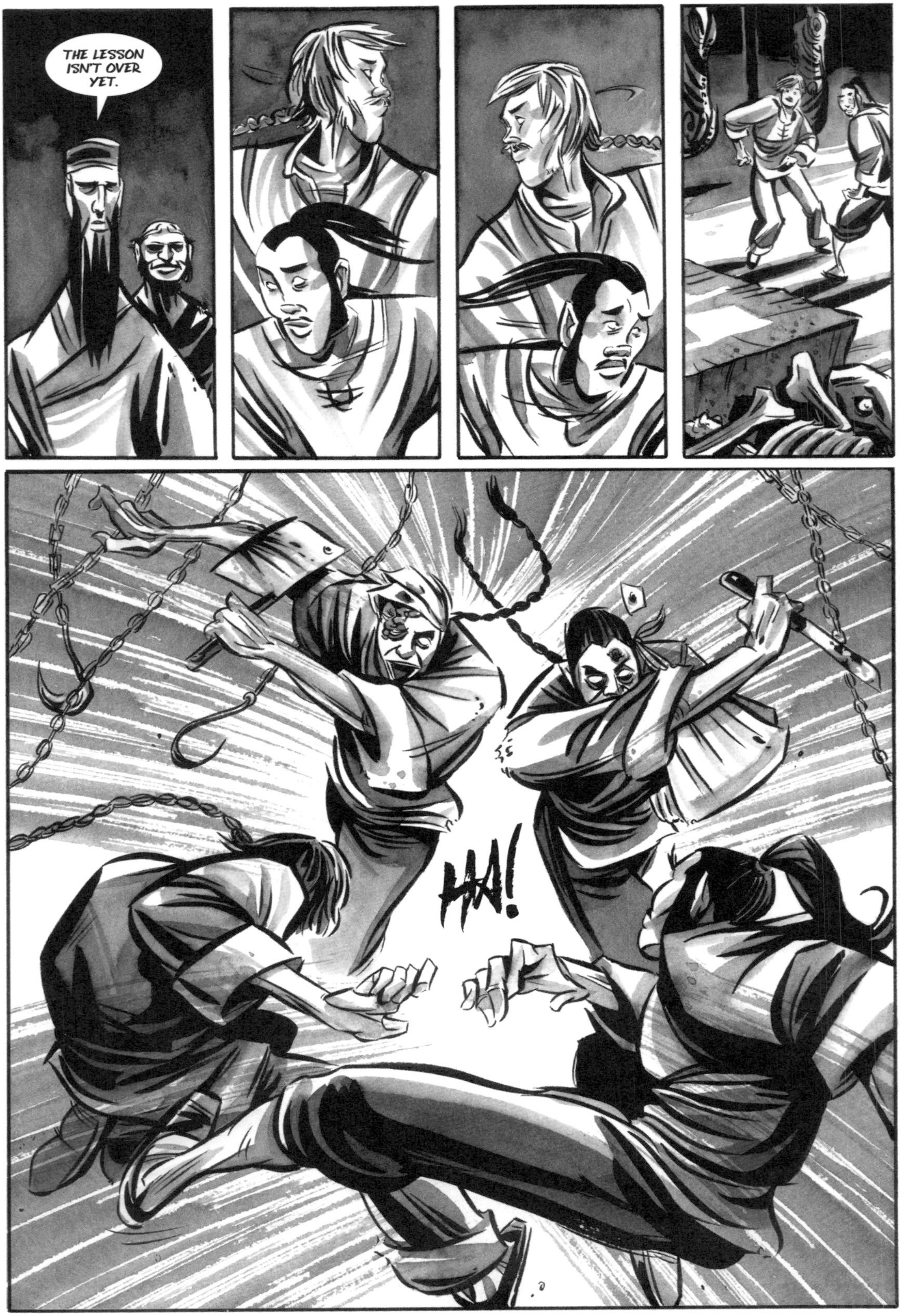
THE LESSON ISN'T OVER YET.
HA!

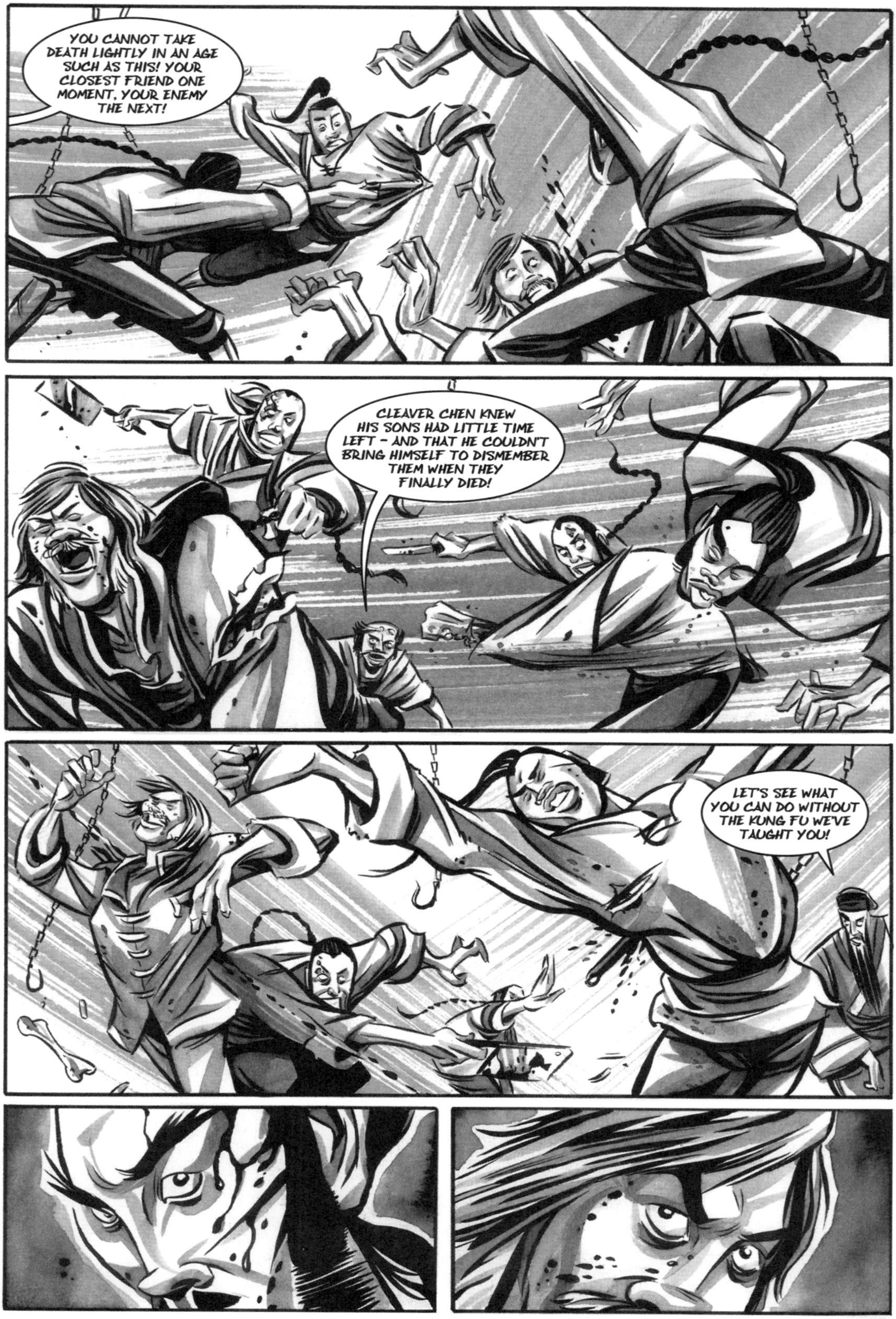
YOU CANNOT TAKE DEATH LIGHTLY IN AN AGE SUCH AS THIS! YOUR CLOSEST FRIEND ONE MOMENT, YOUR ENEMY THE NEXT!
CLEAVER CHEN KNEW HIS SONS HAD LITTLE TIME LEFT – AND THAT HE COULDN'T BRING HIMSELF TO DISMEMBER THEM WHEN THEY FINALLY DIED!
LET'S SEE WHAT YOU CAN DO WITHOUT THE KUNG FU WE'VE TAUGHT YOU!

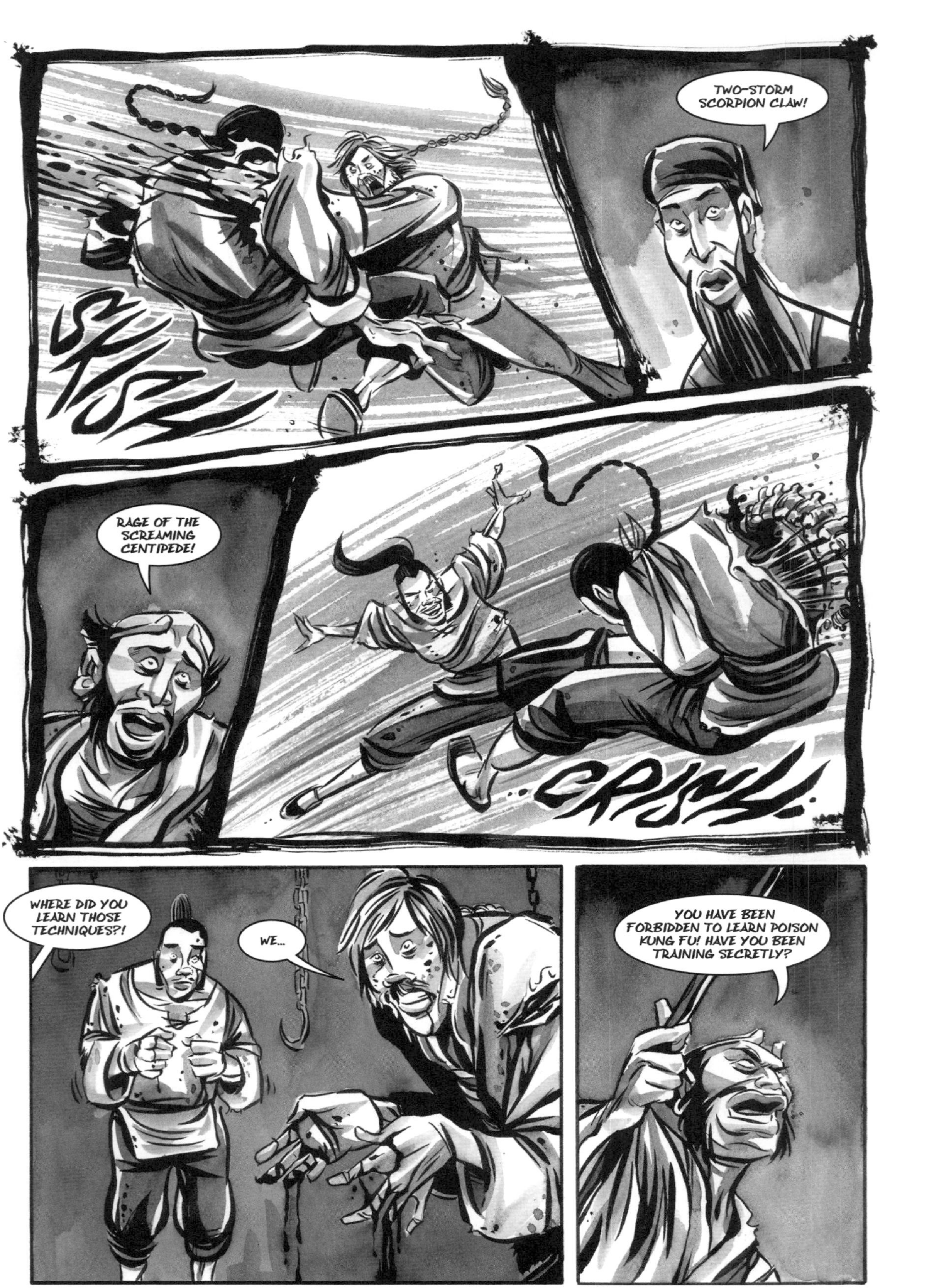
TWO-STORM SCORPION CLAW!
RAGE OF THE SCREAMING CENTIPEDE!
WHERE DID YOU LEARN THOSE TECHNIQUES?!
WE...
YOU HAVE BEEN FORBIDDEN TO LEARN POISON KUNG FU! HAVE YOU BEEN TRAINING SECRETLY?

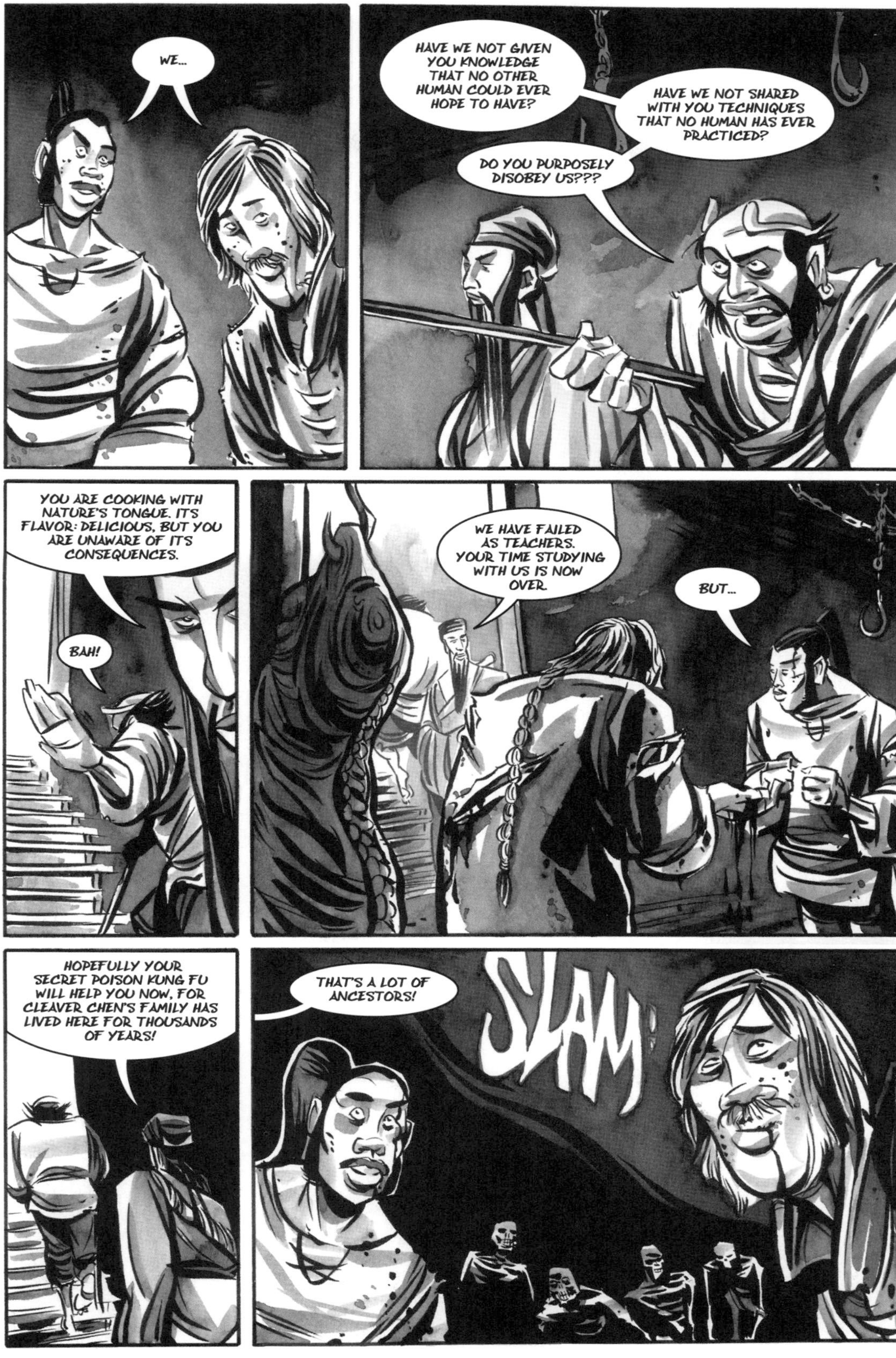
WE...
HAVE WE NOT GIVEN YOU KNOWLEDGE THAT NO OTHER HUMAN COULD EVER HOPE TO HAVE?
HAVE WE NOT SHARED WITH YOU TECHNIQUES THAT NO HUMAN HAS EVER PRACTICED?
DO YOU PURPOSELY DISOBEY US???
YOU ARE COOKING WITH NATURE'S TONGUE. ITS FLAVOR: DELICIOUS, BUT YOU ARE UNAWARE OF ITS CONSEQUENCES.
BAH!
WE HAVE FAILED AS TEACHERS. YOUR TIME STUDYING WITH US IS NOW OVER.
BUT...
HOPEFULLY YOUR SECRET POISON KUNG FU WILL HELP YOU NOW, FOR CLEAVER CHEN'S FAMILY HAS LIVED HERE FOR THOUSANDS OF YEARS!
THAT'S A LOT OF ANCESTORS!
SLAM!

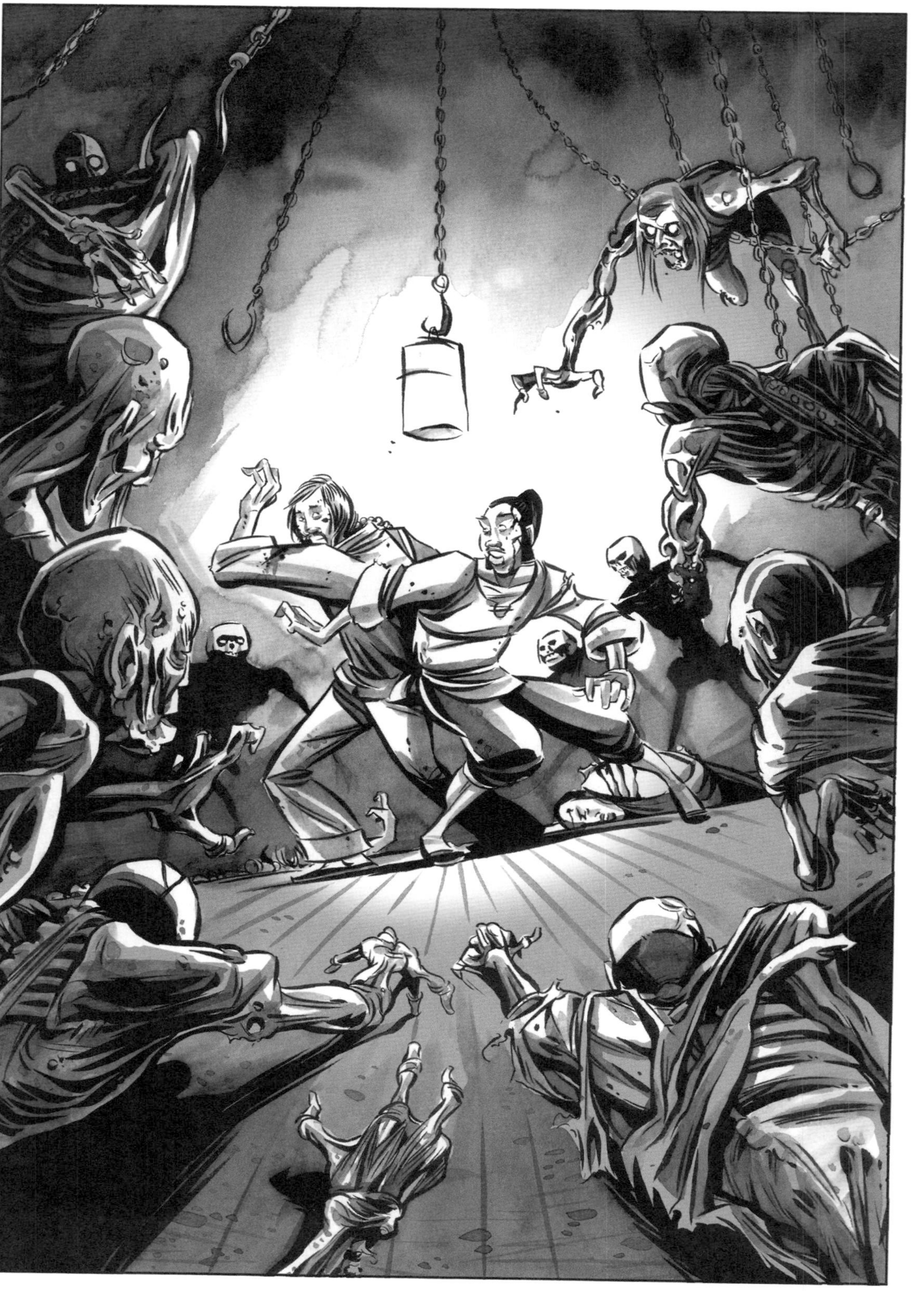

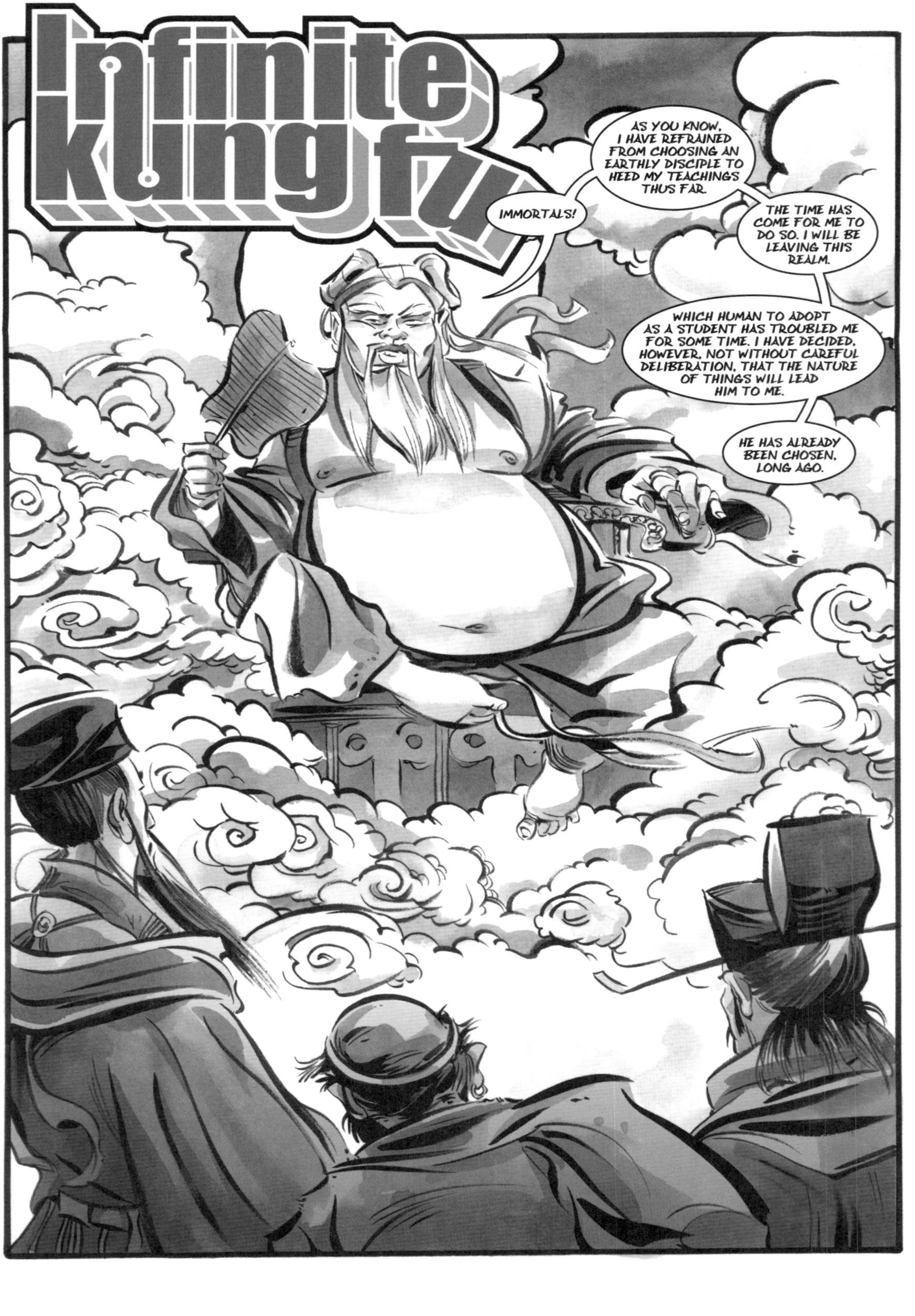
Infinite kung fu
IMMORTALS!
AS YOU KNOW, I HAVE REFRAINED FROM CHOOSING AN EARTHLY DISCIPLE TO HEED MY TEACHINGS THUS FAR.
THE TIME HAS COME FOR ME TO DO SO. I WILL BE LEAVING THIS REALM.
WHICH HUMAN TO ADOPT AS A STUDENT HAS TROUBLED ME FOR SOME TIME. I HAVE DECIDED, HOWEVER, NOT WITHOUT CAREFUL DELIBERATION, THAT THE NATURE OF THINGS WILL LEAD HIM TO ME.
HE HAS ALREADY BEEN CHOSEN, LONG AGO.

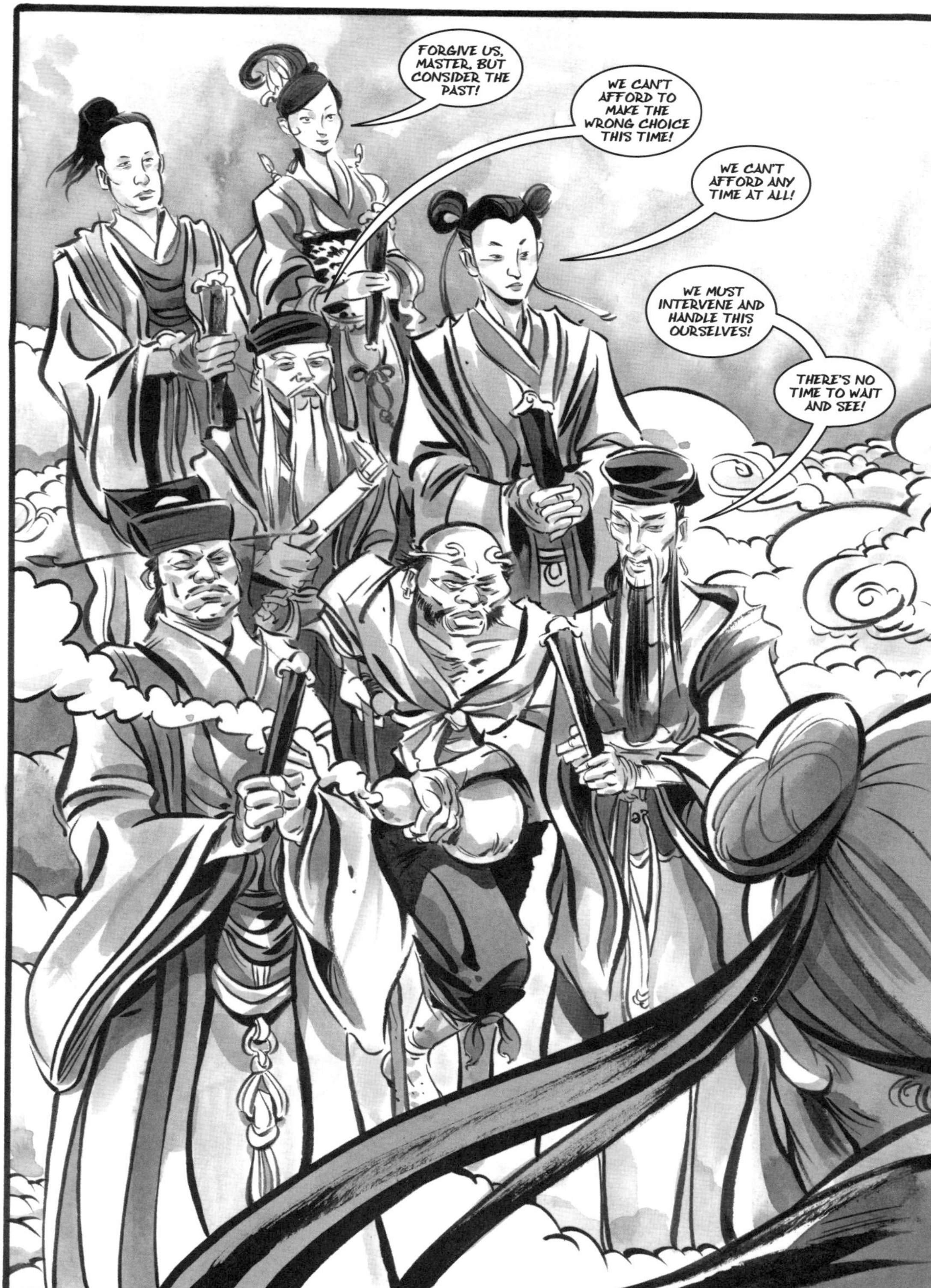
FORGIVE US, MASTER, BUT CONSIDER THE PAST!
WE CAN'T AFFORD TO MAKE THE WRONG CHOICE THIS TIME!
WE CAN'T AFFORD ANY TIME AT ALL!
WE MUST INTERVENE AND HANDLE THIS OURSELVES!
THERE'S NO TIME TO WAIT AND SEE!

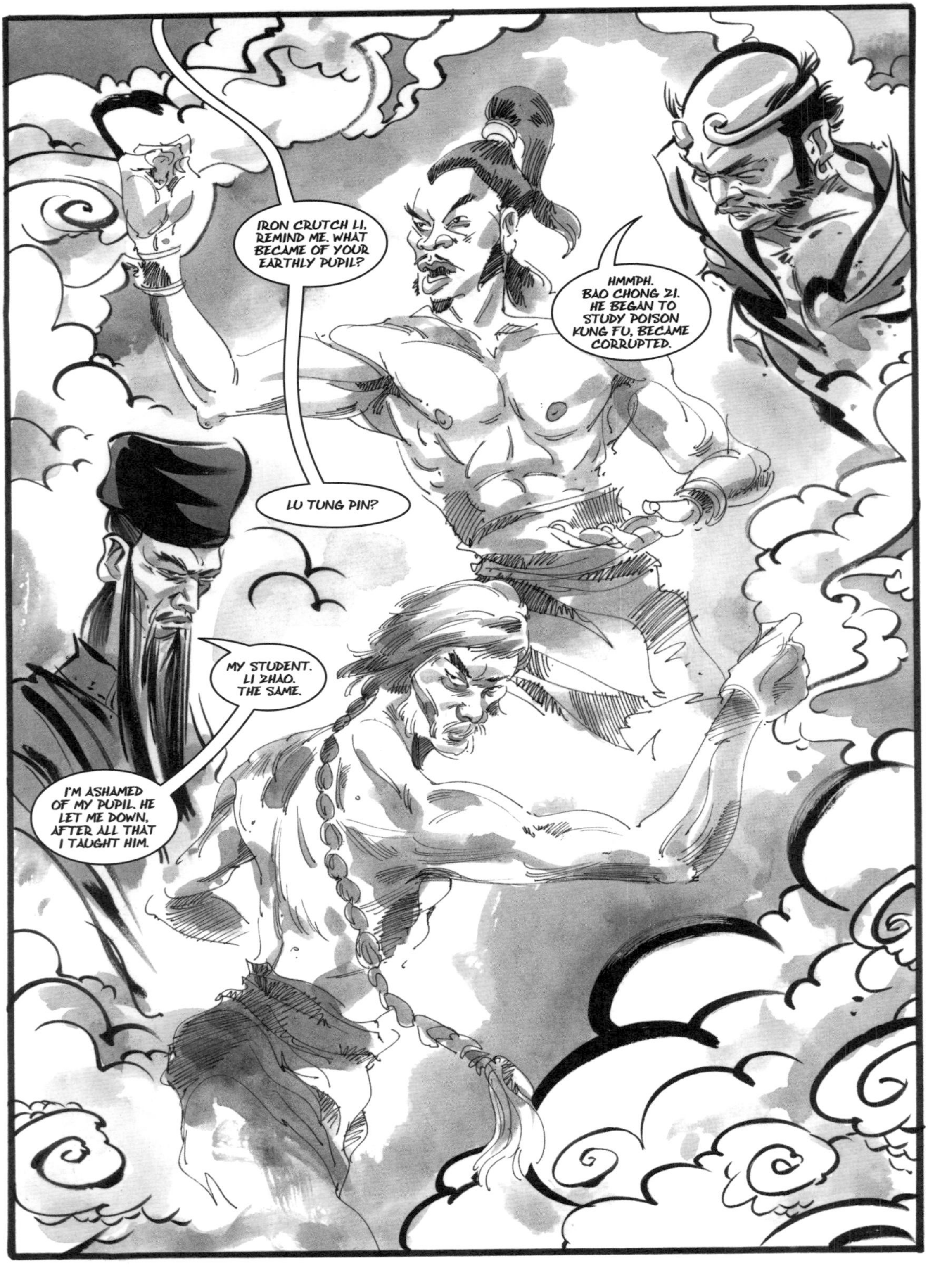
IRON CRUTCH LI. REMIND ME. WHAT BECAME OF YOUR EARTHLY PUPIL?
HMMPH. BAO CHONG ZI. HE BEGAN TO STUDY POISON KUNG FU, BECAME CORRUPTED.
LU TUNG PIN?
MY STUDENT. LI ZHAO. THE SAME.
I'M ASHAMED OF MY PUPIL. HE LET ME DOWN, AFTER ALL THAT I TAUGHT HIM.

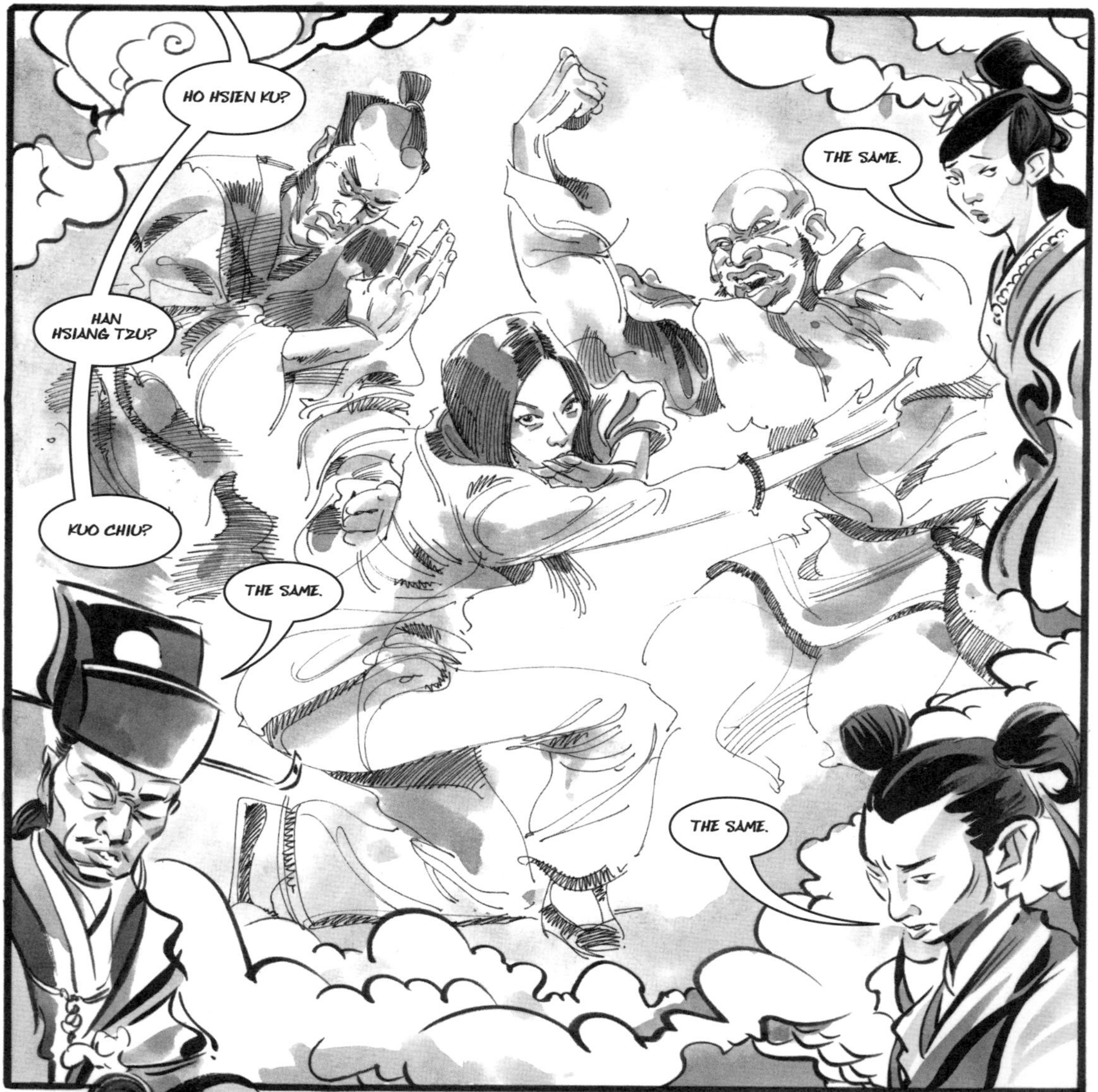
HO HSIEN KU?
THE SAME.
HAN HSIANG TZU?
KUO CHIU?
THE SAME.
THE SAME.

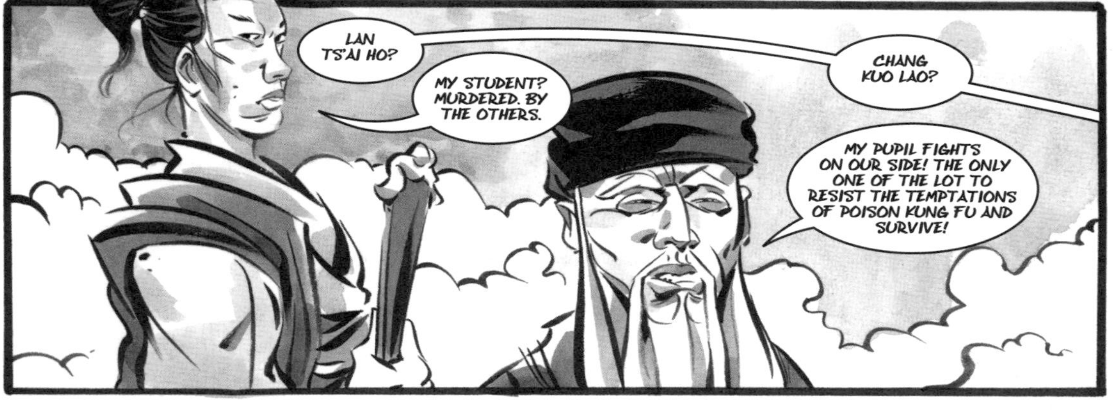
LAN TS'AI HO?
MY STUDENT? MURDERED. BY THE OTHERS.
CHANG KUO LAO?
MY PUPIL FIGHTS ON OUR SIDE! THE ONLY ONE OF THE LOT TO RESIST THE TEMPTATIONS OF POISON KUNG FU AND SURVIVE!

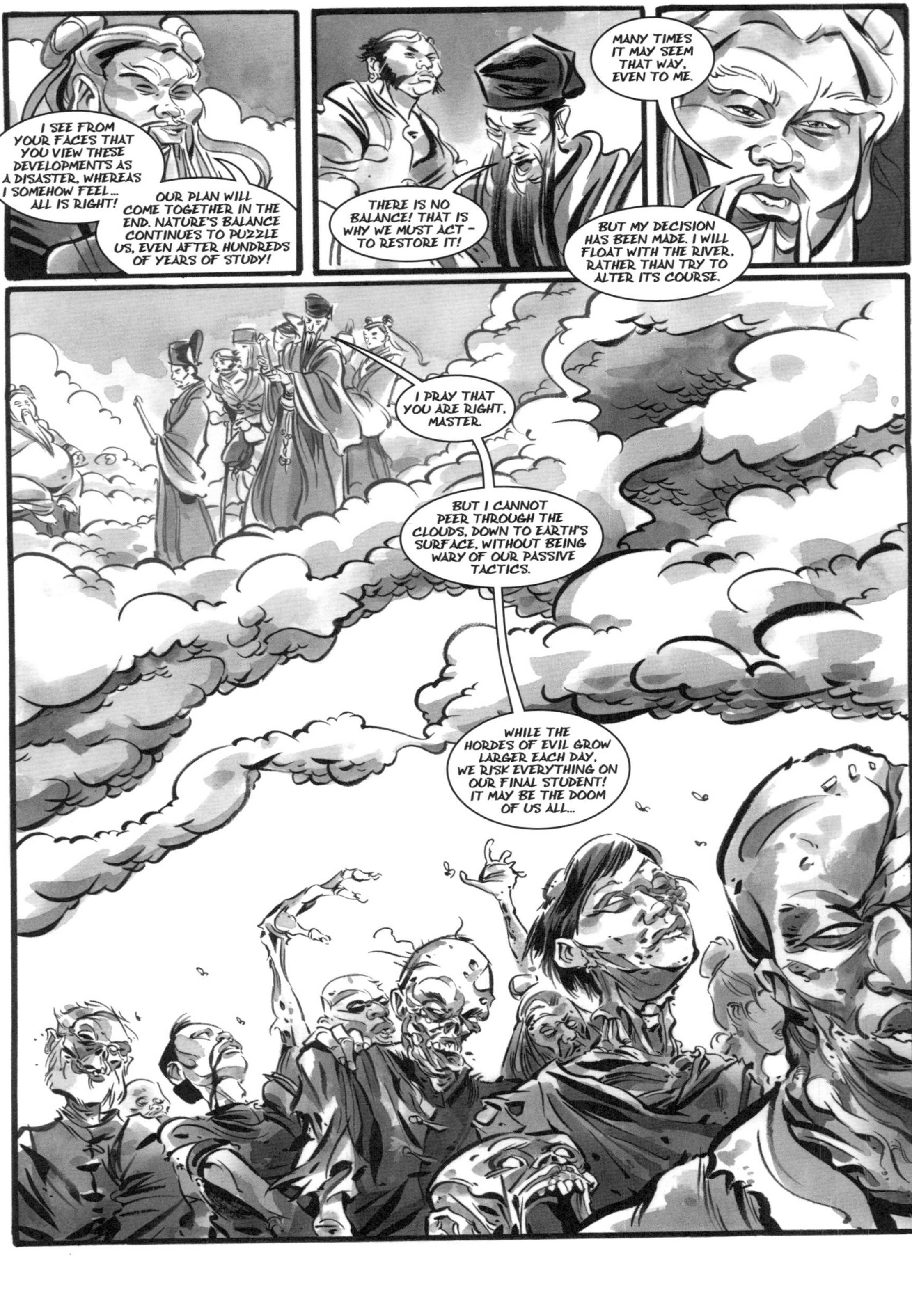
I SEE FROM YOUR FACES THAT YOU VIEW THESE DEVELOPMENTS AS A DISASTER, WHEREAS I SOMEHOW FEEL... ALL IS RIGHT!
OUR PLAN WILL COME TOGETHER IN THE END. NATURE'S BALANCE CONTINUES TO PUZZLE US, EVEN AFTER HUNDREDS OF YEARS OF STUDY!
THERE IS NO BALANCE! THAT IS WHY WE MUST ACT - TO RESTORE IT!
MANY TIMES IT MAY SEEM THAT WAY, EVEN TO ME.
BUT MY DECISION HAS BEEN MADE. I WILL FLOAT WITH THE RIVER, RATHER THAN TRY TO ALTER ITS COURSE.
I PRAY THAT YOU ARE RIGHT, MASTER.
BUT I CANNOT PEER THROUGH THE CLOUDS, DOWN TO EARTH'S SURFACE, WITHOUT BEING WARY OF OUR PASSIVE TACTICS.
WHILE THE HORDES OF EVIL GROW LARGER EACH DAY, WE RISK EVERYTHING ON OUR FINAL STUDENT! IT MAY BE THE DOOM OF US ALL...

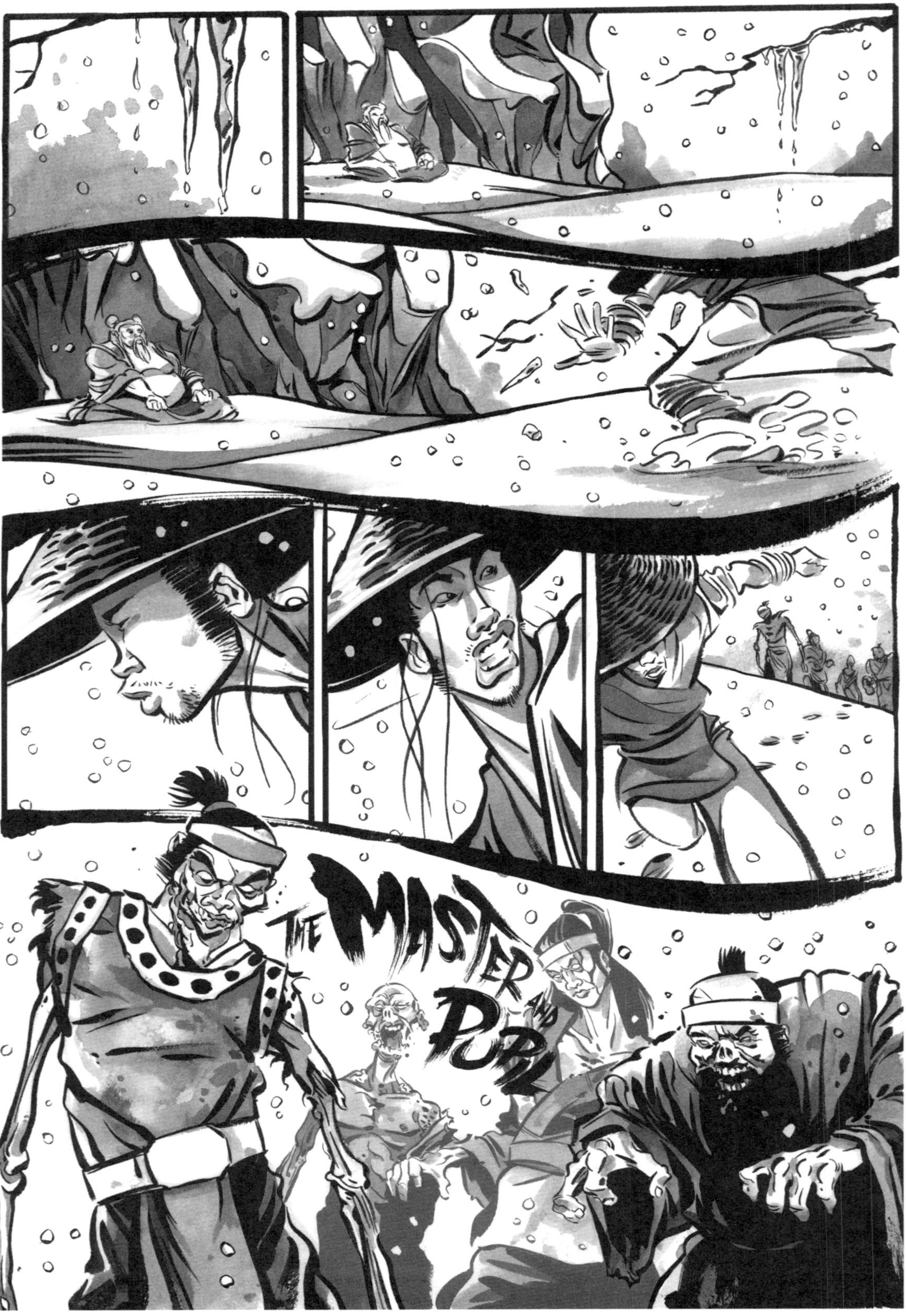
THE MASTER AND PUPIL

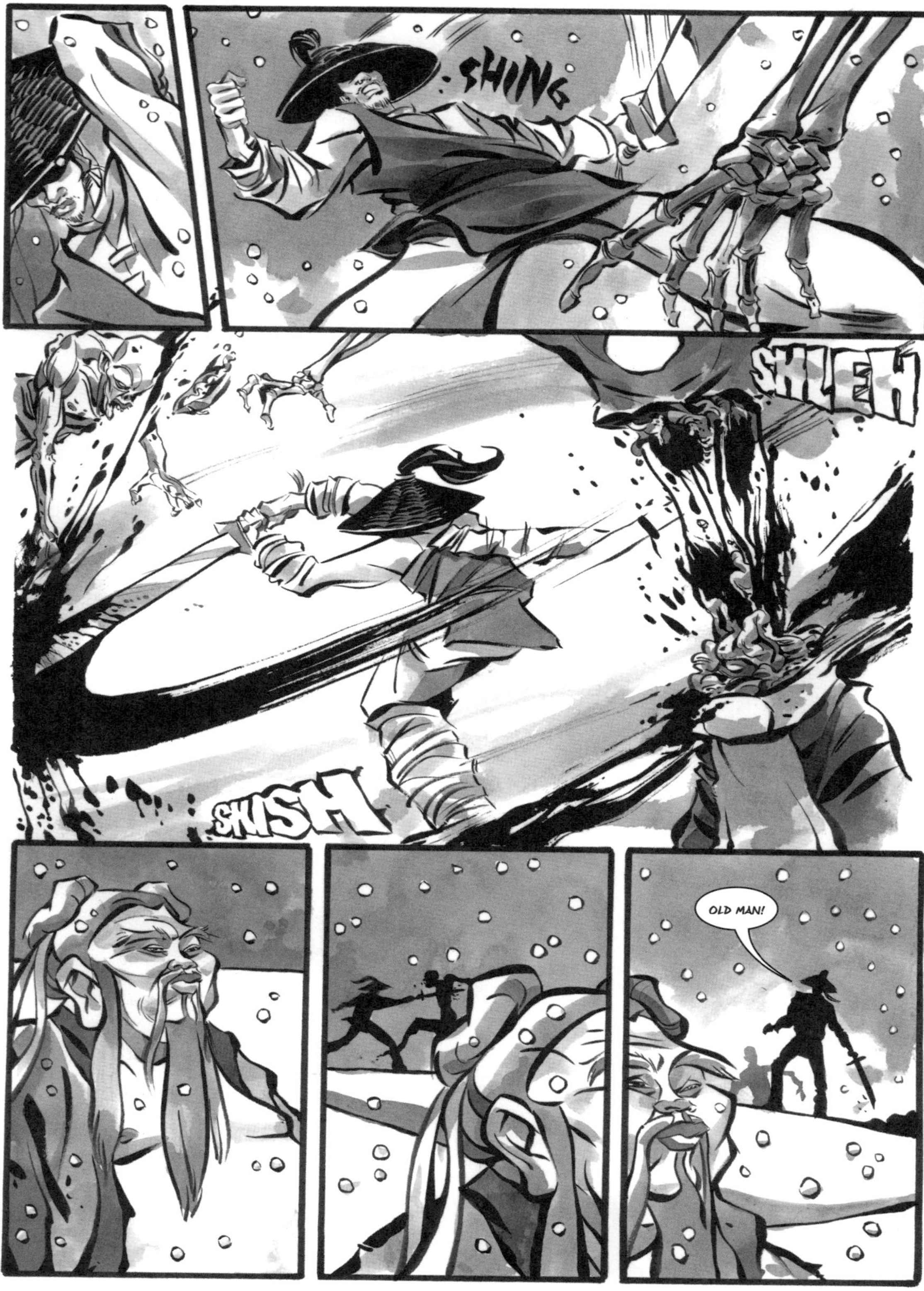
SHING
SHLEH
SHISH
OLD MAN!

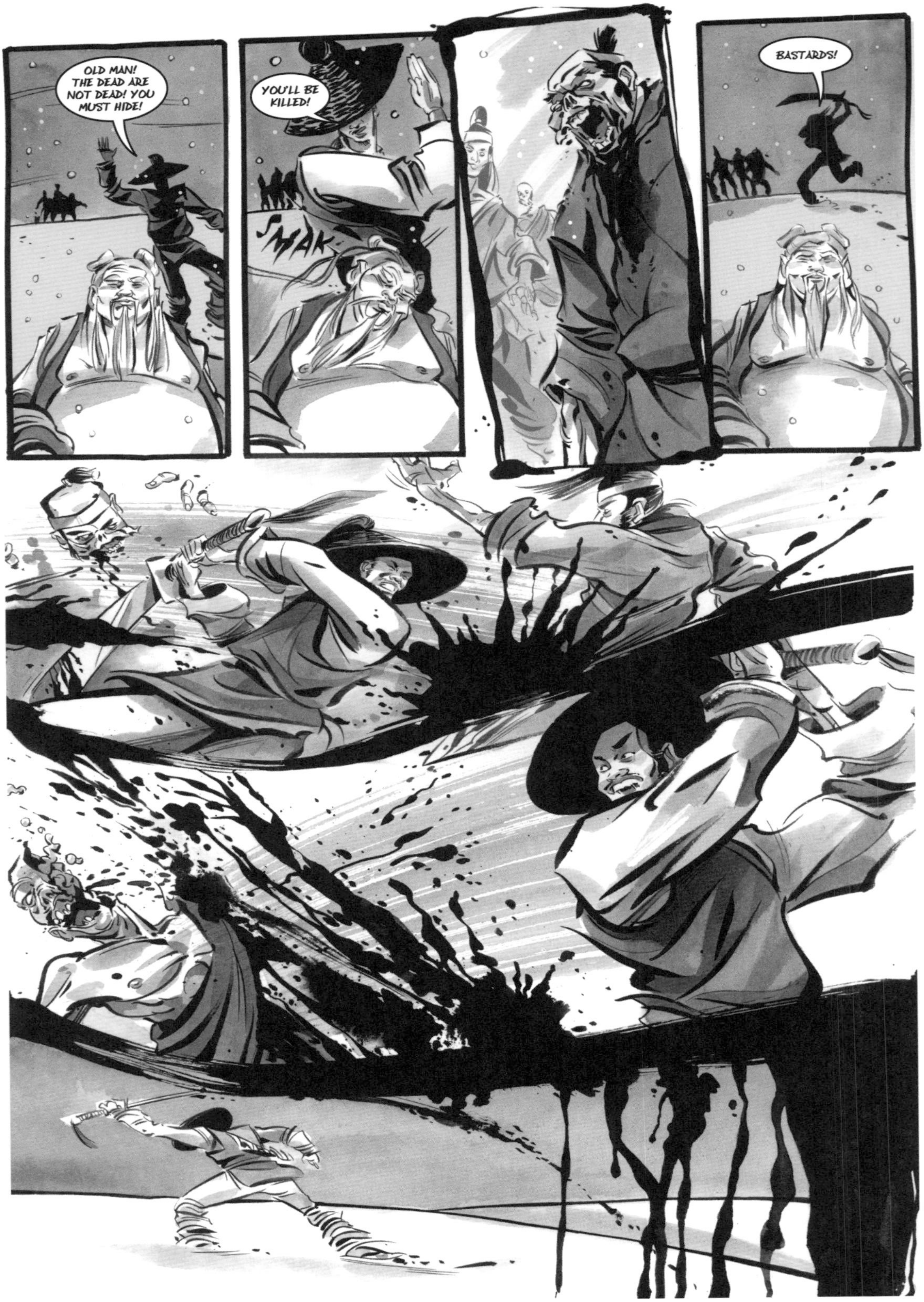
OLD MAN! THE DEAD ARE NOT DEAD! YOU MUST HIDE!
YOU'LL BE KILLED!
SMAK
BASTARDS!

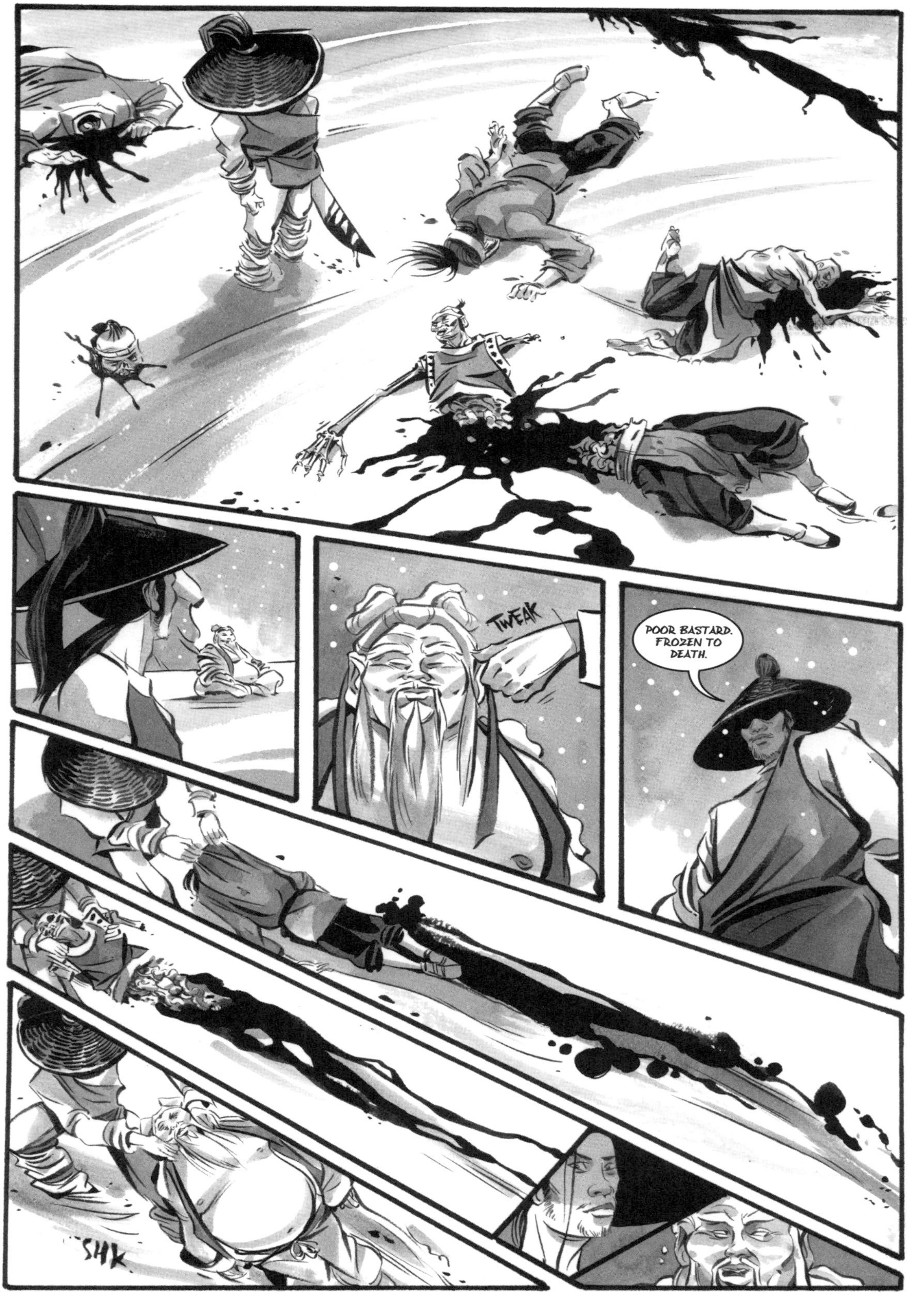
TWEAK
POOR BASTARD. FROZEN TO DEATH.
SHK

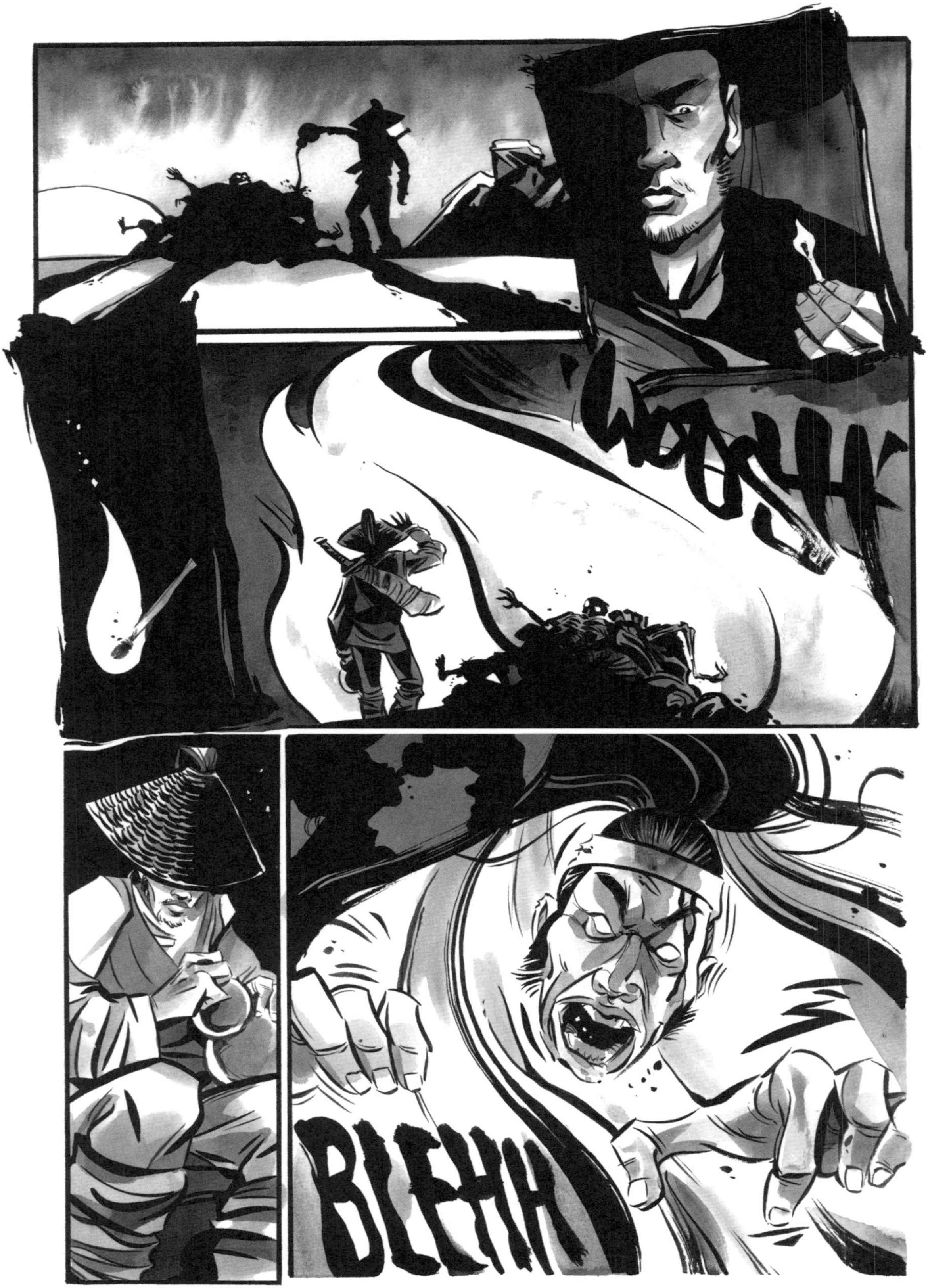
WOOSHK
BLEHH

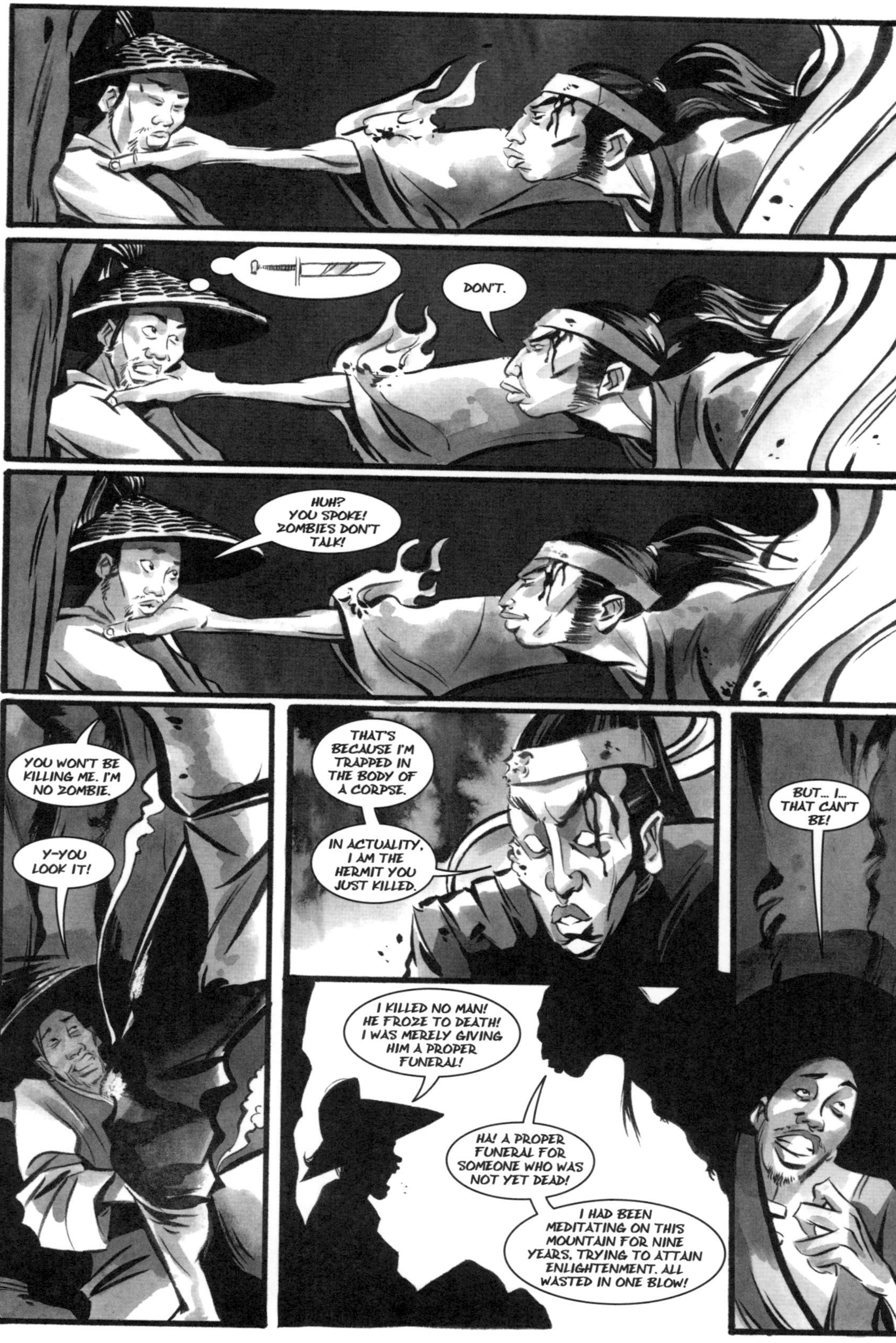
DON'T.
HUH? YOU SPOKE! ZOMBIES DON'T TALK!
YOU WON'T BE KILLING ME. I'M NO ZOMBIE.
Y-YOU LOOK IT!
THAT'S BECAUSE I'M TRAPPED IN THE BODY OF A CORPSE.
IN ACTUALITY, I AM THE HERMIT YOU JUST KILLED.
BUT... I... THAT CAN'T BE!
I KILLED NO MAN! HE FROZE TO DEATH! I WAS MERELY GIVING HIM A PROPER FUNERAL!
HA! A PROPER FUNERAL FOR SOMEONE WHO WAS NOT YET DEAD!
I HAD BEEN MEDITATING ON THIS MOUNTAIN FOR NINE YEARS, TRYING TO ATTAIN ENLIGHTENMENT. ALL WASTED IN ONE BLOW!

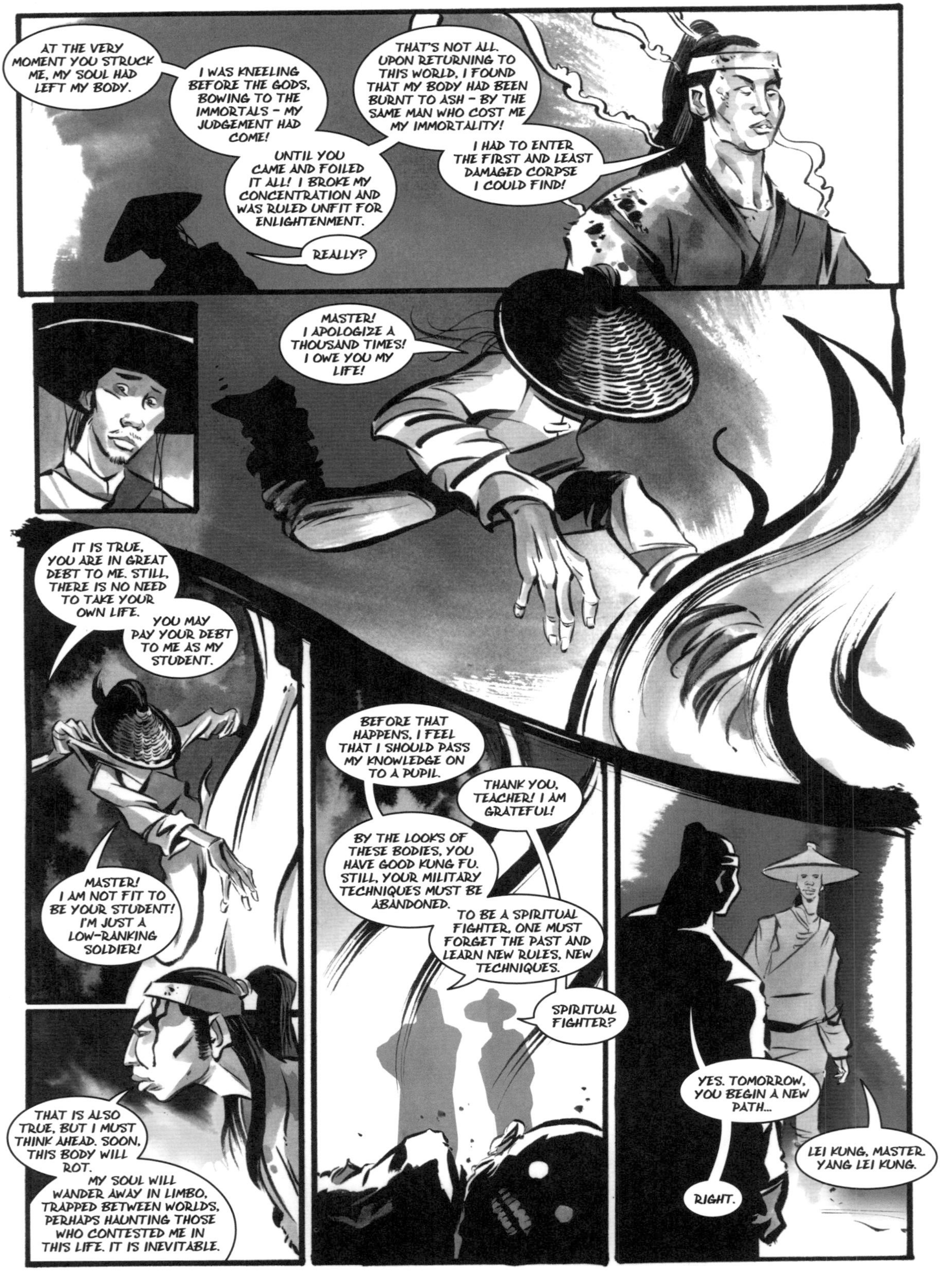
AT THE VERY MOMENT YOU STRUCK ME, MY SOUL HAD LEFT MY BODY.
I WAS KNEELING BEFORE THE GODS, BOWING TO THE IMMORTALS - MY JUDGEMENT HAD COME!
UNTIL YOU CAME AND FOILED IT ALL! I BROKE MY CONCENTRATION AND WAS RULED UNFIT FOR ENLIGHTENMENT.
THAT'S NOT ALL. UPON RETURNING TO THIS WORLD, I FOUND THAT MY BODY HAD BEEN BURNT TO ASH - BY THE SAME MAN WHO COST ME MY IMMORTALITY!
I HAD TO ENTER THE FIRST AND LEAST DAMAGED CORPSE I COULD FIND!
REALLY?
MASTER! I APOLOGIZE A THOUSAND TIMES! I OWE YOU MY LIFE!
IT IS TRUE, YOU ARE IN GREAT DEBT TO ME. STILL, THERE IS NO NEED TO TAKE YOUR OWN LIFE.
YOU MAY PAY YOUR DEBT TO ME AS MY STUDENT.
MASTER! I AM NOT FIT TO BE YOUR STUDENT! I'M JUST A LOW-RANKING SOLDIER!
THAT IS ALSO TRUE, BUT I MUST THINK AHEAD. SOON, THIS BODY WILL ROT.
MY SOUL WILL WANDER AWAY IN LIMBO, TRAPPED BETWEEN WORLDS, PERHAPS HAUNTING THOSE WHO CONTESTED ME IN THIS LIFE. IT IS INEVITABLE.
BEFORE THAT HAPPENS, I FEEL THAT I SHOULD PASS MY KNOWLEDGE ON TO A PUPIL.
THANK YOU, TEACHER! I AM GRATEFUL!
BY THE LOOKS OF THESE BODIES, YOU HAVE GOOD KUNG FU. STILL, YOUR MILITARY TECHNIQUES MUST BE ABANDONED.
TO BE A SPIRITUAL FIGHTER, ONE MUST FORGET THE PAST AND LEARN NEW RULES, NEW TECHNIQUES.
SPIRITUAL FIGHTER?
YES. TOMORROW, YOU BEGIN A NEW PATH...
RIGHT.
LEI KUNG, MASTER. YANG LEI KUNG.

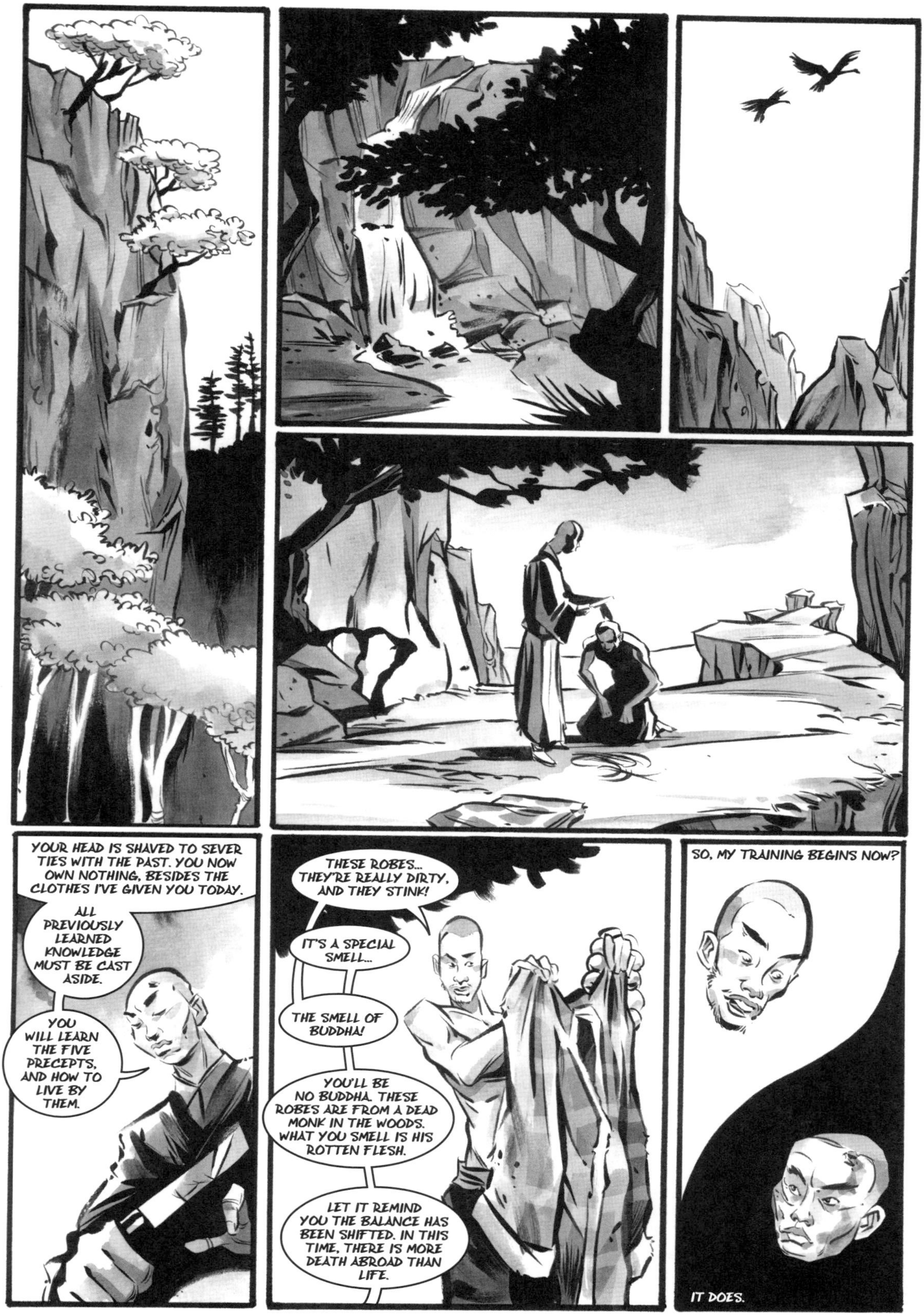
YOUR HEAD IS SHAVED TO SEVER TIES WITH THE PAST. YOU NOW OWN NOTHING, BESIDES THE CLOTHES I'VE GIVEN YOU TODAY.
ALL PREVIOUSLY LEARNED KNOWLEDGE MUST BE CAST ASIDE.
YOU WILL LEARN THE FIVE PRECEPTS, AND HOW TO LIVE BY THEM.
THESE ROBES... THEY'RE REALLY DIRTY, AND THEY STINK!
IT'S A SPECIAL SMELL...
THE SMELL OF BUDDHA!
YOU'LL BE NO BUDDHA. THESE ROBES ARE FROM A DEAD MONK IN THE WOODS. WHAT YOU SMELL IS HIS ROTTEN FLESH.
LET IT REMIND YOU THE BALANCE HAS BEEN SHIFTED. IN THIS TIME, THERE IS MORE DEATH ABROAD THAN LIFE.
SO, MY TRAINING BEGINS NOW?
IT DOES.

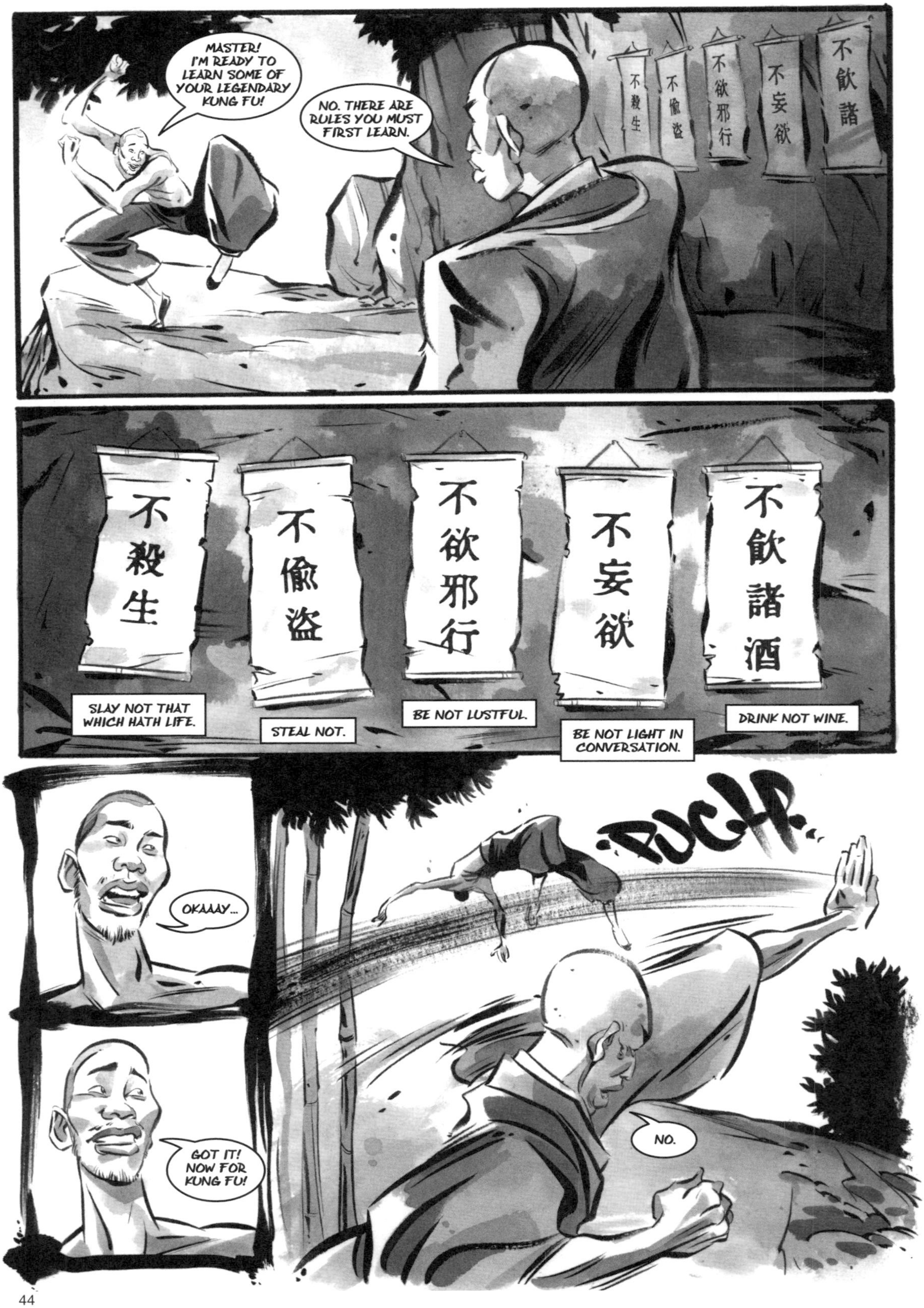
MASTER! I'M READY TO LEARN SOME OF YOUR LEGENDARY KUNG FU!
NO. THERE ARE RULES YOU MUST FIRST LEARN.
不殺生
不偷盗
不欲邪行
不妄欲
不飲諸酒
SLAY NOT THAT WHICH HATH LIFE.
STEAL NOT.
BE NOT LUSTFUL.
BE NOT LIGHT IN CONVERSATION.
DRINK NOT WINE.
OKAAAY...
GOT IT! NOW FOR KUNG FU!
PUGH
NO.

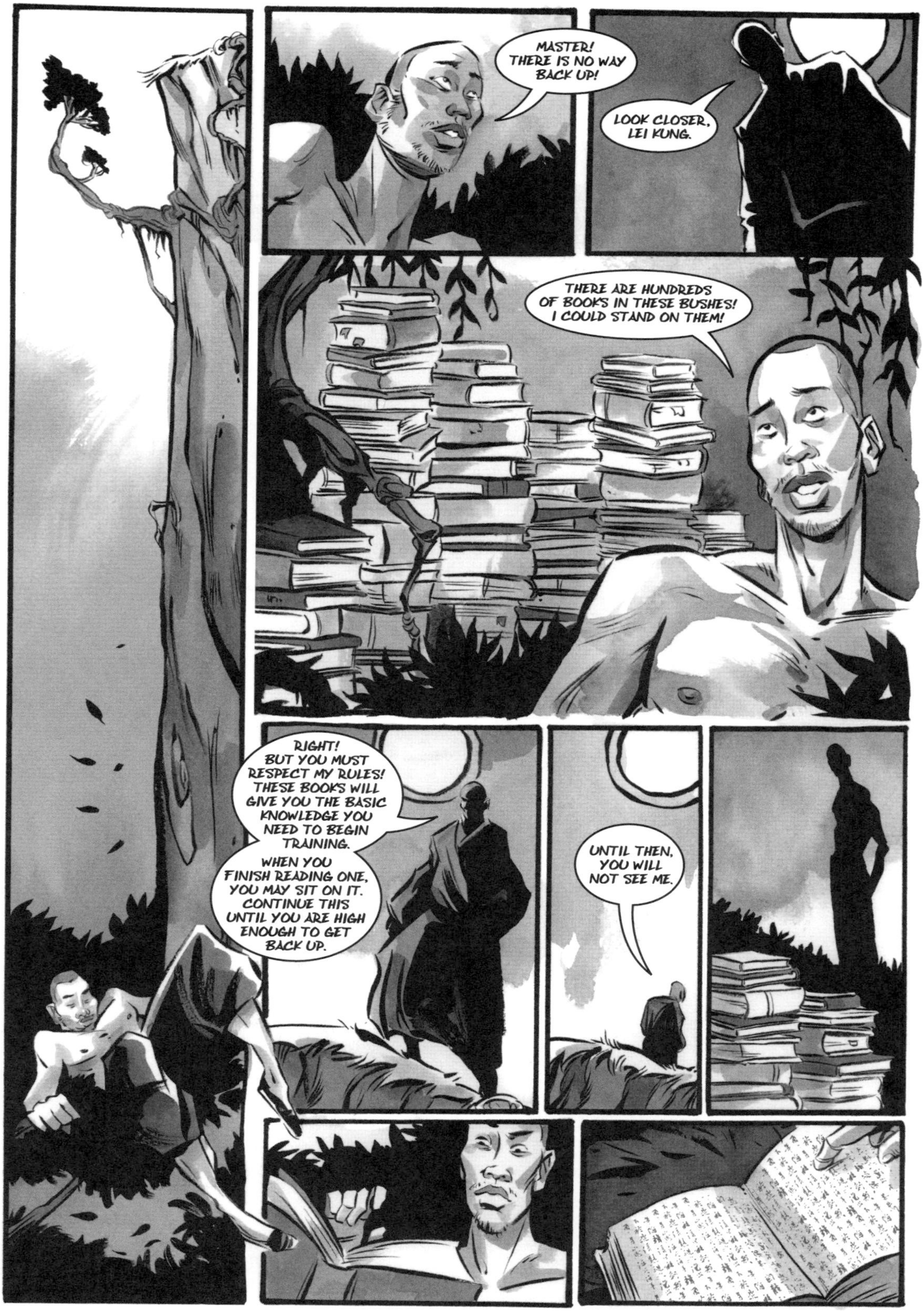
MASTER! THERE IS NO WAY BACK UP!
LOOK CLOSER, LEI KUNG.
THERE ARE HUNDREDS OF BOOKS IN THESE BUSHES! I COULD STAND ON THEM!
RIGHT! BUT YOU MUST RESPECT MY RULES! THESE BOOKS WILL GIVE YOU THE BASIC KNOWLEDGE YOU NEED TO BEGIN TRAINING.
WHEN YOU FINISH READING ONE, YOU MAY SIT ON IT. CONTINUE THIS UNTIL YOU ARE HIGH ENOUGH TO GET BACK UP.
UNTIL THEN, YOU WILL NOT SEE ME.

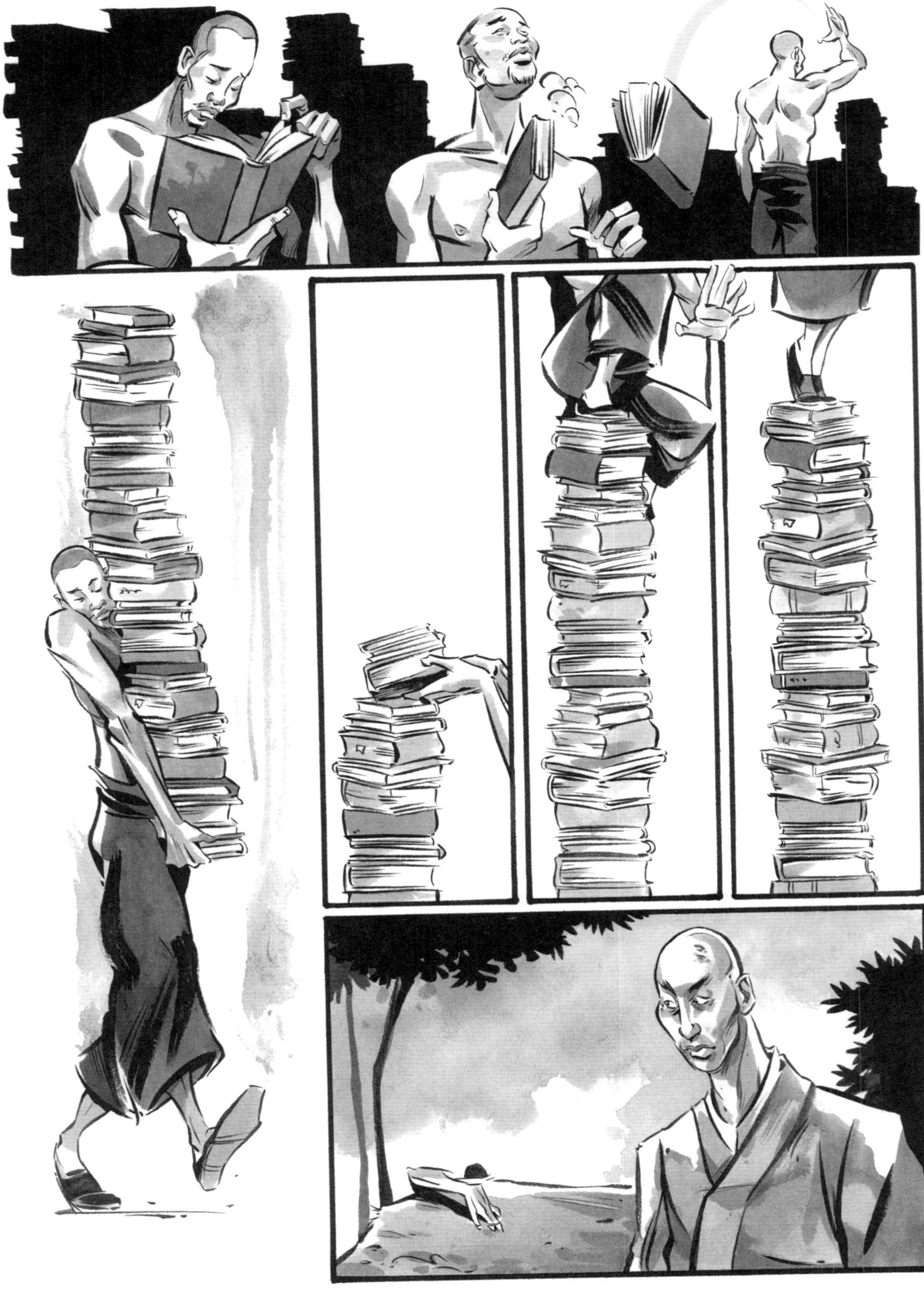

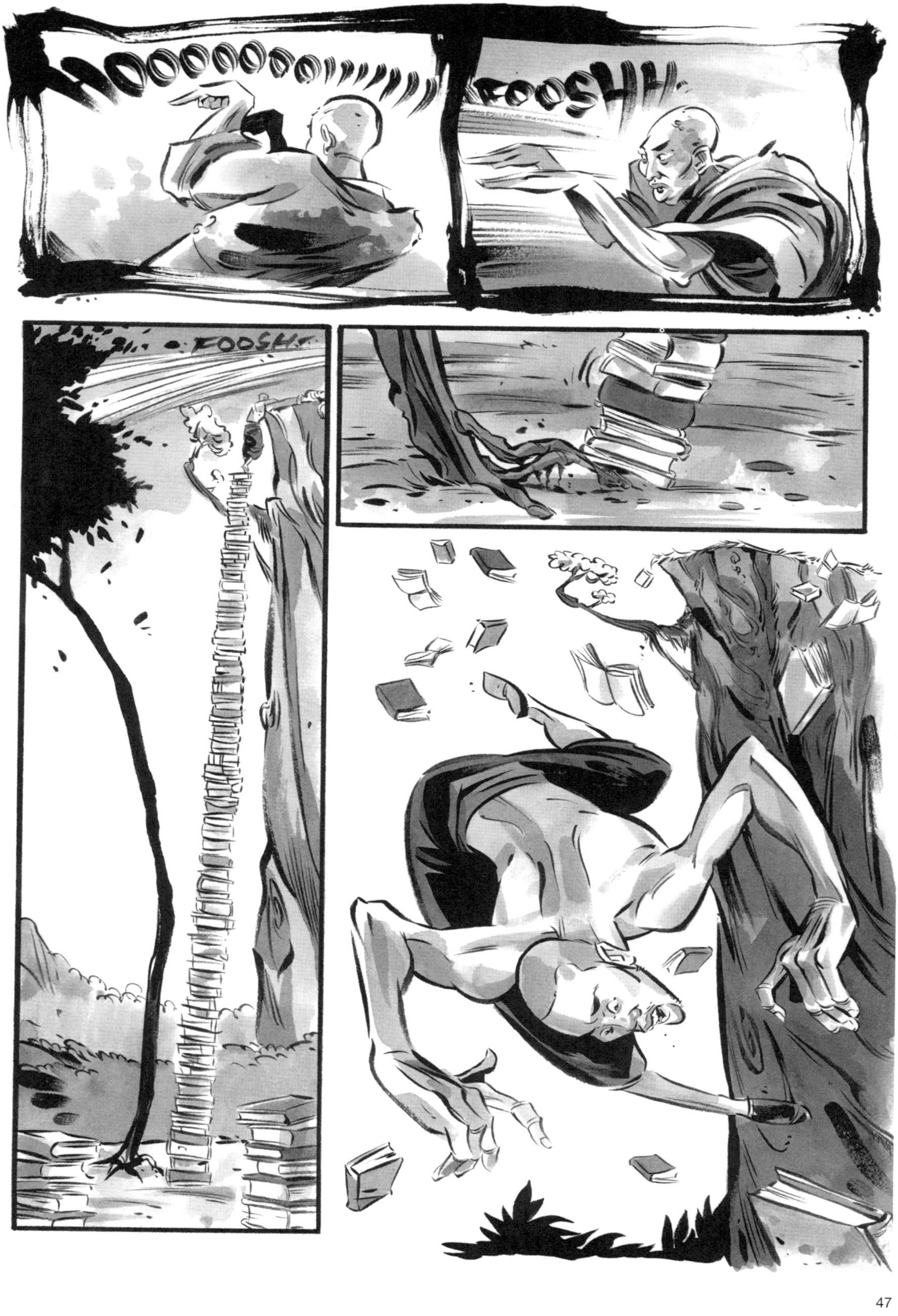
WHOOOOOOOOOOOM
FOOSH
FOOSH

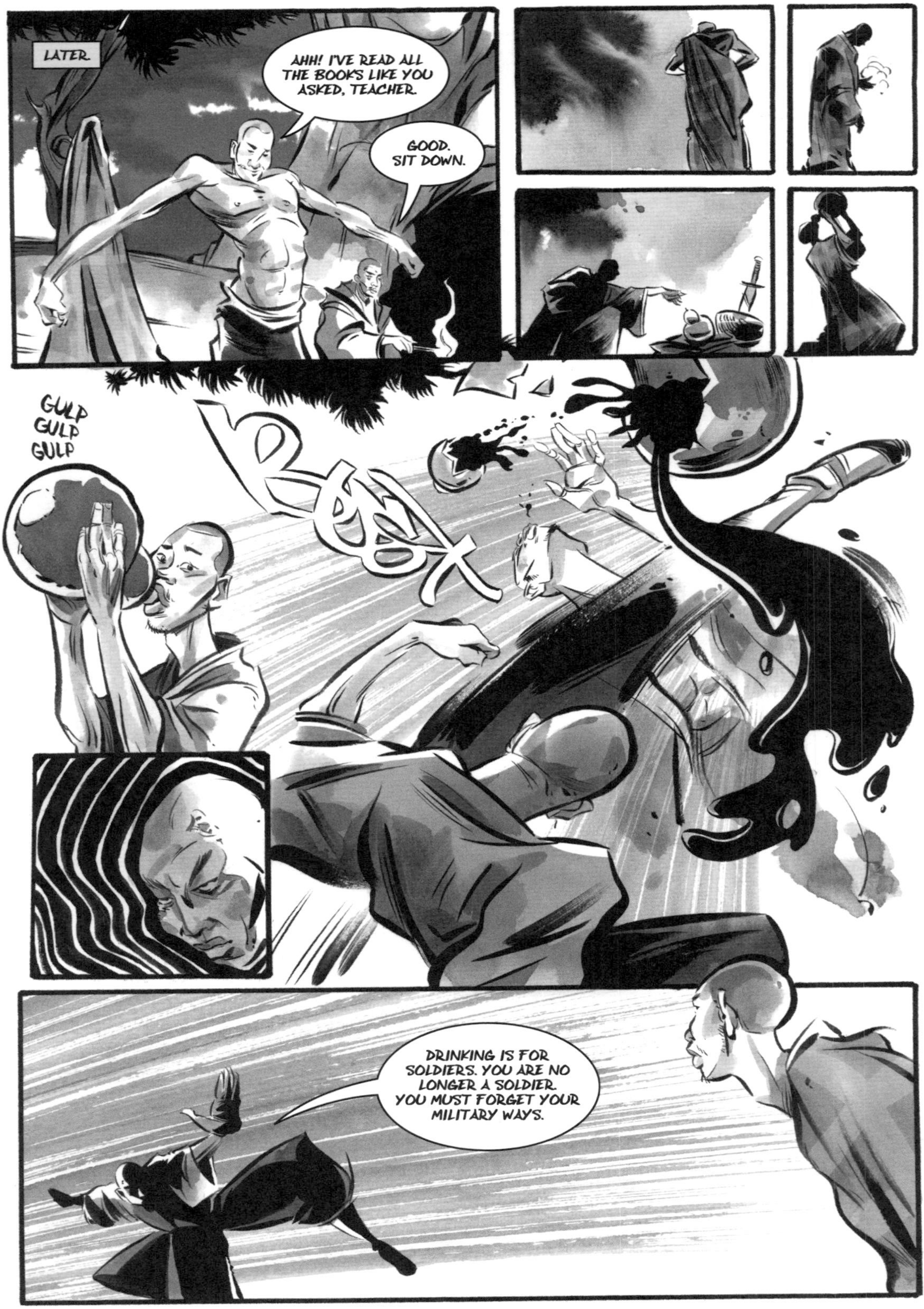
LATER.
AHH! I'VE READ ALL THE BOOKS LIKE YOU ASKED, TEACHER.
GOOD. SIT DOWN.
GULP GULP GULP
DRINKING IS FOR SOLDIERS. YOU ARE NO LONGER A SOLDIER. YOU MUST FORGET YOUR MILITARY WAYS.

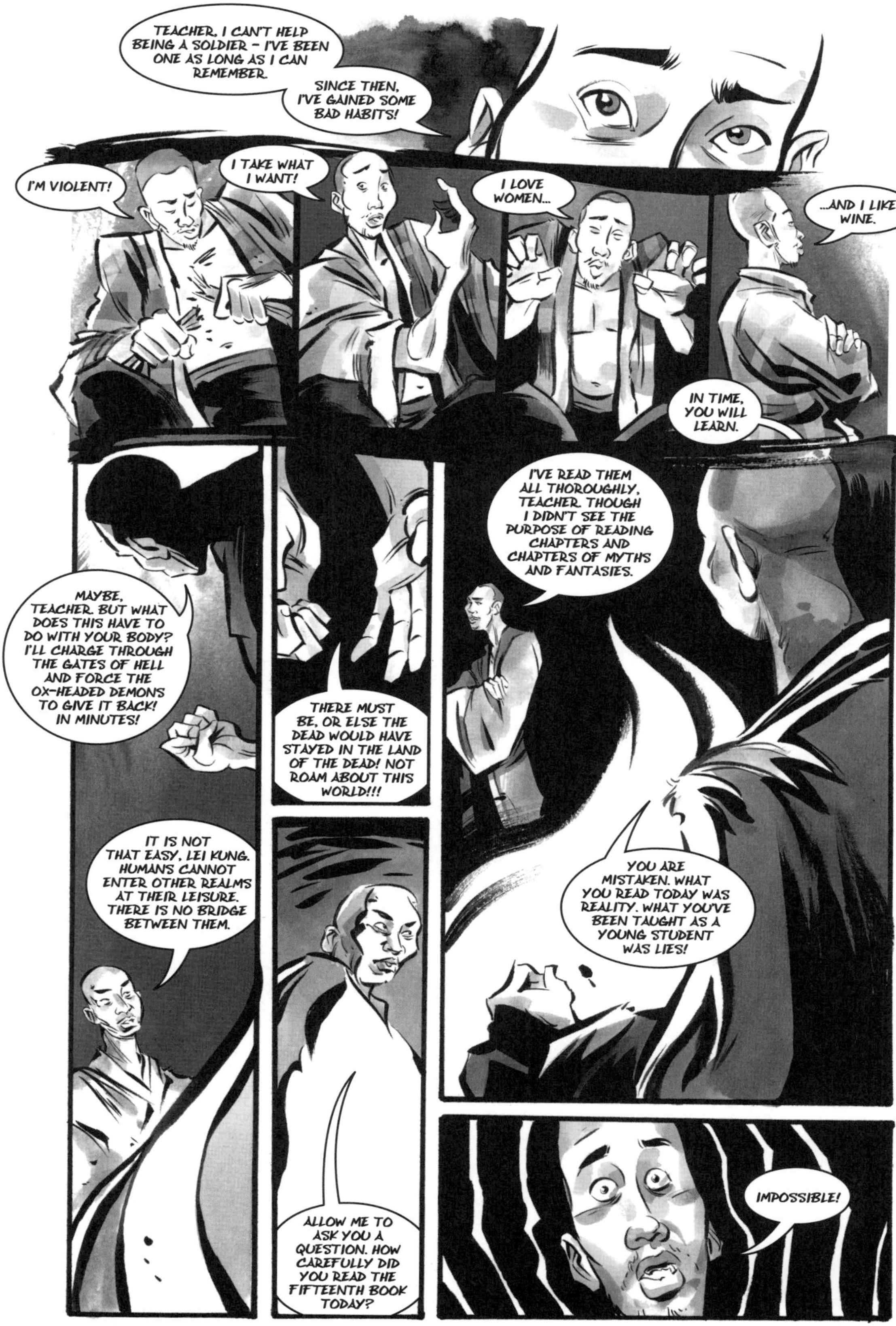
TEACHER. I CAN'T HELP BEING A SOLDIER - I'VE BEEN ONE AS LONG AS I CAN REMEMBER.
SINCE THEN, I'VE GAINED SOME BAD HABITS!
I'M VIOLENT!
I TAKE WHAT I WANT!
I LOVE WOMEN...
...AND I LIKE WINE.
IN TIME, YOU WILL LEARN.
MAYBE, TEACHER. BUT WHAT DOES THIS HAVE TO DO WITH YOUR BODY? I'LL CHARGE THROUGH THE GATES OF HELL AND FORCE THE OX-HEADED DEMONS TO GIVE IT BACK! IN MINUTES!
IT IS NOT THAT EASY, LEI KUNG. HUMANS CANNOT ENTER OTHER REALMS AT THEIR LEISURE. THERE IS NO BRIDGE BETWEEN THEM.
THERE MUST BE, OR ELSE THE DEAD WOULD HAVE STAYED IN THE LAND OF THE DEAD! NOT ROAM ABOUT THIS WORLD!!!
ALLOW ME TO ASK YOU A QUESTION. HOW CAREFULLY DID YOU READ THE FIFTEENTH BOOK TODAY?
I'VE READ THEM ALL THOROUGHLY, TEACHER. THOUGH I DIDN'T SEE THE PURPOSE OF READING CHAPTERS AND CHAPTERS OF MYTHS AND FANTASIES.
YOU ARE MISTAKEN. WHAT YOU READ TODAY WAS REALITY. WHAT YOU'VE BEEN TAUGHT AS A YOUNG STUDENT WAS LIES!
IMPOSSIBLE!

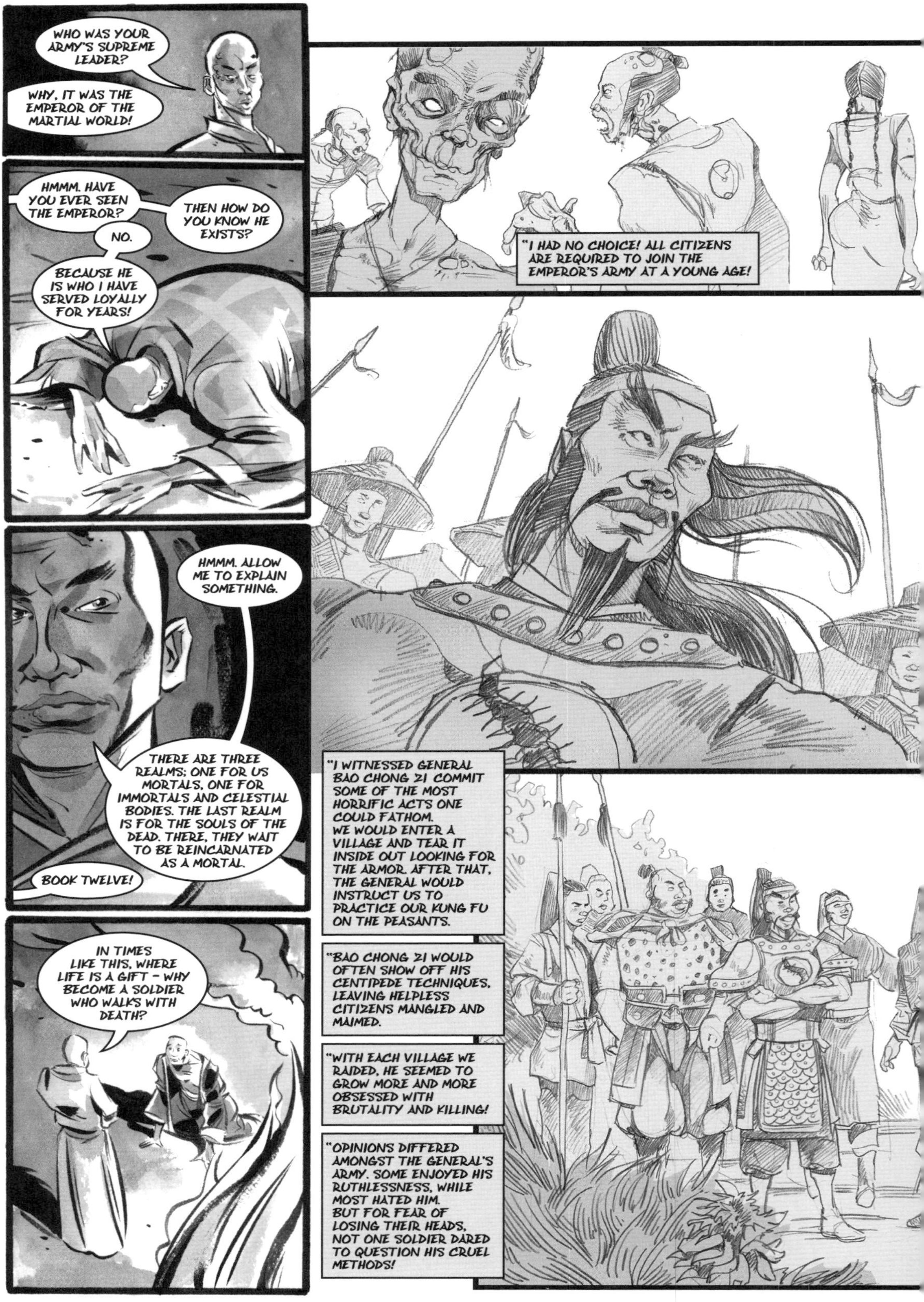
WHO WAS YOUR ARMY'S SUPREME LEADER?
WHY, IT WAS THE EMPEROR OF THE MARTIAL WORLD!
"I HAD NO CHOICE! ALL CITIZENS ARE REQUIRED TO JOIN THE EMPEROR'S ARMY AT A YOUNG AGE!
HMMM. HAVE YOU EVER SEEN THE EMPEROR?
NO.
THEN HOW DO YOU KNOW HE EXISTS?
BECAUSE HE IS WHO I HAVE SERVED LOYALLY FOR YEARS!
HMMM. ALLOW ME TO EXPLAIN SOMETHING.
THERE ARE THREE REALMS; ONE FOR US MORTALS, ONE FOR IMMORTALS AND CELESTIAL BODIES. THE LAST REALM IS FOR THE SOULS OF THE DEAD. THERE, THEY WAIT TO BE REINCARNATED AS A MORTAL.
BOOK TWELVE!
IN TIMES LIKE THIS, WHERE LIFE IS A GIFT - WHY BECOME A SOLDIER WHO WALKS WITH DEATH?
"I WITNESSED GENERAL BAO CHONG ZI COMMIT SOME OF THE MOST HORRIFIC ACTS ONE COULD FATHOM. WE WOULD ENTER A VILLAGE AND TEAR IT INSIDE OUT LOOKING FOR THE ARMOR. AFTER THAT, THE GENERAL WOULD INSTRUCT US TO PRACTICE OUR KUNG FU ON THE PEASANTS.
"BAO CHONG ZI WOULD OFTEN SHOW OFF HIS CENTIPEDE TECHNIQUES, LEAVING HELPLESS CITIZENS MANGLED AND MAIMED.
"WITH EACH VILLAGE WE RAIDED, HE SEEMED TO GROW MORE AND MORE OBSESSED WITH BRUTALITY AND KILLING!
"OPINIONS DIFFERED AMONGST THE GENERAL'S ARMY. SOME ENJOYED HIS RUTHLESSNESS, WHILE MOST HATED HIM. BUT FOR FEAR OF LOSING THEIR HEADS, NOT ONE SOLDIER DARED TO QUESTION HIS CRUEL METHODS!

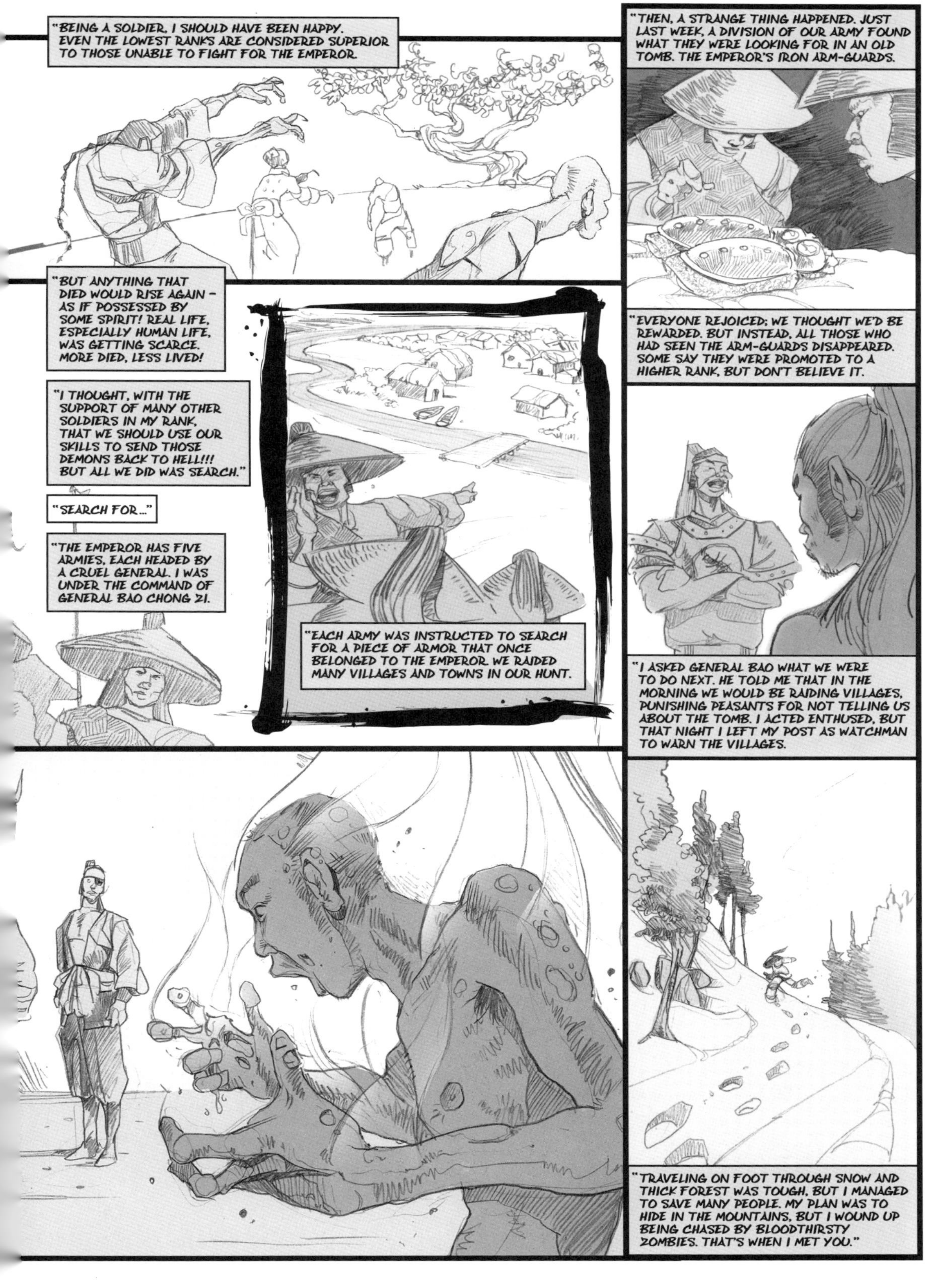
"BEING A SOLDIER, I SHOULD HAVE BEEN HAPPY. EVEN THE LOWEST RANKS ARE CONSIDERED SUPERIOR TO THOSE UNABLE TO FIGHT FOR THE EMPEROR.
"BUT ANYTHING THAT DIED WOULD RISE AGAIN – AS IF POSSESSED BY SOME SPIRIT! REAL LIFE, ESPECIALLY HUMAN LIFE, WAS GETTING SCARCE. MORE DIED, LESS LIVED!
"I THOUGHT, WITH THE SUPPORT OF MANY OTHER SOLDIERS IN MY RANK, THAT WE SHOULD USE OUR SKILLS TO SEND THOSE DEMONS BACK TO HELL!!! BUT ALL WE DID WAS SEARCH."
"SEARCH FOR..."
"THE EMPEROR HAS FIVE ARMIES, EACH HEADED BY A CRUEL GENERAL. I WAS UNDER THE COMMAND OF GENERAL BAO CHONG ZI.
"EACH ARMY WAS INSTRUCTED TO SEARCH FOR A PIECE OF ARMOR THAT ONCE BELONGED TO THE EMPEROR. WE RAIDED MANY VILLAGES AND TOWNS IN OUR HUNT.
"THEN, A STRANGE THING HAPPENED. JUST LAST WEEK, A DIVISION OF OUR ARMY FOUND WHAT THEY WERE LOOKING FOR IN AN OLD TOMB. THE EMPEROR'S IRON ARM-GUARDS.
"EVERYONE REJOICED; WE THOUGHT WE'D BE REWARDED. BUT INSTEAD, ALL THOSE WHO HAD SEEN THE ARM-GUARDS DISAPPEARED. SOME SAY THEY WERE PROMOTED TO A HIGHER RANK, BUT DON'T BELIEVE IT.
"I ASKED GENERAL BAO WHAT WE WERE TO DO NEXT. HE TOLD ME THAT IN THE MORNING WE WOULD BE RAIDING VILLAGES, PUNISHING PEASANTS FOR NOT TELLING US ABOUT THE TOMB. I ACTED ENTHUSED, BUT THAT NIGHT I LEFT MY POST AS WATCHMAN TO WARN THE VILLAGES.
"TRAVELING ON FOOT THROUGH SNOW AND THICK FOREST WAS TOUGH, BUT I MANAGED TO SAVE MANY PEOPLE. MY PLAN WAS TO HIDE IN THE MOUNTAINS, BUT I WOUND UP BEING CHASED BY BLOODTHIRSTY ZOMBIES. THAT'S WHEN I MET YOU."

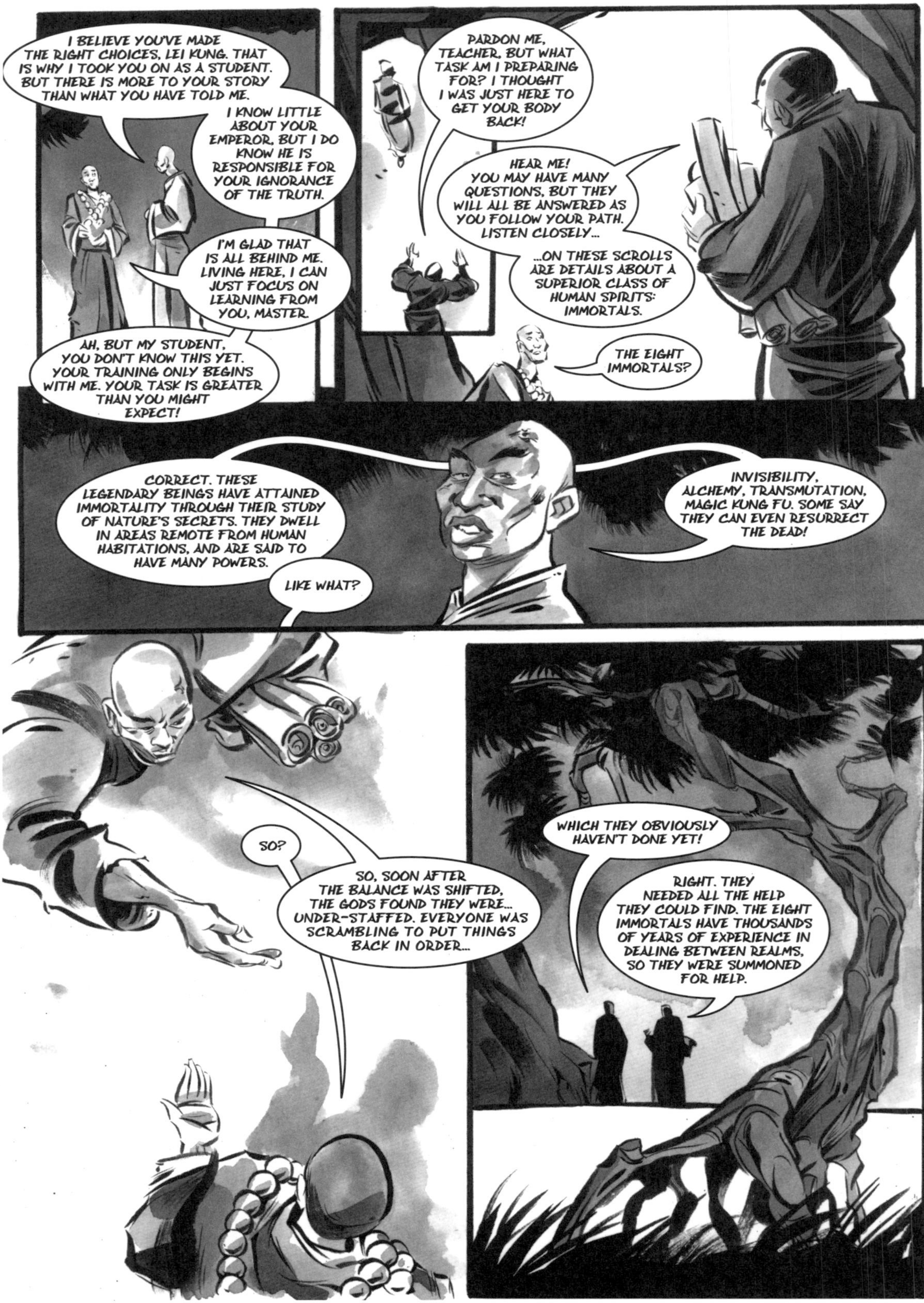
I BELIEVE YOU'VE MADE THE RIGHT CHOICES, LEI KUNG. THAT IS WHY I TOOK YOU ON AS A STUDENT. BUT THERE IS MORE TO YOUR STORY THAN WHAT YOU HAVE TOLD ME.
I KNOW LITTLE ABOUT YOUR EMPEROR, BUT I DO KNOW HE IS RESPONSIBLE FOR YOUR IGNORANCE OF THE TRUTH.
I'M GLAD THAT IS ALL BEHIND ME. LIVING HERE, I CAN JUST FOCUS ON LEARNING FROM YOU, MASTER.
AH, BUT MY STUDENT, YOU DON'T KNOW THIS YET. YOUR TRAINING ONLY BEGINS WITH ME. YOUR TASK IS GREATER THAN YOU MIGHT EXPECT!
PARDON ME, TEACHER, BUT WHAT TASK AM I PREPARING FOR? I THOUGHT I WAS JUST HERE TO GET YOUR BODY BACK!
HEAR ME! YOU MAY HAVE MANY QUESTIONS, BUT THEY WILL ALL BE ANSWERED AS YOU FOLLOW YOUR PATH. LISTEN CLOSELY...
...ON THESE SCROLLS ARE DETAILS ABOUT A SUPERIOR CLASS OF HUMAN SPIRITS: IMMORTALS.
THE EIGHT IMMORTALS?
CORRECT. THESE LEGENDARY BEINGS HAVE ATTAINED IMMORTALITY THROUGH THEIR STUDY OF NATURE'S SECRETS. THEY DWELL IN AREAS REMOTE FROM HUMAN HABITATIONS, AND ARE SAID TO HAVE MANY POWERS.
LIKE WHAT?
INVISIBILITY, ALCHEMY, TRANSMUTATION, MAGIC KUNG FU. SOME SAY THEY CAN EVEN RESURRECT THE DEAD!
SO?
SO, SOON AFTER THE BALANCE WAS SHIFTED, THE GODS FOUND THEY WERE... UNDER-STAFFED. EVERYONE WAS SCRAMBLING TO PUT THINGS BACK IN ORDER...
WHICH THEY OBVIOUSLY HAVEN'T DONE YET!
RIGHT. THEY NEEDED ALL THE HELP THEY COULD FIND. THE EIGHT IMMORTALS HAVE THOUSANDS OF YEARS OF EXPERIENCE IN DEALING BETWEEN REALMS, SO THEY WERE SUMMONED FOR HELP.

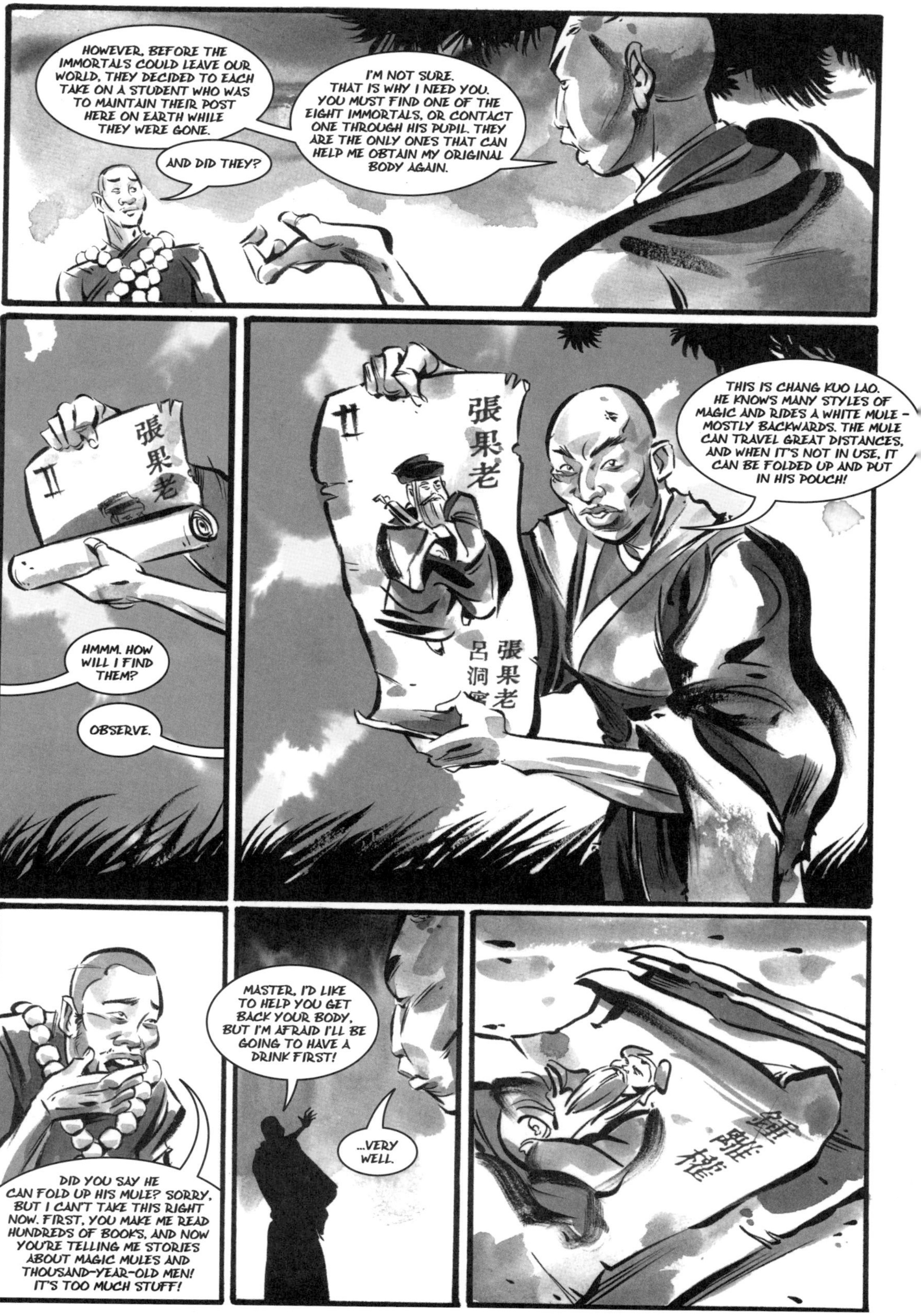
HOWEVER, BEFORE THE IMMORTALS COULD LEAVE OUR WORLD, THEY DECIDED TO EACH TAKE ON A STUDENT WHO WAS TO MAINTAIN THEIR POST HERE ON EARTH WHILE THEY WERE GONE.
AND DID THEY?
I'M NOT SURE. THAT IS WHY I NEED YOU. YOU MUST FIND ONE OF THE EIGHT IMMORTALS, OR CONTACT ONE THROUGH HIS PUPIL. THEY ARE THE ONLY ONES THAT CAN HELP ME OBTAIN MY ORIGINAL BODY AGAIN.
張果老
HMMM. HOW WILL I FIND THEM?
OBSERVE.
張果老
THIS IS CHANG KUO LAO. HE KNOWS MANY STYLES OF MAGIC AND RIDES A WHITE MULE - MOSTLY BACKWARDS. THE MULE CAN TRAVEL GREAT DISTANCES, AND WHEN IT'S NOT IN USE, IT CAN BE FOLDED UP AND PUT IN HIS POUCH!
DID YOU SAY HE CAN FOLD UP HIS MULE? SORRY, BUT I CAN'T TAKE THIS RIGHT NOW. FIRST, YOU MAKE ME READ HUNDREDS OF BOOKS, AND NOW YOU'RE TELLING ME STORIES ABOUT MAGIC MULES AND THOUSAND-YEAR-OLD MEN! IT'S TOO MUCH STUFF!
MASTER, I'D LIKE TO HELP YOU GET BACK YOUR BODY, BUT I'M AFRAID I'LL BE GOING TO HAVE A DRINK FIRST!
...VERY WELL.

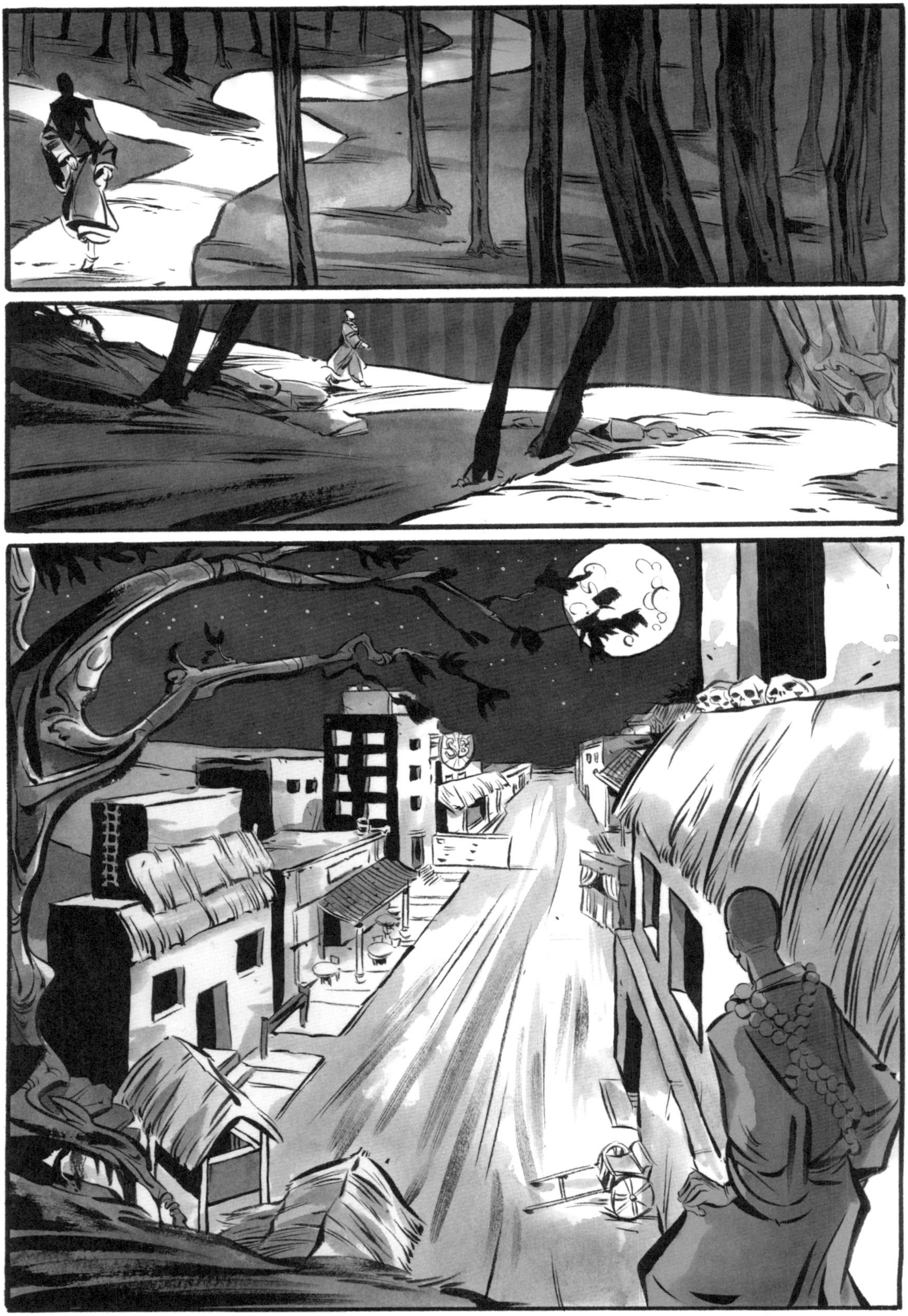

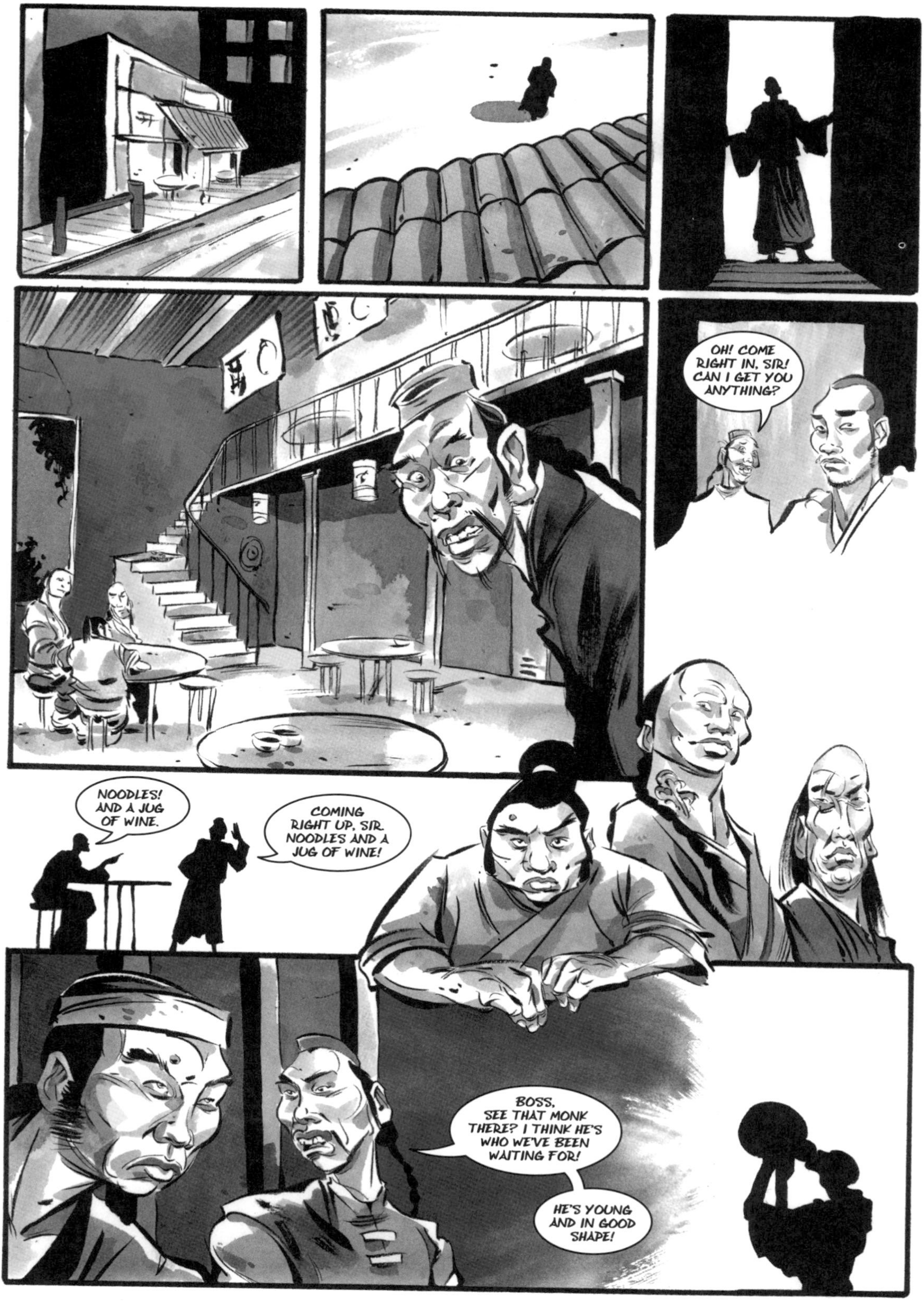
OH! COME RIGHT IN, SIR! CAN I GET YOU ANYTHING?
NOODLES! AND A JUG OF WINE.
COMING RIGHT UP, SIR. NOODLES AND A JUG OF WINE!
BOSS, SEE THAT MONK THERE? I THINK HE'S WHO WE'VE BEEN WAITING FOR!
HE'S YOUNG AND IN GOOD SHAPE!

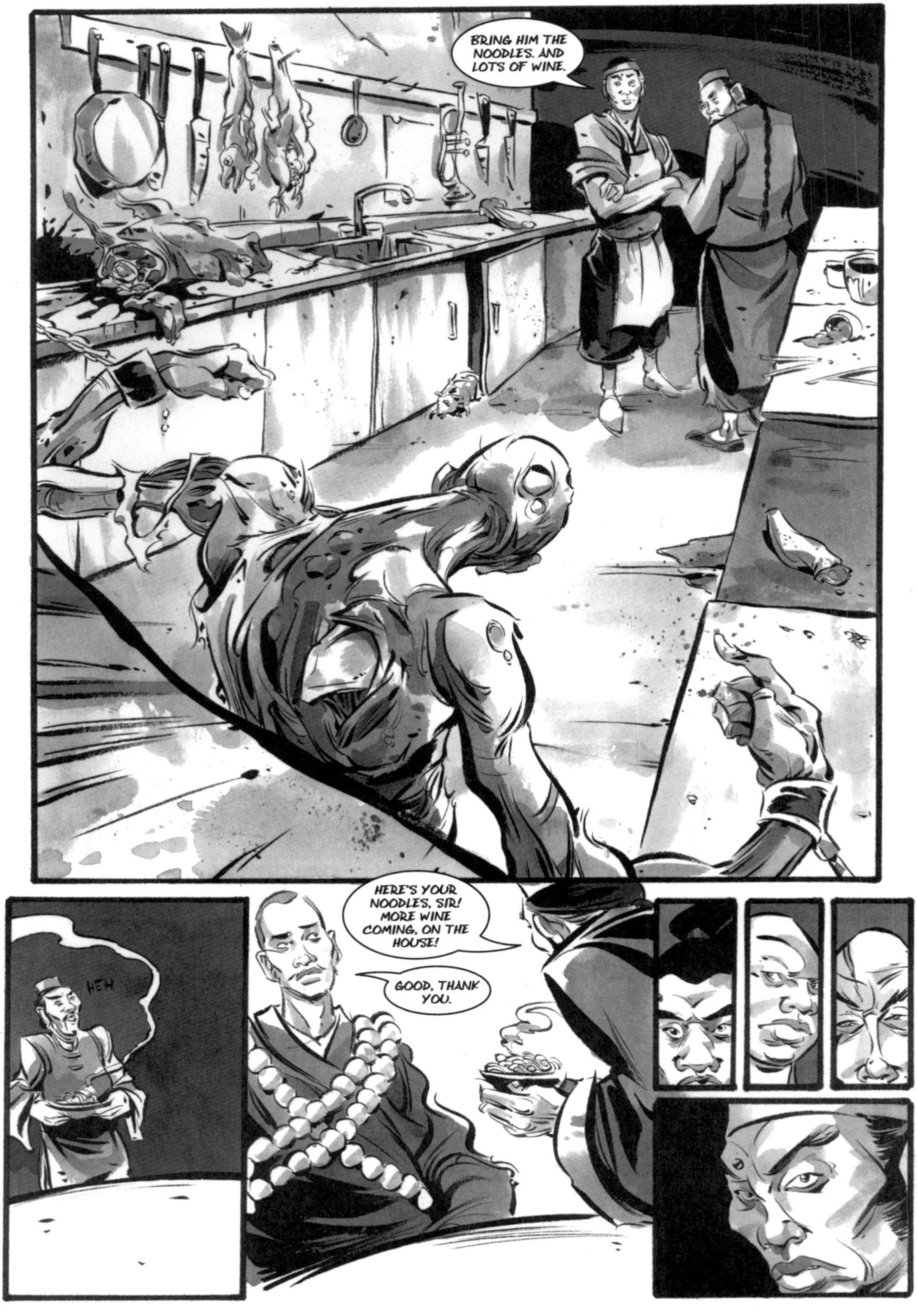
BRING HIM THE NOODLES. AND LOTS OF WINE.
HEH
HERE'S YOUR NOODLES, SIR! MORE WINE COMING, ON THE HOUSE!
GOOD, THANK YOU.

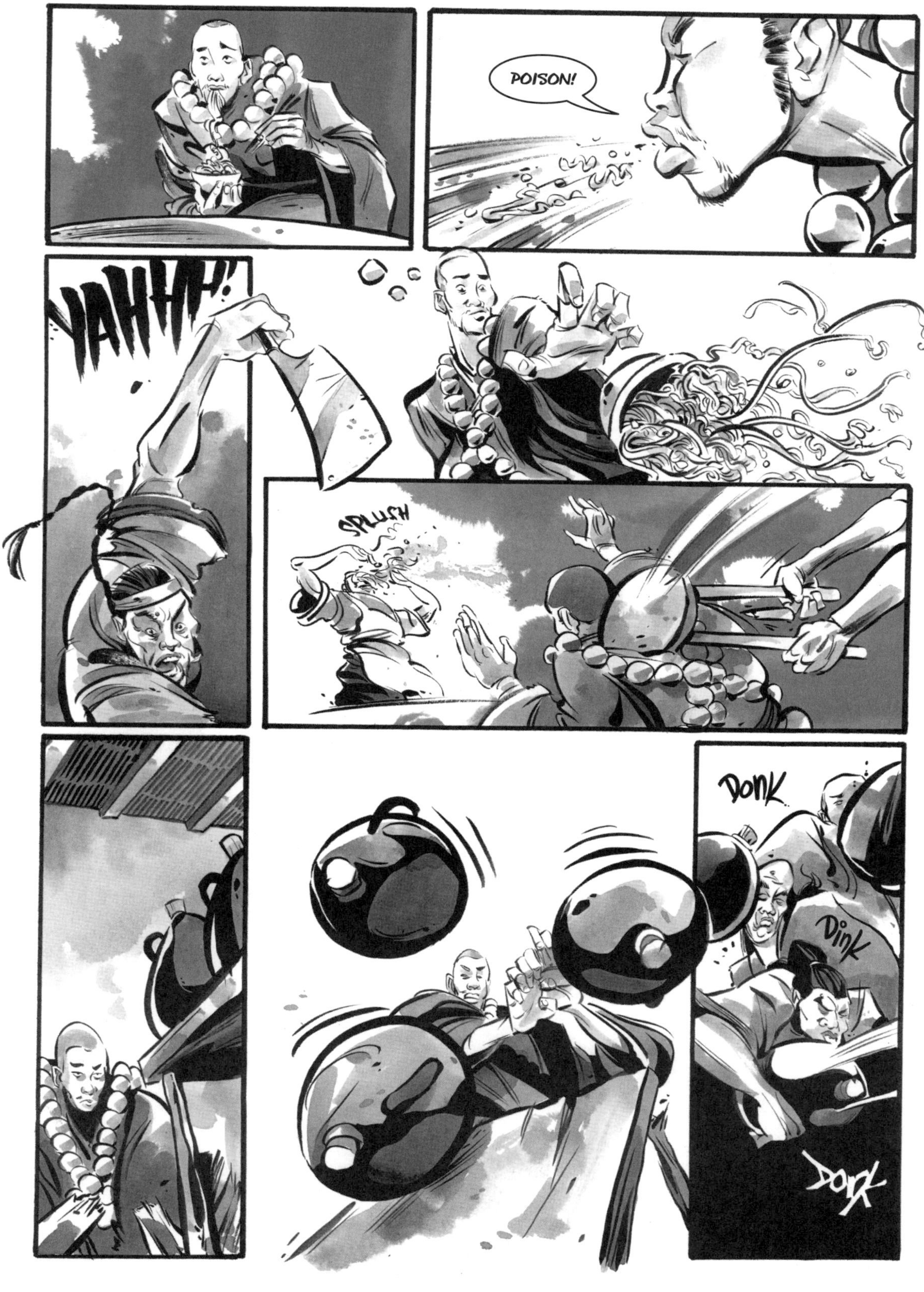
POISON!
YAHHH!
SPLUSH
DONK
DINK
DONK

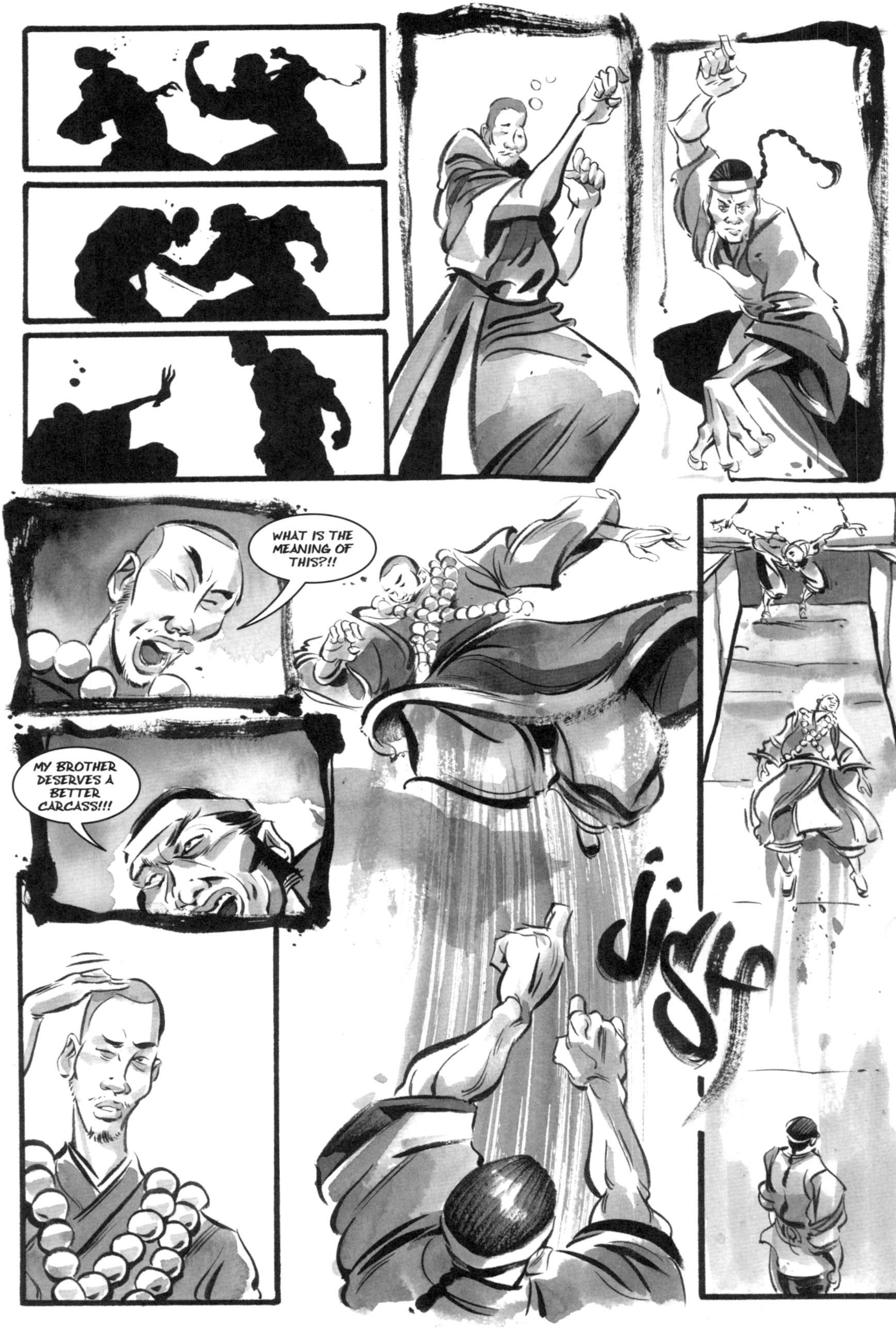
WHAT IS THE MEANING OF THIS?!!
MY BROTHER DESERVES A BETTER CARCASS!!!

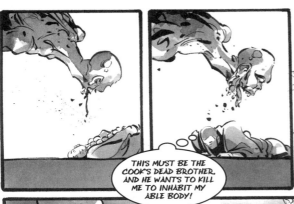

THIS MUST BE THE COOK'S DEAD BROTHER, AND HE WANTS TO KILL ME TO INHABIT MY ABLE BODY!

SCUFF

SCUFF

SCUFF

DINK

CHOK

SNAP

HIC

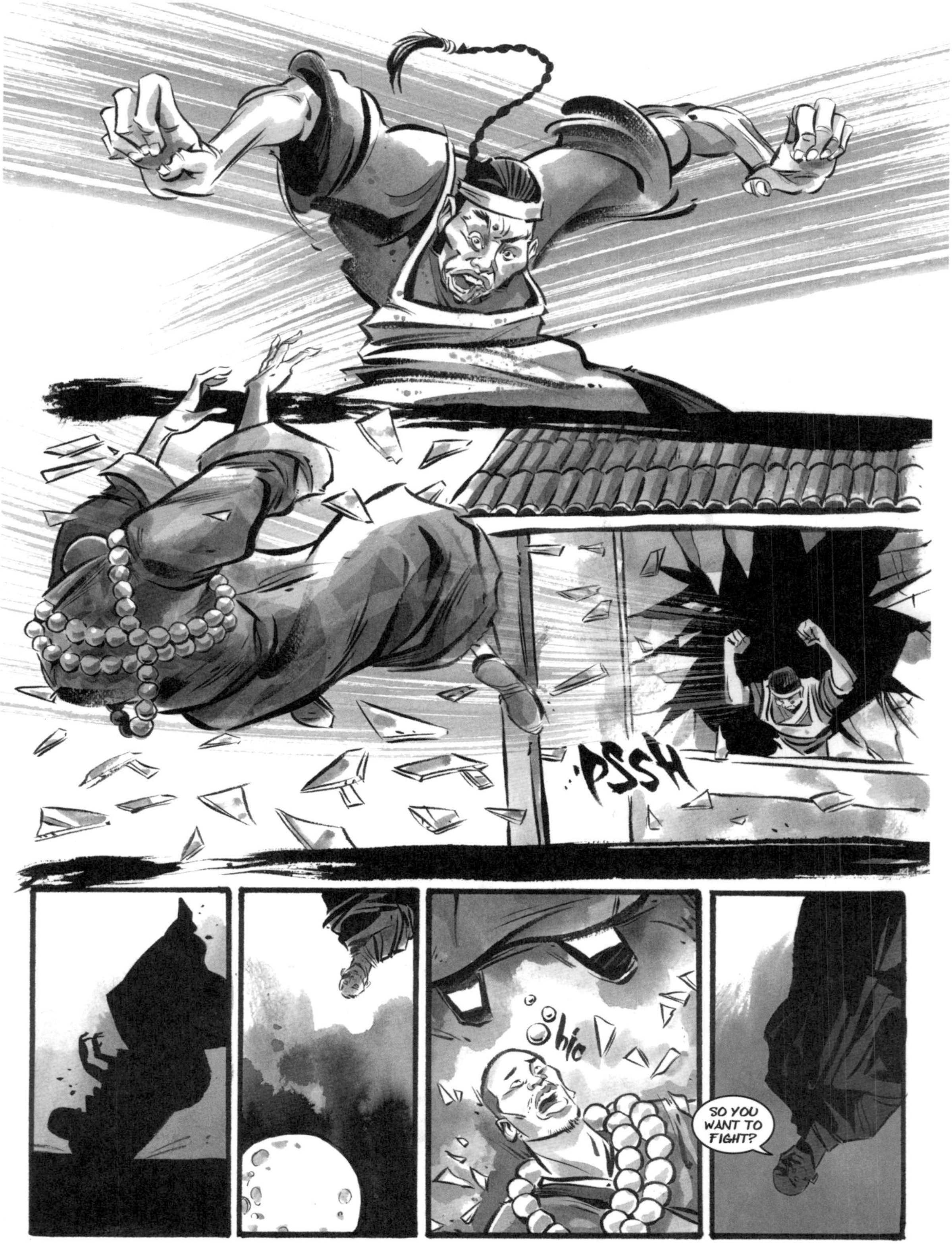
PSSH
hic
SO YOU WANT TO FIGHT?

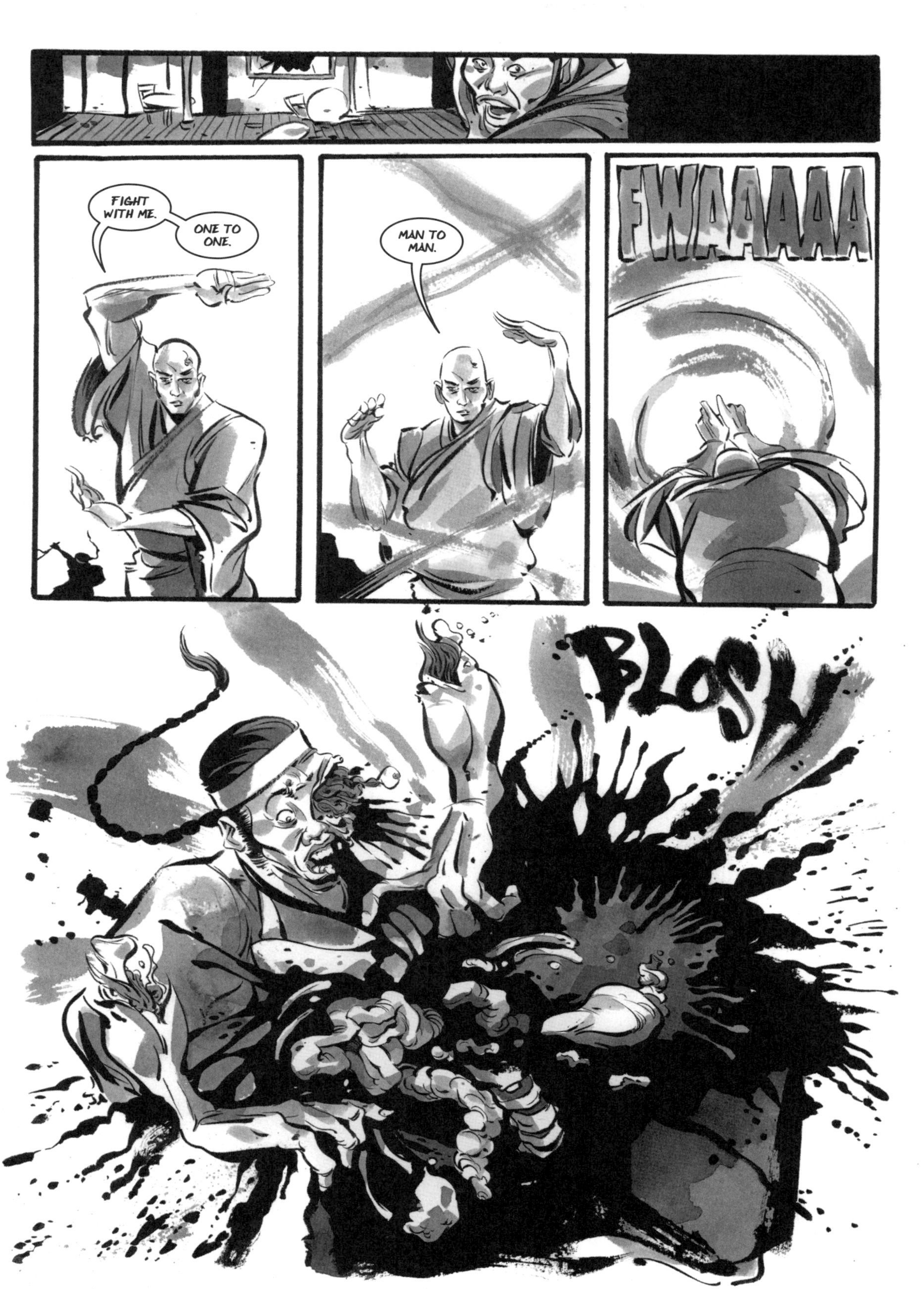
FIGHT WITH ME.
ONE TO ONE.
MAN TO MAN.
FWAAAAA
BLOSH

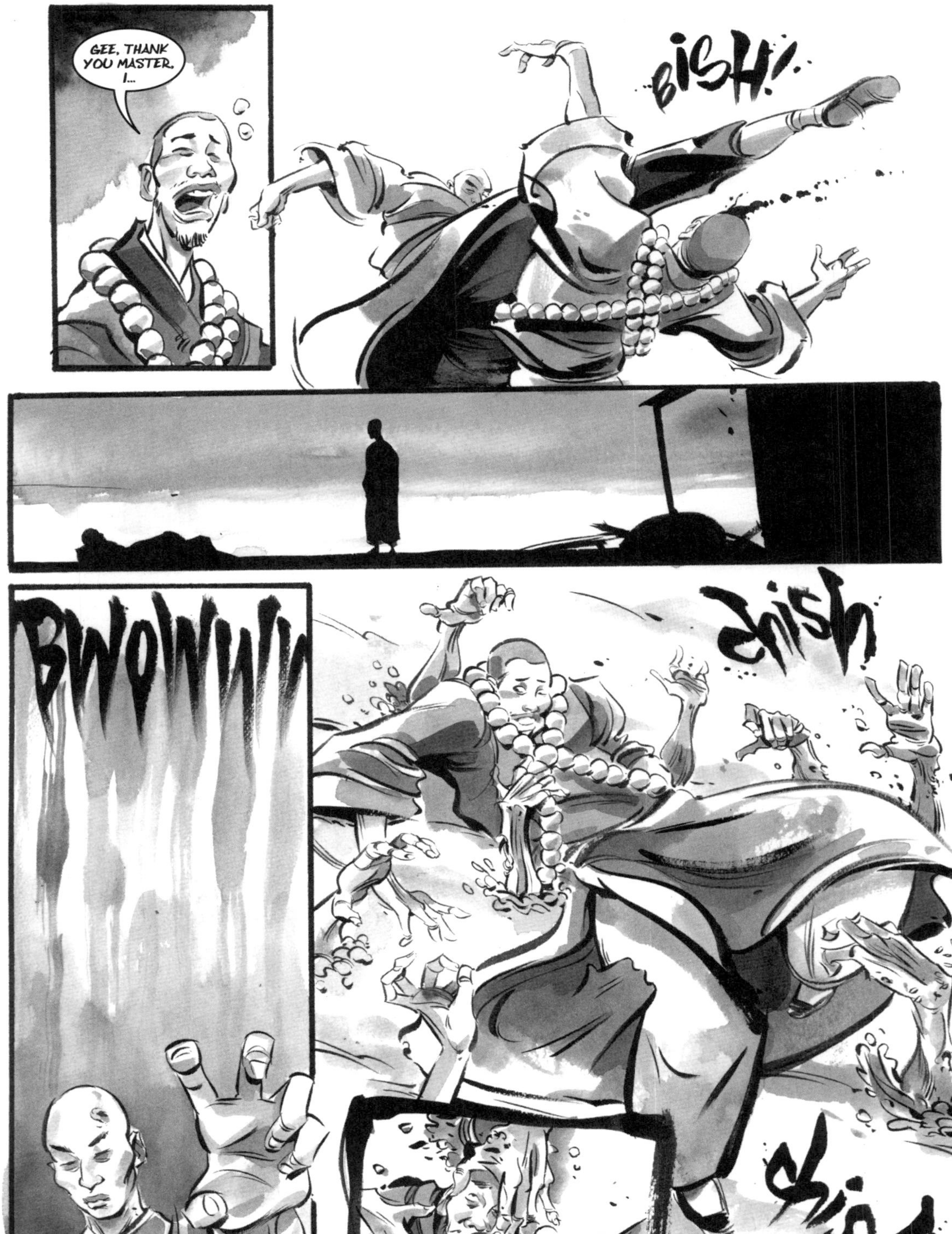
GEE, THANK YOU MASTER, I...
BISH!
BWOWWW
CHISH
CHISH

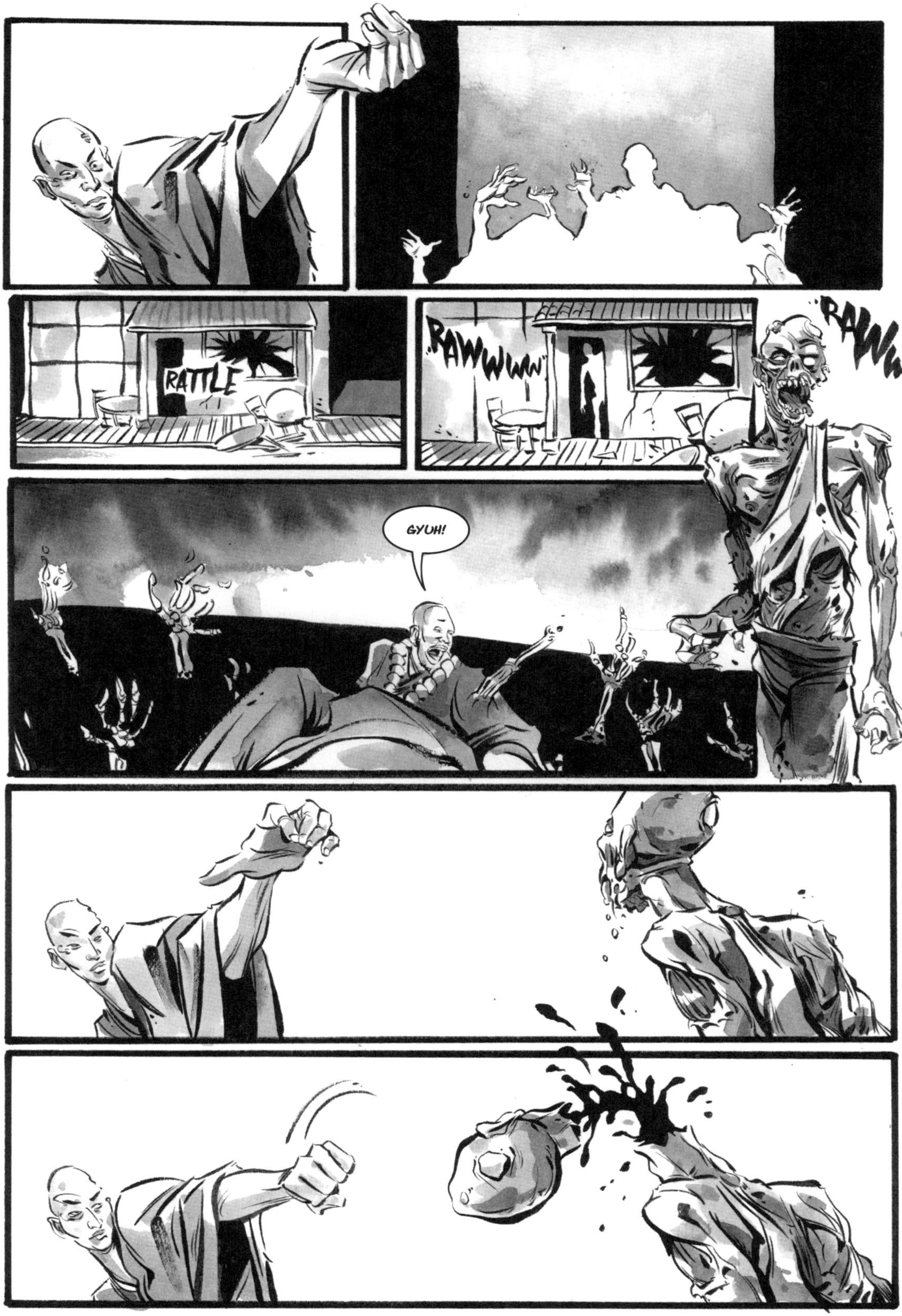
RATTLE
RAWWWWW
RAWW
GYUH!

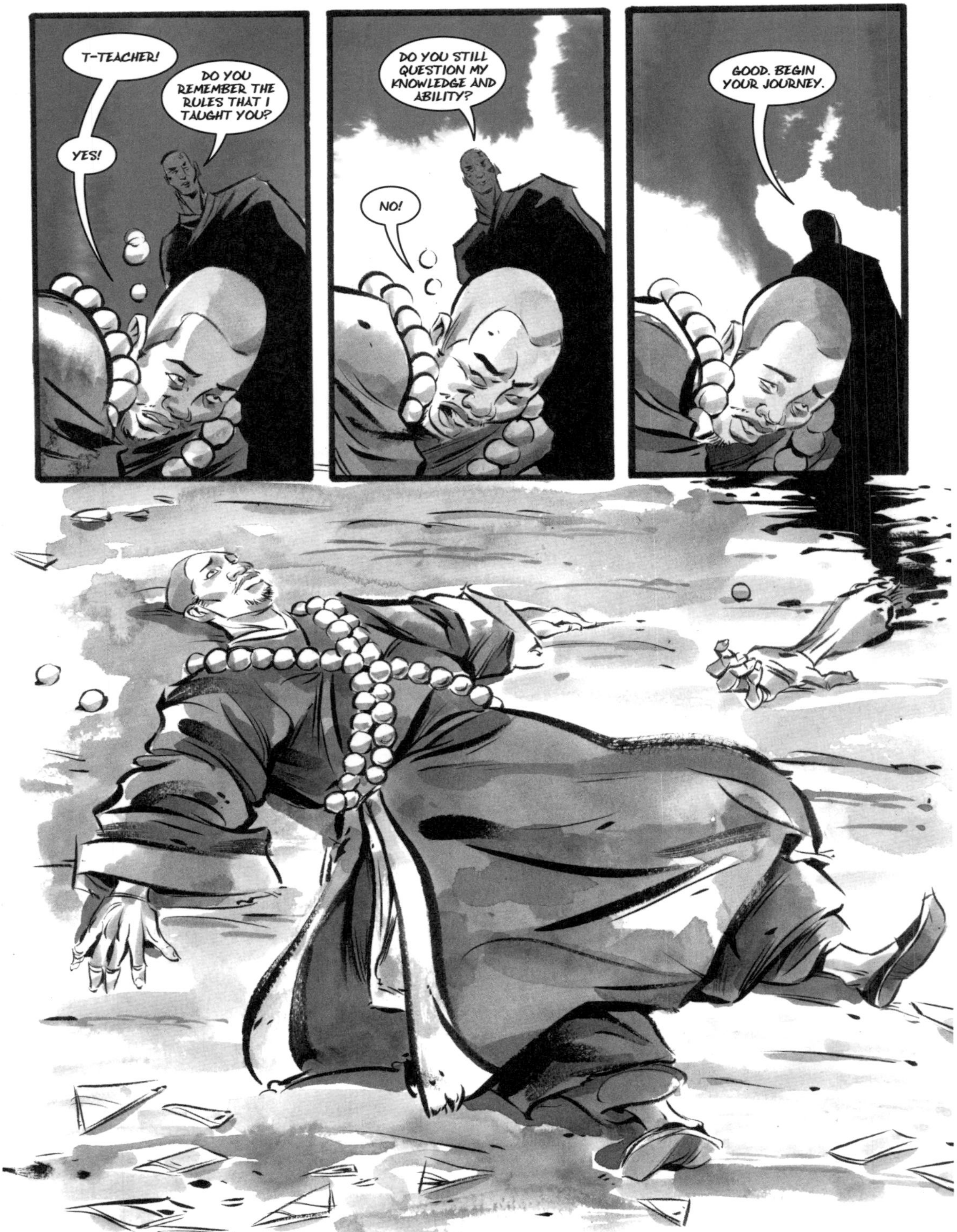
T-TEACHER!
DO YOU REMEMBER THE RULES THAT I TAUGHT YOU?
YES!
DO YOU STILL QUESTION MY KNOWLEDGE AND ABILITY?
NO!
GOOD. BEGIN YOUR JOURNEY.

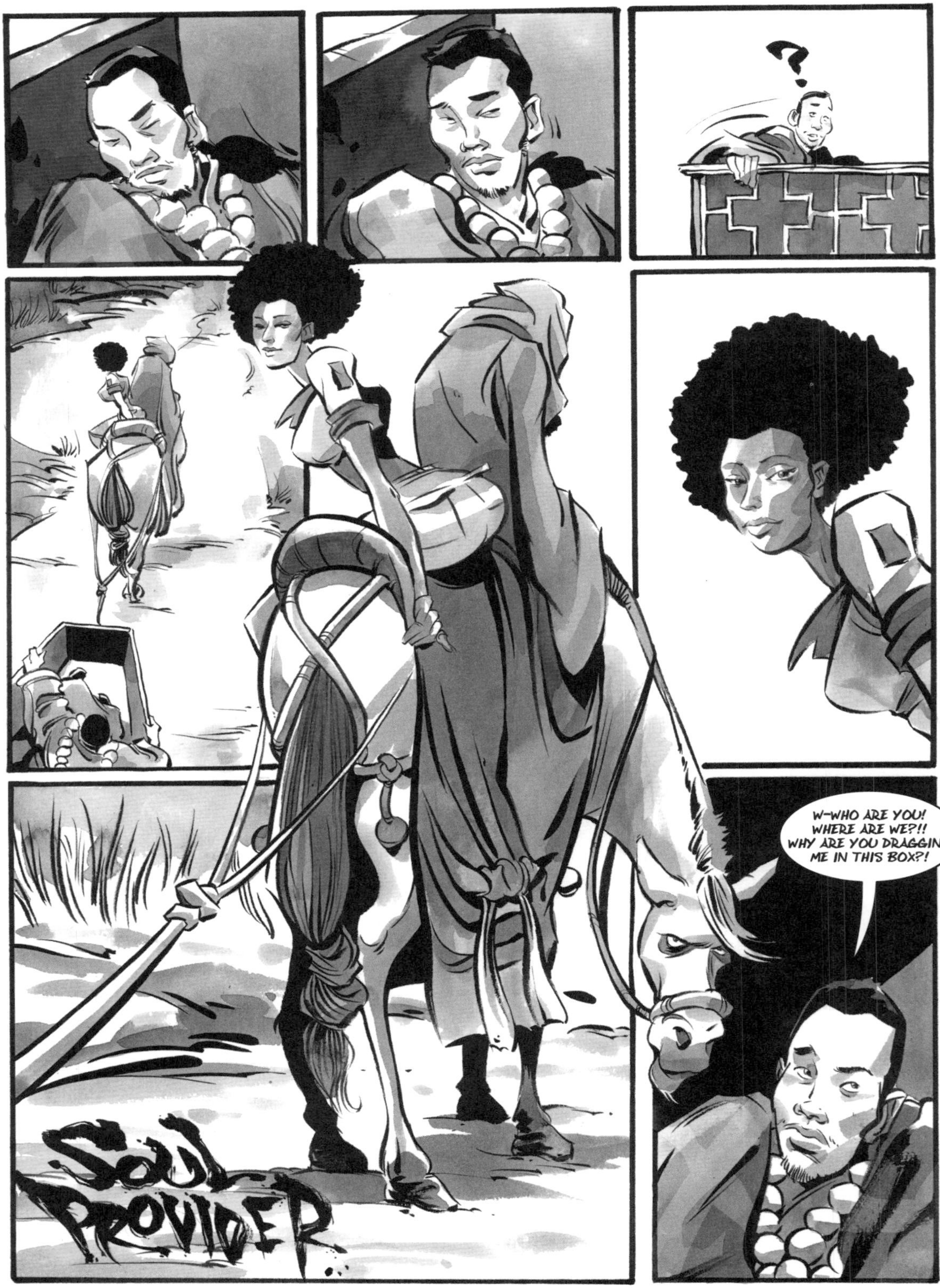
?
W-WHO ARE YOU!
WHERE ARE WE?!!
WHY ARE YOU DRAGGING ME IN THIS BOX?!
SOUL PROVIDER

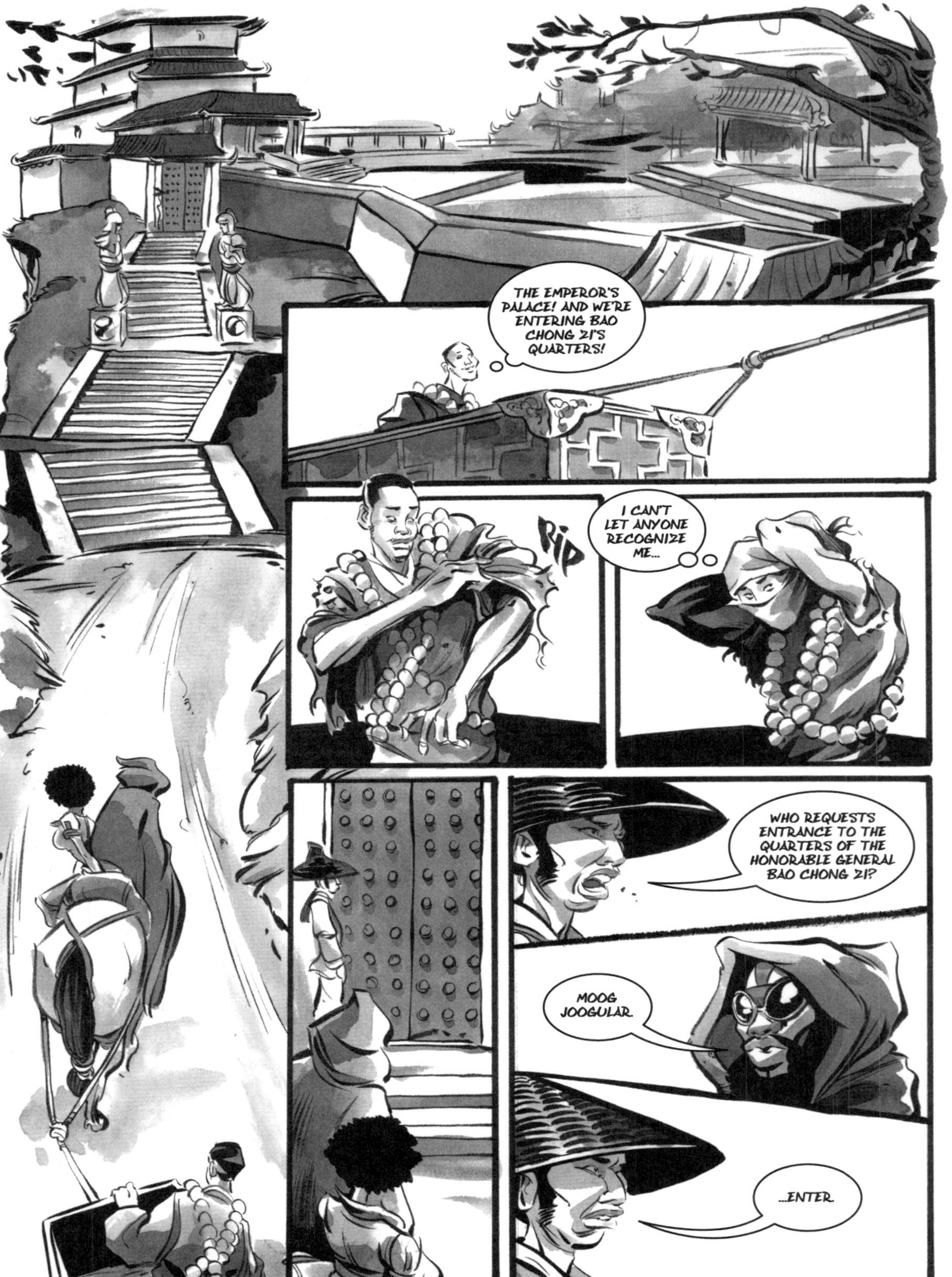
THE EMPEROR'S PALACE! AND WE'RE ENTERING BAO CHONG ZI'S QUARTERS!
RIP
I CAN'T LET ANYONE RECOGNIZE ME...
WHO REQUESTS ENTRANCE TO THE QUARTERS OF THE HONORABLE GENERAL BAO CHONG ZI?
MOOG JOOGULAR.
...ENTER.

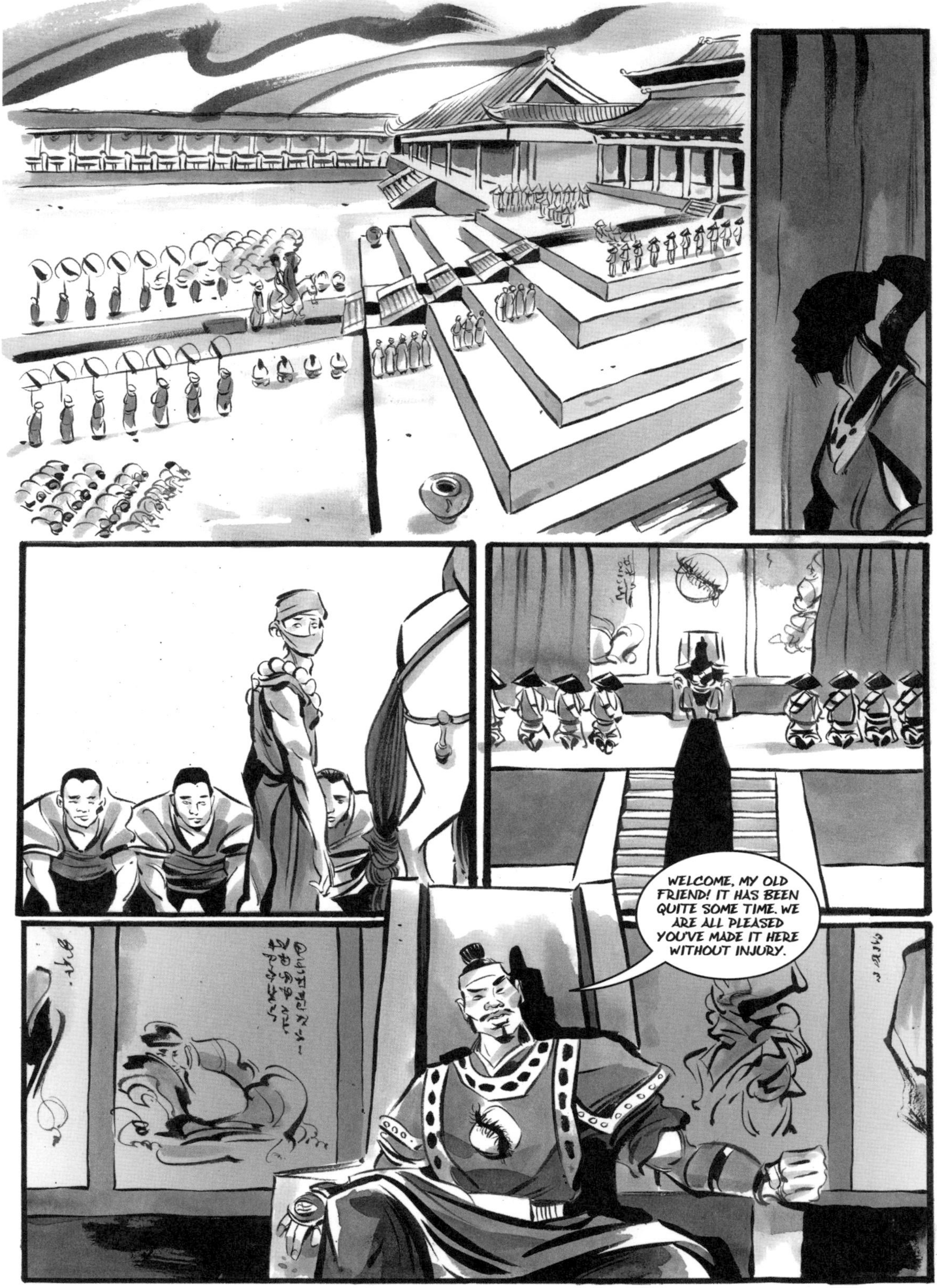
WELCOME, MY OLD FRIEND! IT HAS BEEN QUITE SOME TIME. WE ARE ALL PLEASED YOU'VE MADE IT HERE WITHOUT INJURY.

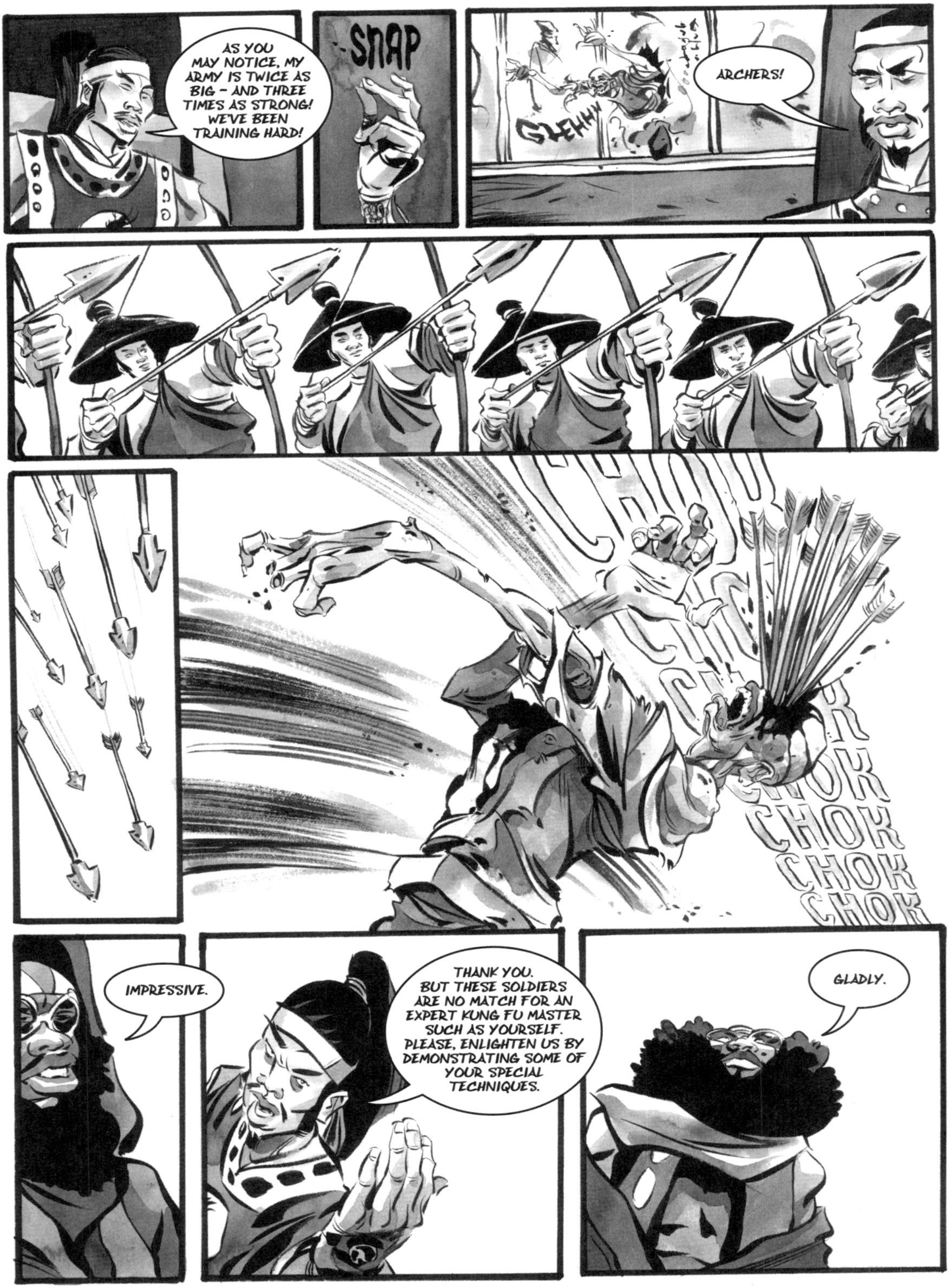
AS YOU MAY NOTICE, MY ARMY IS TWICE AS BIG - AND THREE TIMES AS STRONG! WE'VE BEEN TRAINING HARD!
SNAP
ARCHERS!
GLEHHH
CHOK CHOK CHOK CHOK CHOK
IMPRESSIVE.
THANK YOU. BUT THESE SOLDIERS ARE NO MATCH FOR AN EXPERT KUNG FU MASTER SUCH AS YOURSELF. PLEASE, ENLIGHTEN US BY DEMONSTRATING SOME OF YOUR SPECIAL TECHNIQUES.
GLADLY.

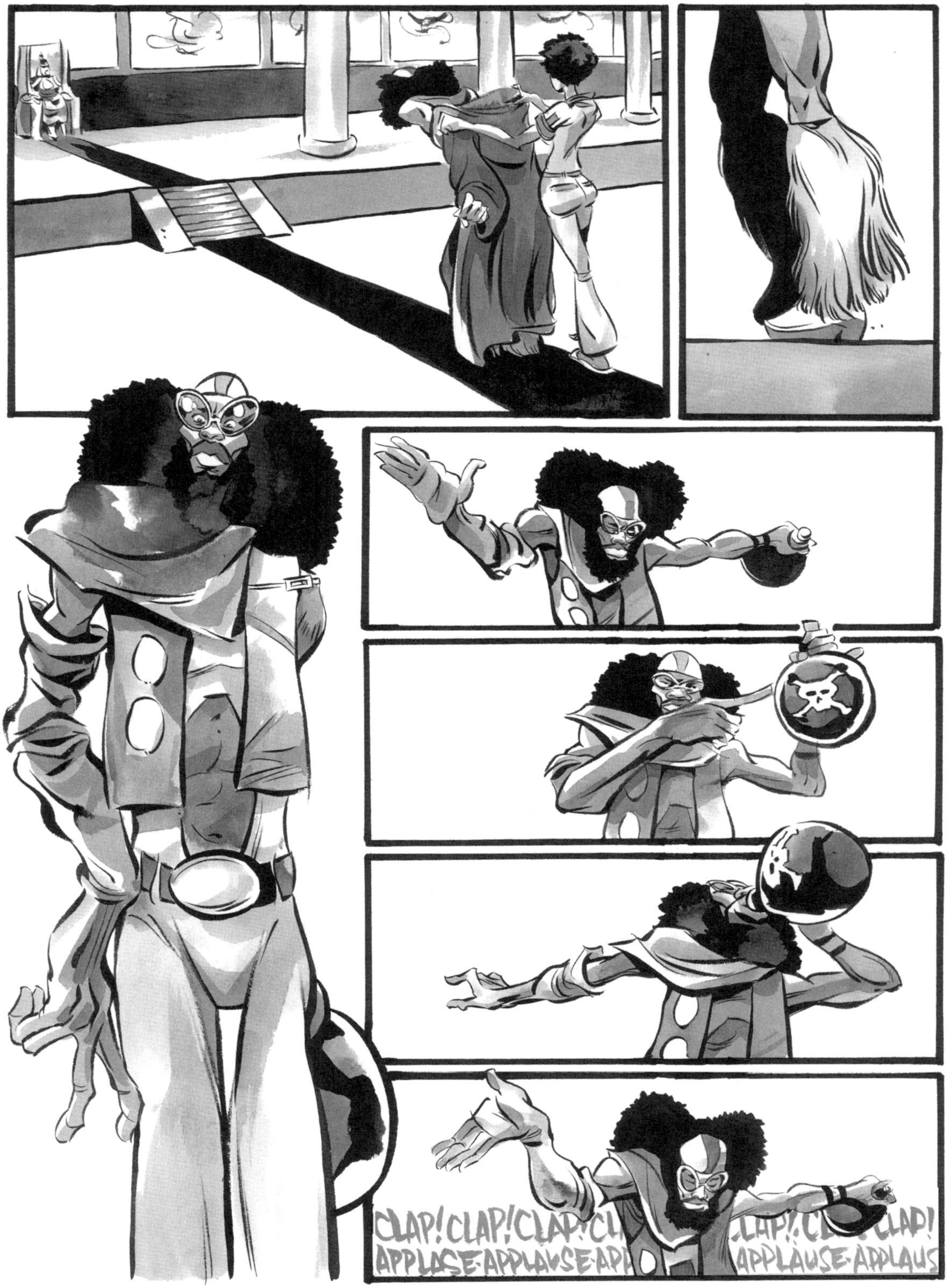
CLAP! CLAP! CLAP!
APPLAUSE APPLAUSE

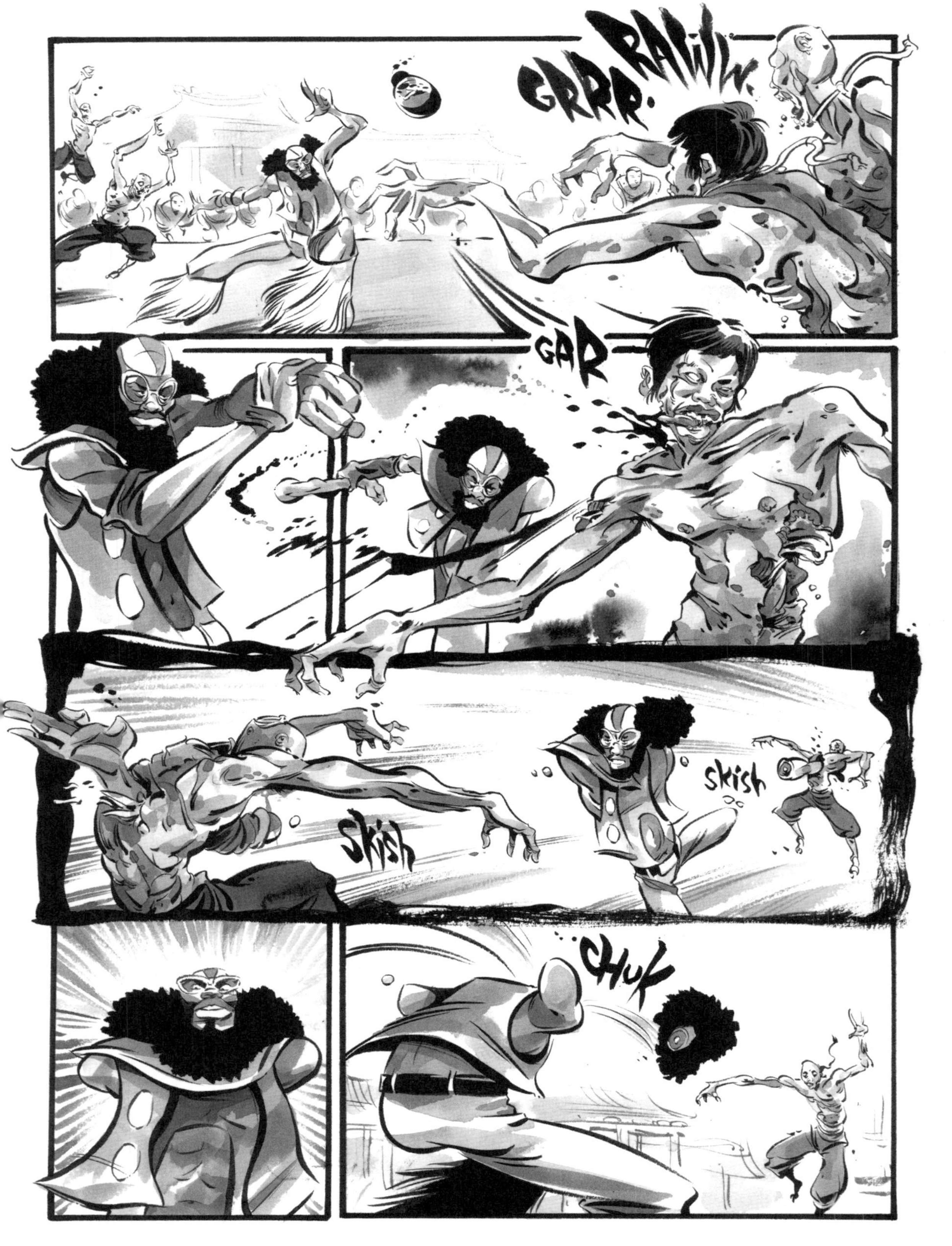
GRRR. RAAWW.
GAR
SKISH
SKISH
CHUK

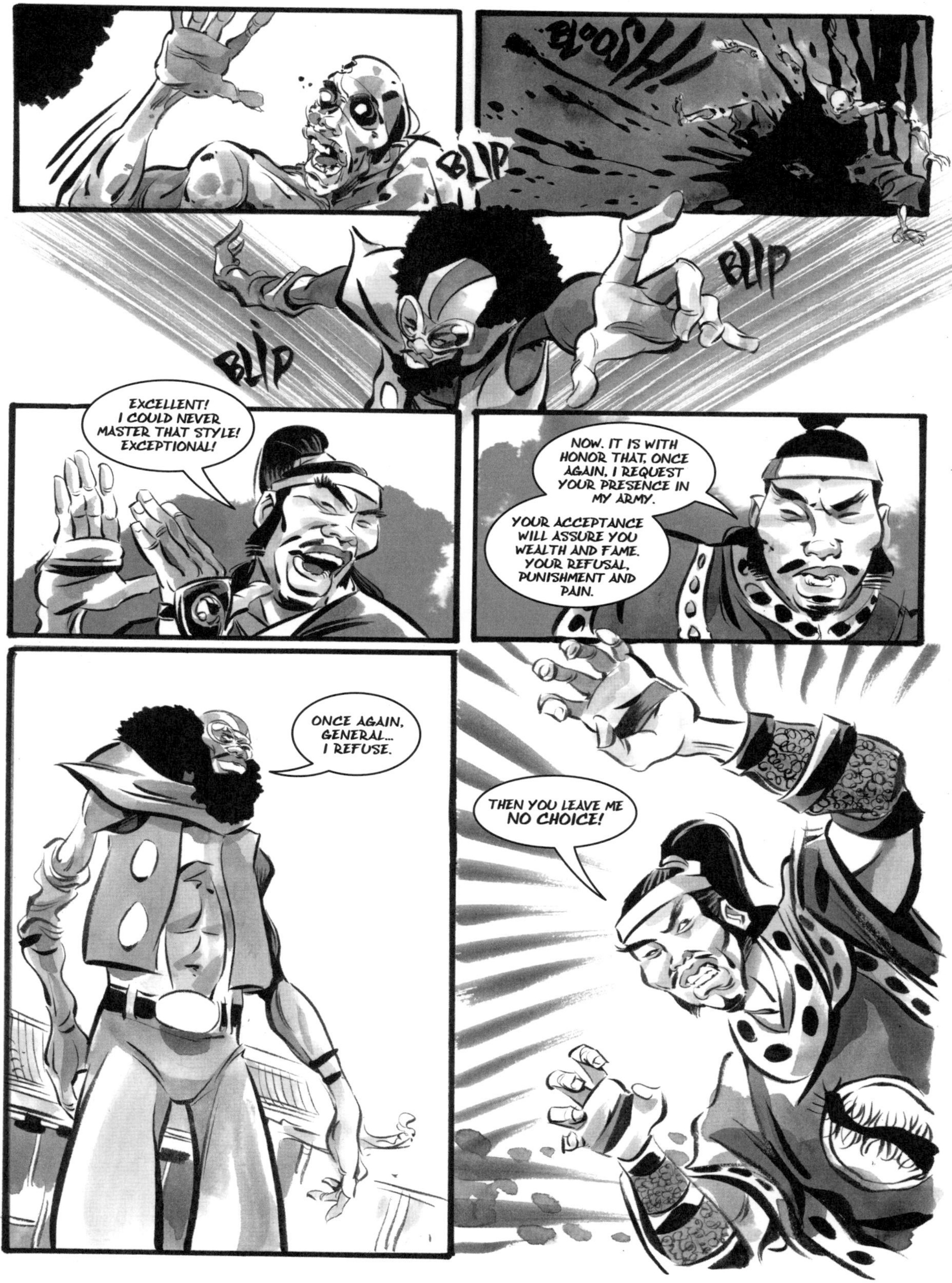
BLOOSH!
BLIP
BLIP
BLIP
EXCELLENT! I COULD NEVER MASTER THAT STYLE! EXCEPTIONAL!
NOW. IT IS WITH HONOR THAT, ONCE AGAIN, I REQUEST YOUR PRESENCE IN MY ARMY.
YOUR ACCEPTANCE WILL ASSURE YOU WEALTH AND FAME. YOUR REFUSAL, PUNISHMENT AND PAIN.
ONCE AGAIN, GENERAL... I REFUSE.
THEN YOU LEAVE ME NO CHOICE!

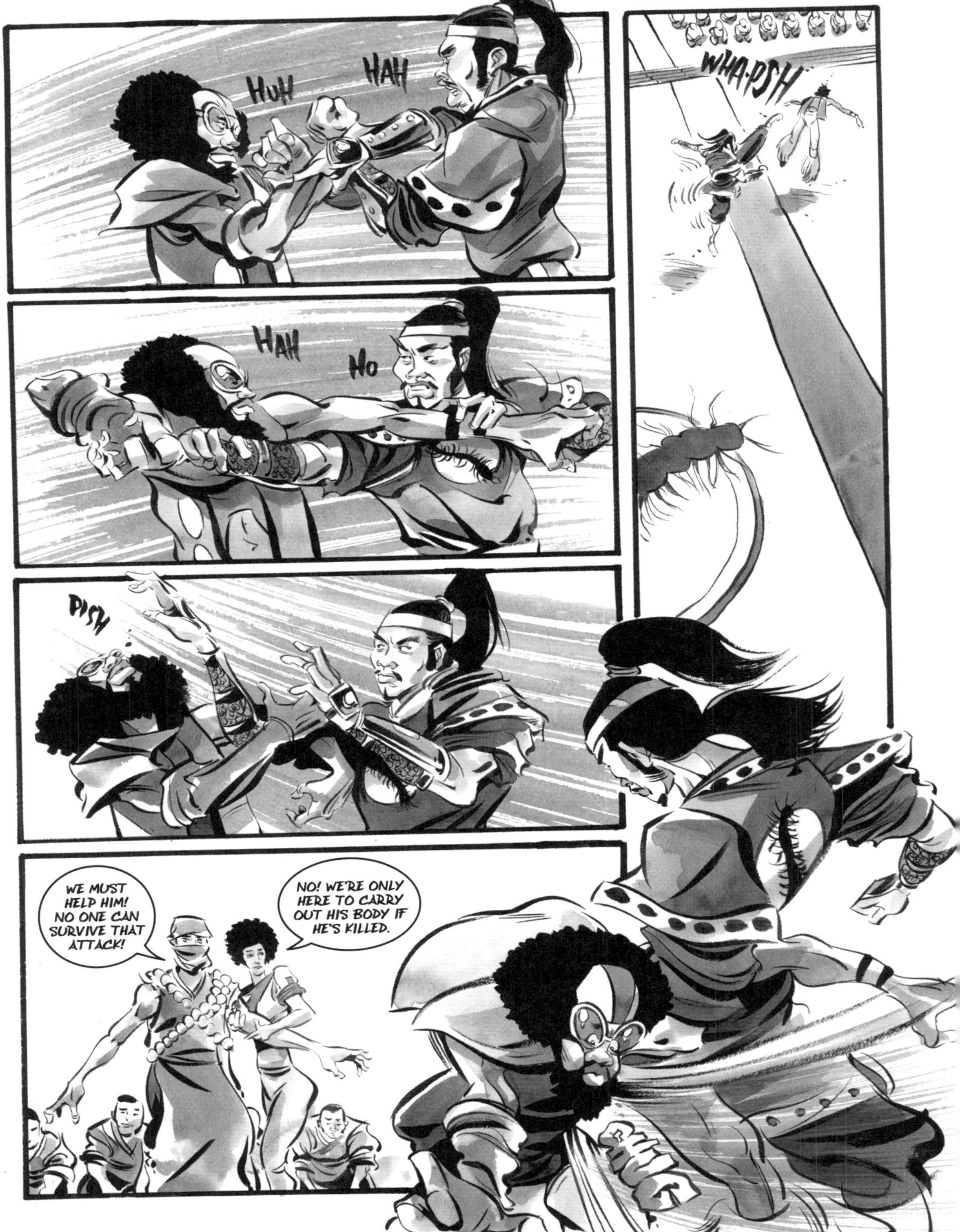
HUH
HAH
WHAPSH
HAH
HO
PISH
WE MUST HELP HIM! NO ONE CAN SURVIVE THAT ATTACK!
NO! WE'RE ONLY HERE TO CARRY OUT HIS BODY IF HE'S KILLED.

WEEEODOWEEEOOO

BLAA

...CENTIPEDE STING-PUNCH... REMARKABLE!

HA HA HA HA

CLAP CLAP CLAP CLAP
CLAP CLAP CLAP CLAP
CLAP CLAP CLAP CLAP

HA HA HA HA

YOU THERE!

MAKE SURE YOUR FRIEND RECEIVES A PROPER BURIAL!

HA HA HA HA HA HA

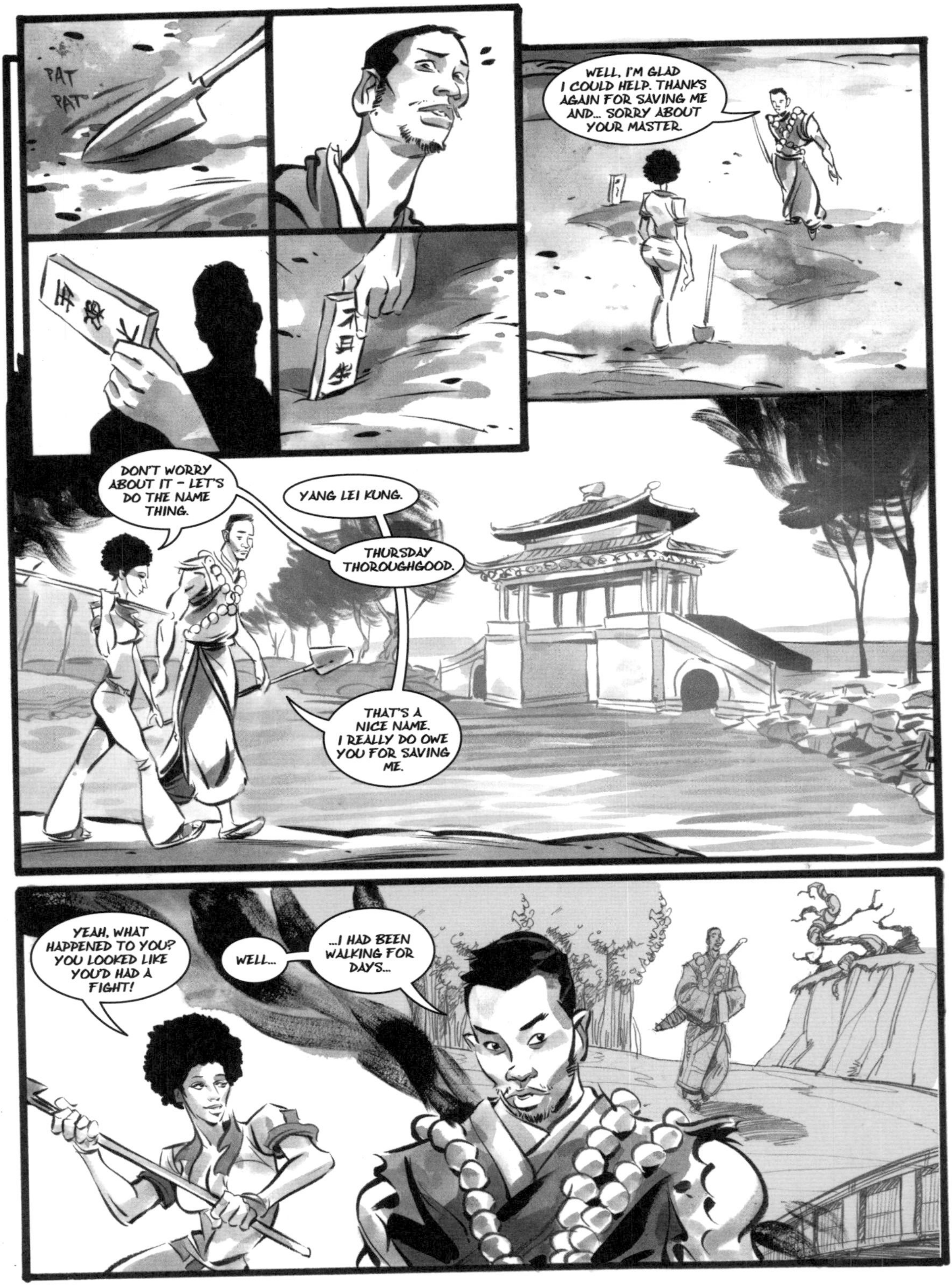
PAT
PAT
WELL, I'M GLAD I COULD HELP. THANKS AGAIN FOR SAVING ME AND... SORRY ABOUT YOUR MASTER.
DON'T WORRY ABOUT IT - LET'S DO THE NAME THING.
YANG LEI KUNG.
THURSDAY THOROUGHGOOD.
THAT'S A NICE NAME. I REALLY DO OWE YOU FOR SAVING ME.
YEAH, WHAT HAPPENED TO YOU? YOU LOOKED LIKE YOU'D HAD A FIGHT!
WELL...
...I HAD BEEN WALKING FOR DAYS...

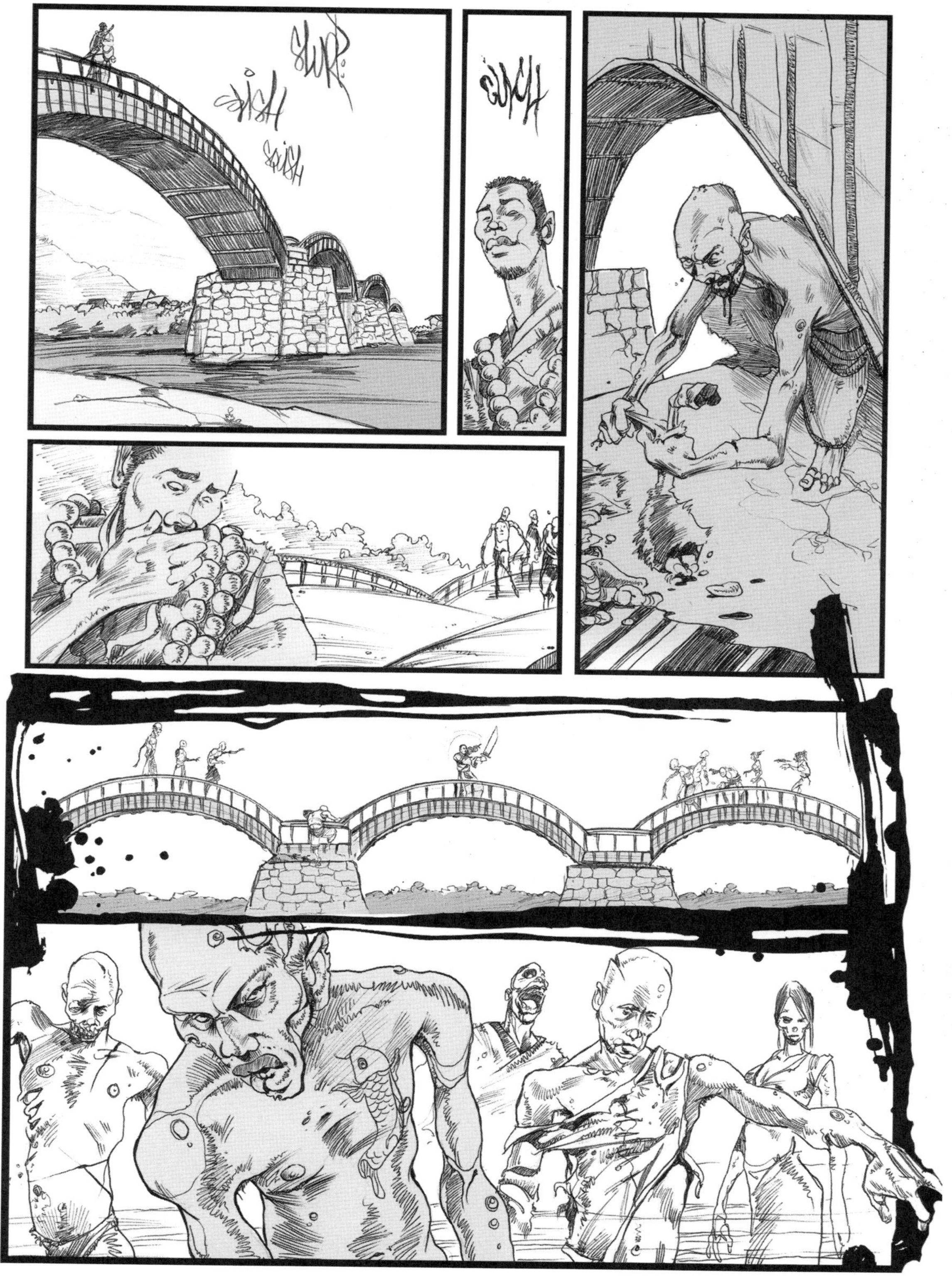
SLURP
SQUISH
SQUISH

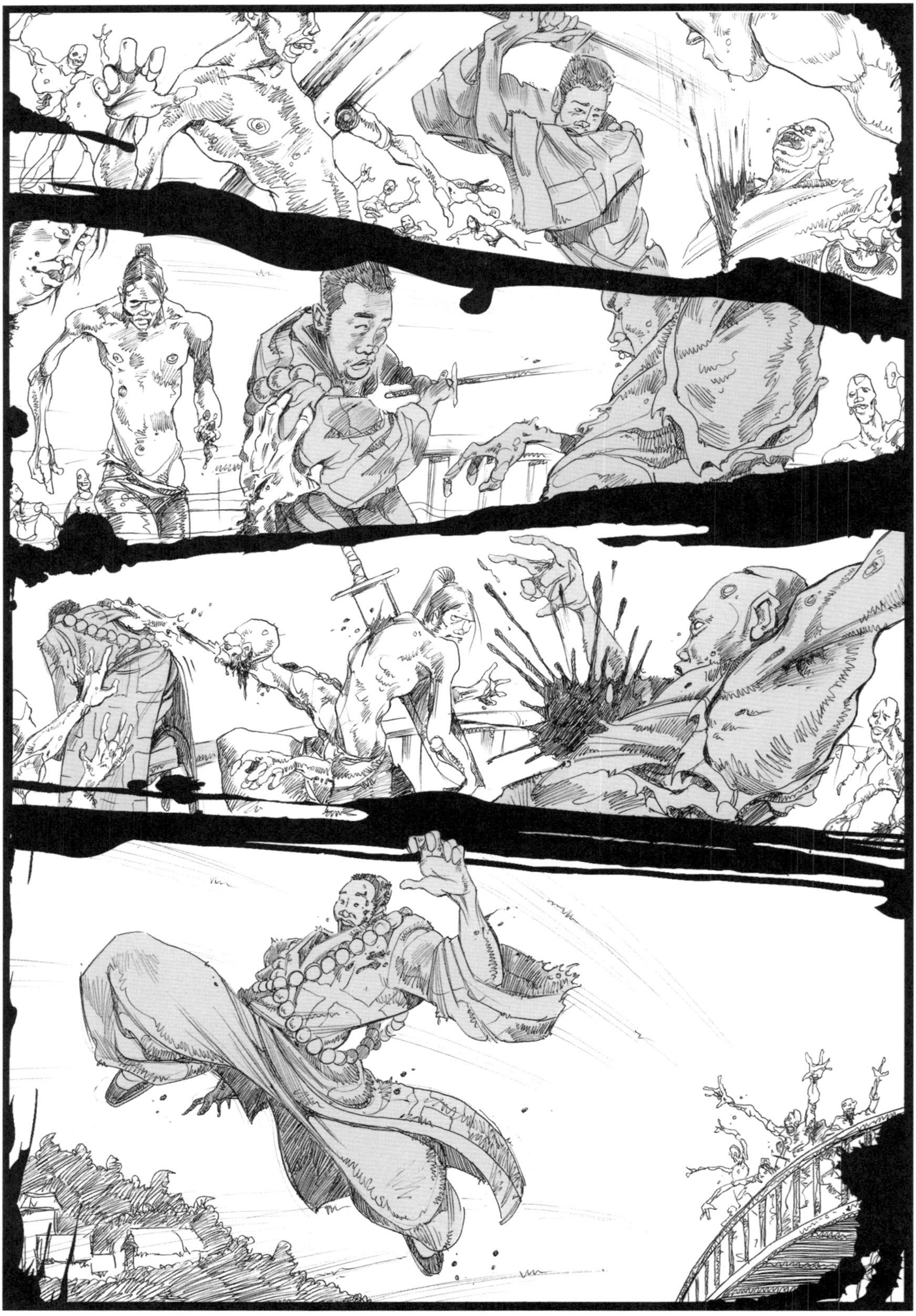

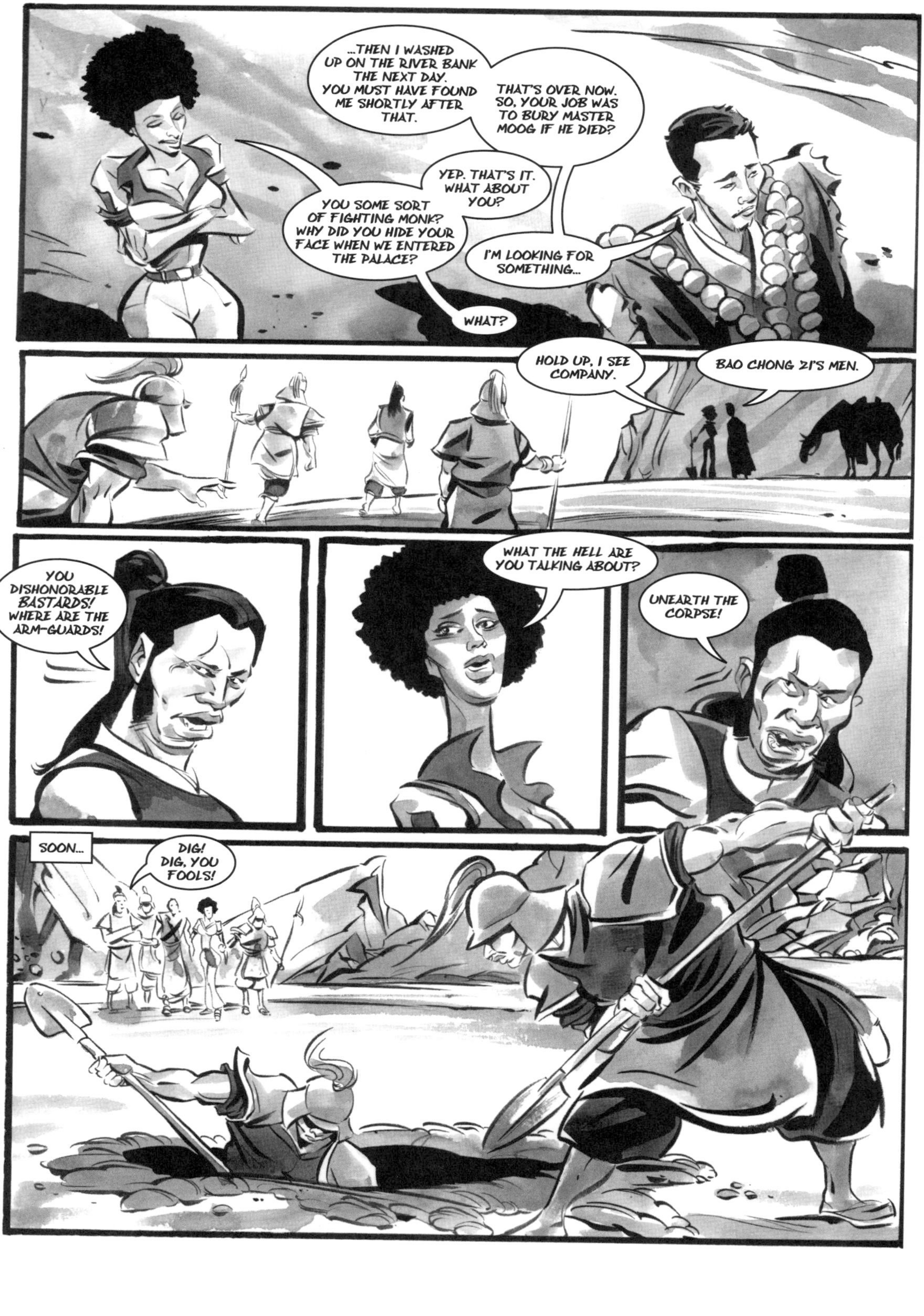
...THEN I WASHED UP ON THE RIVER BANK THE NEXT DAY. YOU MUST HAVE FOUND ME SHORTLY AFTER THAT.
THAT'S OVER NOW. SO, YOUR JOB WAS TO BURY MASTER MOOG IF HE DIED?
YEP. THAT'S IT. WHAT ABOUT YOU?
YOU SOME SORT OF FIGHTING MONK? WHY DID YOU HIDE YOUR FACE WHEN WE ENTERED THE PALACE?
I'M LOOKING FOR SOMETHING...
WHAT?
HOLD UP, I SEE COMPANY.
BAO CHONG ZI'S MEN.
YOU DISHONORABLE BASTARDS! WHERE ARE THE ARM-GUARDS!
WHAT THE HELL ARE YOU TALKING ABOUT?
UNEARTH THE CORPSE!
SOON...
DIG! DIG, YOU FOOLS!

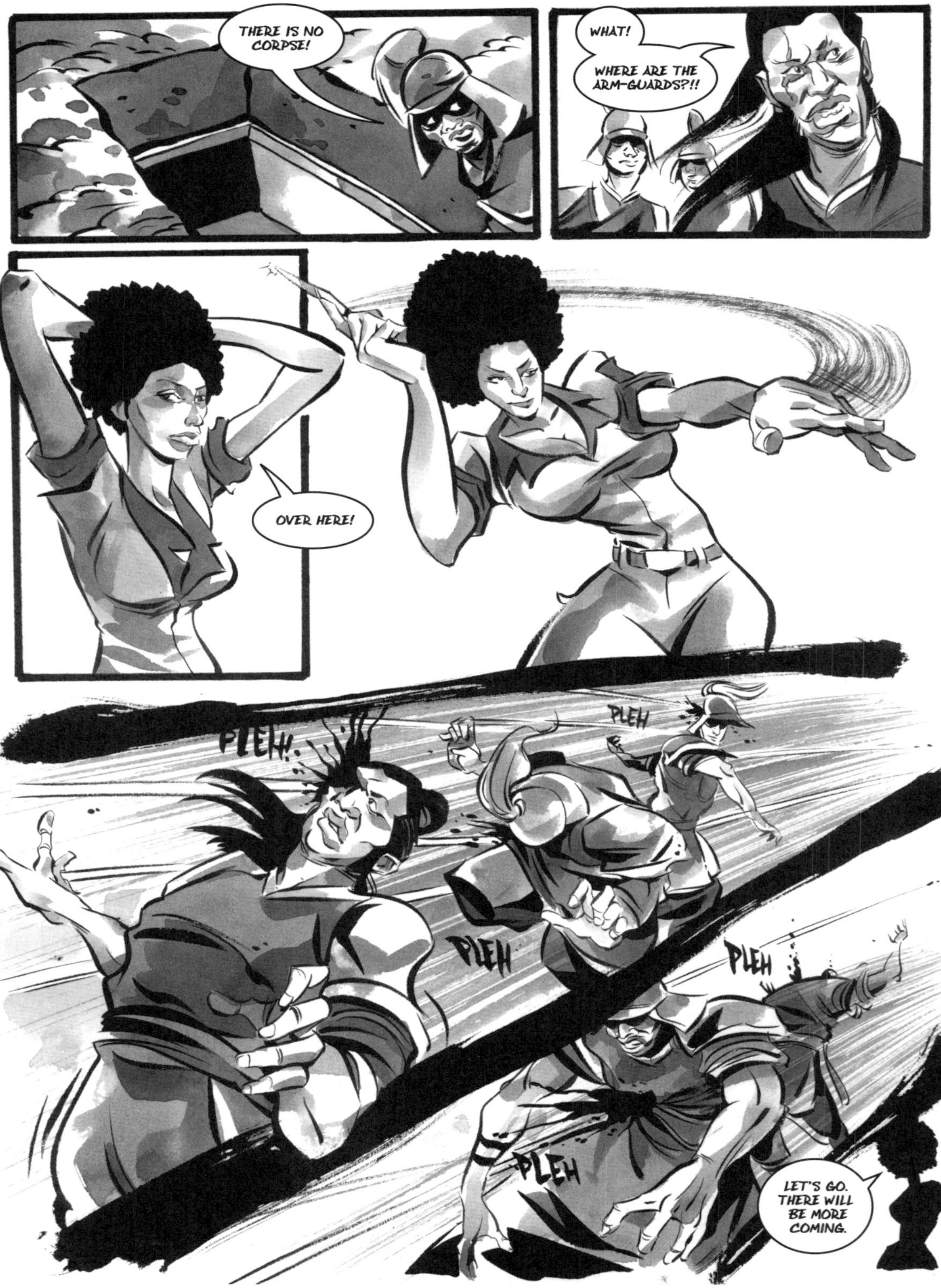
THERE IS NO CORPSE!
WHAT!
WHERE ARE THE ARM-GUARDS?!!
OVER HERE!
PLEH!
PLEH
PLEH
PLEH
PLEH
LET'S GO. THERE WILL BE MORE COMING.

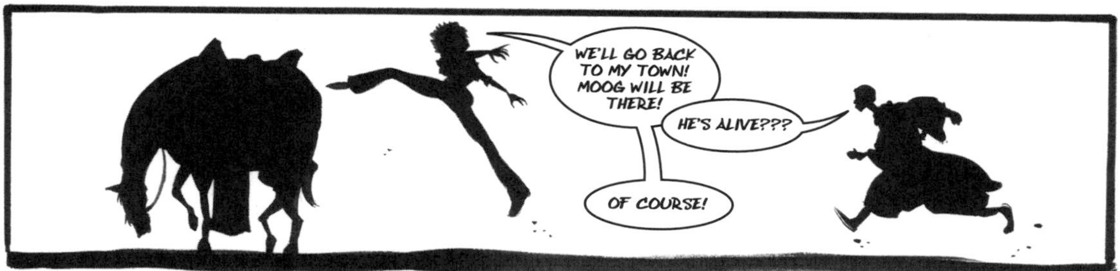
WE'LL GO BACK TO MY TOWN! MOOG WILL BE THERE!
HE'S ALIVE???
OF COURSE!

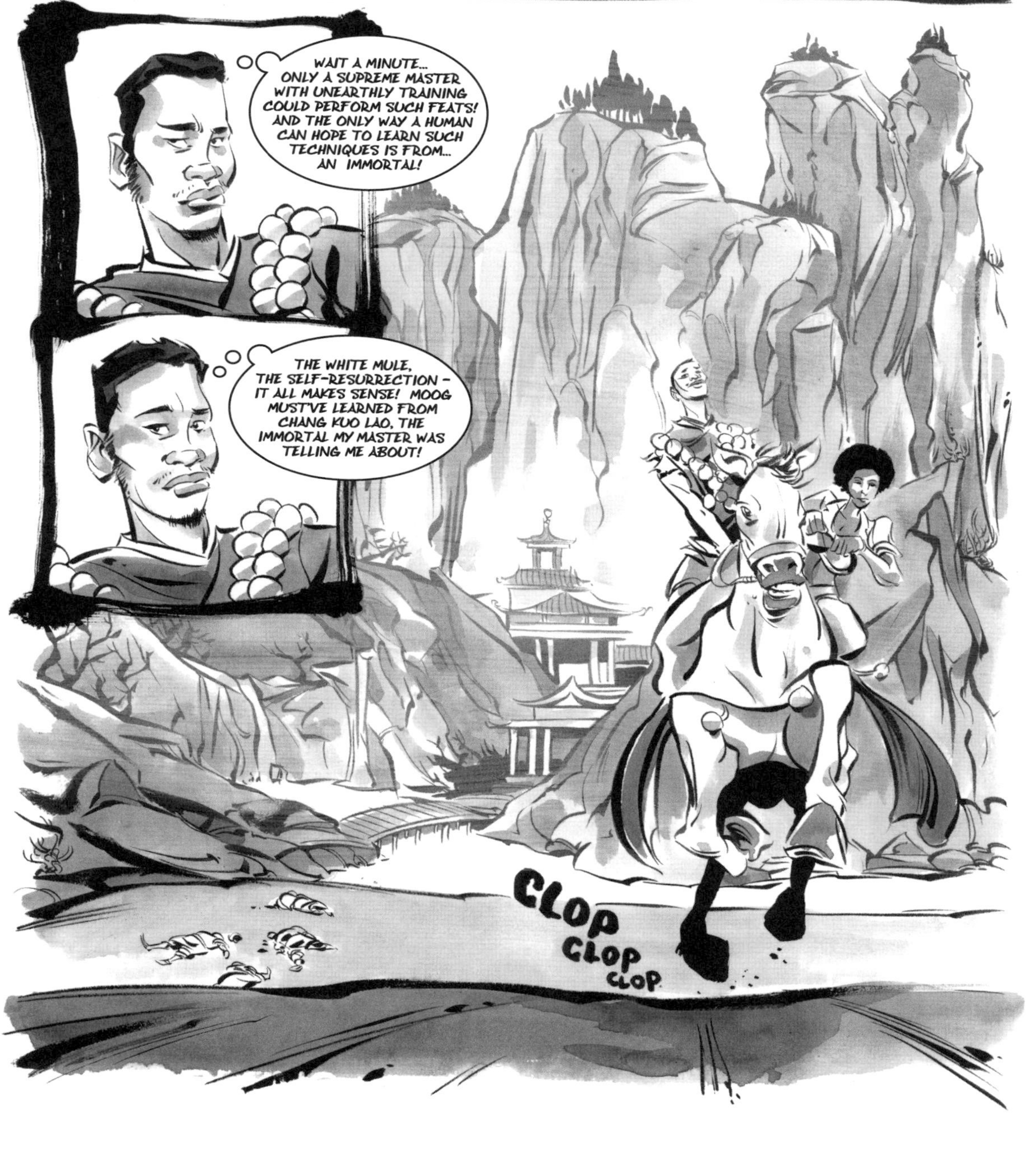
WAIT A MINUTE... ONLY A SUPREME MASTER WITH UNEARTHLY TRAINING COULD PERFORM SUCH FEATS! AND THE ONLY WAY A HUMAN CAN HOPE TO LEARN SUCH TECHNIQUES IS FROM... AN IMMORTAL!
THE WHITE MULE, THE SELF-RESURRECTION - IT ALL MAKES SENSE! MOOG MUST'VE LEARNED FROM CHANG KUO LAO, THE IMMORTAL MY MASTER WAS TELLING ME ABOUT!
CLOP
CLOP
CLOP

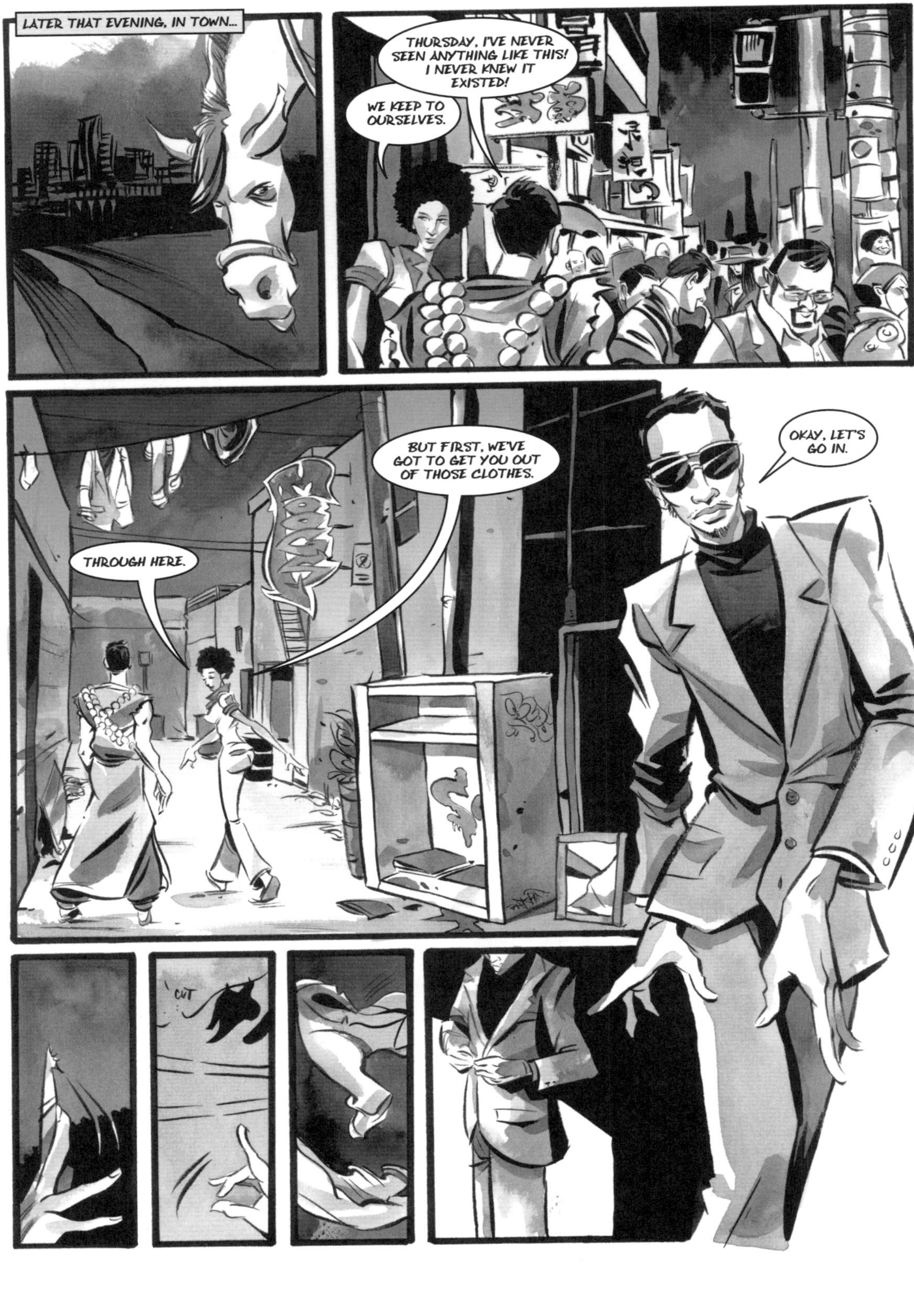

LATER THAT EVENING, IN TOWN...
THURSDAY, I'VE NEVER SEEN ANYTHING LIKE THIS! I NEVER KNEW IT EXISTED!
WE KEEP TO OURSELVES.
BUT FIRST, WE'VE GOT TO GET YOU OUT OF THOSE CLOTHES.
THROUGH HERE.
OKAY, LET'S GO IN.
CUT

CLIK

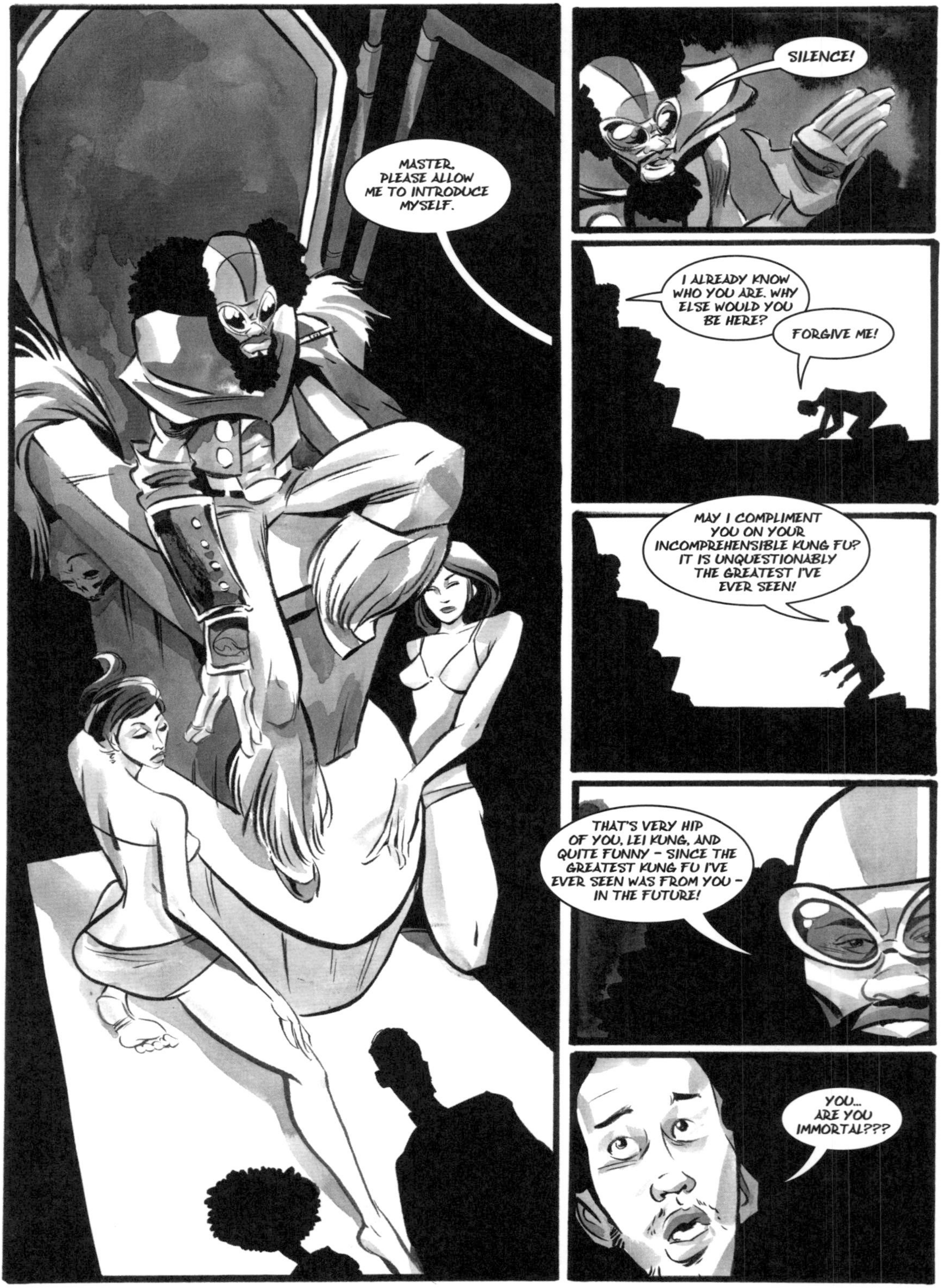
MASTER, PLEASE ALLOW ME TO INTRODUCE MYSELF.
SILENCE!
I ALREADY KNOW WHO YOU ARE. WHY ELSE WOULD YOU BE HERE?
FORGIVE ME!
MAY I COMPLIMENT YOU ON YOUR INCOMPREHENSIBLE KUNG FU? IT IS UNQUESTIONABLY THE GREATEST I'VE EVER SEEN!
THAT'S VERY HIP OF YOU, LEI KUNG, AND QUITE FUNNY - SINCE THE GREATEST KUNG FU I'VE EVER SEEN WAS FROM YOU - IN THE FUTURE!
YOU... ARE YOU IMMORTAL???

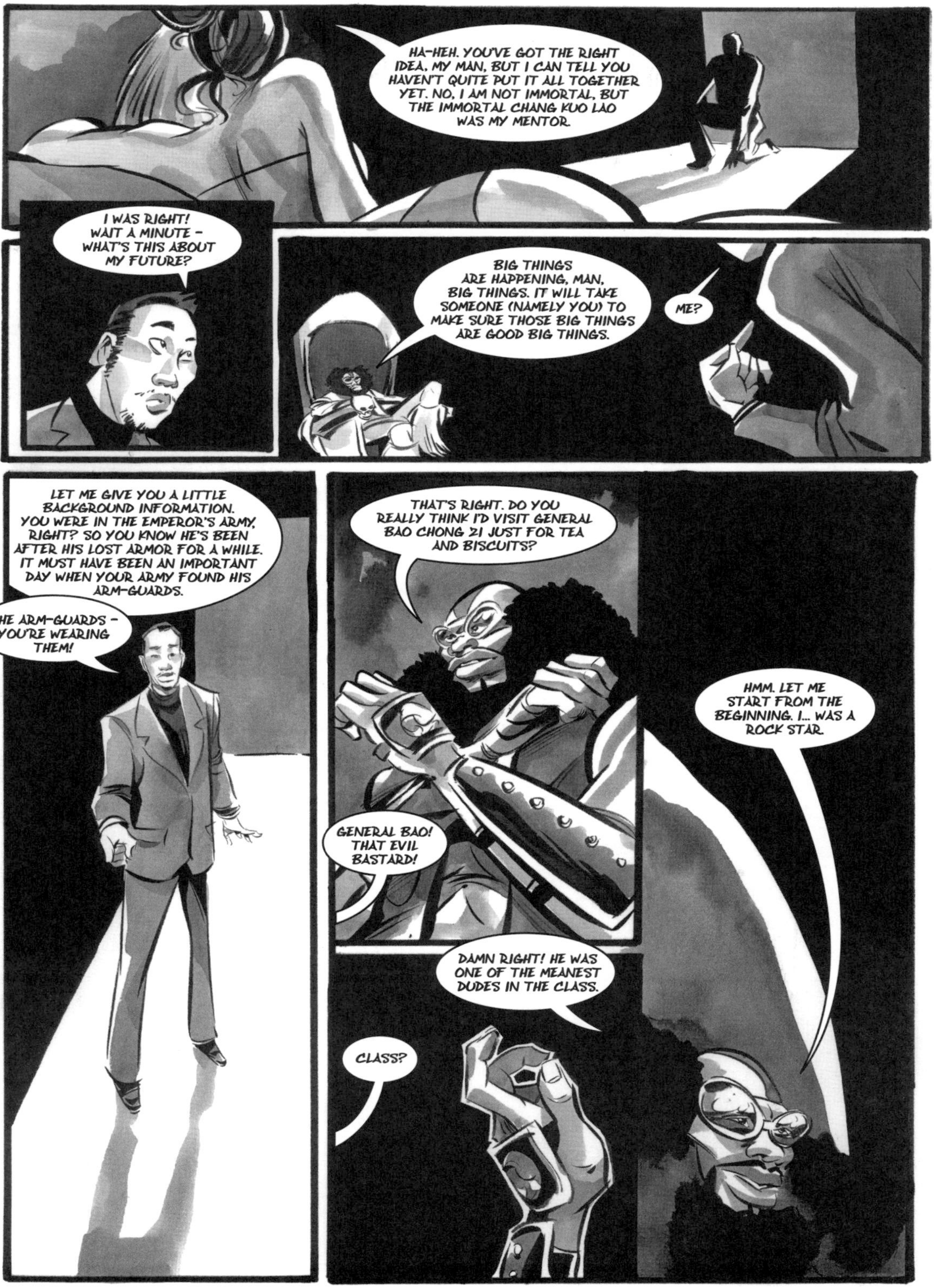
HA-HEH. YOU'VE GOT THE RIGHT IDEA, MY MAN, BUT I CAN TELL YOU HAVEN'T QUITE PUT IT ALL TOGETHER YET. NO, I AM NOT IMMORTAL, BUT THE IMMORTAL CHANG KUO LAO WAS MY MENTOR.
I WAS RIGHT! WAIT A MINUTE - WHAT'S THIS ABOUT MY FUTURE?
BIG THINGS ARE HAPPENING, MAN, BIG THINGS. IT WILL TAKE SOMEONE (NAMELY YOU) TO MAKE SURE THOSE BIG THINGS ARE GOOD BIG THINGS.
ME?
LET ME GIVE YOU A LITTLE BACKGROUND INFORMATION. YOU WERE IN THE EMPEROR'S ARMY, RIGHT? SO YOU KNOW HE'S BEEN AFTER HIS LOST ARMOR FOR A WHILE. IT MUST HAVE BEEN AN IMPORTANT DAY WHEN YOUR ARMY FOUND HIS ARM-GUARDS.
THE ARM-GUARDS - YOU'RE WEARING THEM!
THAT'S RIGHT. DO YOU REALLY THINK I'D VISIT GENERAL BAO CHONG ZI JUST FOR TEA AND BISCUITS?
GENERAL BAO! THAT EVIL BASTARD!
DAMN RIGHT! HE WAS ONE OF THE MEANEST DUDES IN THE CLASS.
CLASS?
HMM. LET ME START FROM THE BEGINNING. I... WAS A ROCK STAR.

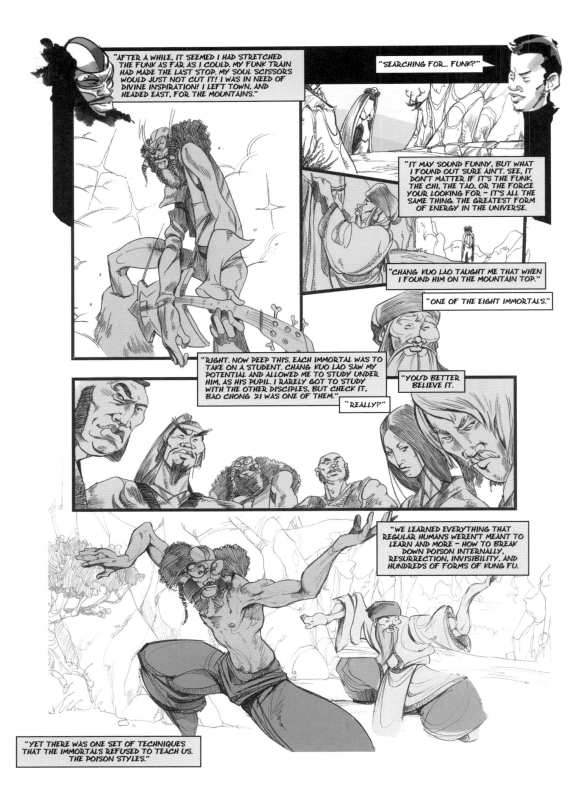

"AFTER A WHILE, IT SEEMED I HAD STRETCHED THE FUNK AS FAR AS I COULD. MY FUNK TRAIN HAD MADE THE LAST STOP. MY SOUL SCISSORS WOULD JUST NOT CUT IT! I WAS IN NEED OF DIVINE INSPIRATION! I LEFT TOWN, AND HEADED EAST, FOR THE MOUNTAINS."

"SEARCHING FOR... FUNK?"

"IT MAY SOUND FUNNY, BUT WHAT I FOUND OUT SURE AIN'T. SEE, IT DON'T MATTER IF IT'S THE FUNK, THE CHI, THE TAO, OR THE FORCE YOUR LOOKING FOR – IT'S ALL THE SAME THING. THE GREATEST FORM OF ENERGY IN THE UNIVERSE.

"CHANG KUO LAO TAUGHT ME THAT WHEN I FOUND HIM ON THE MOUNTAIN TOP."

"ONE OF THE EIGHT IMMORTALS."

"RIGHT. NOW PEEP THIS. EACH IMMORTAL WAS TO TAKE ON A STUDENT. CHANG KUO LAO SAW MY POTENTIAL AND ALLOWED ME TO STUDY UNDER HIM, AS HIS PUPIL. I RARELY GOT TO STUDY WITH THE OTHER DISCIPLES, BUT CHECK IT, BAO CHONG 21 WAS ONE OF THEM."

"YOU'D BETTER BELIEVE IT.

"REALLY?"

"WE LEARNED EVERYTHING THAT REGULAR HUMANS WEREN'T MEANT TO LEARN AND MORE – HOW TO BREAK DOWN POISON INTERNALLY, RESURRECTION, INVISIBILITY, AND HUNDREDS OF FORMS OF KUNG FU.

"YET THERE WAS ONE SET OF TECHNIQUES THAT THE IMMORTALS REFUSED TO TEACH US. THE POISON STYLES."

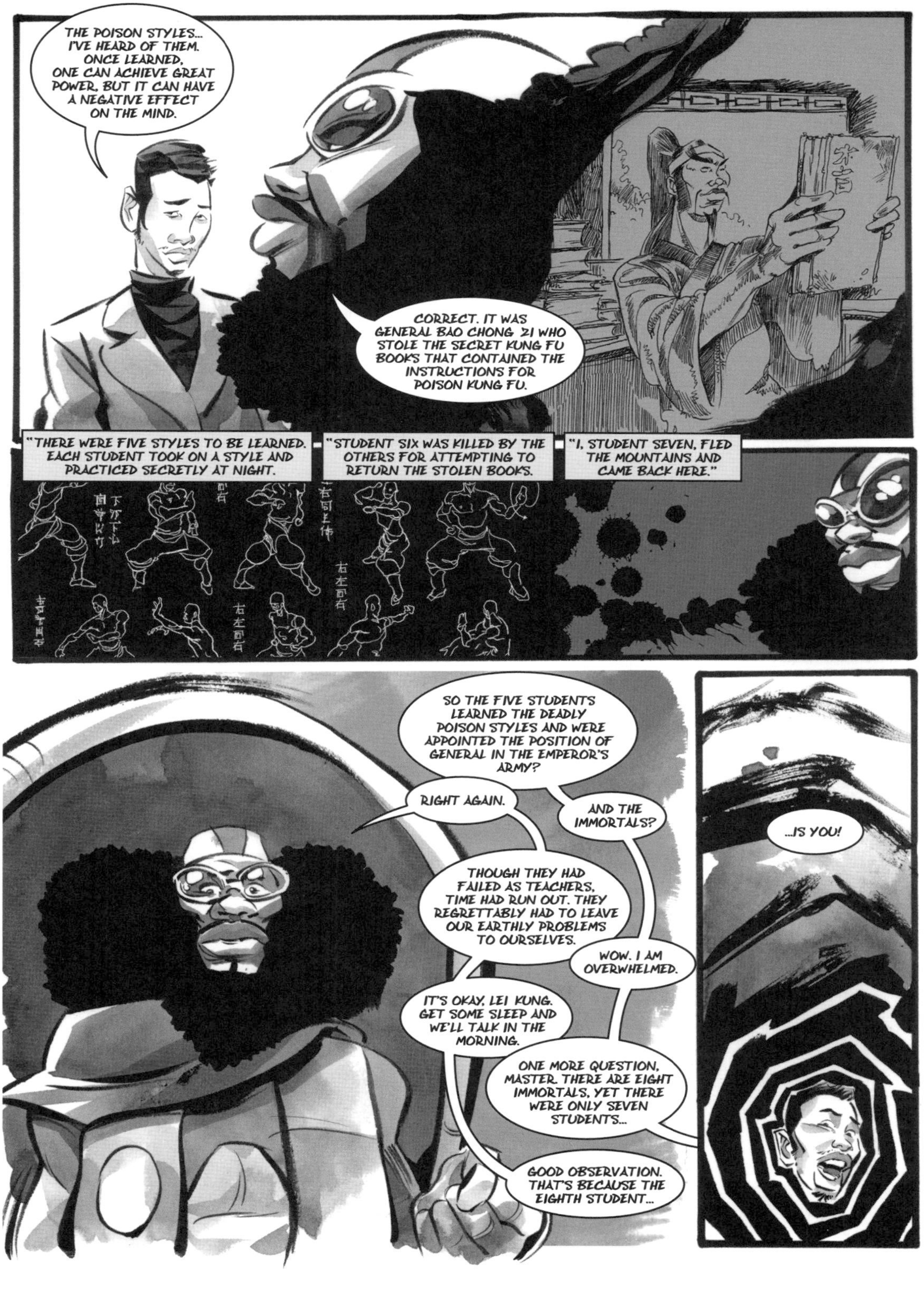
THE POISON STYLES... I'VE HEARD OF THEM. ONCE LEARNED, ONE CAN ACHIEVE GREAT POWER, BUT IT CAN HAVE A NEGATIVE EFFECT ON THE MIND.
CORRECT. IT WAS GENERAL BAO CHONG ZI WHO STOLE THE SECRET KUNG FU BOOKS THAT CONTAINED THE INSTRUCTIONS FOR POISON KUNG FU.
"THERE WERE FIVE STYLES TO BE LEARNED. EACH STUDENT TOOK ON A STYLE AND PRACTICED SECRETLY AT NIGHT.
"STUDENT SIX WAS KILLED BY THE OTHERS FOR ATTEMPTING TO RETURN THE STOLEN BOOKS.
"I, STUDENT SEVEN, FLED THE MOUNTAINS AND CAME BACK HERE."
SO THE FIVE STUDENTS LEARNED THE DEADLY POISON STYLES AND WERE APPOINTED THE POSITION OF GENERAL IN THE EMPEROR'S ARMY?
RIGHT AGAIN.
AND THE IMMORTALS?
THOUGH THEY HAD FAILED AS TEACHERS, TIME HAD RUN OUT. THEY REGRETTABLY HAD TO LEAVE OUR EARTHLY PROBLEMS TO OURSELVES.
WOW. I AM OVERWHELMED.
IT'S OKAY, LEI KUNG. GET SOME SLEEP AND WE'LL TALK IN THE MORNING.
ONE MORE QUESTION, MASTER. THERE ARE EIGHT IMMORTALS, YET THERE WERE ONLY SEVEN STUDENTS...
GOOD OBSERVATION. THAT'S BECAUSE THE EIGHTH STUDENT...
...IS YOU!

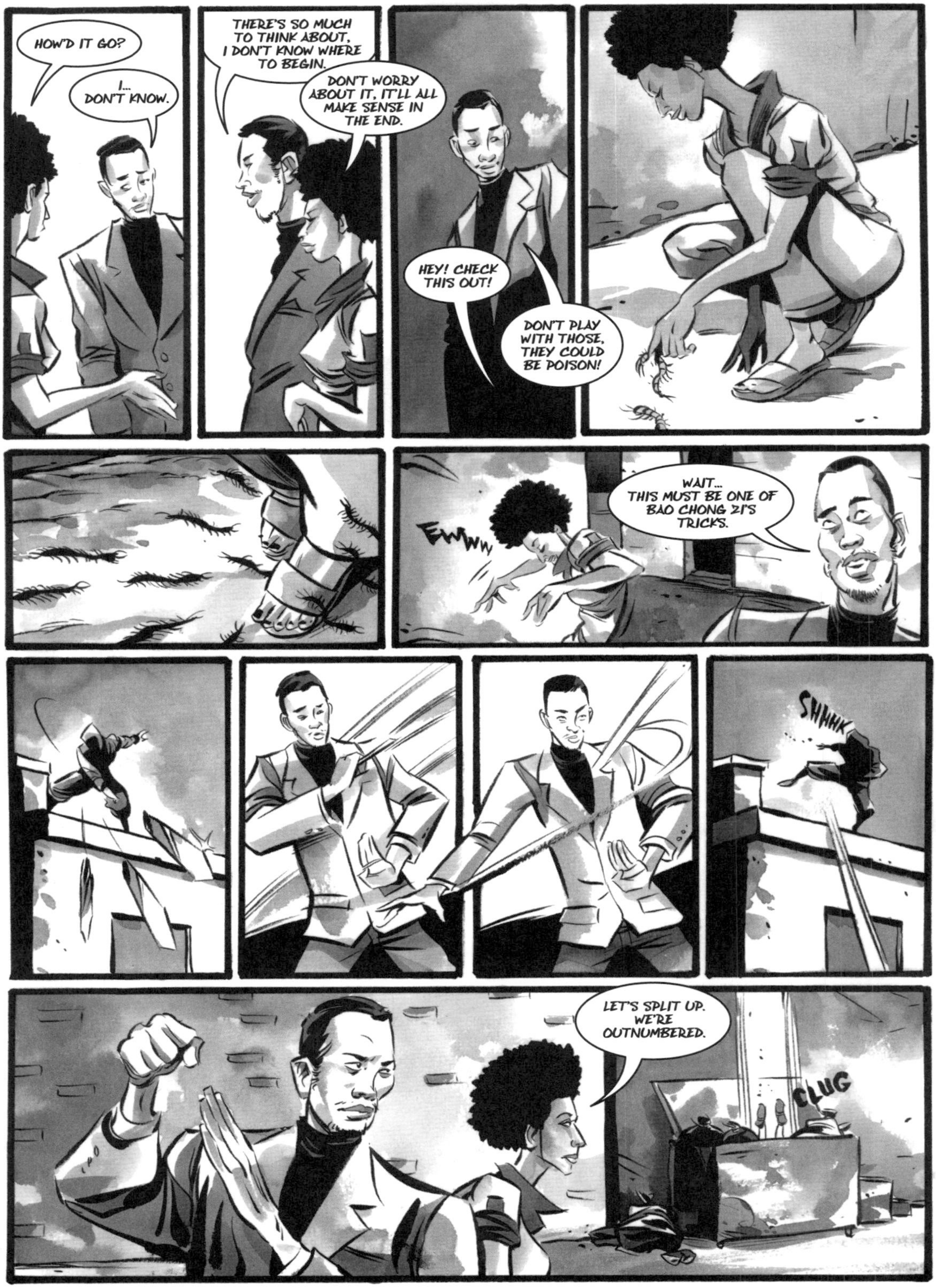
HOW'D IT GO?
I... DON'T KNOW.
THERE'S SO MUCH TO THINK ABOUT, I DON'T KNOW WHERE TO BEGIN.
DON'T WORRY ABOUT IT, IT'LL ALL MAKE SENSE IN THE END.
HEY! CHECK THIS OUT!
DON'T PLAY WITH THOSE, THEY COULD BE POISON!
EWWW
WAIT... THIS MUST BE ONE OF BAO CHONG ZI'S TRICKS.
SHHHK
LET'S SPLIT UP. WE'RE OUTNUMBERED.
CLUG

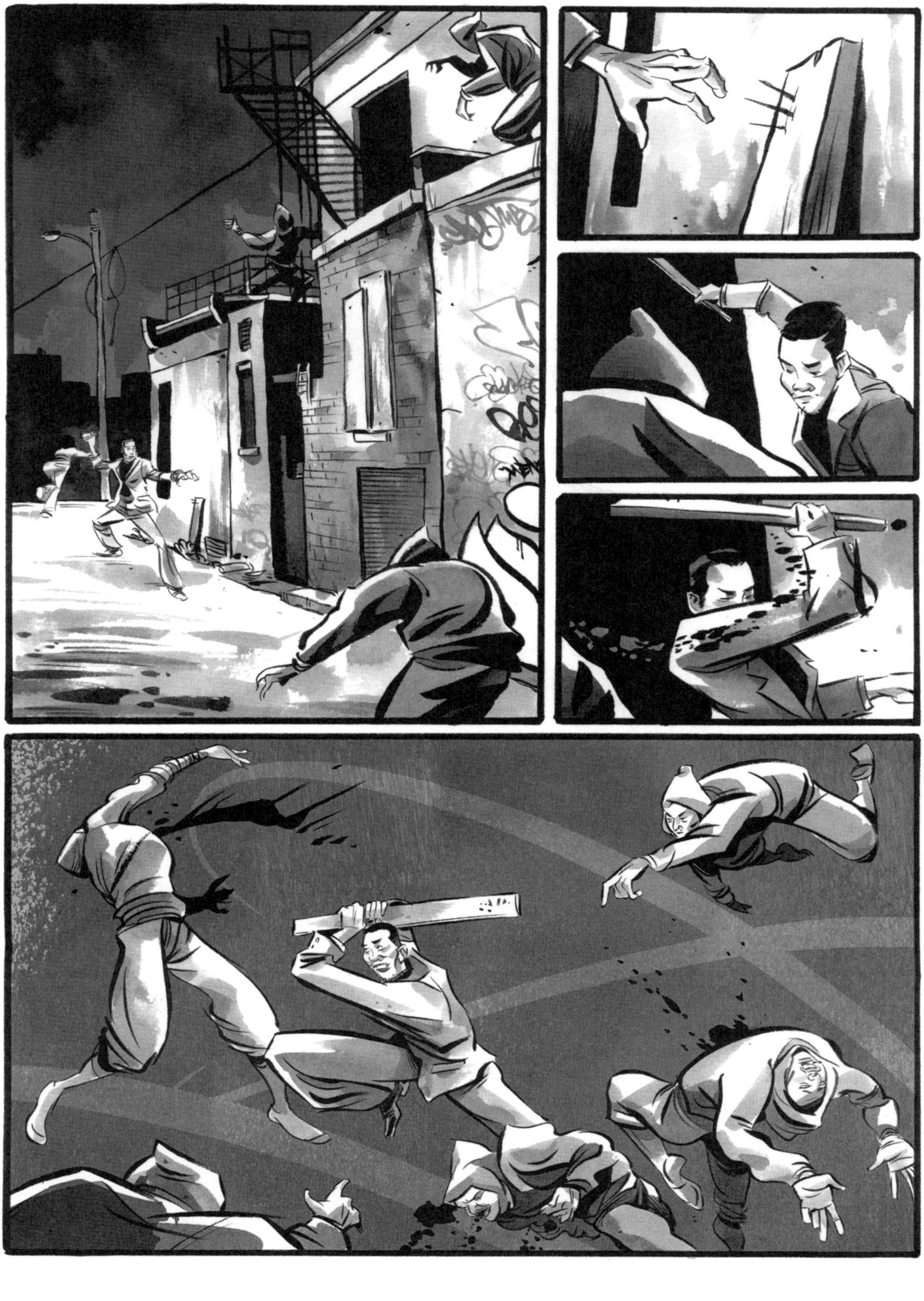

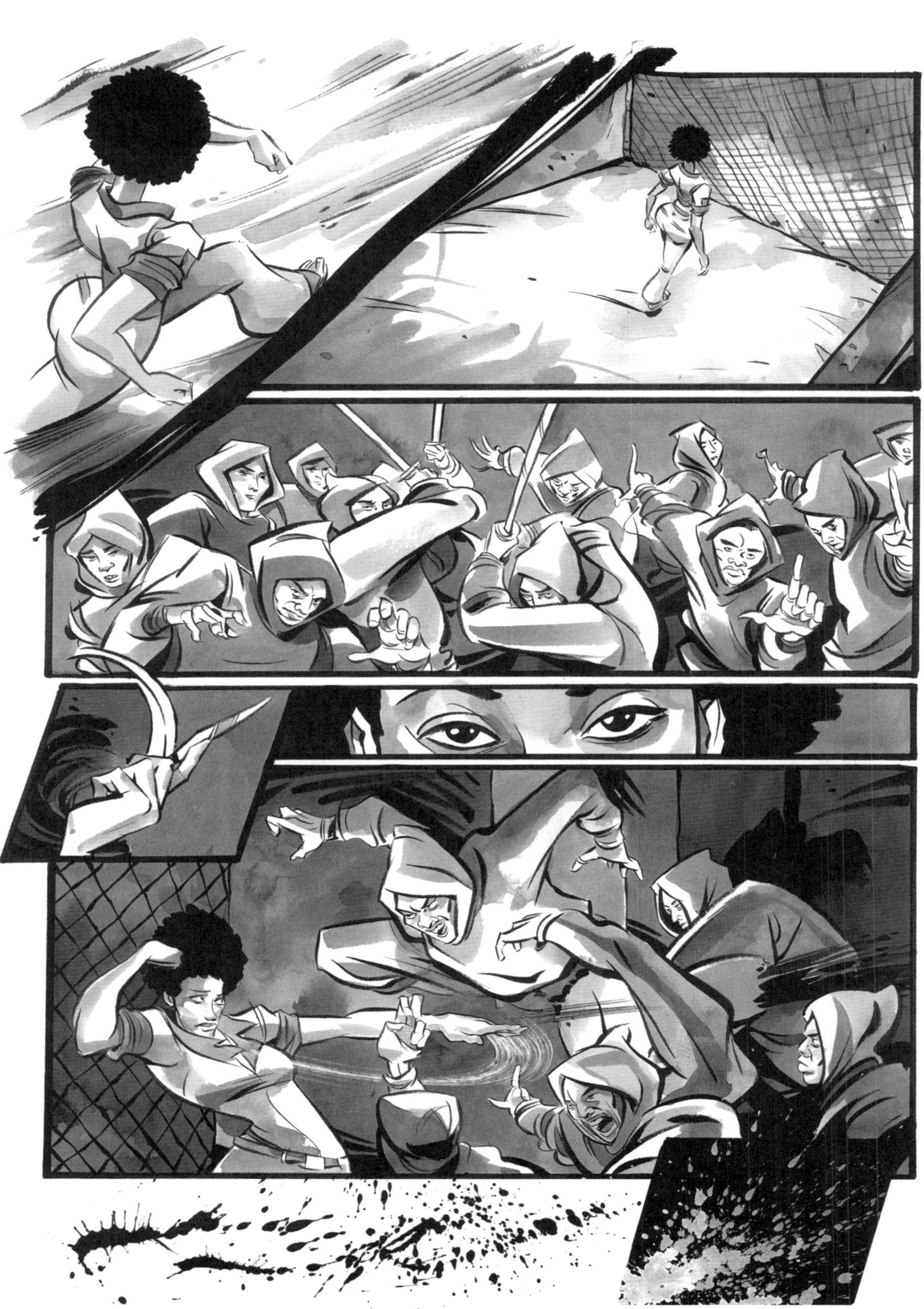

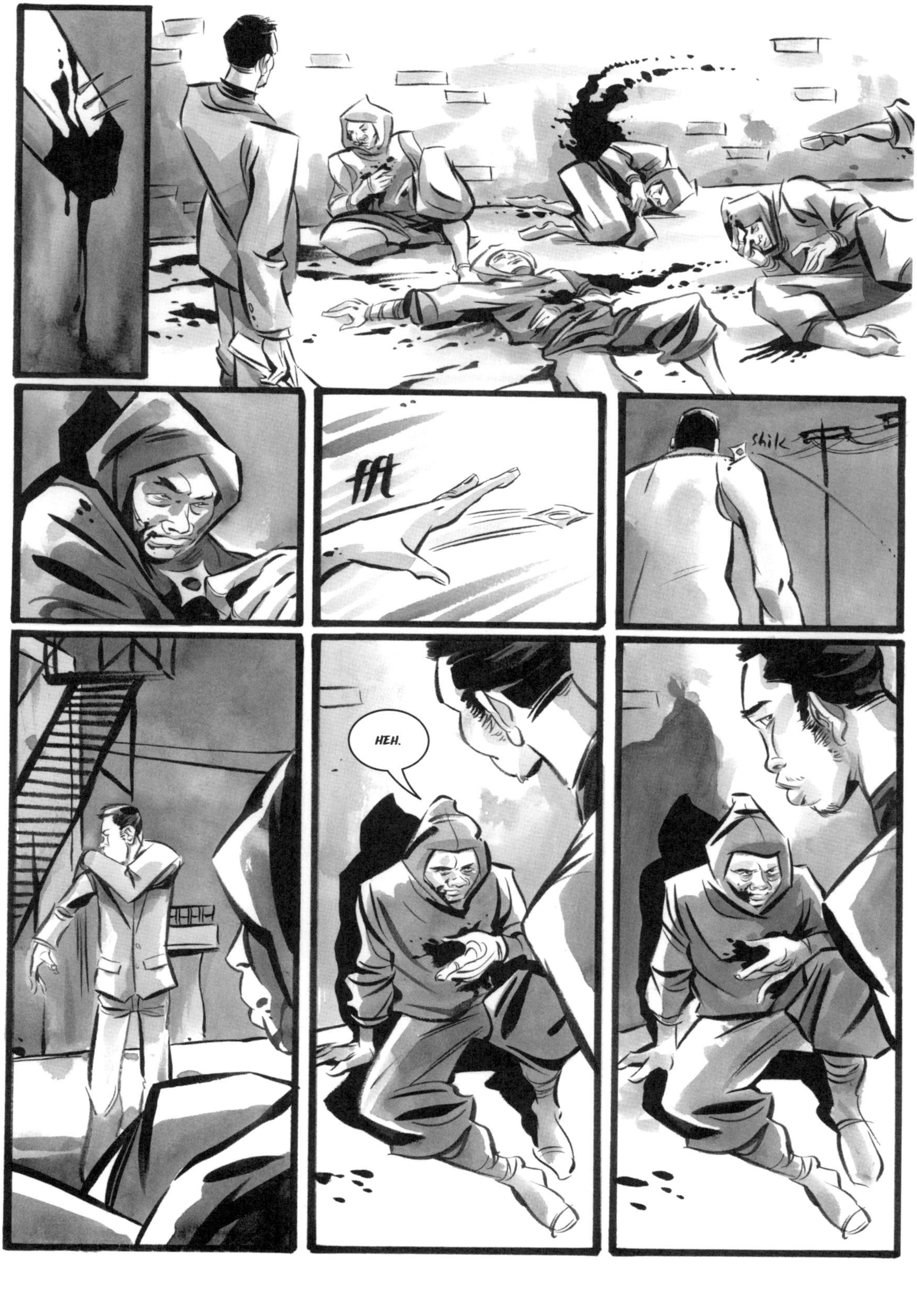
fft
shik
HEH.

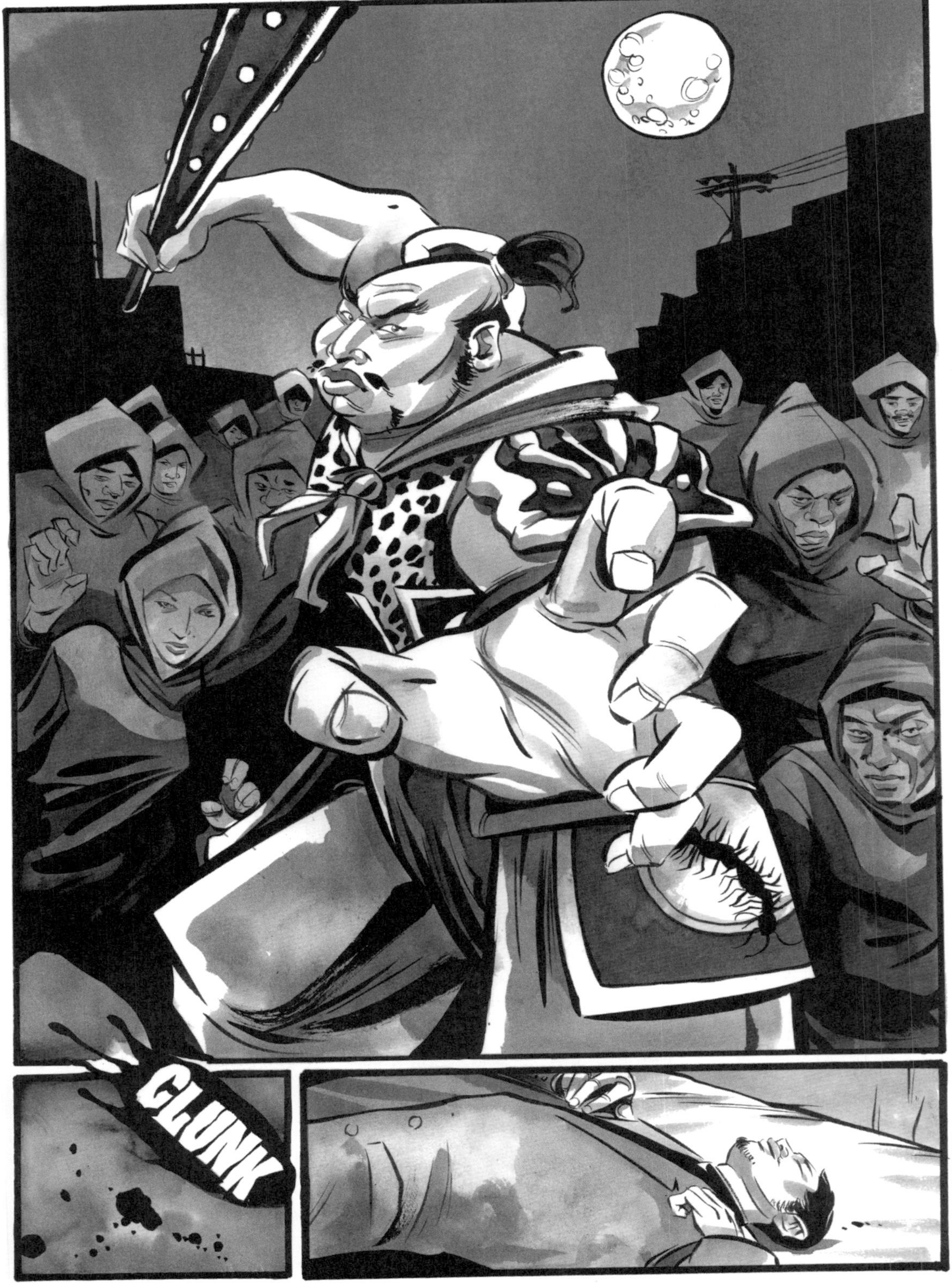
CLUNK

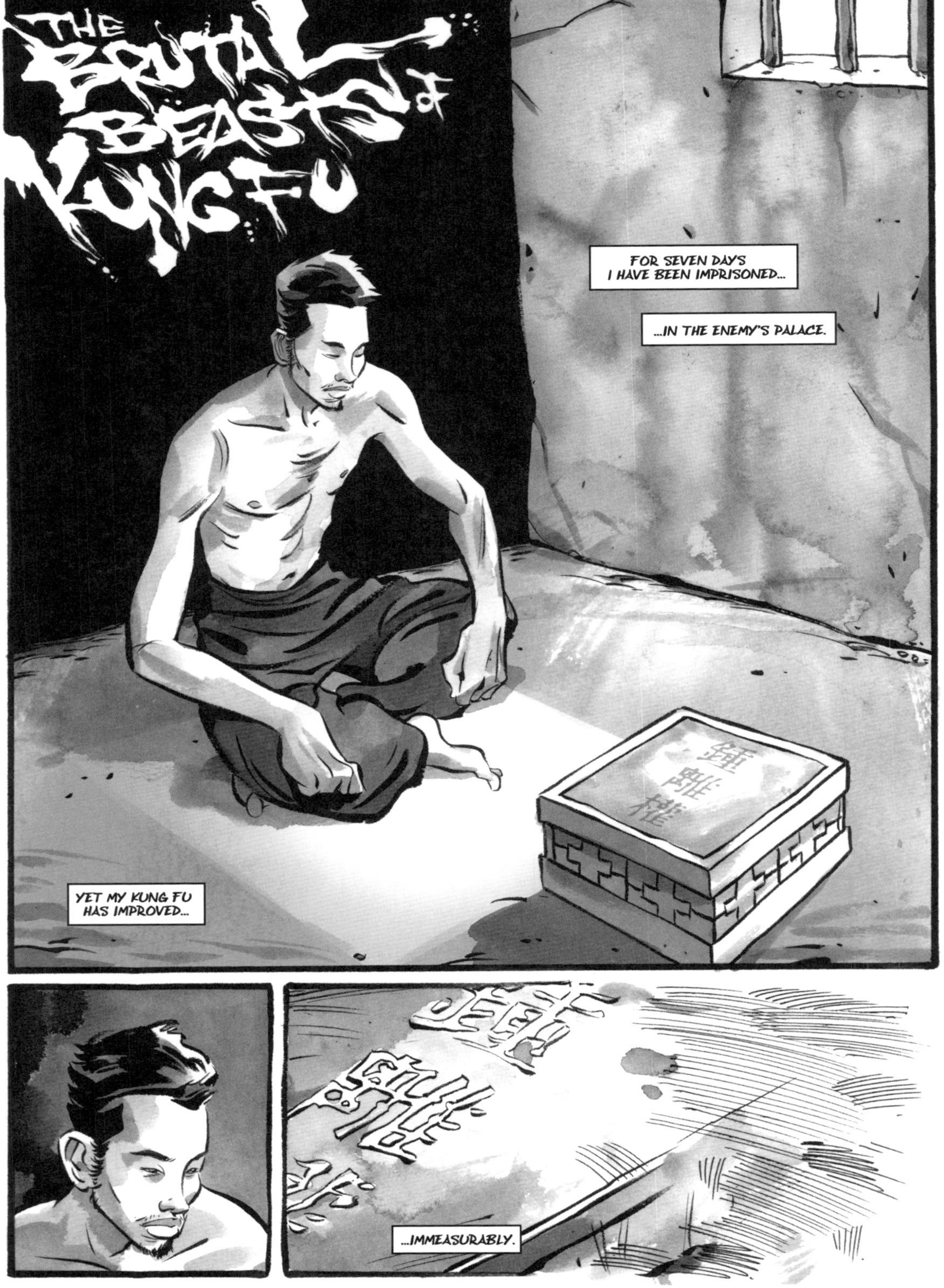
THE BRUTAL BEASTS OF KUNG FU
FOR SEVEN DAYS I HAVE BEEN IMPRISONED...
...IN THE ENEMY'S PALACE.
鍾離權
YET MY KUNG FU HAS IMPROVED...
...IMMEASURABLY.

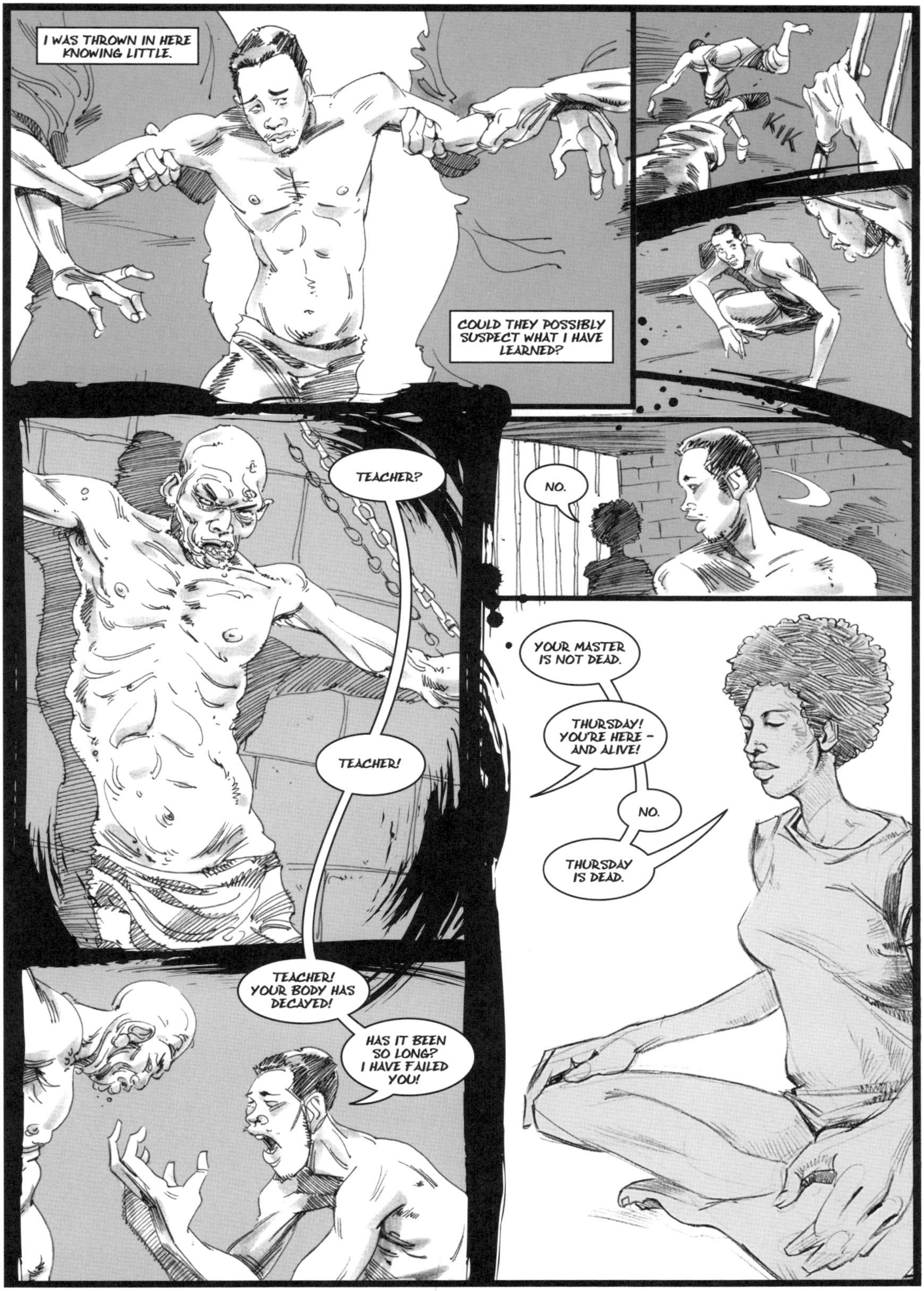
I WAS THROWN IN HERE KNOWING LITTLE.
COULD THEY POSSIBLY SUSPECT WHAT I HAVE LEARNED?
KIK
TEACHER?
TEACHER!
NO.
YOUR MASTER IS NOT DEAD.
THURSDAY! YOU'RE HERE - AND ALIVE!
NO.
THURSDAY IS DEAD.
TEACHER! YOUR BODY HAS DECAYED!
HAS IT BEEN SO LONG? I HAVE FAILED YOU!

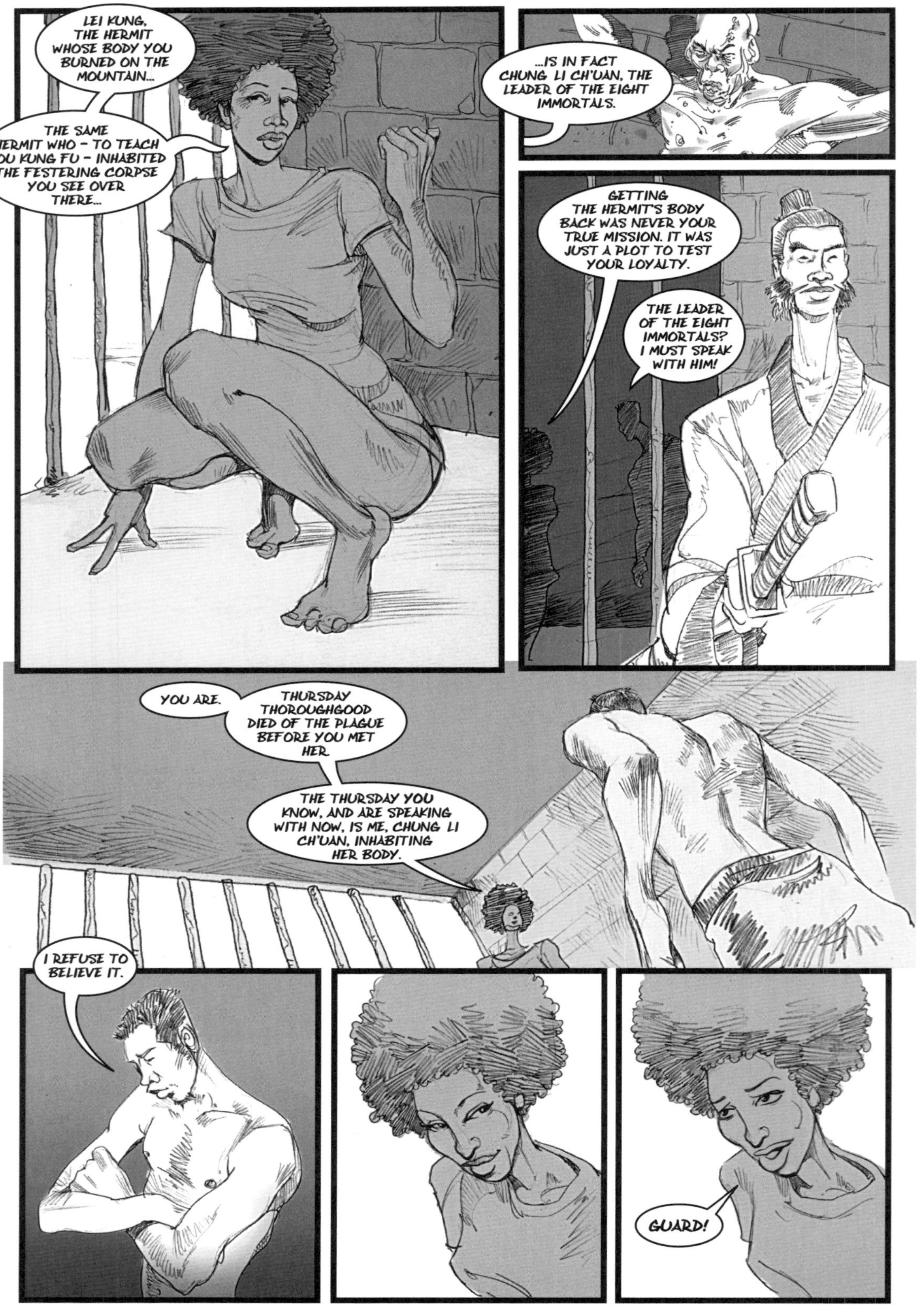
LEI KUNG, THE HERMIT WHOSE BODY YOU BURNED ON THE MOUNTAIN...
THE SAME HERMIT WHO - TO TEACH YOU KUNG FU - INHABITED THE FESTERING CORPSE YOU SEE OVER THERE...
...IS IN FACT CHUNG LI CH'UAN, THE LEADER OF THE EIGHT IMMORTALS.
GETTING THE HERMIT'S BODY BACK WAS NEVER YOUR TRUE MISSION. IT WAS JUST A PLOT TO TEST YOUR LOYALTY.
THE LEADER OF THE EIGHT IMMORTALS? I MUST SPEAK WITH HIM!
YOU ARE.
THURSDAY THOROUGHGOOD DIED OF THE PLAGUE BEFORE YOU MET HER.
THE THURSDAY YOU KNOW, AND ARE SPEAKING WITH NOW, IS ME, CHUNG LI CH'UAN, INHABITING HER BODY.
I REFUSE TO BELIEVE IT.
GUARD!

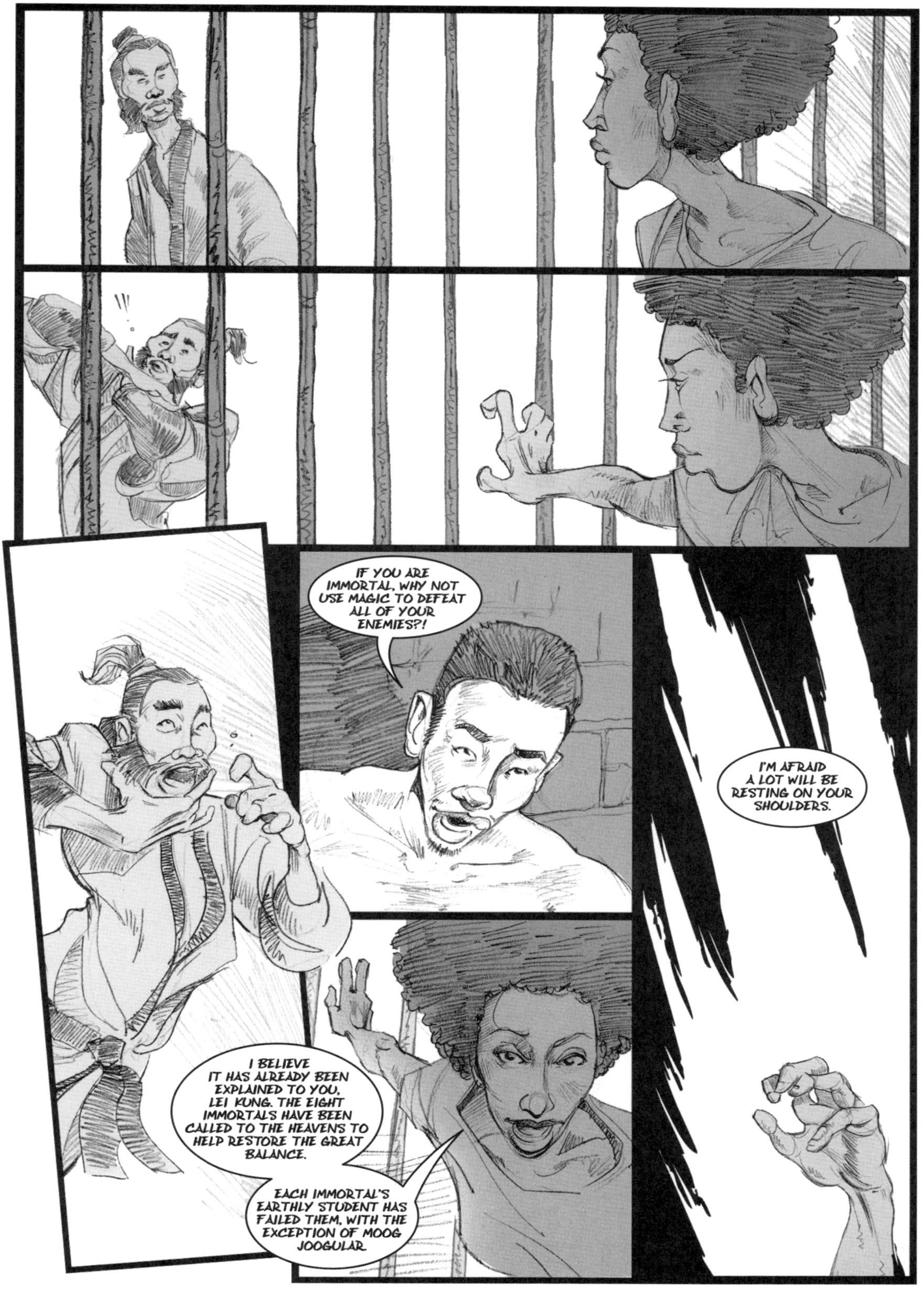

!!
IF YOU ARE IMMORTAL, WHY NOT USE MAGIC TO DEFEAT ALL OF YOUR ENEMIES?!
I'M AFRAID A LOT WILL BE RESTING ON YOUR SHOULDERS.
I BELIEVE IT HAS ALREADY BEEN EXPLAINED TO YOU, LEI KUNG. THE EIGHT IMMORTALS HAVE BEEN CALLED TO THE HEAVENS TO HELP RESTORE THE GREAT BALANCE.
EACH IMMORTAL'S EARTHLY STUDENT HAS FAILED THEM, WITH THE EXCEPTION OF MOOG JOOGULAR.

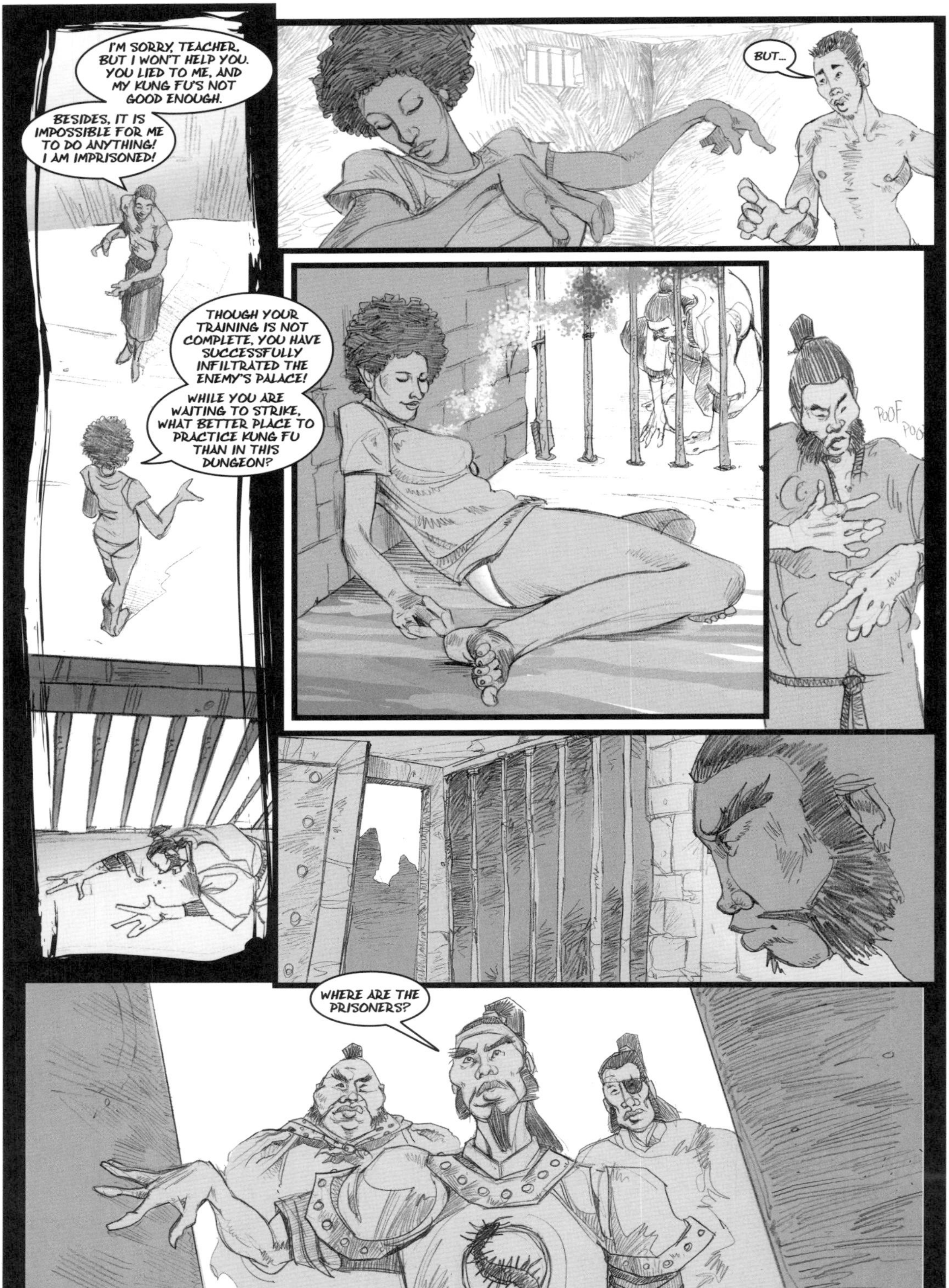

I'M SORRY, TEACHER, BUT I WON'T HELP YOU. YOU LIED TO ME, AND MY KUNG FU'S NOT GOOD ENOUGH.
BESIDES, IT IS IMPOSSIBLE FOR ME TO DO ANYTHING! I AM IMPRISONED!
BUT...
THOUGH YOUR TRAINING IS NOT COMPLETE, YOU HAVE SUCCESSFULLY INFILTRATED THE ENEMY'S PALACE!
WHILE YOU ARE WAITING TO STRIKE, WHAT BETTER PLACE TO PRACTICE KUNG FU THAN IN THIS DUNGEON?
POOF
WHERE ARE THE PRISONERS?

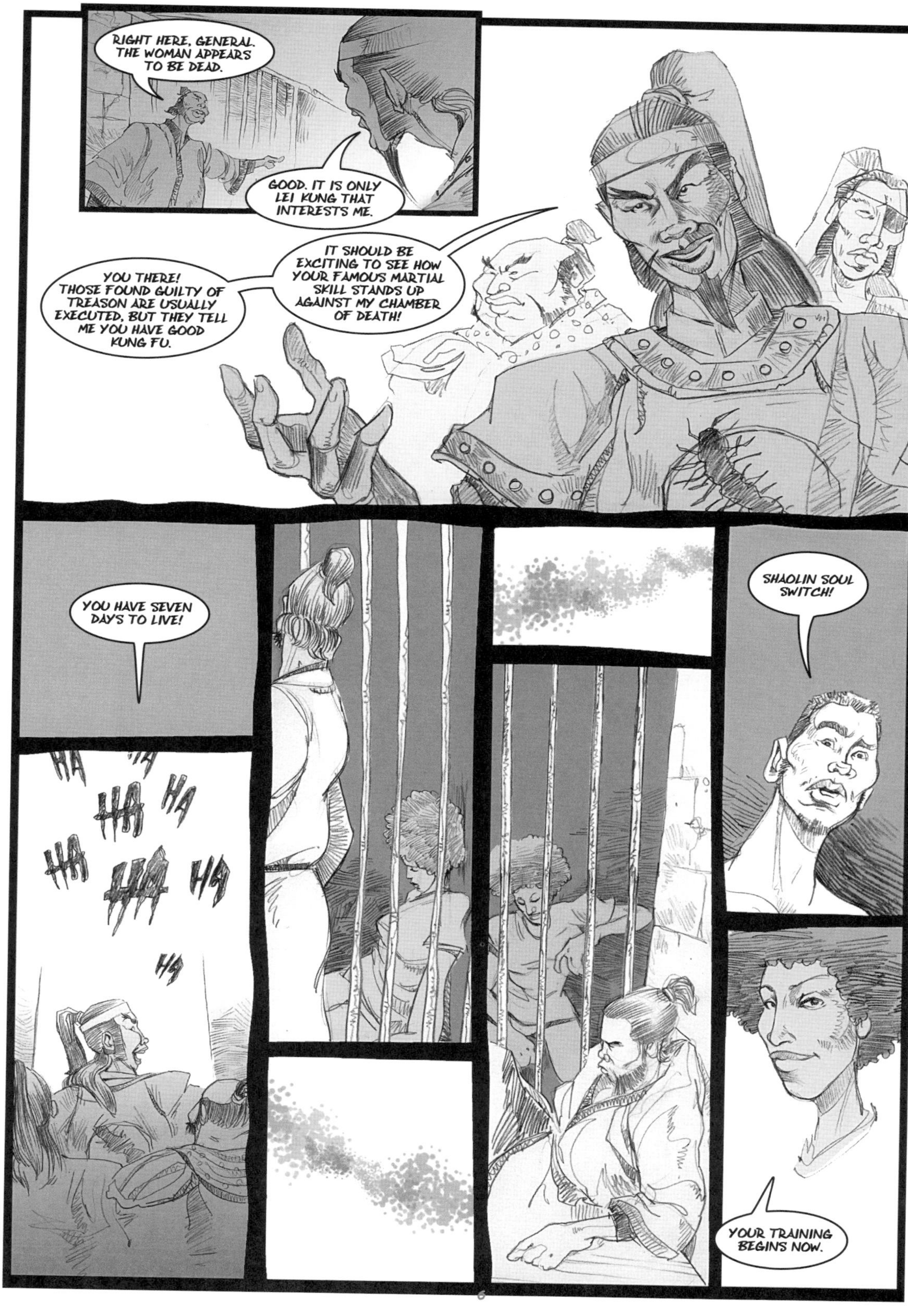
RIGHT HERE, GENERAL. THE WOMAN APPEARS TO BE DEAD.
GOOD. IT IS ONLY LEI KUNG THAT INTERESTS ME.
YOU THERE! THOSE FOUND GUILTY OF TREASON ARE USUALLY EXECUTED, BUT THEY TELL ME YOU HAVE GOOD KUNG FU.
IT SHOULD BE EXCITING TO SEE HOW YOUR FAMOUS MARTIAL SKILL STANDS UP AGAINST MY CHAMBER OF DEATH!
YOU HAVE SEVEN DAYS TO LIVE!
HA HA HA HA HA HA HA HA HA
SHAOLIN SOUL SWITCH!
YOUR TRAINING BEGINS NOW.

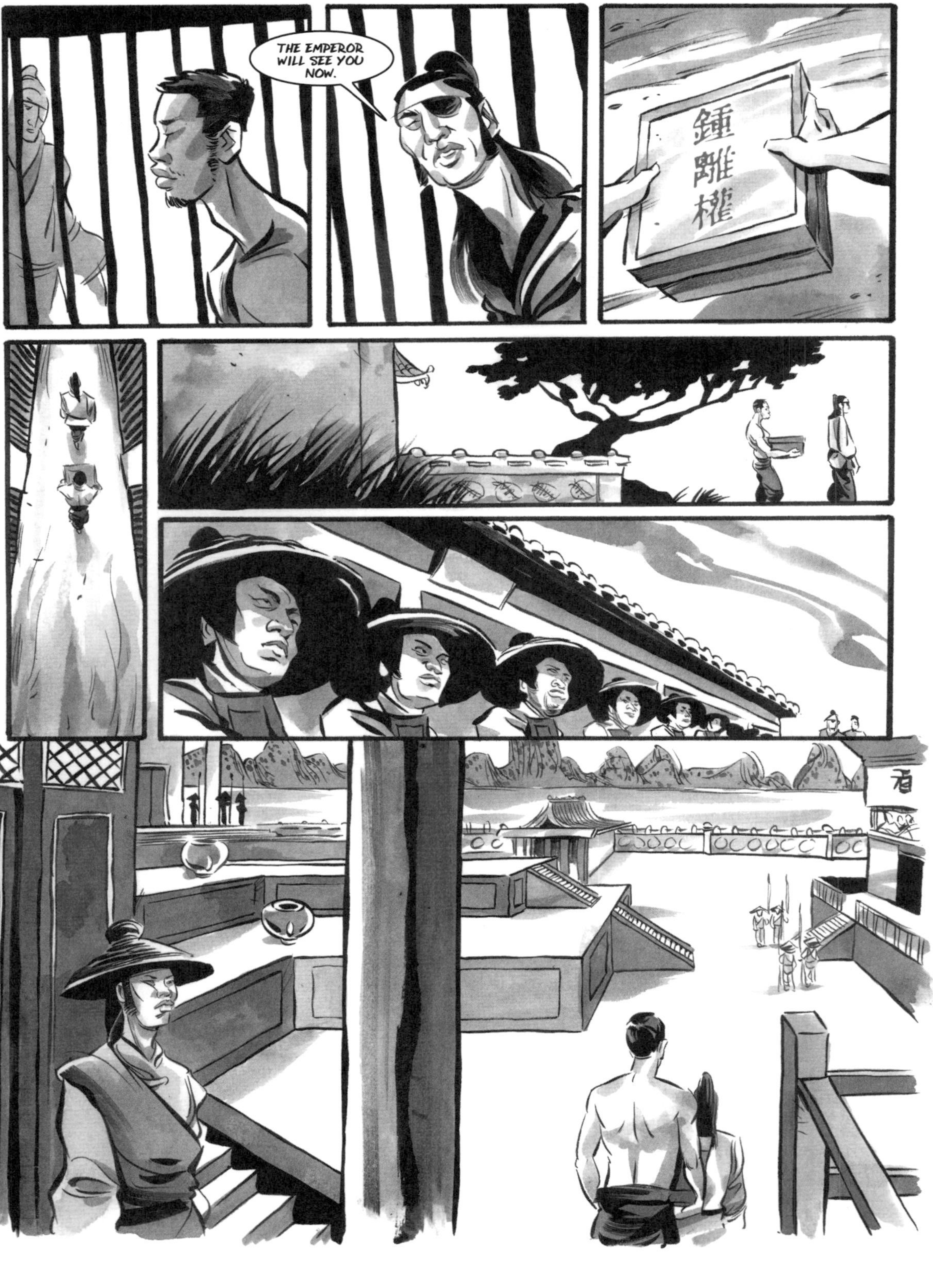
THE EMPEROR WILL SEE YOU NOW.
鍾離權

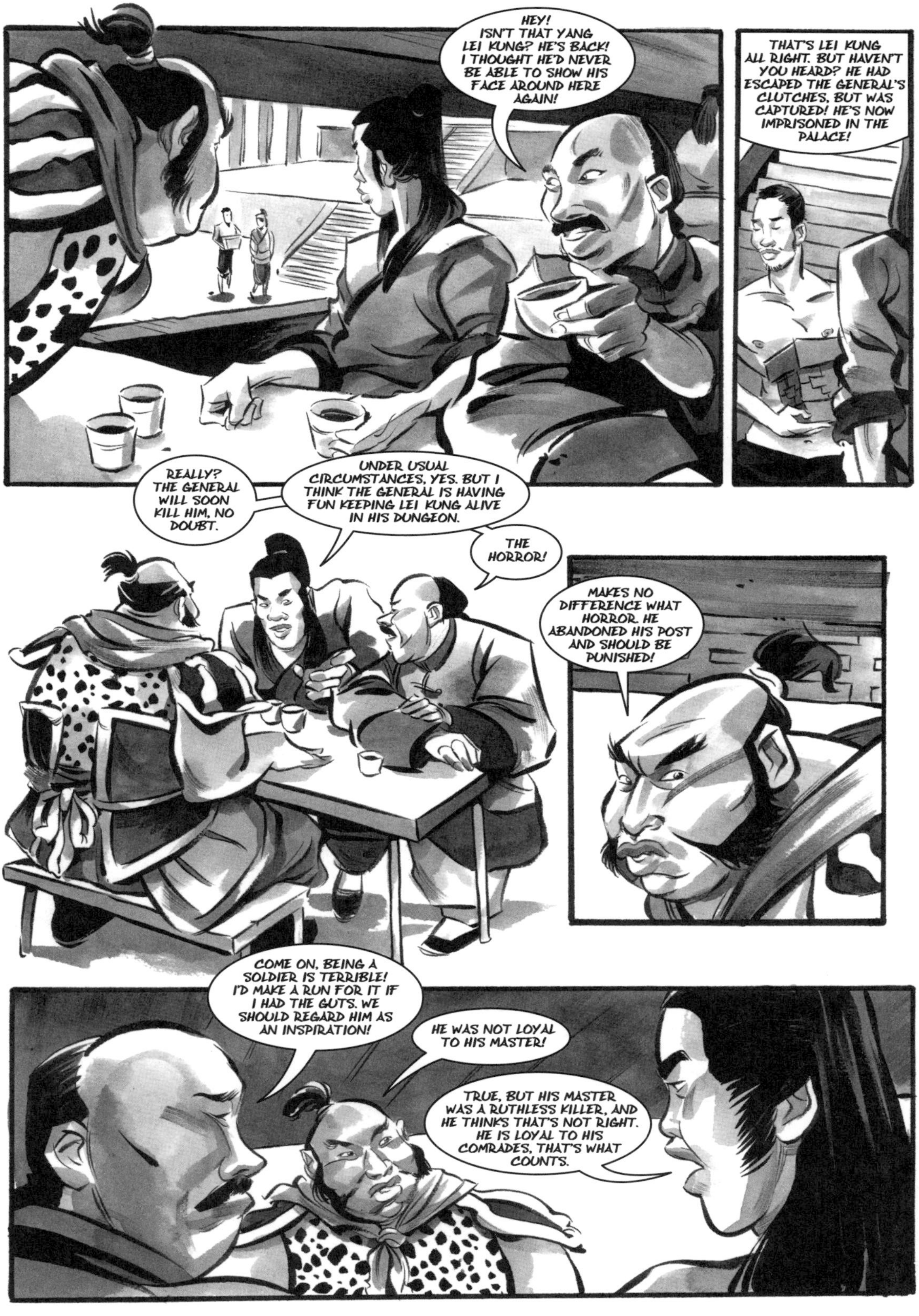
HEY! ISN'T THAT YANG LEI KUNG? HE'S BACK! I THOUGHT HE'D NEVER BE ABLE TO SHOW HIS FACE AROUND HERE AGAIN!
THAT'S LEI KUNG ALL RIGHT. BUT HAVEN'T YOU HEARD? HE HAD ESCAPED THE GENERAL'S CLUTCHES, BUT WAS CAPTURED! HE'S NOW IMPRISONED IN THE PALACE!
REALLY? THE GENERAL WILL SOON KILL HIM, NO DOUBT.
UNDER USUAL CIRCUMSTANCES, YES. BUT I THINK THE GENERAL IS HAVING FUN KEEPING LEI KUNG ALIVE IN HIS DUNGEON.
THE HORROR!
MAKES NO DIFFERENCE WHAT HORROR. HE ABANDONED HIS POST AND SHOULD BE PUNISHED!
COME ON, BEING A SOLDIER IS TERRIBLE! I'D MAKE A RUN FOR IT IF I HAD THE GUTS. WE SHOULD REGARD HIM AS AN INSPIRATION!
HE WAS NOT LOYAL TO HIS MASTER!
TRUE, BUT HIS MASTER WAS A RUTHLESS KILLER, AND HE THINKS THAT'S NOT RIGHT. HE IS LOYAL TO HIS COMRADES, THAT'S WHAT COUNTS.

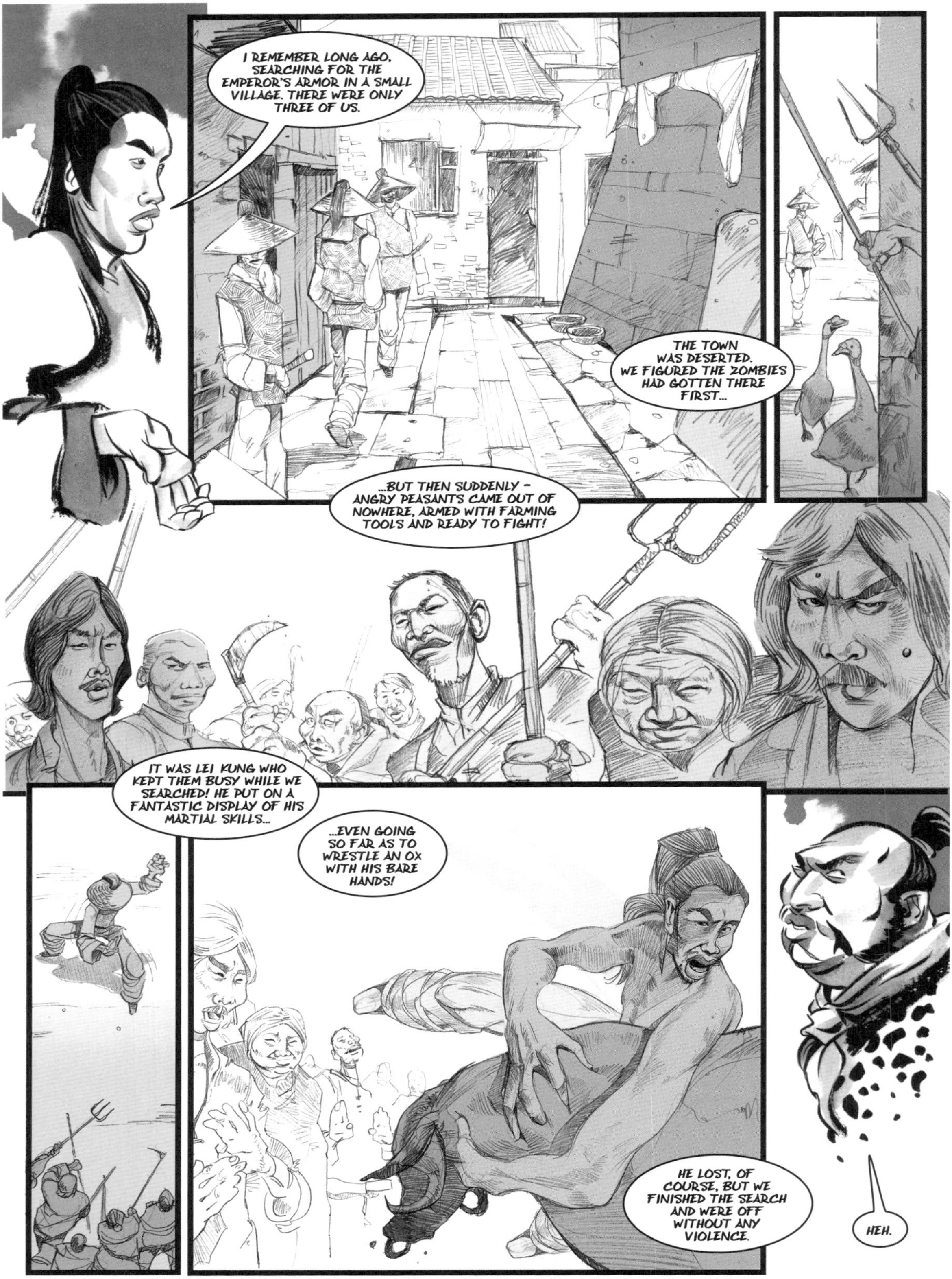
I REMEMBER LONG AGO, SEARCHING FOR THE EMPEROR'S ARMOR IN A SMALL VILLAGE. THERE WERE ONLY THREE OF US.
THE TOWN WAS DESERTED. WE FIGURED THE ZOMBIES HAD GOTTEN THERE FIRST...
...BUT THEN SUDDENLY – ANGRY PEASANTS CAME OUT OF NOWHERE, ARMED WITH FARMING TOOLS AND READY TO FIGHT!
IT WAS LEI KUNG WHO KEPT THEM BUSY WHILE WE SEARCHED! HE PUT ON A FANTASTIC DISPLAY OF HIS MARTIAL SKILLS...
...EVEN GOING SO FAR AS TO WRESTLE AN OX WITH HIS BARE HANDS!
HE LOST, OF COURSE, BUT WE FINISHED THE SEARCH AND WERE OFF WITHOUT ANY VIOLENCE.
HEH.

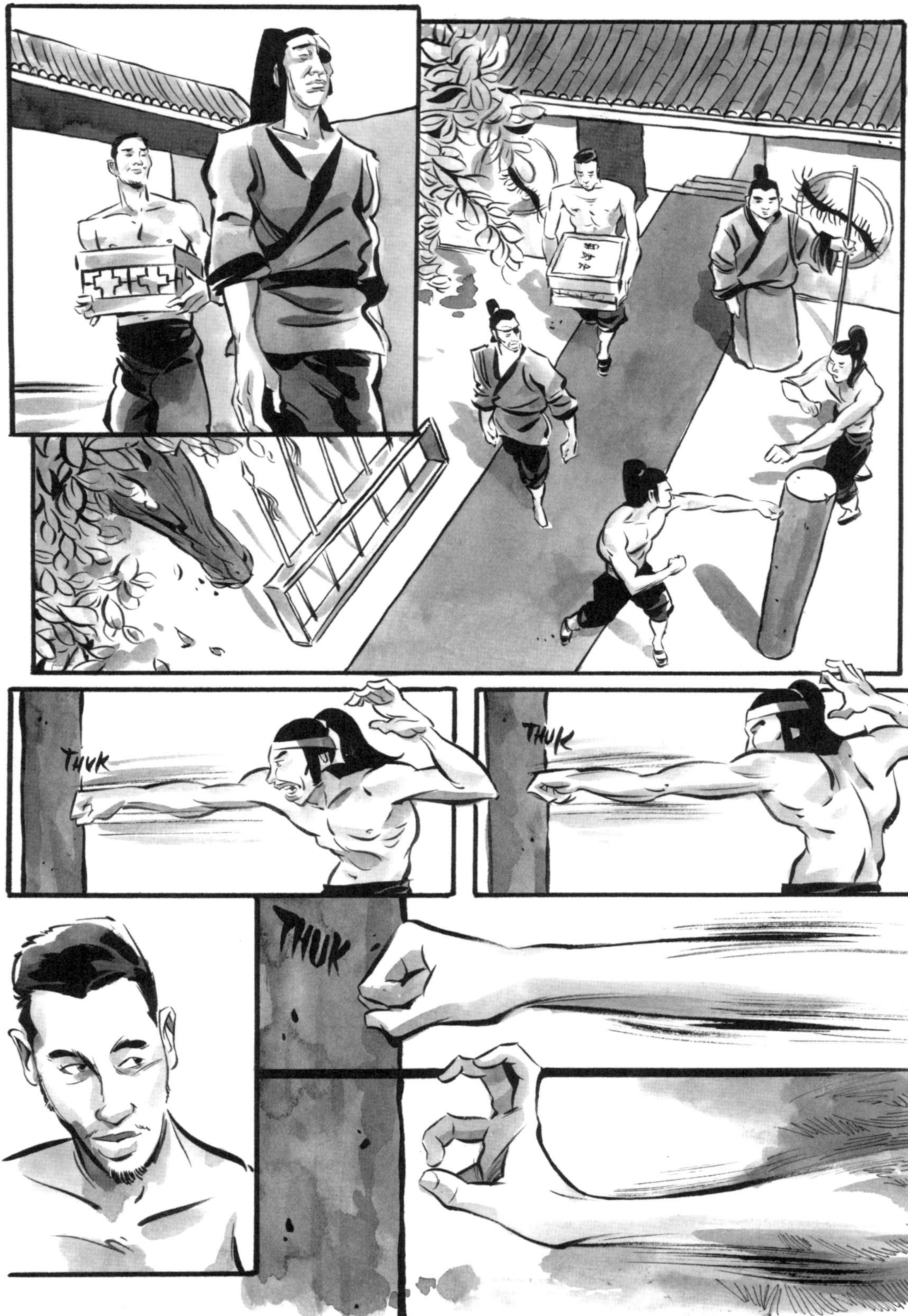
THUK
THUK
THUK

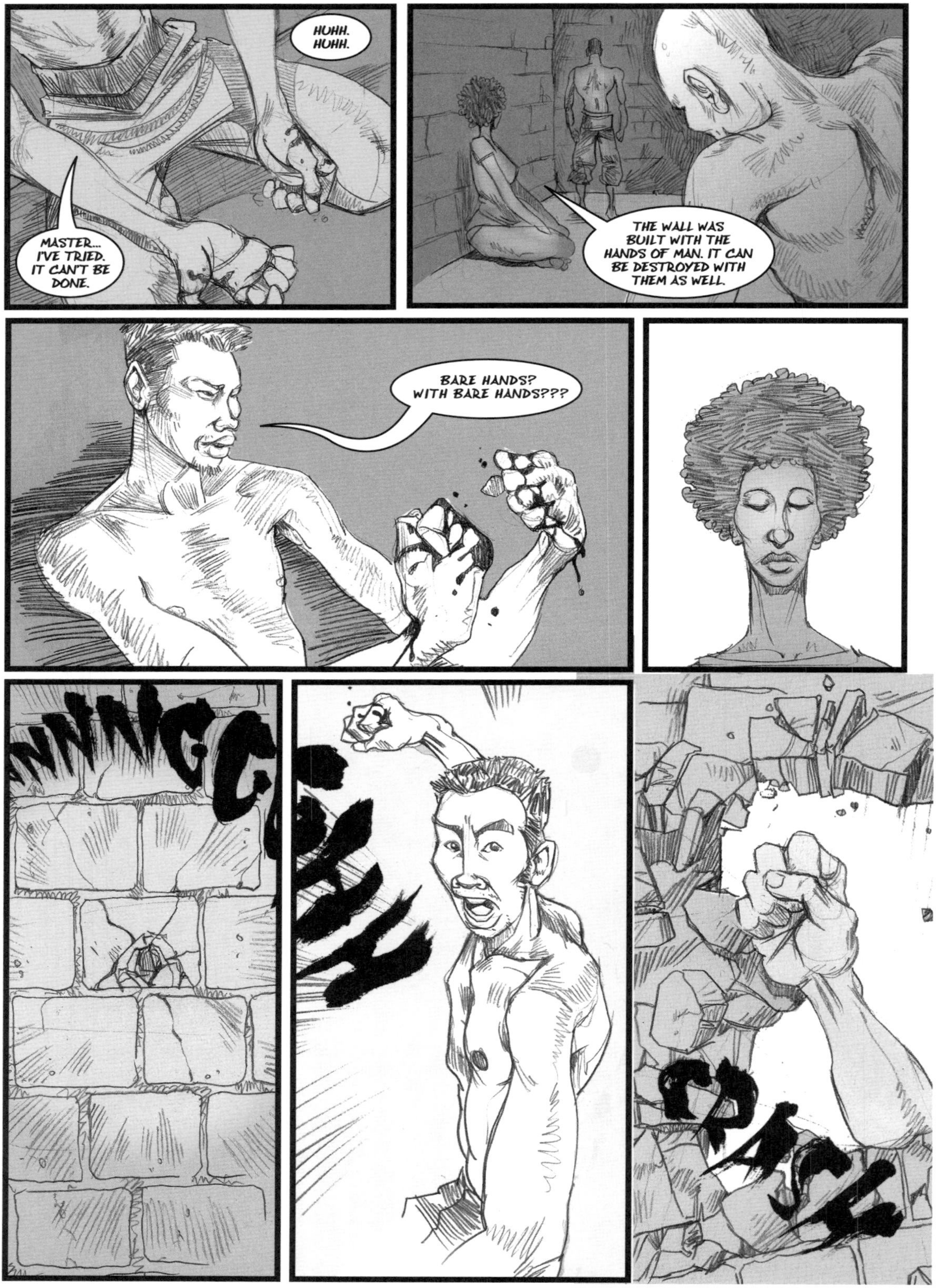
HUHH.
HUHH.
MASTER... I'VE TRIED. IT CAN'T BE DONE.
THE WALL WAS BUILT WITH THE HANDS OF MAN. IT CAN BE DESTROYED WITH THEM AS WELL.
BARE HANDS? WITH BARE HANDS???
CRASH

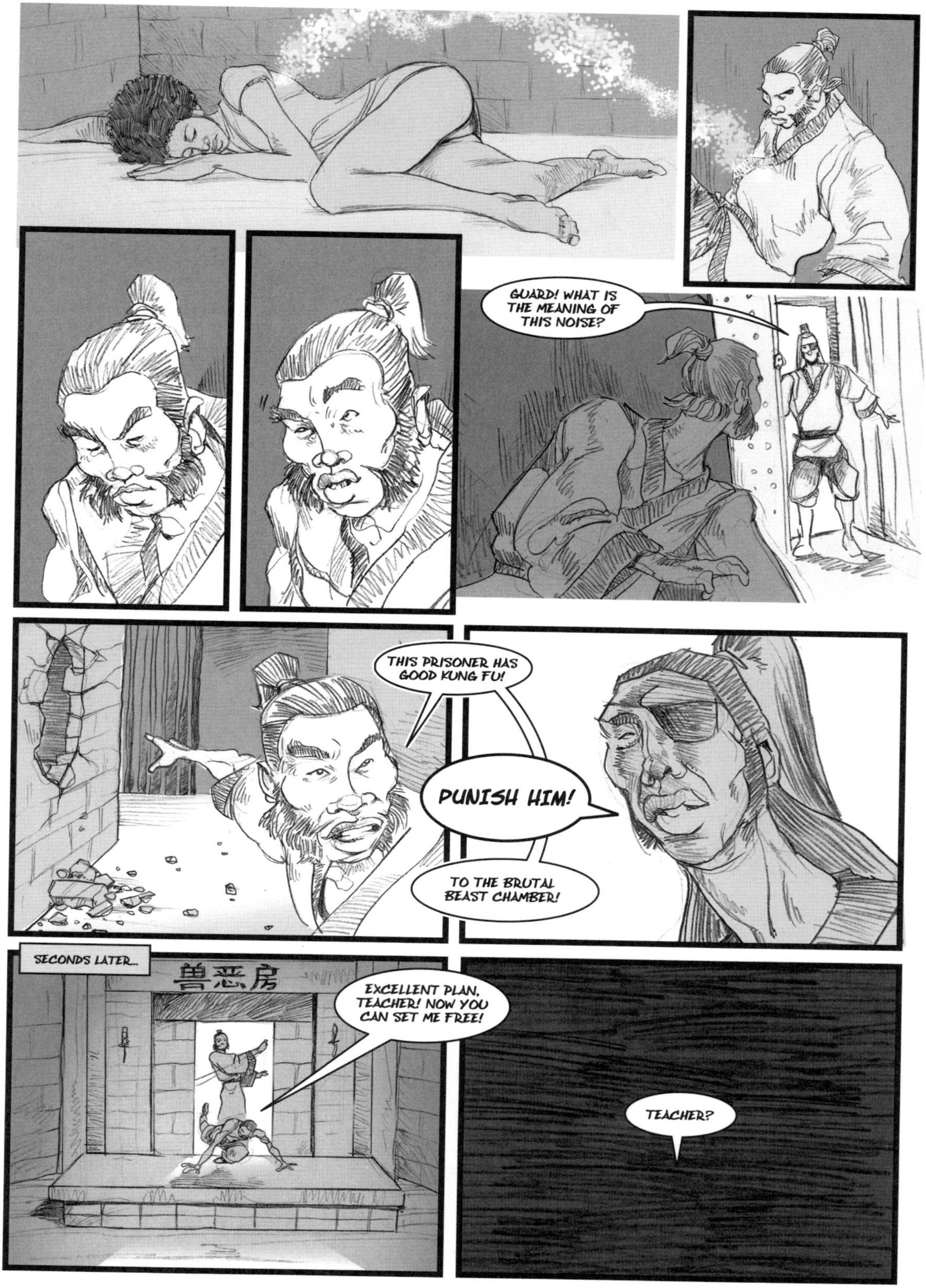
GUARD! WHAT IS THE MEANING OF THIS NOISE?
THIS PRISONER HAS GOOD KUNG FU!
PUNISH HIM!
TO THE BRUTAL BEAST CHAMBER!
SECONDS LATER...
兽恶房
EXCELLENT PLAN, TEACHER! NOW YOU CAN SET ME FREE!
TEACHER?

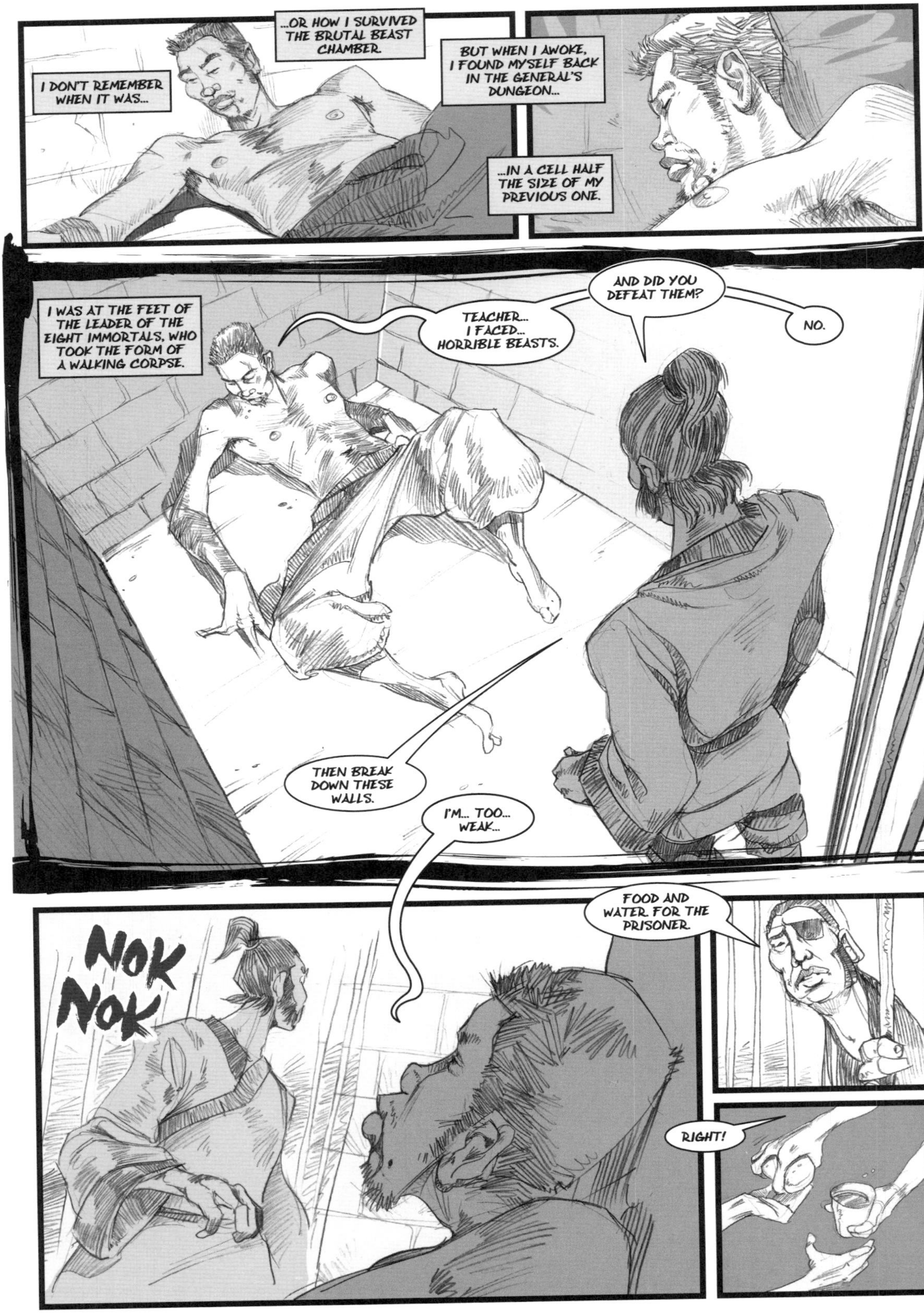
I DON'T REMEMBER WHEN IT WAS...
...OR HOW I SURVIVED THE BRUTAL BEAST CHAMBER.
BUT WHEN I AWOKE, I FOUND MYSELF BACK IN THE GENERAL'S DUNGEON...
...IN A CELL HALF THE SIZE OF MY PREVIOUS ONE.
I WAS AT THE FEET OF THE LEADER OF THE EIGHT IMMORTALS, WHO TOOK THE FORM OF A WALKING CORPSE.
TEACHER... I FACED... HORRIBLE BEASTS.
AND DID YOU DEFEAT THEM?
NO.
THEN BREAK DOWN THESE WALLS.
I'M... TOO... WEAK...
NOK NOK
FOOD AND WATER FOR THE PRISONER.
RIGHT!

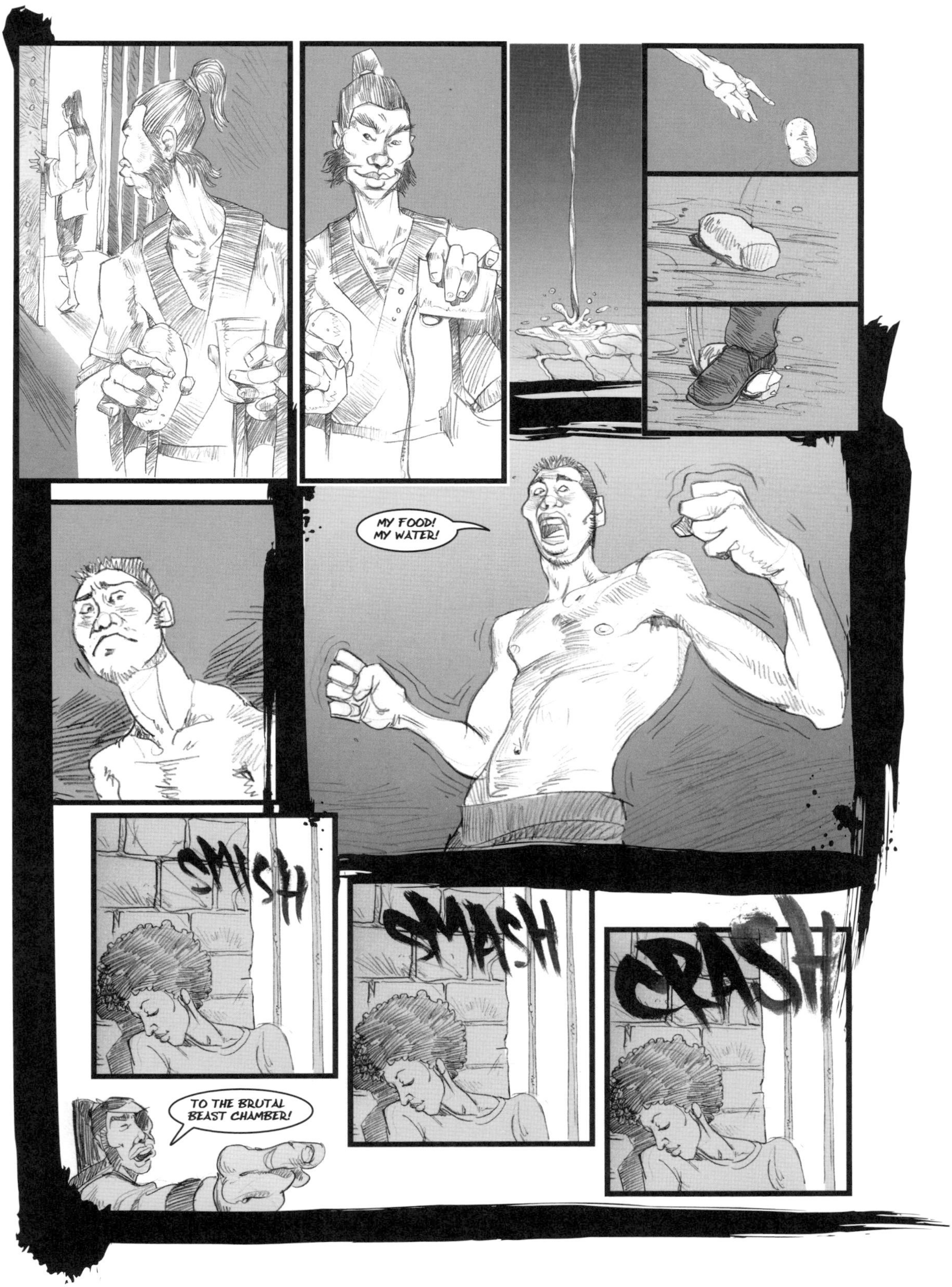
MY FOOD! MY WATER!
SMISH
SMASH
CRASH
TO THE BRUTAL BEAST CHAMBER!

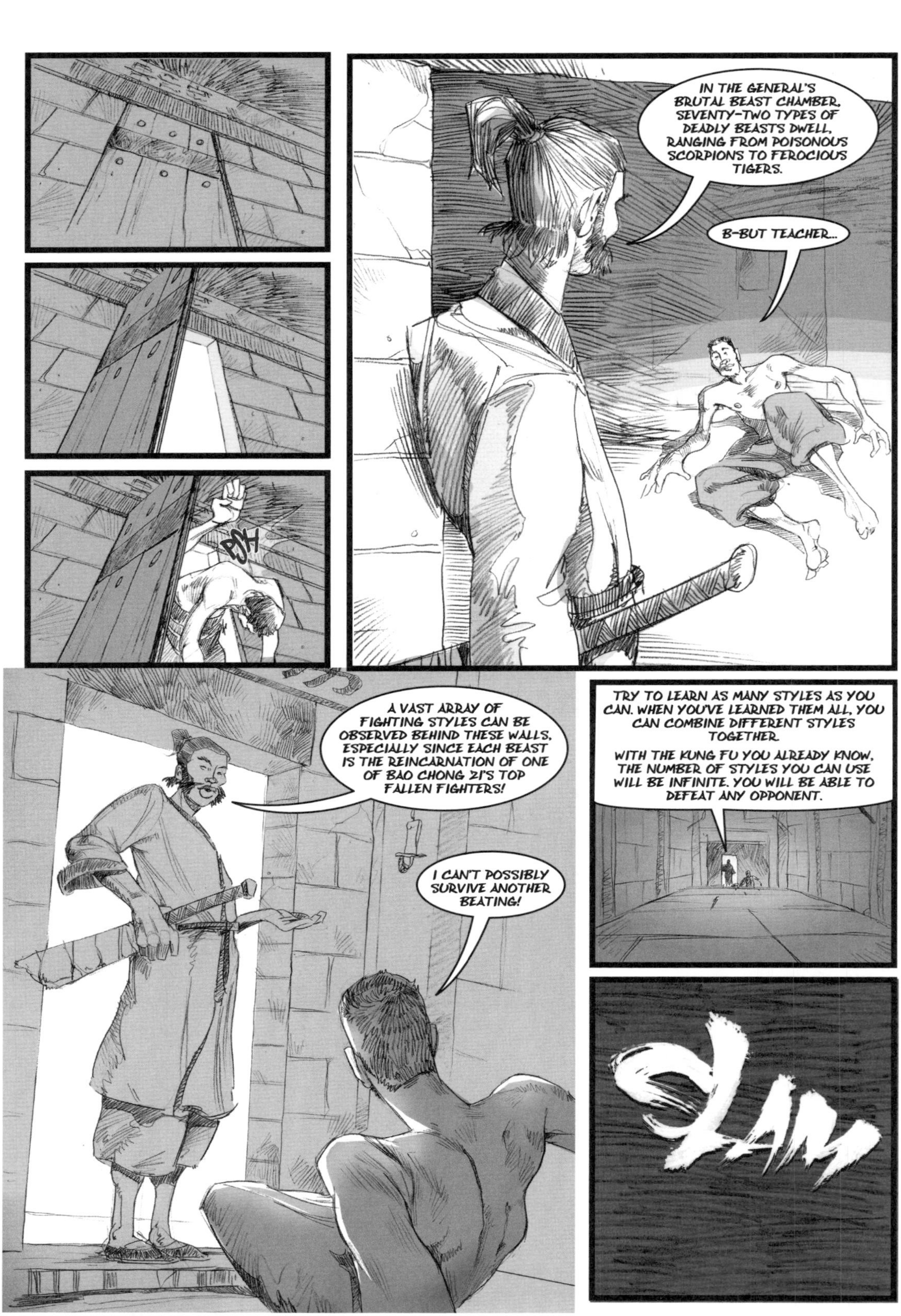
PSH
IN THE GENERAL'S BRUTAL BEAST CHAMBER, SEVENTY-TWO TYPES OF DEADLY BEASTS DWELL, RANGING FROM POISONOUS SCORPIONS TO FEROCIOUS TIGERS.
B-BUT TEACHER...
A VAST ARRAY OF FIGHTING STYLES CAN BE OBSERVED BEHIND THESE WALLS, ESPECIALLY SINCE EACH BEAST IS THE REINCARNATION OF ONE OF BAO CHONG ZI'S TOP FALLEN FIGHTERS!
I CAN'T POSSIBLY SURVIVE ANOTHER BEATING!
TRY TO LEARN AS MANY STYLES AS YOU CAN. WHEN YOU'VE LEARNED THEM ALL, YOU CAN COMBINE DIFFERENT STYLES TOGETHER.
WITH THE KUNG FU YOU ALREADY KNOW, THE NUMBER OF STYLES YOU CAN USE WILL BE INFINITE. YOU WILL BE ABLE TO DEFEAT ANY OPPONENT.
SLAM

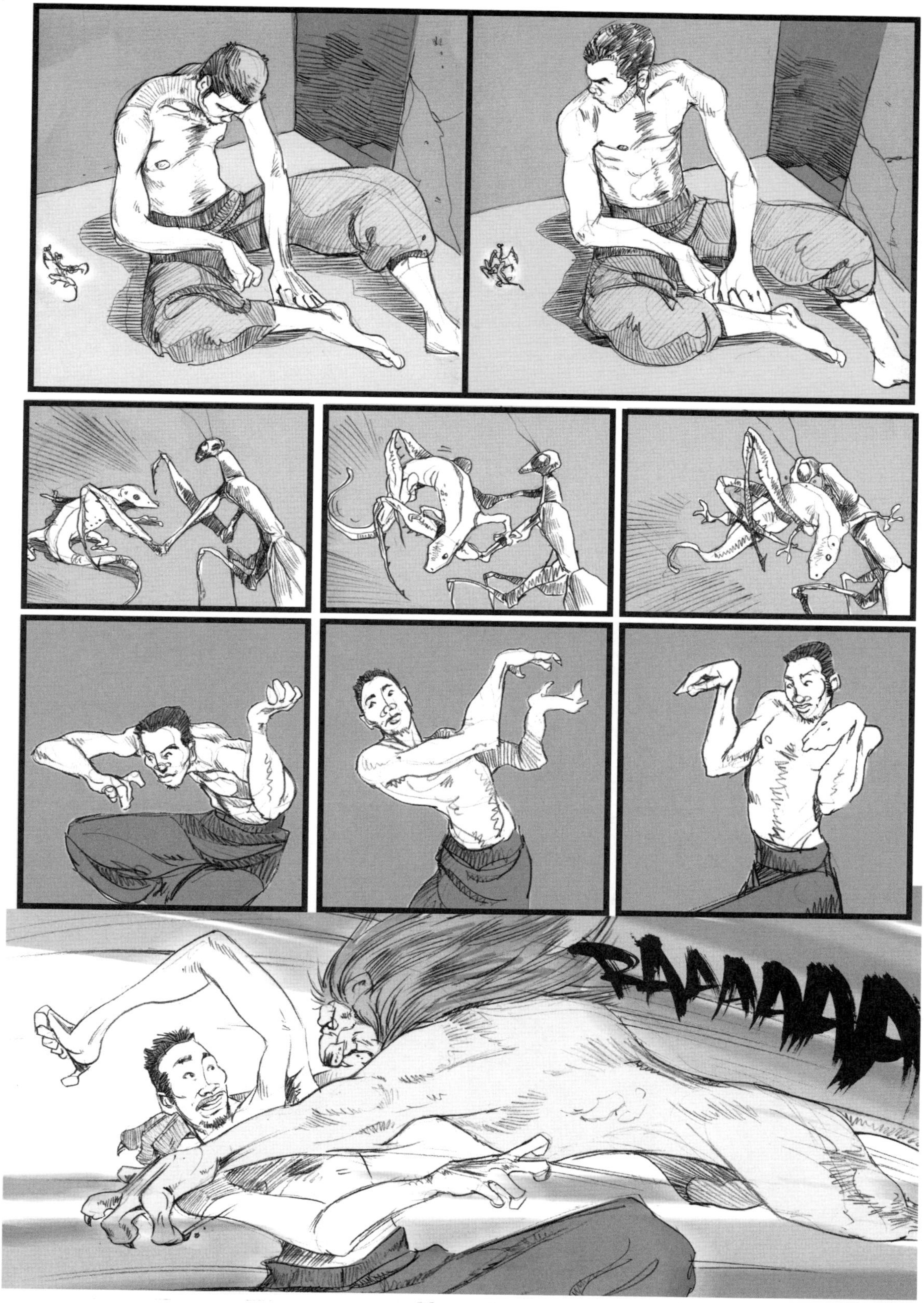
RAAAAAA

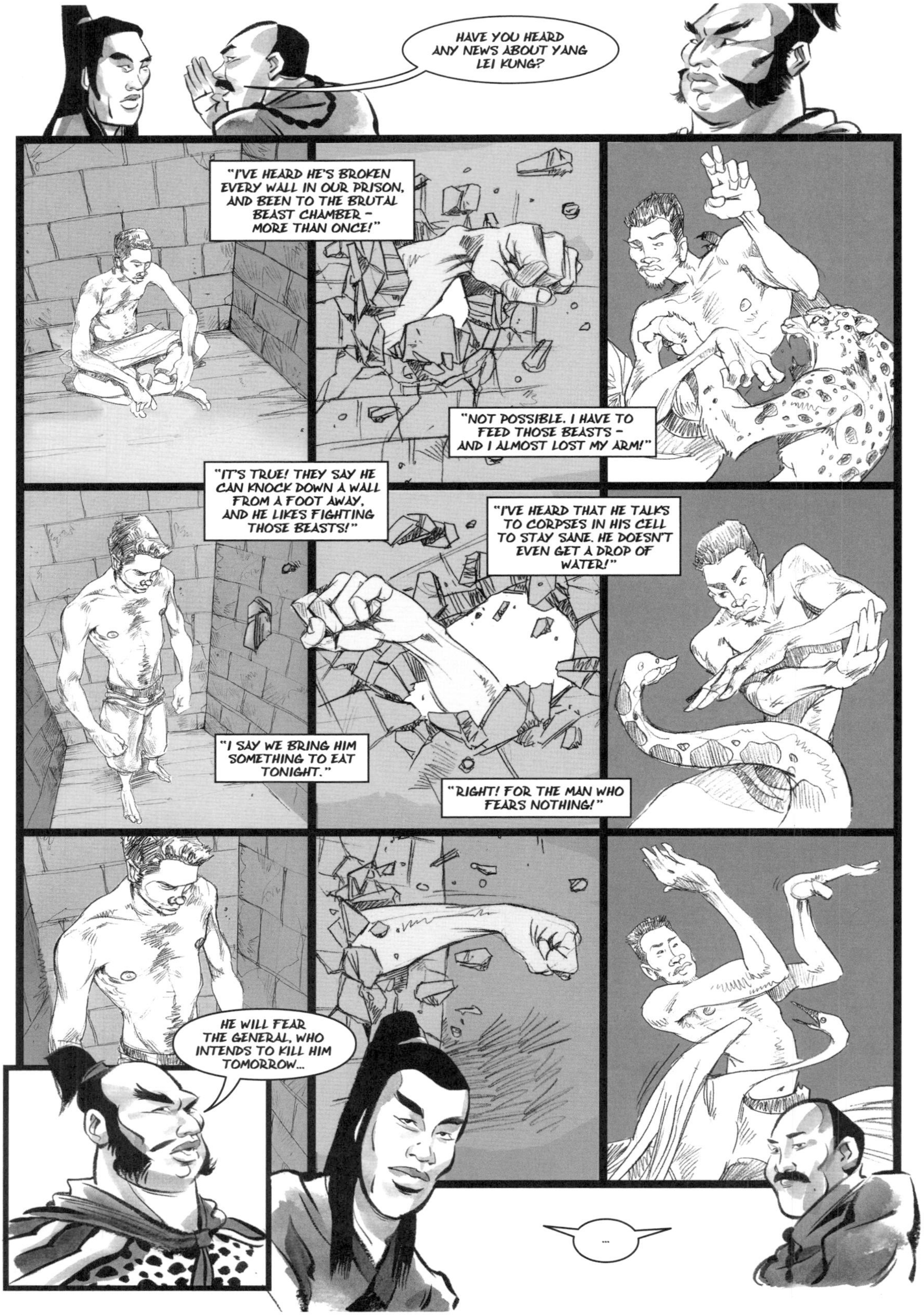
HAVE YOU HEARD ANY NEWS ABOUT YANG LEI KUNG?
"I'VE HEARD HE'S BROKEN EVERY WALL IN OUR PRISON, AND BEEN TO THE BRUTAL BEAST CHAMBER – MORE THAN ONCE!"
"NOT POSSIBLE. I HAVE TO FEED THOSE BEASTS – AND I ALMOST LOST MY ARM!"
"IT'S TRUE! THEY SAY HE CAN KNOCK DOWN A WALL FROM A FOOT AWAY, AND HE LIKES FIGHTING THOSE BEASTS!"
"I'VE HEARD THAT HE TALKS TO CORPSES IN HIS CELL TO STAY SANE. HE DOESN'T EVEN GET A DROP OF WATER!"
"I SAY WE BRING HIM SOMETHING TO EAT TONIGHT."
"RIGHT! FOR THE MAN WHO FEARS NOTHING!"
HE WILL FEAR THE GENERAL, WHO INTENDS TO KILL HIM TOMORROW...
...

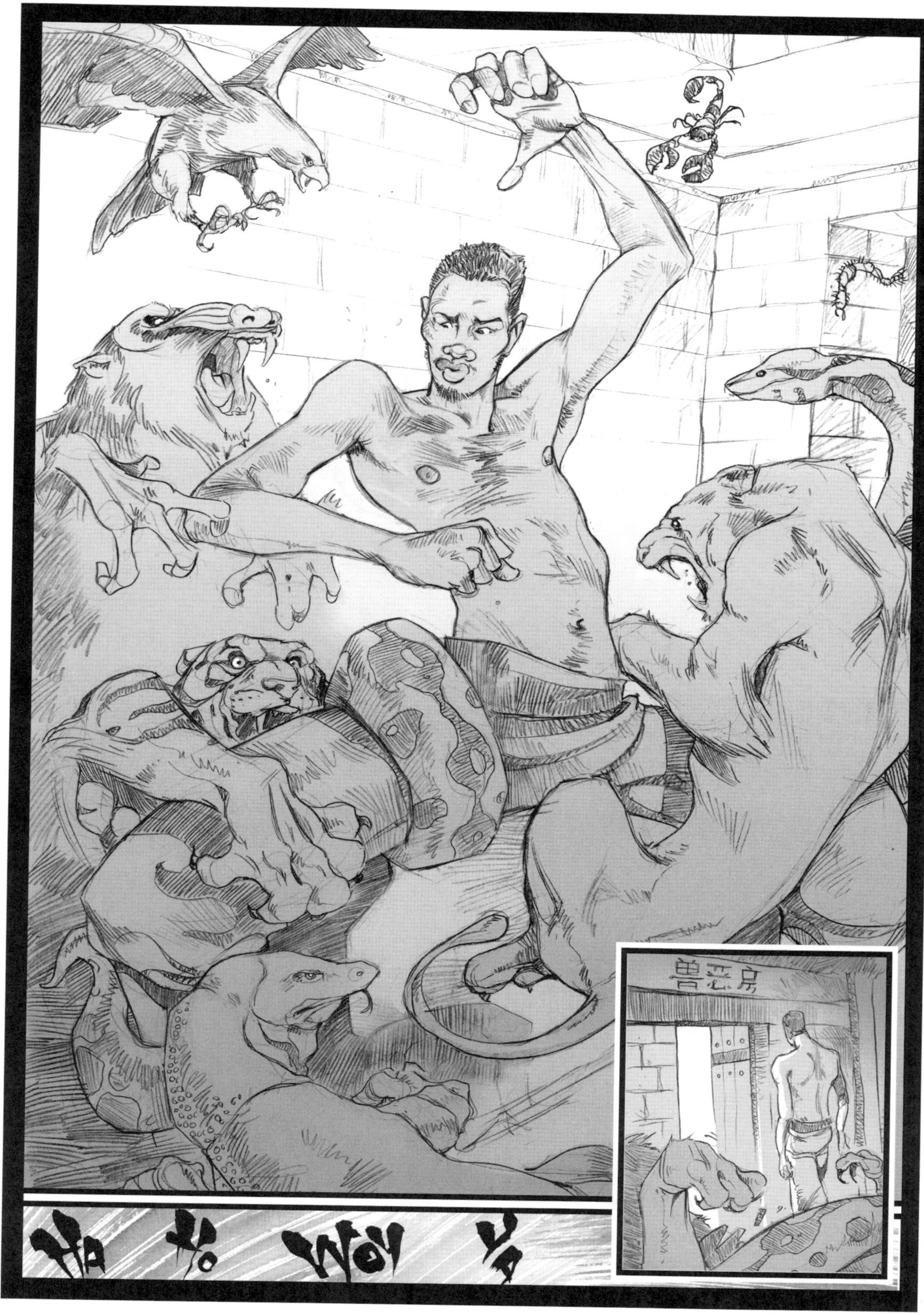

HA HO WOY YA
兽恶房

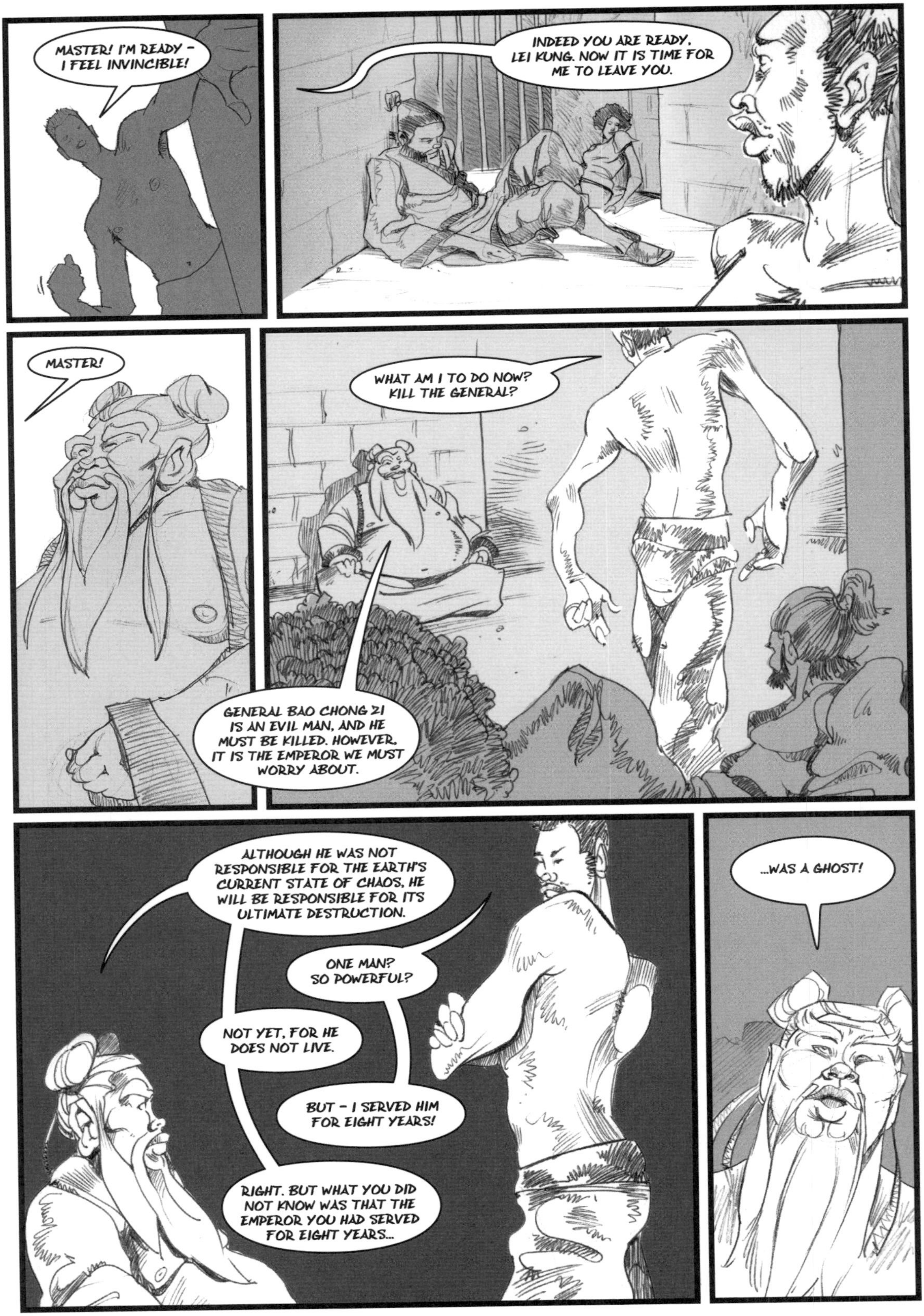
MASTER! I'M READY – I FEEL INVINCIBLE!
INDEED YOU ARE READY, LEI KUNG. NOW IT IS TIME FOR ME TO LEAVE YOU.
MASTER!
WHAT AM I TO DO NOW? KILL THE GENERAL?
GENERAL BAO CHONG ZI IS AN EVIL MAN, AND HE MUST BE KILLED. HOWEVER, IT IS THE EMPEROR WE MUST WORRY ABOUT.
ALTHOUGH HE WAS NOT RESPONSIBLE FOR THE EARTH'S CURRENT STATE OF CHAOS, HE WILL BE RESPONSIBLE FOR ITS ULTIMATE DESTRUCTION.
ONE MAN? SO POWERFUL?
NOT YET, FOR HE DOES NOT LIVE.
BUT – I SERVED HIM FOR EIGHT YEARS!
RIGHT. BUT WHAT YOU DID NOT KNOW WAS THAT THE EMPEROR YOU HAD SERVED FOR EIGHT YEARS...
...WAS A GHOST!

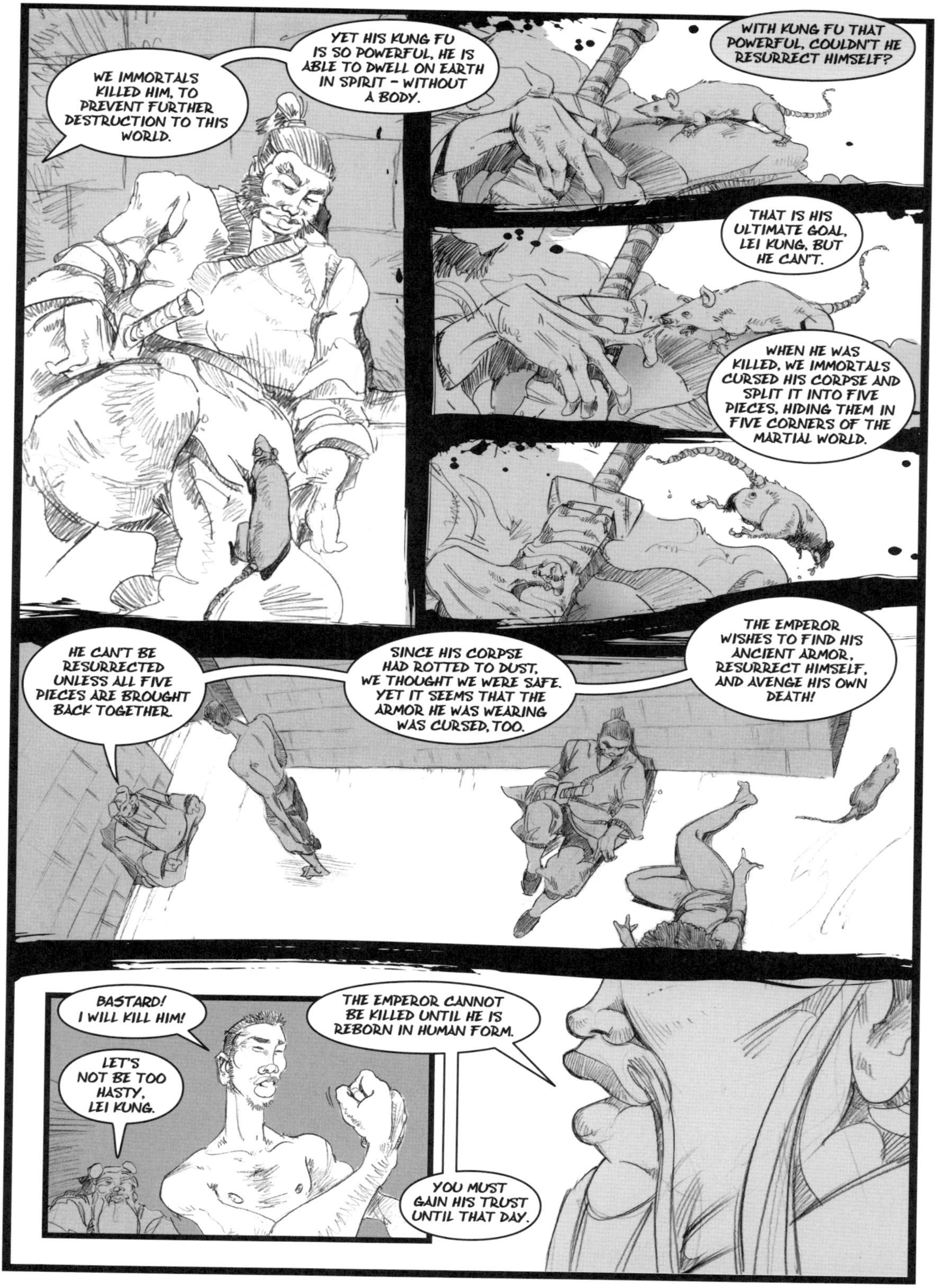
WE IMMORTALS KILLED HIM, TO PREVENT FURTHER DESTRUCTION TO THIS WORLD.
YET HIS KUNG FU IS SO POWERFUL, HE IS ABLE TO DWELL ON EARTH IN SPIRIT - WITHOUT A BODY.
WITH KUNG FU THAT POWERFUL, COULDN'T HE RESURRECT HIMSELF?
THAT IS HIS ULTIMATE GOAL, LEI KUNG, BUT HE CAN'T.
WHEN HE WAS KILLED, WE IMMORTALS CURSED HIS CORPSE AND SPLIT IT INTO FIVE PIECES, HIDING THEM IN FIVE CORNERS OF THE MARTIAL WORLD.
HE CAN'T BE RESURRECTED UNLESS ALL FIVE PIECES ARE BROUGHT BACK TOGETHER.
SINCE HIS CORPSE HAD ROTTED TO DUST, WE THOUGHT WE WERE SAFE. YET IT SEEMS THAT THE ARMOR HE WAS WEARING WAS CURSED, TOO.
THE EMPEROR WISHES TO FIND HIS ANCIENT ARMOR, RESURRECT HIMSELF, AND AVENGE HIS OWN DEATH!
BASTARD! I WILL KILL HIM!
LET'S NOT BE TOO HASTY, LEI KUNG.
THE EMPEROR CANNOT BE KILLED UNTIL HE IS REBORN IN HUMAN FORM.
YOU MUST GAIN HIS TRUST UNTIL THAT DAY.

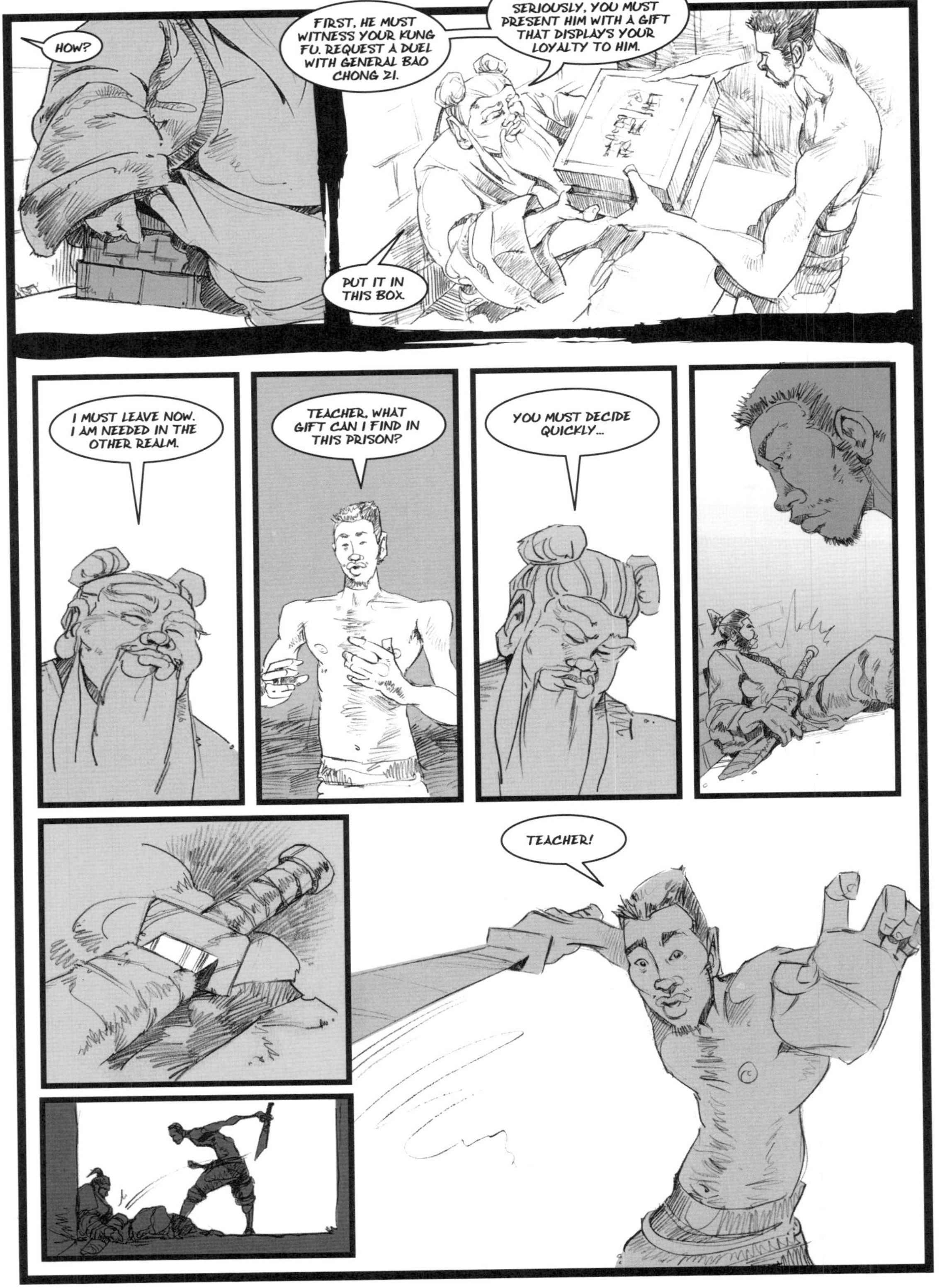
HOW?
FIRST, HE MUST WITNESS YOUR KUNG FU. REQUEST A DUEL WITH GENERAL BAO CHONG ZI.
TO ASSURE THE EMPEROR TAKES YOU SERIOUSLY, YOU MUST PRESENT HIM WITH A GIFT THAT DISPLAYS YOUR LOYALTY TO HIM.
PUT IT IN THIS BOX.
I MUST LEAVE NOW. I AM NEEDED IN THE OTHER REALM.
TEACHER, WHAT GIFT CAN I FIND IN THIS PRISON?
YOU MUST DECIDE QUICKLY...
TEACHER!

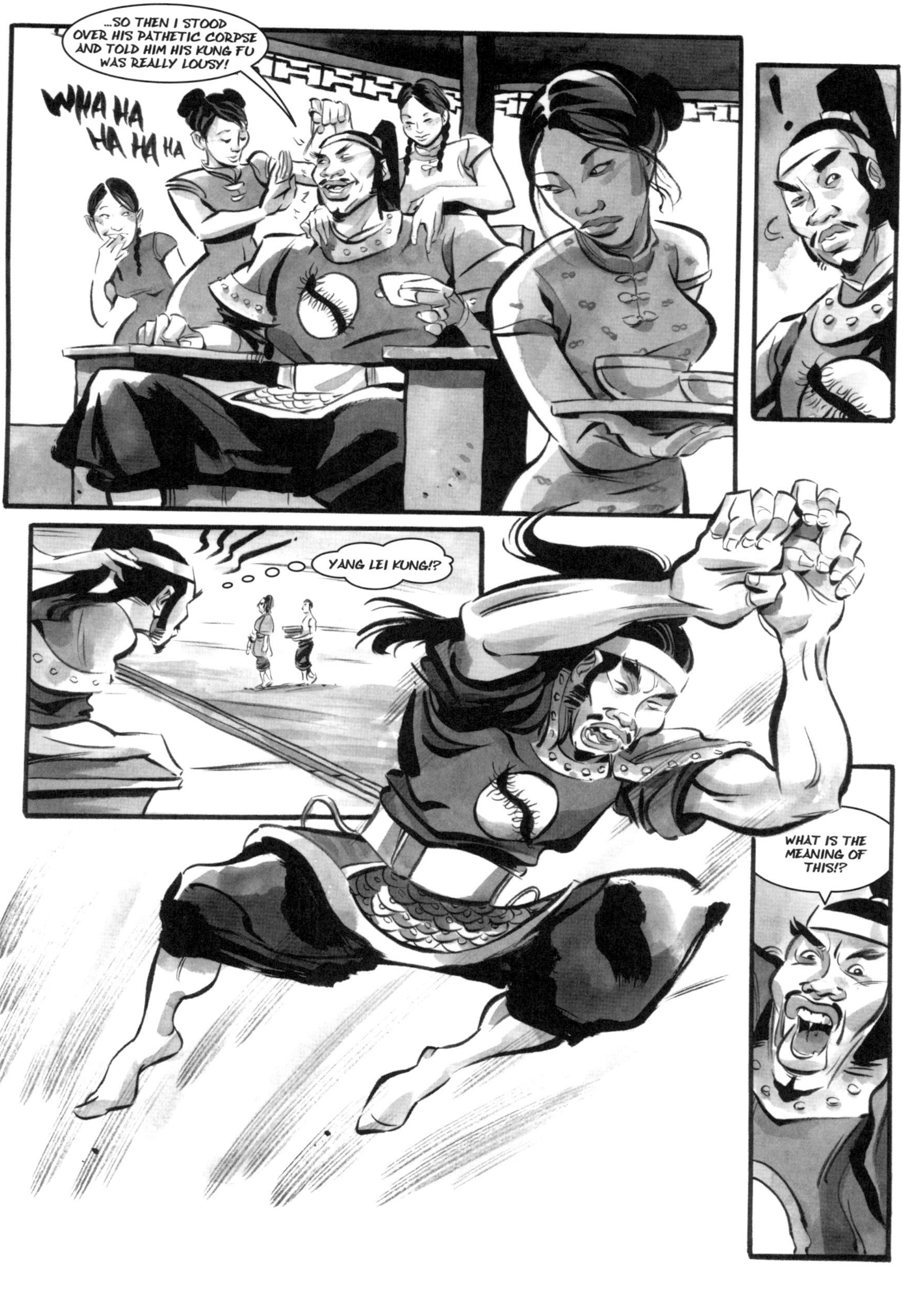
...SO THEN I STOOD OVER HIS PATHETIC CORPSE AND TOLD HIM HIS KUNG FU WAS REALLY LOUSY!
WHA HA HA HA HA
!
YANG LEI KUNG!?
WHAT IS THE MEANING OF THIS!?

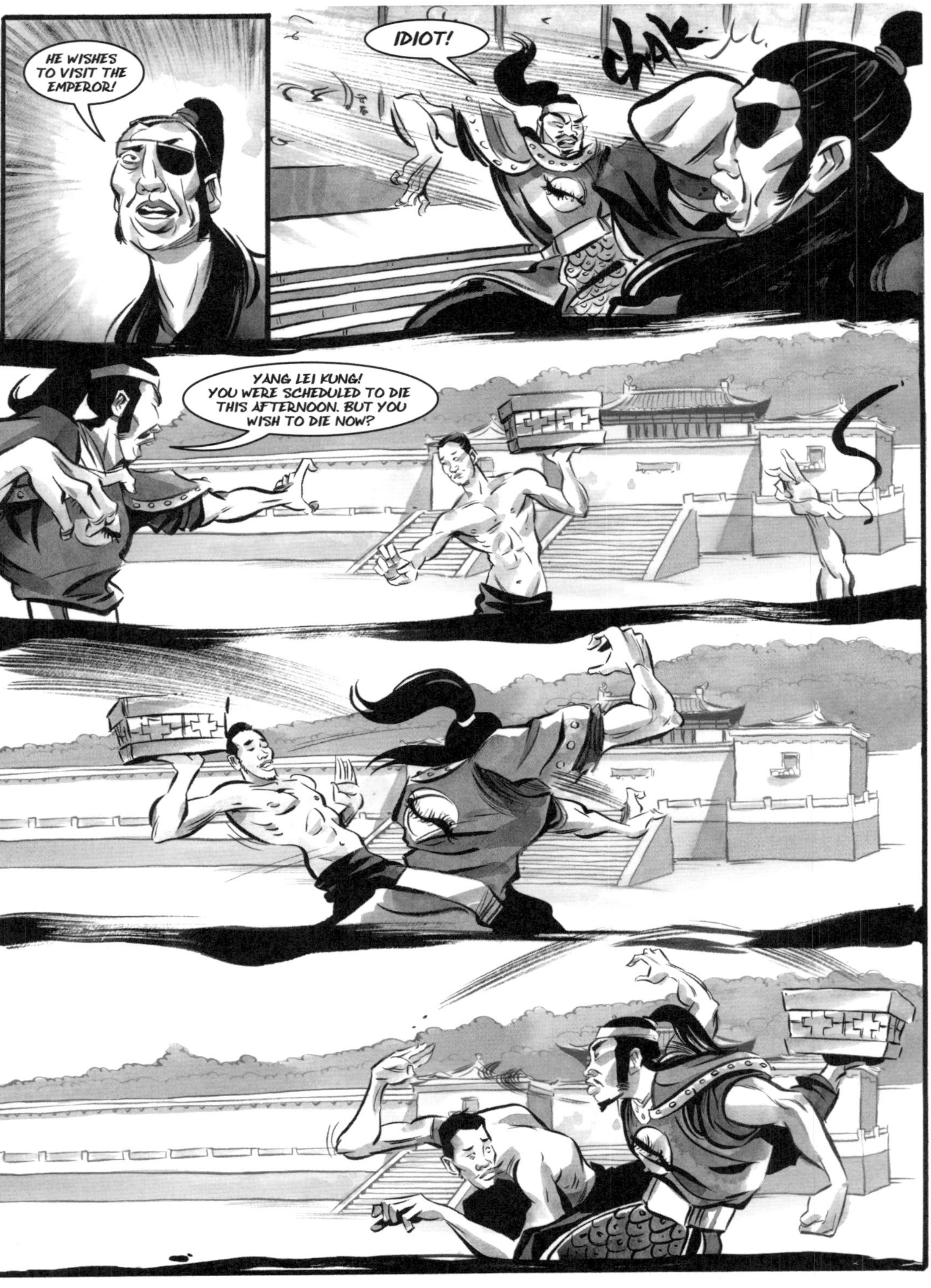
HE WISHES TO VISIT THE EMPEROR!
IDIOT!
CHAK
YANG LEI KUNG! YOU WERE SCHEDULED TO DIE THIS AFTERNOON. BUT YOU WISH TO DIE NOW?

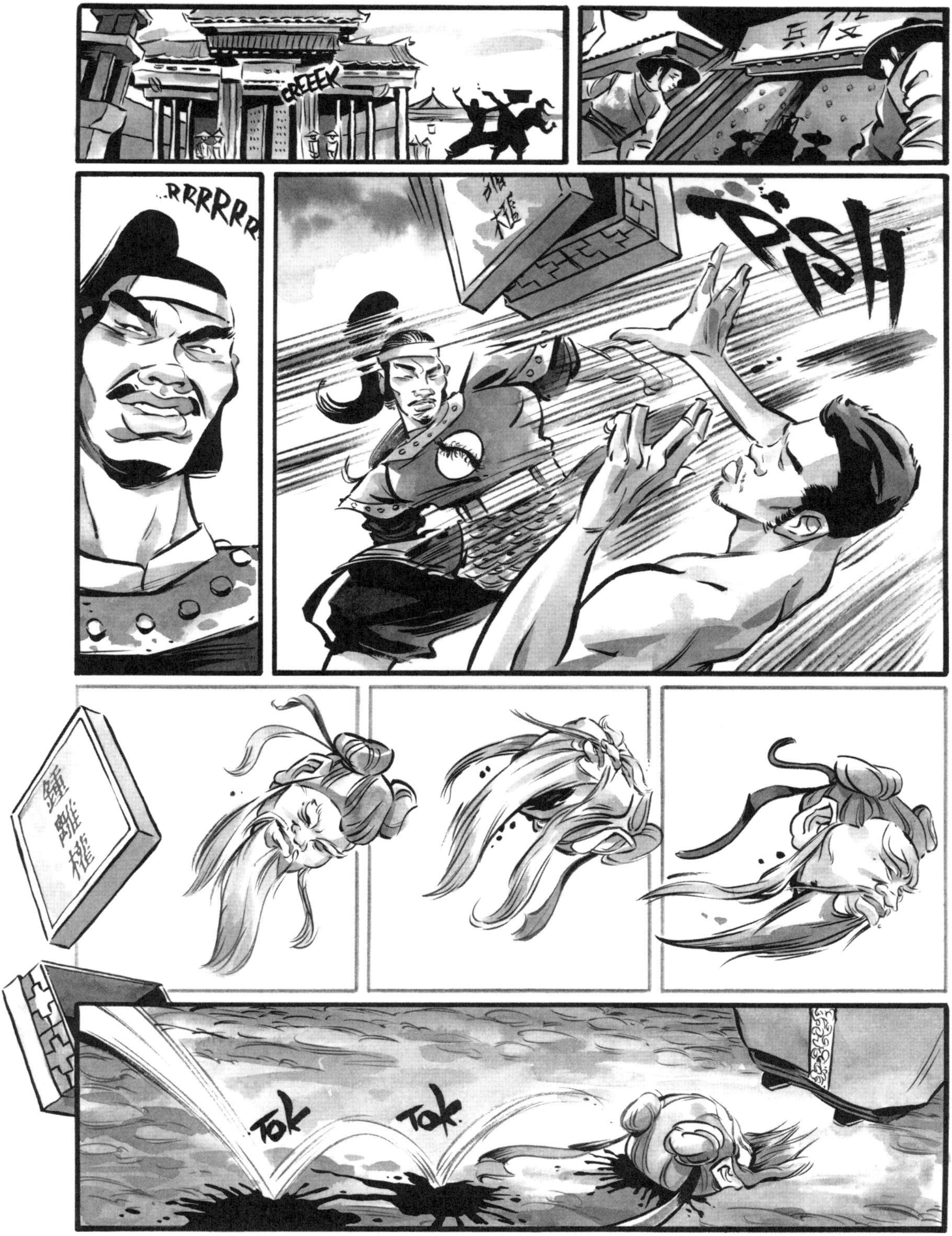
CREEEK
...RRRRRRR
PISH
TOK
TOK

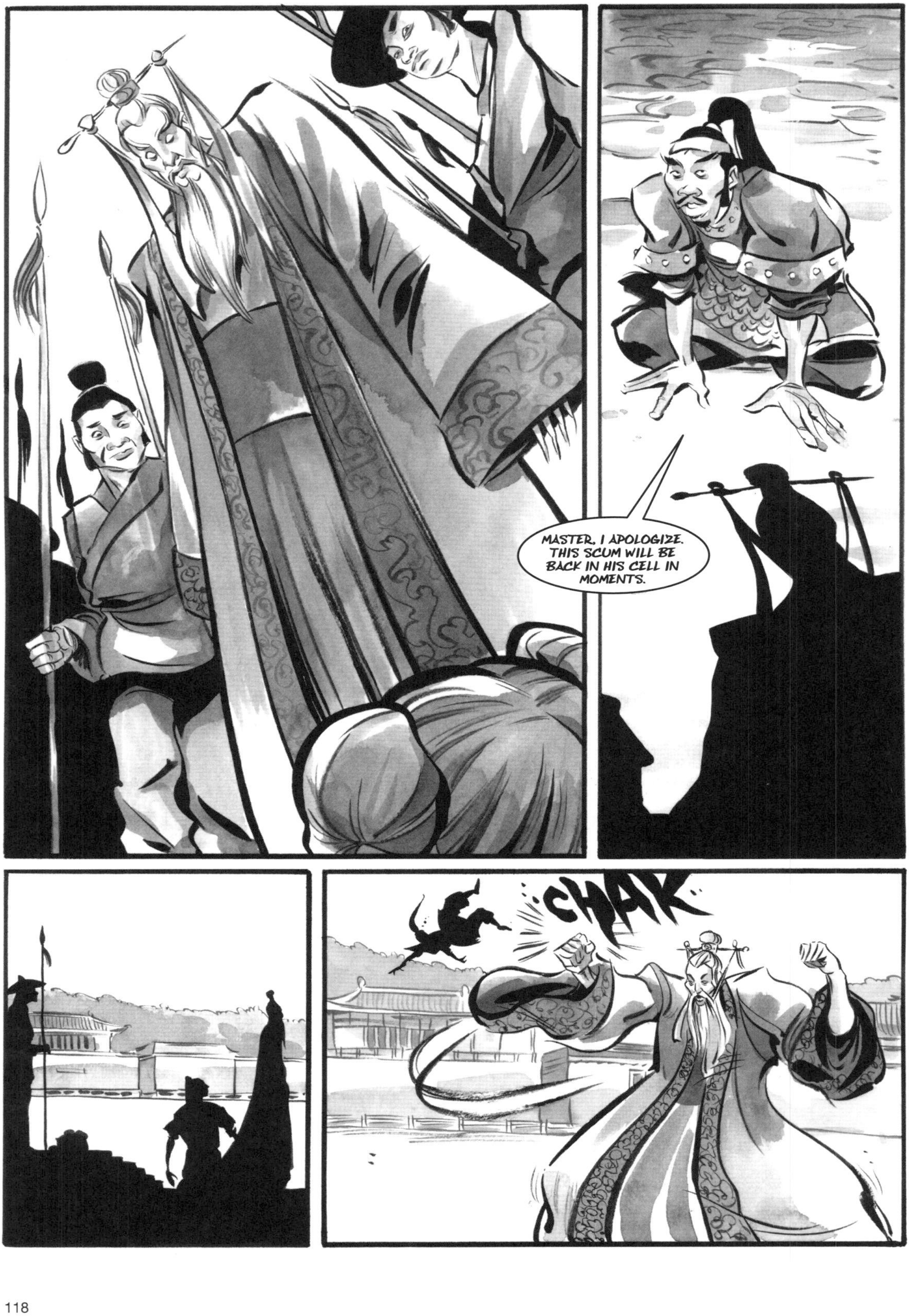
MASTER, I APOLOGIZE. THIS SCUM WILL BE BACK IN HIS CELL IN MOMENTS.
CHAK

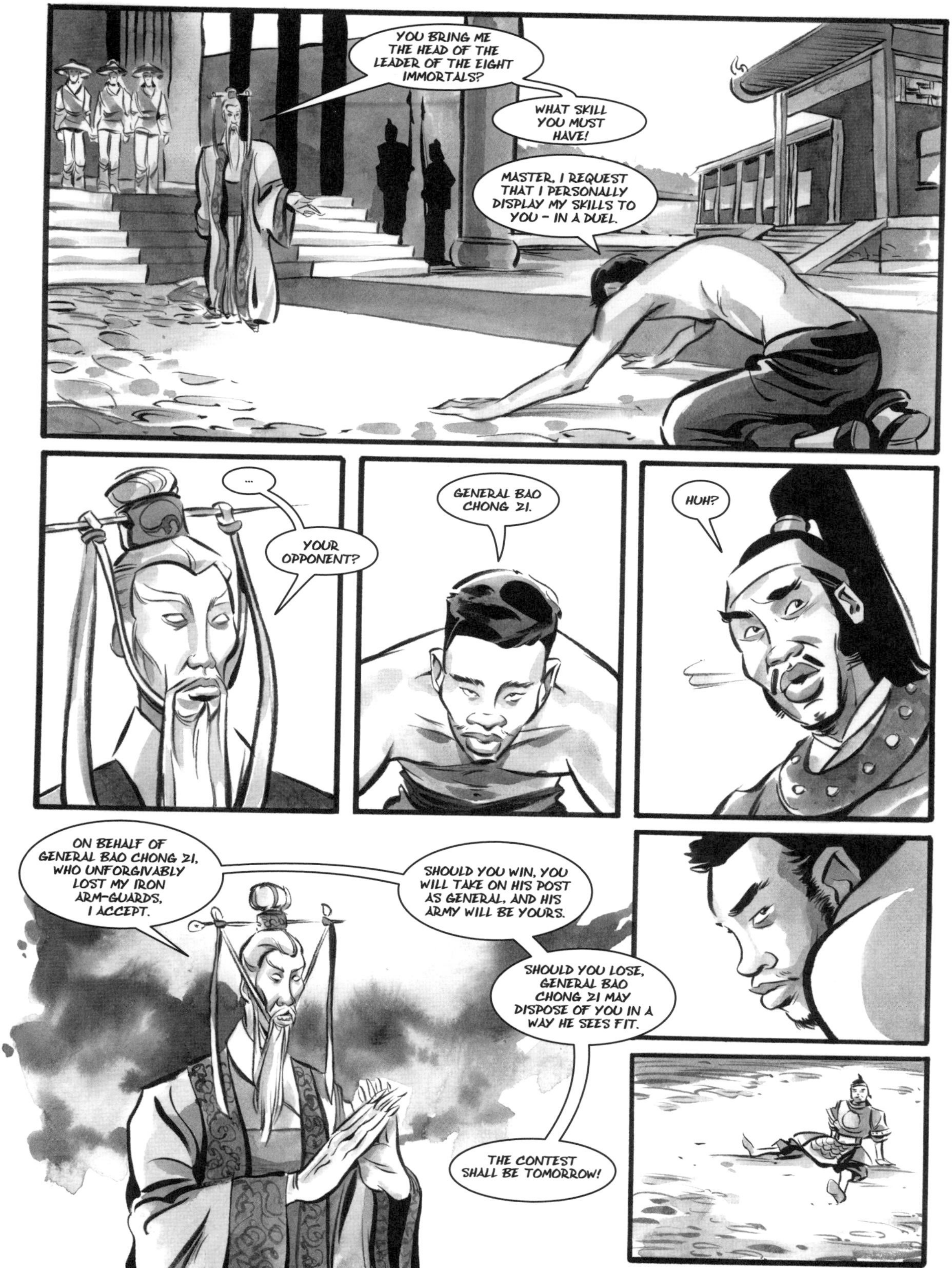
YOU BRING ME THE HEAD OF THE LEADER OF THE EIGHT IMMORTALS?
WHAT SKILL YOU MUST HAVE!
MASTER, I REQUEST THAT I PERSONALLY DISPLAY MY SKILLS TO YOU - IN A DUEL.
...
YOUR OPPONENT?
GENERAL BAO CHONG ZI.
HUH?
ON BEHALF OF GENERAL BAO CHONG ZI, WHO UNFORGIVABLY LOST MY IRON ARM-GUARDS, I ACCEPT.
SHOULD YOU WIN, YOU WILL TAKE ON HIS POST AS GENERAL, AND HIS ARMY WILL BE YOURS.
SHOULD YOU LOSE, GENERAL BAO CHONG ZI MAY DISPOSE OF YOU IN A WAY HE SEES FIT.
THE CONTEST SHALL BE TOMORROW!

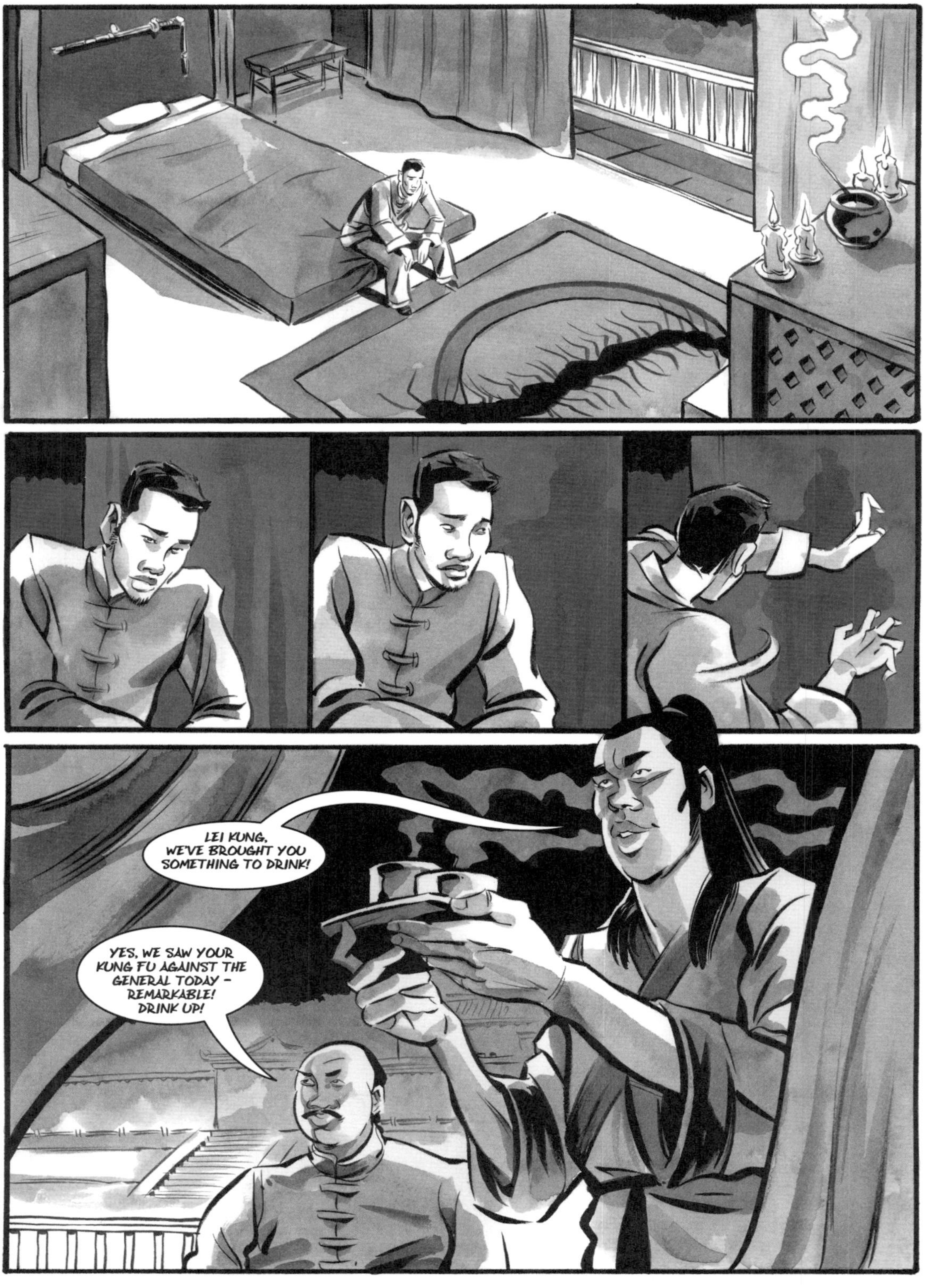
LEI KUNG, WE'VE BROUGHT YOU SOMETHING TO DRINK!
YES, WE SAW YOUR KUNG FU AGAINST THE GENERAL TODAY - REMARKABLE! DRINK UP!

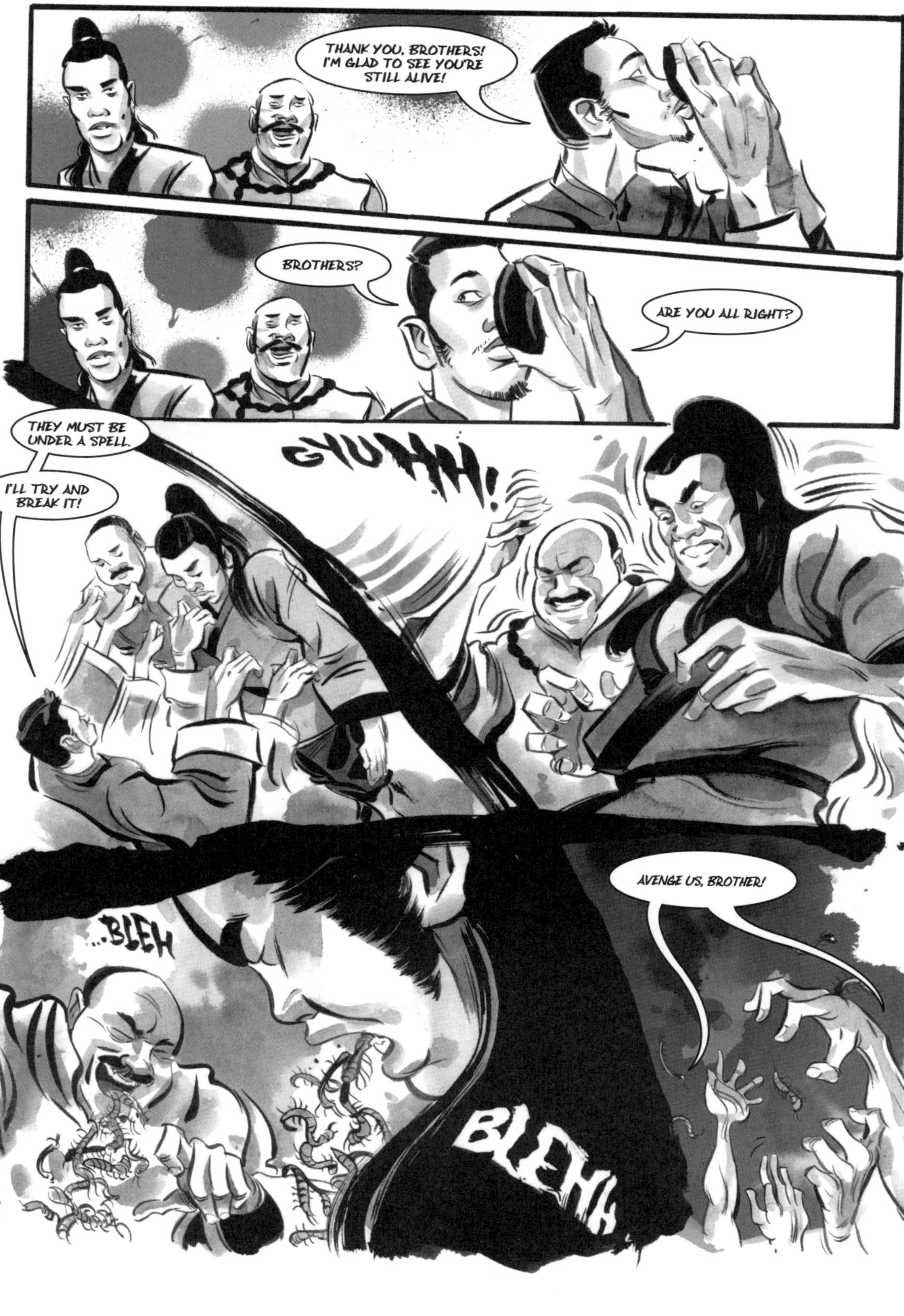
THANK YOU, BROTHERS! I'M GLAD TO SEE YOU'RE STILL ALIVE!
BROTHERS?
ARE YOU ALL RIGHT?
THEY MUST BE UNDER A SPELL.
I'LL TRY AND BREAK IT!
GYUHHH!
AVENGE US, BROTHER!
...BLEH
BLEHH

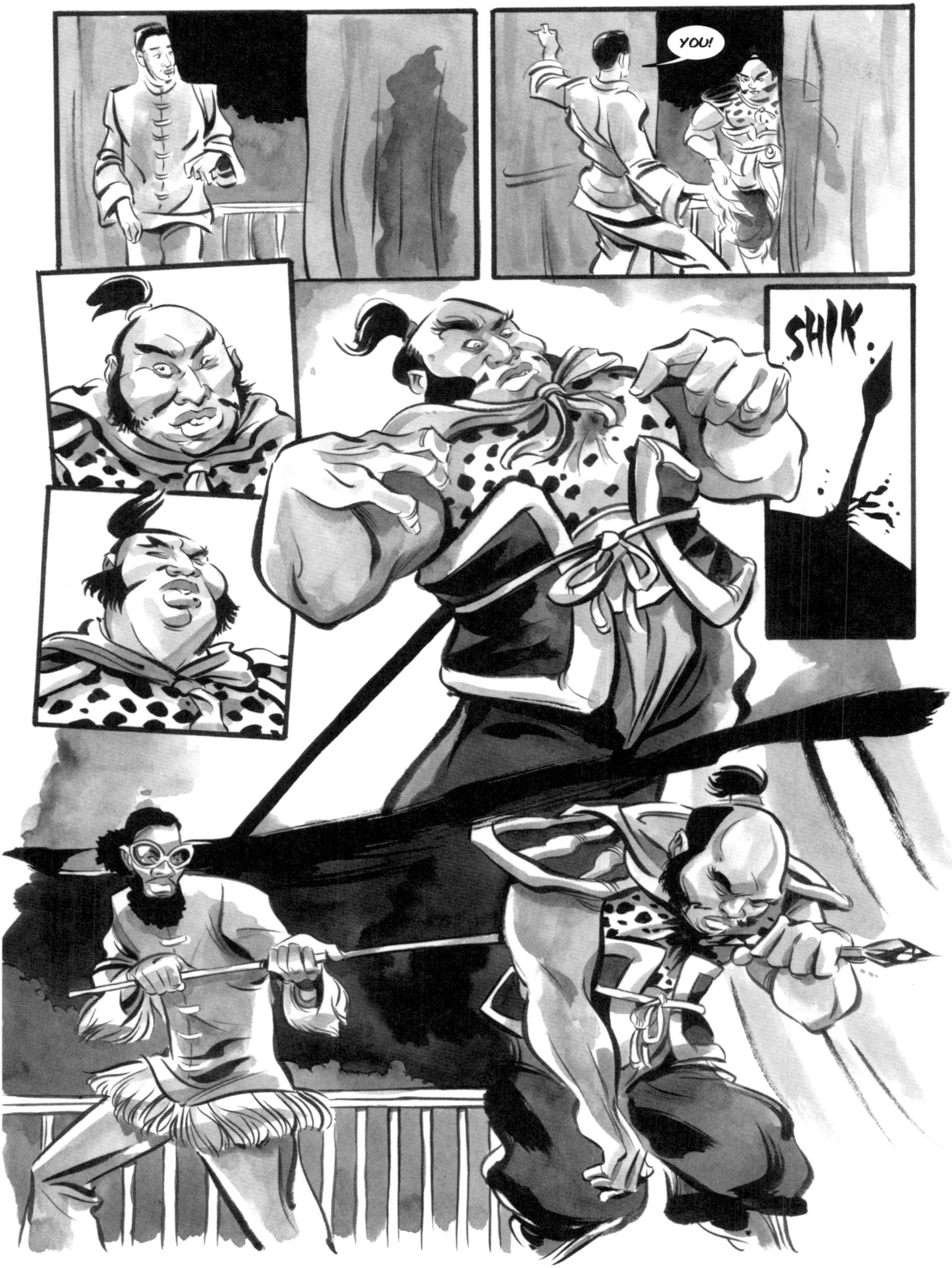
YOU!
SHIK

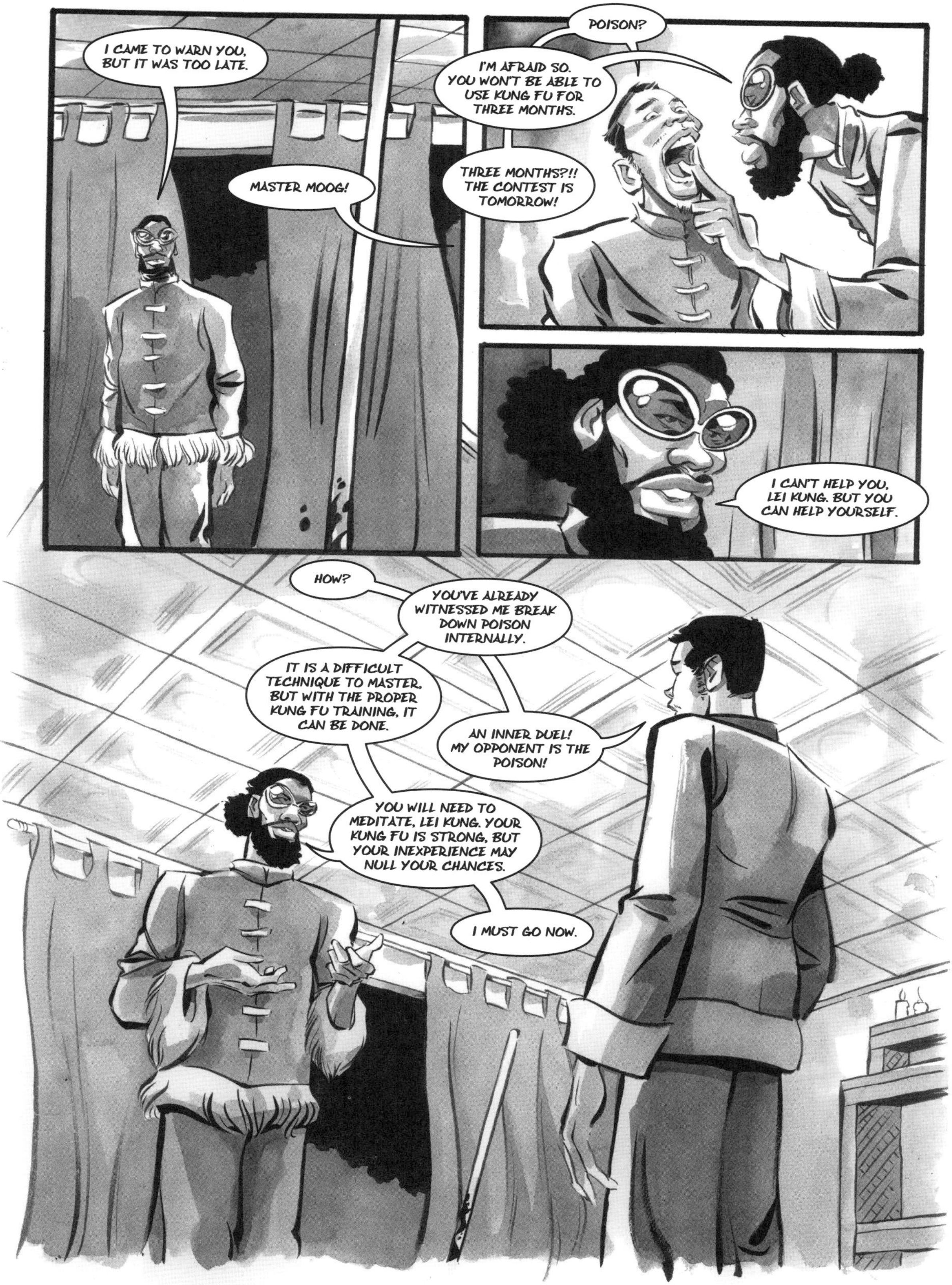
I CAME TO WARN YOU, BUT IT WAS TOO LATE.
MASTER MOOG!
POISON?
I'M AFRAID SO. YOU WON'T BE ABLE TO USE KUNG FU FOR THREE MONTHS.
THREE MONTHS?!! THE CONTEST IS TOMORROW!
I CAN'T HELP YOU, LEI KUNG. BUT YOU CAN HELP YOURSELF.
HOW?
YOU'VE ALREADY WITNESSED ME BREAK DOWN POISON INTERNALLY.
IT IS A DIFFICULT TECHNIQUE TO MASTER, BUT WITH THE PROPER KUNG FU TRAINING, IT CAN BE DONE.
AN INNER DUEL! MY OPPONENT IS THE POISON!
YOU WILL NEED TO MEDITATE, LEI KUNG. YOUR KUNG FU IS STRONG, BUT YOUR INEXPERIENCE MAY NULL YOUR CHANCES.
I MUST GO NOW.

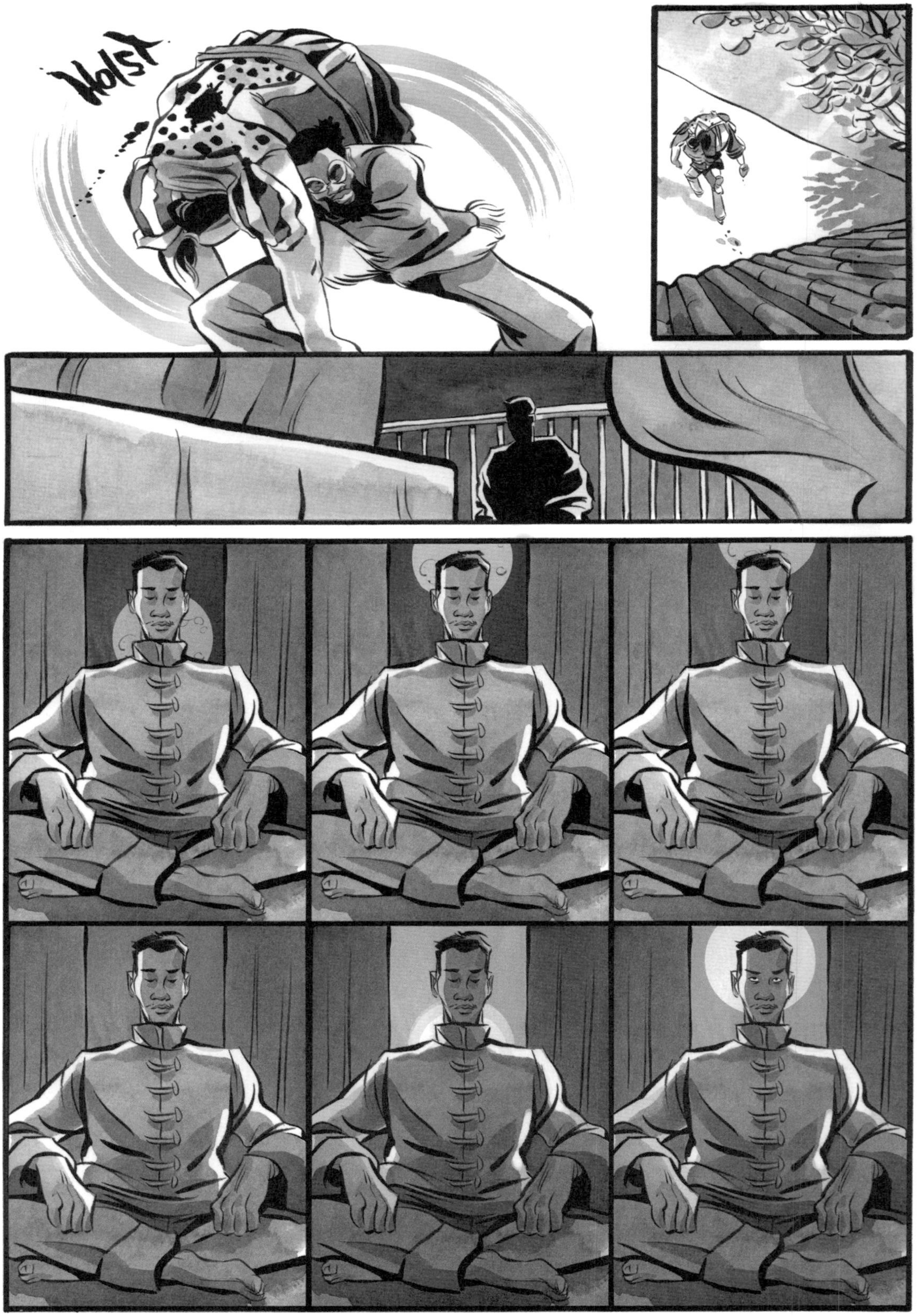
HOIST

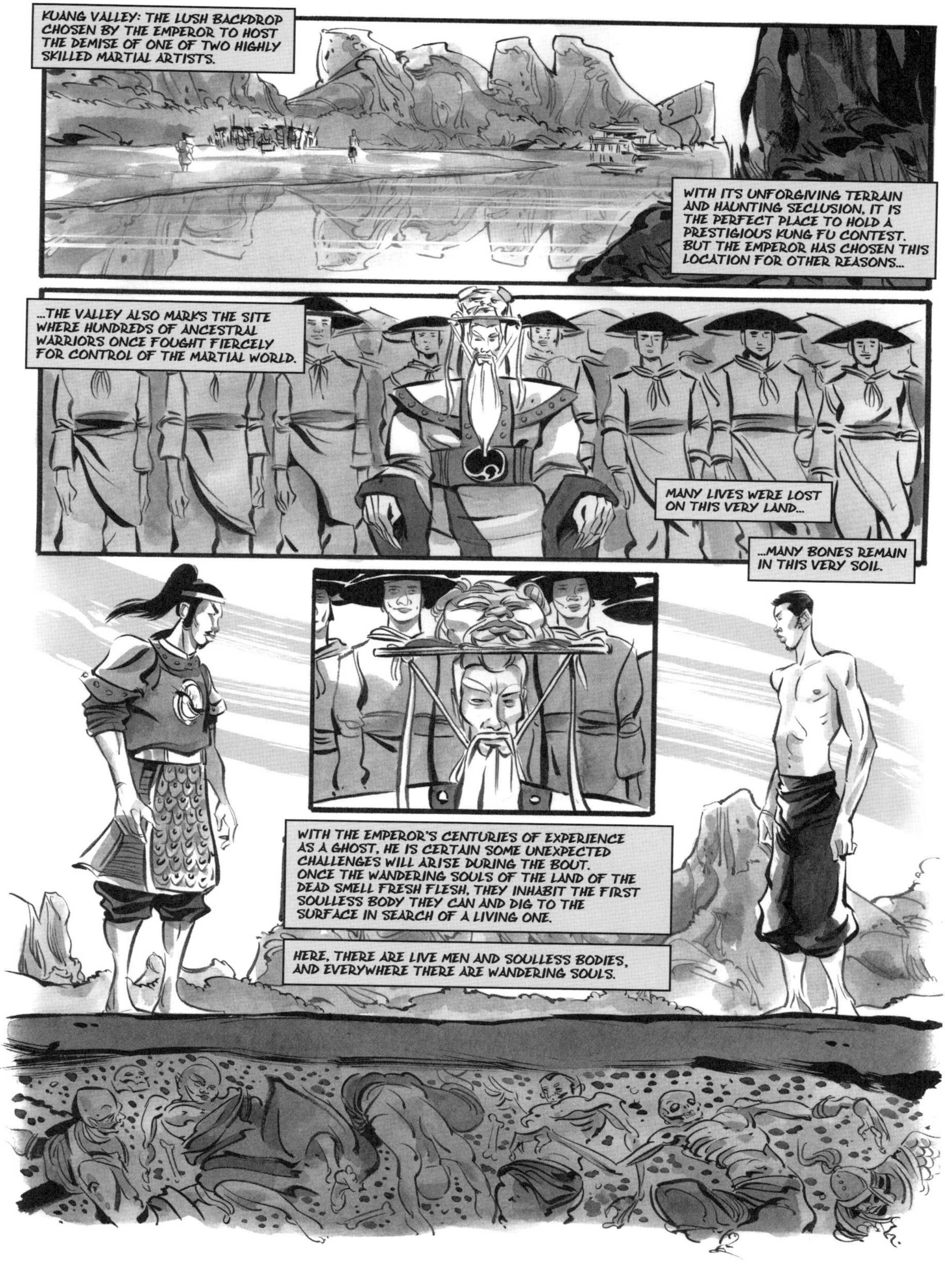
KUANG VALLEY: THE LUSH BACKDROP CHOSEN BY THE EMPEROR TO HOST THE DEMISE OF ONE OF TWO HIGHLY SKILLED MARTIAL ARTISTS.
WITH ITS UNFORGIVING TERRAIN AND HAUNTING SECLUSION, IT IS THE PERFECT PLACE TO HOLD A PRESTIGIOUS KUNG FU CONTEST. BUT THE EMPEROR HAS CHOSEN THIS LOCATION FOR OTHER REASONS...
...THE VALLEY ALSO MARKS THE SITE WHERE HUNDREDS OF ANCESTRAL WARRIORS ONCE FOUGHT FIERCELY FOR CONTROL OF THE MARTIAL WORLD.
MANY LIVES WERE LOST ON THIS VERY LAND...
...MANY BONES REMAIN IN THIS VERY SOIL.
WITH THE EMPEROR'S CENTURIES OF EXPERIENCE AS A GHOST, HE IS CERTAIN SOME UNEXPECTED CHALLENGES WILL ARISE DURING THE BOUT. ONCE THE WANDERING SOULS OF THE LAND OF THE DEAD SMELL FRESH FLESH, THEY INHABIT THE FIRST SOULLESS BODY THEY CAN AND DIG TO THE SURFACE IN SEARCH OF A LIVING ONE.
HERE, THERE ARE LIVE MEN AND SOULLESS BODIES, AND EVERYWHERE THERE ARE WANDERING SOULS.

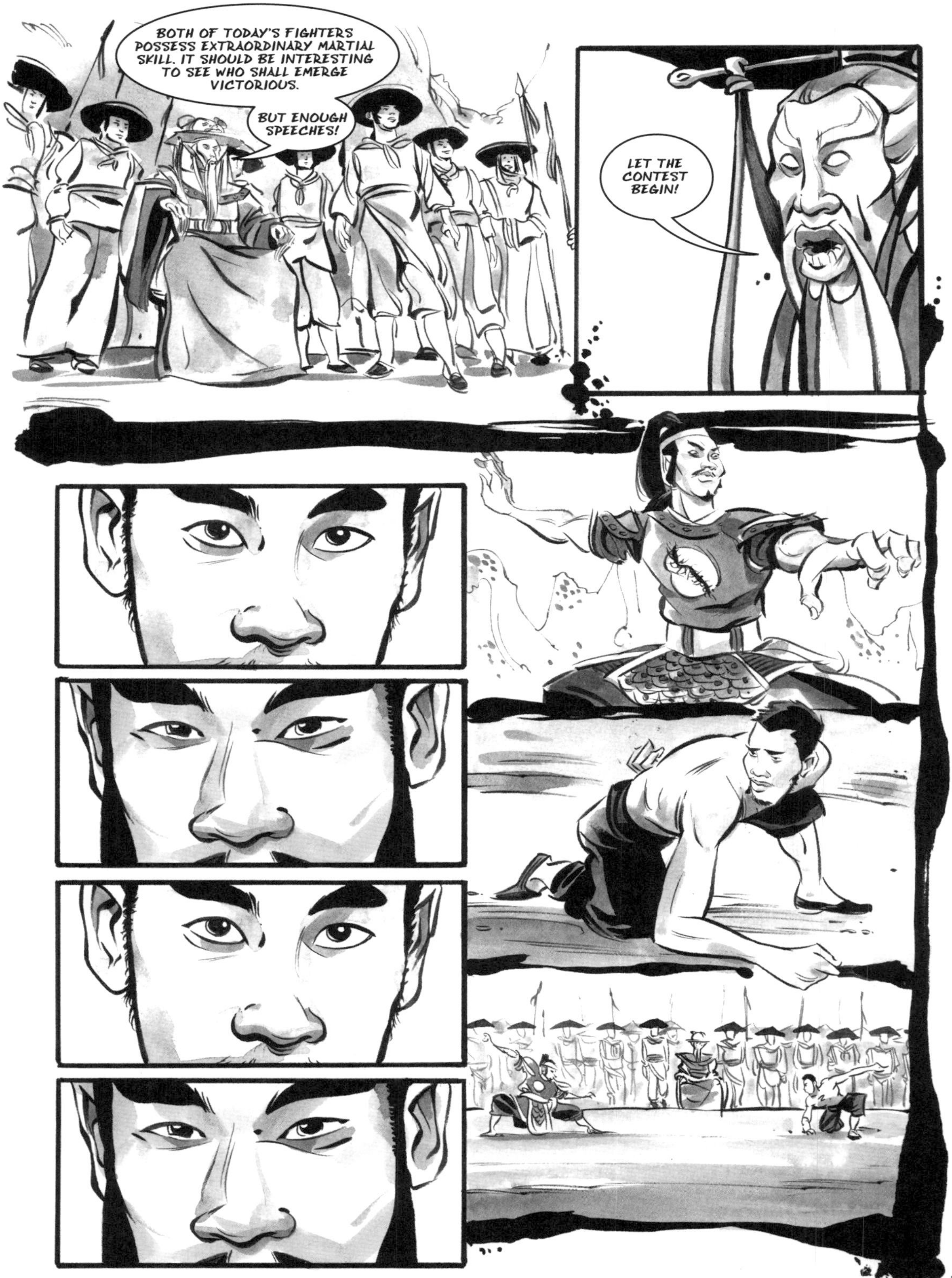
BOTH OF TODAY'S FIGHTERS POSSESS EXTRAORDINARY MARTIAL SKILL. IT SHOULD BE INTERESTING TO SEE WHO SHALL EMERGE VICTORIOUS.
BUT ENOUGH SPEECHES!
LET THE CONTEST BEGIN!

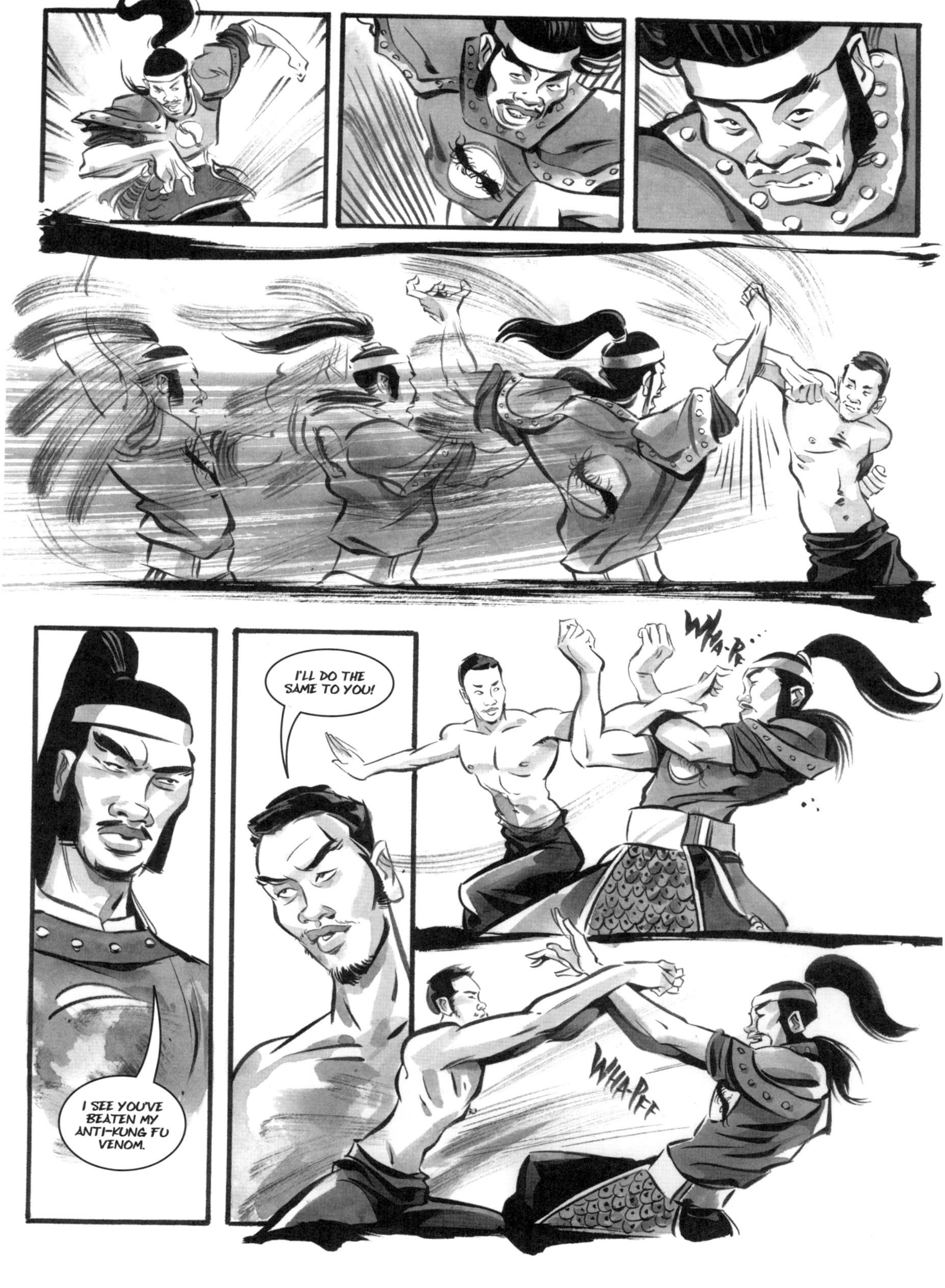
WHA-P...
I'LL DO THE SAME TO YOU!
I SEE YOU'VE BEATEN MY ANTI-KUNG FU VENOM.
WHA-PFF

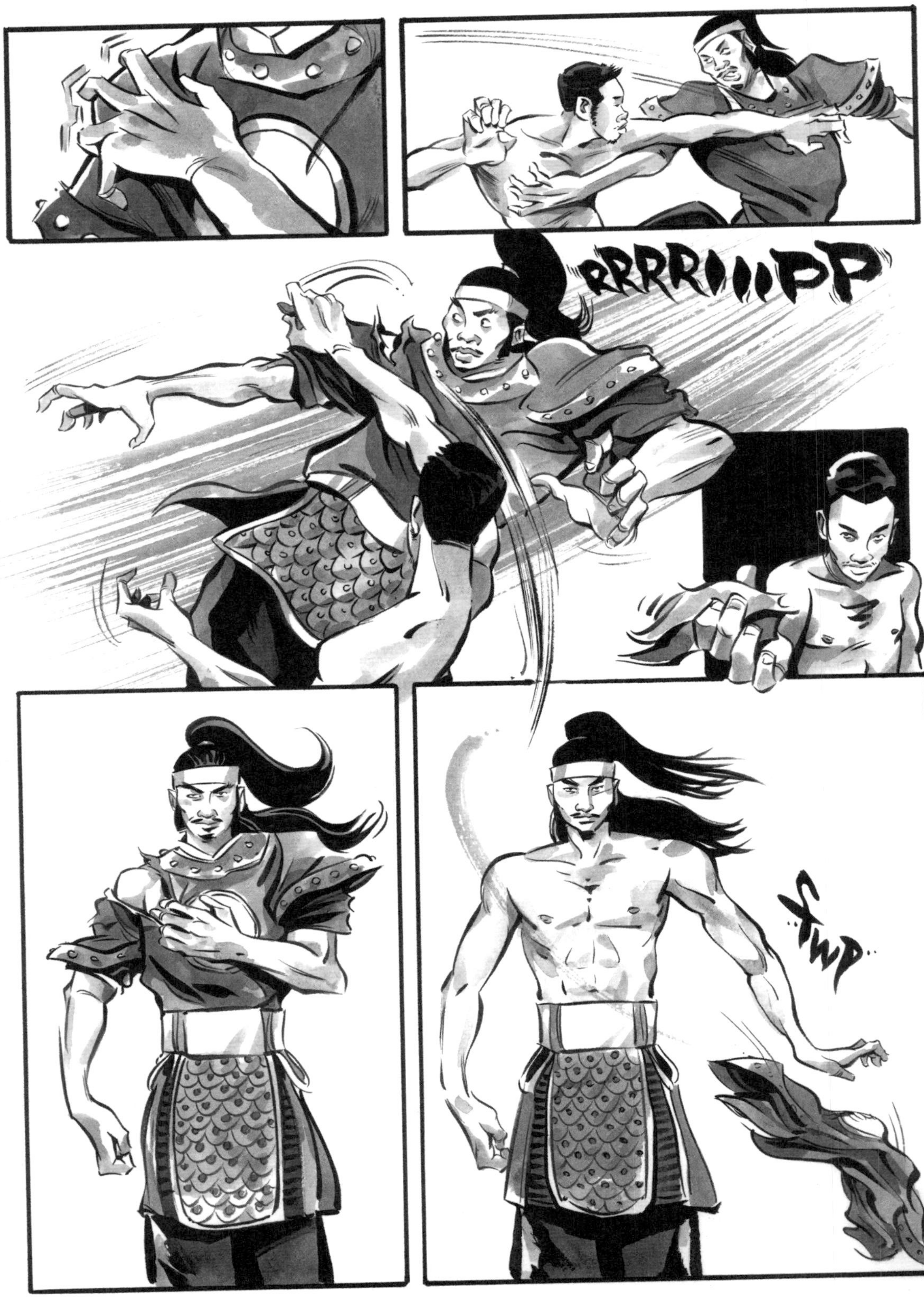
RRRRIIIPP
..FWP..

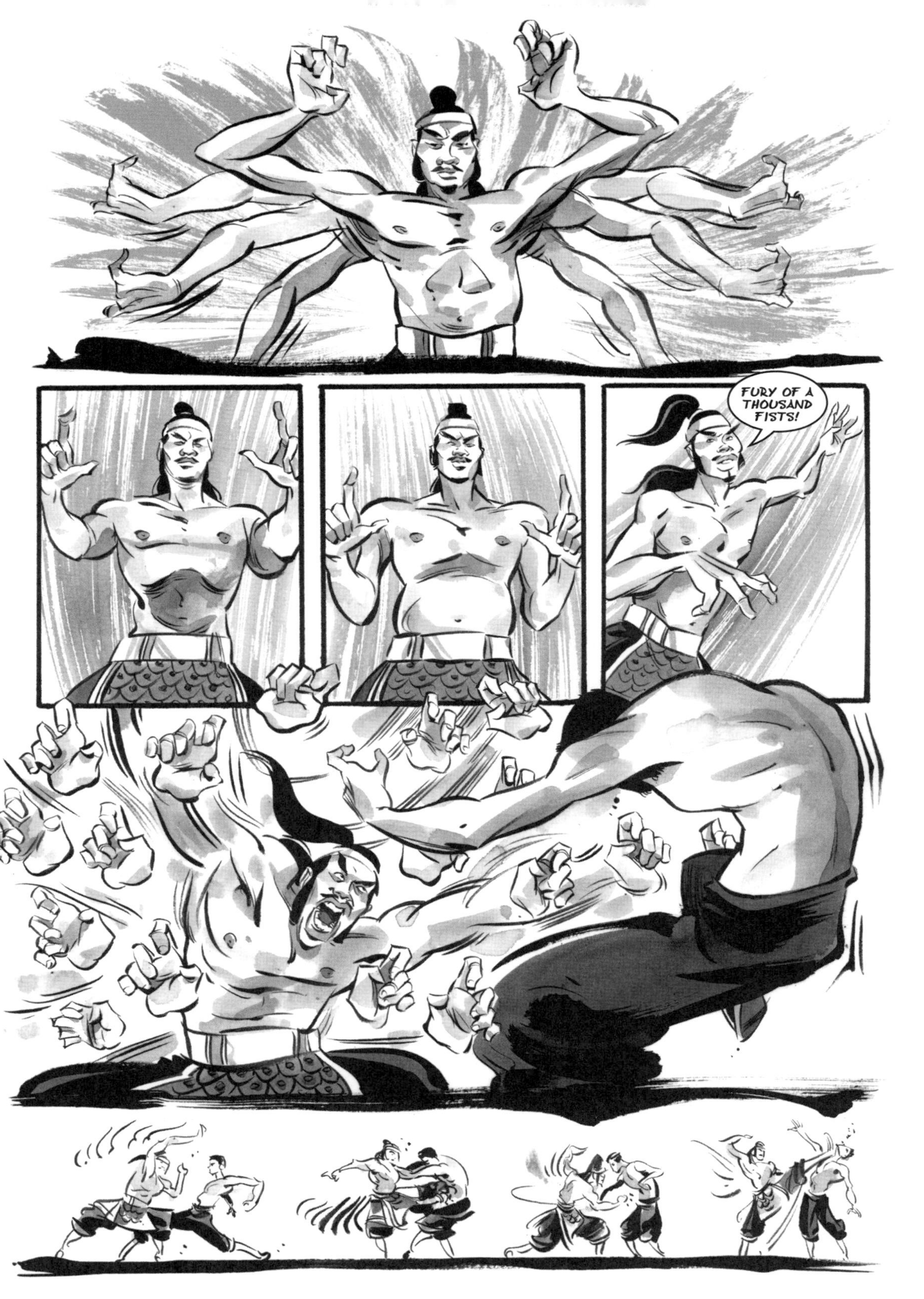
FURY OF A THOUSAND FISTS!

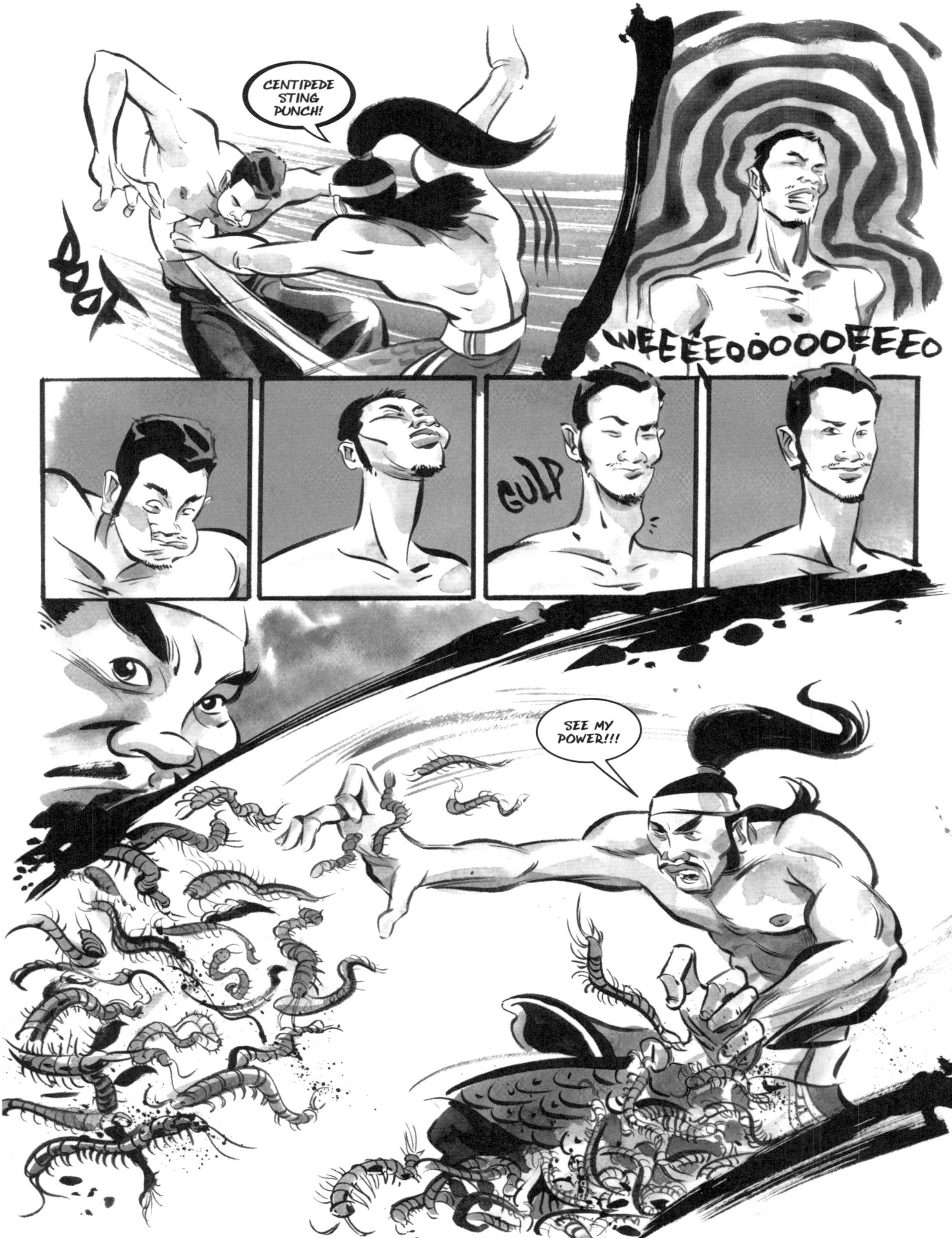
CENTIPEDE STING PUNCH!
WEEEEOOOOOEEEO
GULP
SEE MY POWER!!!

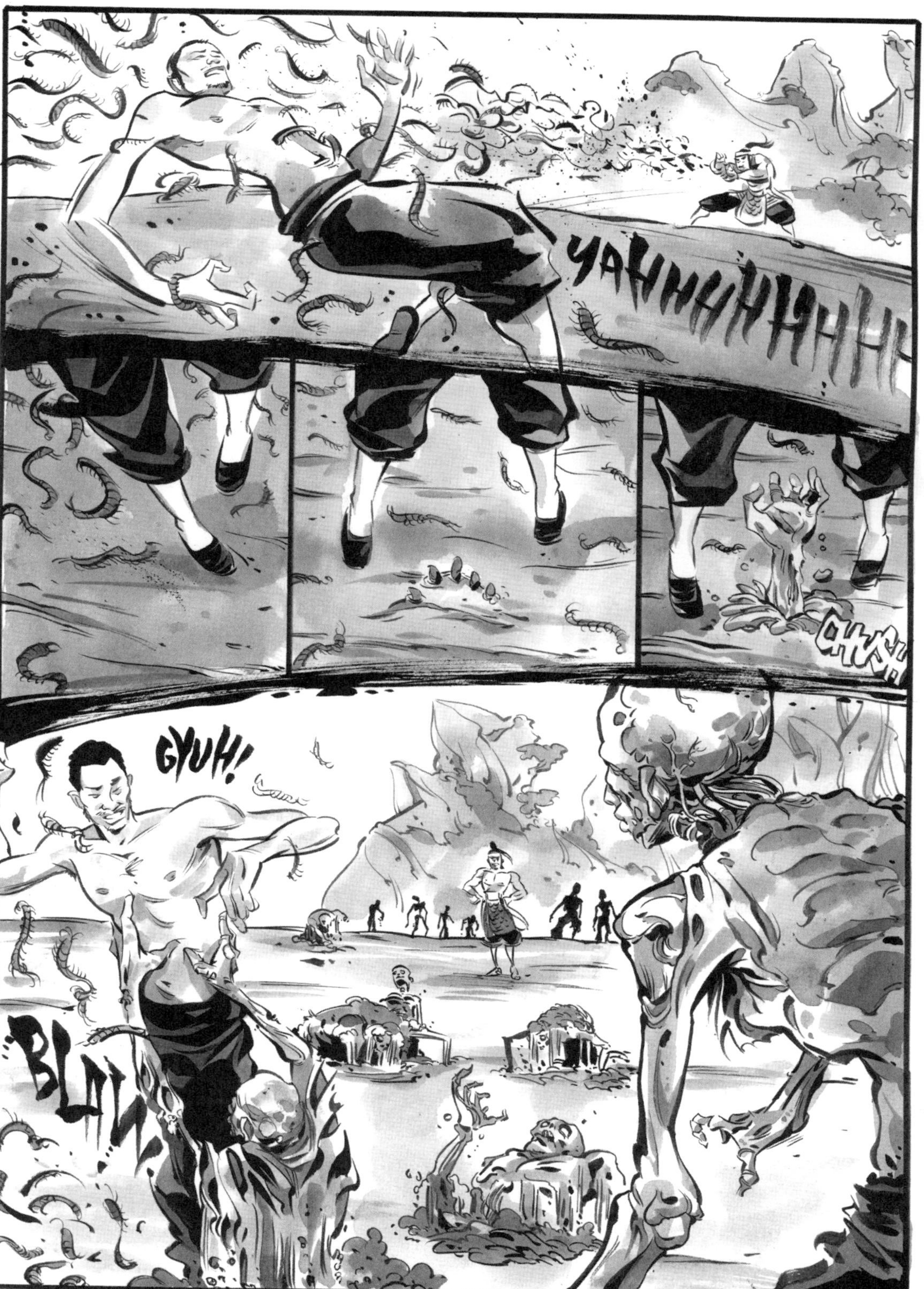
YAHHHHHHHHHH
CHUSH
GYUH!

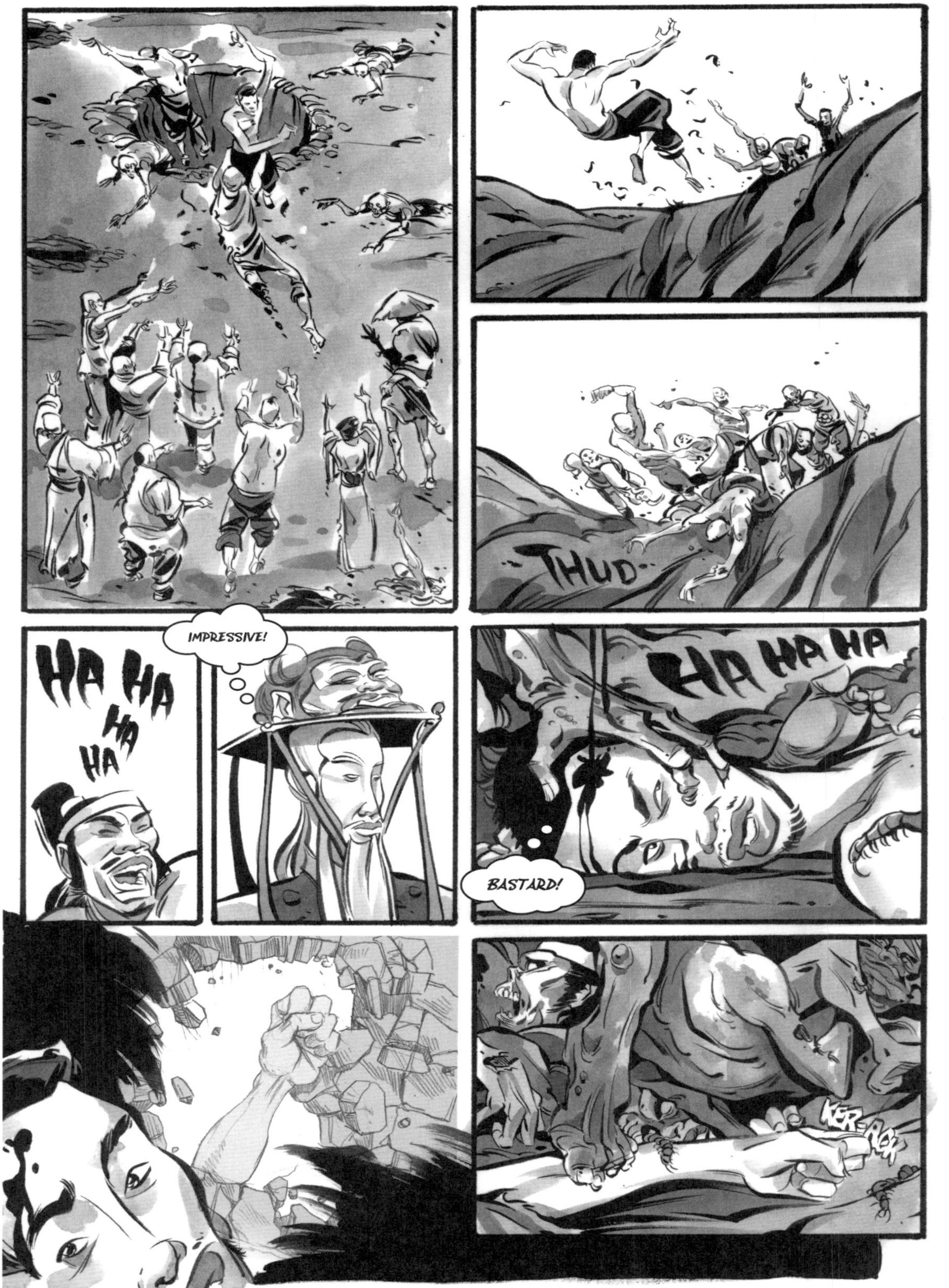
THUD
HA HA
HA
HA
IMPRESSIVE!
HA HA HA
BASTARD!
KER-ACK

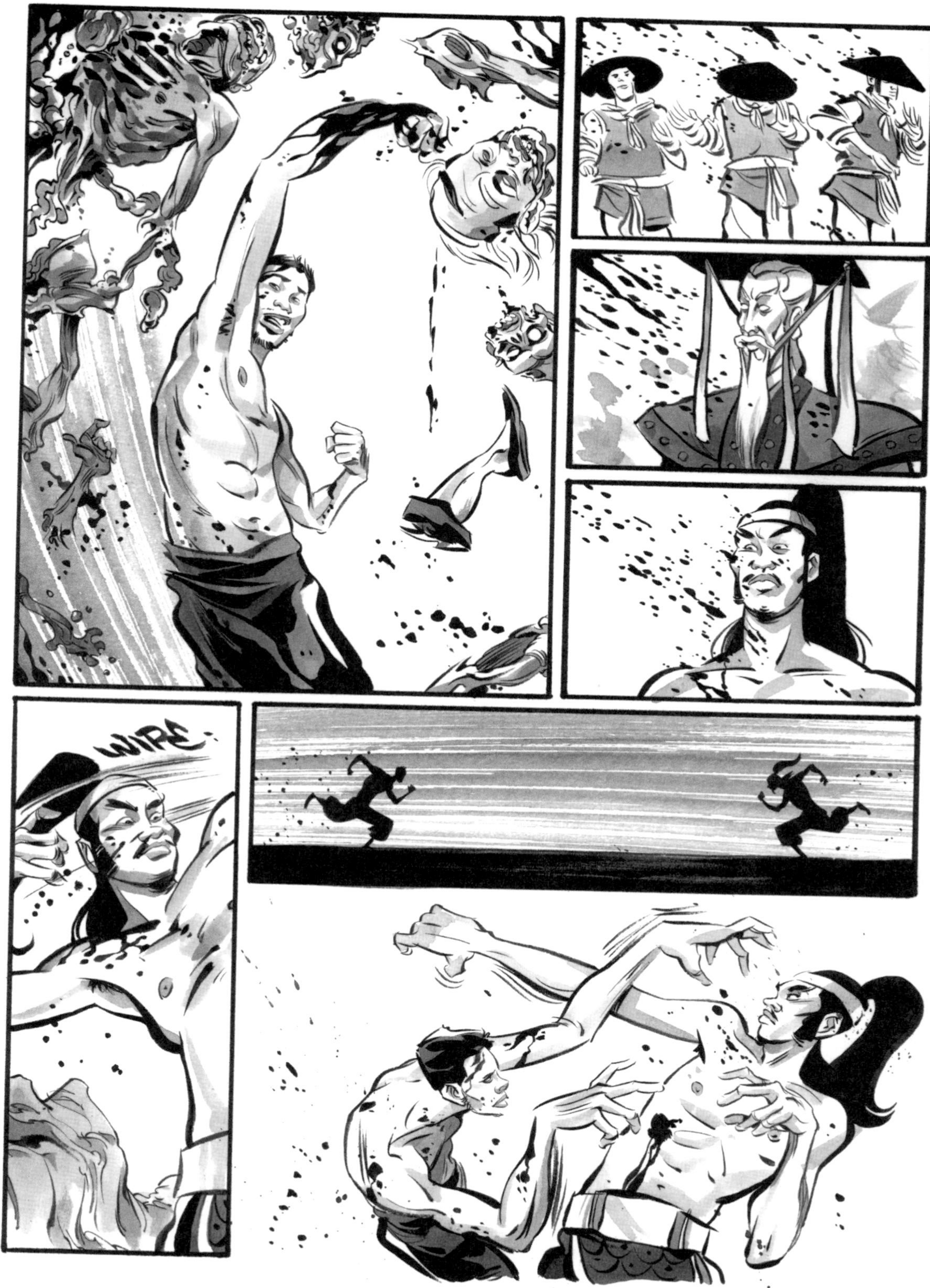
WIRE

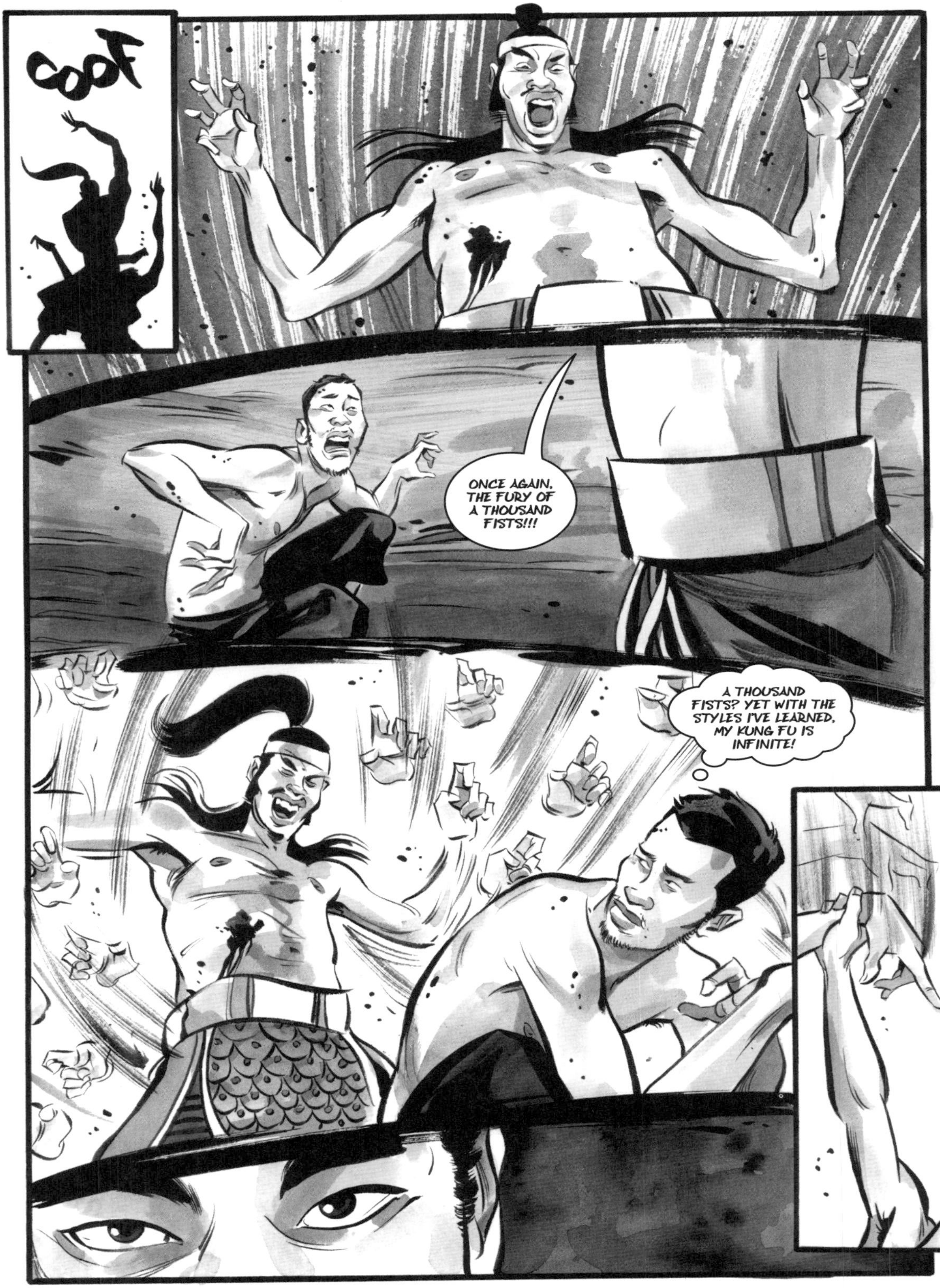
GOOF
ONCE AGAIN, THE FURY OF A THOUSAND FISTS!!!
A THOUSAND FISTS? YET WITH THE STYLES I'VE LEARNED, MY KUNG FU IS INFINITE!

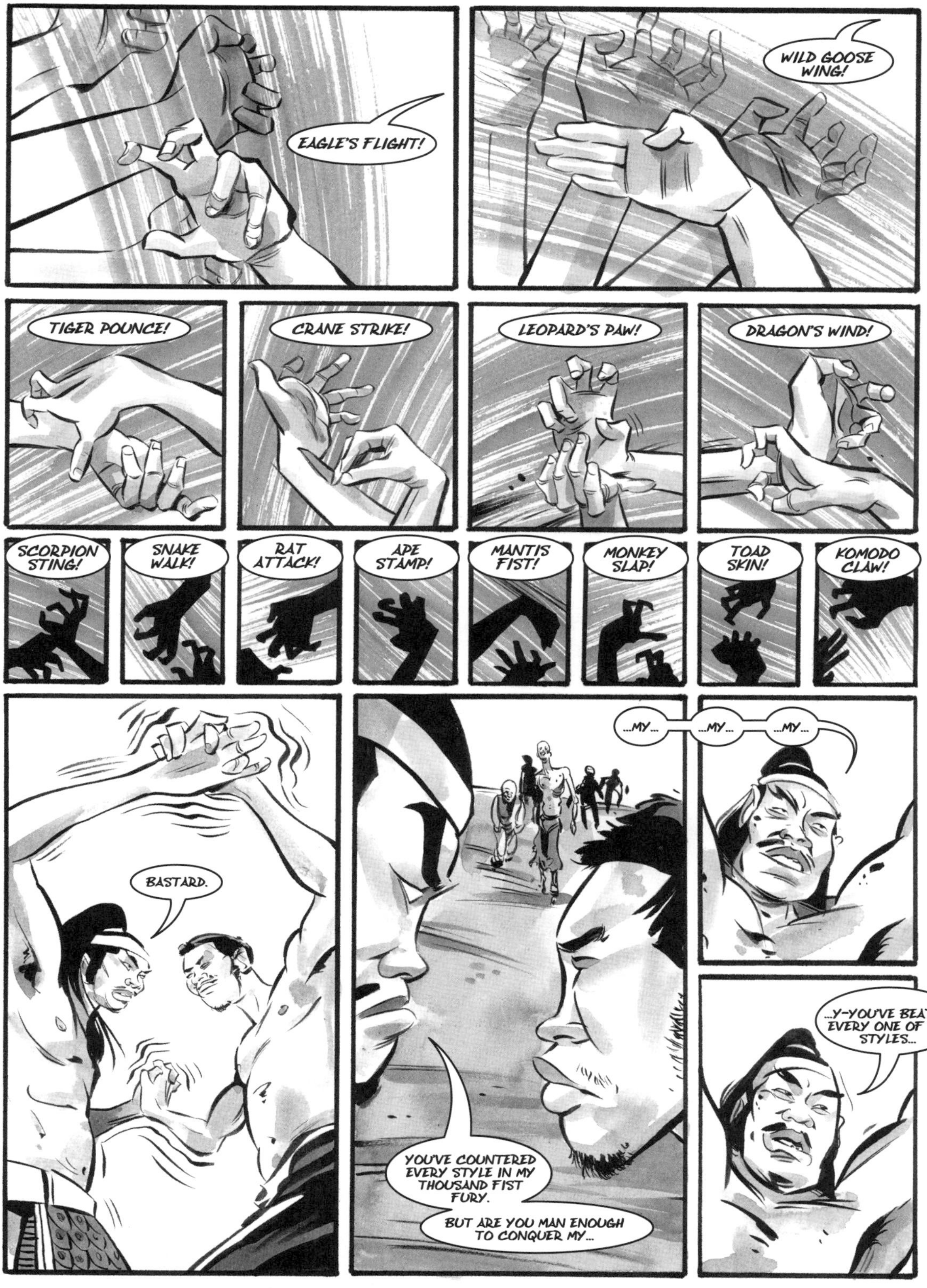
EAGLE'S FLIGHT!
WILD GOOSE WING!
TIGER POUNCE!
CRANE STRIKE!
LEOPARD'S PAW!
DRAGON'S WIND!
SCORPION STING!
SNAKE WALK!
RAT ATTACK!
APE STAMP!
MANTIS FIST!
MONKEY SLAP!
TOAD SKIN!
KOMODO CLAW!
BASTARD.
YOU'VE COUNTERED EVERY STYLE IN MY THOUSAND FIST FURY.
BUT ARE YOU MAN ENOUGH TO CONQUER MY...
...MY... ...MY... ...MY...
...Y-YOU'VE BEATEN EVERY ONE OF MY STYLES...

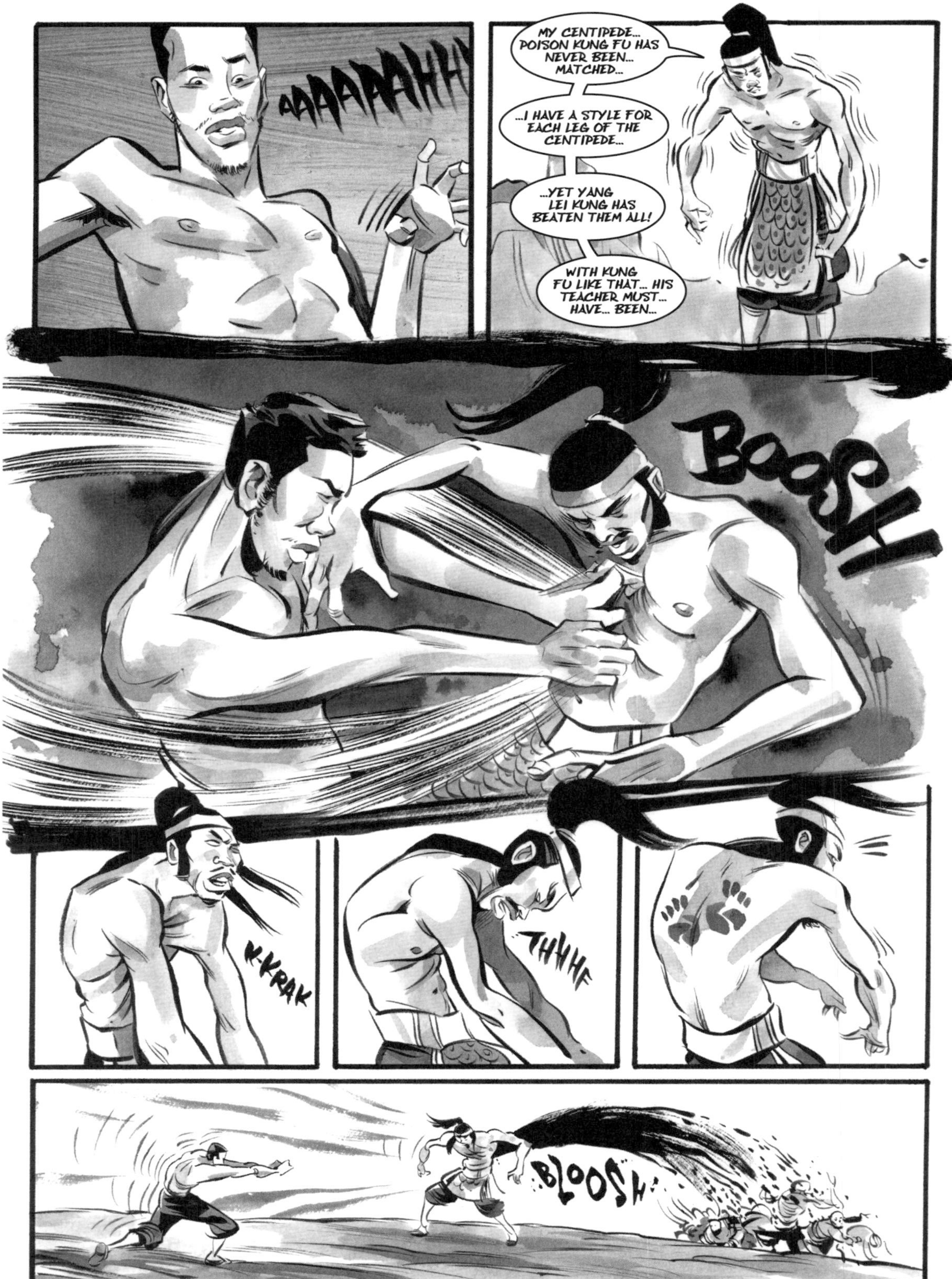
AAAAAAHHH
MY CENTIPEDE... POISON KUNG FU HAS NEVER BEEN... MATCHED...
...I HAVE A STYLE FOR EACH LEG OF THE CENTIPEDE...
...YET YANG LEI KUNG HAS BEATEN THEM ALL!
WITH KUNG FU LIKE THAT... HIS TEACHER MUST... HAVE... BEEN...
BOOSH!
K-KRAK
THUHF
BLOOSH

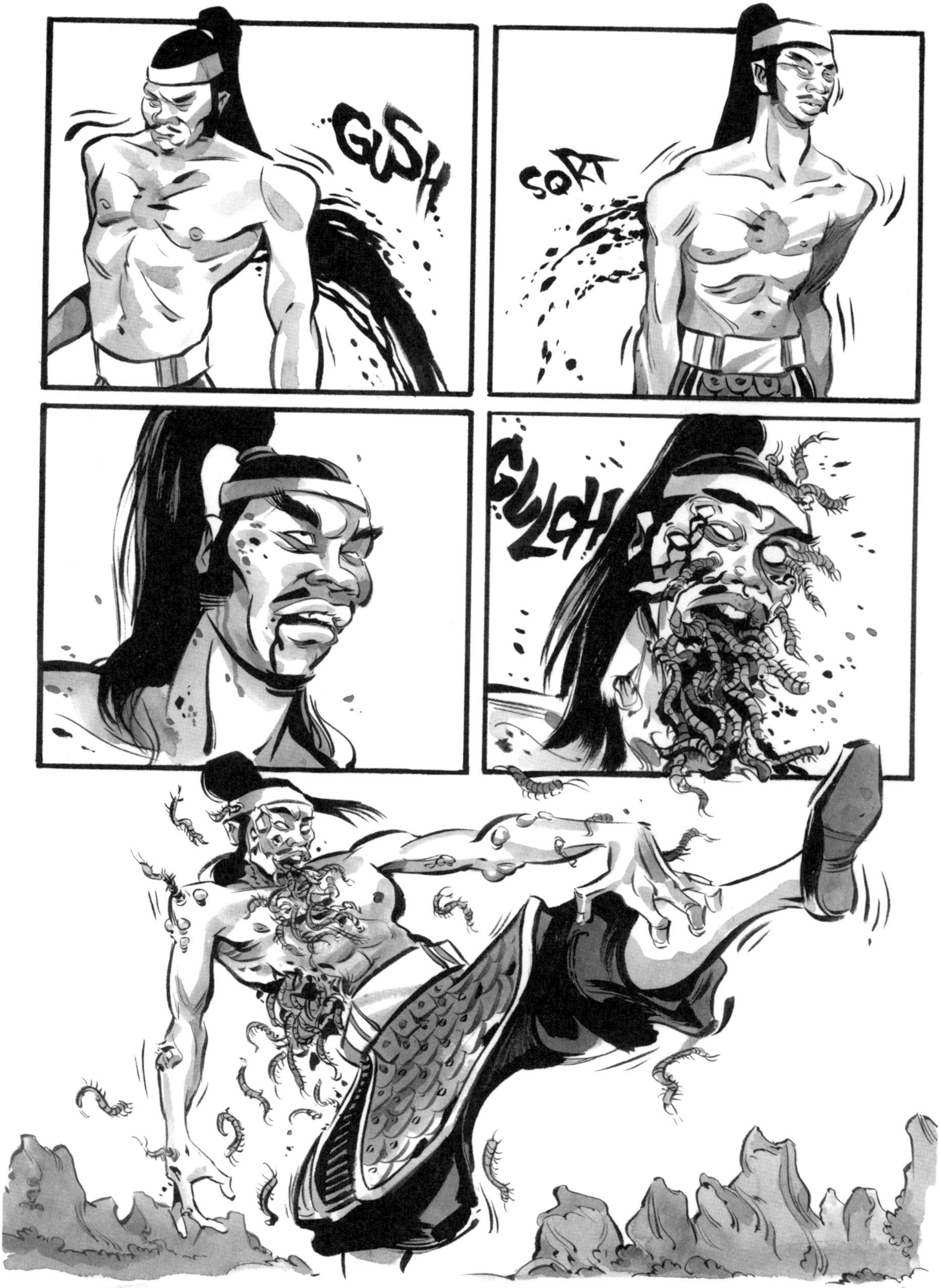
GUSH
SQRT
GULCH

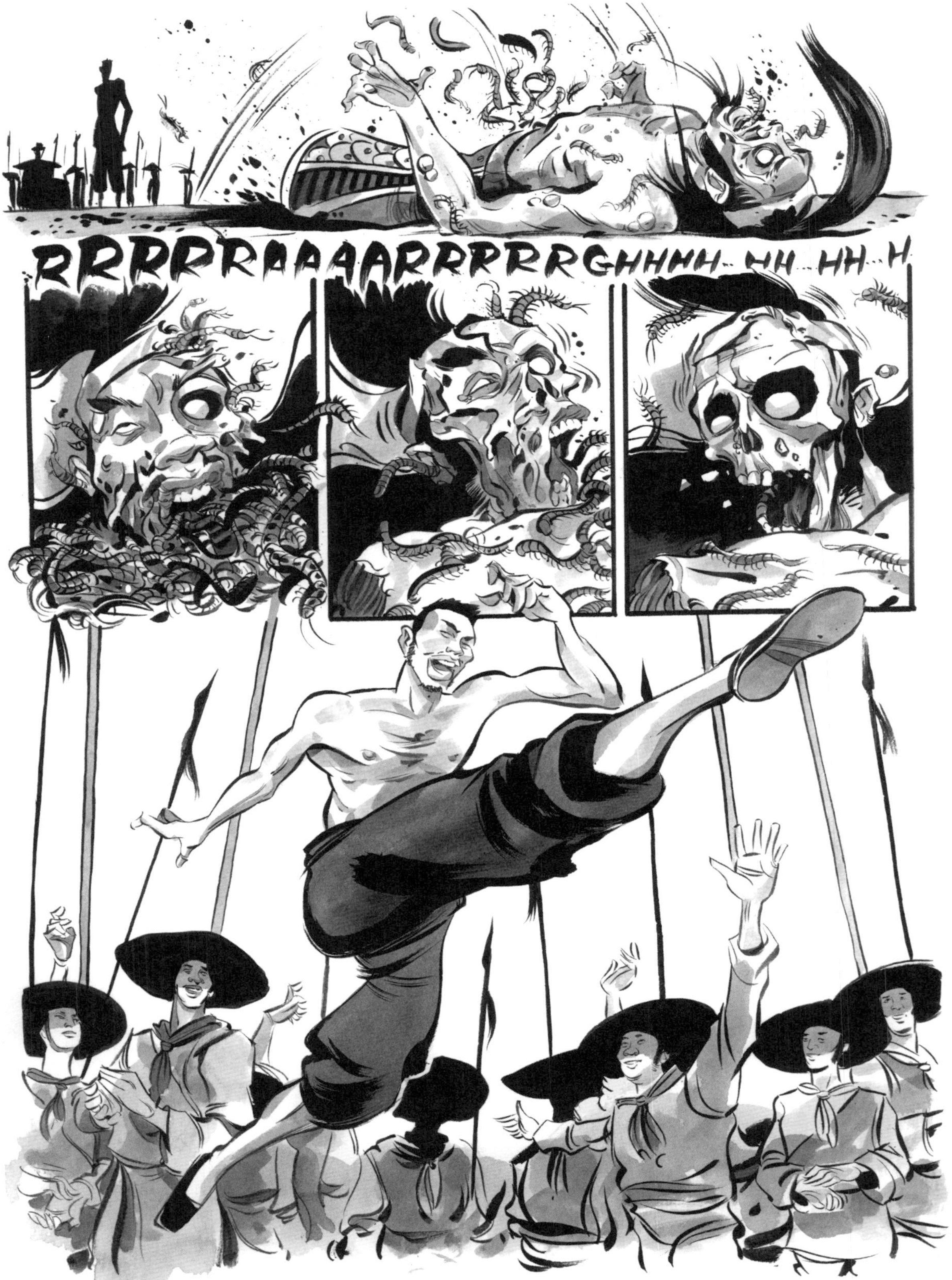
RRRRRAAAARRRRRGHHHH HH HH H

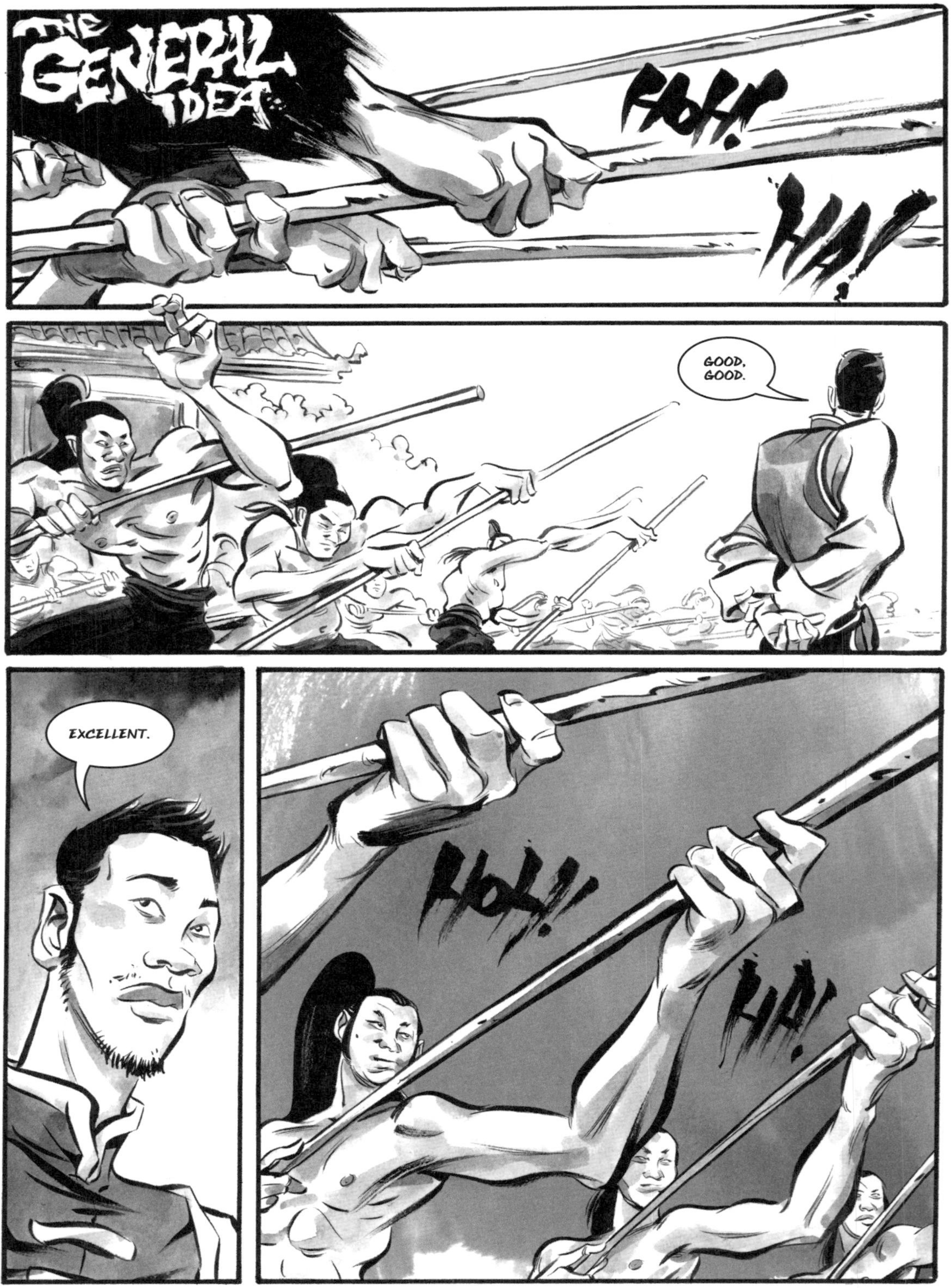
THE GENERAL IDEA
HOH!
HA!
GOOD. GOOD.
EXCELLENT.
HOH!!
HA!

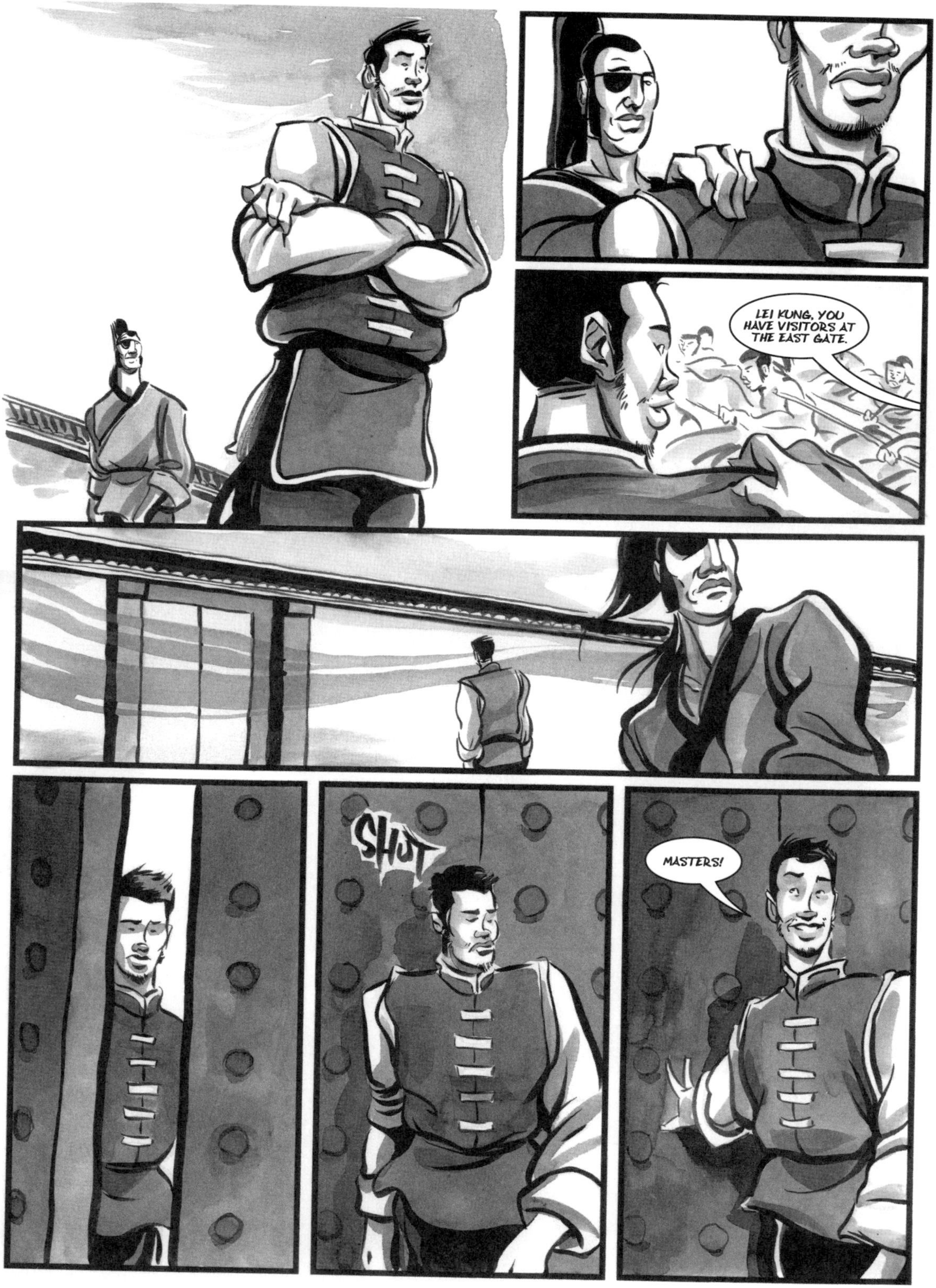
LEI KUNG, YOU HAVE VISITORS AT THE EAST GATE.
SHUT
MASTERS!

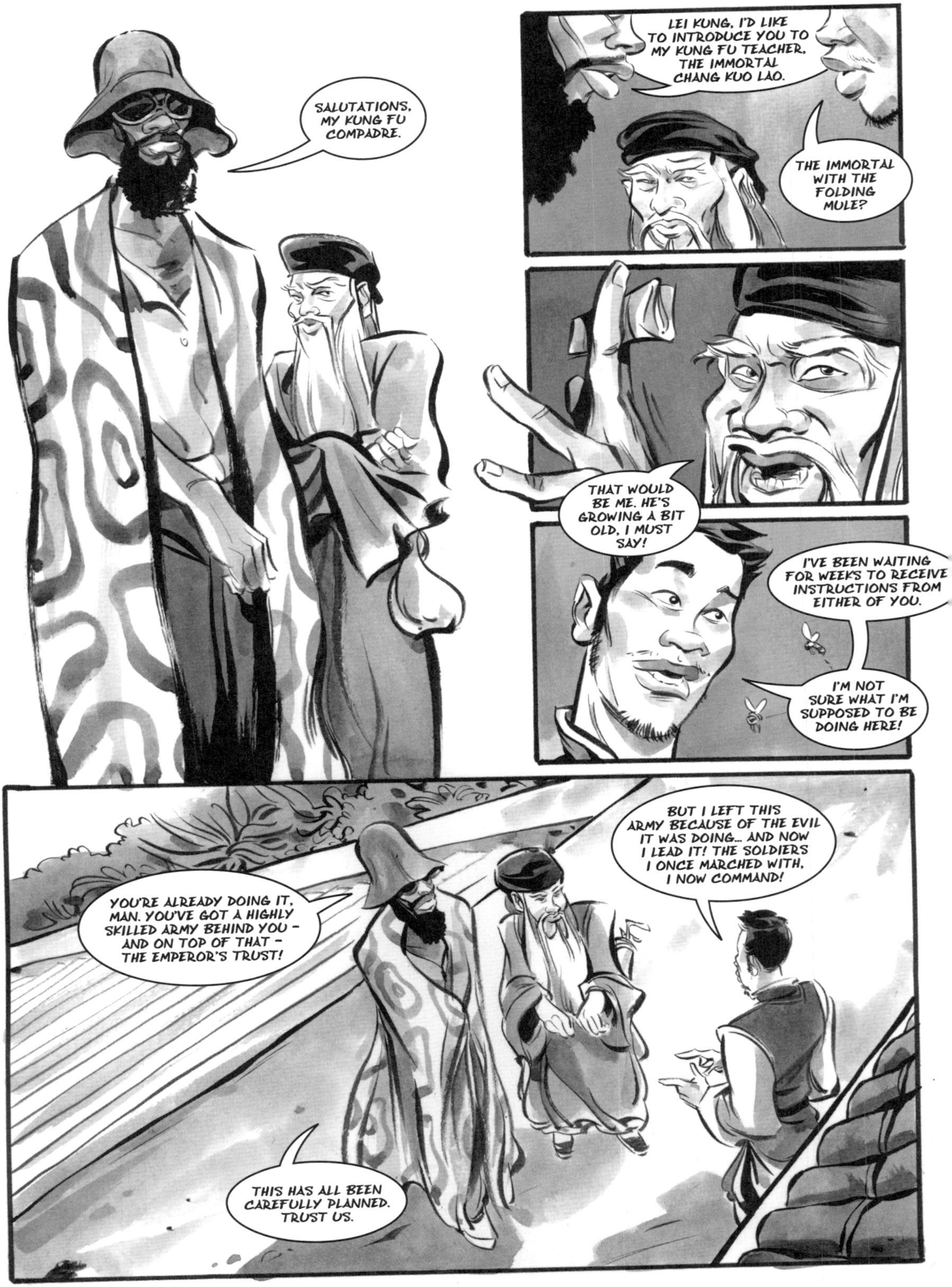
SALUTATIONS, MY KUNG FU COMPADRE.
LEI KUNG, I'D LIKE TO INTRODUCE YOU TO MY KUNG FU TEACHER, THE IMMORTAL CHANG KUO LAO.
THE IMMORTAL WITH THE FOLDING MULE?
THAT WOULD BE ME. HE'S GROWING A BIT OLD, I MUST SAY!
I'VE BEEN WAITING FOR WEEKS TO RECEIVE INSTRUCTIONS FROM EITHER OF YOU.
I'M NOT SURE WHAT I'M SUPPOSED TO BE DOING HERE!
YOU'RE ALREADY DOING IT, MAN. YOU'VE GOT A HIGHLY SKILLED ARMY BEHIND YOU - AND ON TOP OF THAT - THE EMPEROR'S TRUST!
BUT I LEFT THIS ARMY BECAUSE OF THE EVIL IT WAS DOING... AND NOW I LEAD IT! THE SOLDIERS I ONCE MARCHED WITH, I NOW COMMAND!
THIS HAS ALL BEEN CAREFULLY PLANNED. TRUST US.

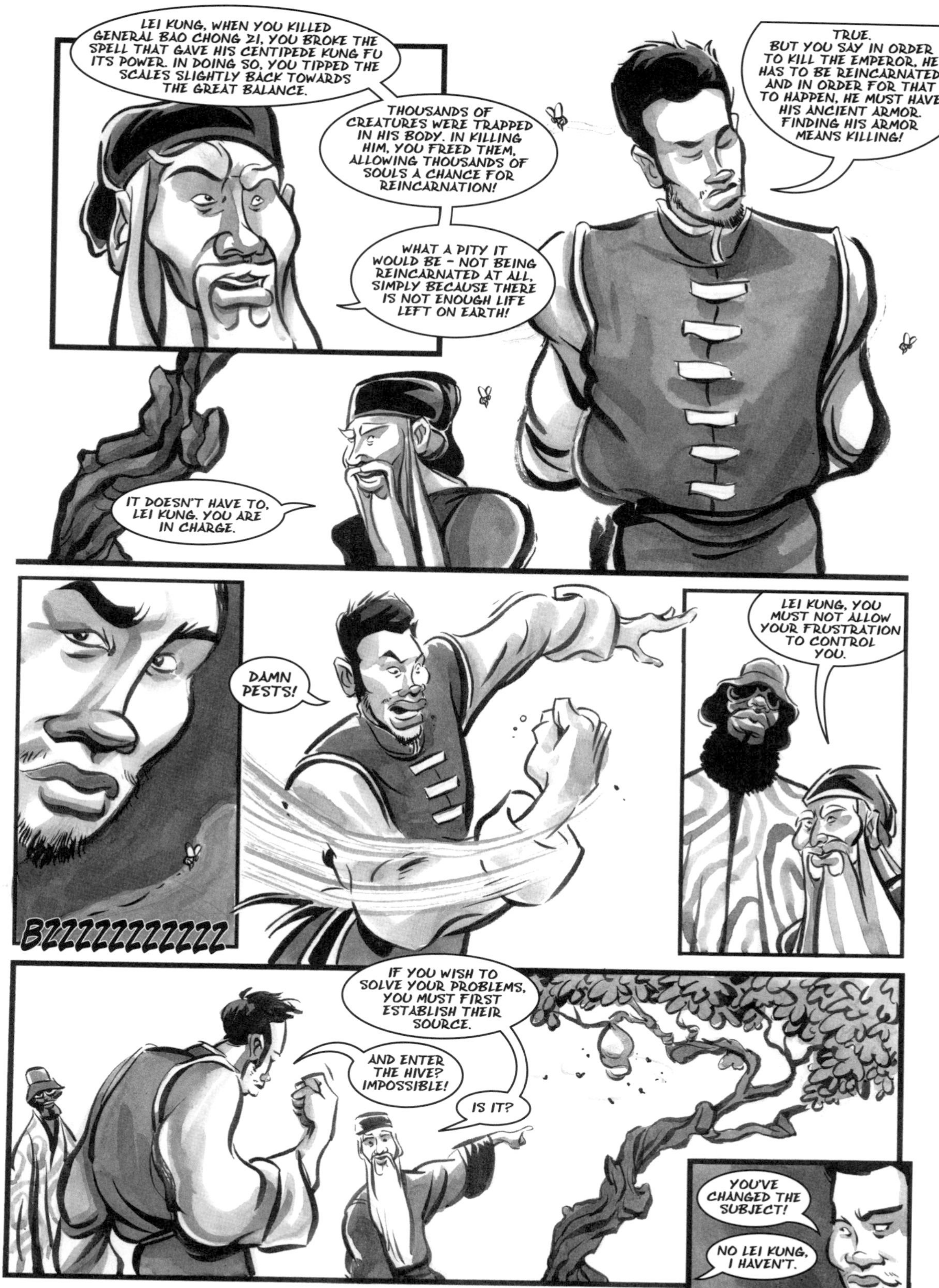

LEI KUNG, WHEN YOU KILLED GENERAL BAO CHONG ZI, YOU BROKE THE SPELL THAT GAVE HIS CENTIPEDE KUNG FU ITS POWER. IN DOING SO, YOU TIPPED THE SCALES SLIGHTLY BACK TOWARDS THE GREAT BALANCE.
THOUSANDS OF CREATURES WERE TRAPPED IN HIS BODY. IN KILLING HIM, YOU FREED THEM, ALLOWING THOUSANDS OF SOULS A CHANCE FOR REINCARNATION!
TRUE. BUT YOU SAY IN ORDER TO KILL THE EMPEROR, HE HAS TO BE REINCARNATED. AND IN ORDER FOR THAT TO HAPPEN, HE MUST HAVE HIS ANCIENT ARMOR. FINDING HIS ARMOR MEANS KILLING!
WHAT A PITY IT WOULD BE - NOT BEING REINCARNATED AT ALL, SIMPLY BECAUSE THERE IS NOT ENOUGH LIFE LEFT ON EARTH!
IT DOESN'T HAVE TO, LEI KUNG. YOU ARE IN CHARGE.
BZZZZZZZZZZZ
DAMN PESTS!
LEI KUNG, YOU MUST NOT ALLOW YOUR FRUSTRATION TO CONTROL YOU.
IF YOU WISH TO SOLVE YOUR PROBLEMS, YOU MUST FIRST ESTABLISH THEIR SOURCE.
AND ENTER THE HIVE? IMPOSSIBLE!
IS IT?
YOU'VE CHANGED THE SUBJECT!
NO LEI KUNG, I HAVEN'T.

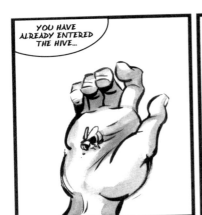

YOU HAVE ALREADY ENTERED THE HIVE...

...AND MANY OF THE BEES ARE ON YOUR SIDE.

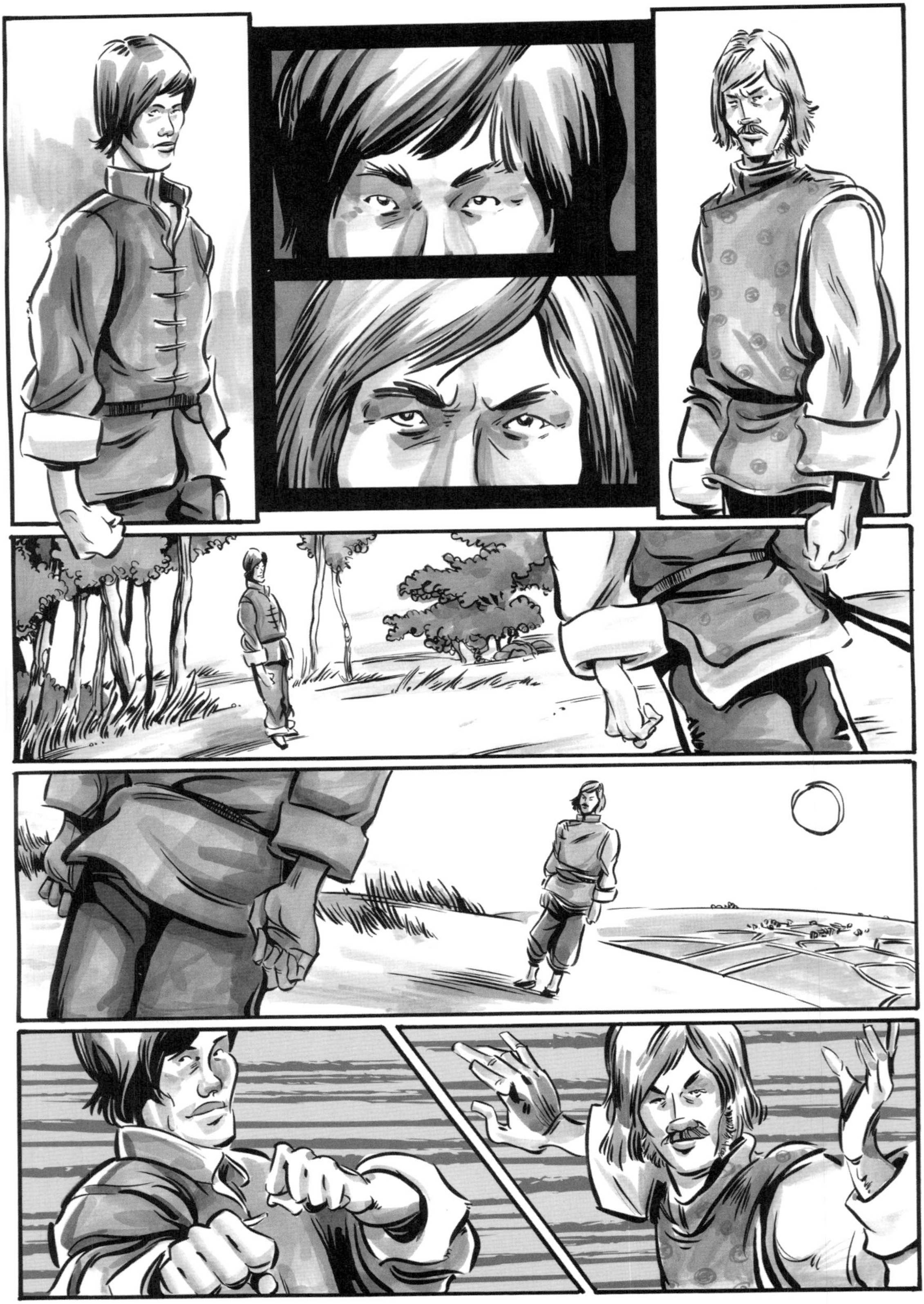

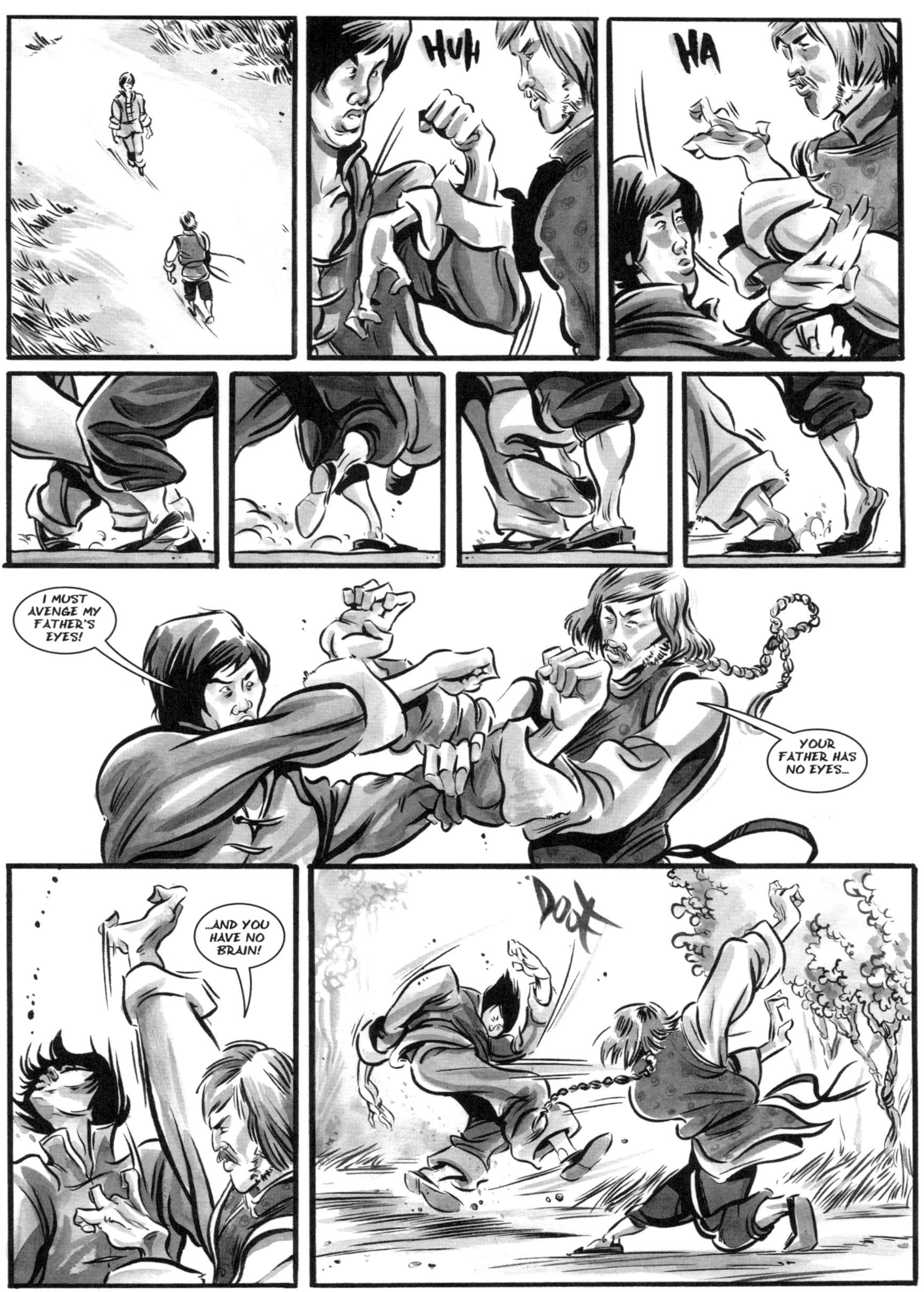
HUH
HA
I MUST AVENGE MY FATHER'S EYES!
YOUR FATHER HAS NO EYES...
...AND YOU HAVE NO BRAIN!

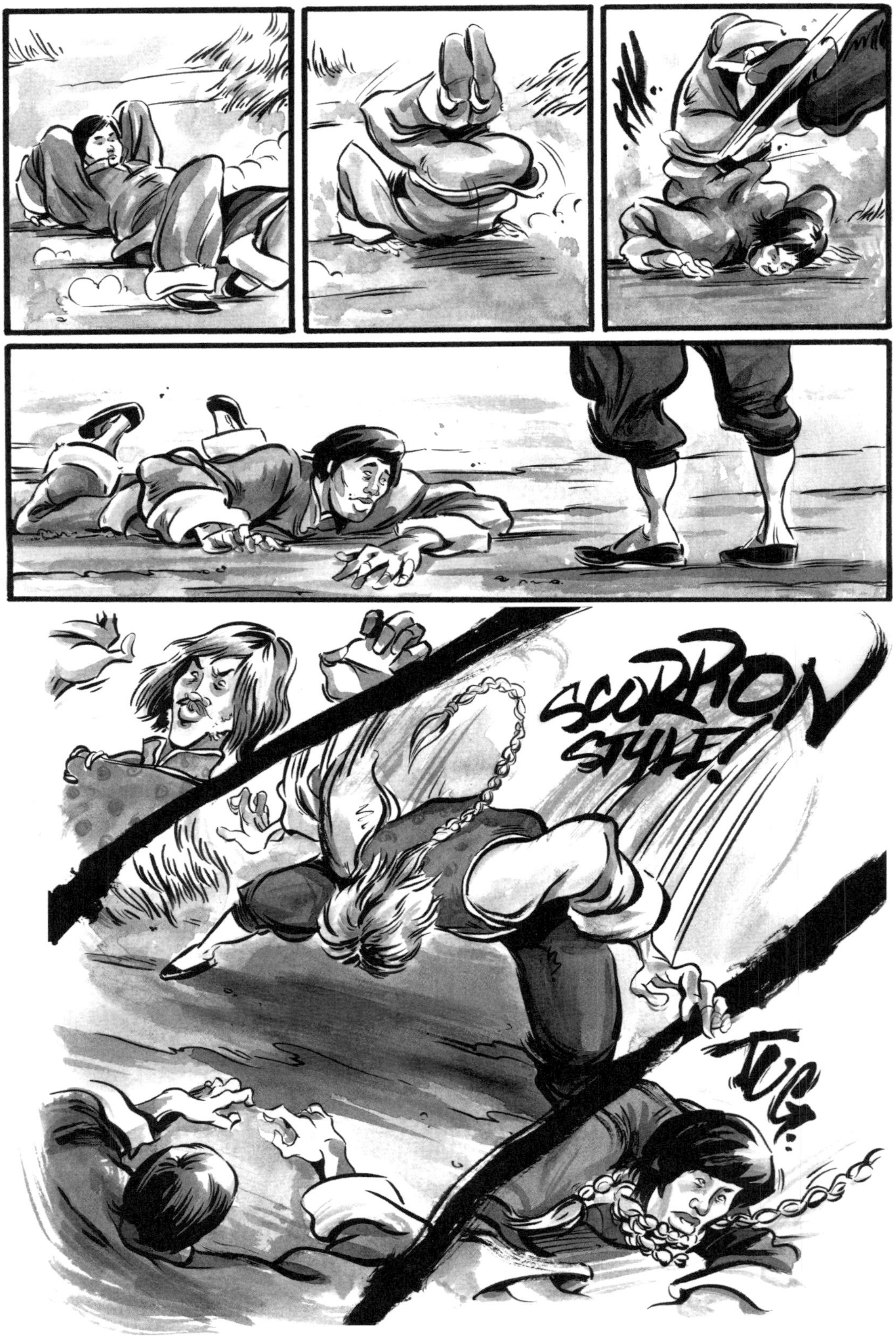
SCORPION STYLE!
TUG..

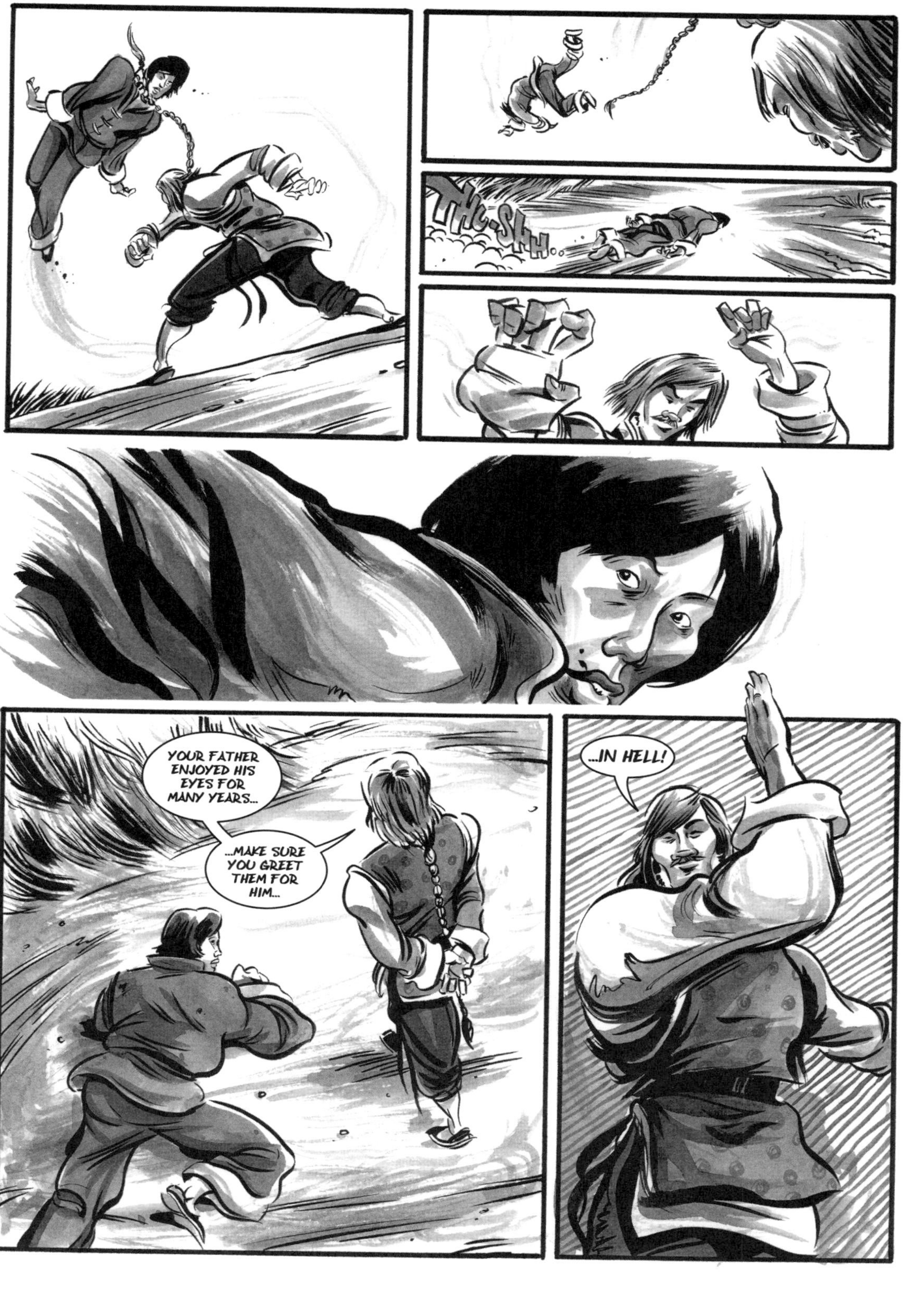
THU-SHH..
YOUR FATHER ENJOYED HIS EYES FOR MANY YEARS...
...MAKE SURE YOU GREET THEM FOR HIM...
...IN HELL!

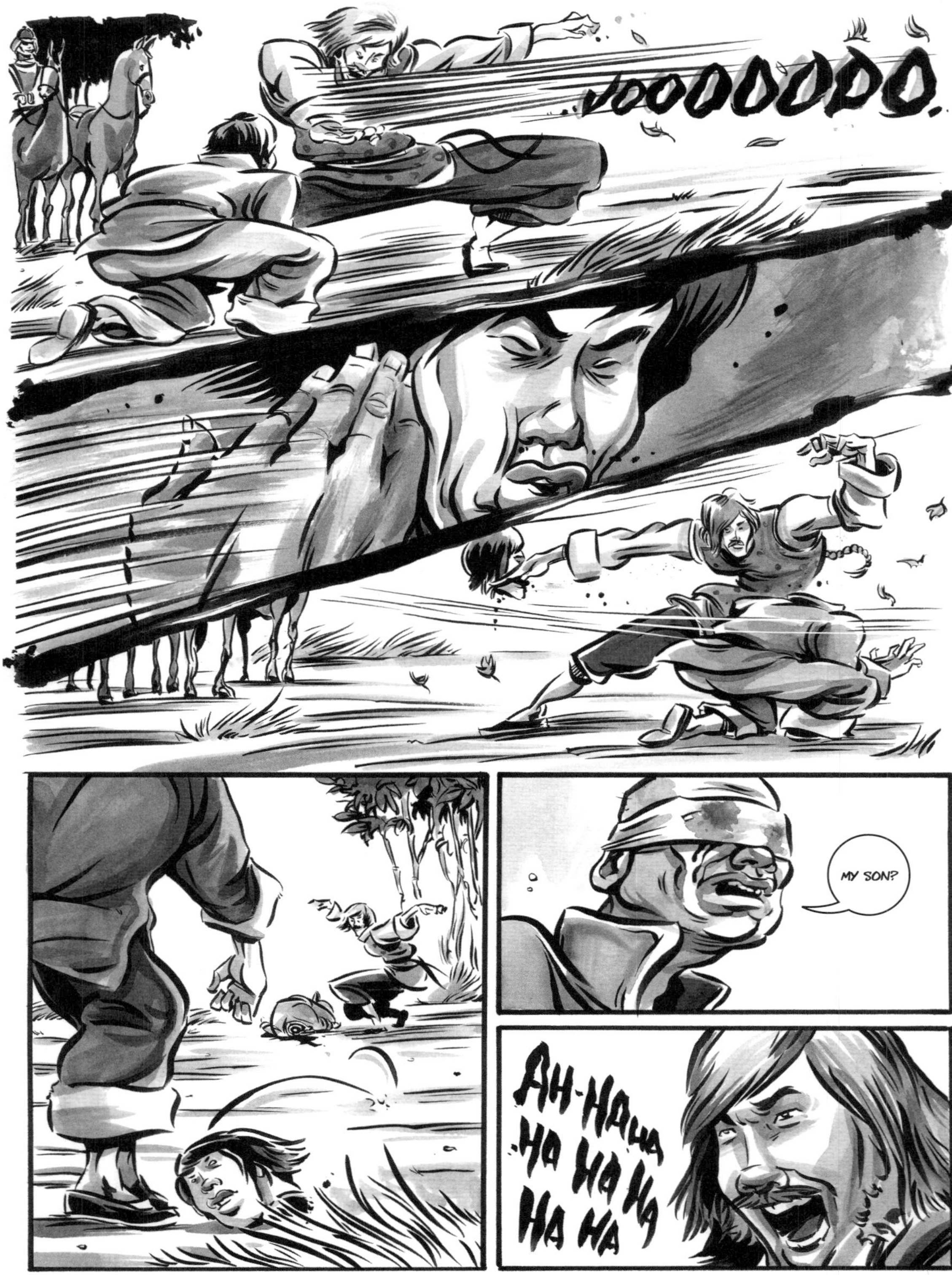
VOOOOOOOO
MY SON?
AH-HAHA HA HA HA HA HA

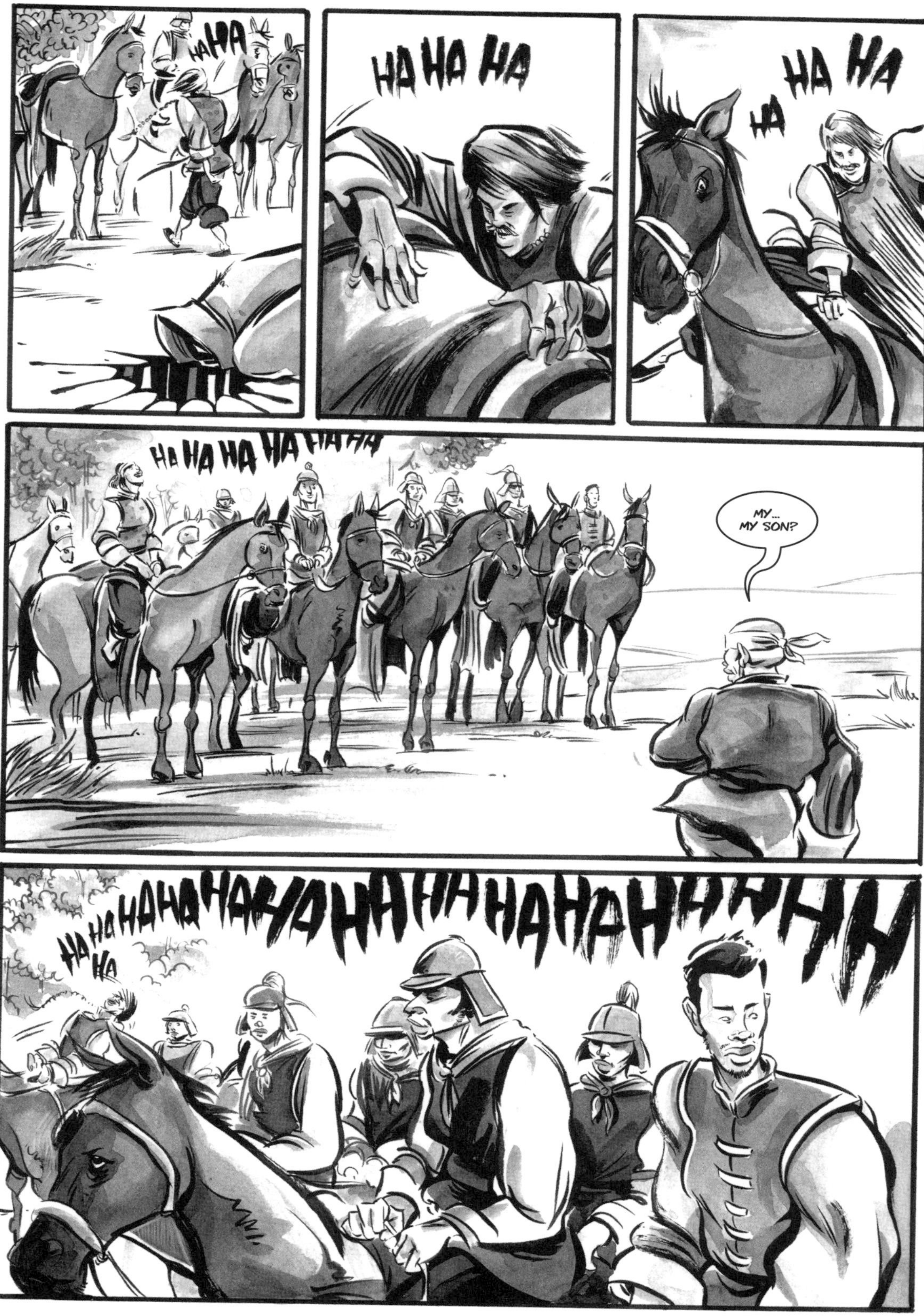
HA HA
HA HA HA
HA HA HA
HA HA HA HA HA HA
MY... MY SON?
HA HA HA HA HA HA HA HA HA HA HA HA HA HA

# DEAD OR A RIVAL

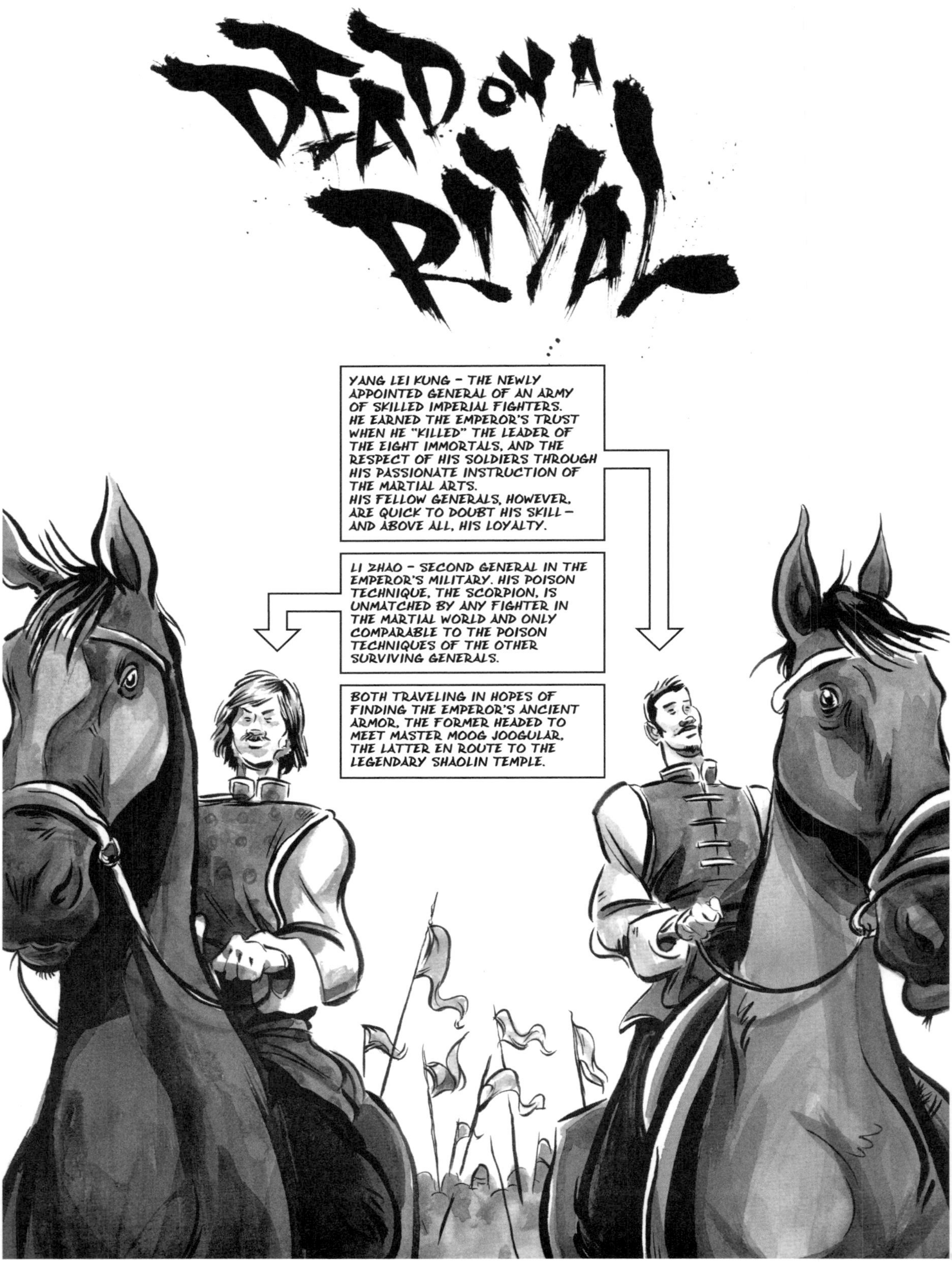
YANG LEI KUNG – THE NEWLY APPOINTED GENERAL OF AN ARMY OF SKILLED IMPERIAL FIGHTERS. HE EARNED THE EMPEROR'S TRUST WHEN HE "KILLED" THE LEADER OF THE EIGHT IMMORTALS, AND THE RESPECT OF HIS SOLDIERS THROUGH HIS PASSIONATE INSTRUCTION OF THE MARTIAL ARTS. HIS FELLOW GENERALS, HOWEVER, ARE QUICK TO DOUBT HIS SKILL – AND ABOVE ALL, HIS LOYALTY.
LI ZHAO – SECOND GENERAL IN THE EMPEROR'S MILITARY. HIS POISON TECHNIQUE, THE SCORPION, IS UNMATCHED BY ANY FIGHTER IN THE MARTIAL WORLD AND ONLY COMPARABLE TO THE POISON TECHNIQUES OF THE OTHER SURVIVING GENERALS.
BOTH TRAVELING IN HOPES OF FINDING THE EMPEROR'S ANCIENT ARMOR, THE FORMER HEADED TO MEET MASTER MOOG JOOGULAR, THE LATTER EN ROUTE TO THE LEGENDARY SHAOLIN TEMPLE.

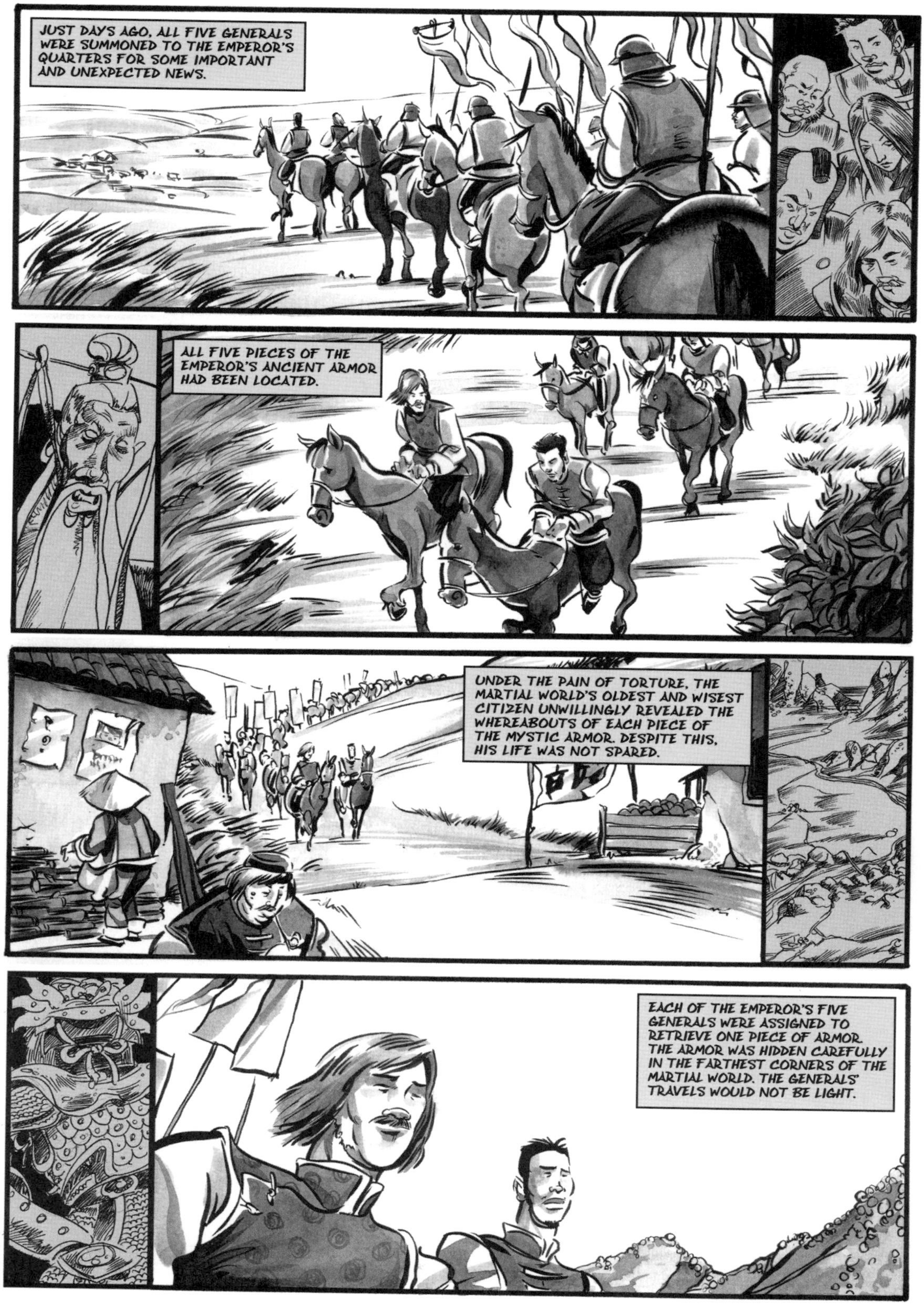
JUST DAYS AGO, ALL FIVE GENERALS WERE SUMMONED TO THE EMPEROR'S QUARTERS FOR SOME IMPORTANT AND UNEXPECTED NEWS.
ALL FIVE PIECES OF THE EMPEROR'S ANCIENT ARMOR HAD BEEN LOCATED.
UNDER THE PAIN OF TORTURE, THE MARTIAL WORLD'S OLDEST AND WISEST CITIZEN UNWILLINGLY REVEALED THE WHEREABOUTS OF EACH PIECE OF THE MYSTIC ARMOR. DESPITE THIS, HIS LIFE WAS NOT SPARED.
EACH OF THE EMPEROR'S FIVE GENERALS WERE ASSIGNED TO RETRIEVE ONE PIECE OF ARMOR. THE ARMOR WAS HIDDEN CAREFULLY IN THE FARTHEST CORNERS OF THE MARTIAL WORLD. THE GENERALS' TRAVELS WOULD NOT BE LIGHT.

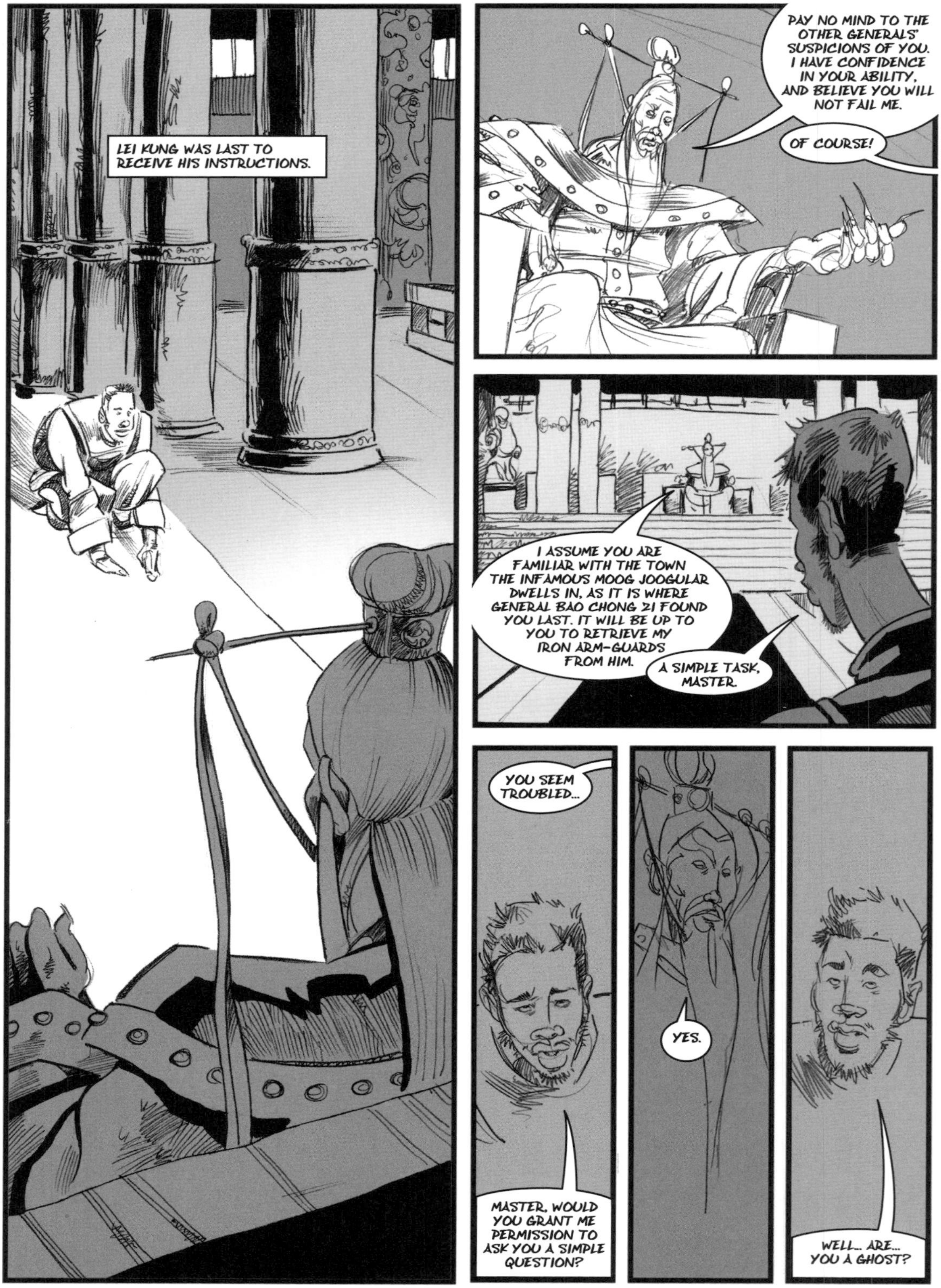
LEI KUNG WAS LAST TO RECEIVE HIS INSTRUCTIONS.
PAY NO MIND TO THE OTHER GENERALS' SUSPICIONS OF YOU. I HAVE CONFIDENCE IN YOUR ABILITY, AND BELIEVE YOU WILL NOT FAIL ME.
OF COURSE!
I ASSUME YOU ARE FAMILIAR WITH THE TOWN THE INFAMOUS MOOG JOOGULAR DWELLS IN, AS IT IS WHERE GENERAL BAO CHONG ZI FOUND YOU LAST. IT WILL BE UP TO YOU TO RETRIEVE MY IRON ARM-GUARDS FROM HIM.
A SIMPLE TASK, MASTER.
YOU SEEM TROUBLED...
MASTER, WOULD YOU GRANT ME PERMISSION TO ASK YOU A SIMPLE QUESTION?
YES.
WELL... ARE... YOU A GHOST?

HA

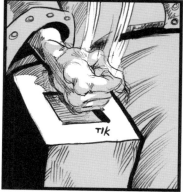

TIK

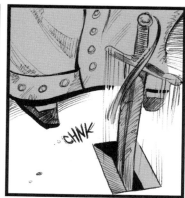

CHNK

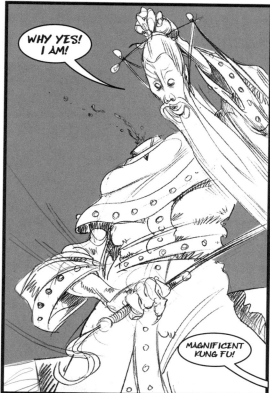

WHY YES! I AM!

MAGNIFICENT KUNG FU!

INDEED, MY KUNG FU IS IMPRESSIVE. YET AS A GHOST, MY POWER IS LIMITED.

I HAVE LITTLE CONTROL OVER THINGS IN THIS REALM, WHICH IS WHY I MUST RESURRECT MYSELF IN HUMAN FORM!

BUT WHAT WILL BE THE DIFFERENCE? EITHER WAY, YOU ARE STILL THE EMPEROR!

DEAD... I AM UNBEATABLE, YET MY SOUL IS TORMENTED.

ALIVE... I AM UNBEATABLE.

YOU MUST GO NOW.

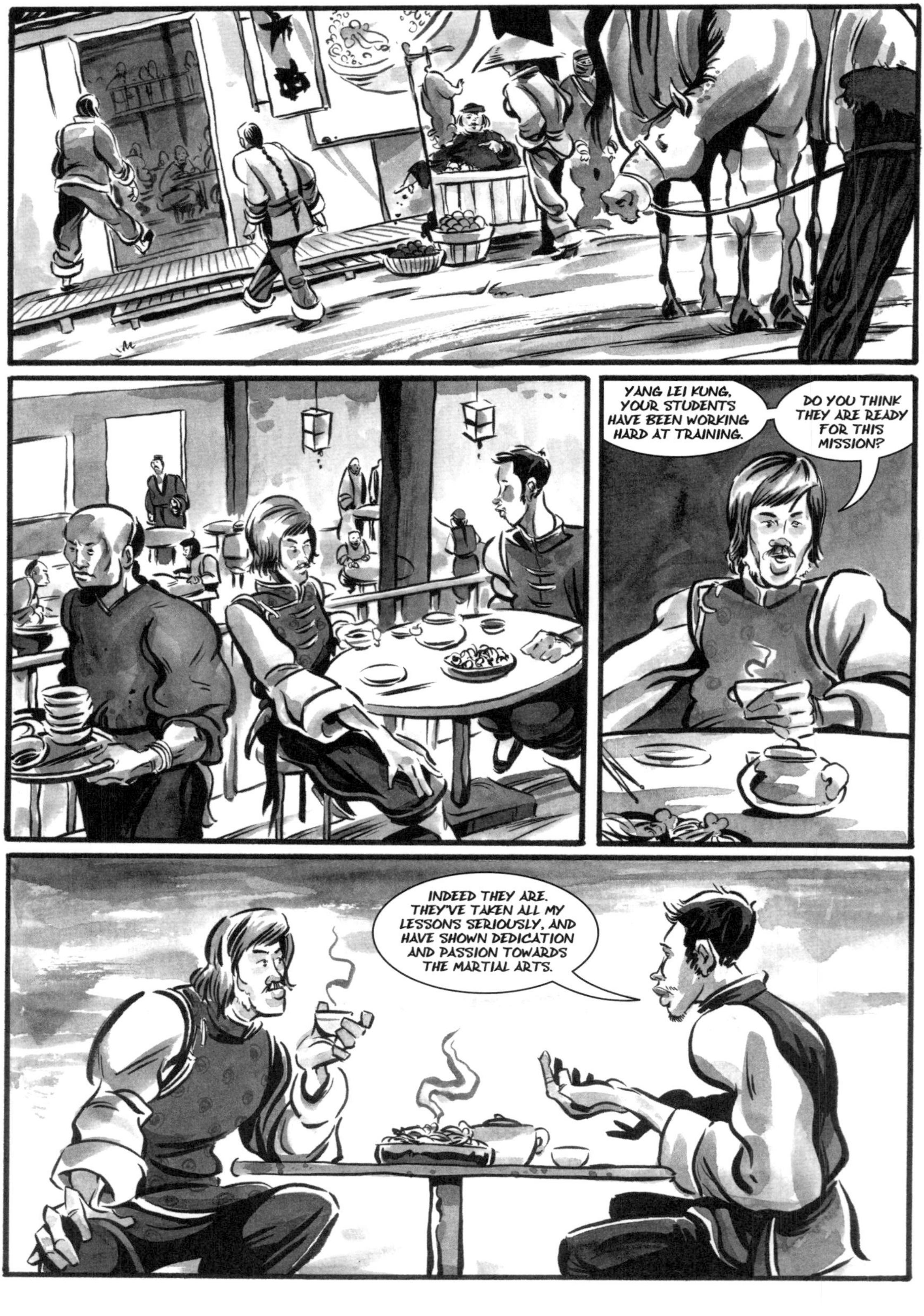
YANG LEI KUNG, YOUR STUDENTS HAVE BEEN WORKING HARD AT TRAINING.
DO YOU THINK THEY ARE READY FOR THIS MISSION?
INDEED THEY ARE. THEY'VE TAKEN ALL MY LESSONS SERIOUSLY, AND HAVE SHOWN DEDICATION AND PASSION TOWARDS THE MARTIAL ARTS.

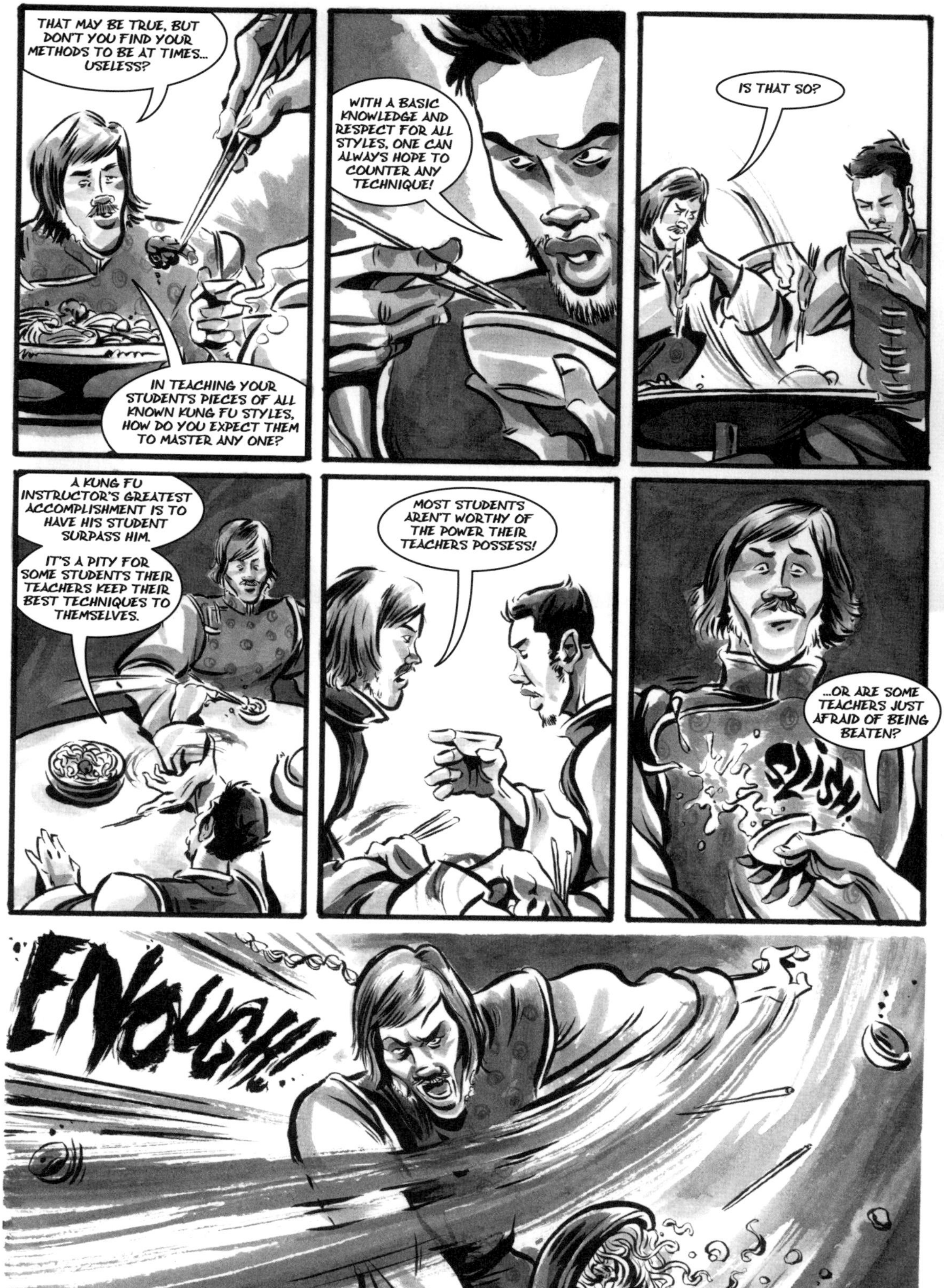
THAT MAY BE TRUE, BUT DON'T YOU FIND YOUR METHODS TO BE AT TIMES... USELESS?
IN TEACHING YOUR STUDENTS PIECES OF ALL KNOWN KUNG FU STYLES, HOW DO YOU EXPECT THEM TO MASTER ANY ONE?
WITH A BASIC KNOWLEDGE AND RESPECT FOR ALL STYLES, ONE CAN ALWAYS HOPE TO COUNTER ANY TECHNIQUE!
IS THAT SO?
A KUNG FU INSTRUCTOR'S GREATEST ACCOMPLISHMENT IS TO HAVE HIS STUDENT SURPASS HIM.
IT'S A PITY FOR SOME STUDENTS THEIR TEACHERS KEEP THEIR BEST TECHNIQUES TO THEMSELVES.
MOST STUDENTS AREN'T WORTHY OF THE POWER THEIR TEACHERS POSSESS!
SPLISH!
...OR ARE SOME TEACHERS JUST AFRAID OF BEING BEATEN?
ENOUGH!!

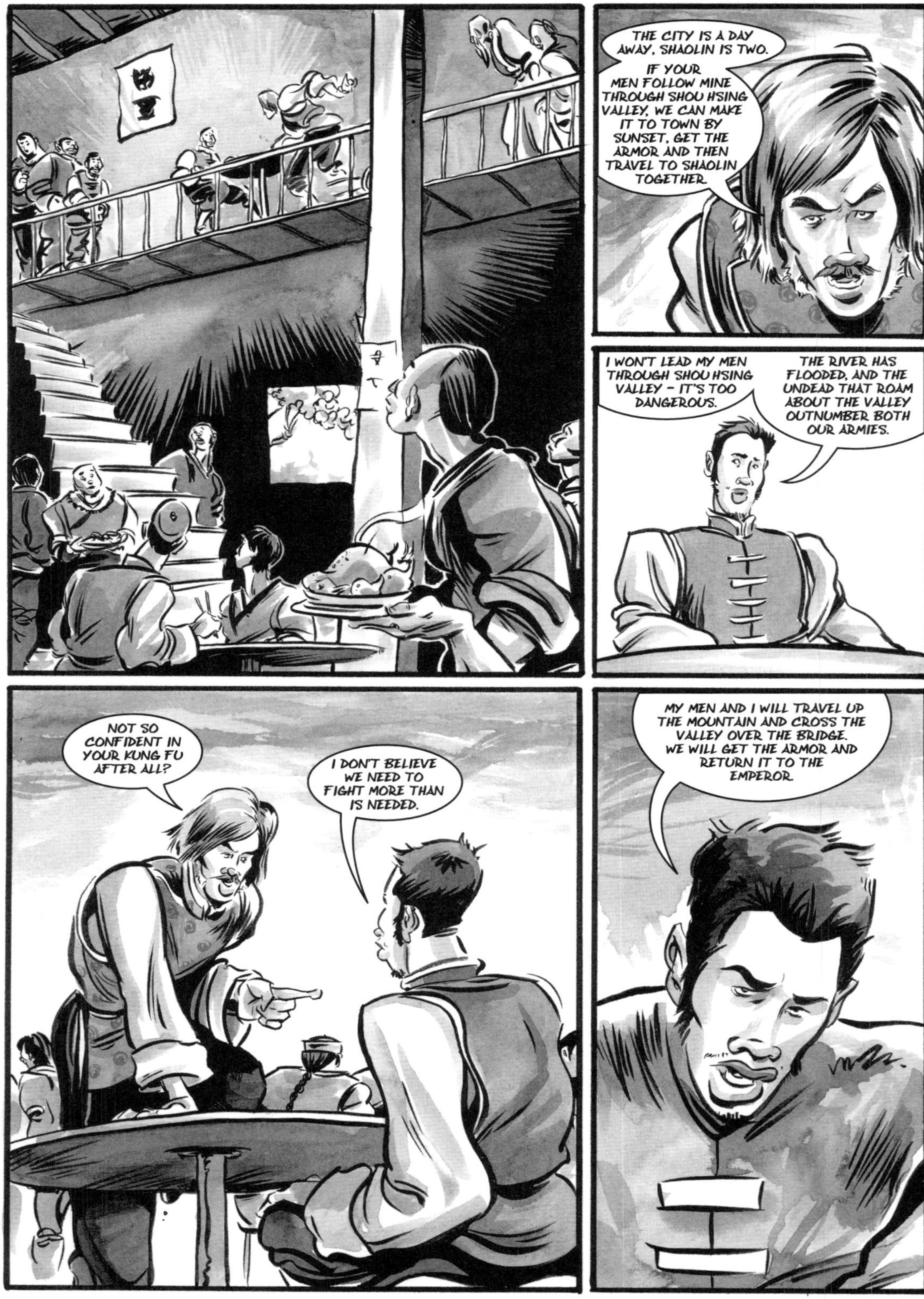
THE CITY IS A DAY AWAY, SHAOLIN IS TWO.
IF YOUR MEN FOLLOW MINE THROUGH SHOU H'SING VALLEY, WE CAN MAKE IT TO TOWN BY SUNSET, GET THE ARMOR AND THEN TRAVEL TO SHAOLIN TOGETHER.
I WON'T LEAD MY MEN THROUGH SHOU H'SING VALLEY - IT'S TOO DANGEROUS.
THE RIVER HAS FLOODED, AND THE UNDEAD THAT ROAM ABOUT THE VALLEY OUTNUMBER BOTH OUR ARMIES.
NOT SO CONFIDENT IN YOUR KUNG FU AFTER ALL?
I DON'T BELIEVE WE NEED TO FIGHT MORE THAN IS NEEDED.
MY MEN AND I WILL TRAVEL UP THE MOUNTAIN AND CROSS THE VALLEY OVER THE BRIDGE. WE WILL GET THE ARMOR AND RETURN IT TO THE EMPEROR.

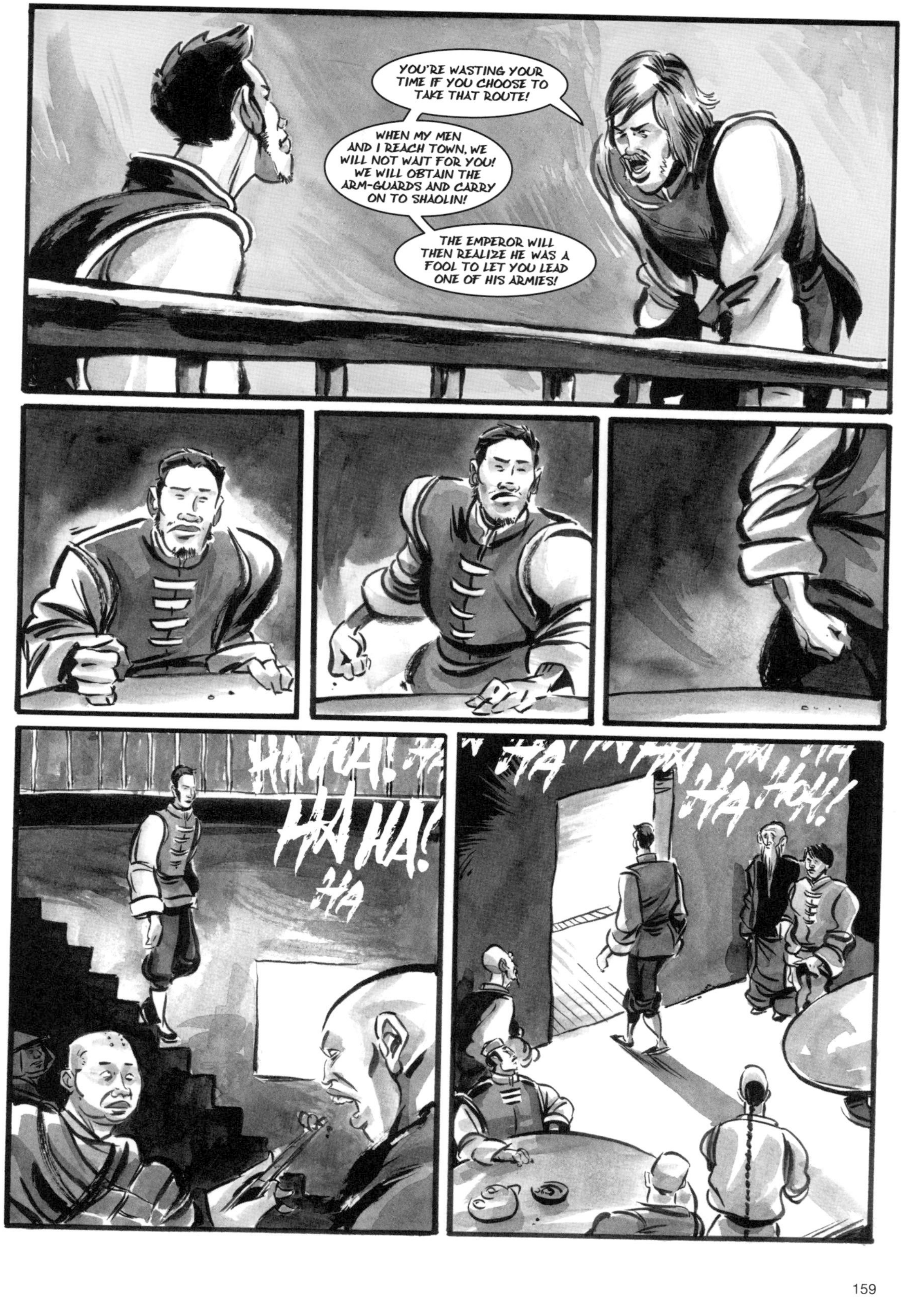
YOU'RE WASTING YOUR TIME IF YOU CHOOSE TO TAKE THAT ROUTE!
WHEN MY MEN AND I REACH TOWN, WE WILL NOT WAIT FOR YOU! WE WILL OBTAIN THE ARM-GUARDS AND CARRY ON TO SHAOLIN!
THE EMPEROR WILL THEN REALIZE HE WAS A FOOL TO LET YOU LEAD ONE OF HIS ARMIES!
HA HA!
HA HA!
HA
HA
HA
HA HOH!

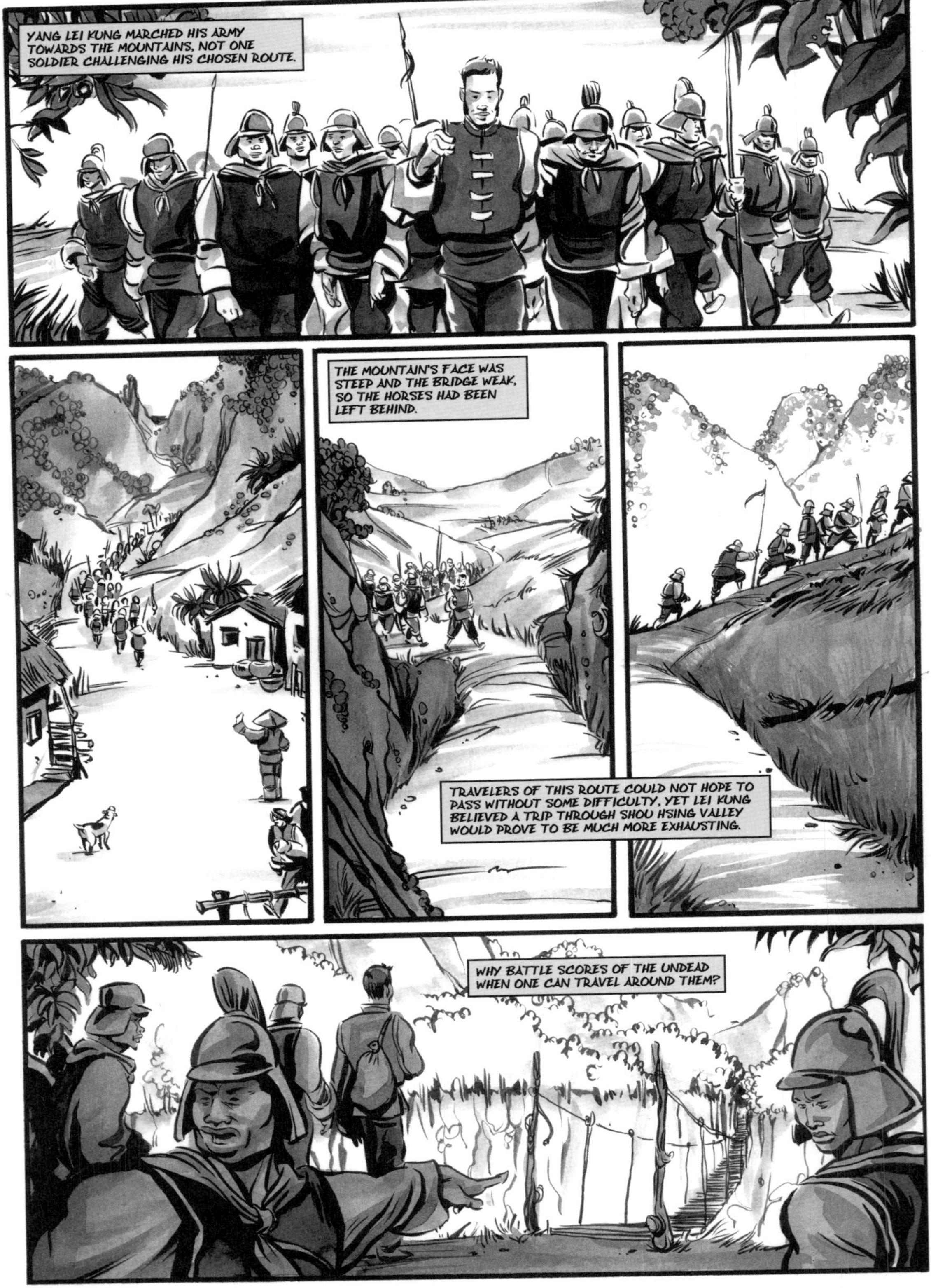
YANG LEI KUNG MARCHED HIS ARMY TOWARDS THE MOUNTAINS, NOT ONE SOLDIER CHALLENGING HIS CHOSEN ROUTE.
THE MOUNTAIN'S FACE WAS STEEP AND THE BRIDGE WEAK, SO THE HORSES HAD BEEN LEFT BEHIND.
TRAVELERS OF THIS ROUTE COULD NOT HOPE TO PASS WITHOUT SOME DIFFICULTY, YET LEI KUNG BELIEVED A TRIP THROUGH SHOU HSING VALLEY WOULD PROVE TO BE MUCH MORE EXHAUSTING.
WHY BATTLE SCORES OF THE UNDEAD WHEN ONE CAN TRAVEL AROUND THEM?

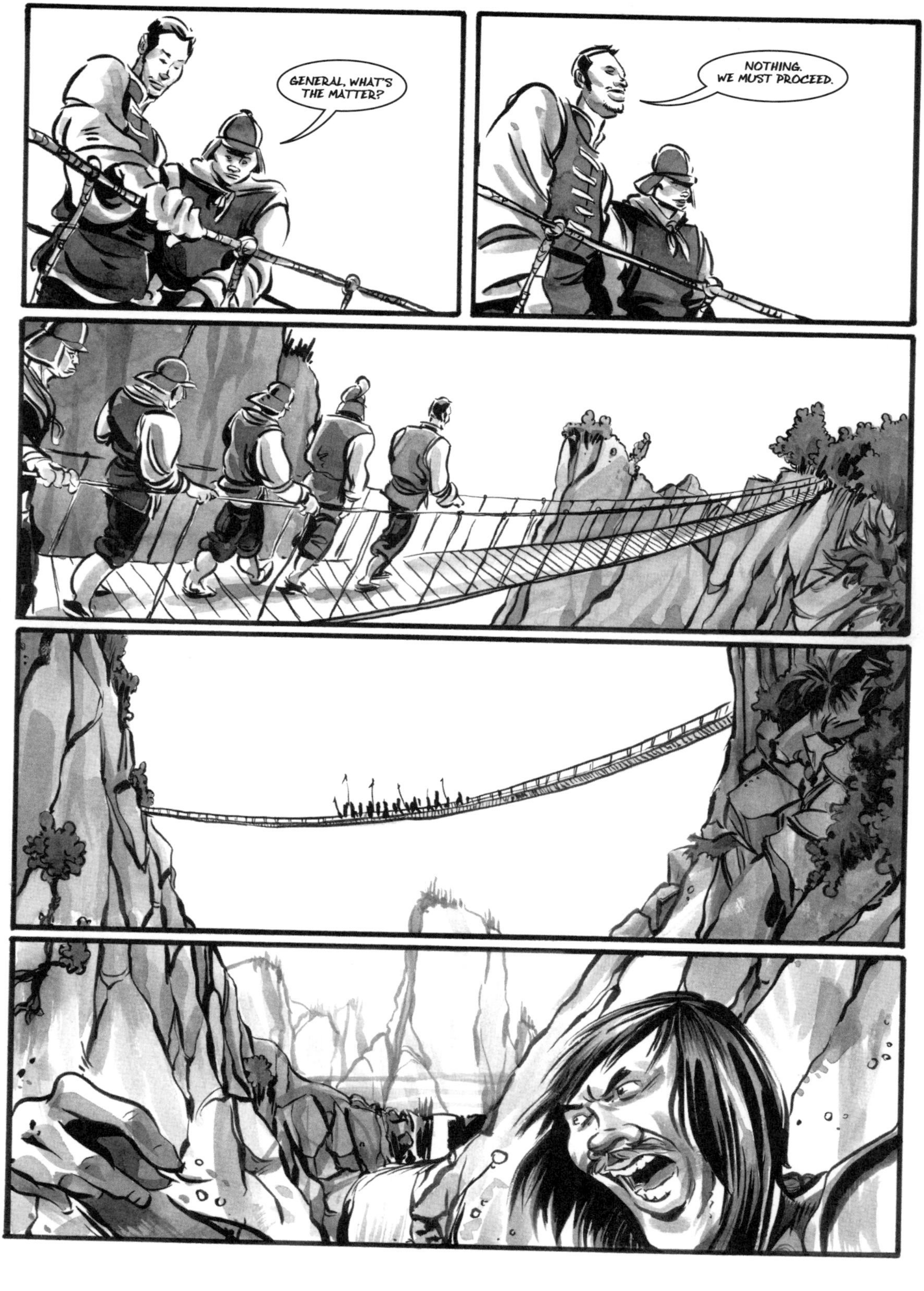
GENERAL, WHAT'S THE MATTER?
NOTHING. WE MUST PROCEED.

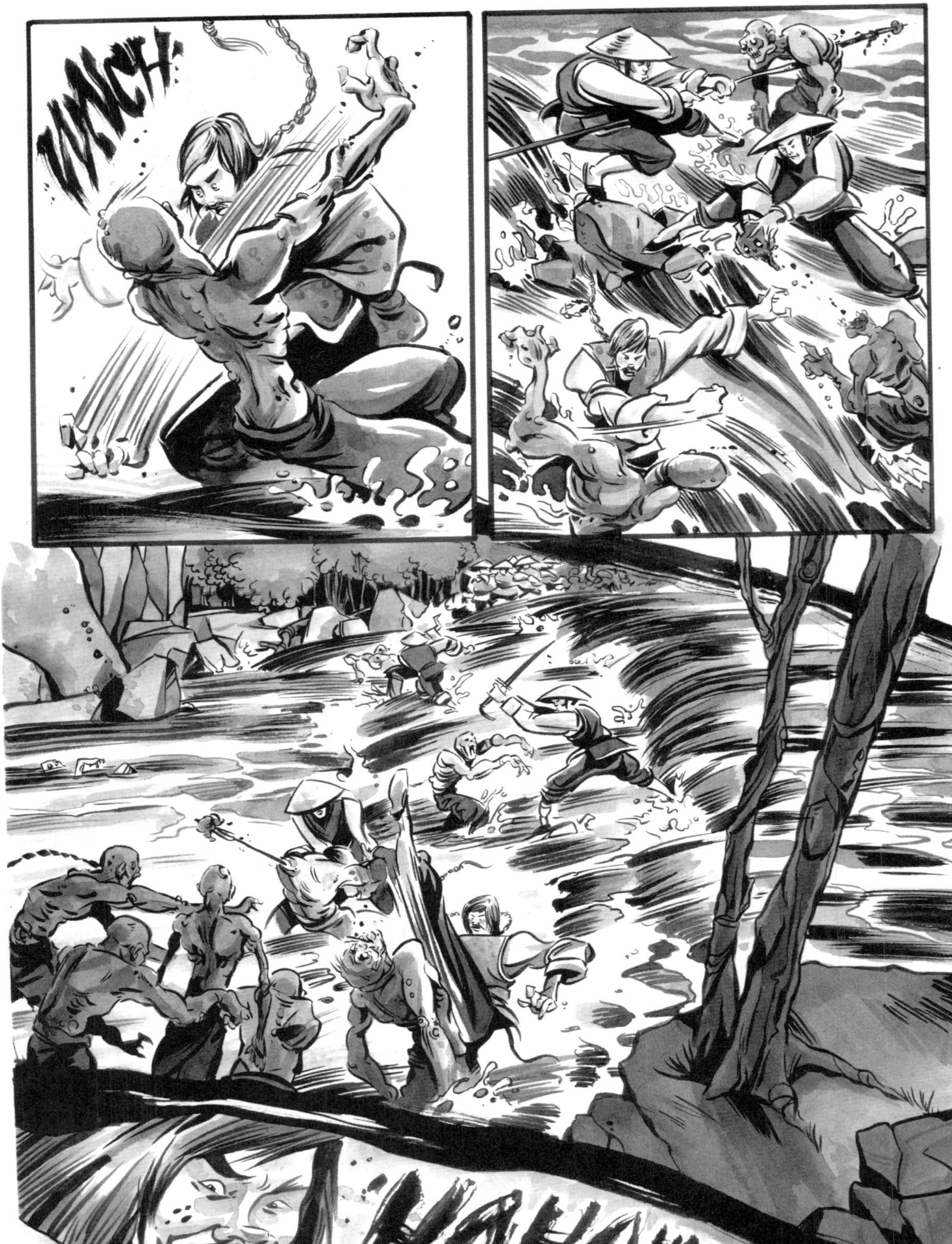
HAHAHA!

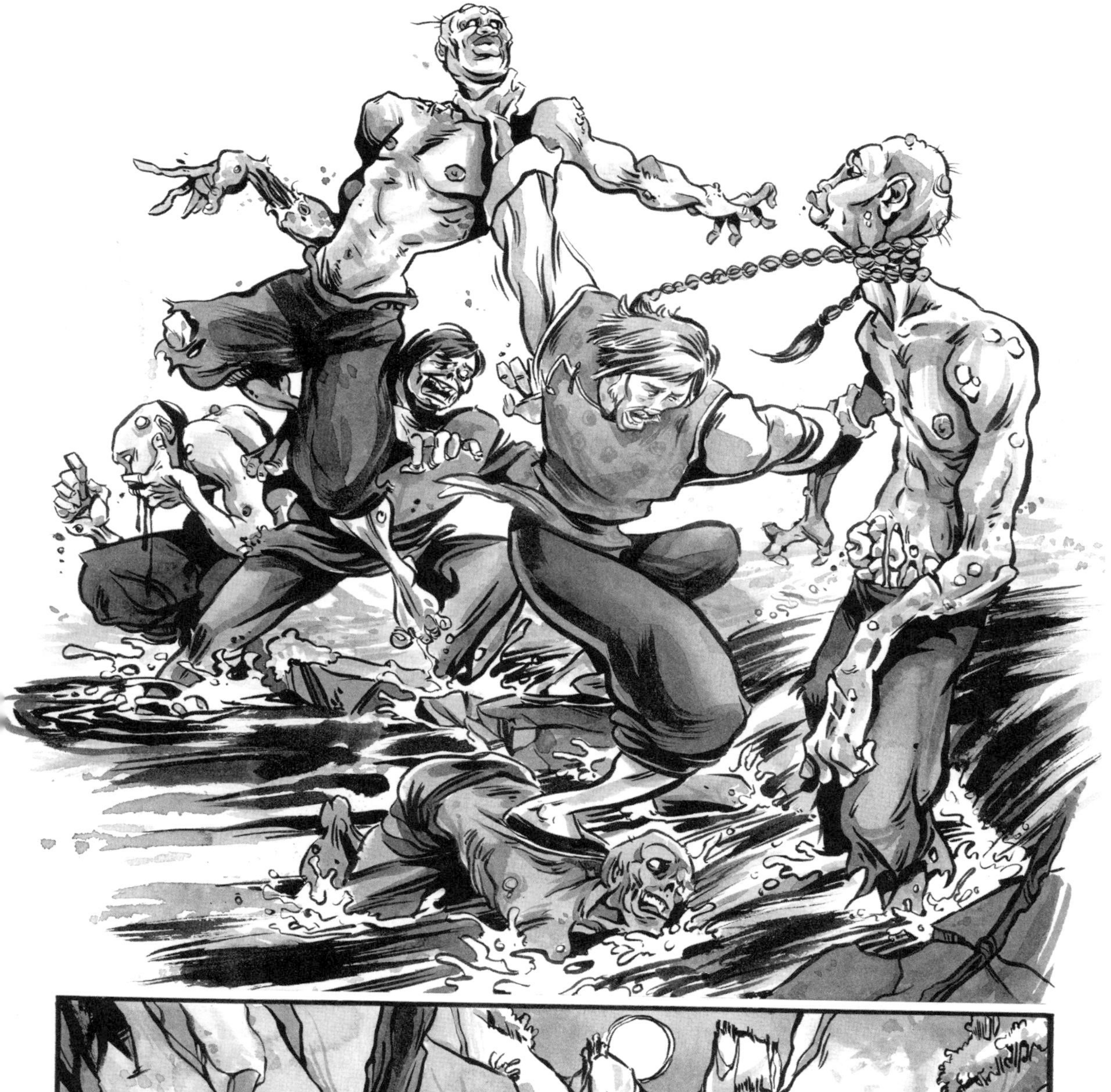

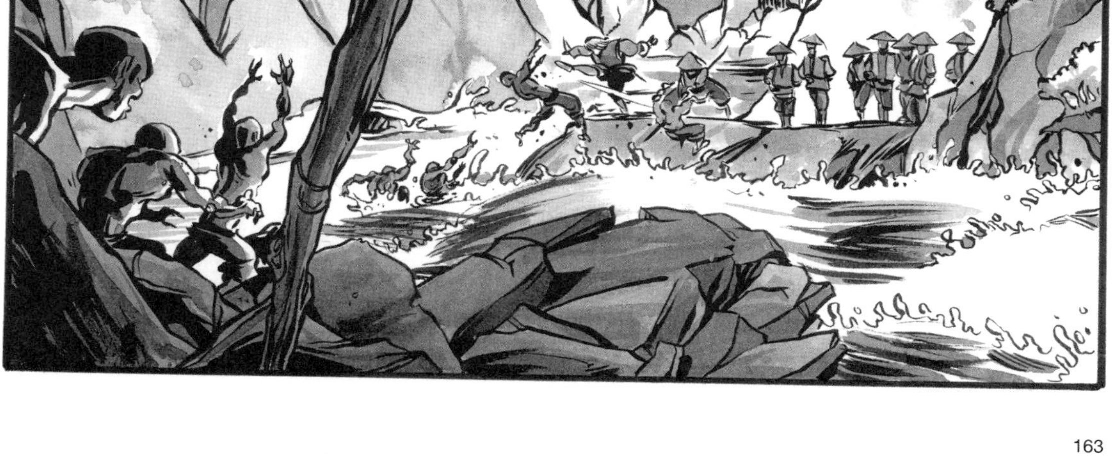

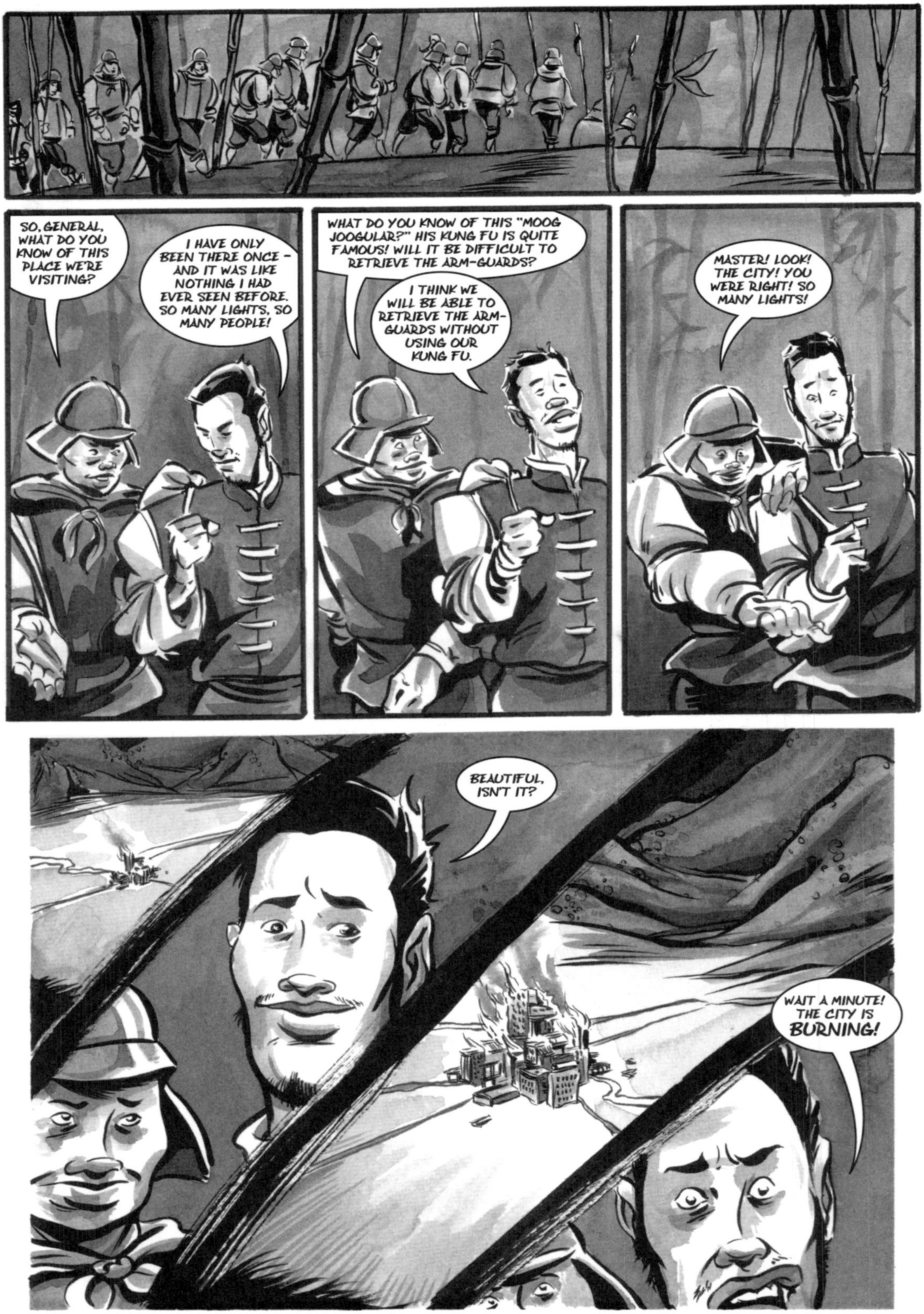

SO, GENERAL, WHAT DO YOU KNOW OF THIS PLACE WE'RE VISITING?
I HAVE ONLY BEEN THERE ONCE - AND IT WAS LIKE NOTHING I HAD EVER SEEN BEFORE. SO MANY LIGHTS, SO MANY PEOPLE!
WHAT DO YOU KNOW OF THIS "MOOG JOOGULAR?" HIS KUNG FU IS QUITE FAMOUS! WILL IT BE DIFFICULT TO RETRIEVE THE ARM-GUARDS?
I THINK WE WILL BE ABLE TO RETRIEVE THE ARM-GUARDS WITHOUT USING OUR KUNG FU.
MASTER! LOOK! THE CITY! YOU WERE RIGHT! SO MANY LIGHTS!
BEAUTIFUL, ISN'T IT?
WAIT A MINUTE! THE CITY IS BURNING!

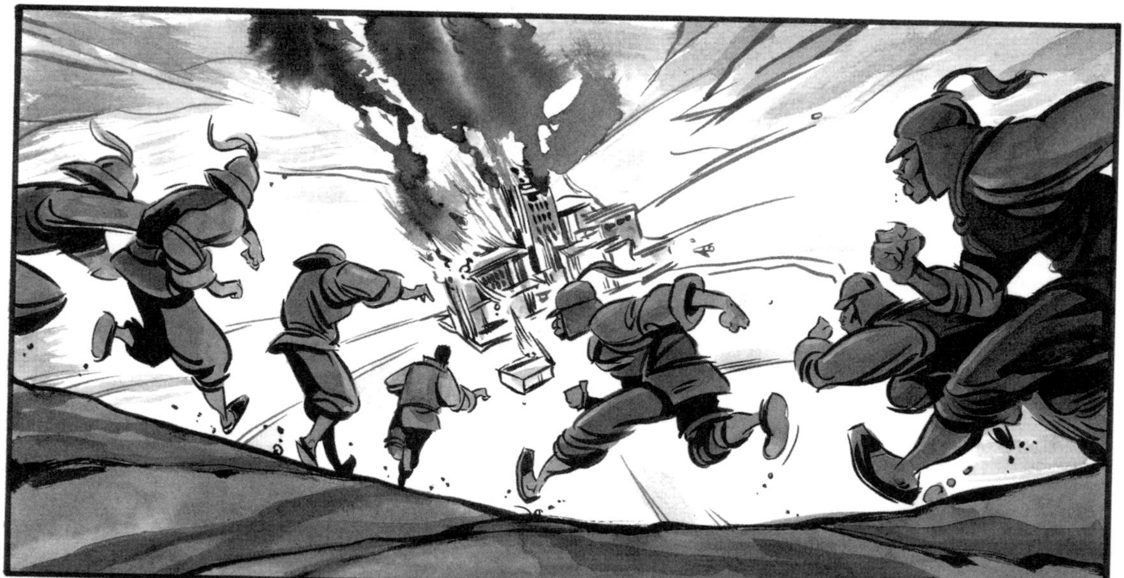

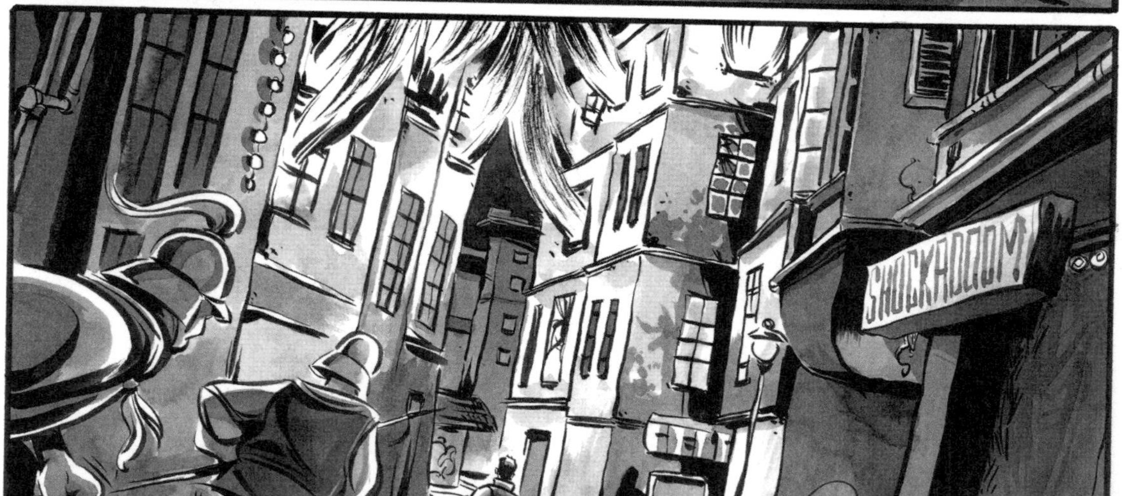
SHOCKADOOM!

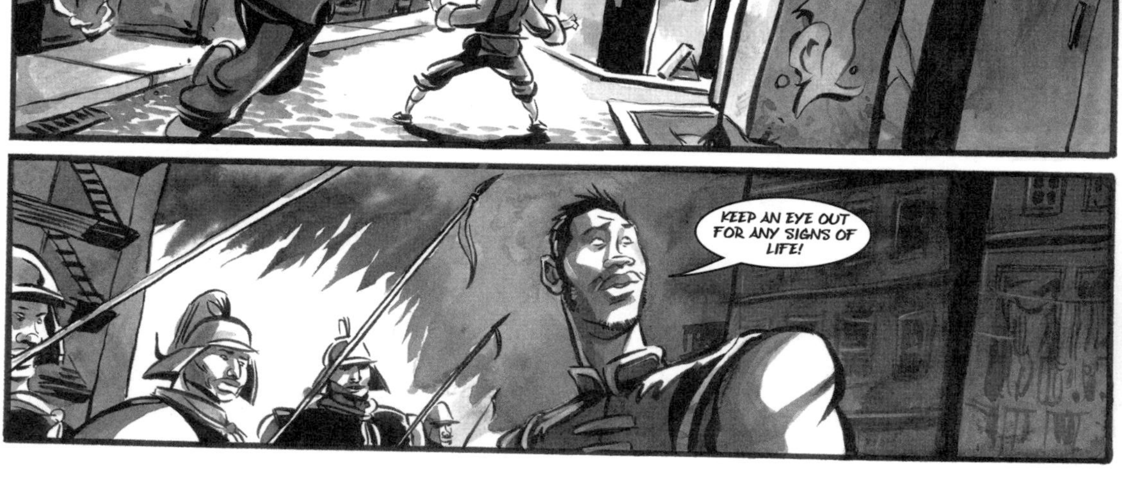
KEEP AN EYE OUT FOR ANY SIGNS OF LIFE!

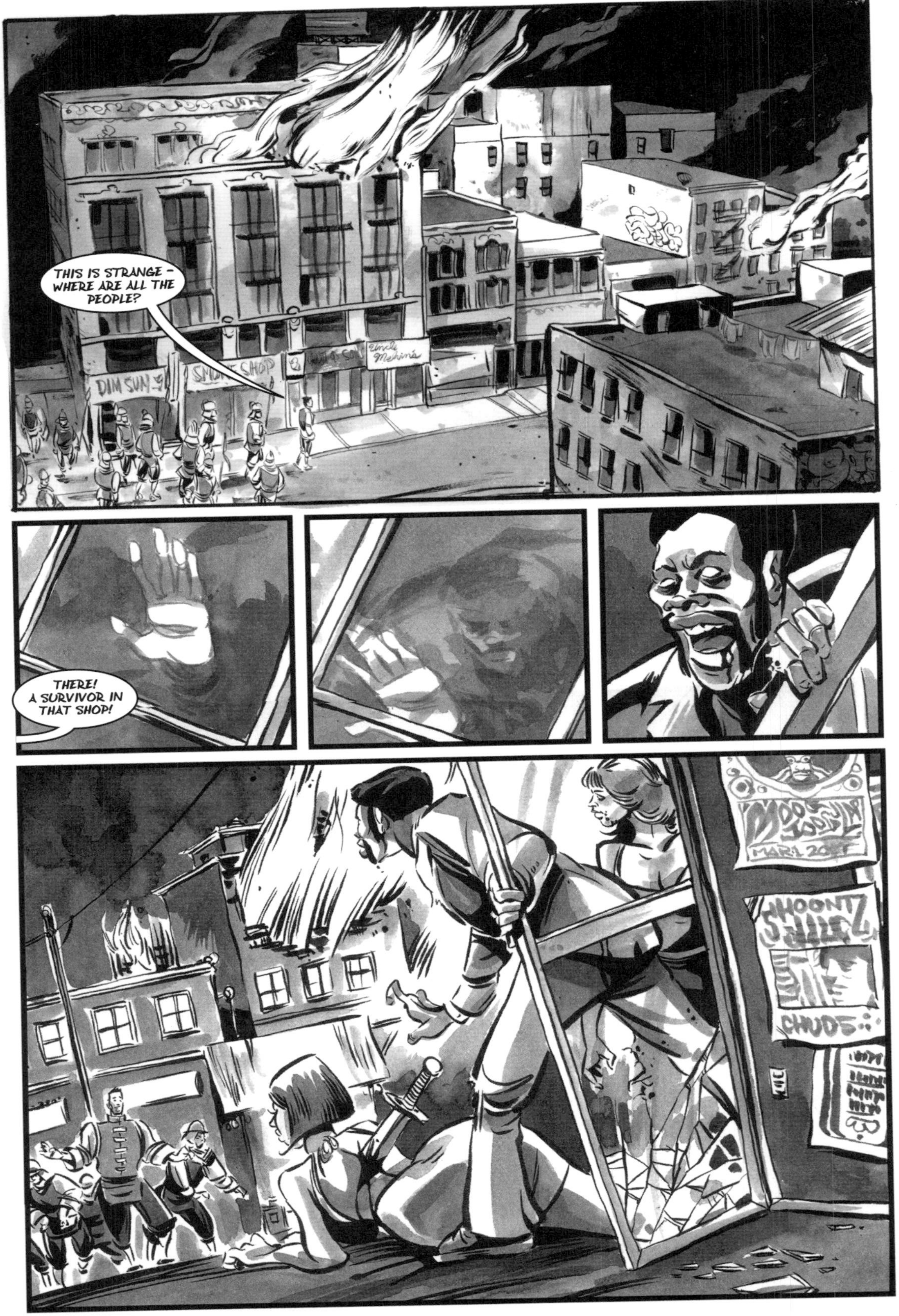
THIS IS STRANGE - WHERE ARE ALL THE PEOPLE?
THERE! A SURVIVOR IN THAT SHOP!

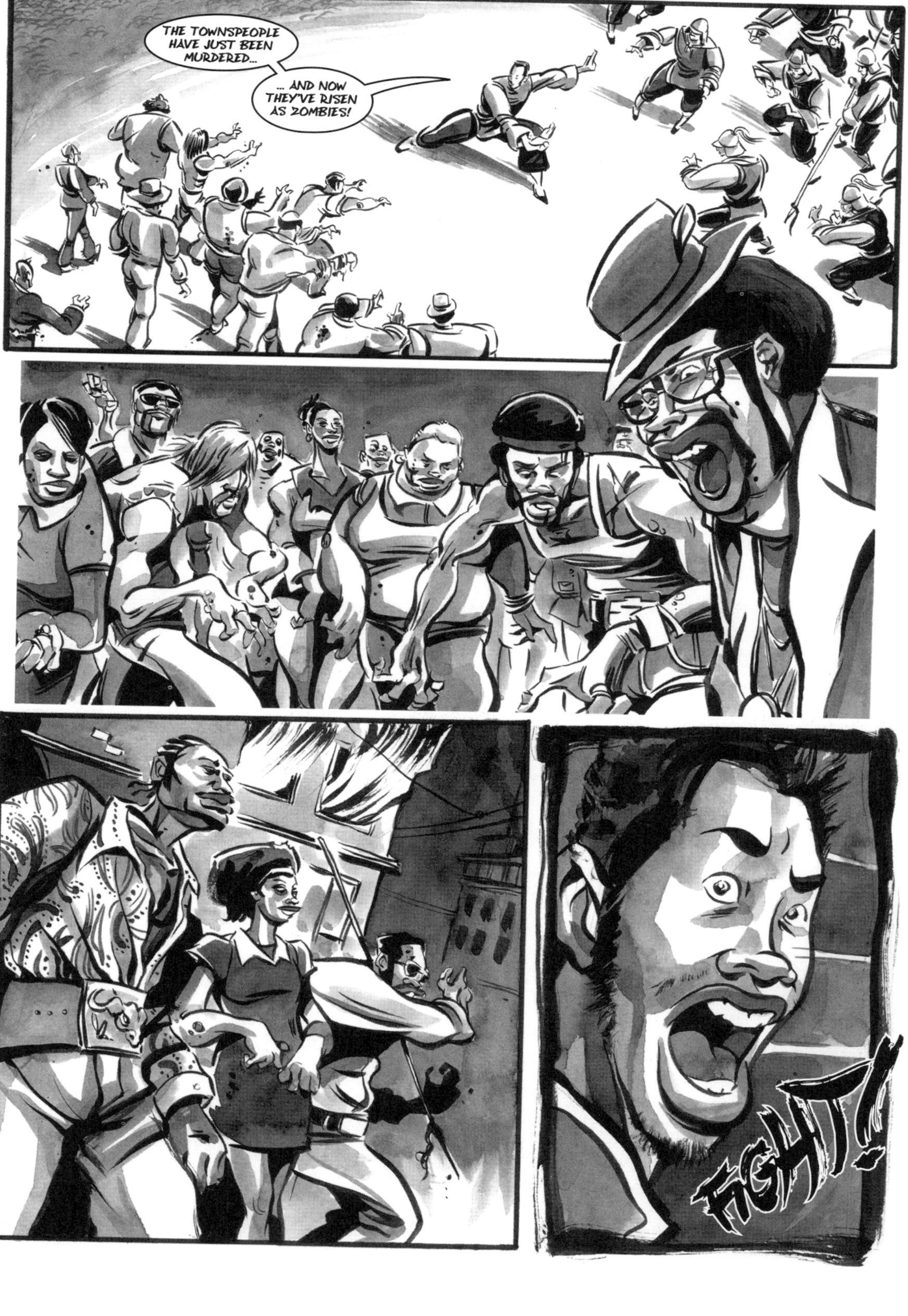
THE TOWNSPEOPLE HAVE JUST BEEN MURDERED...
... AND NOW THEY'VE RISEN AS ZOMBIES!
FIGHT!

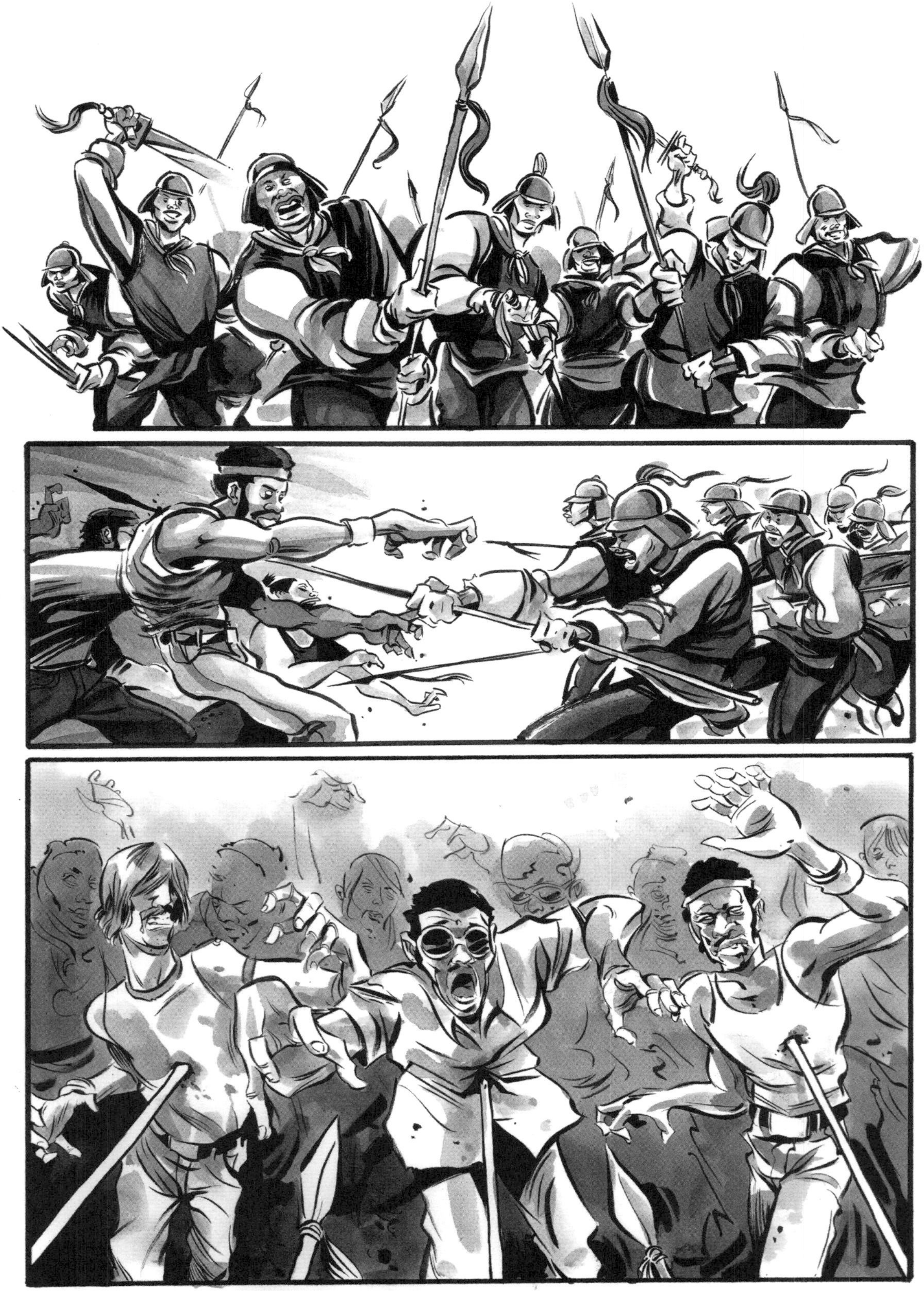

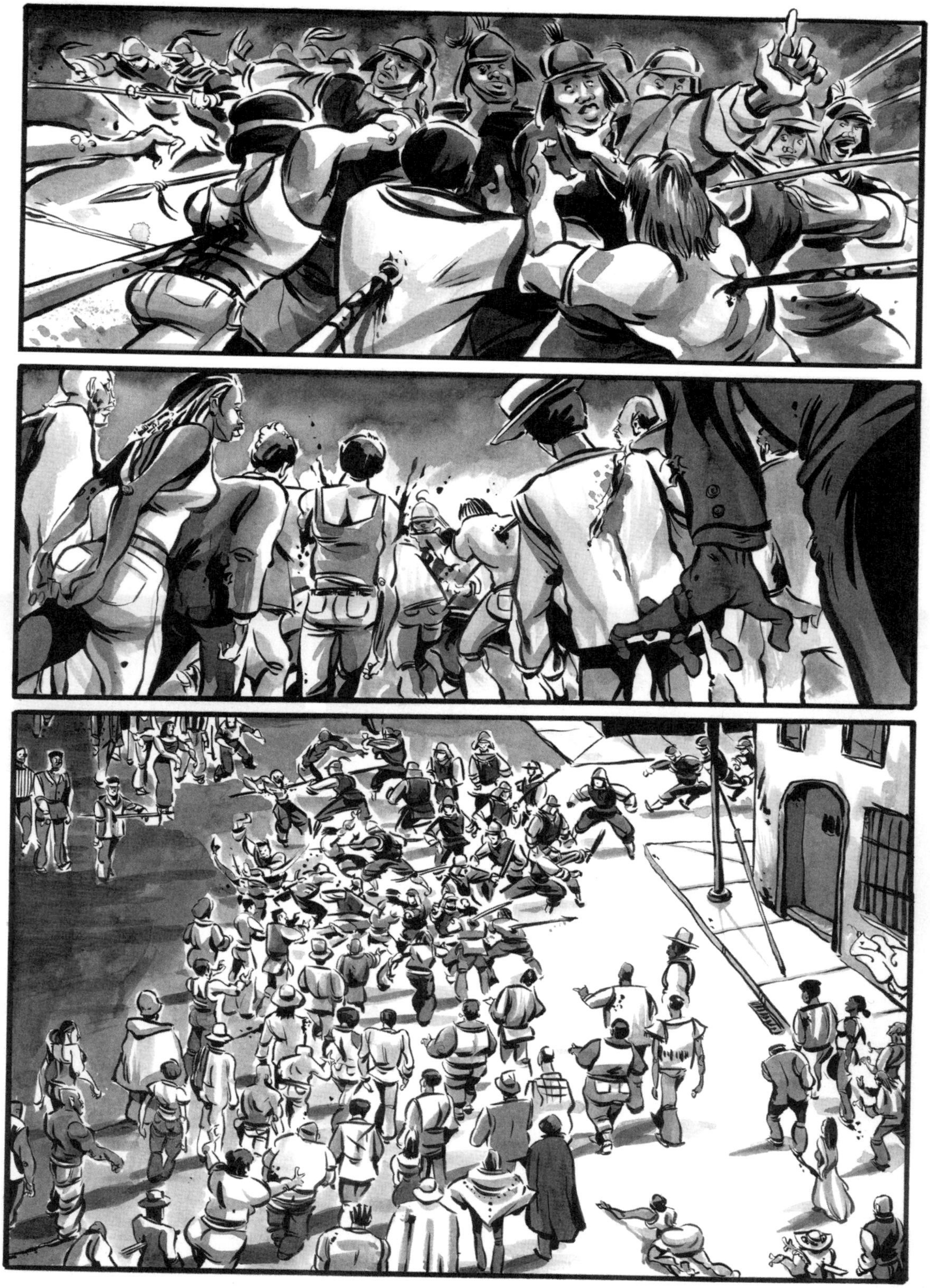

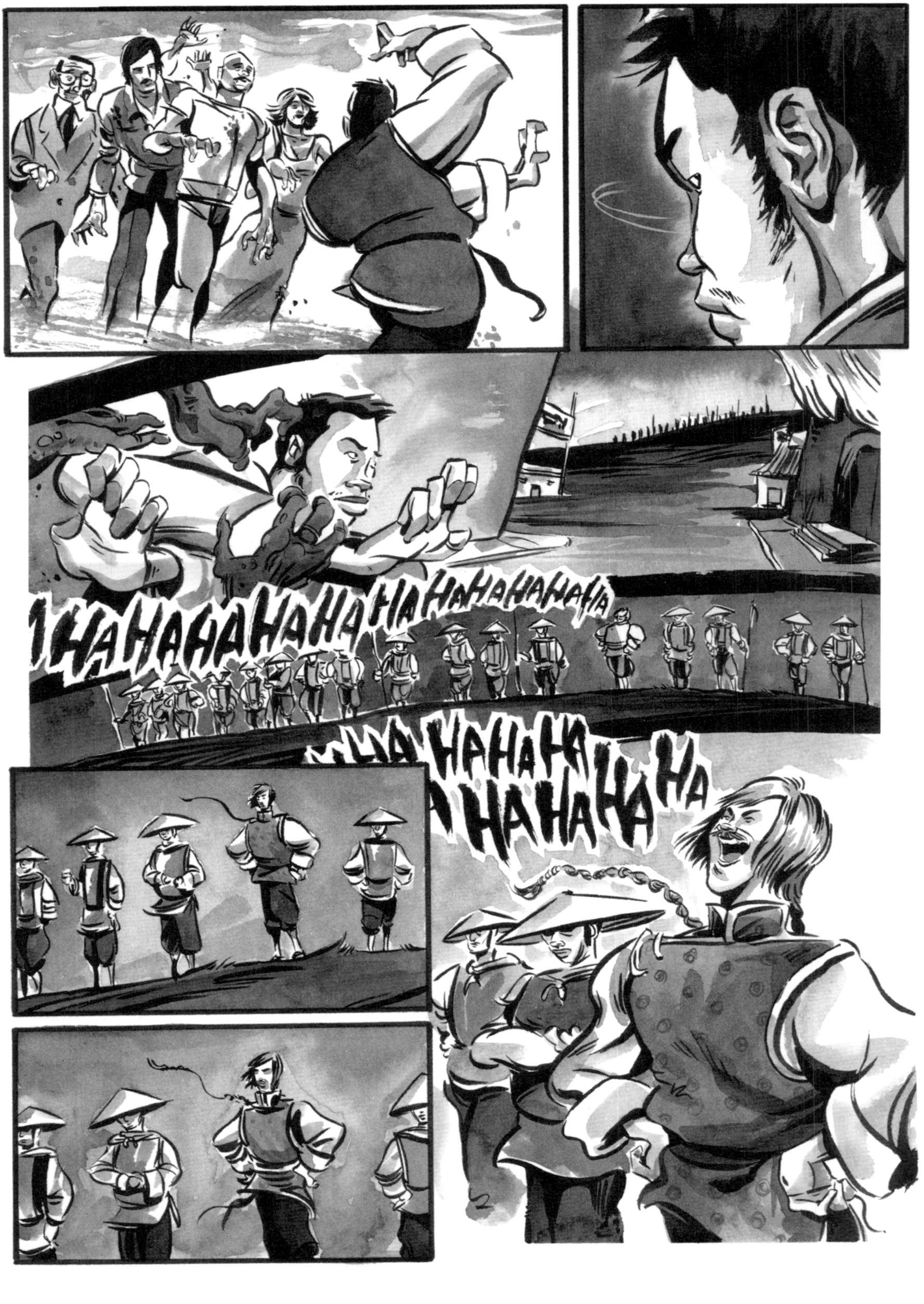
HAHAHAHAHAHAHAHAHAHA
HAHAHAHAHA
HAHAHAHA

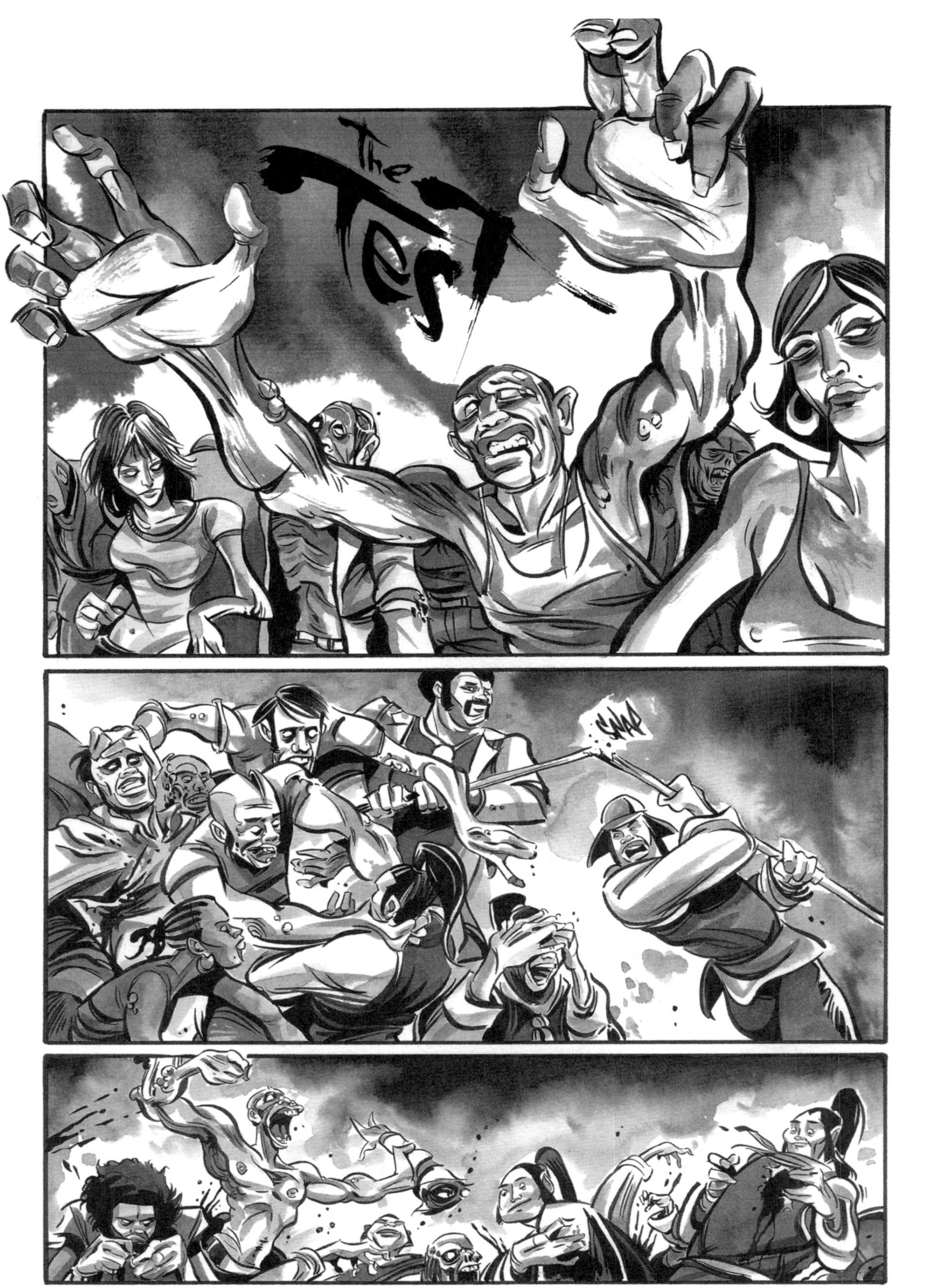
The Test
SNAP

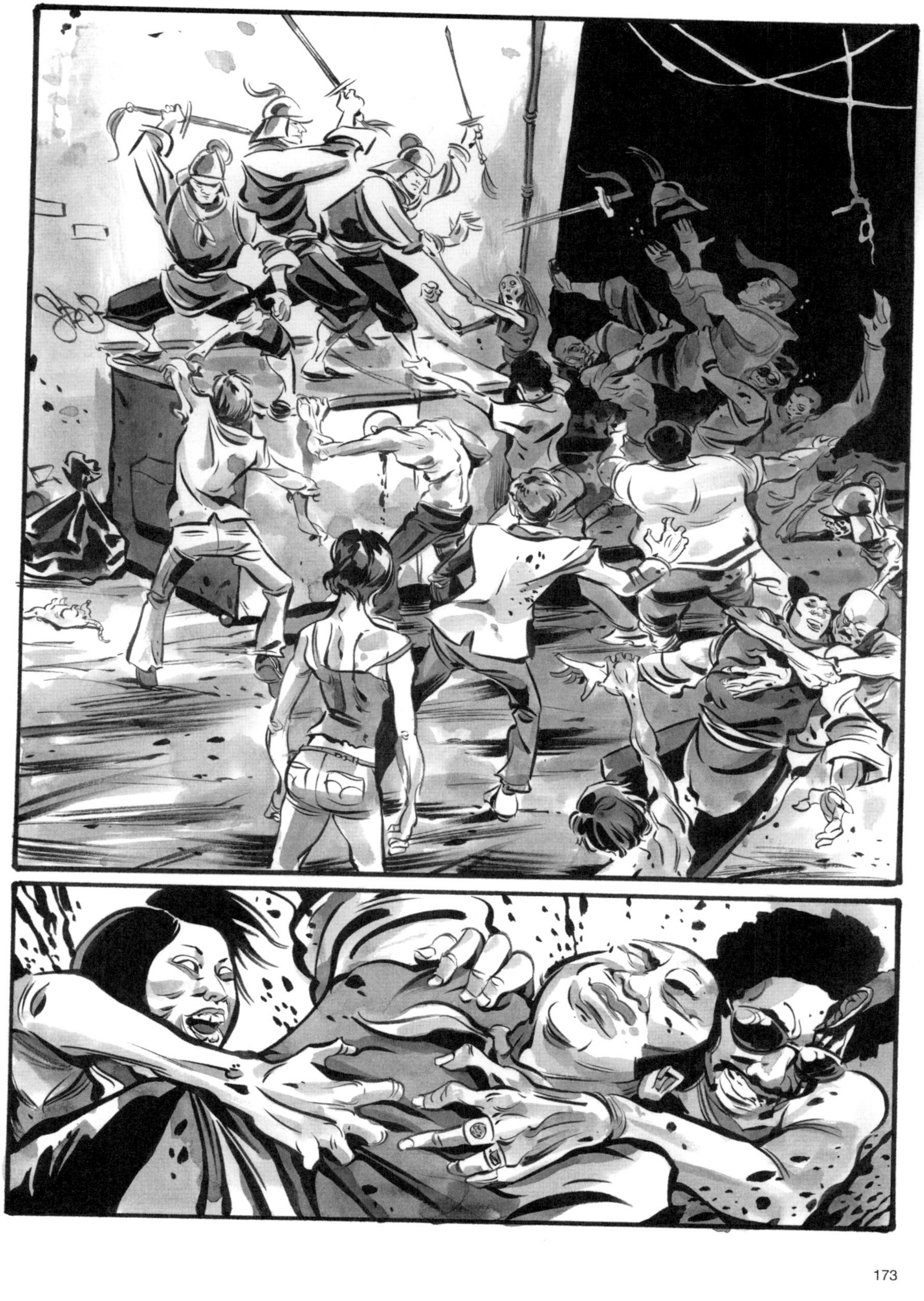

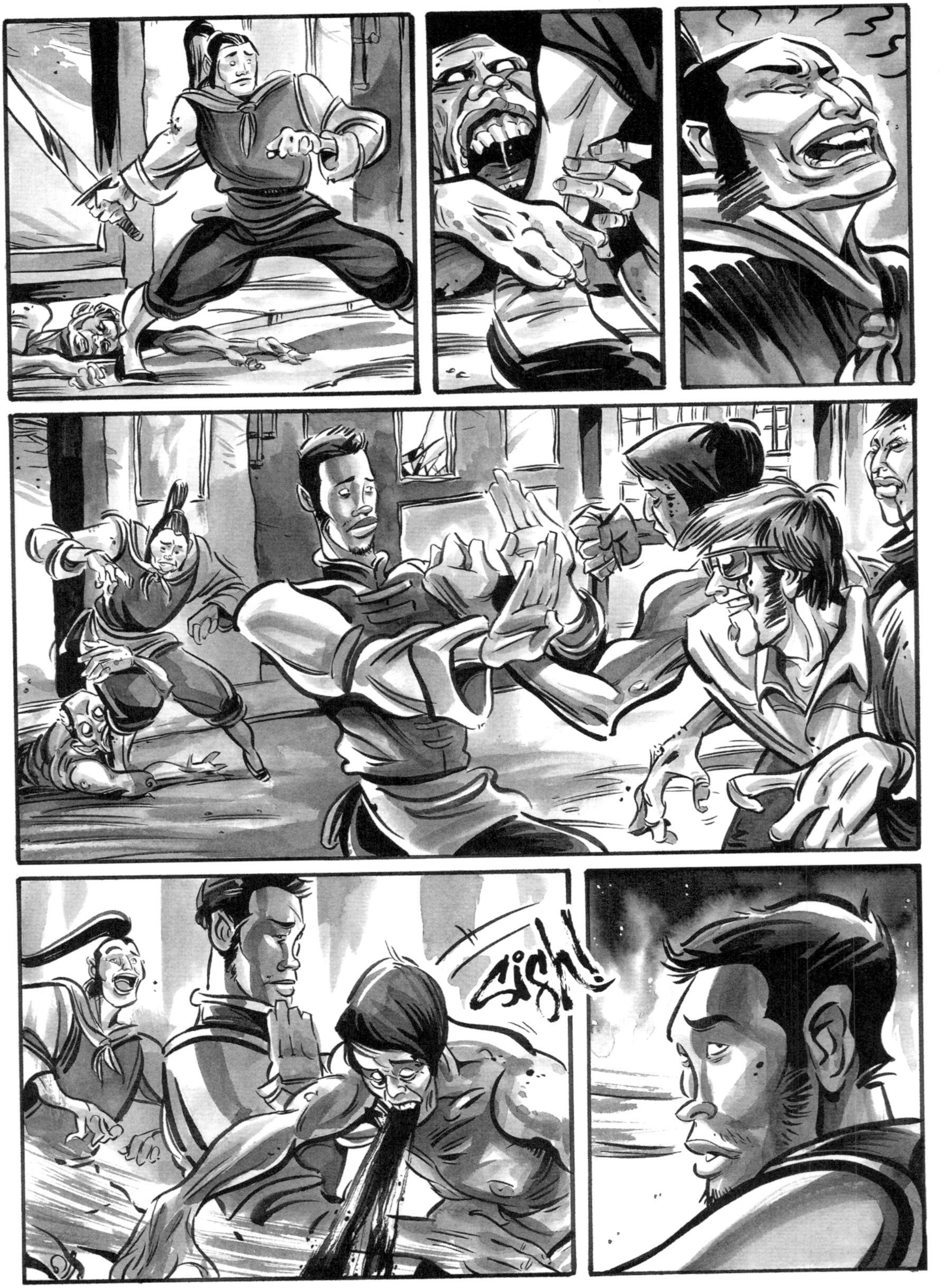
Sish!

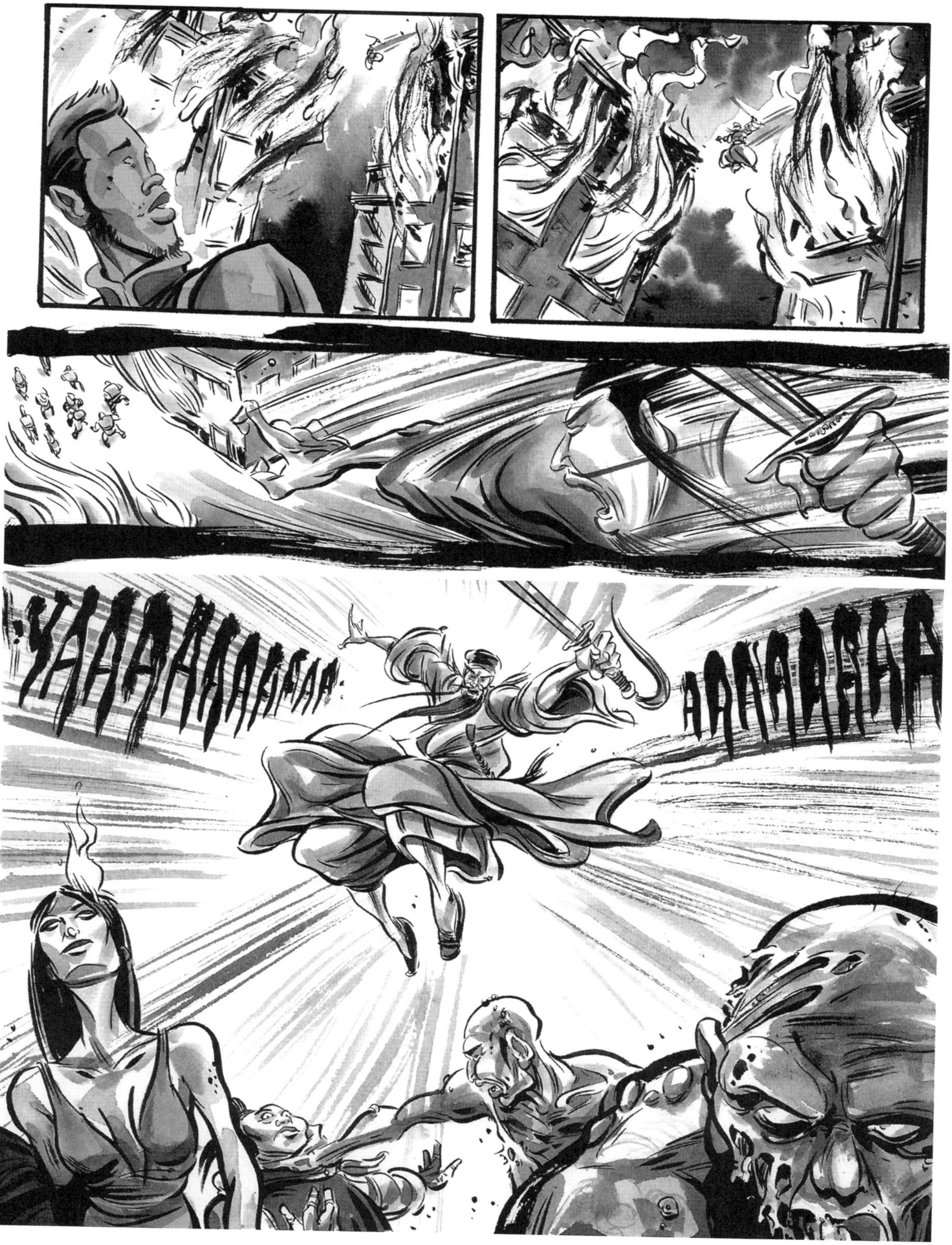

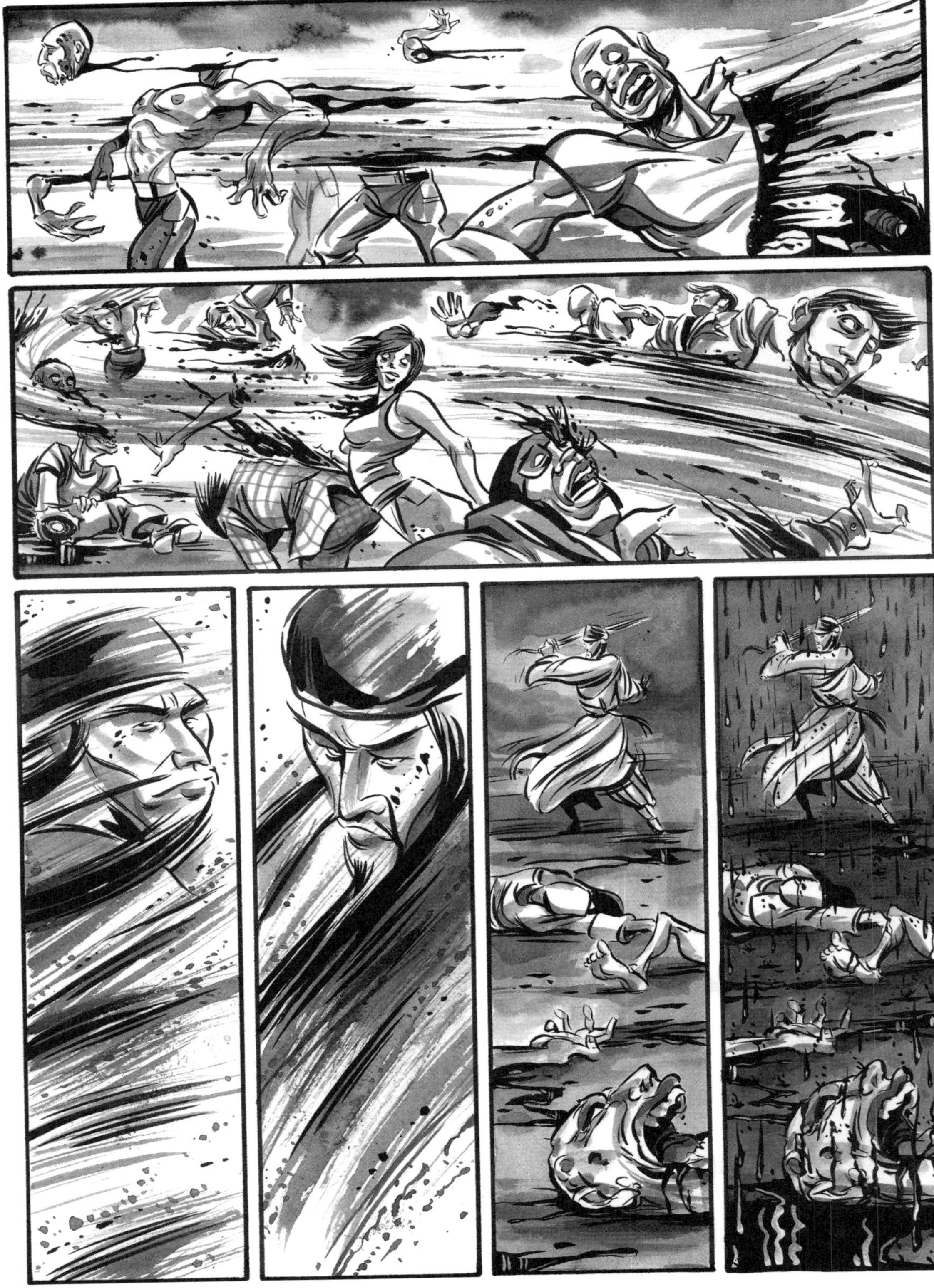

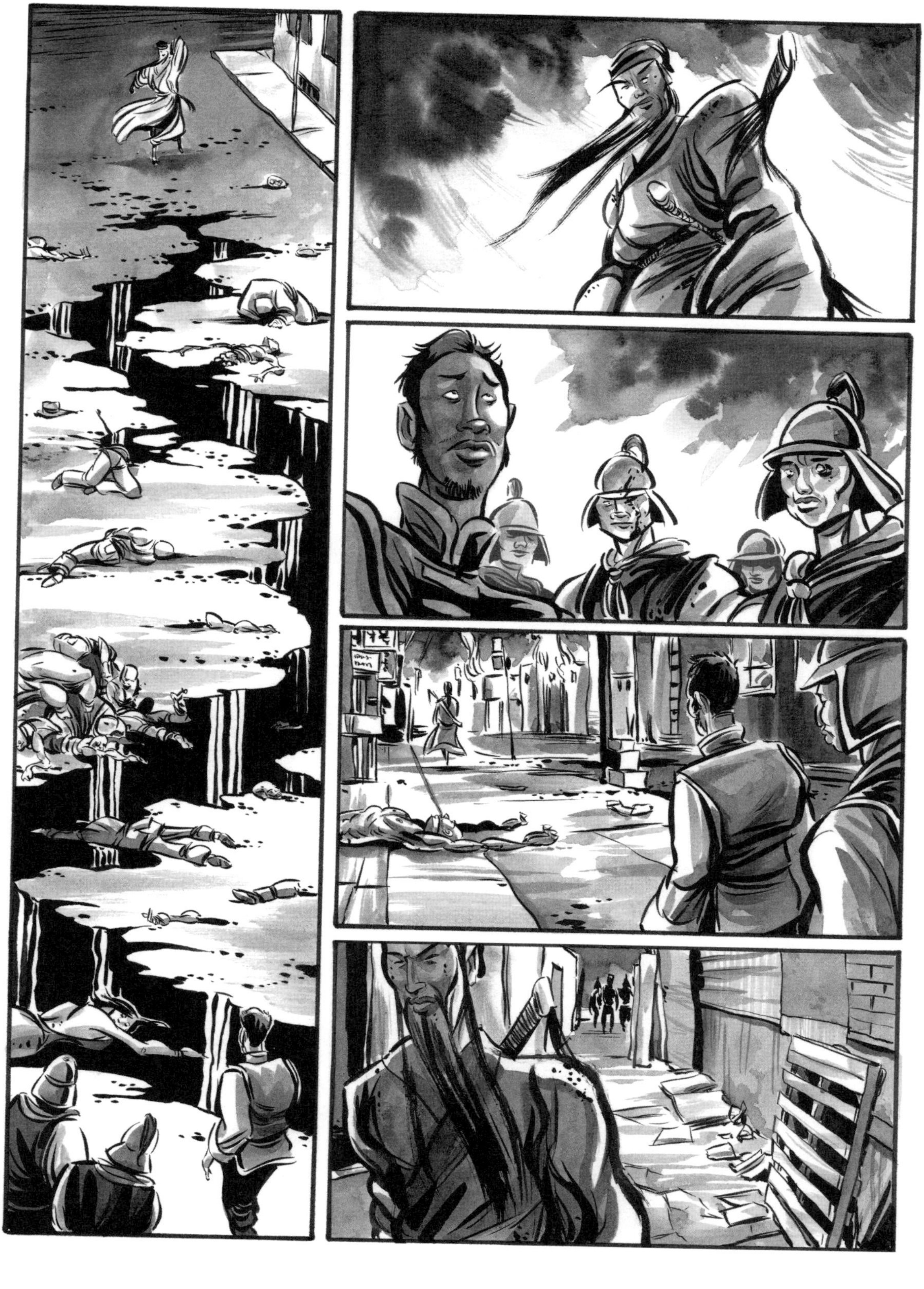

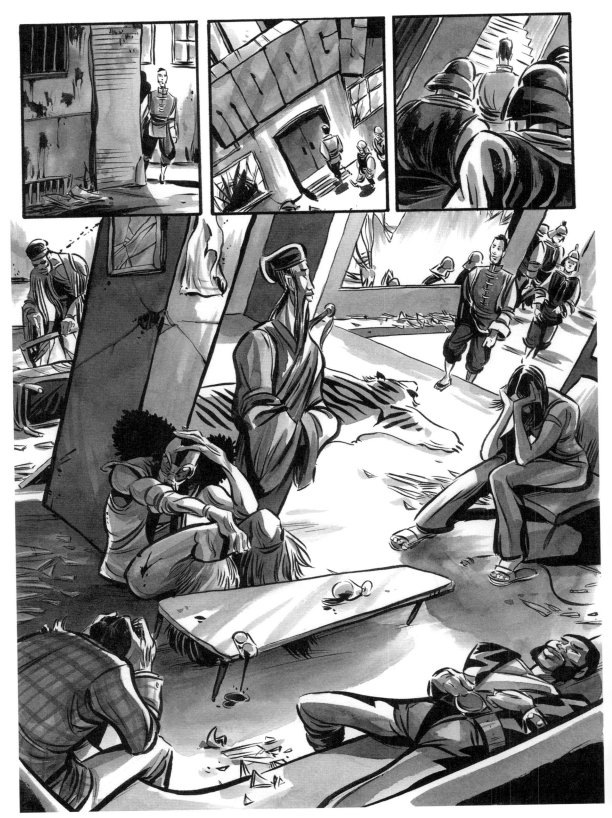

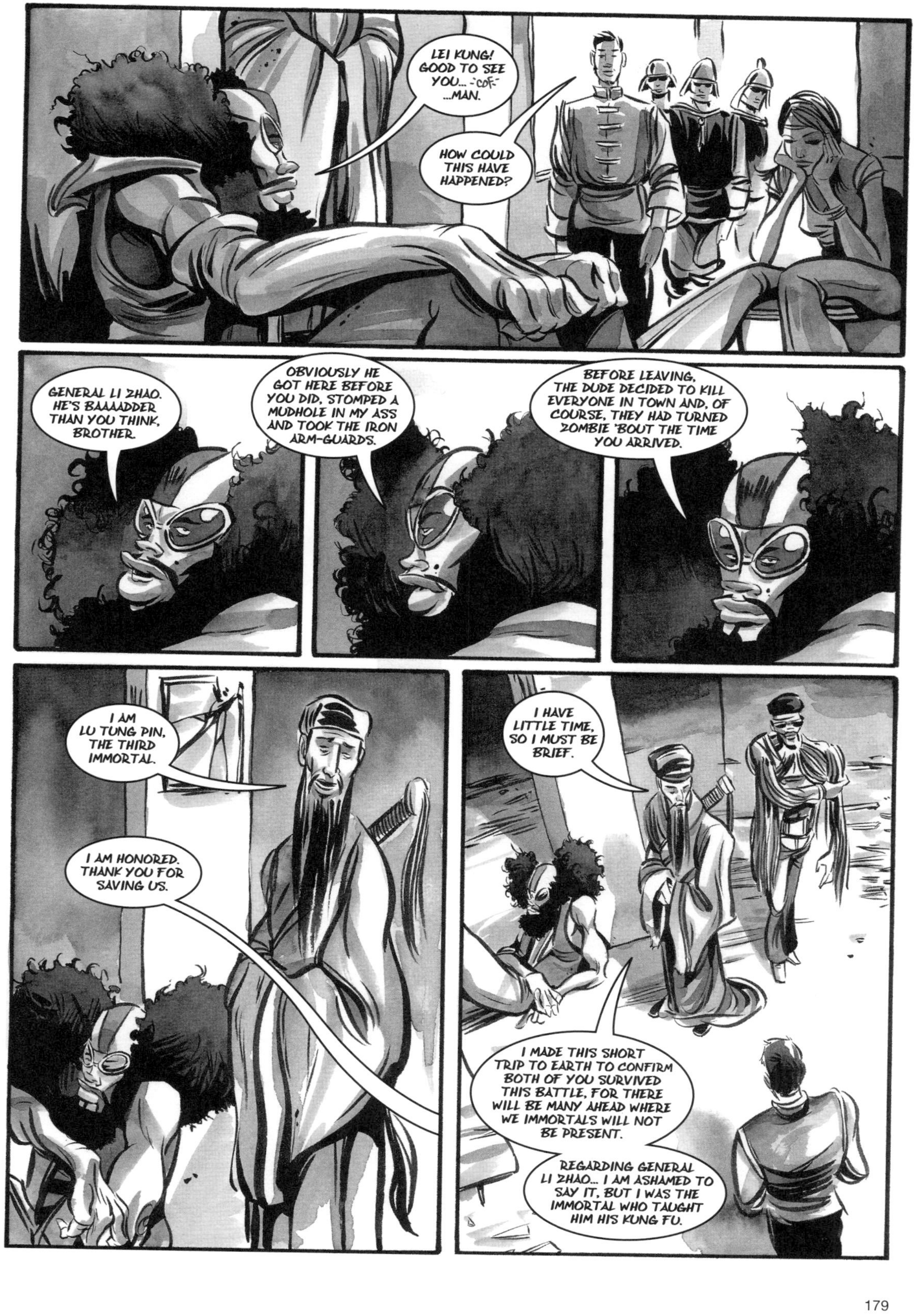
LEI KUNG! GOOD TO SEE YOU... -COF- ...MAN.
HOW COULD THIS HAVE HAPPENED?
GENERAL LI ZHAO. HE'S BAAAADDER THAN YOU THINK, BROTHER.
OBVIOUSLY HE GOT HERE BEFORE YOU DID, STOMPED A MUDHOLE IN MY ASS AND TOOK THE IRON ARM-GUARDS.
BEFORE LEAVING, THE DUDE DECIDED TO KILL EVERYONE IN TOWN AND, OF COURSE, THEY HAD TURNED ZOMBIE 'BOUT THE TIME YOU ARRIVED.
I AM LU TUNG PIN, THE THIRD IMMORTAL.
I AM HONORED. THANK YOU FOR SAVING US.
I HAVE LITTLE TIME, SO I MUST BE BRIEF.
I MADE THIS SHORT TRIP TO EARTH TO CONFIRM BOTH OF YOU SURVIVED THIS BATTLE, FOR THERE WILL BE MANY AHEAD WHERE WE IMMORTALS WILL NOT BE PRESENT.
REGARDING GENERAL LI ZHAO... I AM ASHAMED TO SAY IT, BUT I WAS THE IMMORTAL WHO TAUGHT HIM HIS KUNG FU.

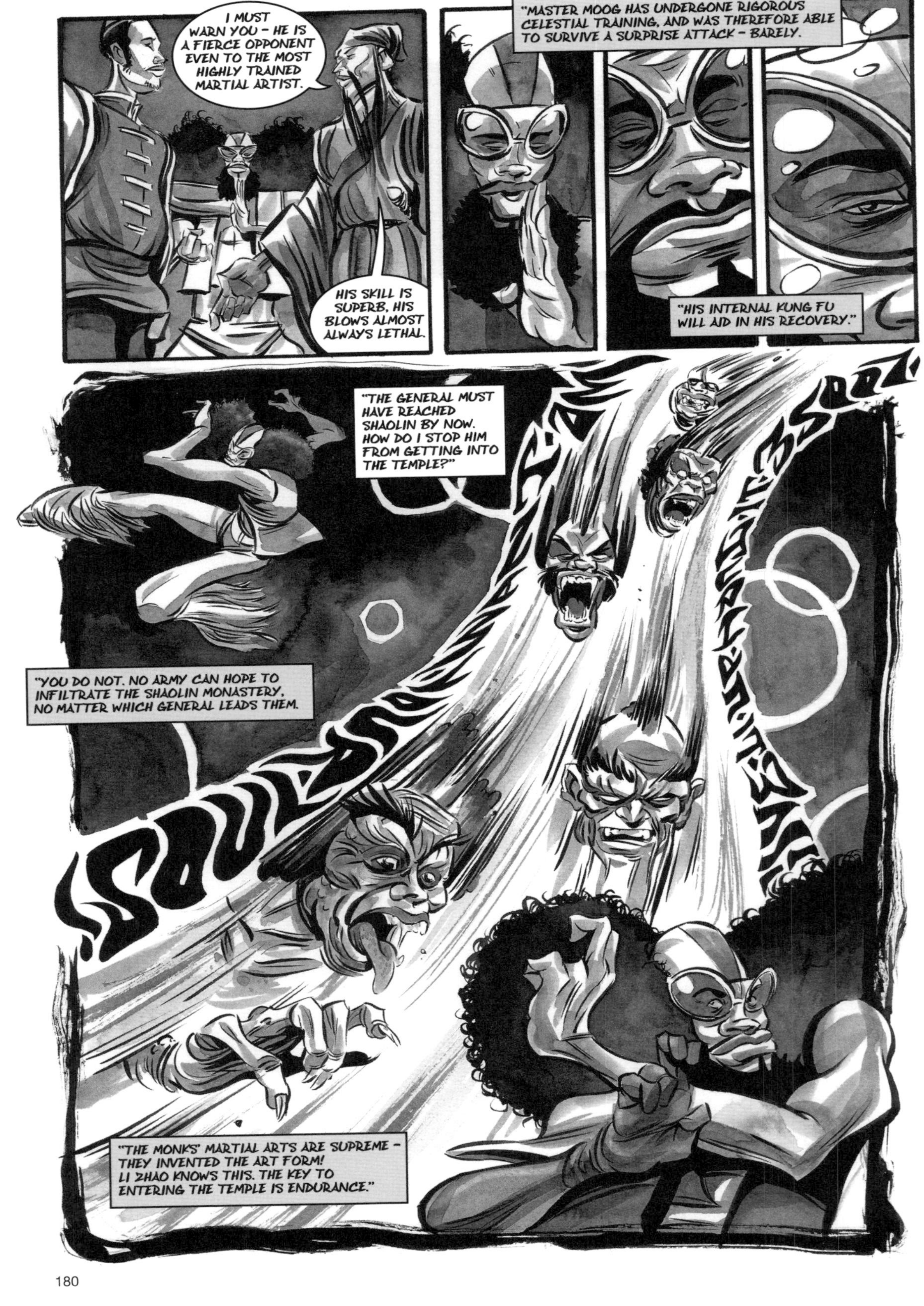

I MUST WARN YOU - HE IS A FIERCE OPPONENT EVEN TO THE MOST HIGHLY TRAINED MARTIAL ARTIST.
HIS SKILL IS SUPERB, HIS BLOWS ALMOST ALWAYS LETHAL.
"MASTER MOOG HAS UNDERGONE RIGOROUS CELESTIAL TRAINING, AND WAS THEREFORE ABLE TO SURVIVE A SURPRISE ATTACK - BARELY.
"HIS INTERNAL KUNG FU WILL AID IN HIS RECOVERY."
"THE GENERAL MUST HAVE REACHED SHAOLIN BY NOW. HOW DO I STOP HIM FROM GETTING INTO THE TEMPLE?"
"YOU DO NOT. NO ARMY CAN HOPE TO INFILTRATE THE SHAOLIN MONASTERY, NO MATTER WHICH GENERAL LEADS THEM.
"THE MONKS' MARTIAL ARTS ARE SUPREME - THEY INVENTED THE ART FORM! LI ZHAO KNOWS THIS. THE KEY TO ENTERING THE TEMPLE IS ENDURANCE."

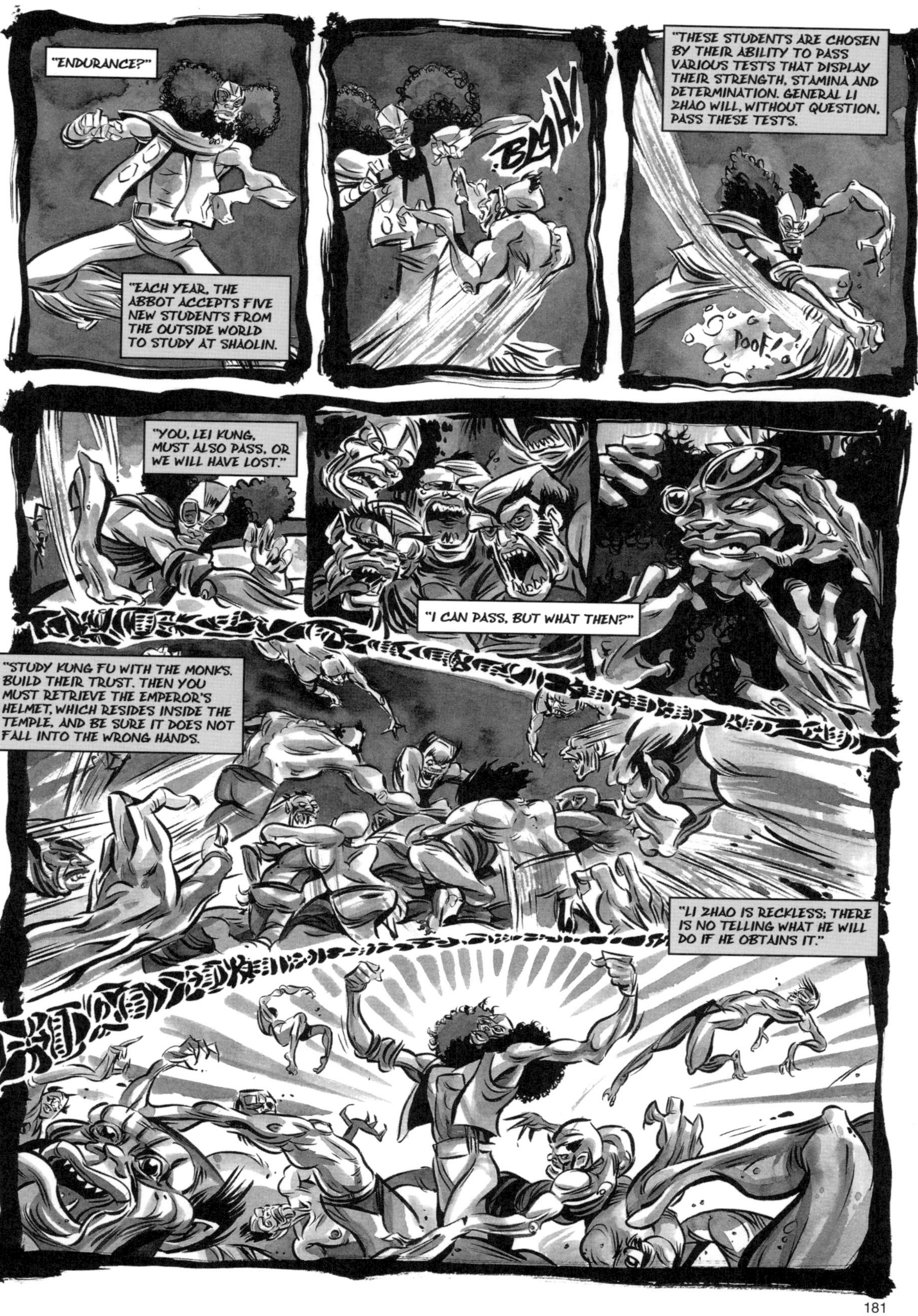
"ENDURANCE?"
"EACH YEAR, THE ABBOT ACCEPTS FIVE NEW STUDENTS FROM THE OUTSIDE WORLD TO STUDY AT SHAOLIN.
BLAH!
"THESE STUDENTS ARE CHOSEN BY THEIR ABILITY TO PASS VARIOUS TESTS THAT DISPLAY THEIR STRENGTH, STAMINA AND DETERMINATION. GENERAL LI ZHAO WILL, WITHOUT QUESTION, PASS THESE TESTS.
POOF!
"YOU, LEI KUNG, MUST ALSO PASS, OR WE WILL HAVE LOST."
"I CAN PASS, BUT WHAT THEN?"
"STUDY KUNG FU WITH THE MONKS. BUILD THEIR TRUST. THEN YOU MUST RETRIEVE THE EMPEROR'S HELMET, WHICH RESIDES INSIDE THE TEMPLE, AND BE SURE IT DOES NOT FALL INTO THE WRONG HANDS.
"LI ZHAO IS RECKLESS; THERE IS NO TELLING WHAT HE WILL DO IF HE OBTAINS IT."

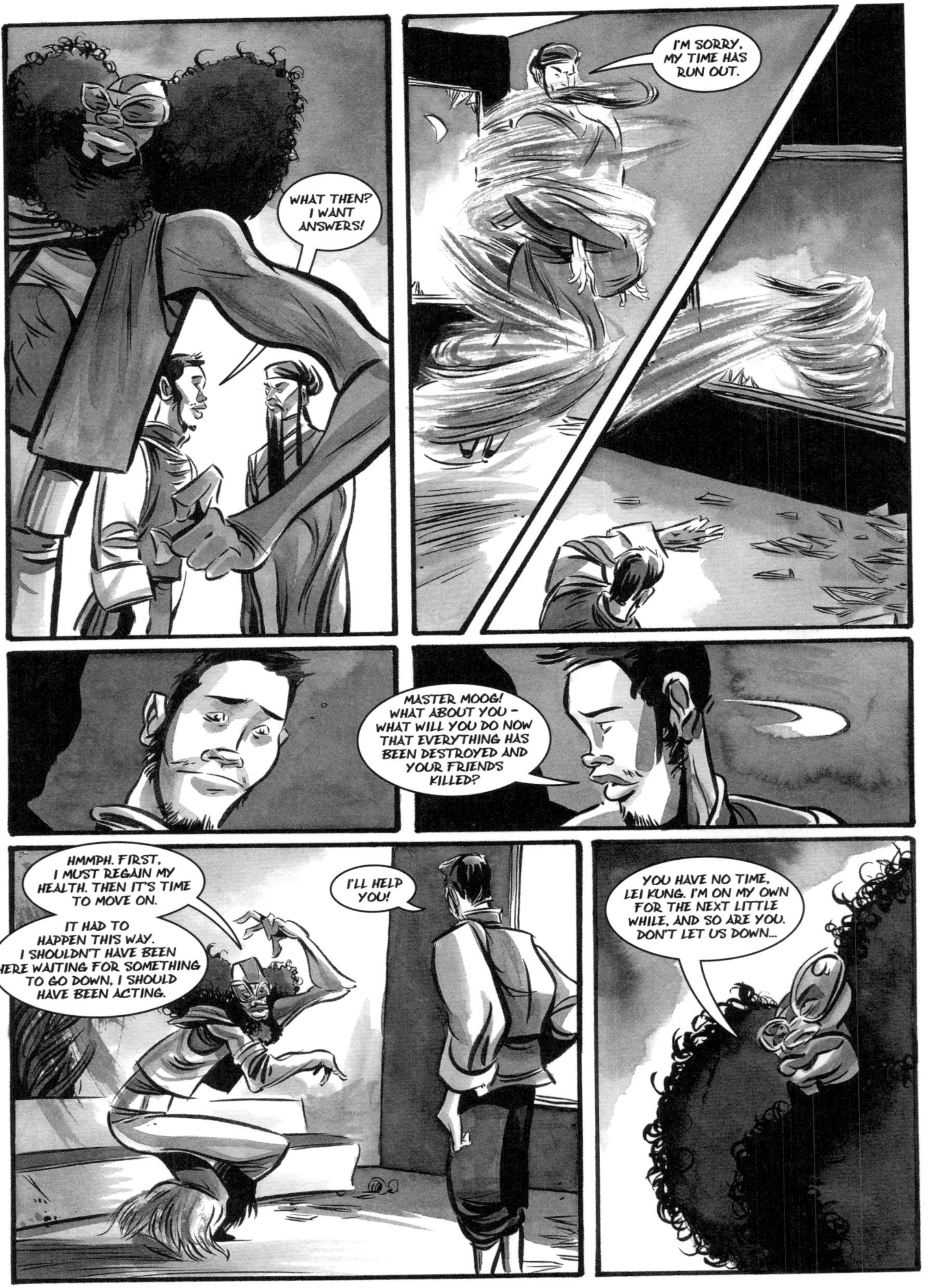
WHAT THEN? I WANT ANSWERS!
I'M SORRY, MY TIME HAS RUN OUT.
MASTER MOOG! WHAT ABOUT YOU - WHAT WILL YOU DO NOW THAT EVERYTHING HAS BEEN DESTROYED AND YOUR FRIENDS KILLED?
HMMPH. FIRST, I MUST REGAIN MY HEALTH. THEN IT'S TIME TO MOVE ON.
IT HAD TO HAPPEN THIS WAY. I SHOULDN'T HAVE BEEN HERE WAITING FOR SOMETHING TO GO DOWN. I SHOULD HAVE BEEN ACTING.
I'LL HELP YOU!
YOU HAVE NO TIME, LEI KUNG. I'M ON MY OWN FOR THE NEXT LITTLE WHILE, AND SO ARE YOU. DON'T LET US DOWN...

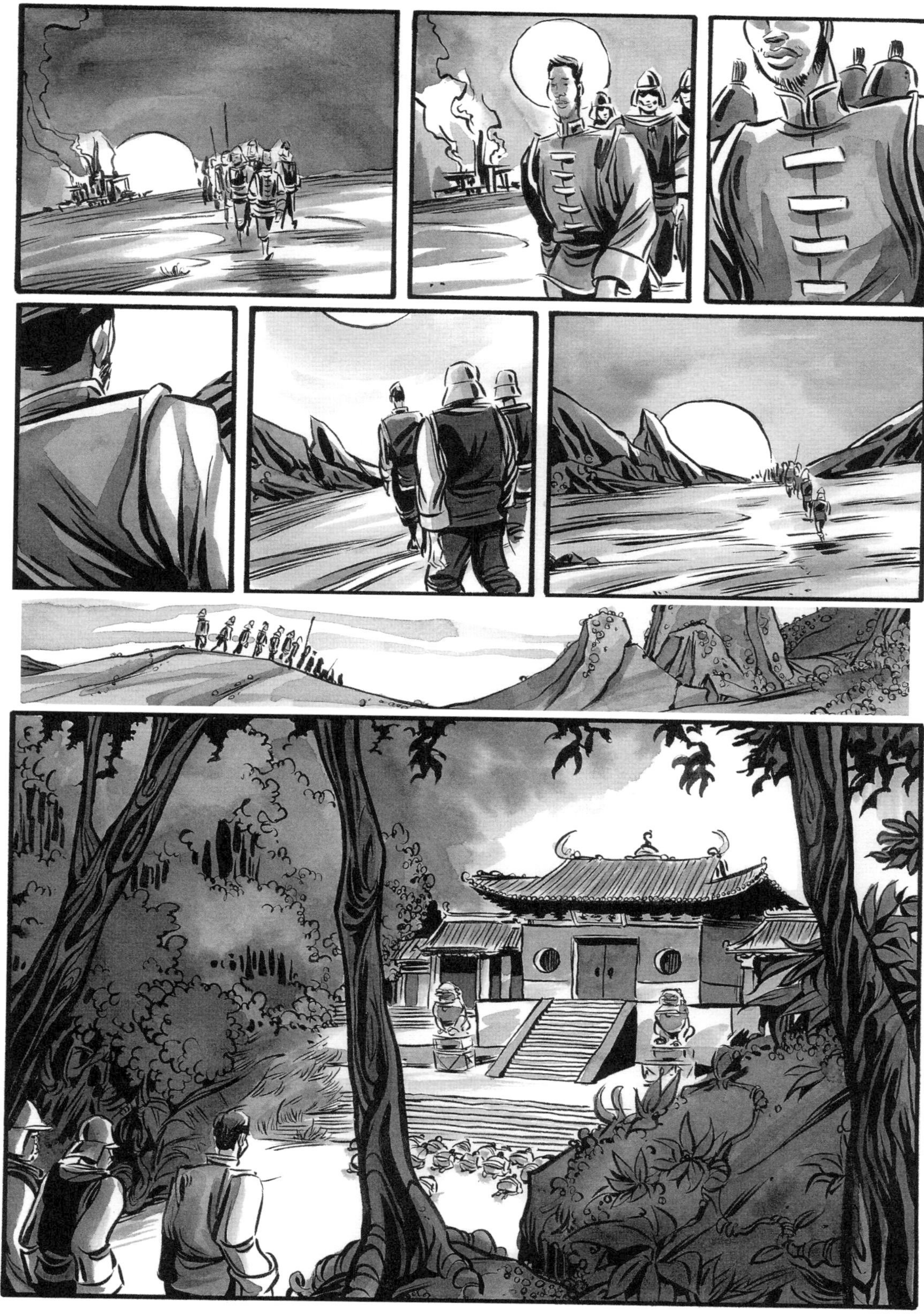

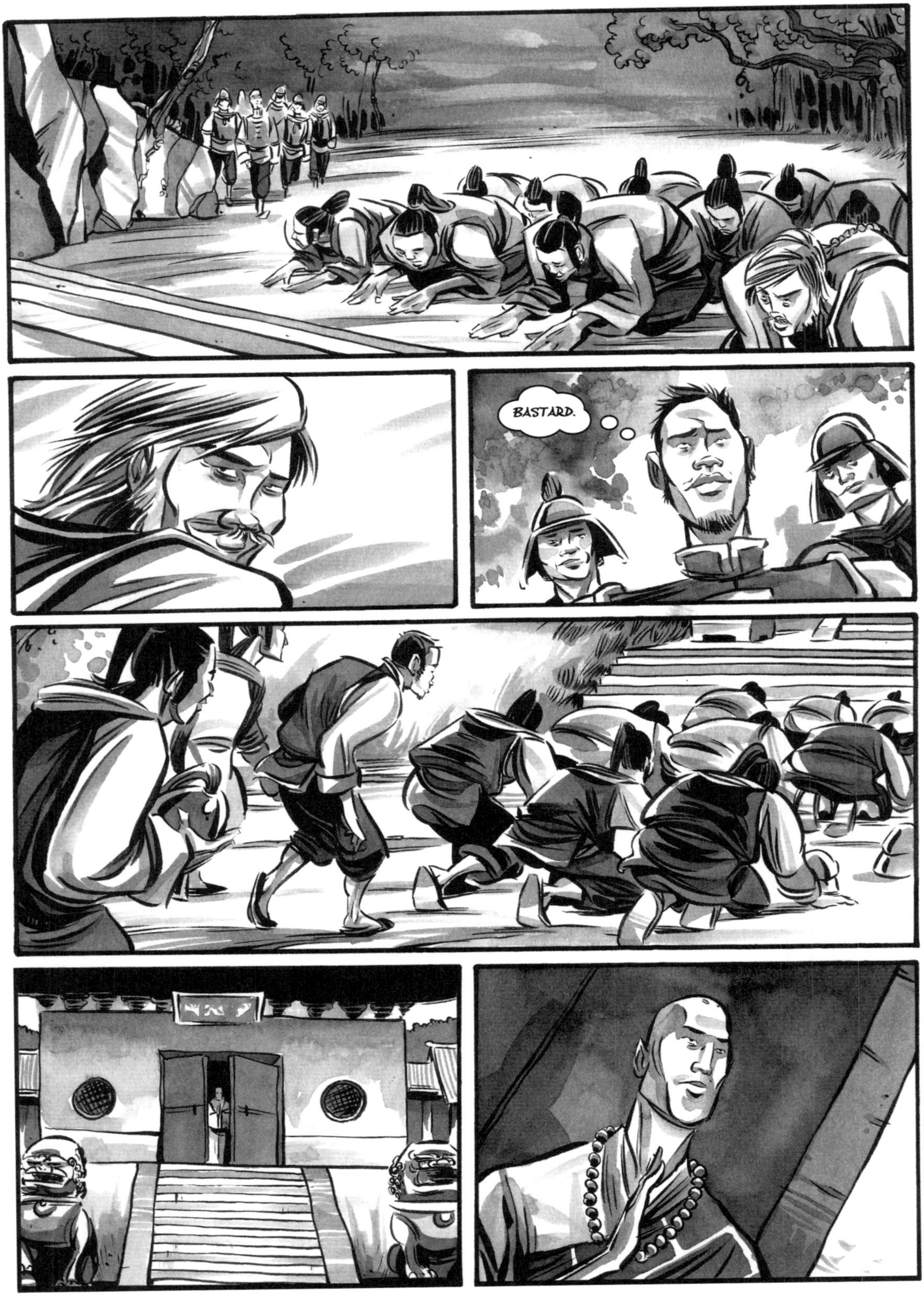
BASTARD.

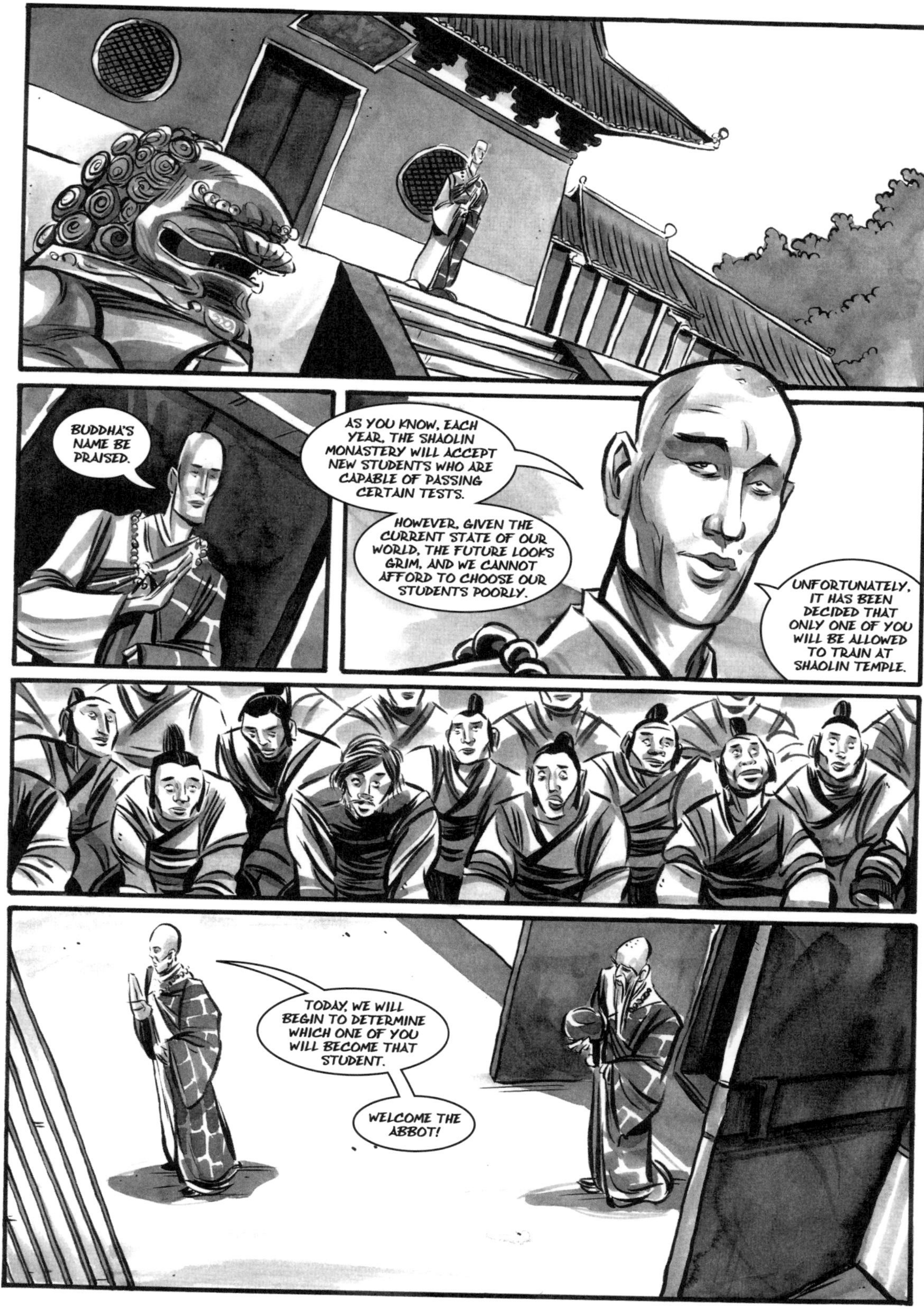
BUDDHA'S NAME BE PRAISED.
AS YOU KNOW, EACH YEAR, THE SHAOLIN MONASTERY WILL ACCEPT NEW STUDENTS WHO ARE CAPABLE OF PASSING CERTAIN TESTS.
HOWEVER, GIVEN THE CURRENT STATE OF OUR WORLD, THE FUTURE LOOKS GRIM, AND WE CANNOT AFFORD TO CHOOSE OUR STUDENTS POORLY.
UNFORTUNATELY, IT HAS BEEN DECIDED THAT ONLY ONE OF YOU WILL BE ALLOWED TO TRAIN AT SHAOLIN TEMPLE.
TODAY, WE WILL BEGIN TO DETERMINE WHICH ONE OF YOU WILL BECOME THAT STUDENT.
WELCOME THE ABBOT!

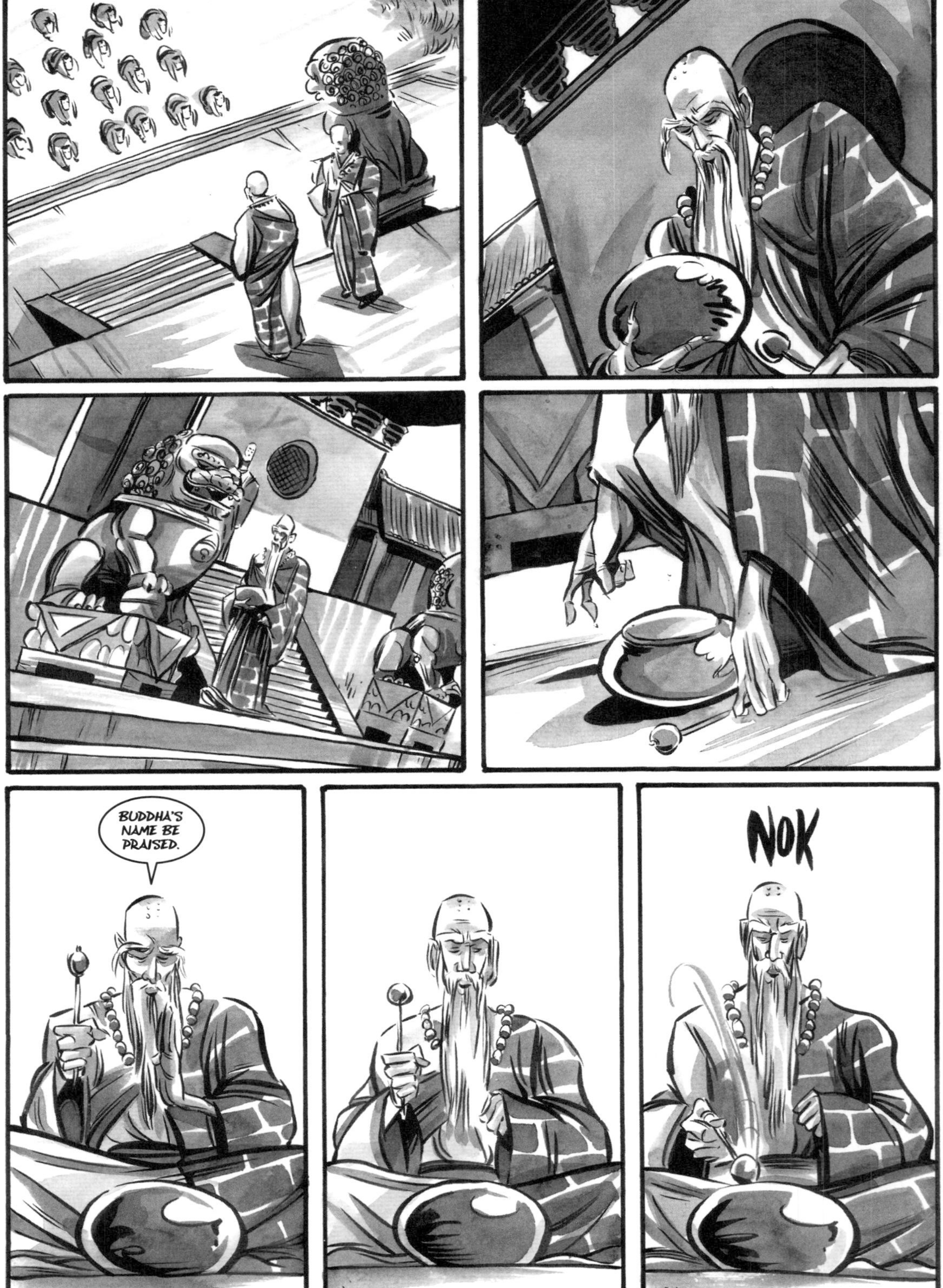
BUDDHA'S NAME BE PRAISED.
NOK

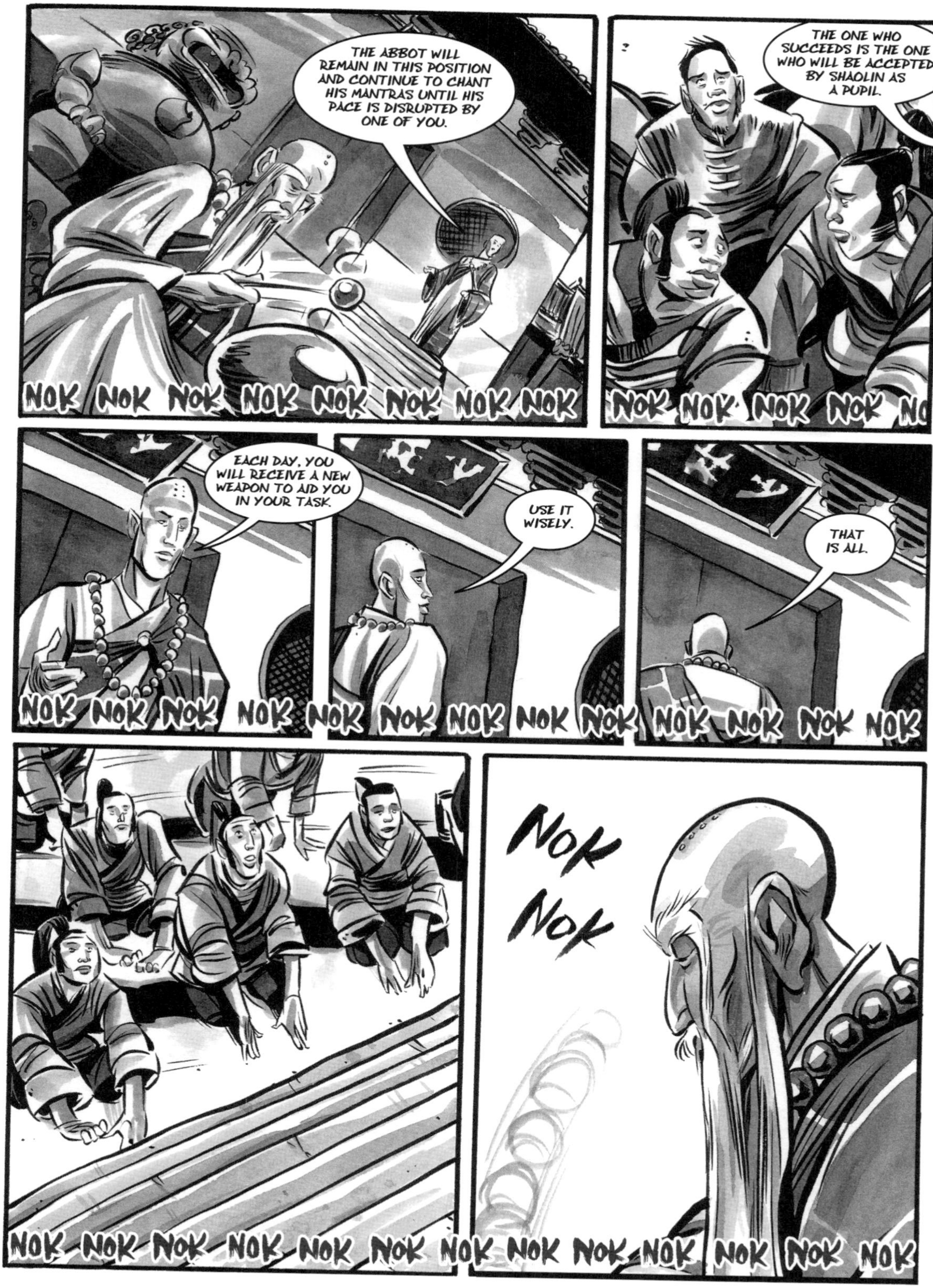

THE ABBOT WILL REMAIN IN THIS POSITION AND CONTINUE TO CHANT HIS MANTRAS UNTIL HIS PACE IS DISRUPTED BY ONE OF YOU.
NOK NOK NOK NOK NOK NOK NOK NOK
THE ONE WHO SUCCEEDS IS THE ONE WHO WILL BE ACCEPTED BY SHAOLIN AS A PUPIL.
NOK NOK NOK NOK NO
EACH DAY, YOU WILL RECEIVE A NEW WEAPON TO AID YOU IN YOUR TASK.
NOK NOK NOK
USE IT WISELY.
NOK NOK NOK NOK NOK
THAT IS ALL.
NOK NOK NOK NOK NOK
NOK NOK NOK NOK NOK NOK NOK
NOK NOK
NOK NOK NOK NOK NOK NOK

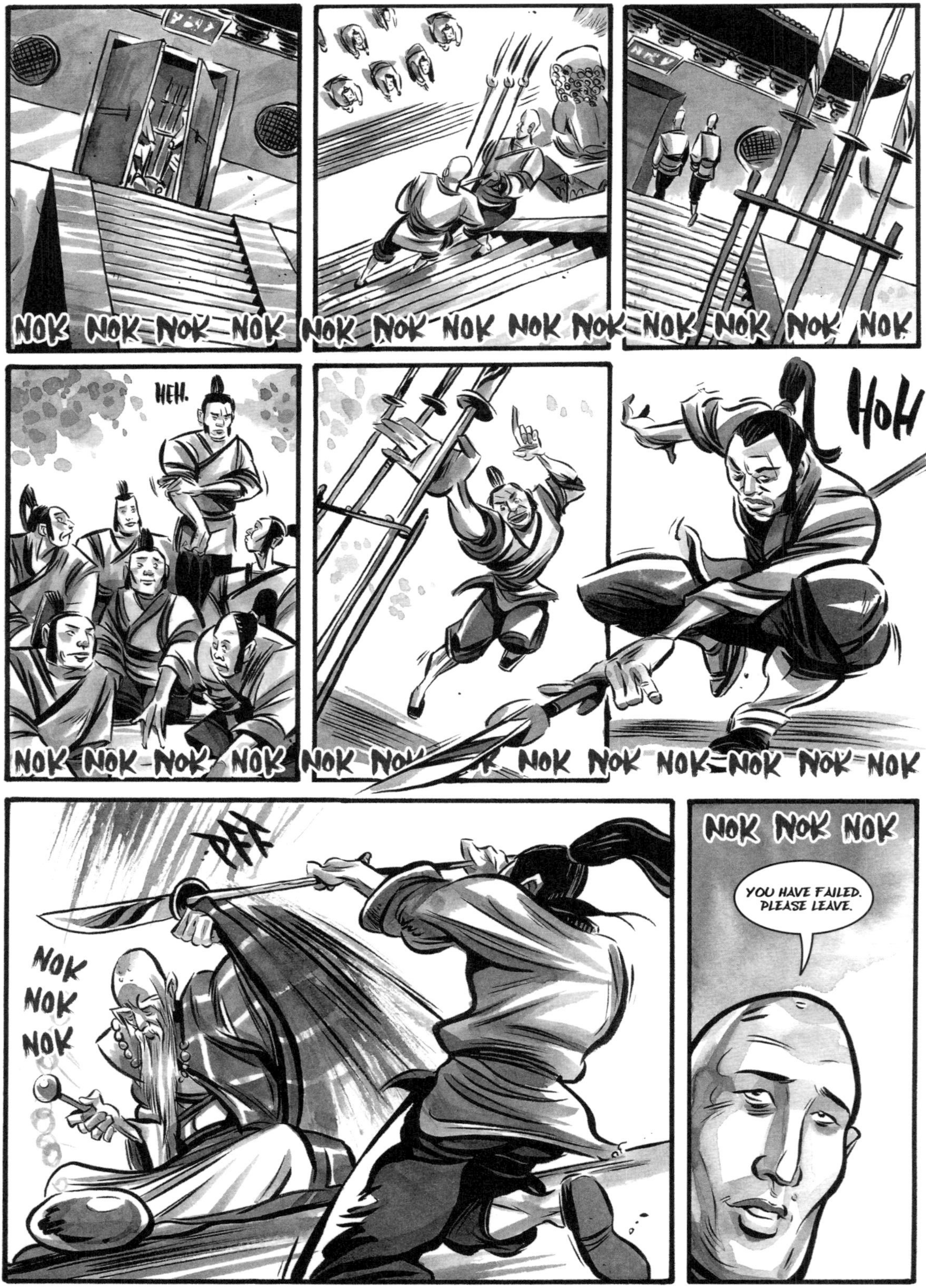
NOK NOK NOK NOK NOK NOK NOK NOK NOK NOK NOK NOK NOK
HEH.
HOH
NOK NOK NOK NOK NOK NOK NOK NOK NOK NOK NOK NOK
NOK NOK NOK
NOK NOK NOK
YOU HAVE FAILED. PLEASE LEAVE.

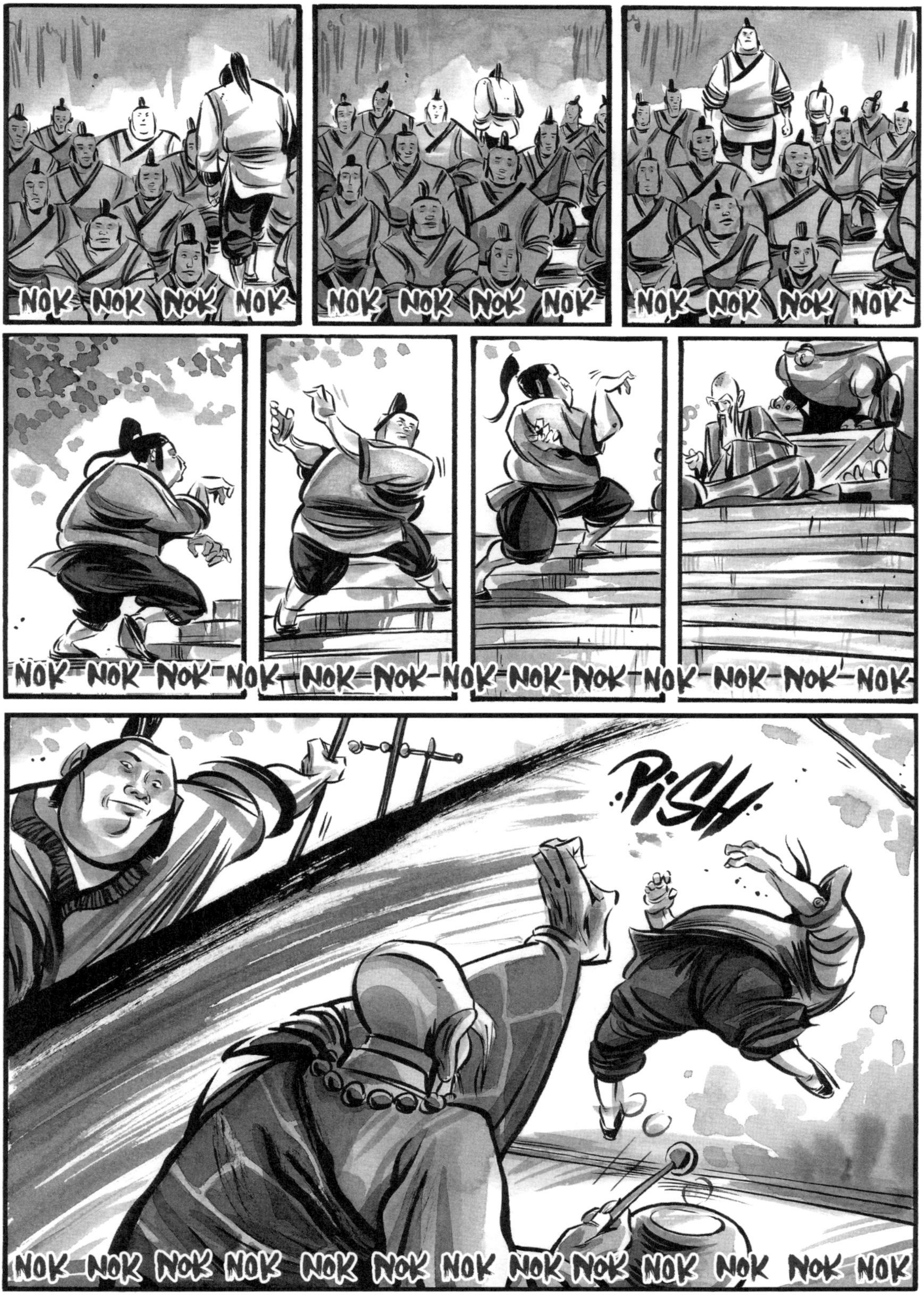
NOK NOK NOK NOK
NOK NOK NOK NOK
NOK NOK NOK NOK
NOK NOK NOK NOK NOK NOK NOK NOK NOK NOK NOK NOK NOK
PISH
NOK NOK NOK NOK NOK NOK NOK NOK NOK NOK NOK NOK NOK

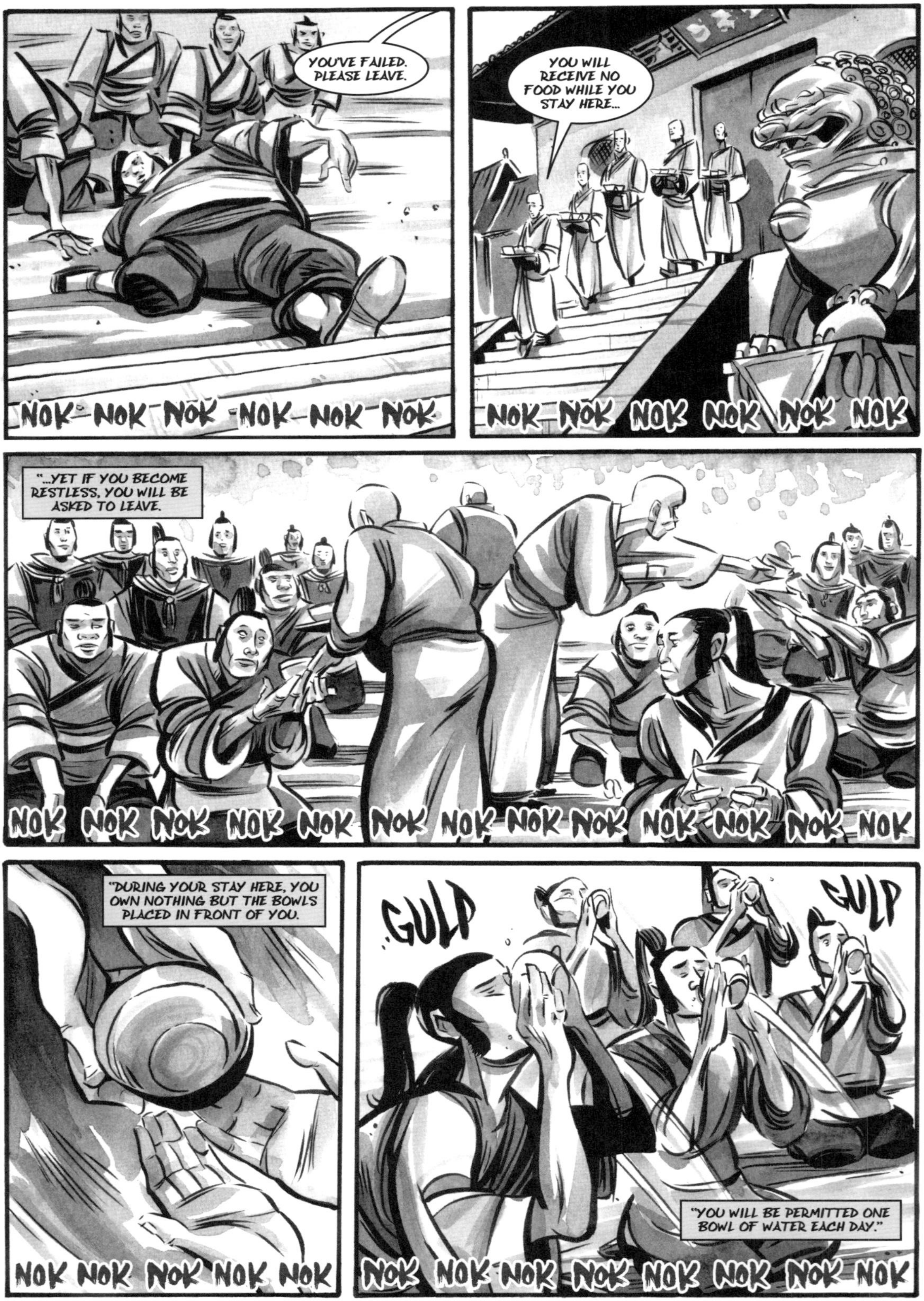
YOU'VE FAILED. PLEASE LEAVE.
NOK NOK NOK NOK NOK NOK
YOU WILL RECEIVE NO FOOD WHILE YOU STAY HERE...
NOK NOK NOK NOK NOK NOK
"...YET IF YOU BECOME RESTLESS, YOU WILL BE ASKED TO LEAVE.
NOK NOK NOK NOK NOK NOK NOK NOK NOK NOK NOK NOK NOK
"DURING YOUR STAY HERE, YOU OWN NOTHING BUT THE BOWLS PLACED IN FRONT OF YOU.
NOK NOK NOK NOK NOK
GULP
GULP
"YOU WILL BE PERMITTED ONE BOWL OF WATER EACH DAY."
NOK NOK NOK NOK NOK NOK NOK NOK

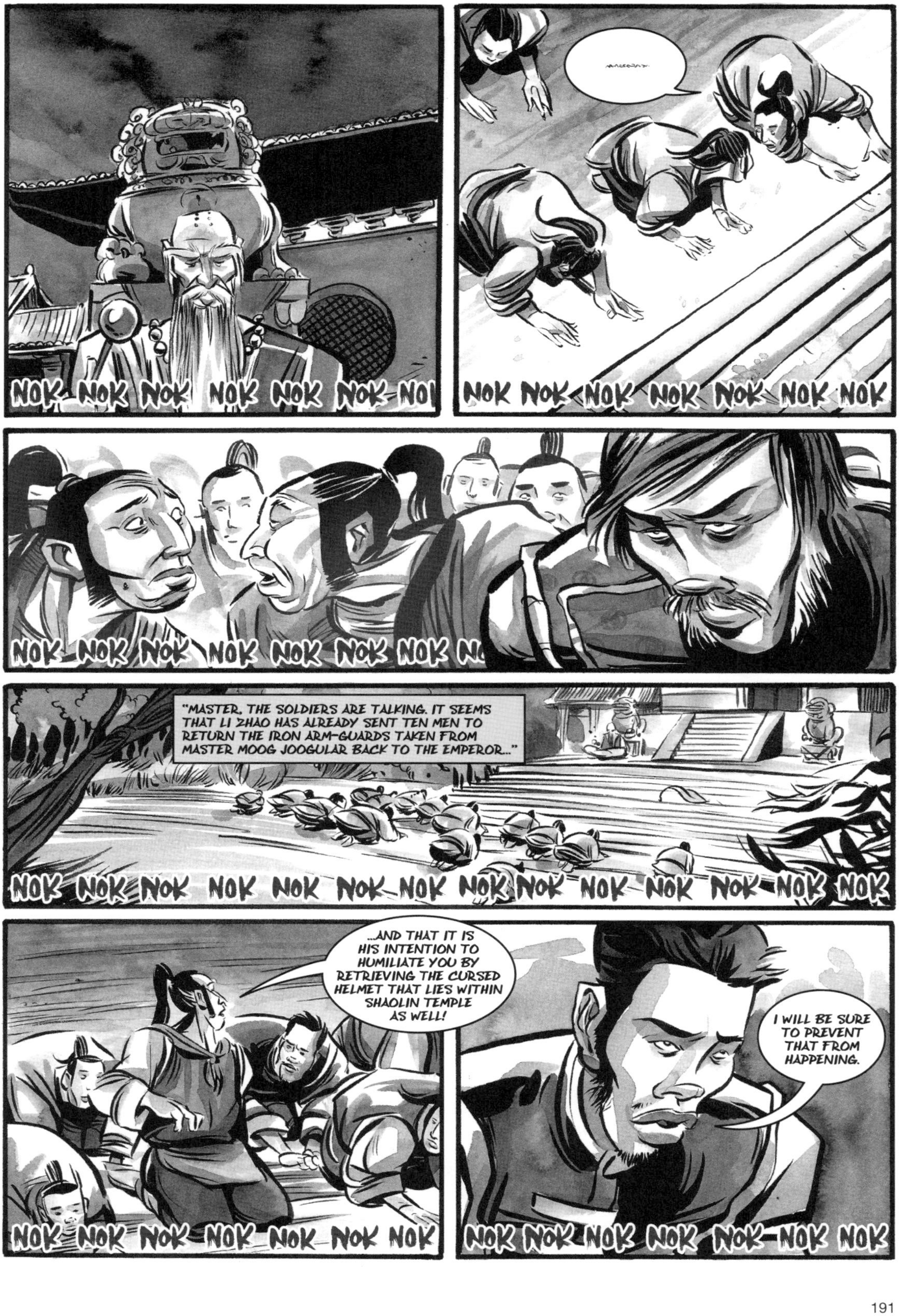
NOK NOK NOK NOK NOK NOK NOK
NOK NOK NOK NOK NOK NOK NOK
NOK NOK NOK NOK NOK NOK NOK
"MASTER, THE SOLDIERS ARE TALKING. IT SEEMS THAT LI ZHAO HAS ALREADY SENT TEN MEN TO RETURN THE IRON ARM-GUARDS TAKEN FROM MASTER MOOG JOOGULAR BACK TO THE EMPEROR..."
NOK NOK NOK NOK NOK NOK NOK NOK NOK NOK NOK NOK NOK NOK
...AND THAT IT IS HIS INTENTION TO HUMILIATE YOU BY RETRIEVING THE CURSED HELMET THAT LIES WITHIN SHAOLIN TEMPLE AS WELL!
NOK NOK NOK NOK NOK NOK NOK
I WILL BE SURE TO PREVENT THAT FROM HAPPENING.
NOK NOK NOK NOK NOK NOK NOK

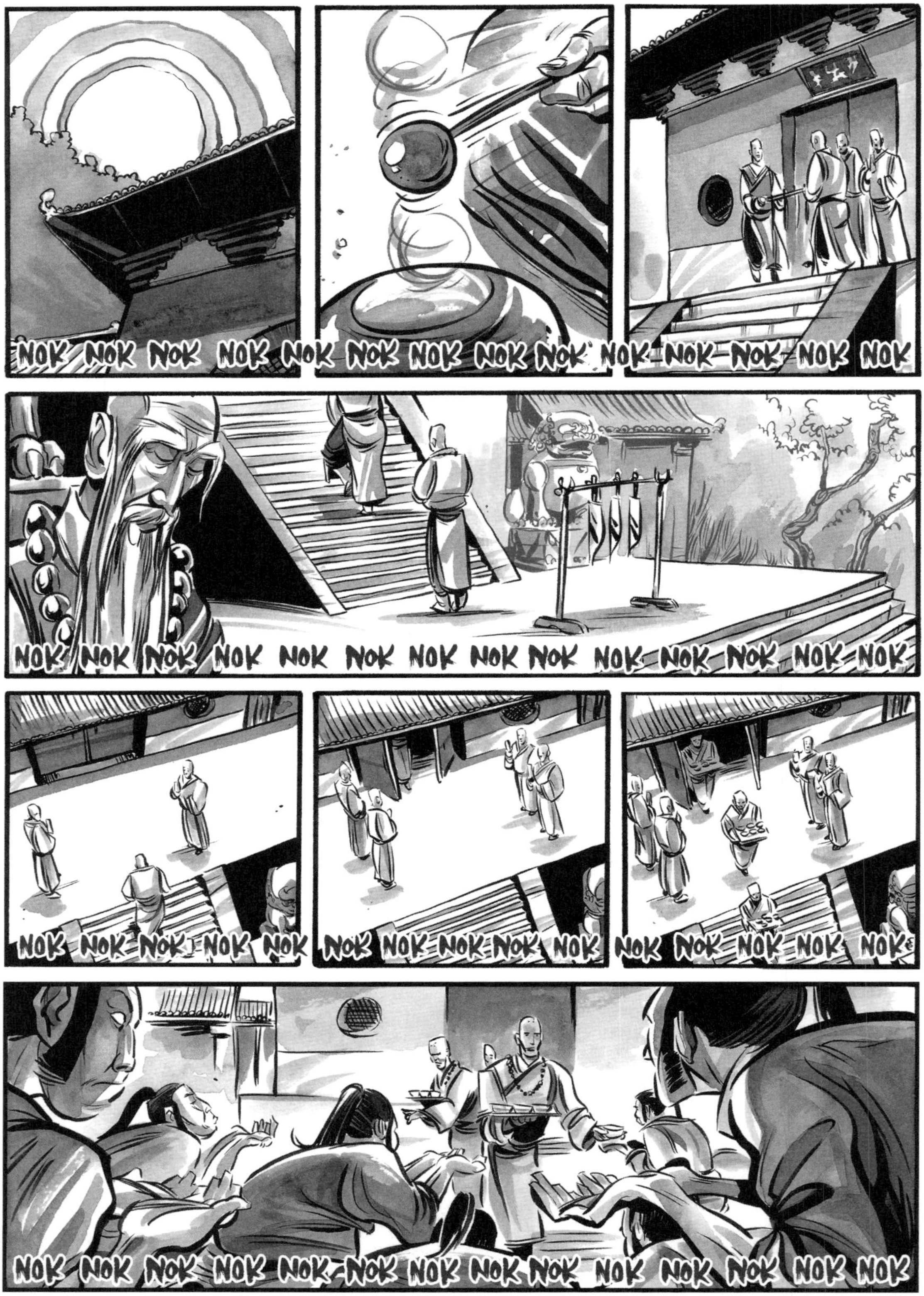
NOK NOK NOK NOK NOK NOK NOK NOK NOK NOK NOK NOK NOK NOK
NOK NOK NOK NOK NOK NOK NOK NOK NOK NOK NOK NOK NOK NOK
NOK NOK NOK NOK NOK
NOK NOK NOK NOK NOK
NOK NOK NOK NOK NOK
NOK NOK NOK NOK NOK NOK NOK NOK NOK NOK NOK NOK NOK NOK

NOK NOK NOK NOK NOK NOK N

CHING
NOK NOK NOK NOK NOK NOK NOK

NOK NOK NOK NOK NOK

NOK NOK NOK NOK NOK NOK NOK NOK NOK

NOK NOK NOK

NOK NOK NOK

NOK NOK WHUD

NOK NOK NOK

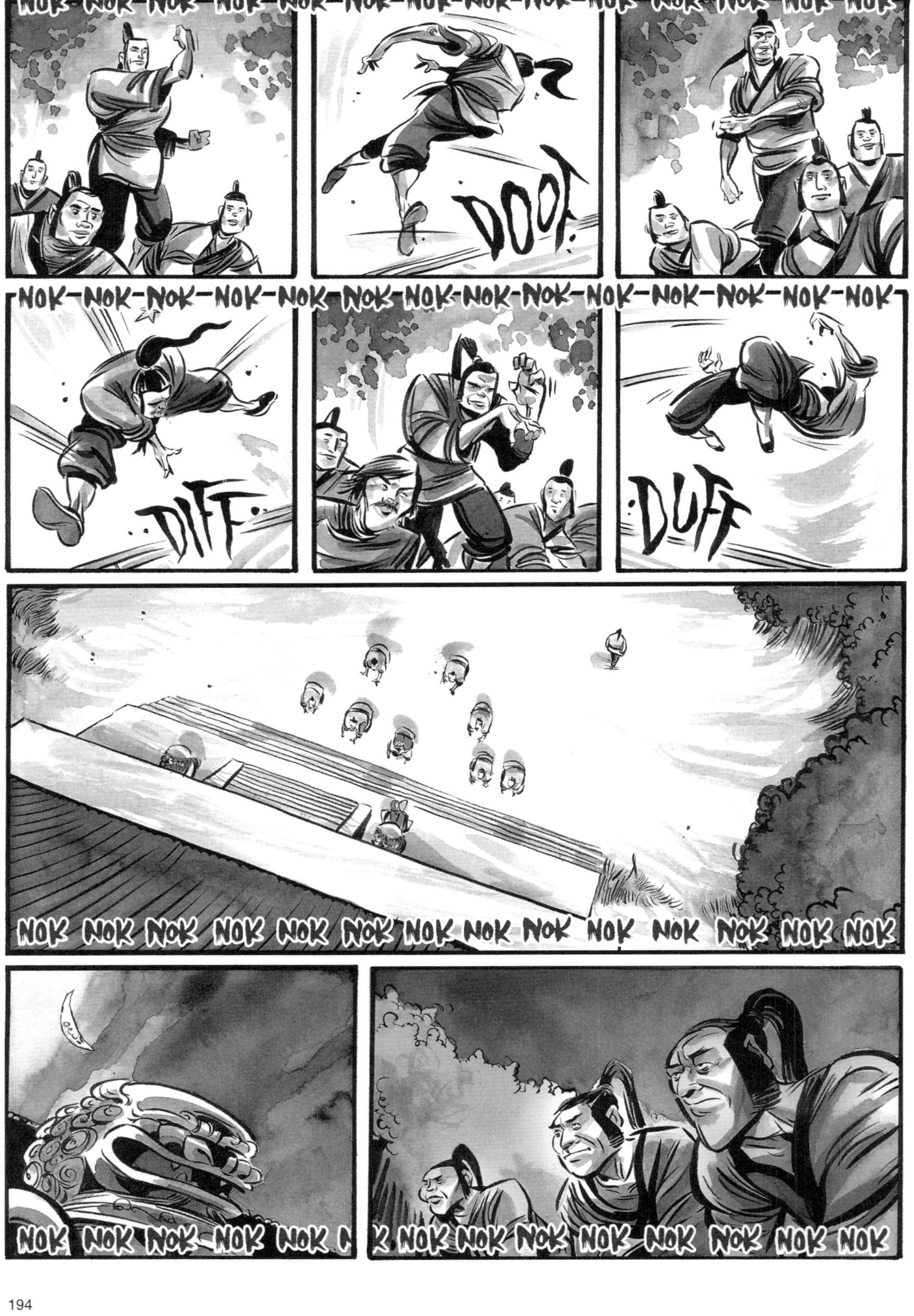
NOK-NOK-NOK-NOK-NOK-NOK-NOK-NOK-NOK-NOK-NOK-NOK-NOK-NOK
DOOF
NOK-NOK-NOK-NOK-NOK-NOK-NOK-NOK-NOK-NOK-NOK-NOK-NOK-NOK
DIFF
DUFF
NOK NOK NOK NOK NOK NOK NOK NOK NOK NOK NOK NOK NOK NOK
NOK NOK NOK NOK NOK
NOK NOK NOK NOK NOK NOK NOK

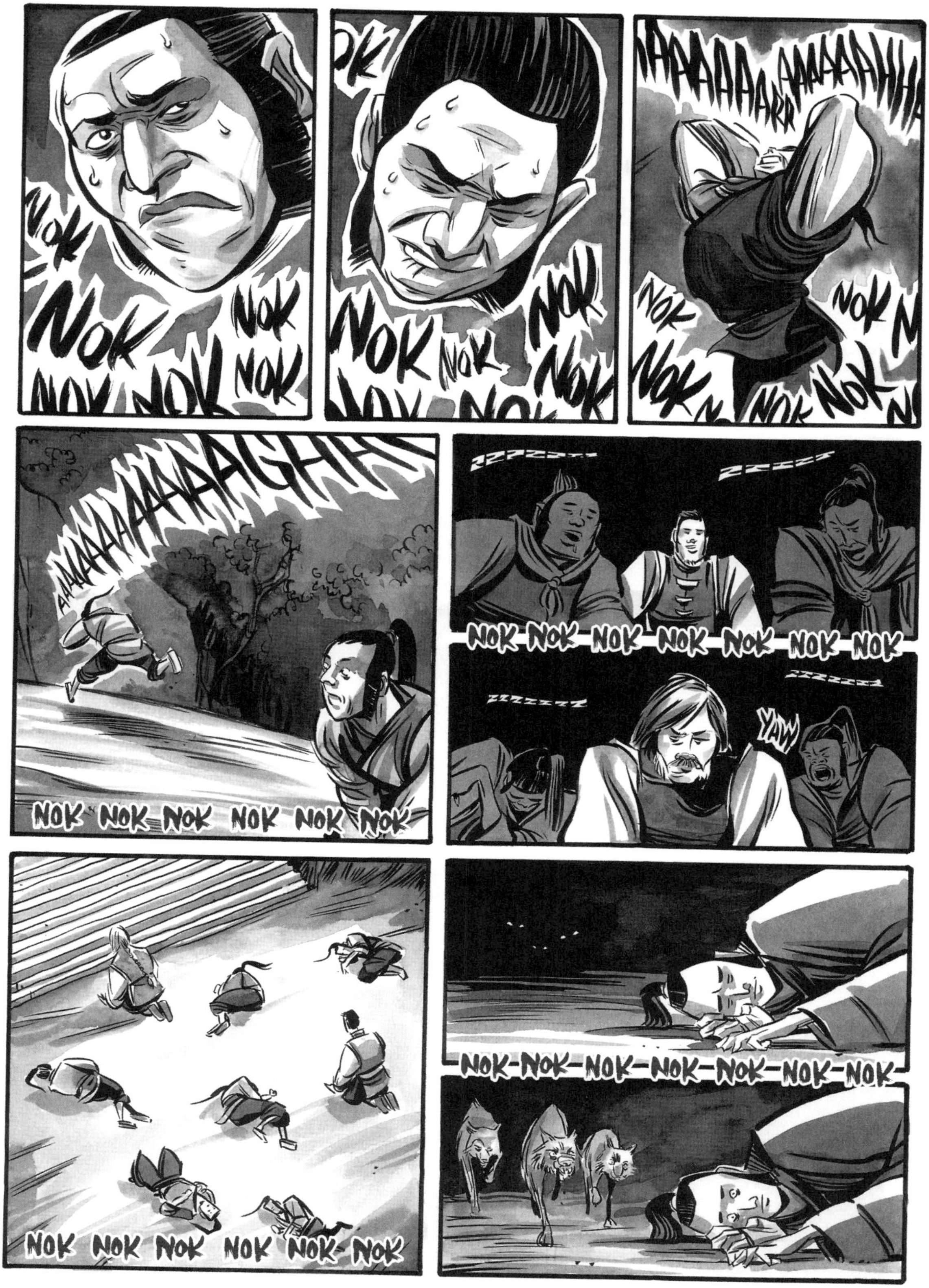
NOK NOK NOK NOK NOK NOK
NOK NOK NOK NOK NOK NOK
AAAAAAARR AAAAAAAHH
NOK NOK NOK NOK NOK NOK NOK
AAAAAAAAAAAAAGH
NOK NOK NOK NOK NOK NOK
ZZZZZZ
ZZZZZ
NOK NOK NOK NOK NOK NOK NOK
ZZZZZZZ
ZZZZZZ
YAW
NOK NOK NOK NOK NOK NOK
NOK-NOK-NOK-NOK-NOK-NOK-NOK

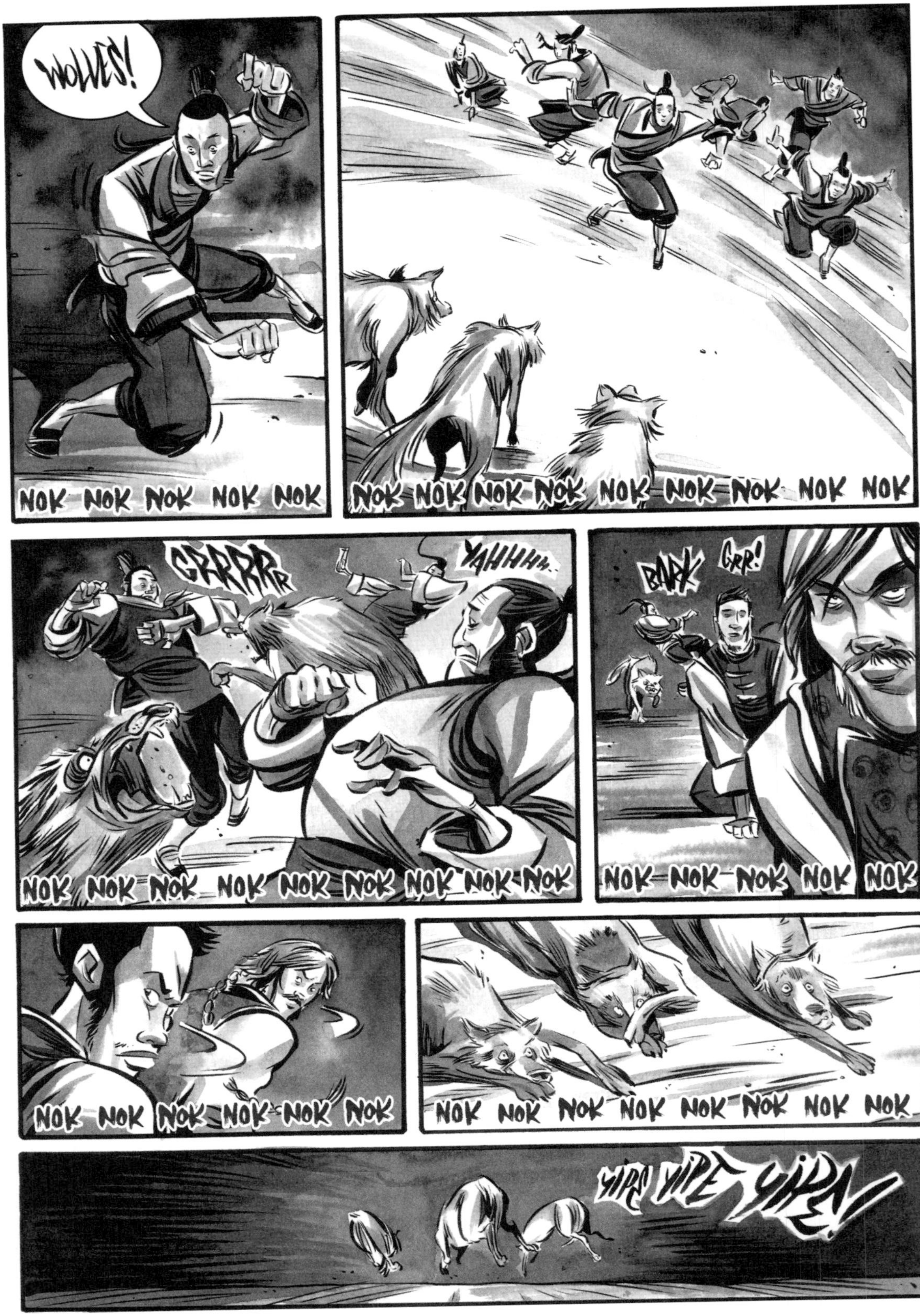
WOLVES!
NOK NOK NOK NOK NOK
NOK NOK NOK NOK NOK NOK NOK NOK NOK
GRRRRr
YAHHHH...
NOK NOK NOK NOK NOK NOK NOK NOK NOK
BARK
GRR!
NOK NOK NOK NOK NOK
NOK NOK NOK NOK NOK NOK
NOK NOK NOK NOK NOK NOK NOK NOK
YIPS YIPE YIPE!

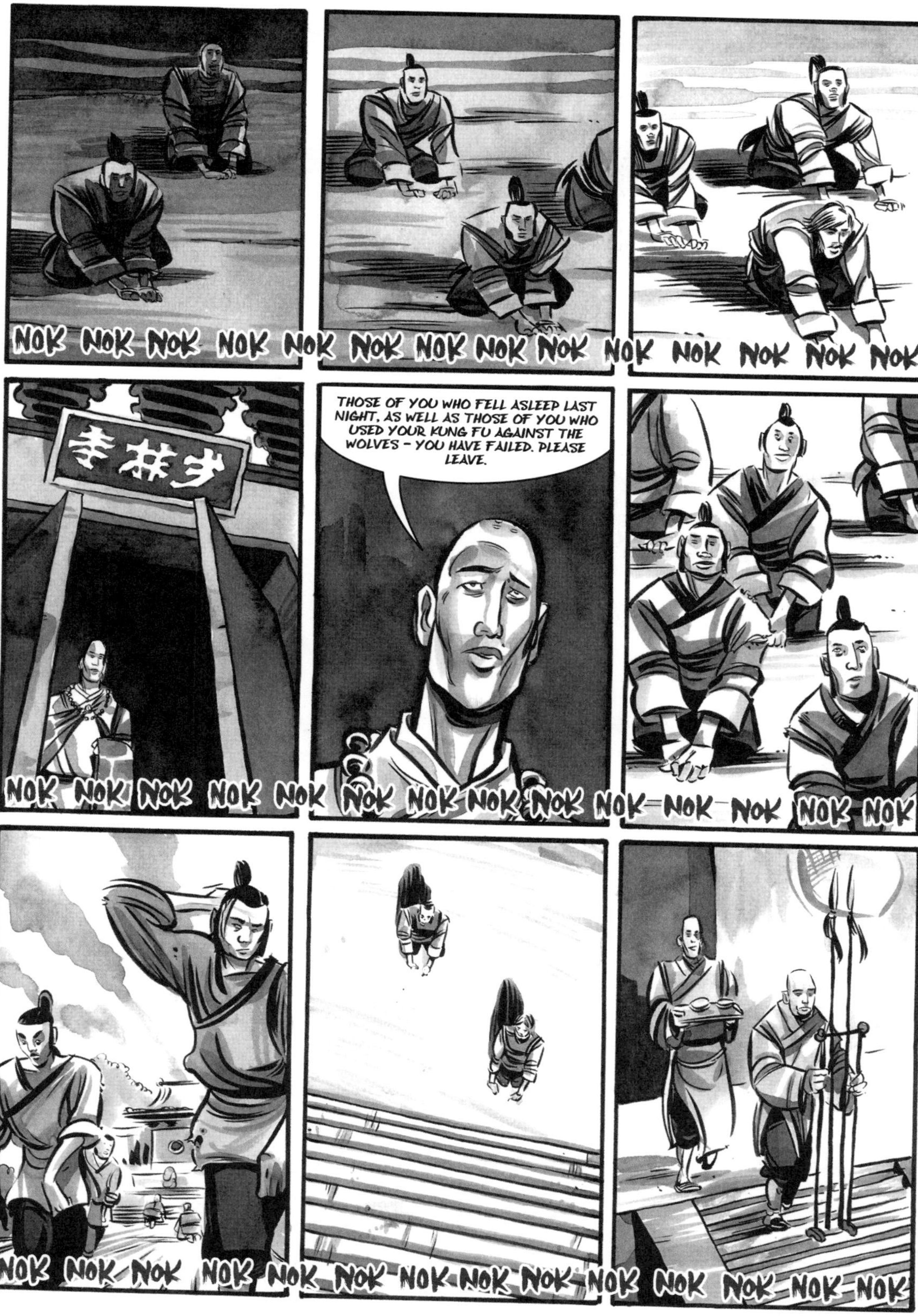
NOK NOK NOK NOK NOK NOK NOK NOK NOK NOK NOK NOK NOK NOK
THOSE OF YOU WHO FELL ASLEEP LAST NIGHT, AS WELL AS THOSE OF YOU WHO USED YOUR KUNG FU AGAINST THE WOLVES – YOU HAVE FAILED. PLEASE LEAVE.
NOK NOK NOK NOK NOK NOK NOK NOK NOK NOK NOK NOK NOK NOK
NOK NOK NOK NOK NOK NOK NOK NOK NOK NOK NOK NOK NOK NOK

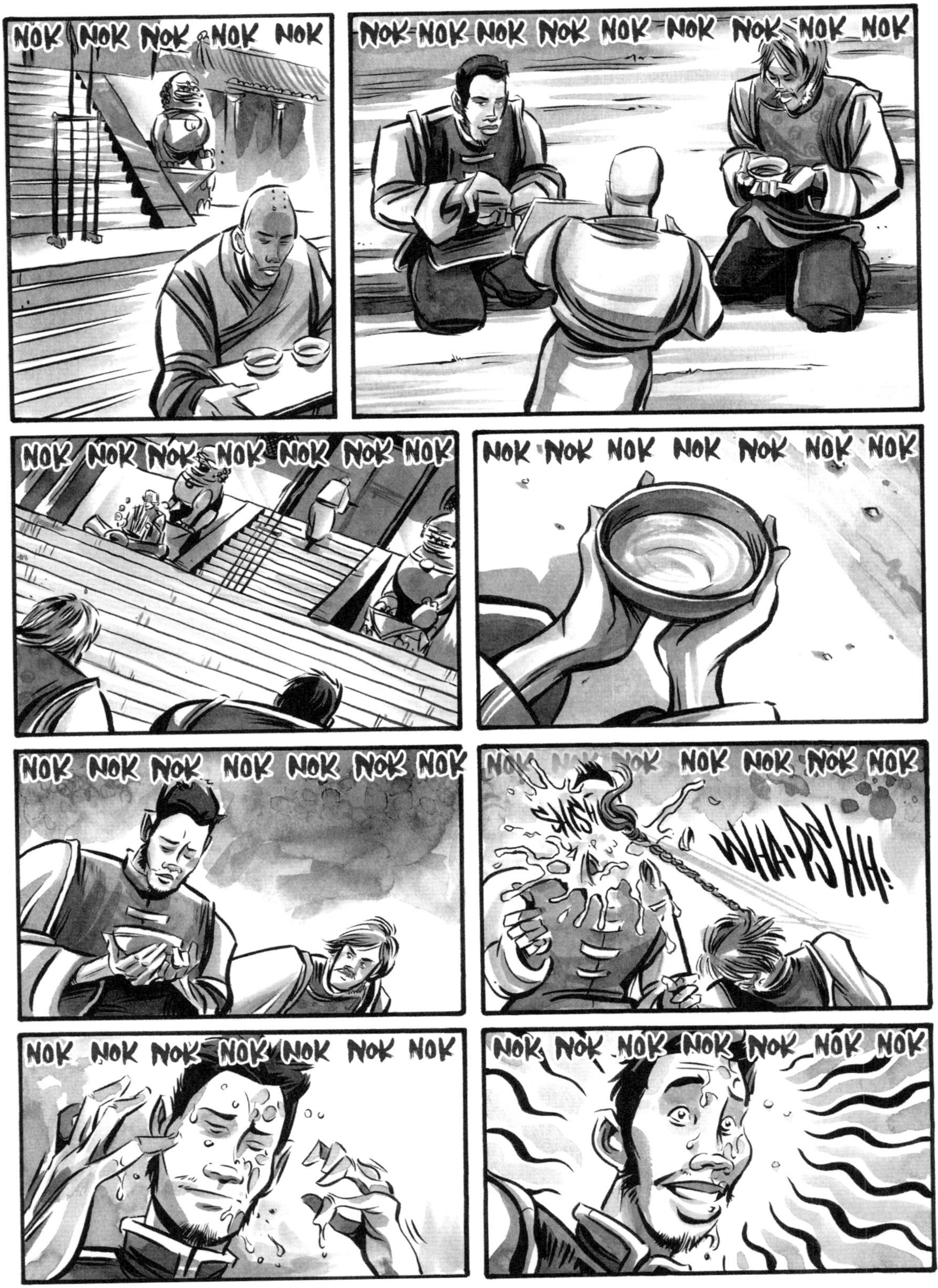
NOK NOK NOK NOK NOK
NOK NOK NOK NOK NOK NOK NOK NOK NOK
NOK NOK NOK NOK NOK NOK NOK
NOK NOK NOK NOK NOK NOK NOK
NOK NOK NOK NOK NOK NOK NOK
NOK NOK NOK NOK
WHA-PSHH!
NOK NOK NOK NOK NOK NOK NOK
NOK NOK NOK NOK NOK NOK NOK

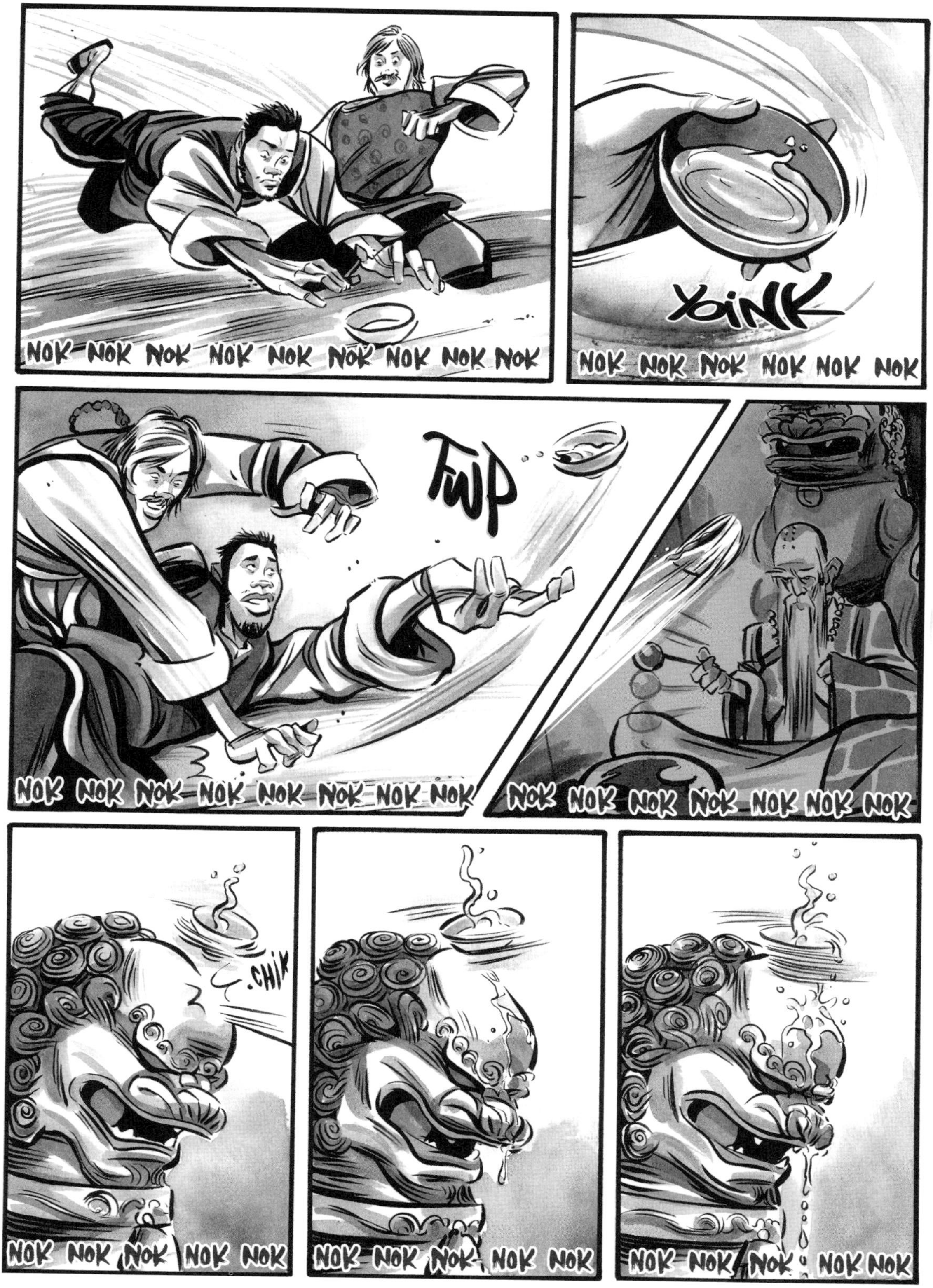
NOK NOK NOK NOK NOK NOK NOK NOK NOK
YOINK
NOK NOK NOK NOK NOK NOK
TWIP
NOK NOK NOK NOK NOK NOK NOK NOK
NOK NOK NOK NOK NOK NOK NOK
CHIK
NOK NOK NOK NOK NOK
NOK NOK NOK NOK NOK
NOK NOK NOK NOK NOK

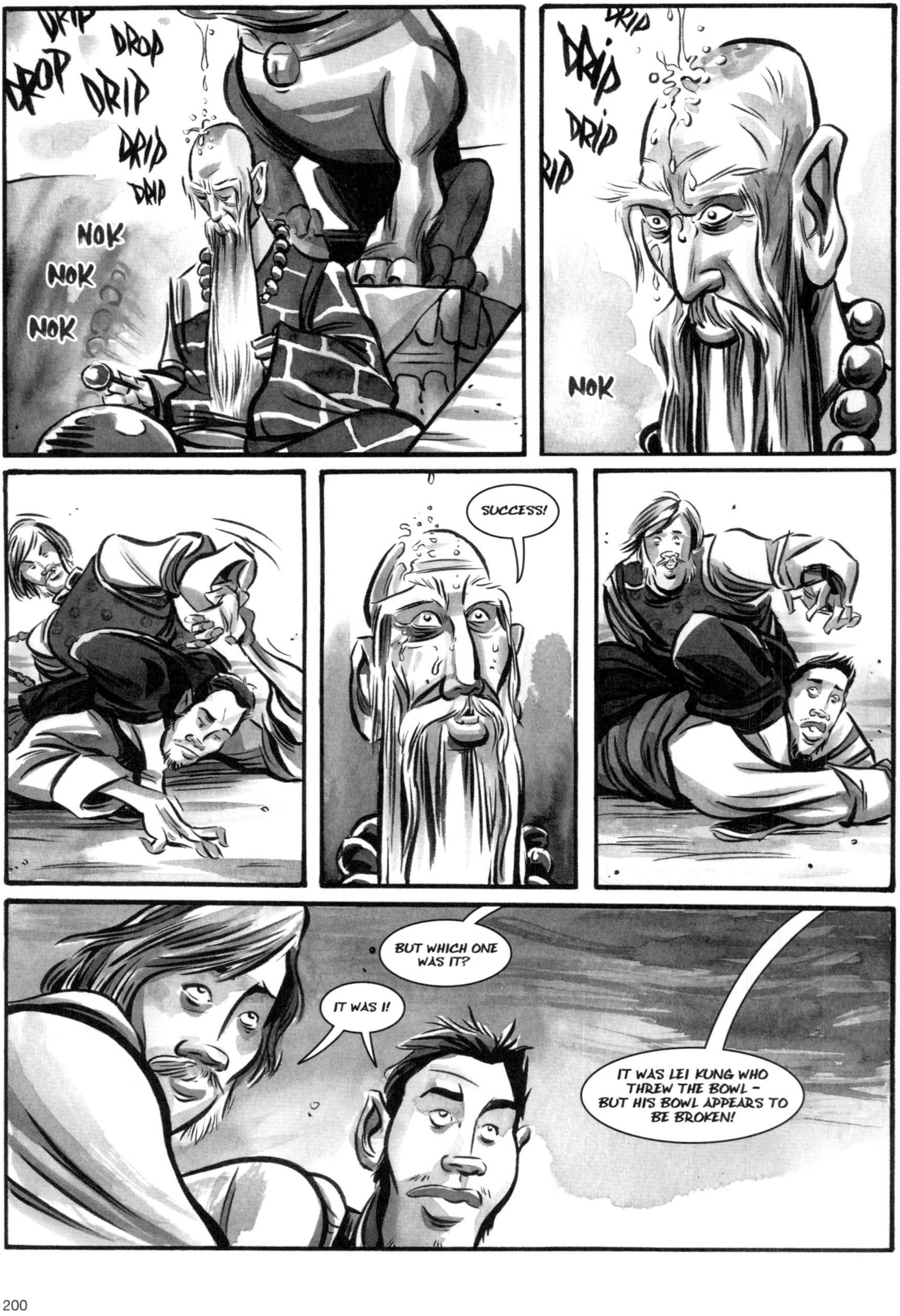
DRIP
DROP
DROP
DRIP
DRIP
DRIP
NOK
NOK
NOK
DRIP
DRIP
DRIP
DRIP
NOK
SUCCESS!
BUT WHICH ONE WAS IT?
IT WAS I!
IT WAS LEI KUNG WHO THREW THE BOWL - BUT HIS BOWL APPEARS TO BE BROKEN!

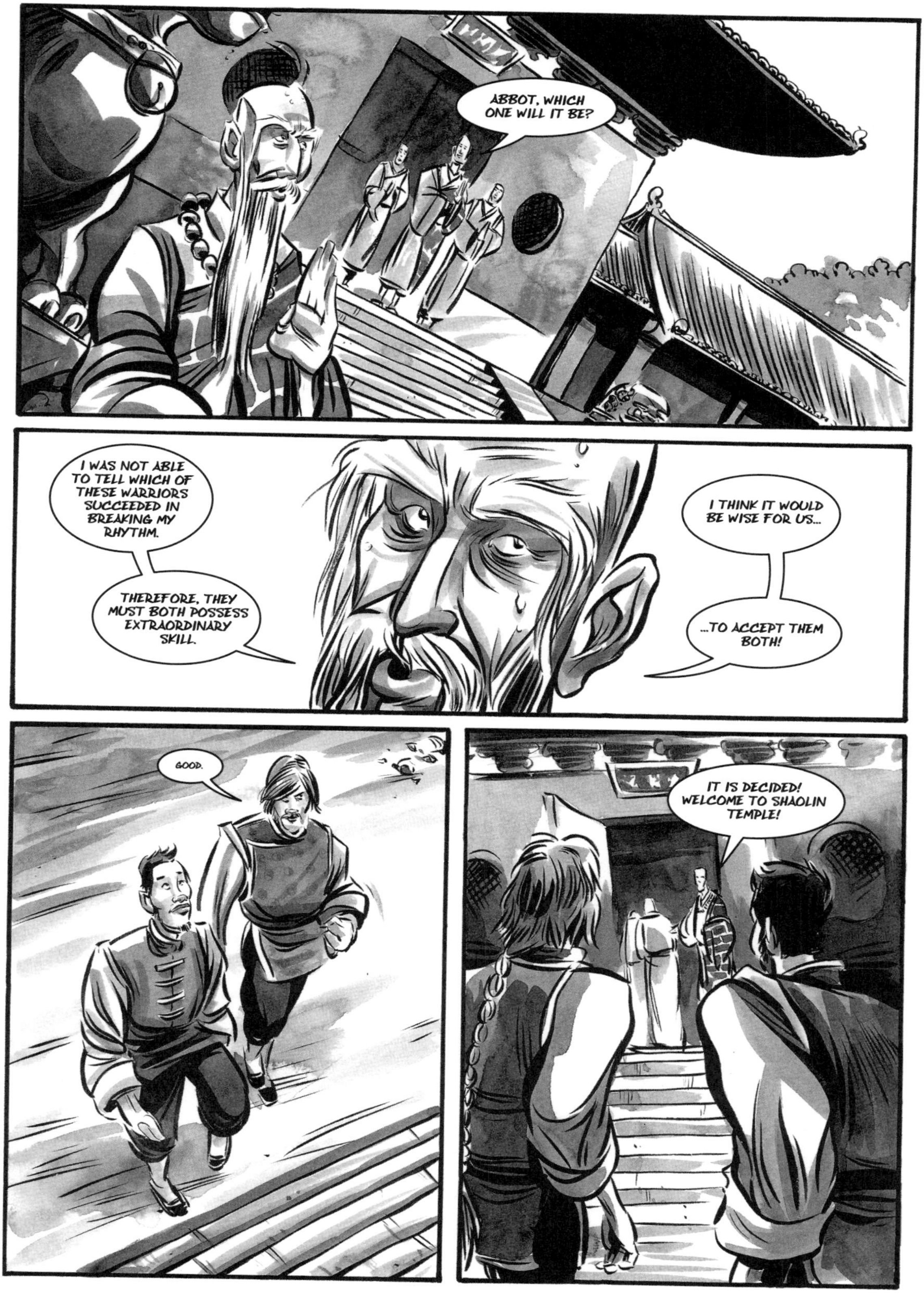
ABBOT, WHICH ONE WILL IT BE?
I WAS NOT ABLE TO TELL WHICH OF THESE WARRIORS SUCCEEDED IN BREAKING MY RHYTHM.
THEREFORE, THEY MUST BOTH POSSESS EXTRAORDINARY SKILL.
I THINK IT WOULD BE WISE FOR US...
...TO ACCEPT THEM BOTH!
GOOD.
IT IS DECIDED! WELCOME TO SHAOLIN TEMPLE!

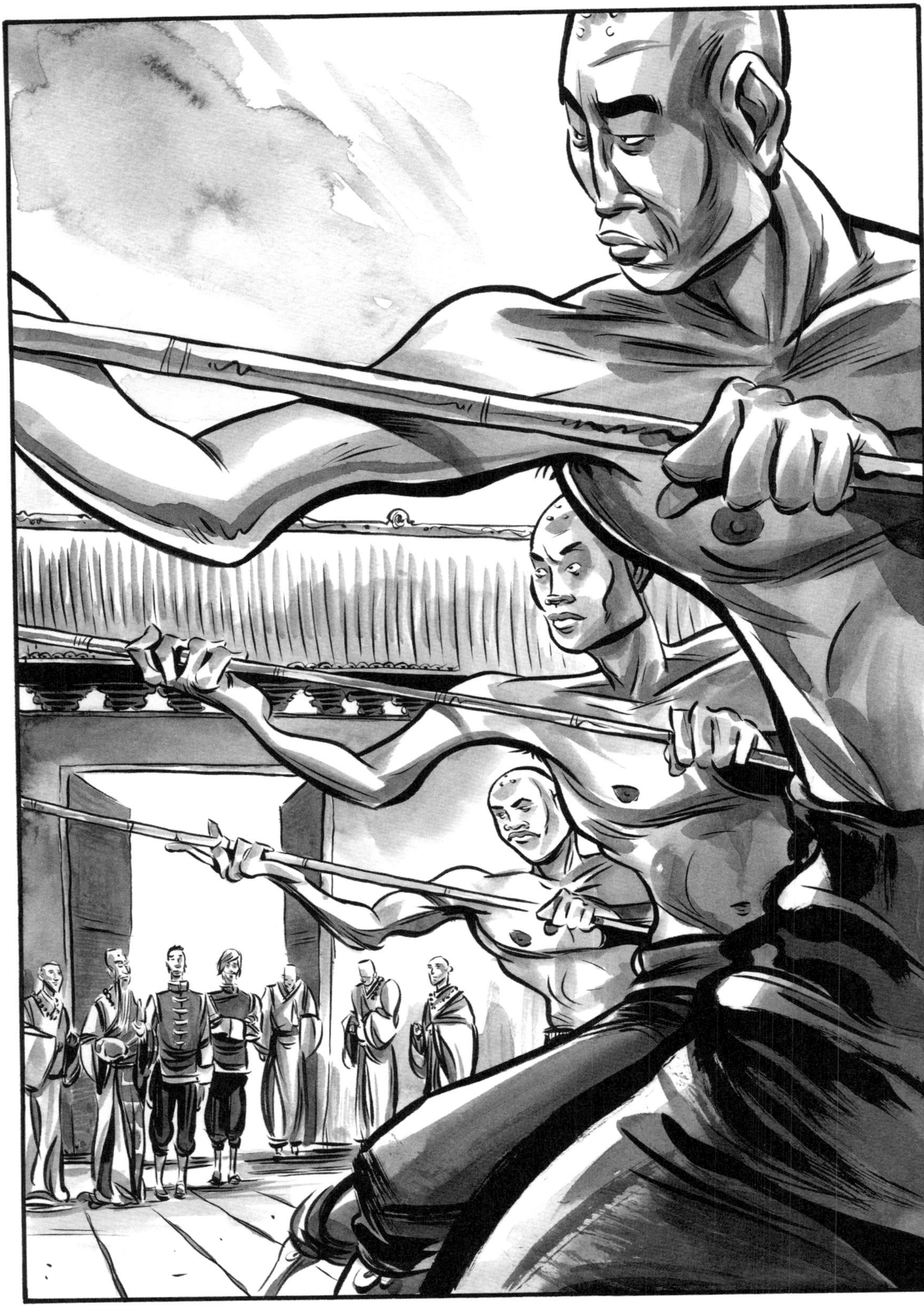

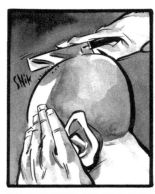

# CHARLES'S BRONZEMEN

SSSSSSSSSSS

SSSSSSS

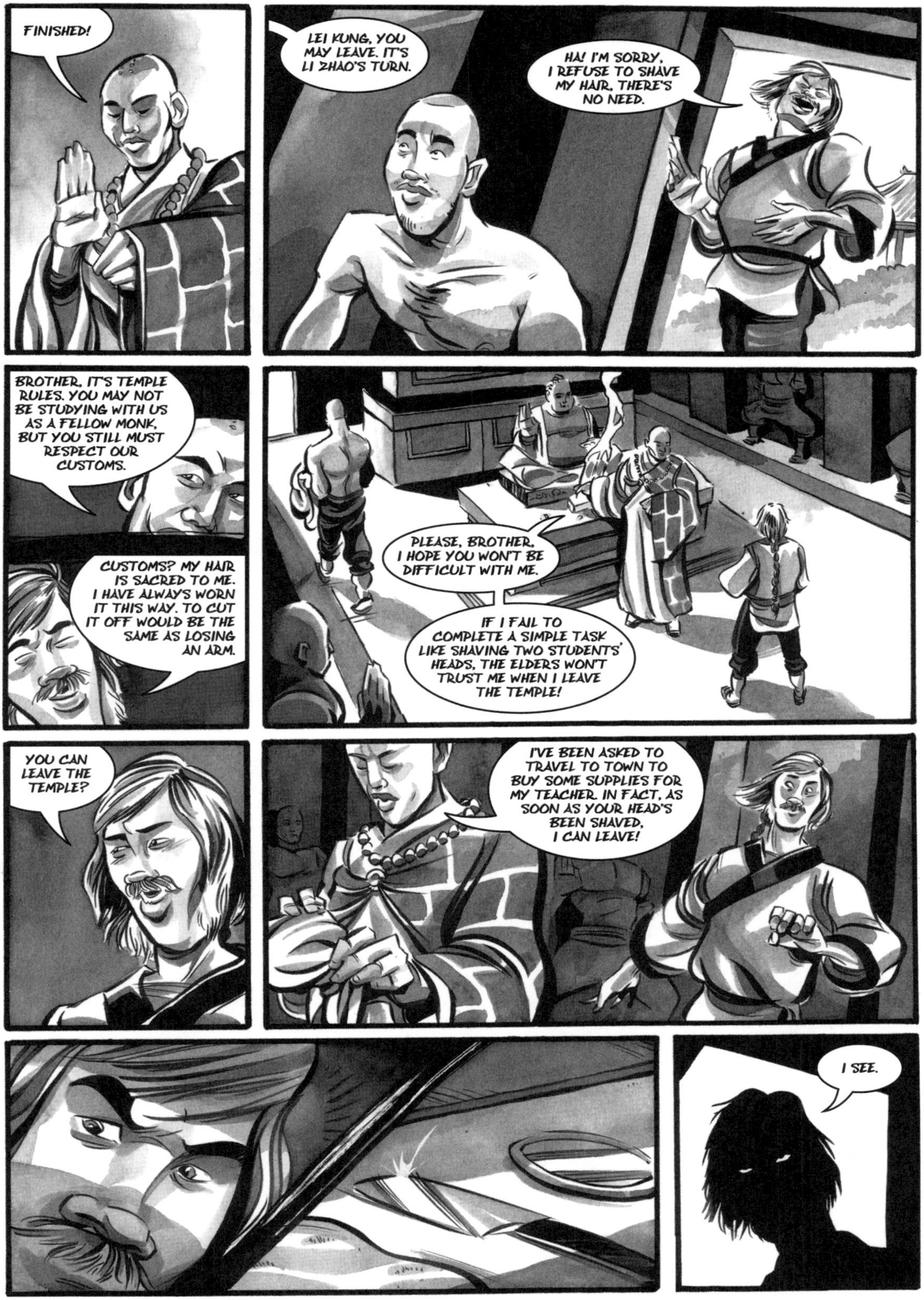
FINISHED!
LEI KUNG, YOU MAY LEAVE. IT'S LI ZHAO'S TURN.
HA! I'M SORRY, I REFUSE TO SHAVE MY HAIR. THERE'S NO NEED.
BROTHER, IT'S TEMPLE RULES. YOU MAY NOT BE STUDYING WITH US AS A FELLOW MONK, BUT YOU STILL MUST RESPECT OUR CUSTOMS.
CUSTOMS? MY HAIR IS SACRED TO ME. I HAVE ALWAYS WORN IT THIS WAY. TO CUT IT OFF WOULD BE THE SAME AS LOSING AN ARM.
PLEASE, BROTHER. I HOPE YOU WON'T BE DIFFICULT WITH ME.
IF I FAIL TO COMPLETE A SIMPLE TASK LIKE SHAVING TWO STUDENTS' HEADS, THE ELDERS WON'T TRUST ME WHEN I LEAVE THE TEMPLE!
YOU CAN LEAVE THE TEMPLE?
I'VE BEEN ASKED TO TRAVEL TO TOWN TO BUY SOME SUPPLIES FOR MY TEACHER. IN FACT, AS SOON AS YOUR HEAD'S BEEN SHAVED, I CAN LEAVE!
I SEE.

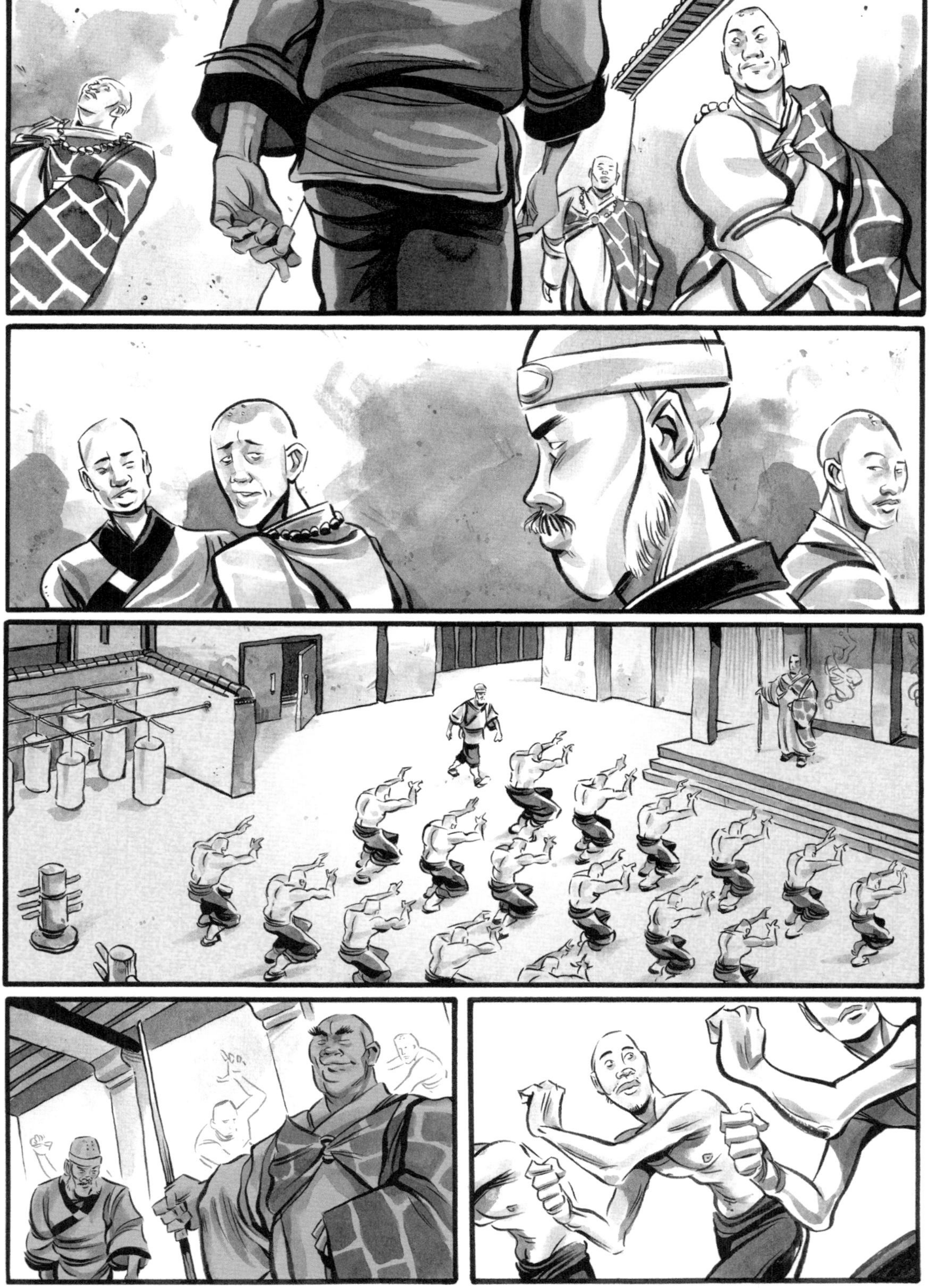

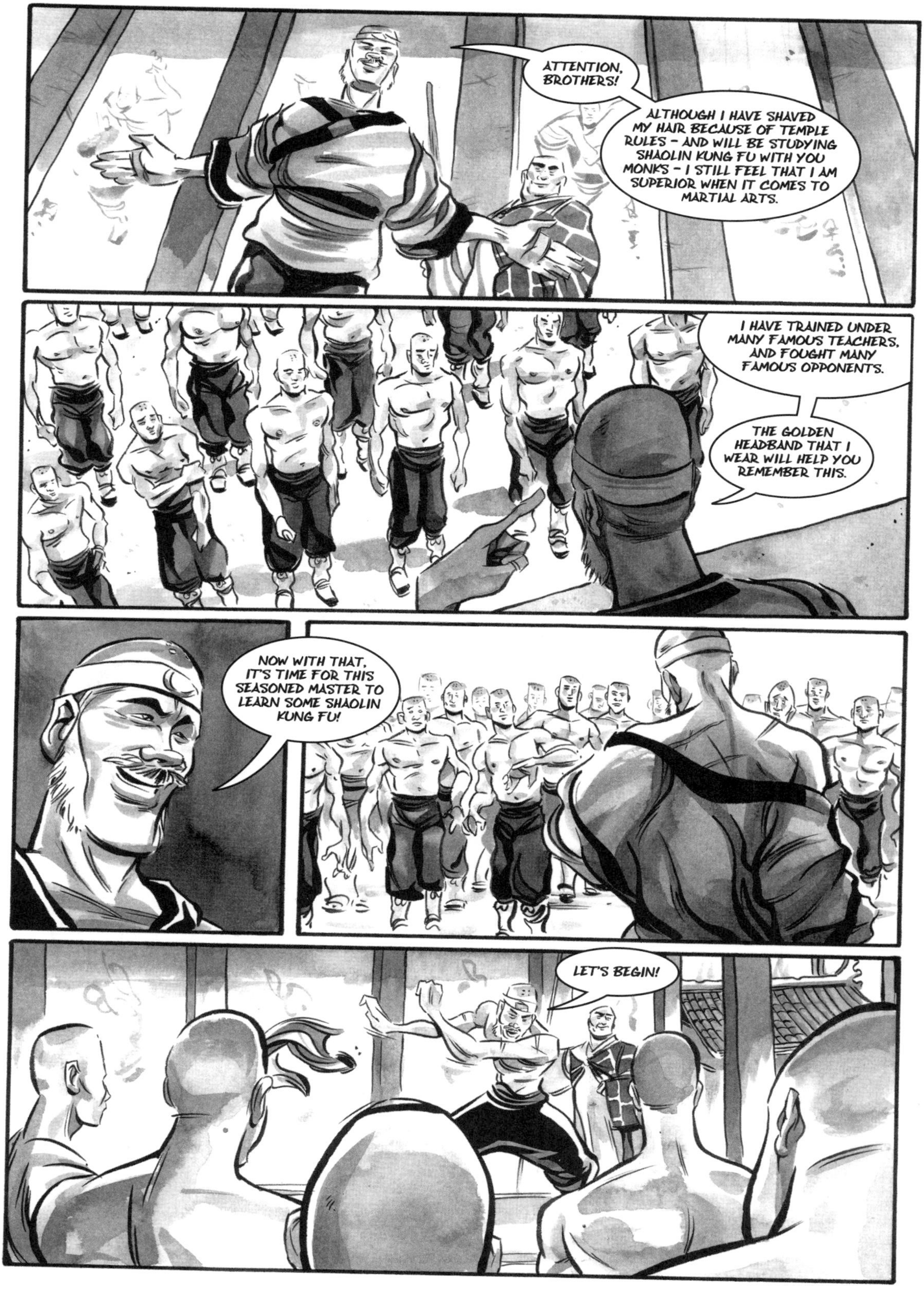
ATTENTION, BROTHERS!
ALTHOUGH I HAVE SHAVED MY HAIR BECAUSE OF TEMPLE RULES - AND WILL BE STUDYING SHAOLIN KUNG FU WITH YOU MONKS - I STILL FEEL THAT I AM SUPERIOR WHEN IT COMES TO MARTIAL ARTS.
I HAVE TRAINED UNDER MANY FAMOUS TEACHERS, AND FOUGHT MANY FAMOUS OPPONENTS.
THE GOLDEN HEADBAND THAT I WEAR WILL HELP YOU REMEMBER THIS.
NOW WITH THAT, IT'S TIME FOR THIS SEASONED MASTER TO LEARN SOME SHAOLIN KUNG FU!
LET'S BEGIN!

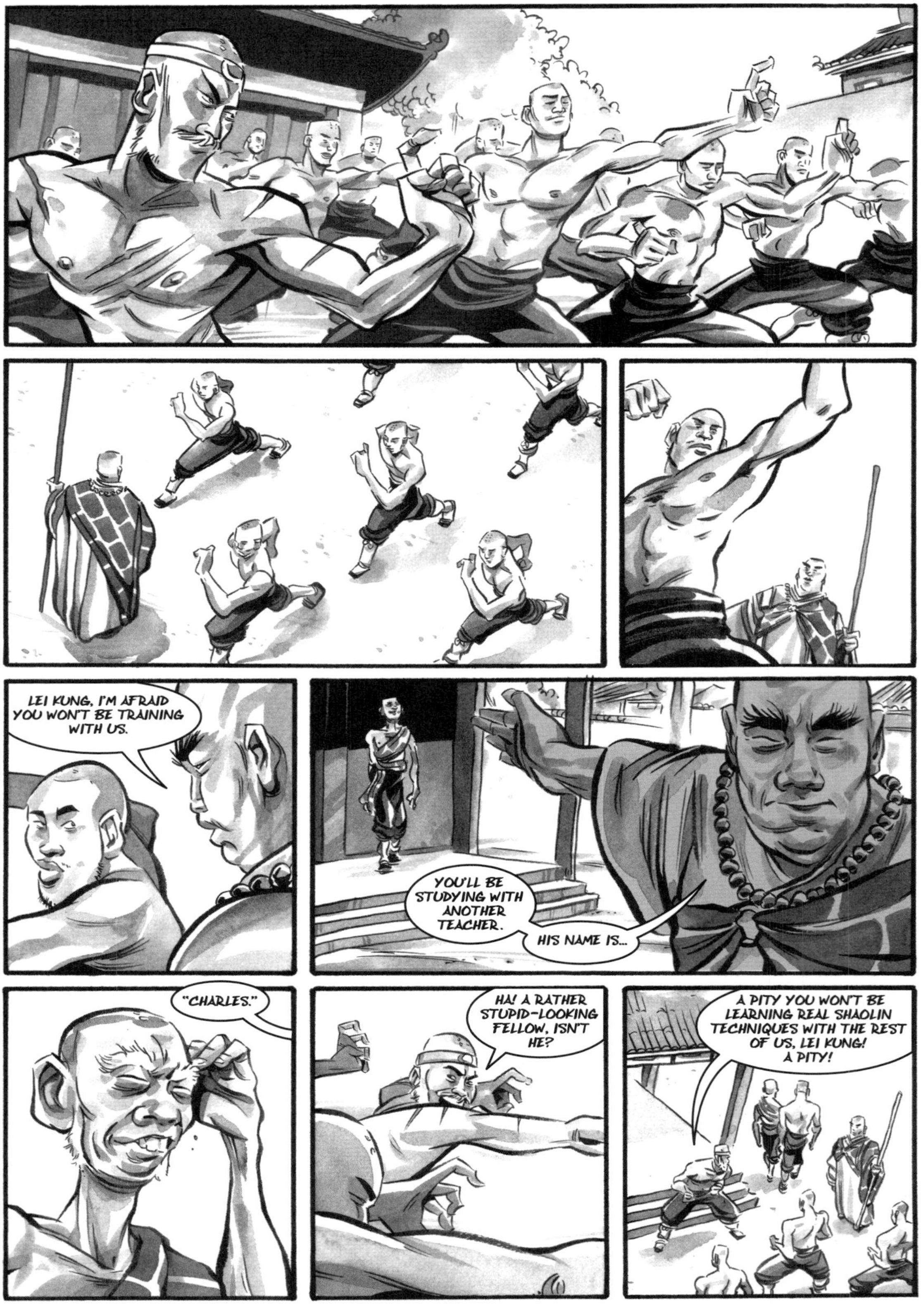

LEI KUNG, I'M AFRAID YOU WON'T BE TRAINING WITH US.
YOU'LL BE STUDYING WITH ANOTHER TEACHER.
HIS NAME IS...
"CHARLES."
HA! A RATHER STUPID-LOOKING FELLOW, ISN'T HE?
A PITY YOU WON'T BE LEARNING REAL SHAOLIN TECHNIQUES WITH THE REST OF US, LEI KUNG! A PITY!

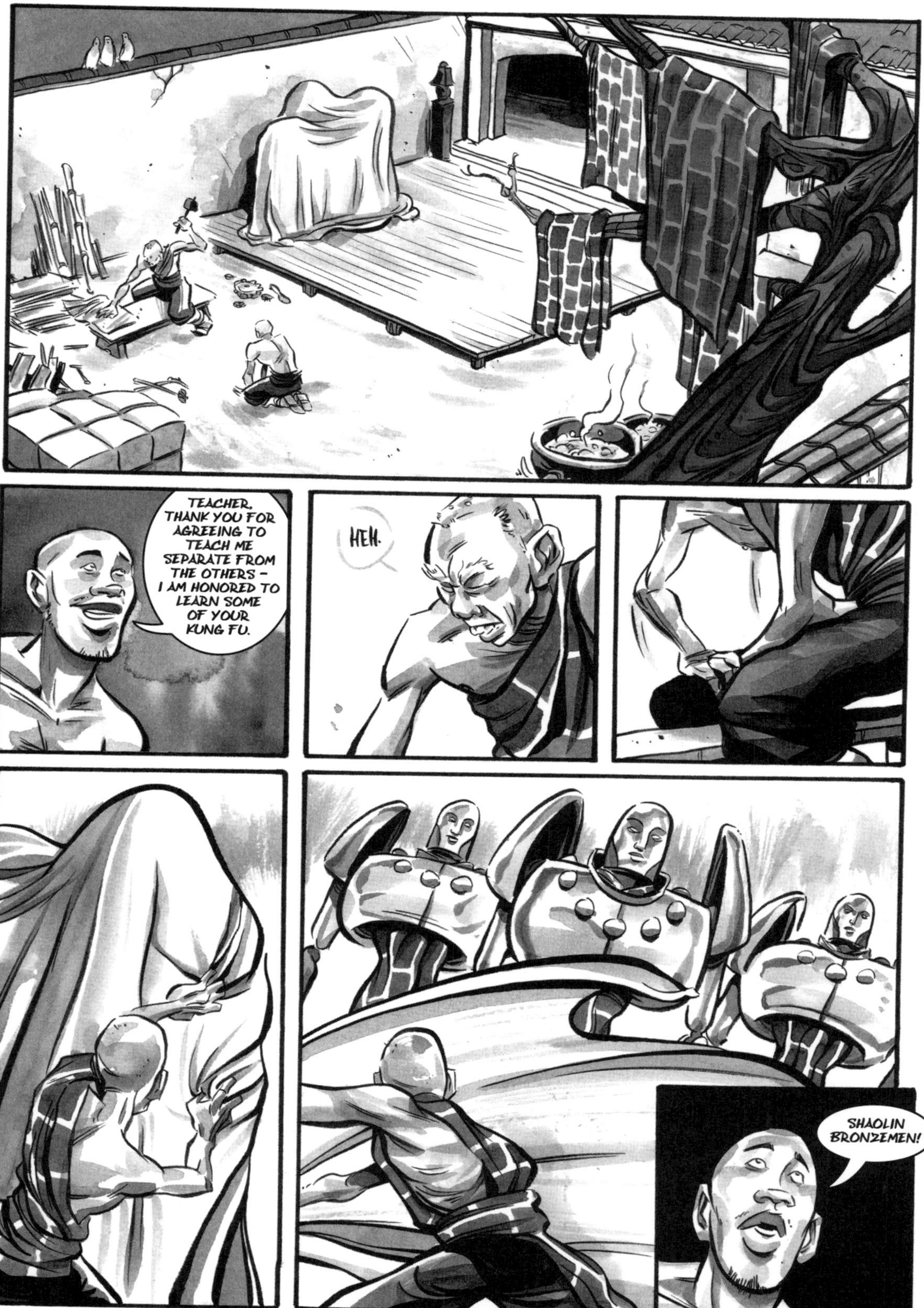
TEACHER. THANK YOU FOR AGREEING TO TEACH ME SEPARATE FROM THE OTHERS - I AM HONORED TO LEARN SOME OF YOUR KUNG FU.
HEH.
SHAOLIN BRONZEMEN!

HERE IN THE TEMPLE, I BUILD ALL OF THE VARIOUS CONTRAPTIONS WE USE FOR TRAINING OUR MONKS.

THE SHAOLIN HAND WHEEL, THE RIVER OF PERSEVERANCE, AND THE WRATH OF 10,000 BUDDHAS – ALL MINE!

AND NOW YOU'RE WORKING ON A NEW SET OF BRONZEMEN?

CORRECT. AS YOU MAY KNOW, IN ORDER TO LEAVE SHAOLIN TEMPLE, ONE MUST FACE MY 18 BRONZEMEN.

MY EARLIER MODELS HAVE BECOME OUTDATED, AND I'VE DECIDED TO REBUILD THEM!

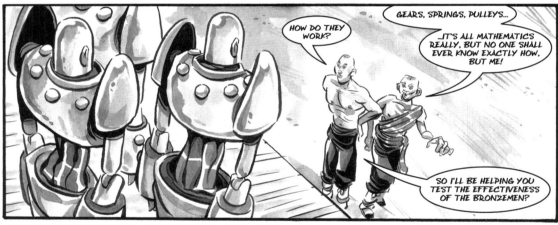

HOW DO THEY WORK?

GEARS, SPRINGS, PULLEYS...

...IT'S ALL MATHEMATICS REALLY, BUT NO ONE SHALL EVER KNOW EXACTLY HOW, BUT ME!

SO I'LL BE HELPING YOU TEST THE EFFECTIVENESS OF THE BRONZEMEN?

HA! I'M SORRY, LEI KUNG, BUT YOUR TASK WILL BE A BIT DIFFERENT.

"THE ABBOT HAS ALLOWED ME SOLITUDE IN THIS COURTYARD TO COMPLETE MY WORK. HOWEVER, BEING IN THE OPEN AIR CREATES SOME PROBLEMS.

I'LL NEED YOU TO KEEP THE PIGEONS FROM SHITTING ON MY BRONZEMEN.

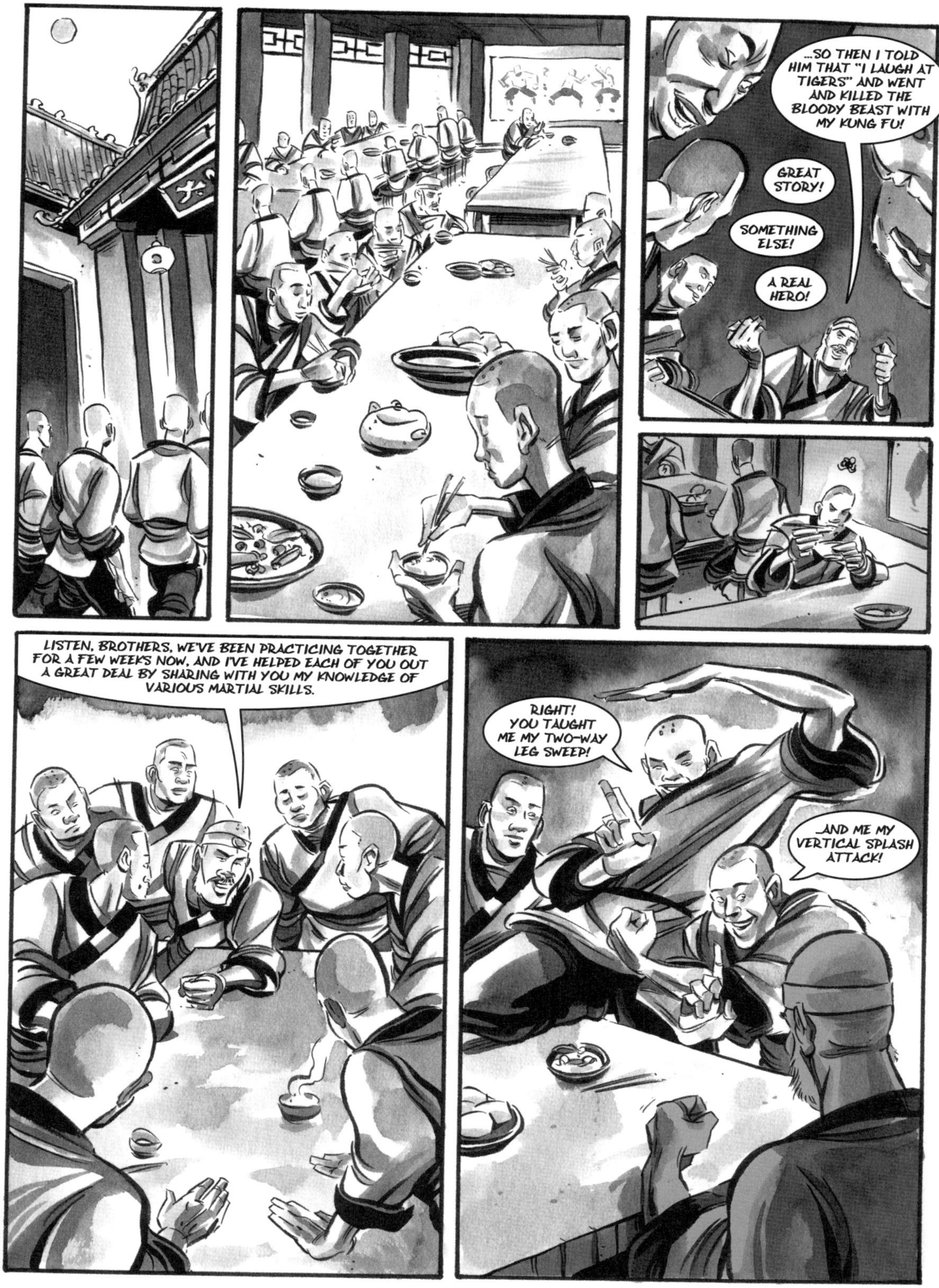
...SO THEN I TOLD HIM THAT "I LAUGH AT TIGERS" AND WENT AND KILLED THE BLOODY BEAST WITH MY KUNG FU!
GREAT STORY!
SOMETHING ELSE!
A REAL HERO!
LISTEN, BROTHERS, WE'VE BEEN PRACTICING TOGETHER FOR A FEW WEEKS NOW, AND I'VE HELPED EACH OF YOU OUT A GREAT DEAL BY SHARING WITH YOU MY KNOWLEDGE OF VARIOUS MARTIAL SKILLS.
RIGHT! YOU TAUGHT ME MY TWO-WAY LEG SWEEP!
...AND ME MY VERTICAL SPLASH ATTACK!

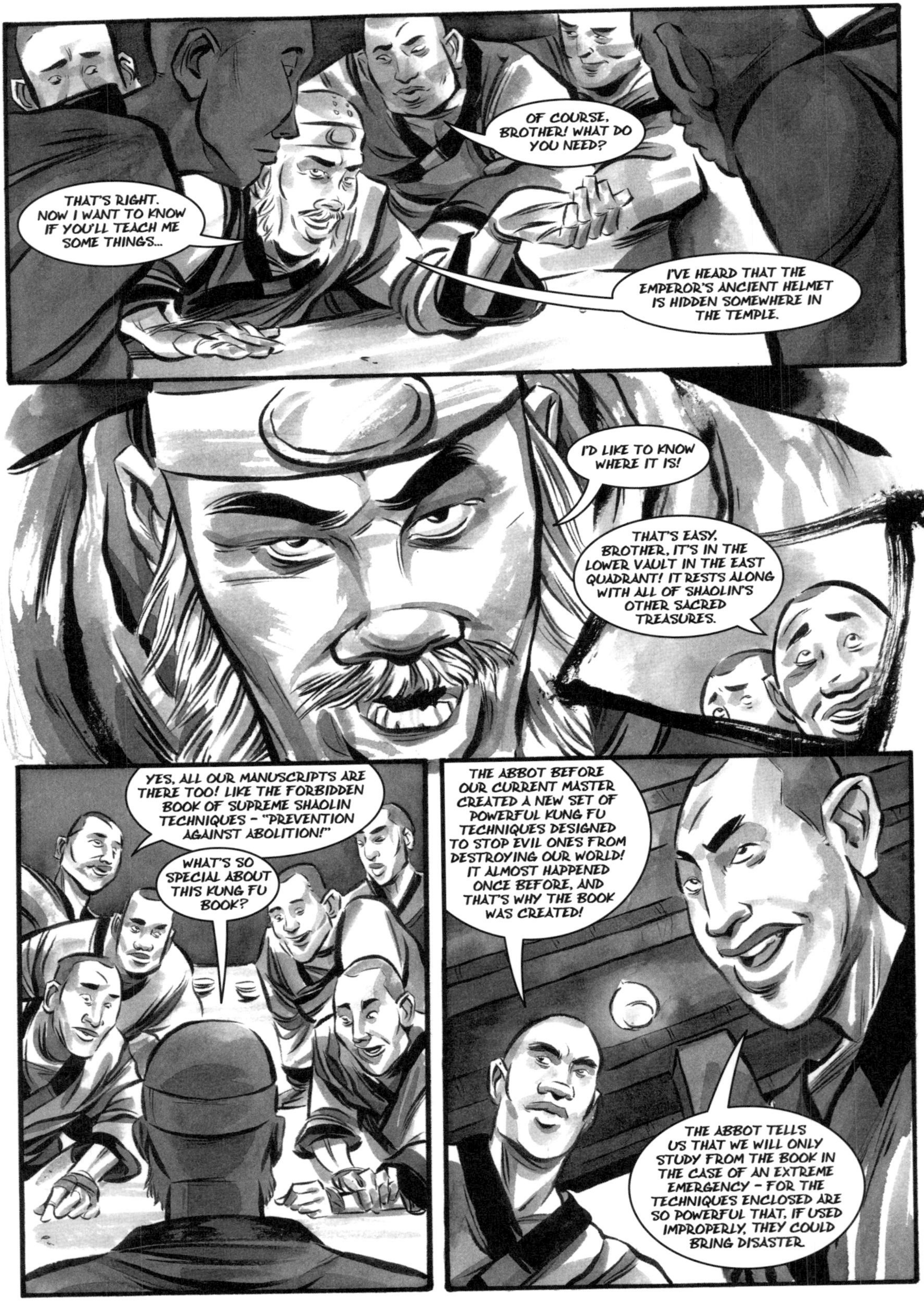

OF COURSE, BROTHER! WHAT DO YOU NEED?
THAT'S RIGHT. NOW I WANT TO KNOW IF YOU'LL TEACH ME SOME THINGS...
I'VE HEARD THAT THE EMPEROR'S ANCIENT HELMET IS HIDDEN SOMEWHERE IN THE TEMPLE.
I'D LIKE TO KNOW WHERE IT IS!
THAT'S EASY, BROTHER, IT'S IN THE LOWER VAULT IN THE EAST QUADRANT! IT RESTS ALONG WITH ALL OF SHAOLIN'S OTHER SACRED TREASURES.
YES, ALL OUR MANUSCRIPTS ARE THERE TOO! LIKE THE FORBIDDEN BOOK OF SUPREME SHAOLIN TECHNIQUES – "PREVENTION AGAINST ABOLITION!"
WHAT'S SO SPECIAL ABOUT THIS KUNG FU BOOK?
THE ABBOT BEFORE OUR CURRENT MASTER CREATED A NEW SET OF POWERFUL KUNG FU TECHNIQUES DESIGNED TO STOP EVIL ONES FROM DESTROYING OUR WORLD! IT ALMOST HAPPENED ONCE BEFORE, AND THAT'S WHY THE BOOK WAS CREATED!
THE ABBOT TELLS US THAT WE WILL ONLY STUDY FROM THE BOOK IN THE CASE OF AN EXTREME EMERGENCY – FOR THE TECHNIQUES ENCLOSED ARE SO POWERFUL THAT, IF USED IMPROPERLY, THEY COULD BRING DISASTER.

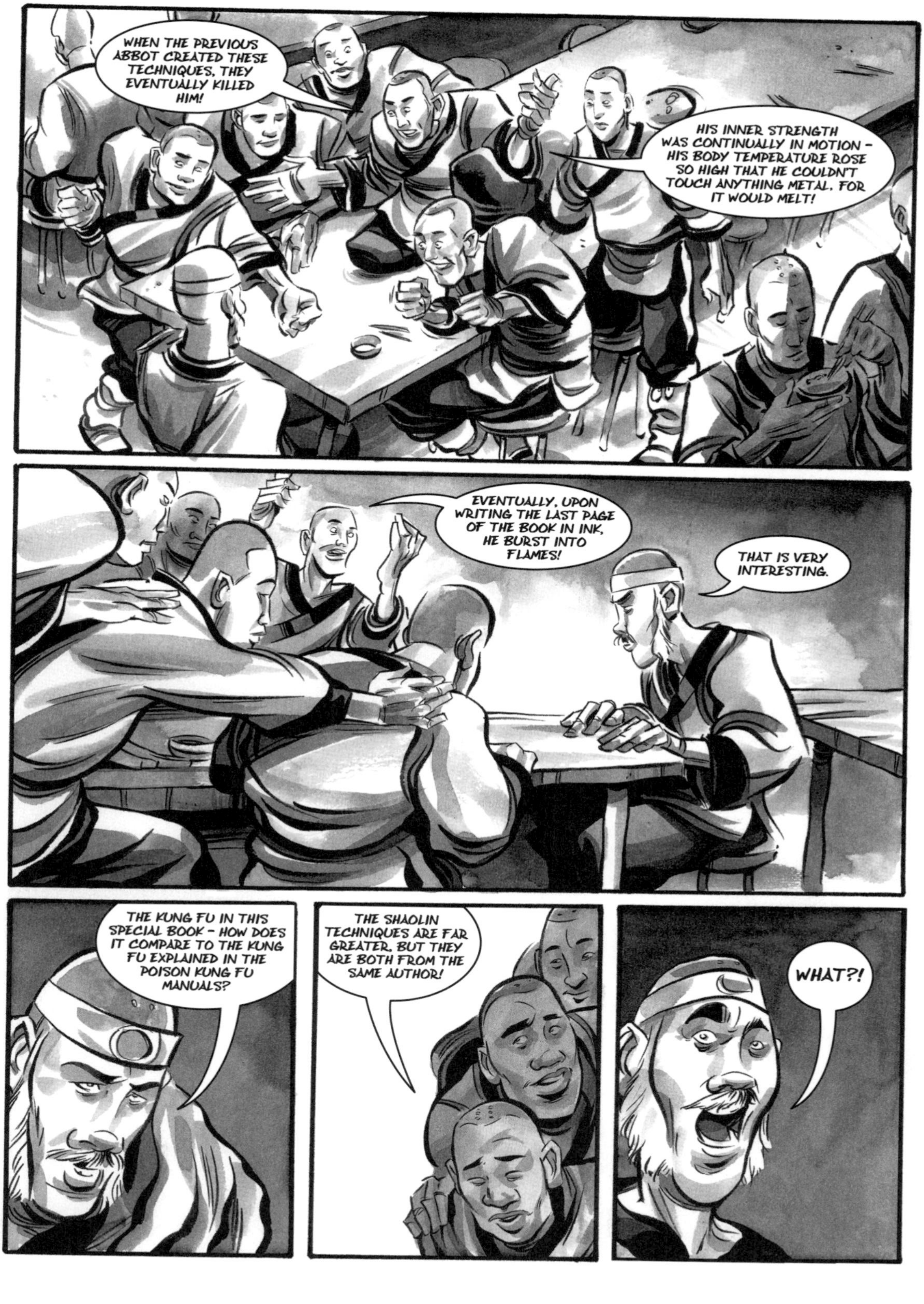
WHEN THE PREVIOUS ABBOT CREATED THESE TECHNIQUES, THEY EVENTUALLY KILLED HIM!
HIS INNER STRENGTH WAS CONTINUALLY IN MOTION - HIS BODY TEMPERATURE ROSE SO HIGH THAT HE COULDN'T TOUCH ANYTHING METAL, FOR IT WOULD MELT!
EVENTUALLY, UPON WRITING THE LAST PAGE OF THE BOOK IN INK, HE BURST INTO FLAMES!
THAT IS VERY INTERESTING.
THE KUNG FU IN THIS SPECIAL BOOK - HOW DOES IT COMPARE TO THE KUNG FU EXPLAINED IN THE POISON KUNG FU MANUALS?
THE SHAOLIN TECHNIQUES ARE FAR GREATER, BUT THEY ARE BOTH FROM THE SAME AUTHOR!
WHAT?!

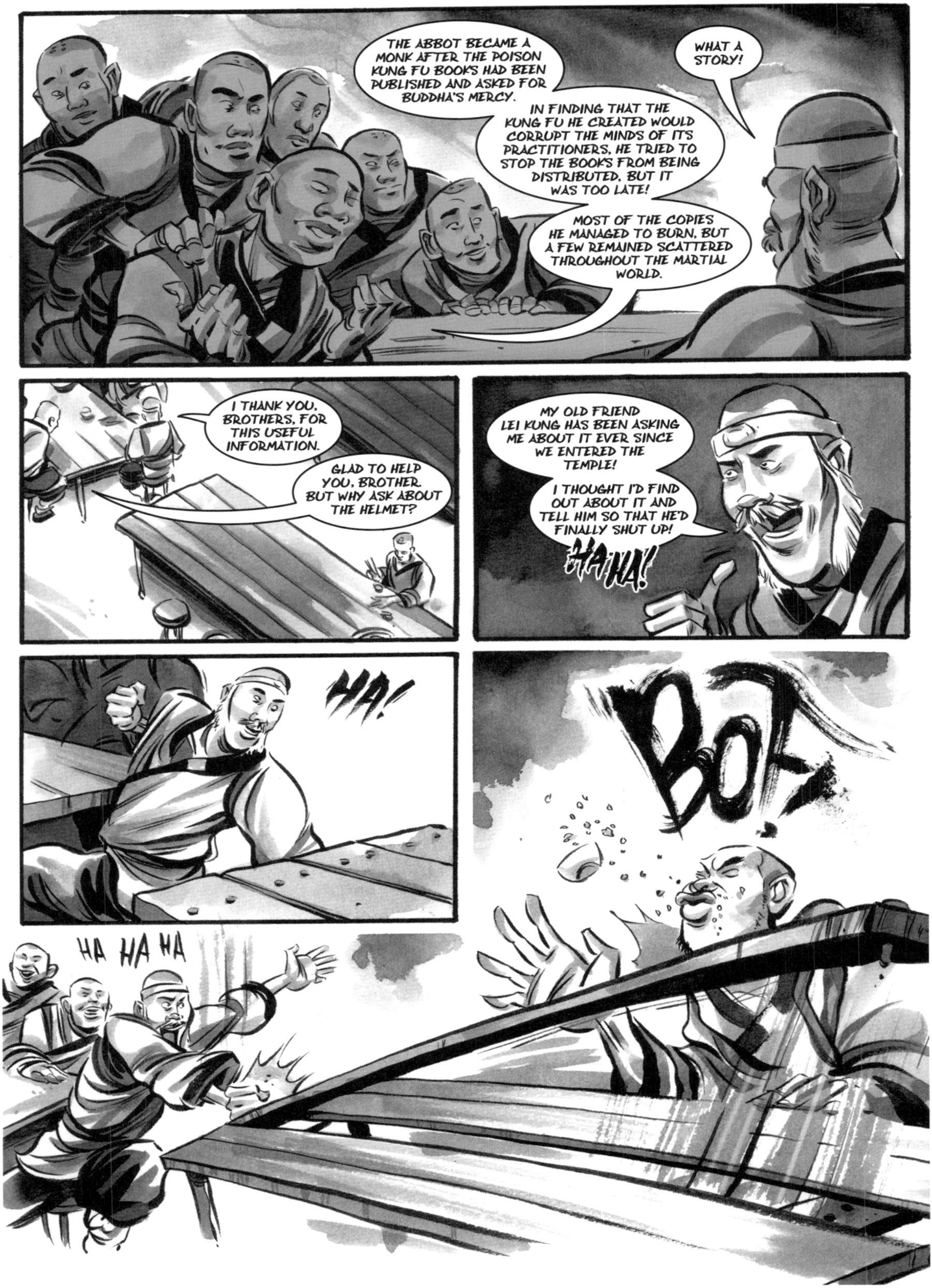
THE ABBOT BECAME A MONK AFTER THE POISON KUNG FU BOOKS HAD BEEN PUBLISHED AND ASKED FOR BUDDHA'S MERCY.
IN FINDING THAT THE KUNG FU HE CREATED WOULD CORRUPT THE MINDS OF ITS PRACTITIONERS, HE TRIED TO STOP THE BOOKS FROM BEING DISTRIBUTED, BUT IT WAS TOO LATE!
MOST OF THE COPIES HE MANAGED TO BURN, BUT A FEW REMAINED SCATTERED THROUGHOUT THE MARTIAL WORLD.
WHAT A STORY!
I THANK YOU, BROTHERS, FOR THIS USEFUL INFORMATION.
GLAD TO HELP YOU, BROTHER. BUT WHY ASK ABOUT THE HELMET?
MY OLD FRIEND LEI KUNG HAS BEEN ASKING ME ABOUT IT EVER SINCE WE ENTERED THE TEMPLE!
I THOUGHT I'D FIND OUT ABOUT IT AND TELL HIM SO THAT HE'D FINALLY SHUT UP!
HA HA!
HA!
BOF
HA HA HA

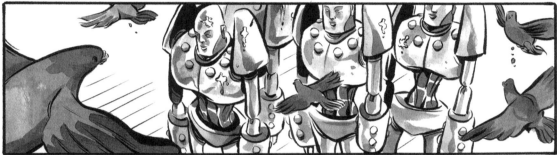

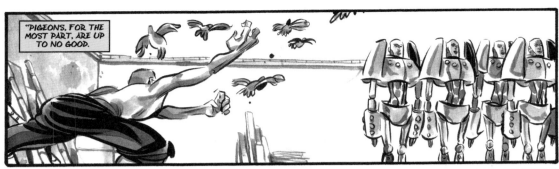

"PIGEONS, FOR THE MOST PART, ARE UP TO NO GOOD.

"HOWEVER, THEY ARE LIVING CREATURES, AND BUDDHA TEACHES US WE SHOULDN'T KILL THEM.

BISH!

"I WANT YOU TO FIND A WAY TO KEEP THOSE FILTHY BIRDS AWAY FROM MY BRONZEMEN AS I WORK...

"...REFRAINING FROM HARMING THEM...

"...UNTIL THE 18TH WARRIOR IS COMPLETED."

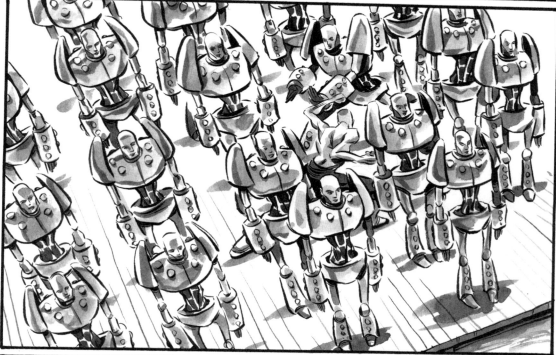

CHANG.

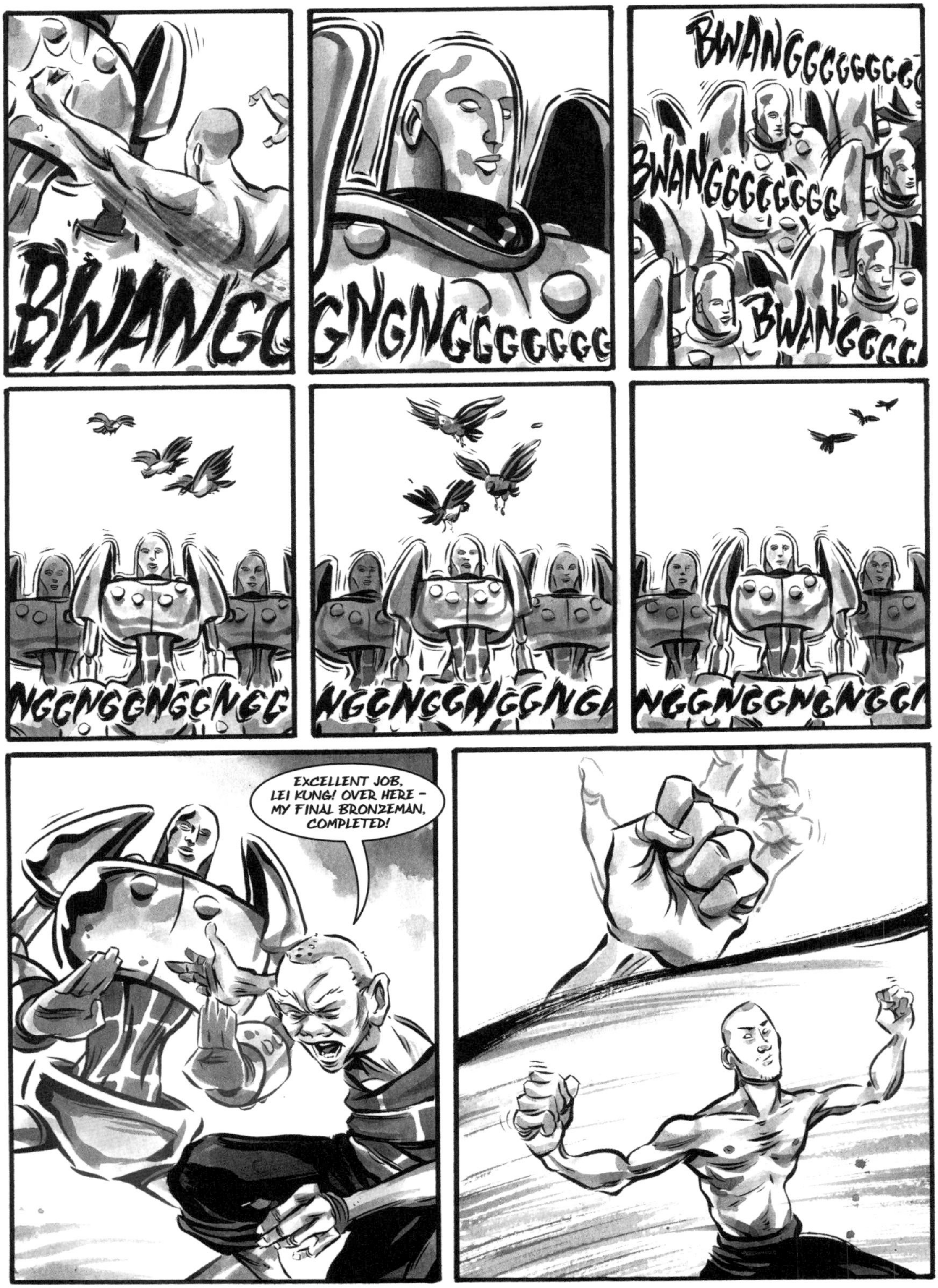
BWANGG
GNGNGGGGGG
BWANGGGGGGGG
BWANGGGGGGGG
BWANGGGG
NGGNGGNGGNGG
NGGNGGNGGNG
NGGNGGNGNGG
EXCELLENT JOB, LEI KUNG! OVER HERE - MY FINAL BRONZEMAN, COMPLETED!

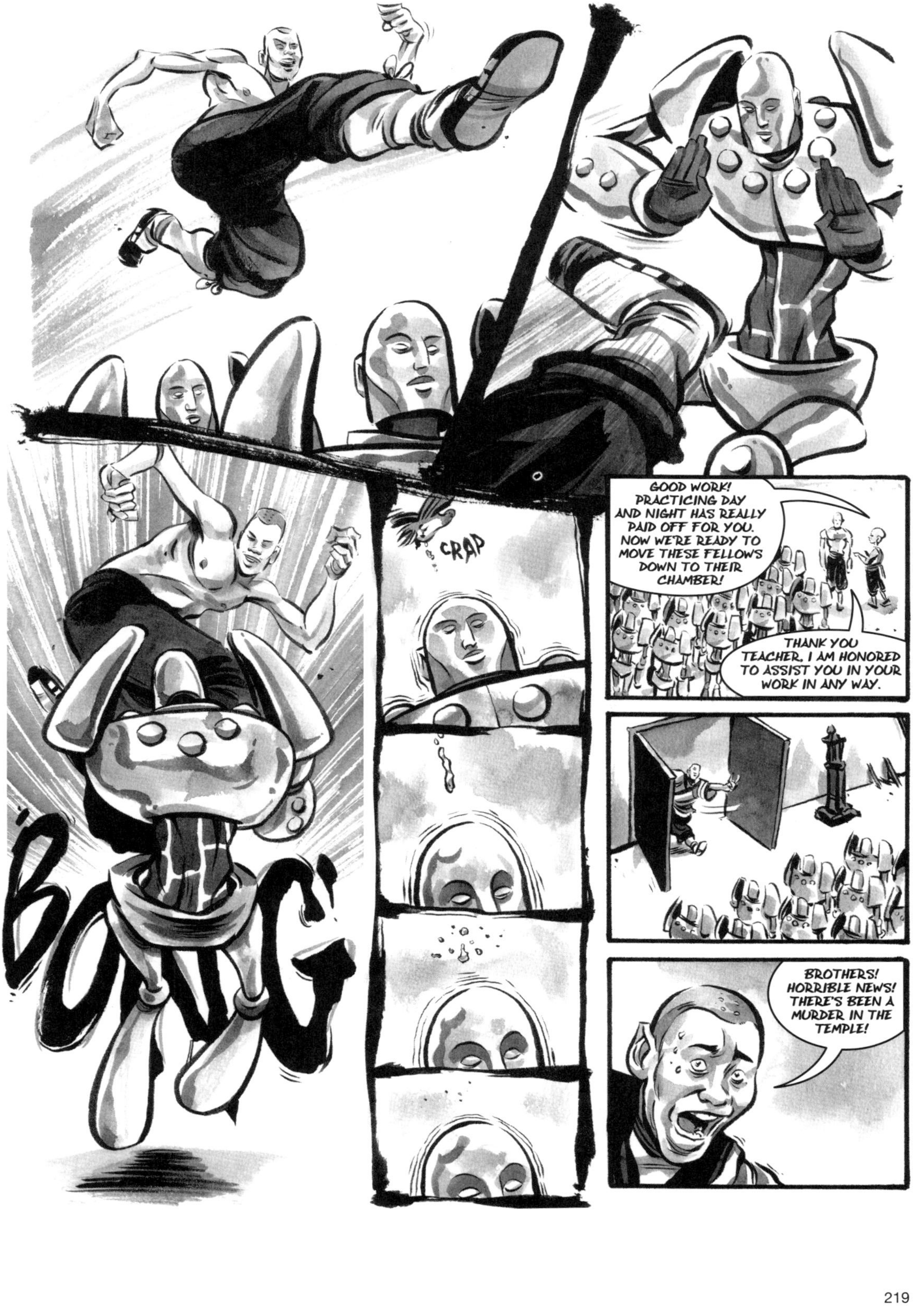
CRAP
BONG!
GOOD WORK! PRACTICING DAY AND NIGHT HAS REALLY PAID OFF FOR YOU. NOW WE'RE READY TO MOVE THESE FELLOWS DOWN TO THEIR CHAMBER!
THANK YOU TEACHER. I AM HONORED TO ASSIST YOU IN YOUR WORK IN ANY WAY.
BROTHERS! HORRIBLE NEWS! THERE'S BEEN A MURDER IN THE TEMPLE!

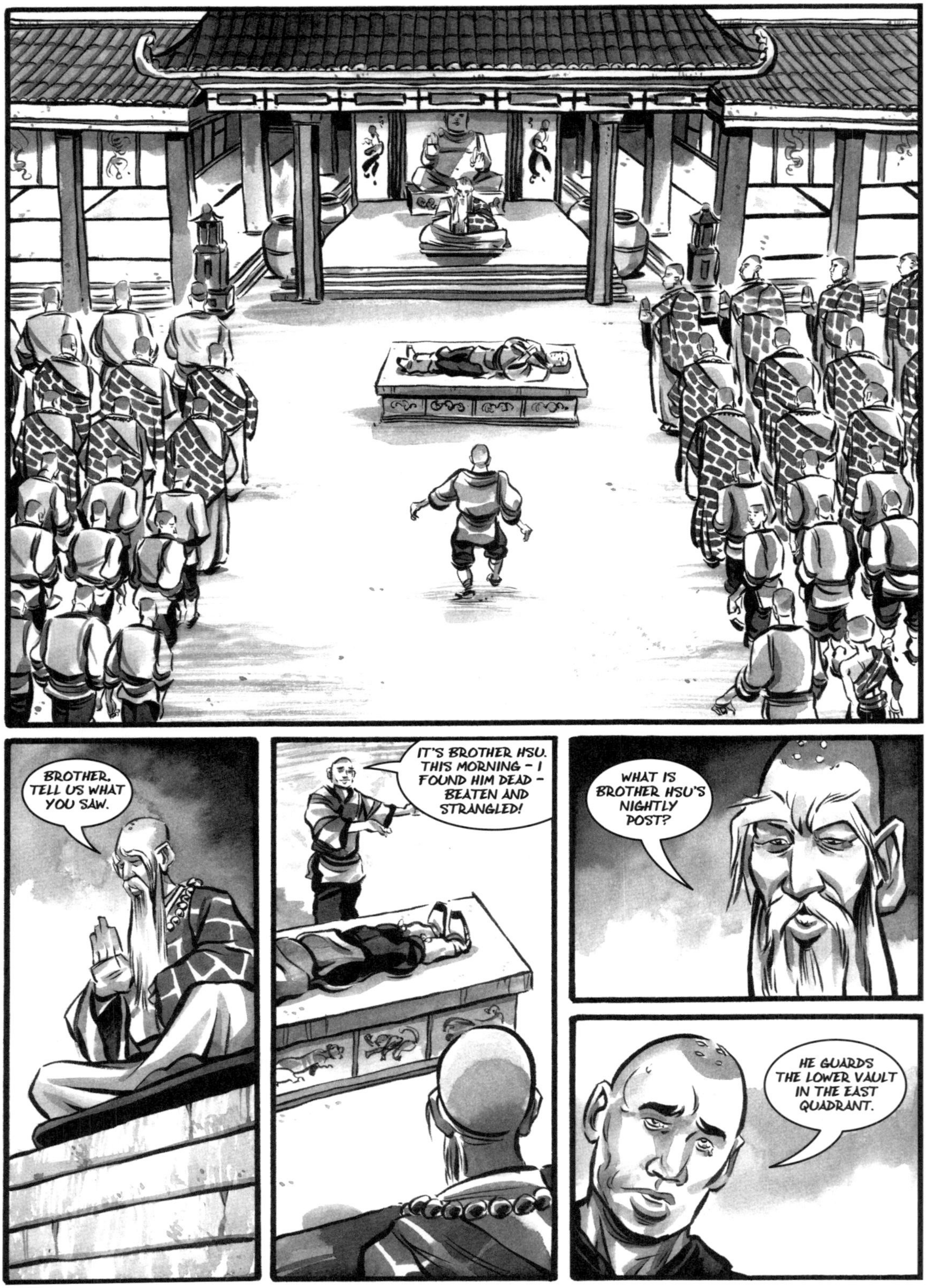
BROTHER. TELL US WHAT YOU SAW.
IT'S BROTHER HSU. THIS MORNING - I FOUND HIM DEAD - BEATEN AND STRANGLED!
WHAT IS BROTHER HSU'S NIGHTLY POST?
HE GUARDS THE LOWER VAULT IN THE EAST QUADRANT.

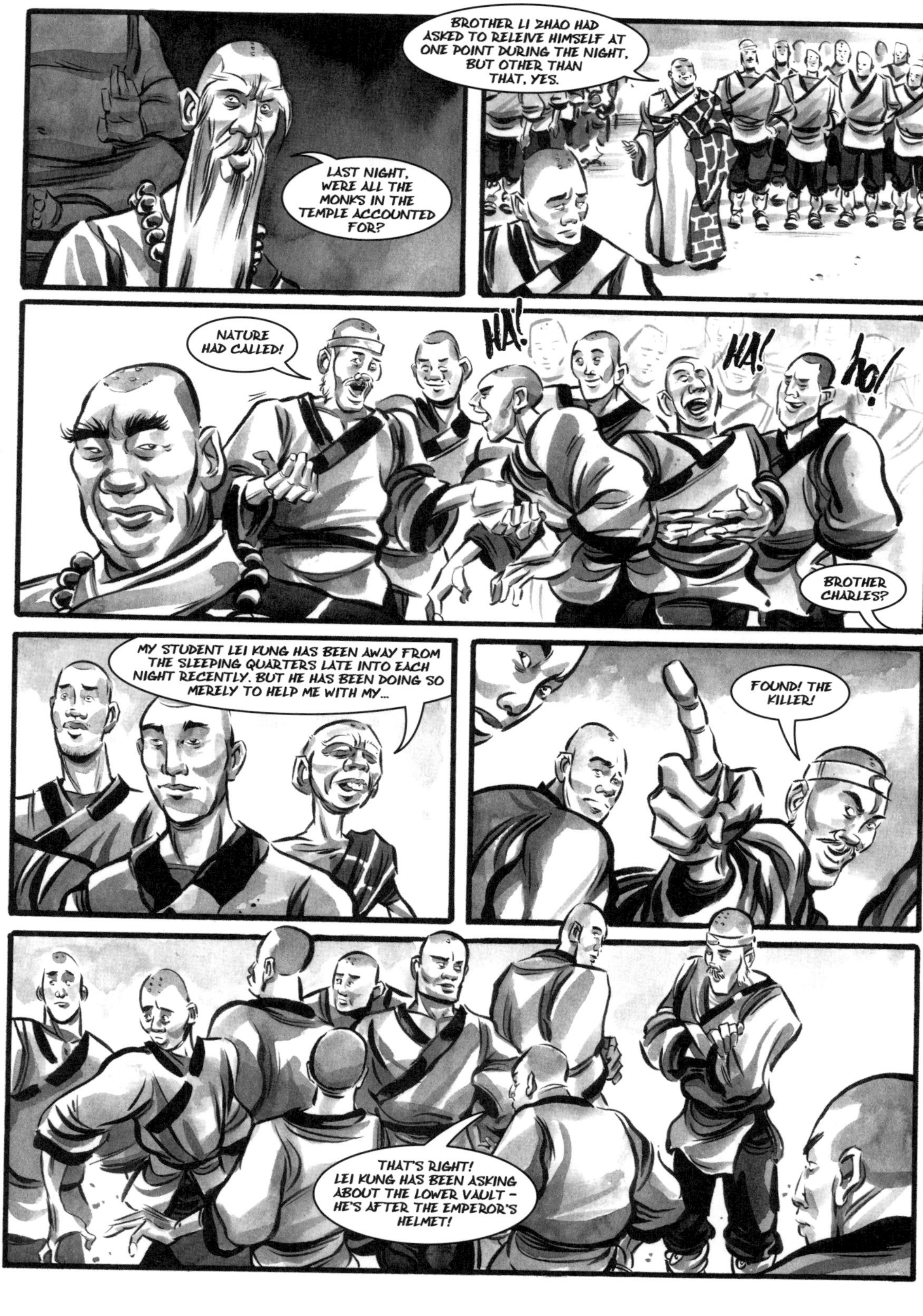
LAST NIGHT, WERE ALL THE MONKS IN THE TEMPLE ACCOUNTED FOR?
BROTHER LI ZHAO HAD ASKED TO RELEIVE HIMSELF AT ONE POINT DURING THE NIGHT, BUT OTHER THAN THAT, YES.
NATURE HAD CALLED!
HA!
HA!
ho!
BROTHER CHARLES?
MY STUDENT LEI KUNG HAS BEEN AWAY FROM THE SLEEPING QUARTERS LATE INTO EACH NIGHT RECENTLY. BUT HE HAS BEEN DOING SO MERELY TO HELP ME WITH MY...
FOUND! THE KILLER!
THAT'S RIGHT! LEI KUNG HAS BEEN ASKING ABOUT THE LOWER VAULT – HE'S AFTER THE EMPEROR'S HELMET!

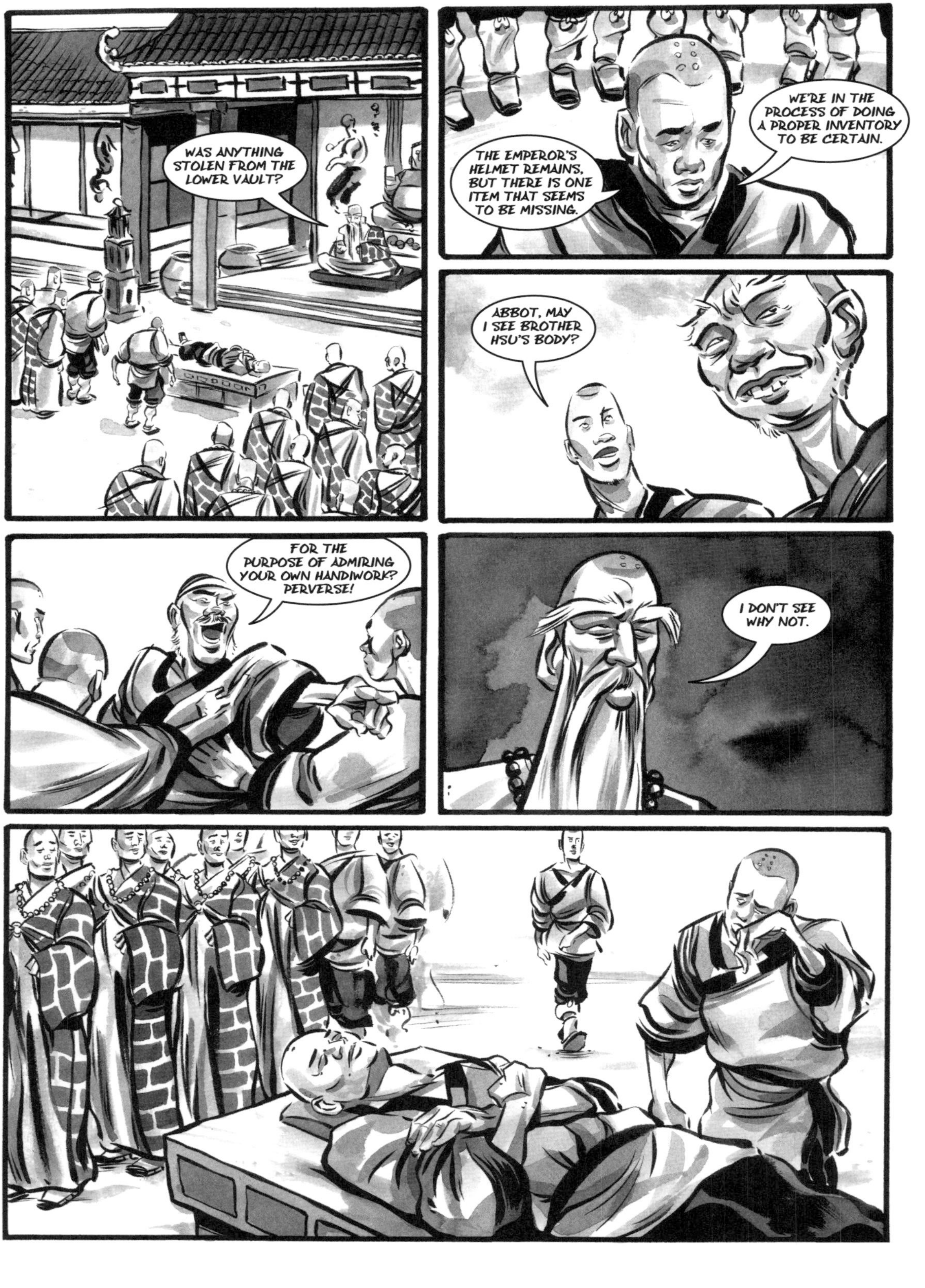
WAS ANYTHING STOLEN FROM THE LOWER VAULT?
THE EMPEROR'S HELMET REMAINS, BUT THERE IS ONE ITEM THAT SEEMS TO BE MISSING.
WE'RE IN THE PROCESS OF DOING A PROPER INVENTORY TO BE CERTAIN.
ABBOT, MAY I SEE BROTHER HSU'S BODY?
FOR THE PURPOSE OF ADMIRING YOUR OWN HANDIWORK? PERVERSE!
I DON'T SEE WHY NOT.

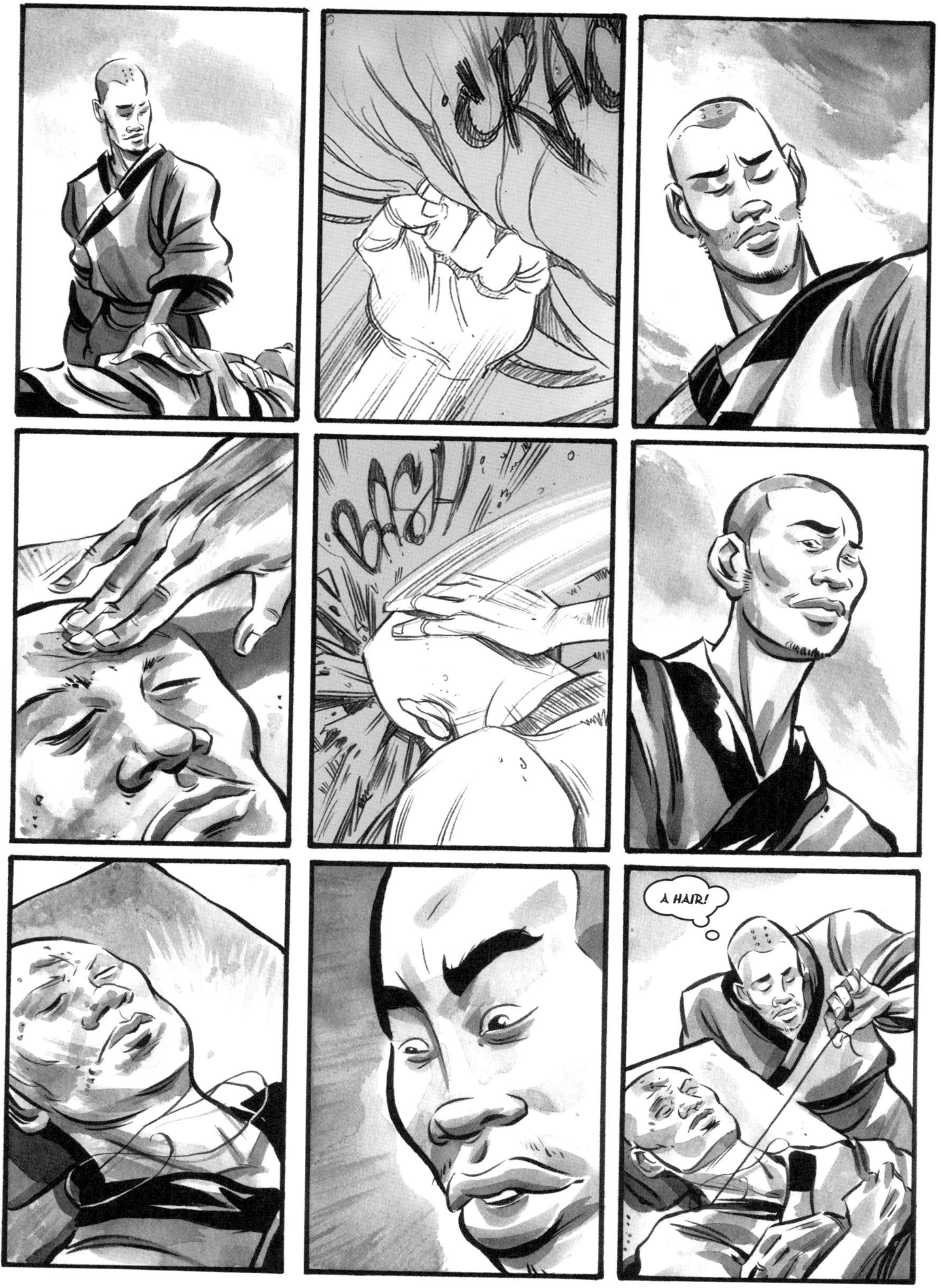
CRAC
BASH
A HAIR!

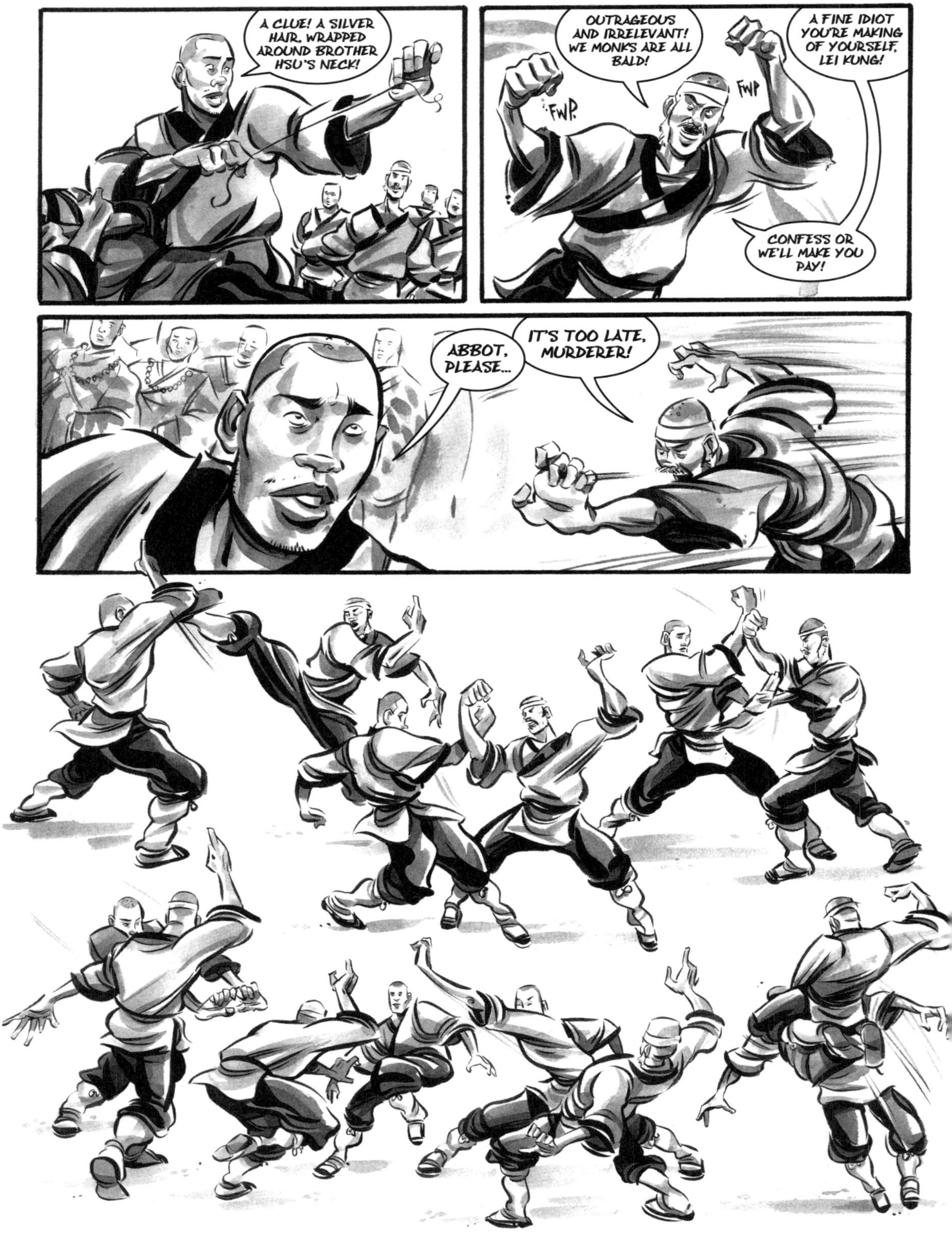
A CLUE! A SILVER HAIR, WRAPPED AROUND BROTHER HSU'S NECK!
OUTRAGEOUS AND IRRELEVANT! WE MONKS ARE ALL BALD!
FWP.
FWP
A FINE IDIOT YOU'RE MAKING OF YOURSELF, LEI KUNG!
CONFESS OR WE'LL MAKE YOU PAY!
ABBOT, PLEASE...
IT'S TOO LATE, MURDERER!

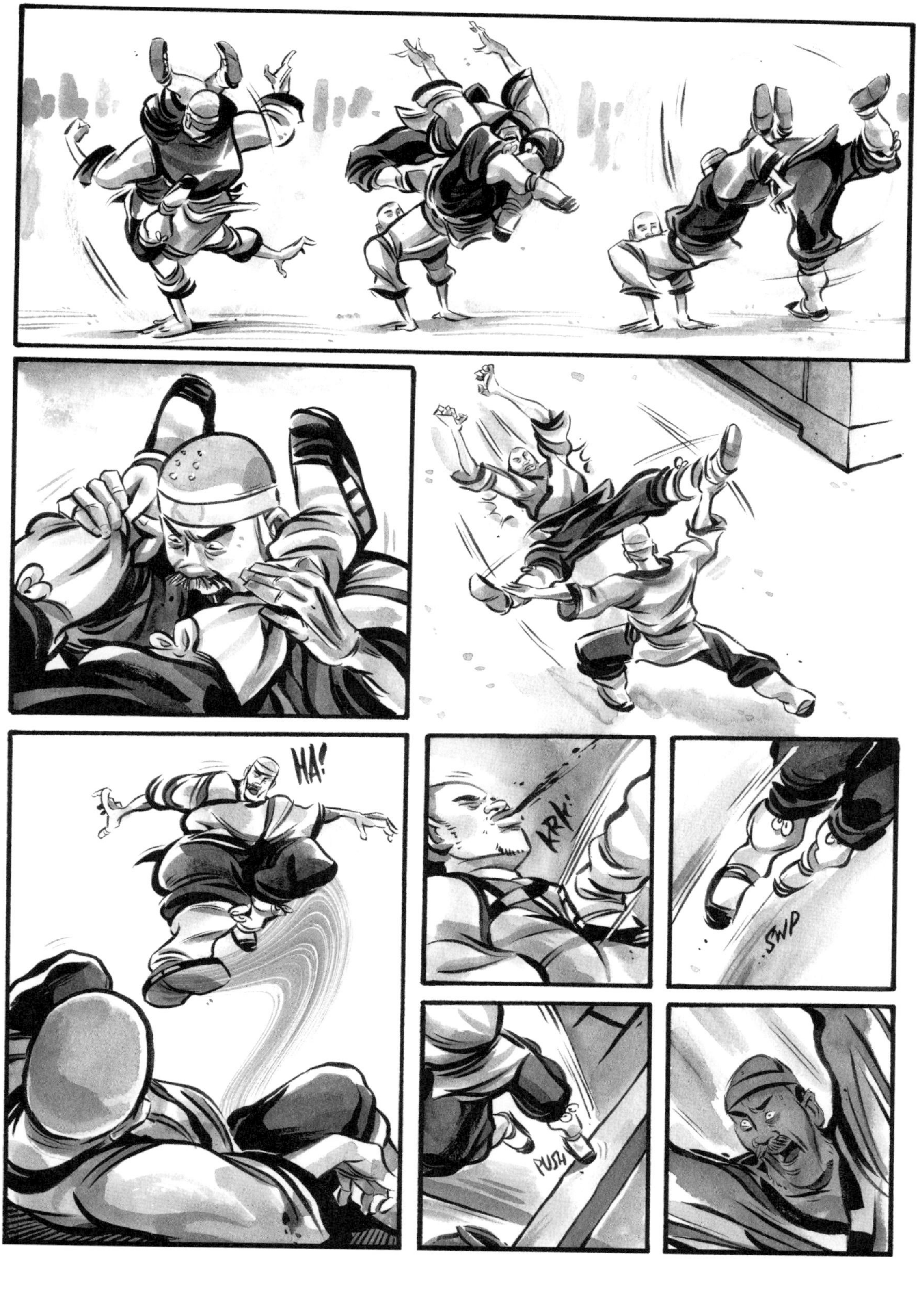
HA!
KRK!
SWP
PUSH

BOOM

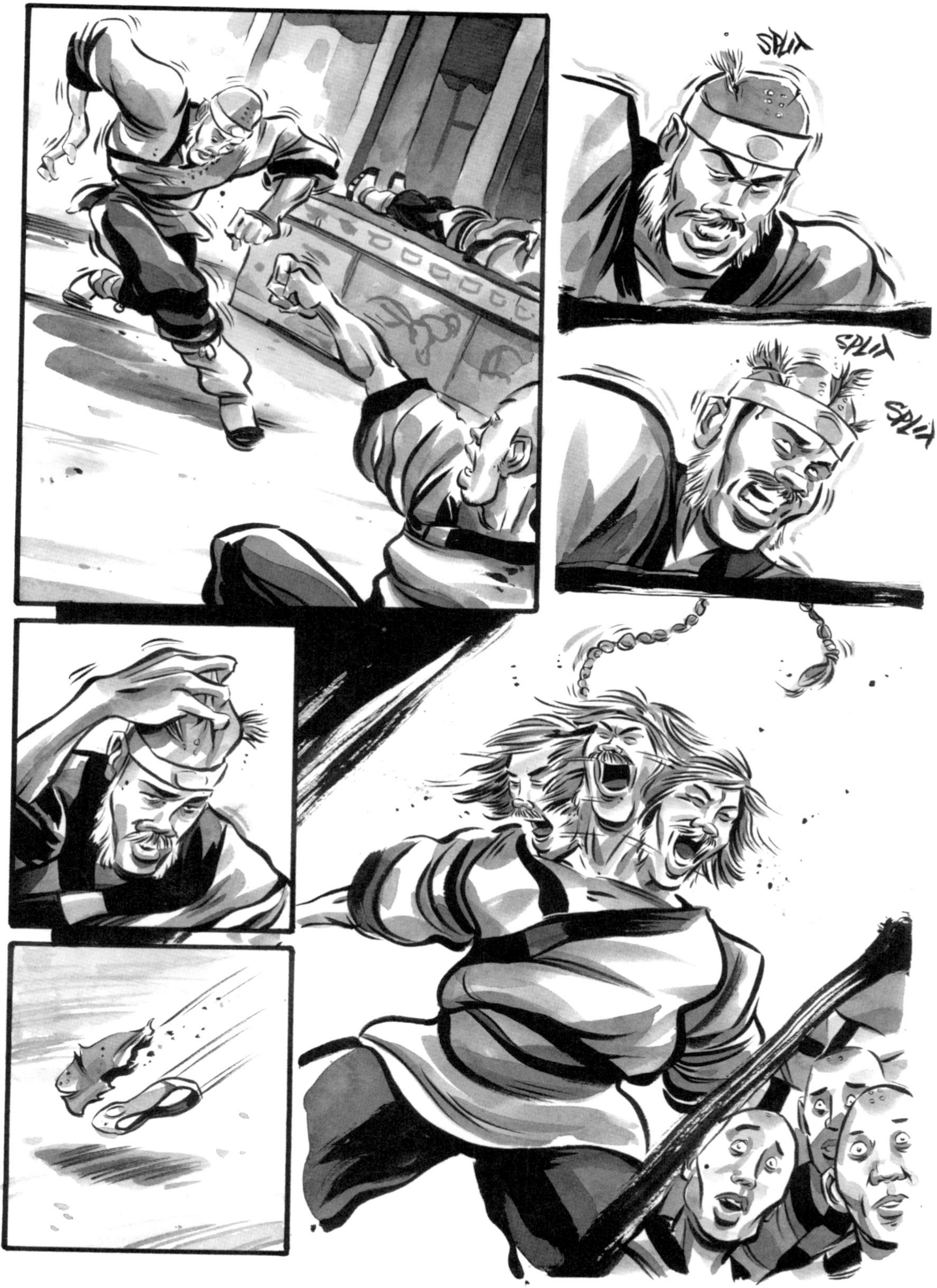
SPLIT
SPLIT
SPLIT

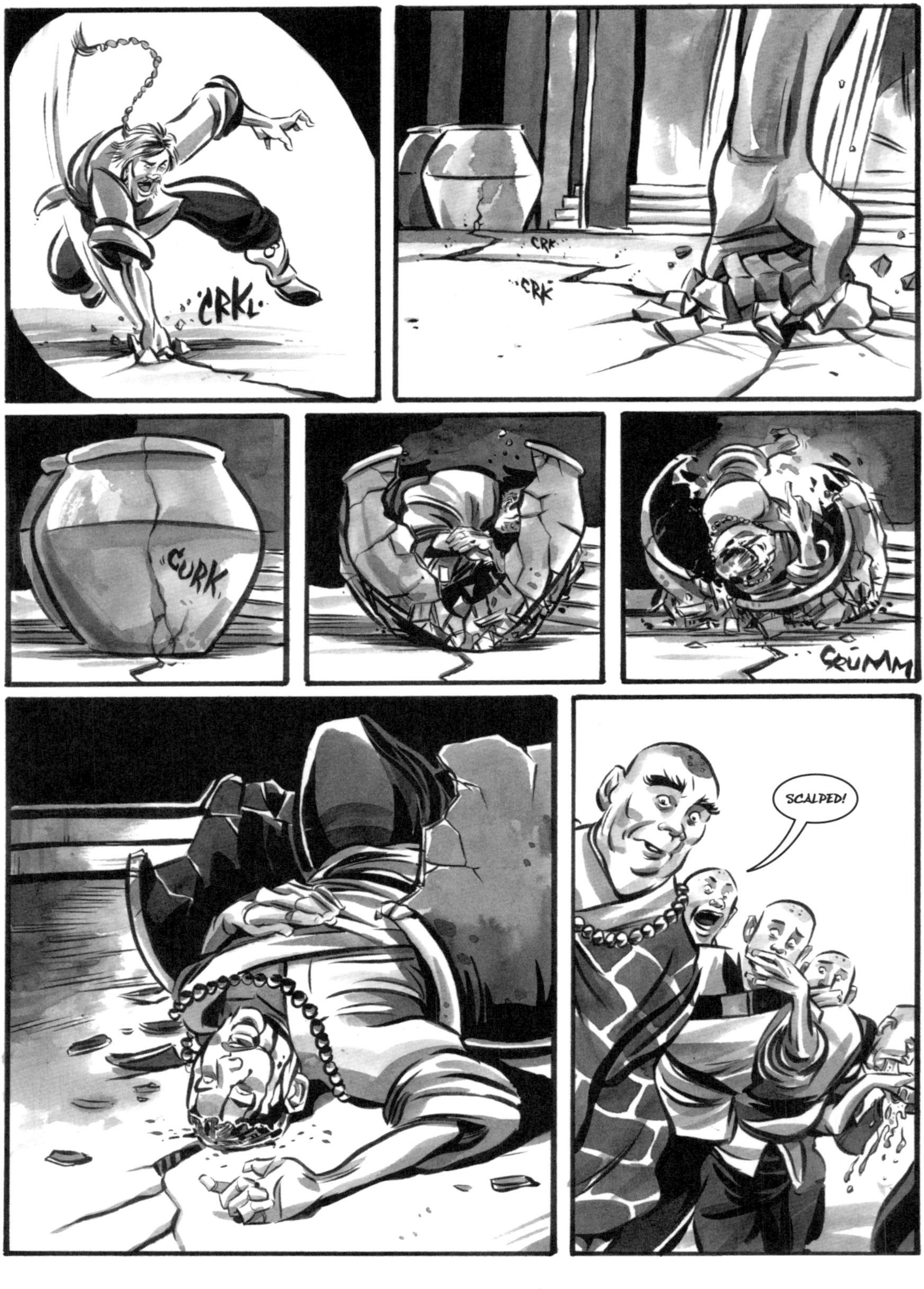
CRKL
CRK
CRK
CURK
CRUMM
SCALPED!

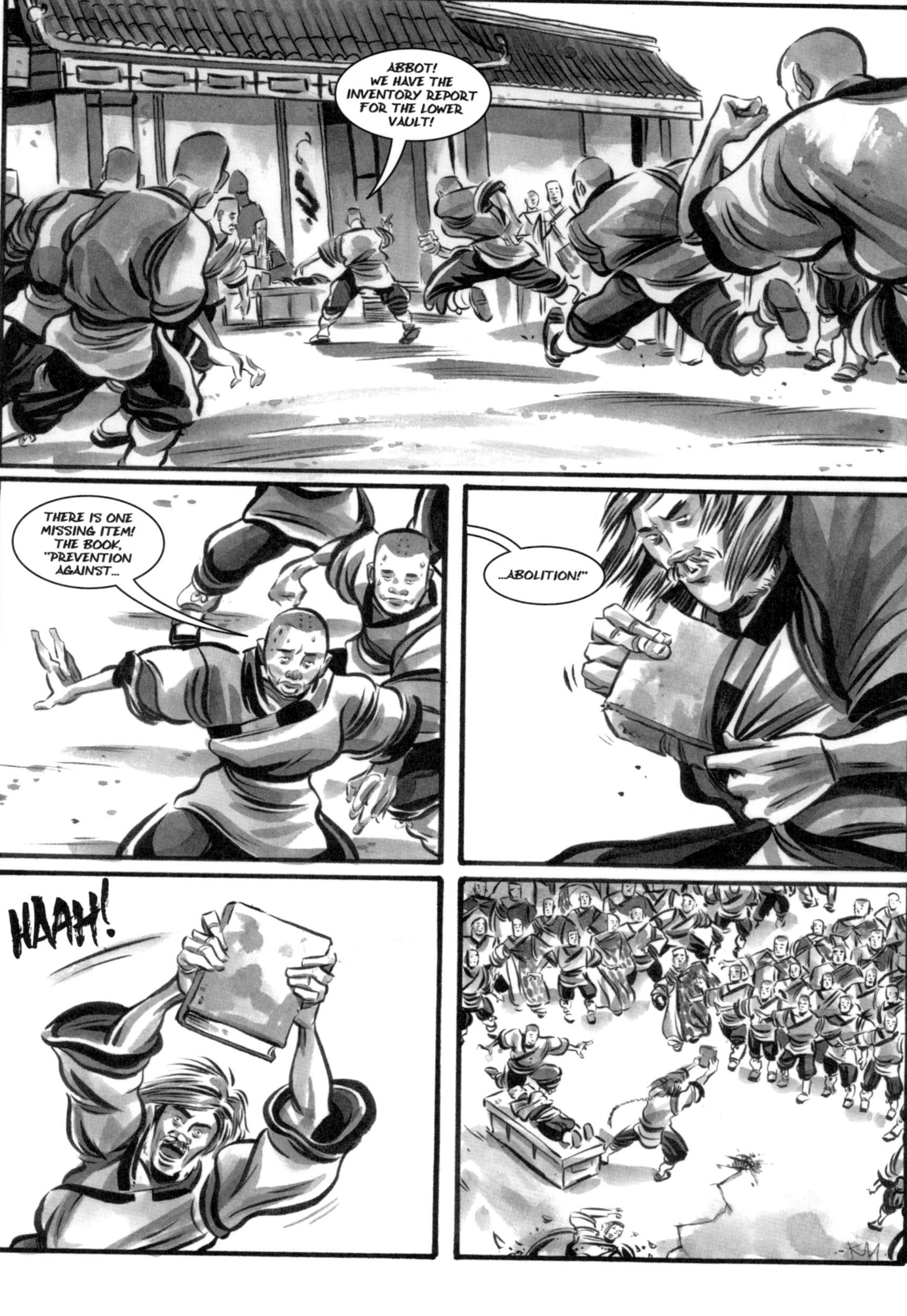
ABBOT! WE HAVE THE INVENTORY REPORT FOR THE LOWER VAULT!
THERE IS ONE MISSING ITEM! THE BOOK, "PREVENTION AGAINST...
...ABOLITION!"
HAAH!

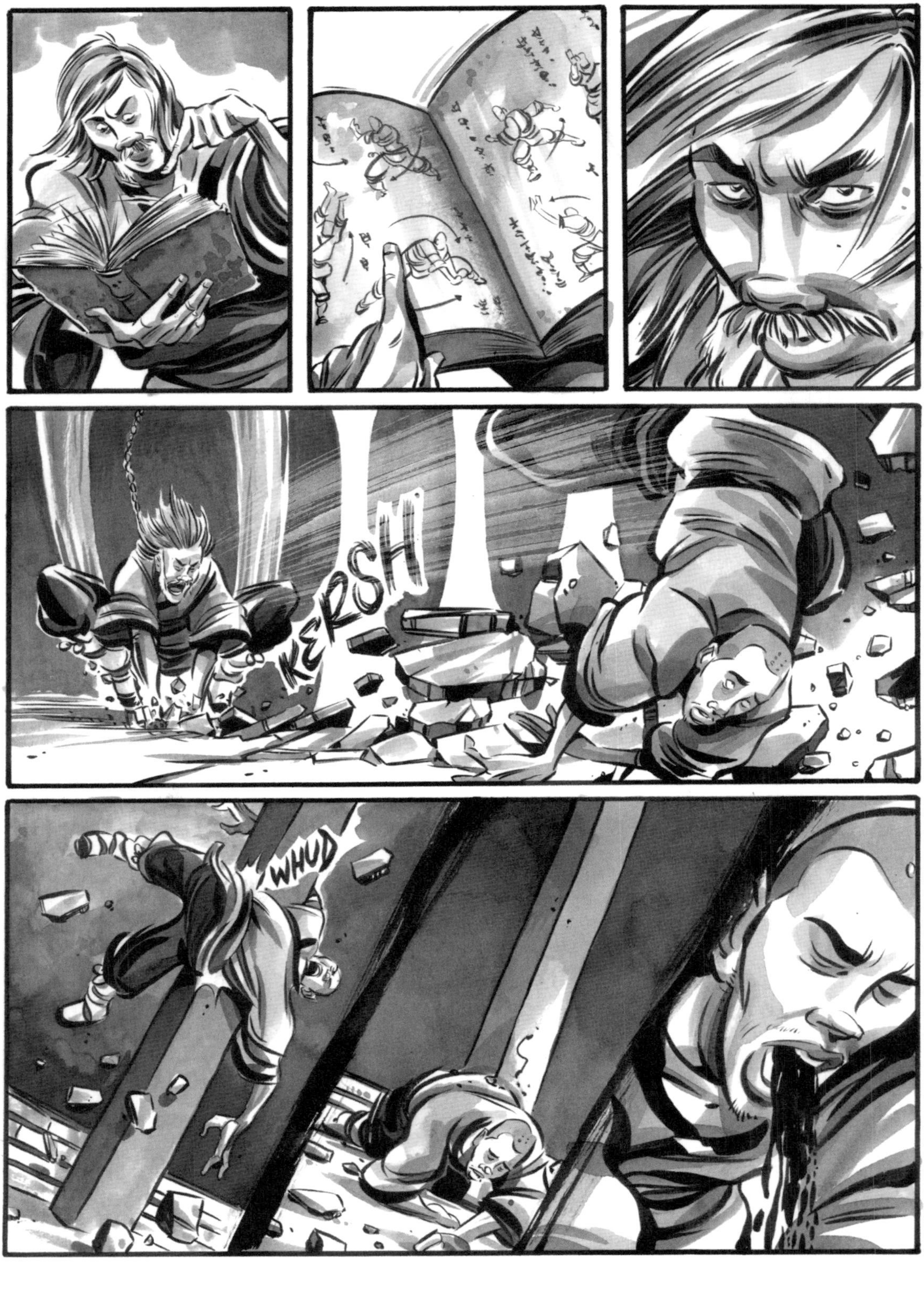
KERSH
WHUD

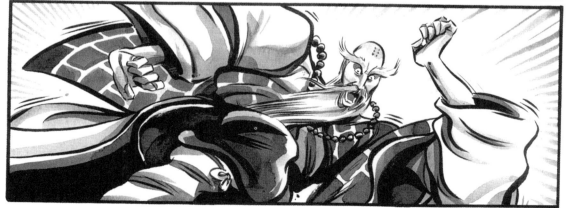

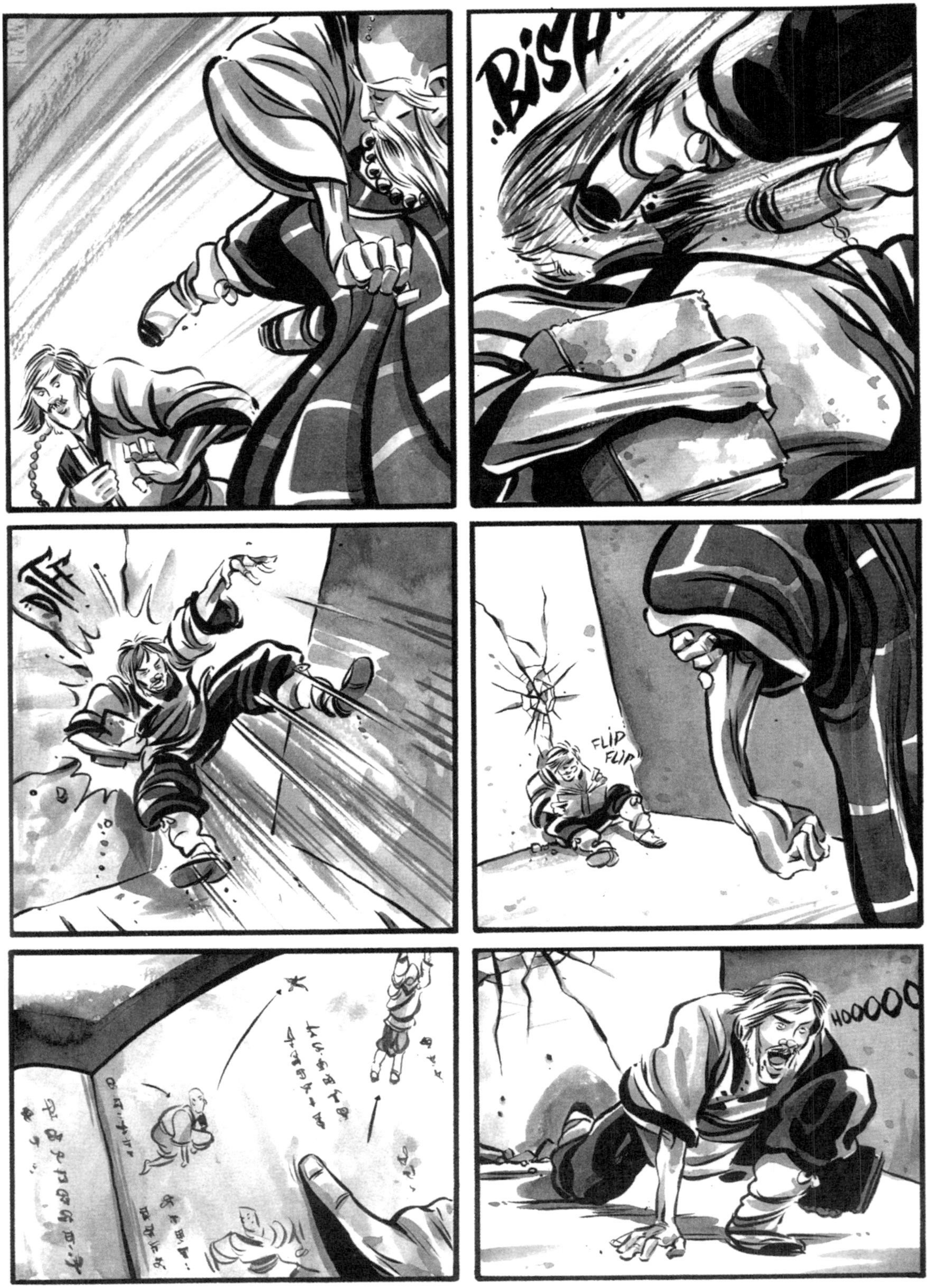
BISH
DIFF
FLIP
FLIP
HOOOOO

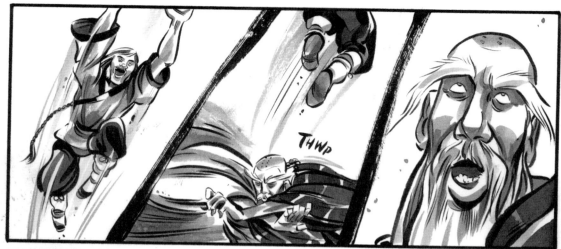

THWP

SQUACK

I...
I DON'T KNOW.

ABBOT,
WHAT ARE WE
GOING TO DO?

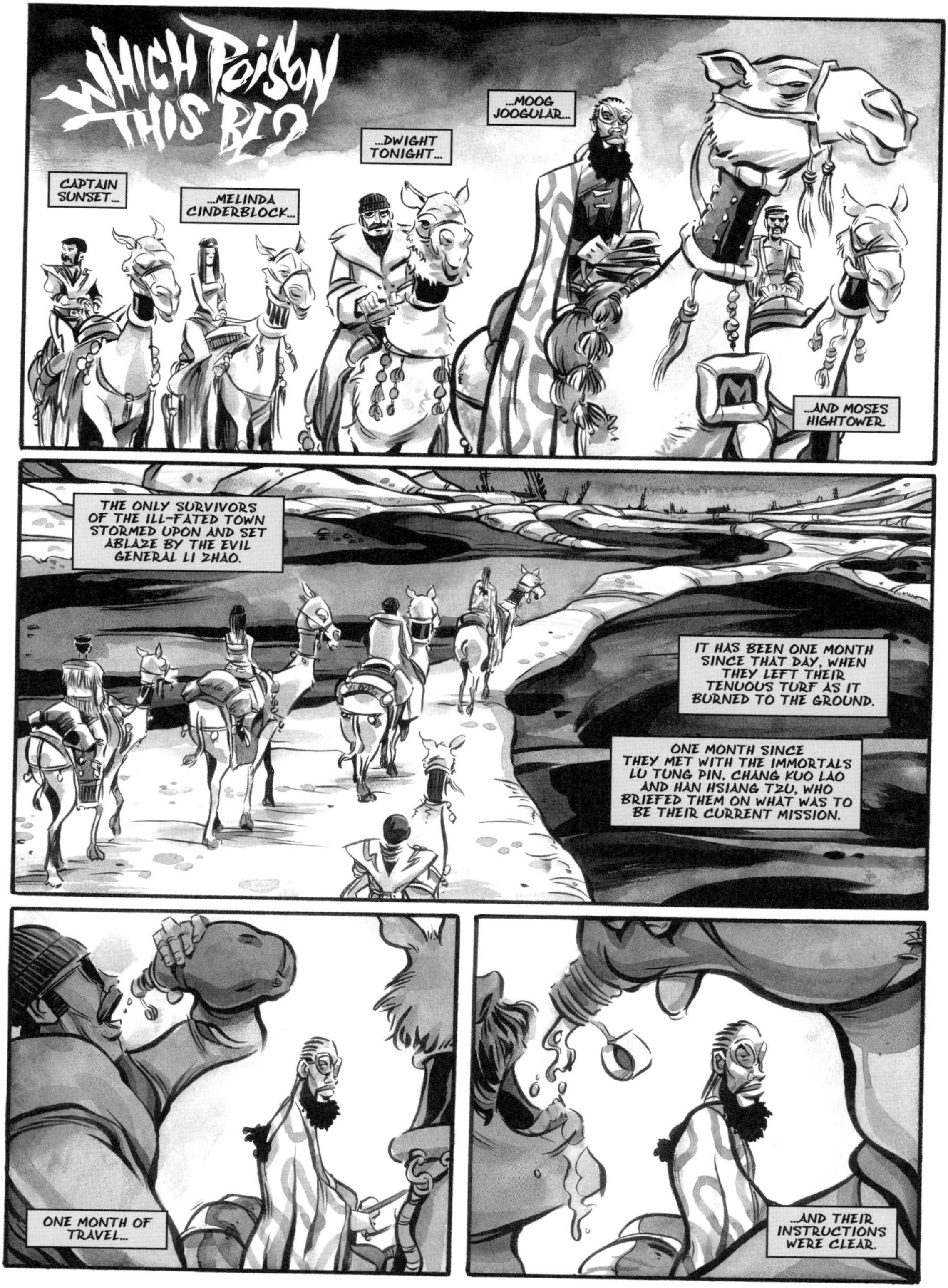
WHICH POISON THIS BE?
CAPTAIN SUNSET...
...MELINDA CINDERBLOCK...
...DWIGHT TONIGHT...
...MOOG JOOGULAR...
...AND MOSES HIGHTOWER
THE ONLY SURVIVORS OF THE ILL-FATED TOWN STORMED UPON AND SET ABLAZE BY THE EVIL GENERAL LI ZHAO.
IT HAS BEEN ONE MONTH SINCE THAT DAY, WHEN THEY LEFT THEIR TENUOUS TURF AS IT BURNED TO THE GROUND.
ONE MONTH SINCE THEY MET WITH THE IMMORTALS LU TUNG PIN, CHANG KUO LAO AND HAN HSIANG TZU, WHO BRIEFED THEM ON WHAT WAS TO BE THEIR CURRENT MISSION.
ONE MONTH OF TRAVEL...
...AND THEIR INSTRUCTIONS WERE CLEAR.

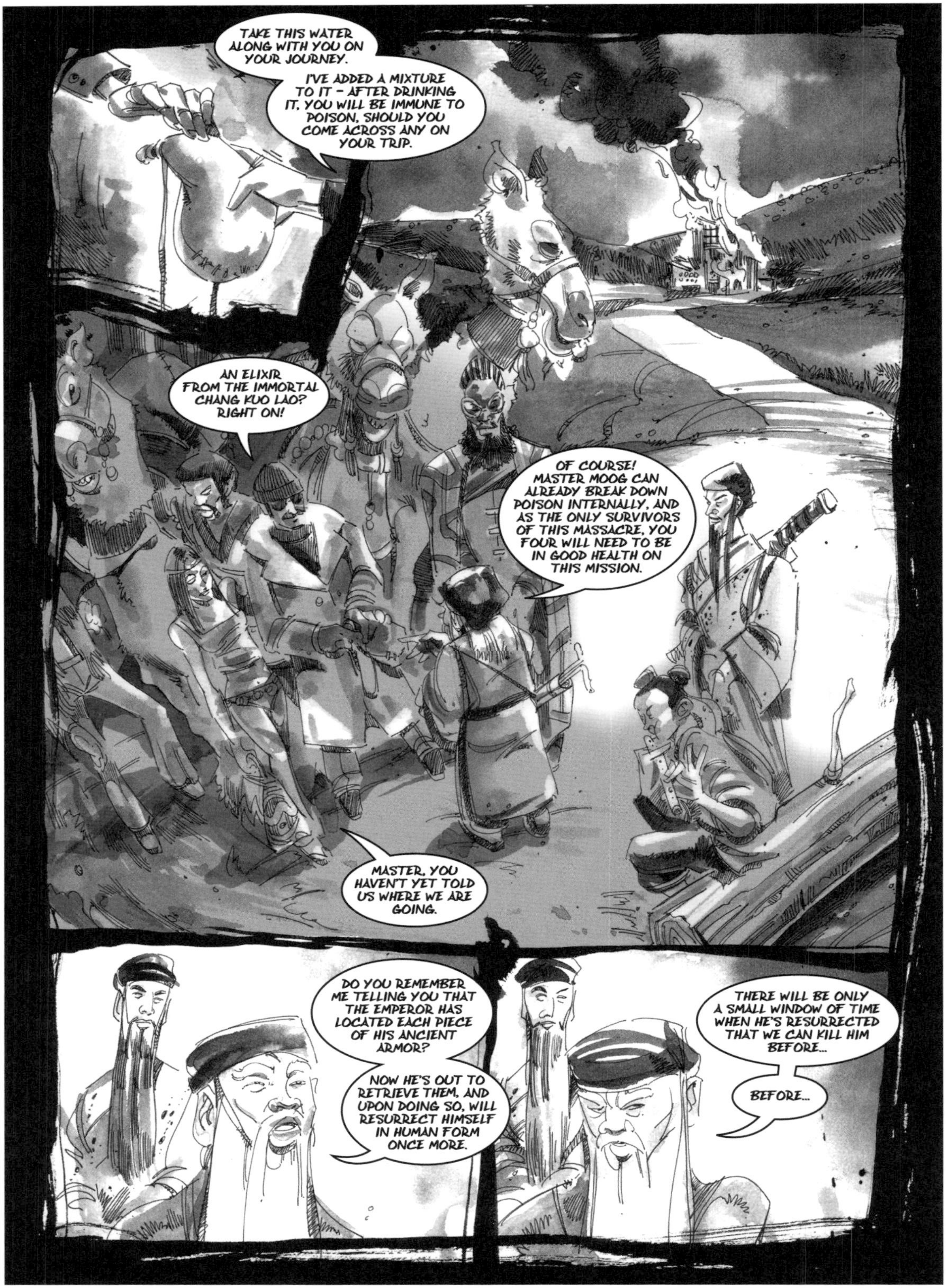
TAKE THIS WATER ALONG WITH YOU ON YOUR JOURNEY.
I'VE ADDED A MIXTURE TO IT - AFTER DRINKING IT, YOU WILL BE IMMUNE TO POISON, SHOULD YOU COME ACROSS ANY ON YOUR TRIP.
AN ELIXIR FROM THE IMMORTAL CHANG KUO LAO? RIGHT ON!
OF COURSE! MASTER MOOG CAN ALREADY BREAK DOWN POISON INTERNALLY, AND AS THE ONLY SURVIVORS OF THIS MASSACRE, YOU FOUR WILL NEED TO BE IN GOOD HEALTH ON THIS MISSION.
MASTER, YOU HAVEN'T YET TOLD US WHERE WE ARE GOING.
DO YOU REMEMBER ME TELLING YOU THAT THE EMPEROR HAS LOCATED EACH PIECE OF HIS ANCIENT ARMOR?
NOW HE'S OUT TO RETRIEVE THEM, AND UPON DOING SO, WILL RESURRECT HIMSELF IN HUMAN FORM ONCE MORE.
THERE WILL BE ONLY A SMALL WINDOW OF TIME WHEN HE'S RESURRECTED THAT WE CAN KILL HIM BEFORE...
BEFORE...

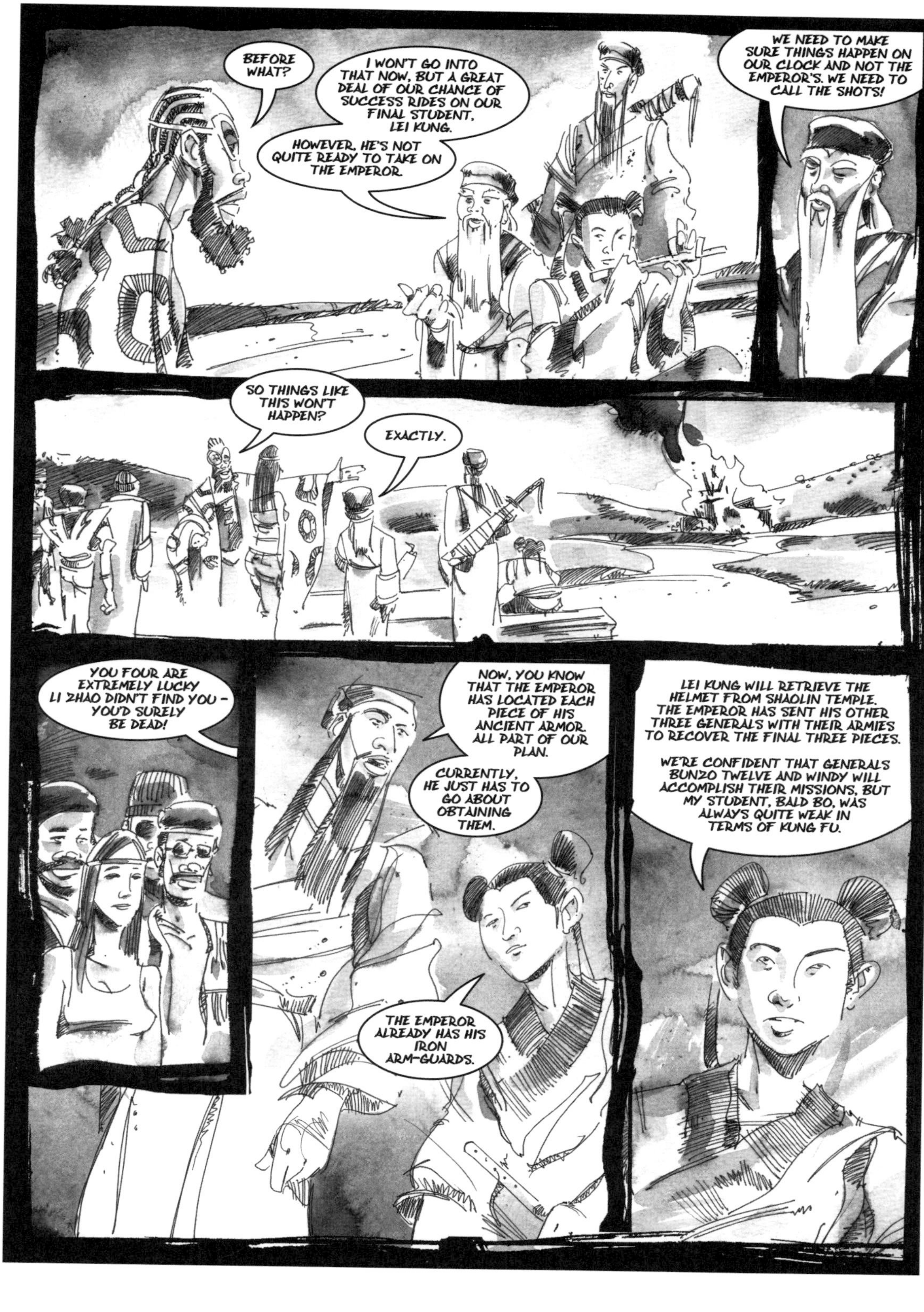
BEFORE WHAT?
I WON'T GO INTO THAT NOW, BUT A GREAT DEAL OF OUR CHANCE OF SUCCESS RIDES ON OUR FINAL STUDENT, LEI KUNG.
HOWEVER, HE'S NOT QUITE READY TO TAKE ON THE EMPEROR.
WE NEED TO MAKE SURE THINGS HAPPEN ON OUR CLOCK AND NOT THE EMPEROR'S. WE NEED TO CALL THE SHOTS!
SO THINGS LIKE THIS WON'T HAPPEN?
EXACTLY.
YOU FOUR ARE EXTREMELY LUCKY LI ZHAO DIDN'T FIND YOU - YOU'D SURELY BE DEAD!
NOW, YOU KNOW THAT THE EMPEROR HAS LOCATED EACH PIECE OF HIS ANCIENT ARMOR. ALL PART OF OUR PLAN.
CURRENTLY, HE JUST HAS TO GO ABOUT OBTAINING THEM.
THE EMPEROR ALREADY HAS HIS IRON ARM-GUARDS.
LEI KUNG WILL RETRIEVE THE HELMET FROM SHAOLIN TEMPLE. THE EMPEROR HAS SENT HIS OTHER THREE GENERALS WITH THEIR ARMIES TO RECOVER THE FINAL THREE PIECES.
WE'RE CONFIDENT THAT GENERALS BUNZO TWELVE AND WINDY WILL ACCOMPLISH THEIR MISSIONS, BUT MY STUDENT, BALD BO, WAS ALWAYS QUITE WEAK IN TERMS OF KUNG FU.

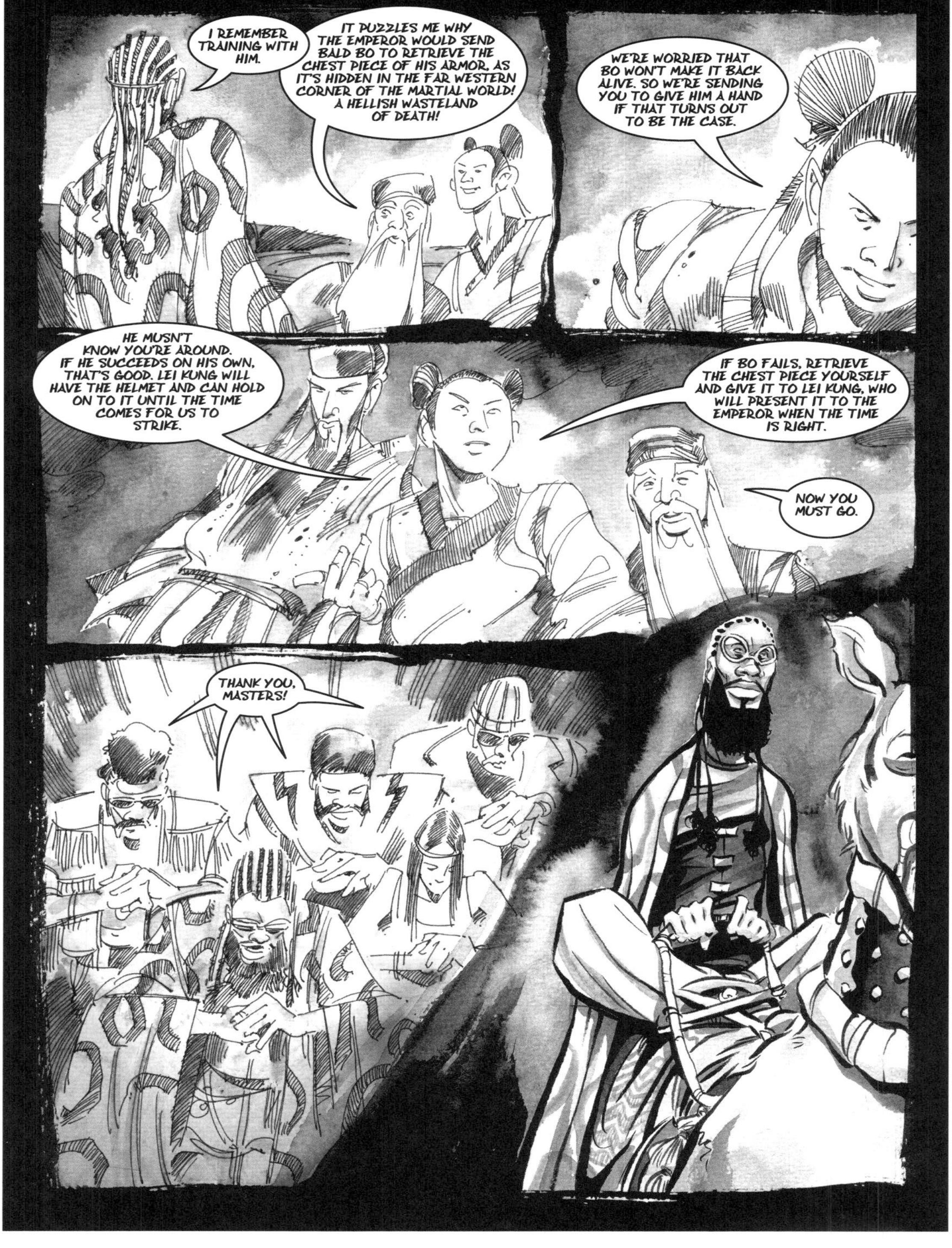
I REMEMBER TRAINING WITH HIM.
IT PUZZLES ME WHY THE EMPEROR WOULD SEND BALD BO TO RETRIEVE THE CHEST PIECE OF HIS ARMOR, AS IT'S HIDDEN IN THE FAR WESTERN CORNER OF THE MARTIAL WORLD! A HELLISH WASTELAND OF DEATH!
WE'RE WORRIED THAT BO WON'T MAKE IT BACK ALIVE. SO WE'RE SENDING YOU TO GIVE HIM A HAND IF THAT TURNS OUT TO BE THE CASE.
HE MUSN'T KNOW YOU'RE AROUND. IF HE SUCCEEDS ON HIS OWN, THAT'S GOOD. LEI KUNG WILL HAVE THE HELMET AND CAN HOLD ON TO IT UNTIL THE TIME COMES FOR US TO STRIKE.
IF BO FAILS, RETRIEVE THE CHEST PIECE YOURSELF AND GIVE IT TO LEI KUNG, WHO WILL PRESENT IT TO THE EMPEROR WHEN THE TIME IS RIGHT.
NOW YOU MUST GO.
THANK YOU, MASTERS!

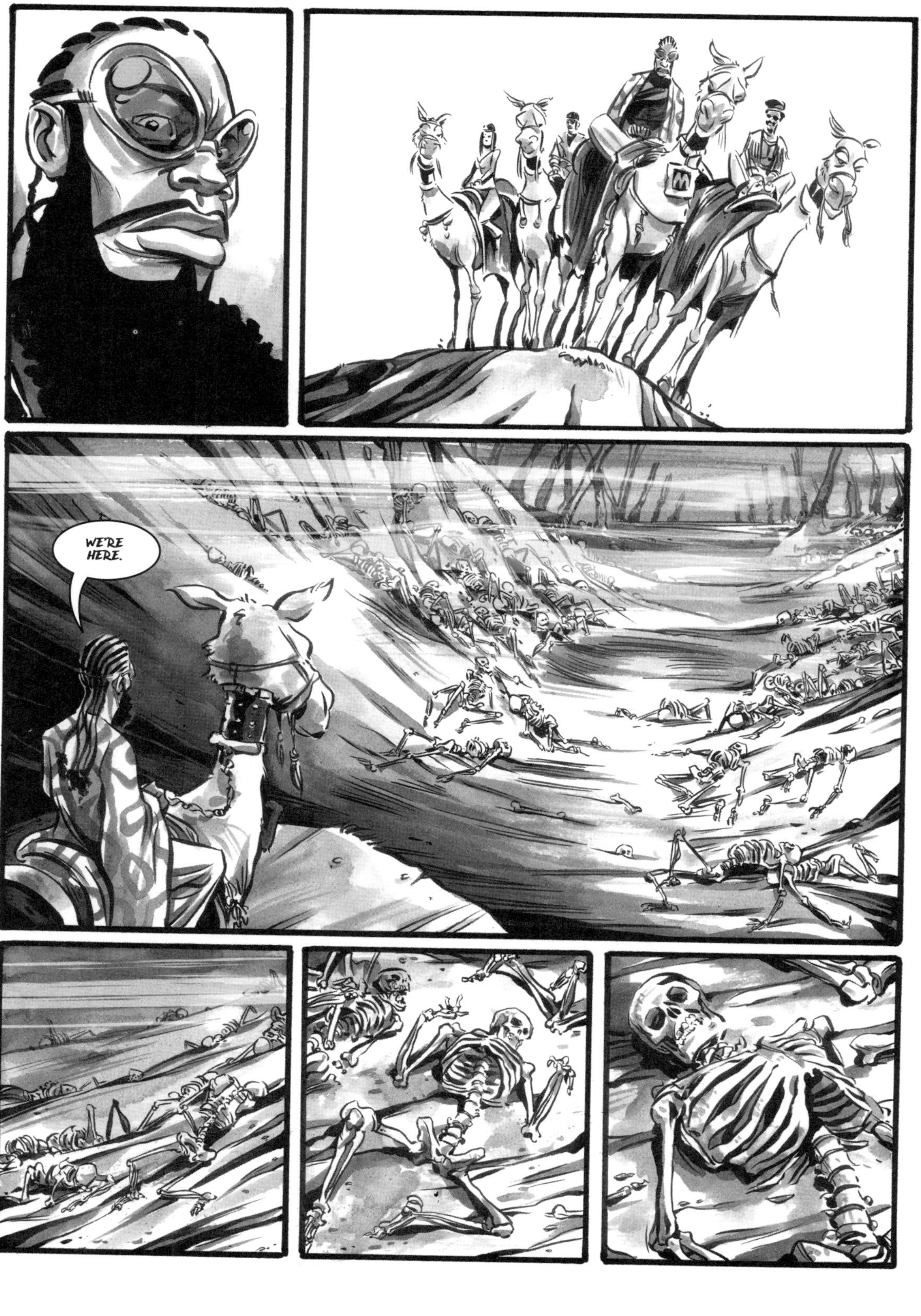
WE'RE HERE.

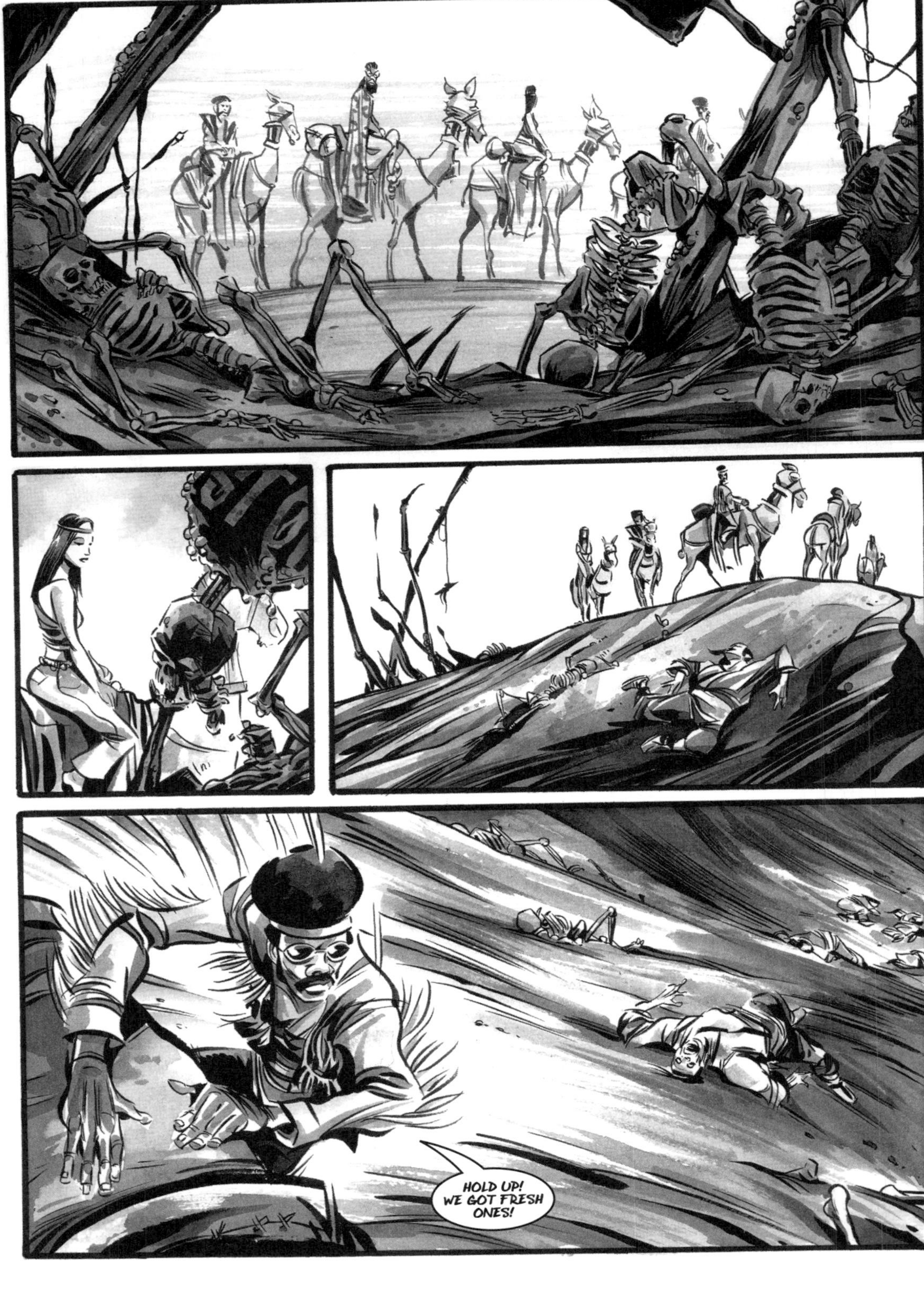
HOLD UP! WE GOT FRESH ONES!

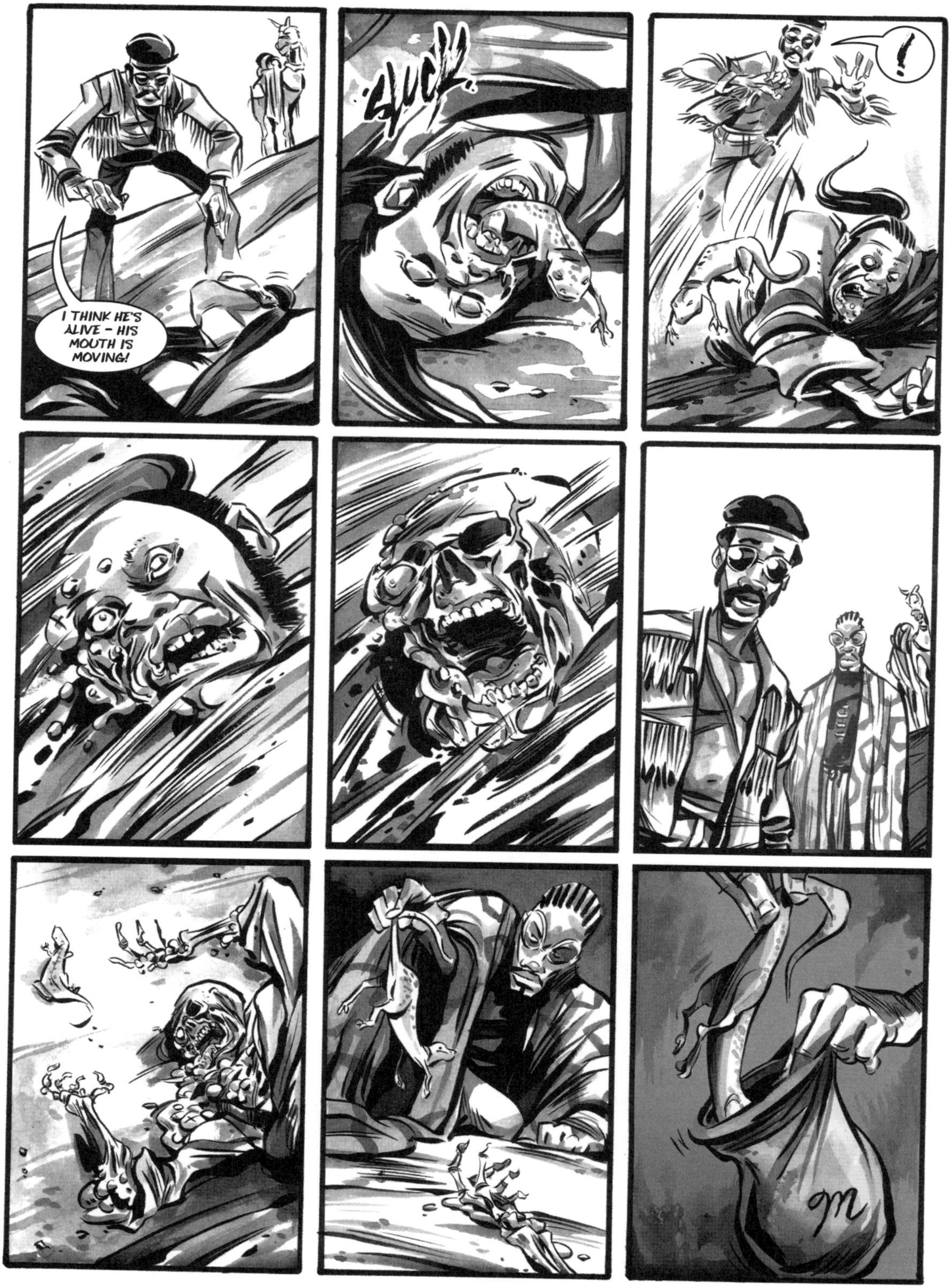
I THINK HE'S ALIVE - HIS MOUTH IS MOVING!
SLUCK!
!

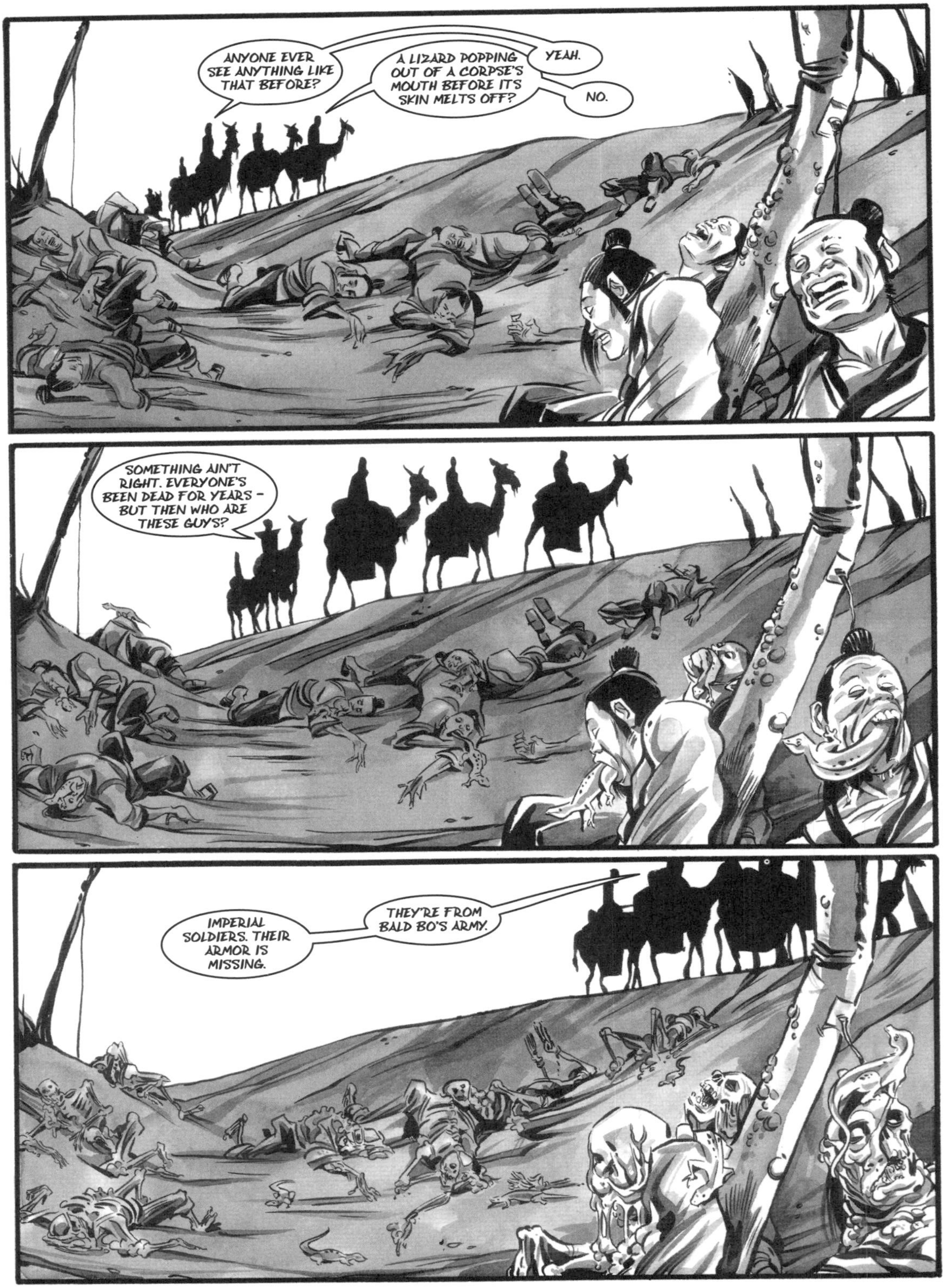
ANYONE EVER SEE ANYTHING LIKE THAT BEFORE?
YEAH.
A LIZARD POPPING OUT OF A CORPSE'S MOUTH BEFORE ITS SKIN MELTS OFF?
NO.
SOMETHING AIN'T RIGHT. EVERYONE'S BEEN DEAD FOR YEARS - BUT THEN WHO ARE THESE GUYS?
IMPERIAL SOLDIERS. THEIR ARMOR IS MISSING.
THEY'RE FROM BALD BO'S ARMY.

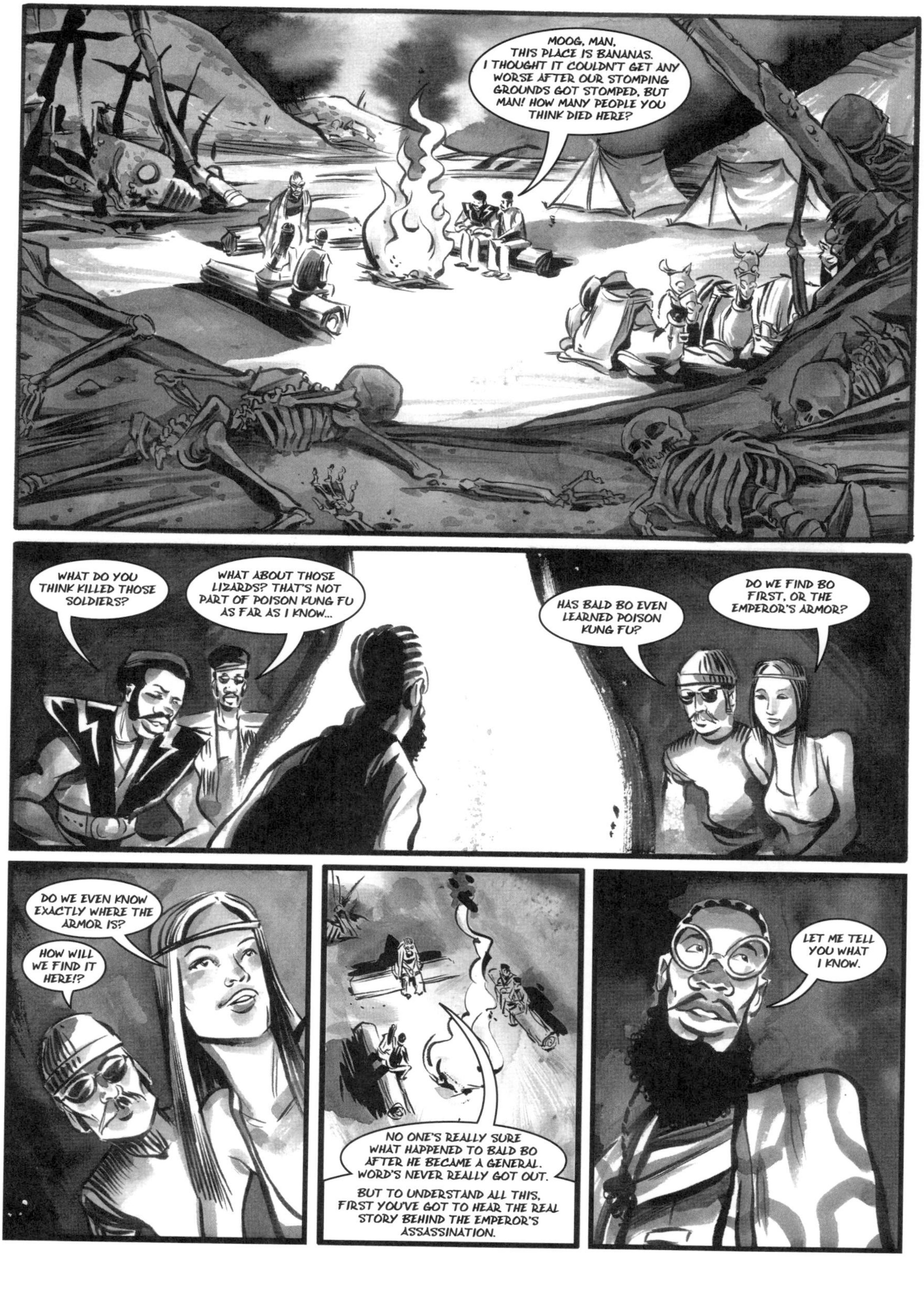
MOOG, MAN, THIS PLACE IS BANANAS. I THOUGHT IT COULDN'T GET ANY WORSE AFTER OUR STOMPING GROUNDS GOT STOMPED, BUT MAN! HOW MANY PEOPLE YOU THINK DIED HERE?
WHAT DO YOU THINK KILLED THOSE SOLDIERS?
WHAT ABOUT THOSE LIZARDS? THAT'S NOT PART OF POISON KUNG FU AS FAR AS I KNOW...
HAS BALD BO EVEN LEARNED POISON KUNG FU?
DO WE FIND BO FIRST, OR THE EMPEROR'S ARMOR?
DO WE EVEN KNOW EXACTLY WHERE THE ARMOR IS?
HOW WILL WE FIND IT HERE!?
NO ONE'S REALLY SURE WHAT HAPPENED TO BALD BO AFTER HE BECAME A GENERAL. WORD'S NEVER REALLY GOT OUT.
BUT TO UNDERSTAND ALL THIS, FIRST YOU'VE GOT TO HEAR THE REAL STORY BEHIND THE EMPEROR'S ASSASSINATION.
LET ME TELL YOU WHAT I KNOW.

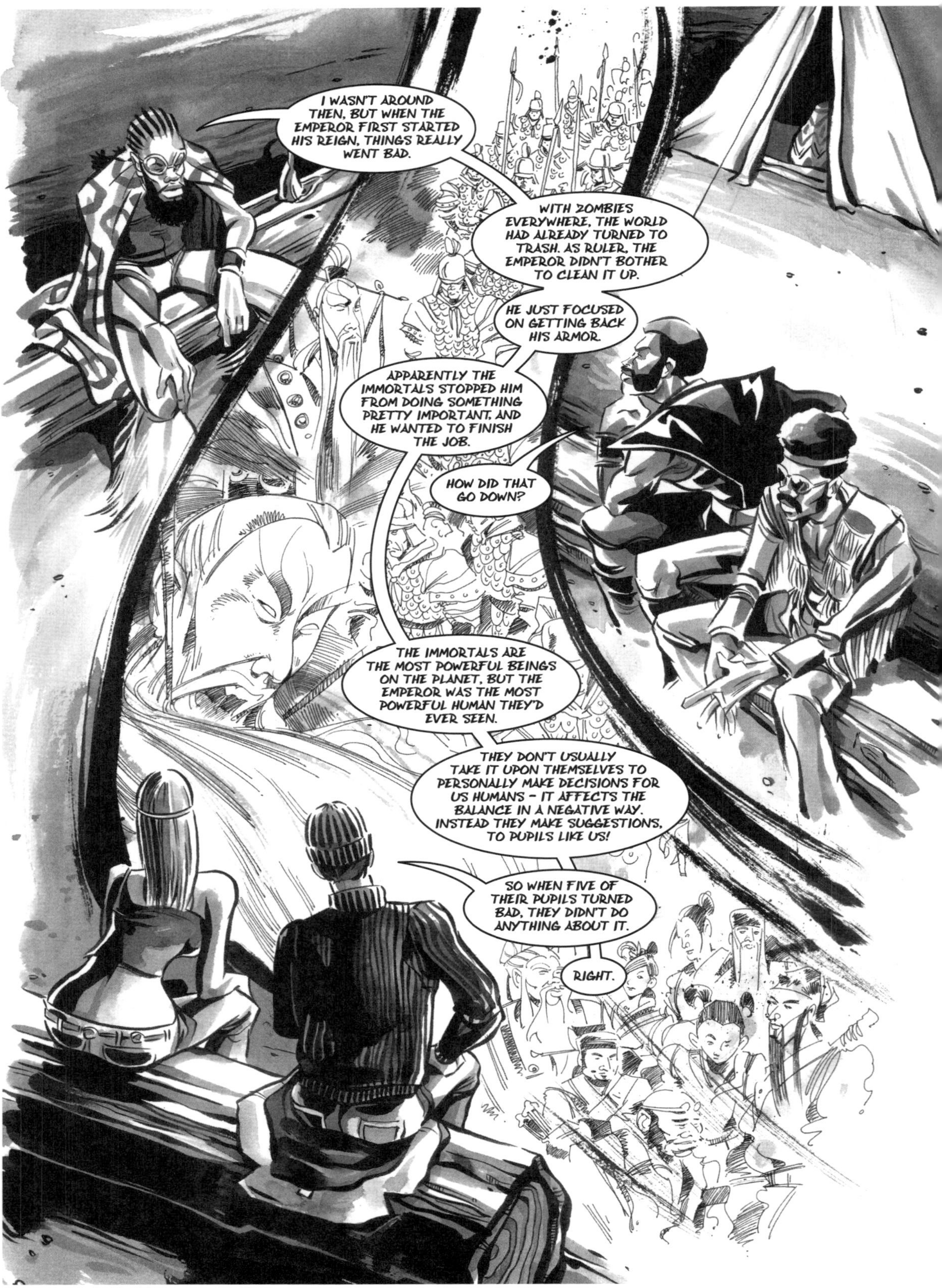
I WASN'T AROUND THEN, BUT WHEN THE EMPEROR FIRST STARTED HIS REIGN, THINGS REALLY WENT BAD.
WITH ZOMBIES EVERYWHERE, THE WORLD HAD ALREADY TURNED TO TRASH. AS RULER, THE EMPEROR DIDN'T BOTHER TO CLEAN IT UP.
HE JUST FOCUSED ON GETTING BACK HIS ARMOR.
APPARENTLY THE IMMORTALS STOPPED HIM FROM DOING SOMETHING PRETTY IMPORTANT, AND HE WANTED TO FINISH THE JOB.
HOW DID THAT GO DOWN?
THE IMMORTALS ARE THE MOST POWERFUL BEINGS ON THE PLANET, BUT THE EMPEROR WAS THE MOST POWERFUL HUMAN THEY'D EVER SEEN.
THEY DON'T USUALLY TAKE IT UPON THEMSELVES TO PERSONALLY MAKE DECISIONS FOR US HUMANS - IT AFFECTS THE BALANCE IN A NEGATIVE WAY. INSTEAD THEY MAKE SUGGESTIONS, TO PUPILS LIKE US!
SO WHEN FIVE OF THEIR PUPILS TURNED BAD, THEY DIDN'T DO ANYTHING ABOUT IT.
RIGHT.

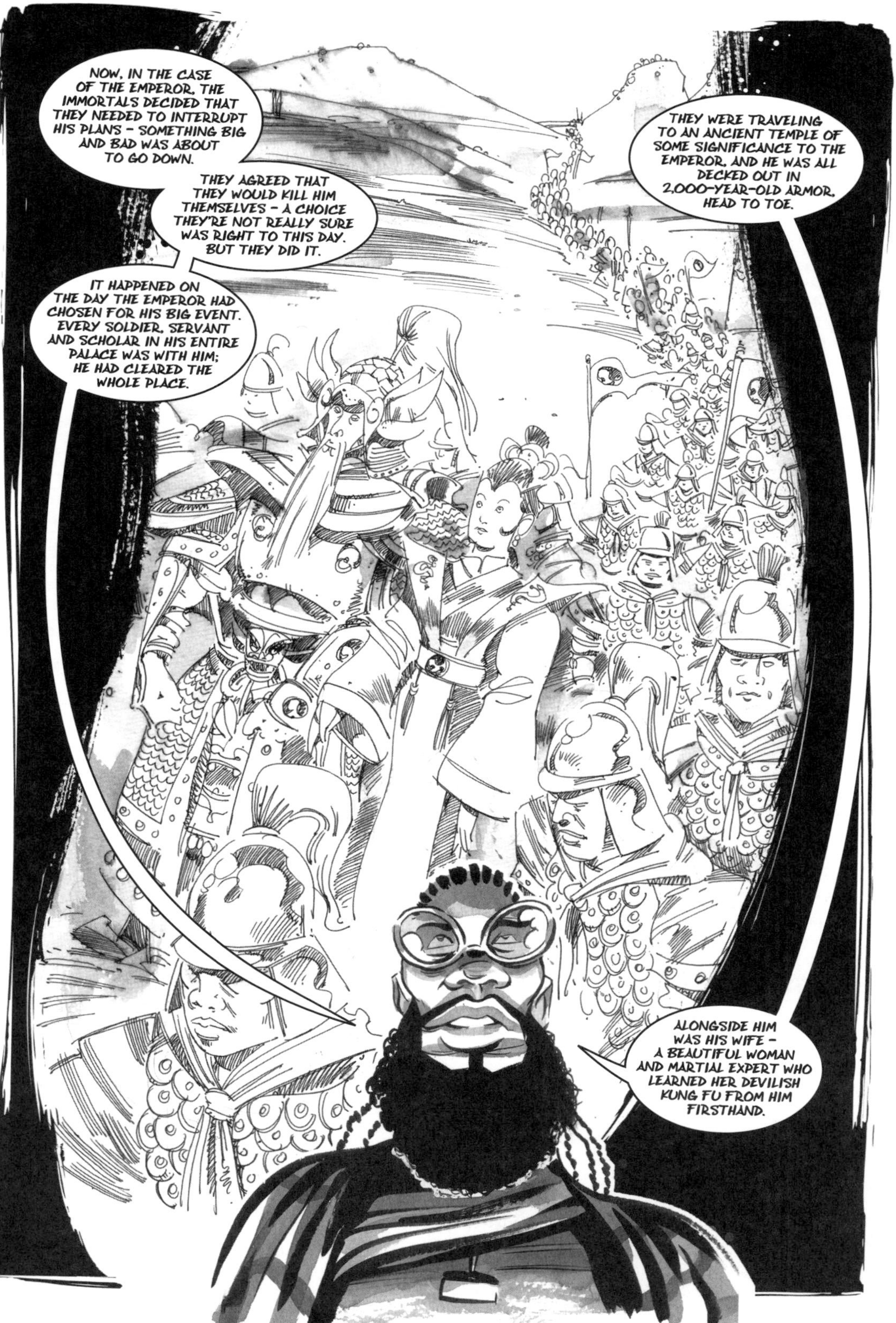
NOW, IN THE CASE OF THE EMPEROR, THE IMMORTALS DECIDED THAT THEY NEEDED TO INTERRUPT HIS PLANS - SOMETHING BIG AND BAD WAS ABOUT TO GO DOWN.
THEY AGREED THAT THEY WOULD KILL HIM THEMSELVES - A CHOICE THEY'RE NOT REALLY SURE WAS RIGHT TO THIS DAY. BUT THEY DID IT.
IT HAPPENED ON THE DAY THE EMPEROR HAD CHOSEN FOR HIS BIG EVENT. EVERY SOLDIER, SERVANT AND SCHOLAR IN HIS ENTIRE PALACE WAS WITH HIM; HE HAD CLEARED THE WHOLE PLACE.
THEY WERE TRAVELING TO AN ANCIENT TEMPLE OF SOME SIGNIFICANCE TO THE EMPEROR, AND HE WAS ALL DECKED OUT IN 2,000-YEAR-OLD ARMOR, HEAD TO TOE.
ALONGSIDE HIM WAS HIS WIFE - A BEAUTIFUL WOMAN AND MARTIAL EXPERT WHO LEARNED HER DEVILISH KUNG FU FROM HIM FIRSTHAND.

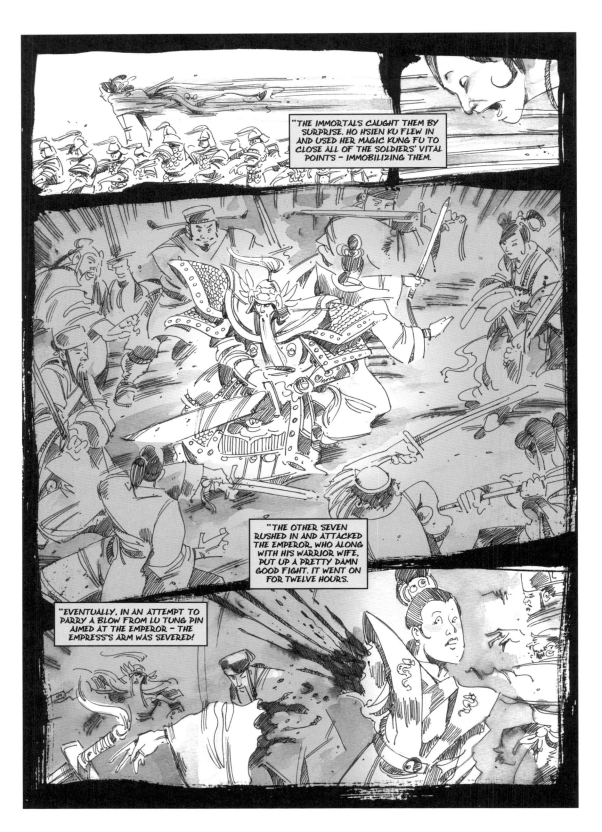

"THE IMMORTALS CAUGHT THEM BY SURPRISE. HO HSIEN KU FLEW IN AND USED HER MAGIC KUNG FU TO CLOSE ALL OF THE SOLDIERS' VITAL POINTS – IMMOBILIZING THEM.

"THE OTHER SEVEN RUSHED IN AND ATTACKED THE EMPEROR, WHO ALONG WITH HIS WARRIOR WIFE, PUT UP A PRETTY DAMN GOOD FIGHT. IT WENT ON FOR TWELVE HOURS.

"EVENTUALLY, IN AN ATTEMPT TO PARRY A BLOW FROM LU TUNG PIN AIMED AT THE EMPEROR – THE EMPRESS'S ARM WAS SEVERED!

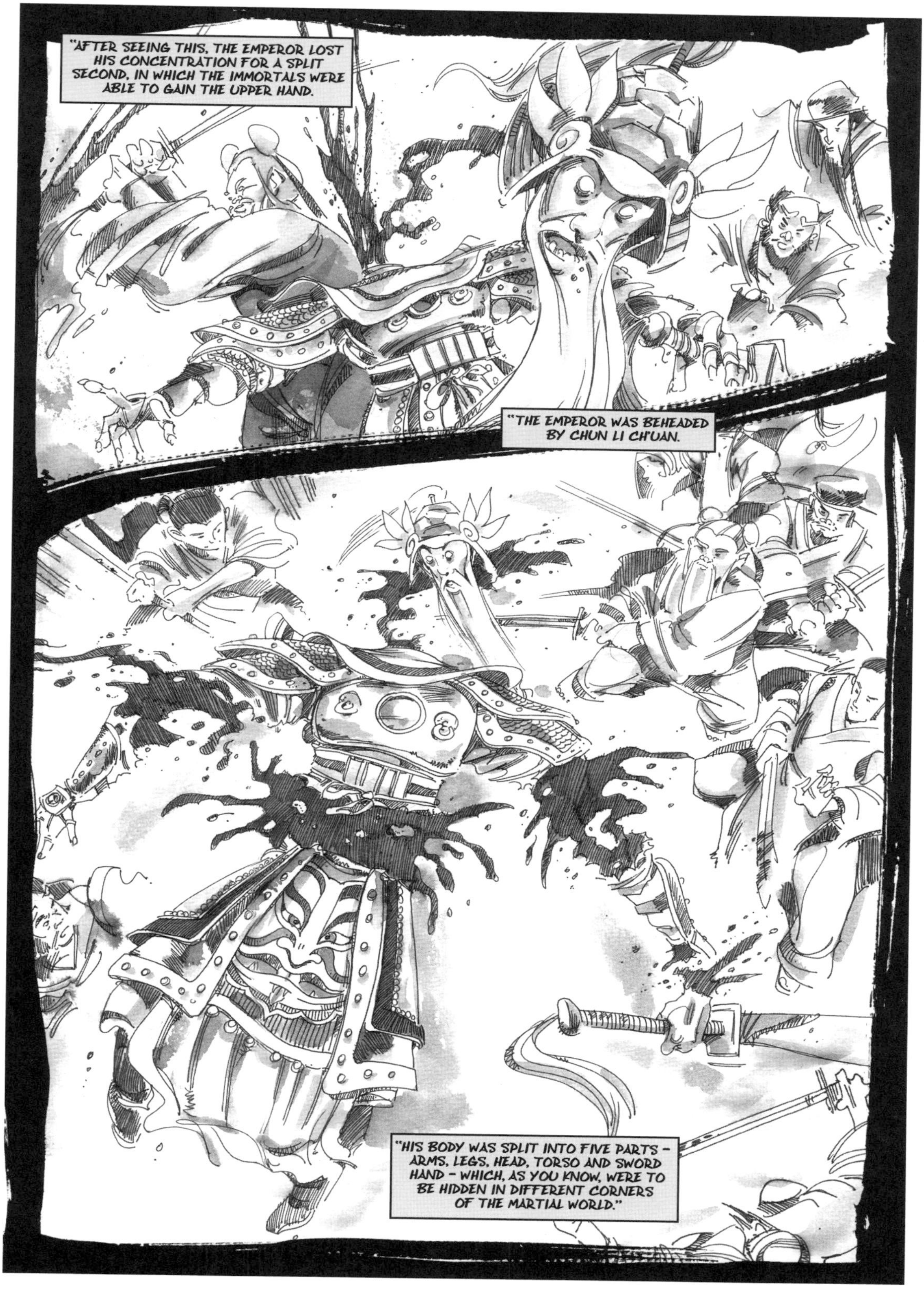
"AFTER SEEING THIS, THE EMPEROR LOST HIS CONCENTRATION FOR A SPLIT SECOND, IN WHICH THE IMMORTALS WERE ABLE TO GAIN THE UPPER HAND.
"THE EMPEROR WAS BEHEADED BY CHUN LI CH'UAN.
"HIS BODY WAS SPLIT INTO FIVE PARTS – ARMS, LEGS, HEAD, TORSO AND SWORD HAND – WHICH, AS YOU KNOW, WERE TO BE HIDDEN IN DIFFERENT CORNERS OF THE MARTIAL WORLD."

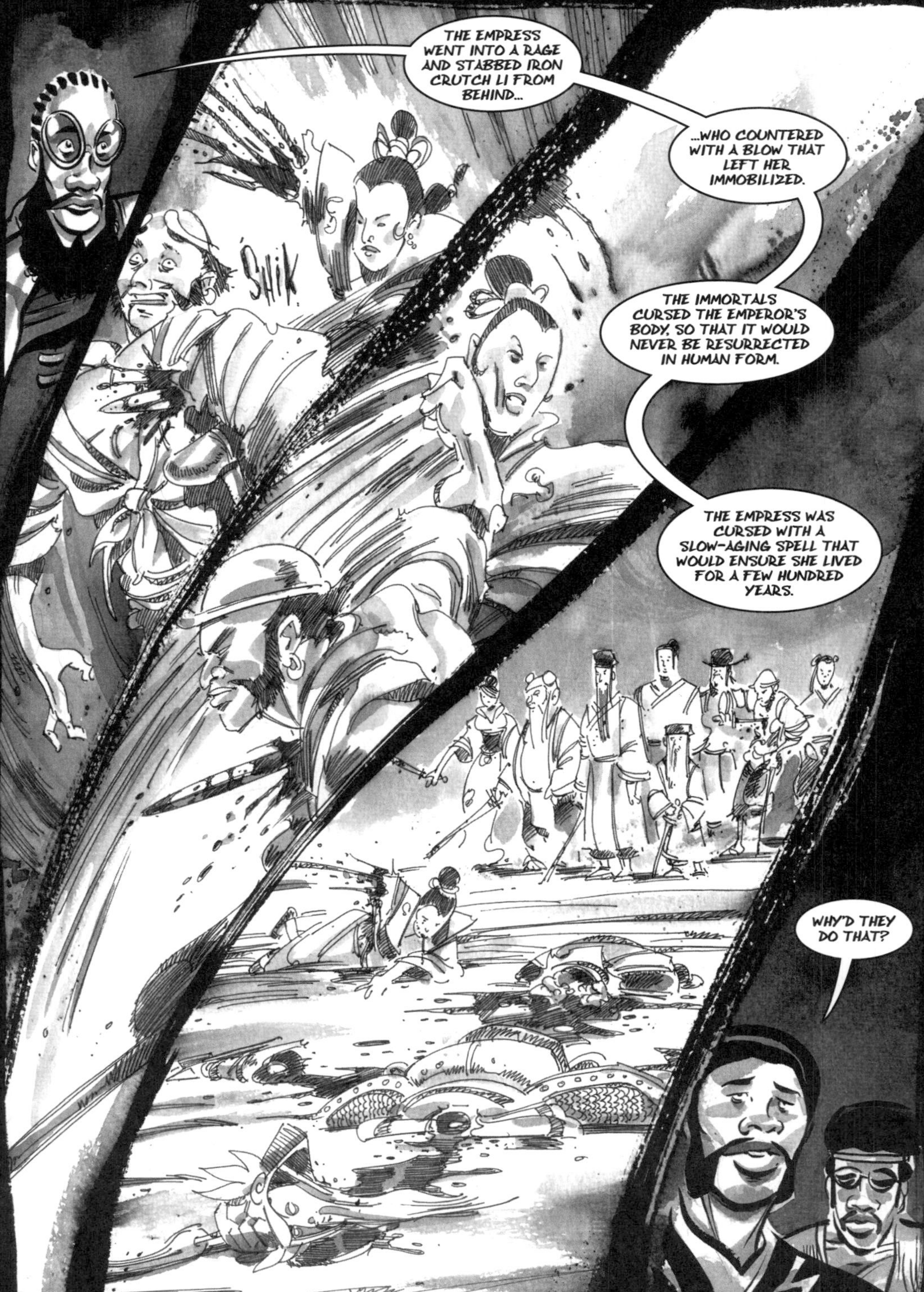
THE EMPRESS WENT INTO A RAGE AND STABBED IRON CRUTCH LI FROM BEHIND...
SHIK
...WHO COUNTERED WITH A BLOW THAT LEFT HER IMMOBILIZED.
THE IMMORTALS CURSED THE EMPEROR'S BODY, SO THAT IT WOULD NEVER BE RESURRECTED IN HUMAN FORM.
THE EMPRESS WAS CURSED WITH A SLOW-AGING SPELL THAT WOULD ENSURE SHE LIVED FOR A FEW HUNDRED YEARS.
WHY'D THEY DO THAT?

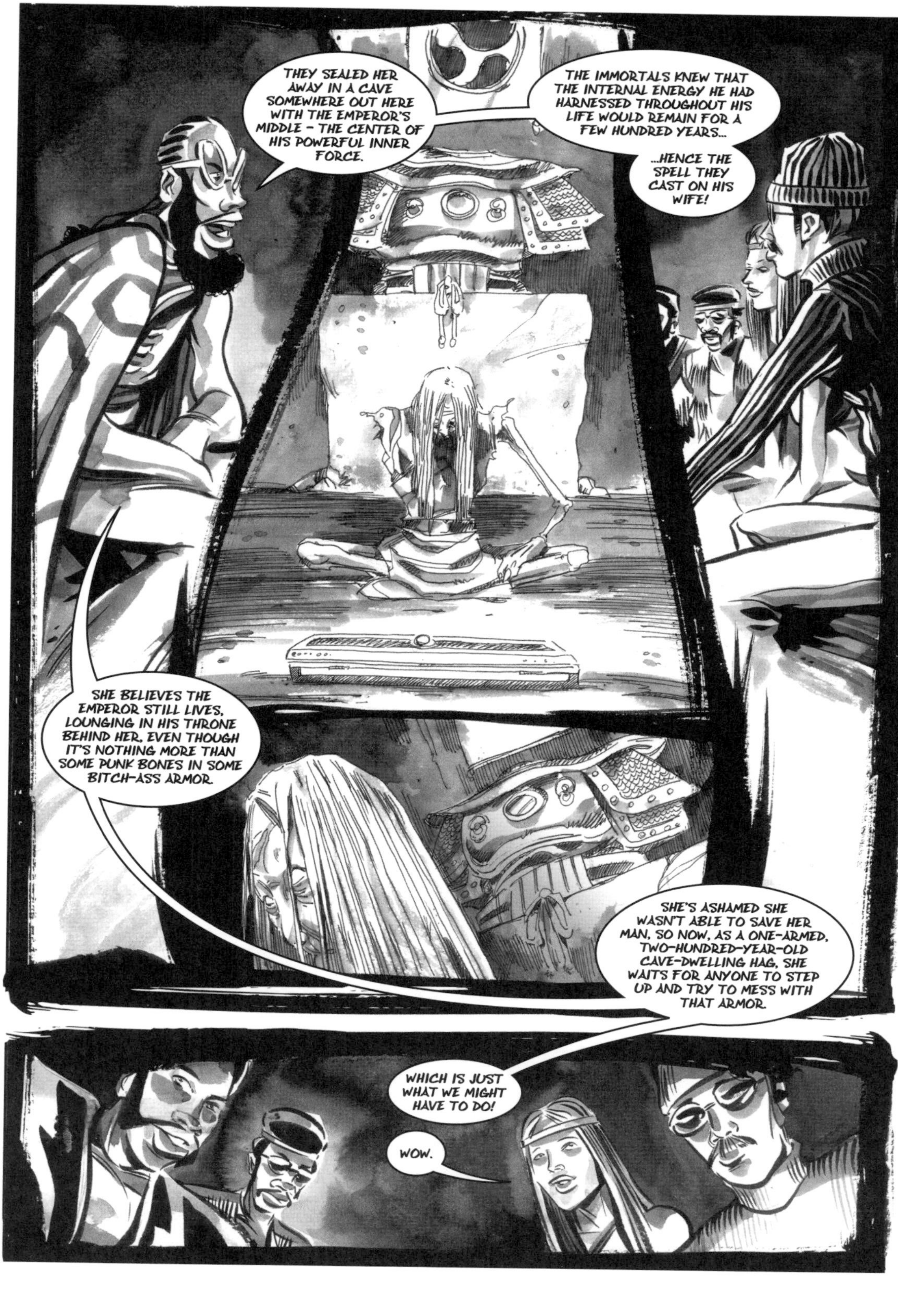
THEY SEALED HER AWAY IN A CAVE SOMEWHERE OUT HERE WITH THE EMPEROR'S MIDDLE - THE CENTER OF HIS POWERFUL INNER FORCE.
THE IMMORTALS KNEW THAT THE INTERNAL ENERGY HE HAD HARNESSED THROUGHOUT HIS LIFE WOULD REMAIN FOR A FEW HUNDRED YEARS...
...HENCE THE SPELL THEY CAST ON HIS WIFE!
SHE BELIEVES THE EMPEROR STILL LIVES, LOUNGING IN HIS THRONE BEHIND HER, EVEN THOUGH IT'S NOTHING MORE THAN SOME PUNK BONES IN SOME BITCH-ASS ARMOR.
SHE'S ASHAMED SHE WASN'T ABLE TO SAVE HER MAN, SO NOW, AS A ONE-ARMED, TWO-HUNDRED-YEAR-OLD CAVE-DWELLING HAG, SHE WAITS FOR ANYONE TO STEP UP AND TRY TO MESS WITH THAT ARMOR.
WHICH IS JUST WHAT WE MIGHT HAVE TO DO!
WOW.

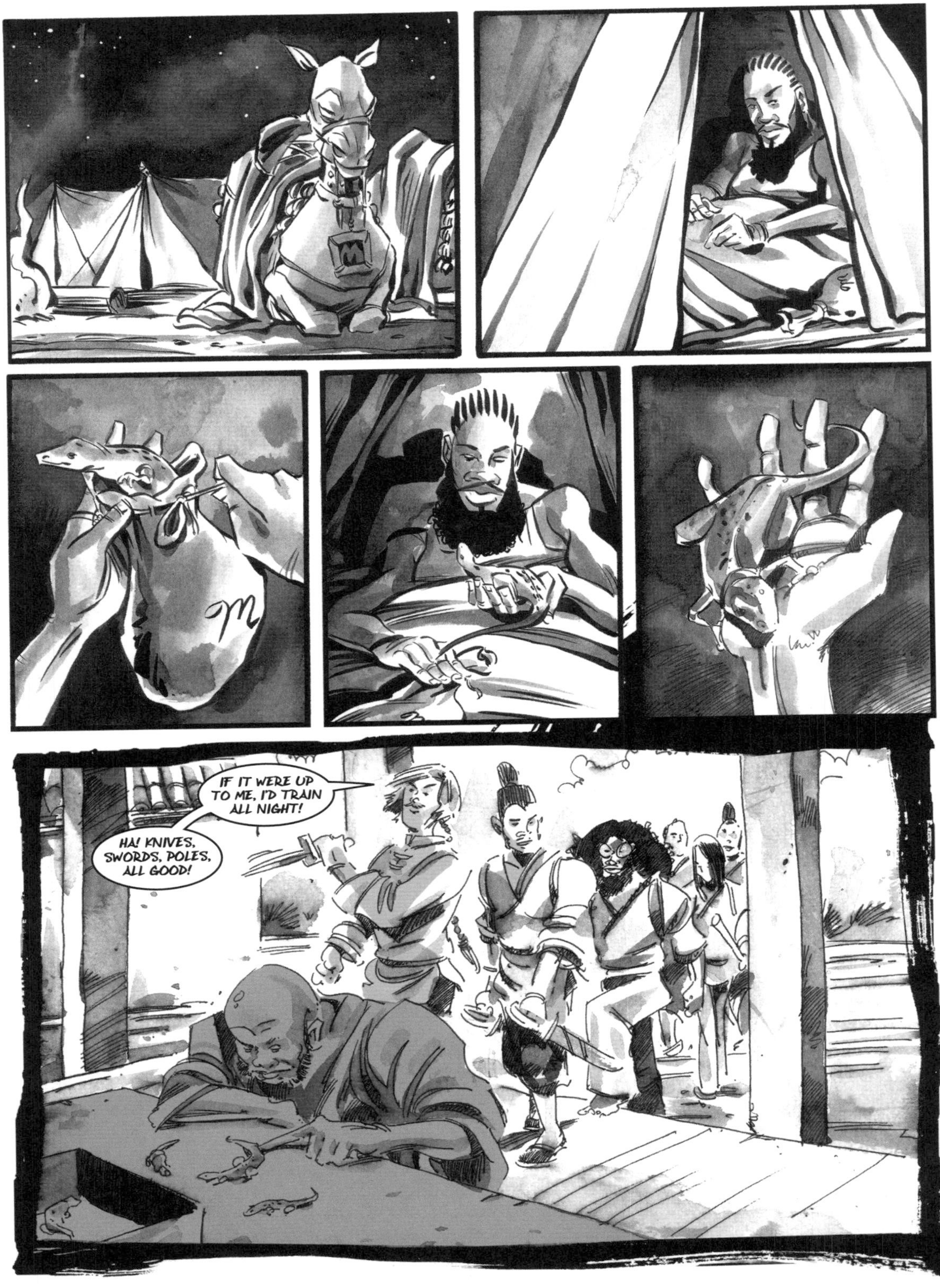
IF IT WERE UP TO ME, I'D TRAIN ALL NIGHT!
HA! KNIVES, SWORDS, POLES, ALL GOOD!

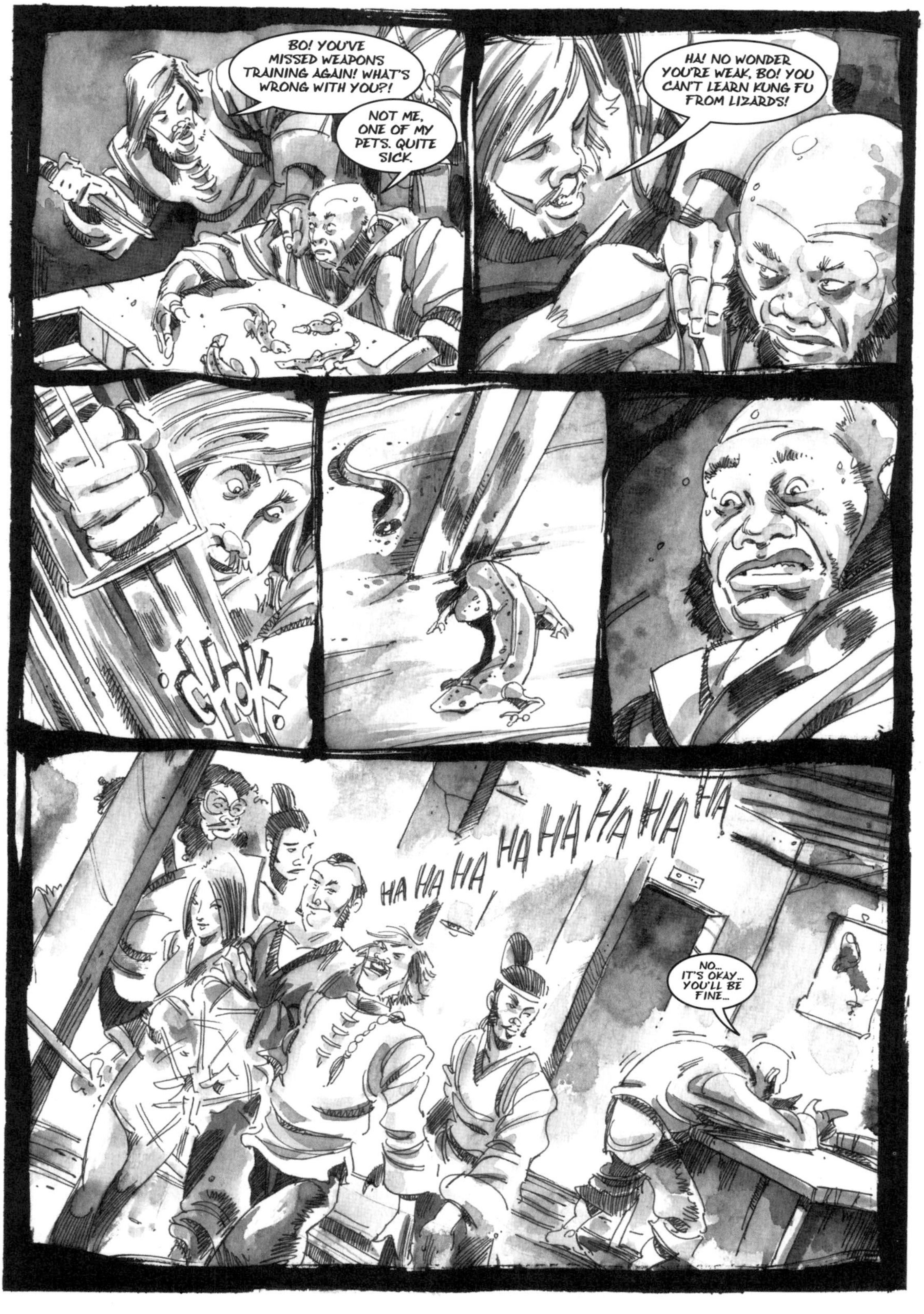
BO! YOU'VE MISSED WEAPONS TRAINING AGAIN! WHAT'S WRONG WITH YOU?!
NOT ME, ONE OF MY PETS. QUITE SICK.
HA! NO WONDER YOU'RE WEAK, BO! YOU CAN'T LEARN KUNG FU FROM LIZARDS!
CHOK
HA HA HA HA HA HA HA HA HA
NO... IT'S OKAY... YOU'LL BE FINE...

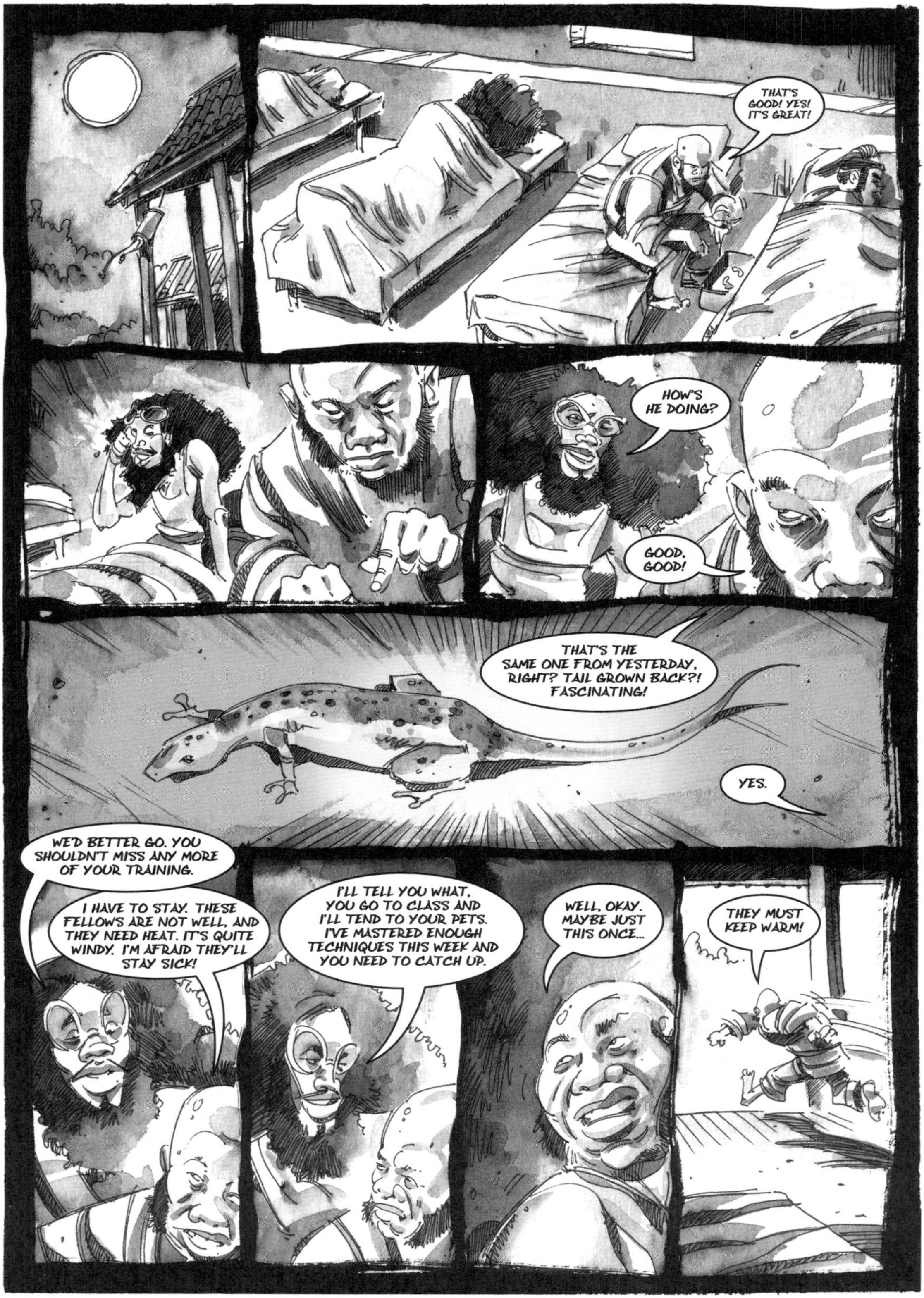
THAT'S GOOD! YES! IT'S GREAT!
HOW'S HE DOING?
GOOD, GOOD!
THAT'S THE SAME ONE FROM YESTERDAY, RIGHT? TAIL GROWN BACK?! FASCINATING!
YES.
WE'D BETTER GO. YOU SHOULDN'T MISS ANY MORE OF YOUR TRAINING.
I HAVE TO STAY. THESE FELLOWS ARE NOT WELL, AND THEY NEED HEAT. IT'S QUITE WINDY. I'M AFRAID THEY'LL STAY SICK!
I'LL TELL YOU WHAT, YOU GO TO CLASS AND I'LL TEND TO YOUR PETS. I'VE MASTERED ENOUGH TECHNIQUES THIS WEEK AND YOU NEED TO CATCH UP.
WELL, OKAY. MAYBE JUST THIS ONCE...
THEY MUST KEEP WARM!

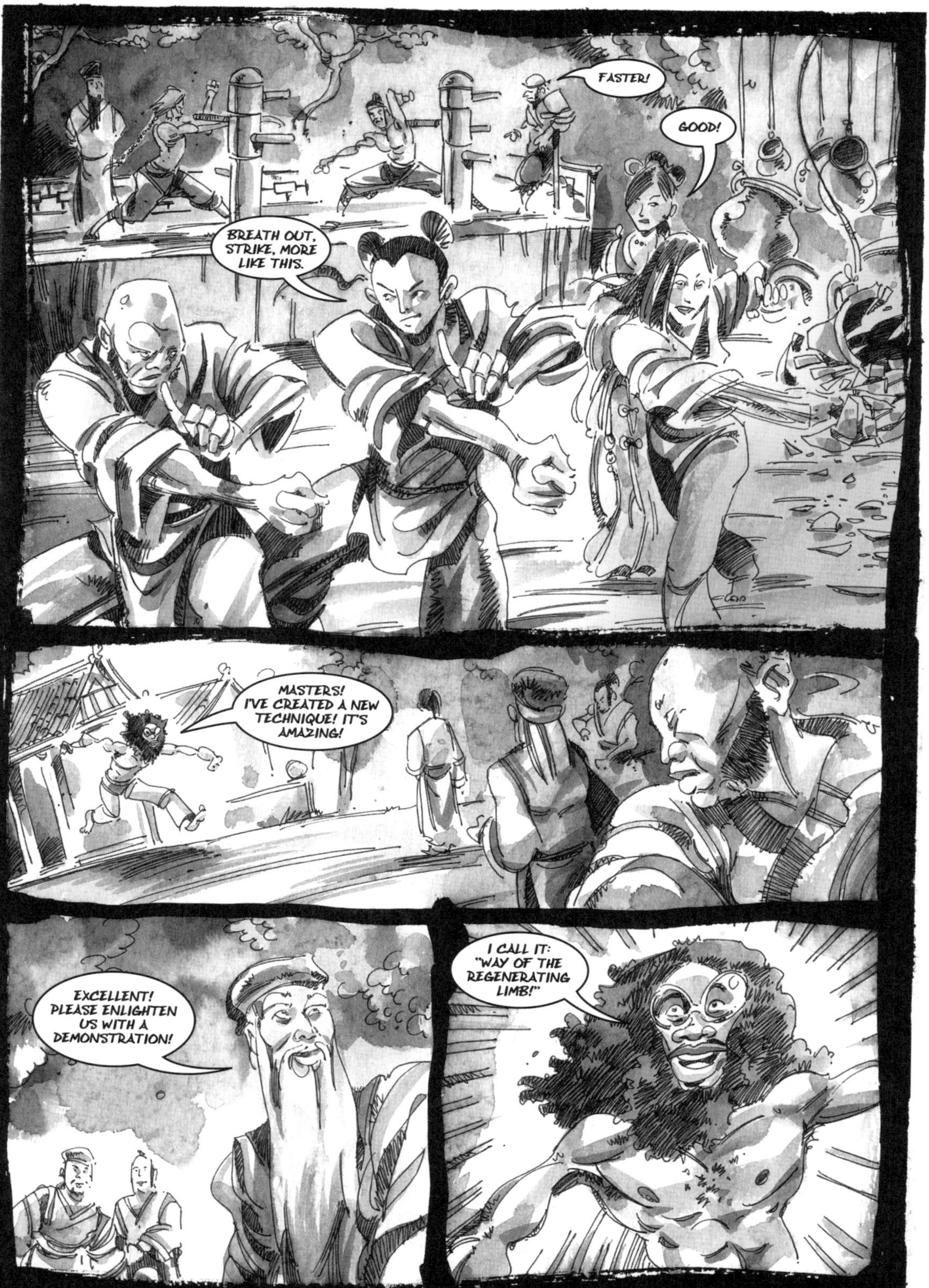
FASTER!
GOOD!
BREATH OUT, STRIKE, MORE LIKE THIS.
MASTERS! I'VE CREATED A NEW TECHNIQUE! IT'S AMAZING!
EXCELLENT! PLEASE ENLIGHTEN US WITH A DEMONSTRATION!
I CALL IT: "WAY OF THE REGENERATING LIMB!"

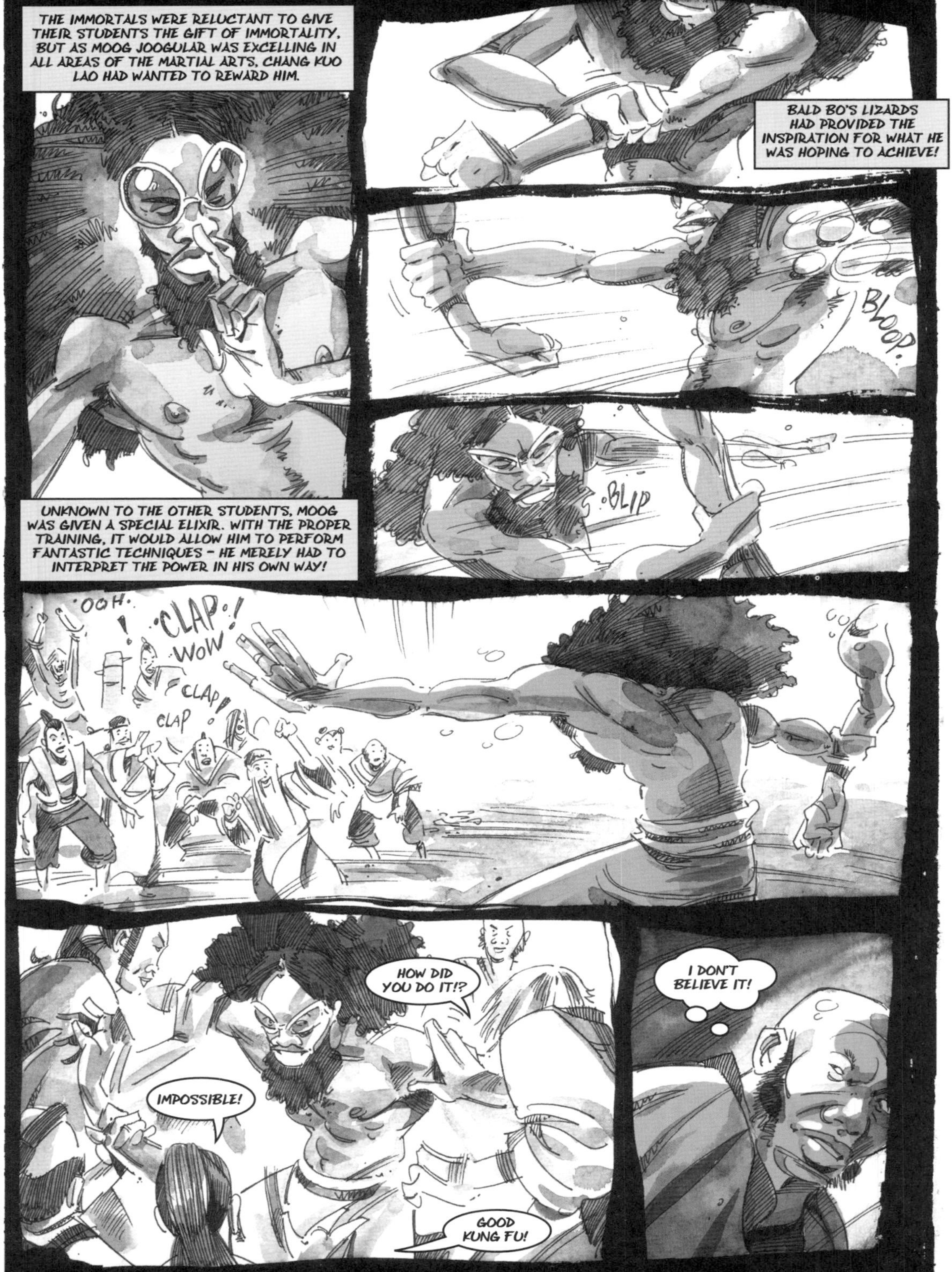
THE IMMORTALS WERE RELUCTANT TO GIVE THEIR STUDENTS THE GIFT OF IMMORTALITY. BUT AS MOOG JOOGULAR WAS EXCELLING IN ALL AREAS OF THE MARTIAL ARTS, CHANG KUO LAO HAD WANTED TO REWARD HIM.
BALD BO'S LIZARDS HAD PROVIDED THE INSPIRATION FOR WHAT HE WAS HOPING TO ACHIEVE!
BLOOP.
UNKNOWN TO THE OTHER STUDENTS, MOOG WAS GIVEN A SPECIAL ELIXIR. WITH THE PROPER TRAINING, IT WOULD ALLOW HIM TO PERFORM FANTASTIC TECHNIQUES - HE MERELY HAD TO INTERPRET THE POWER IN HIS OWN WAY!
BLIP
OOH.
CLAP!
WOW
CLAP!
CLAP
HOW DID YOU DO IT!?
IMPOSSIBLE!
GOOD KUNG FU!
I DON'T BELIEVE IT!

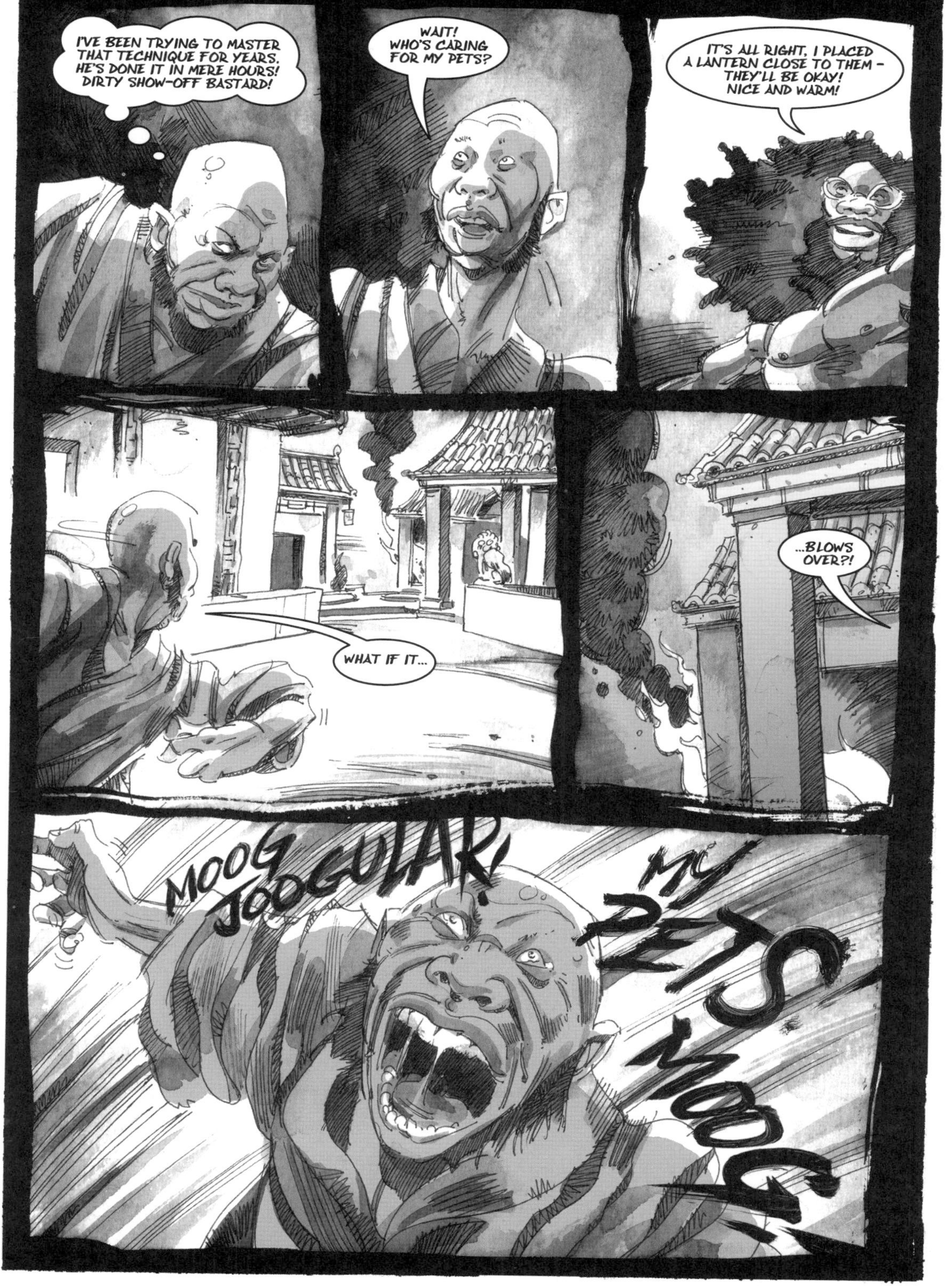
I'VE BEEN TRYING TO MASTER THAT TECHNIQUE FOR YEARS. HE'S DONE IT IN MERE HOURS! DIRTY SHOW-OFF BASTARD!
WAIT! WHO'S CARING FOR MY PETS?
IT'S ALL RIGHT. I PLACED A LANTERN CLOSE TO THEM – THEY'LL BE OKAY! NICE AND WARM!
WHAT IF IT...
...BLOWS OVER?!
MOOG JOOGULAR!
MY PETS MOOG!

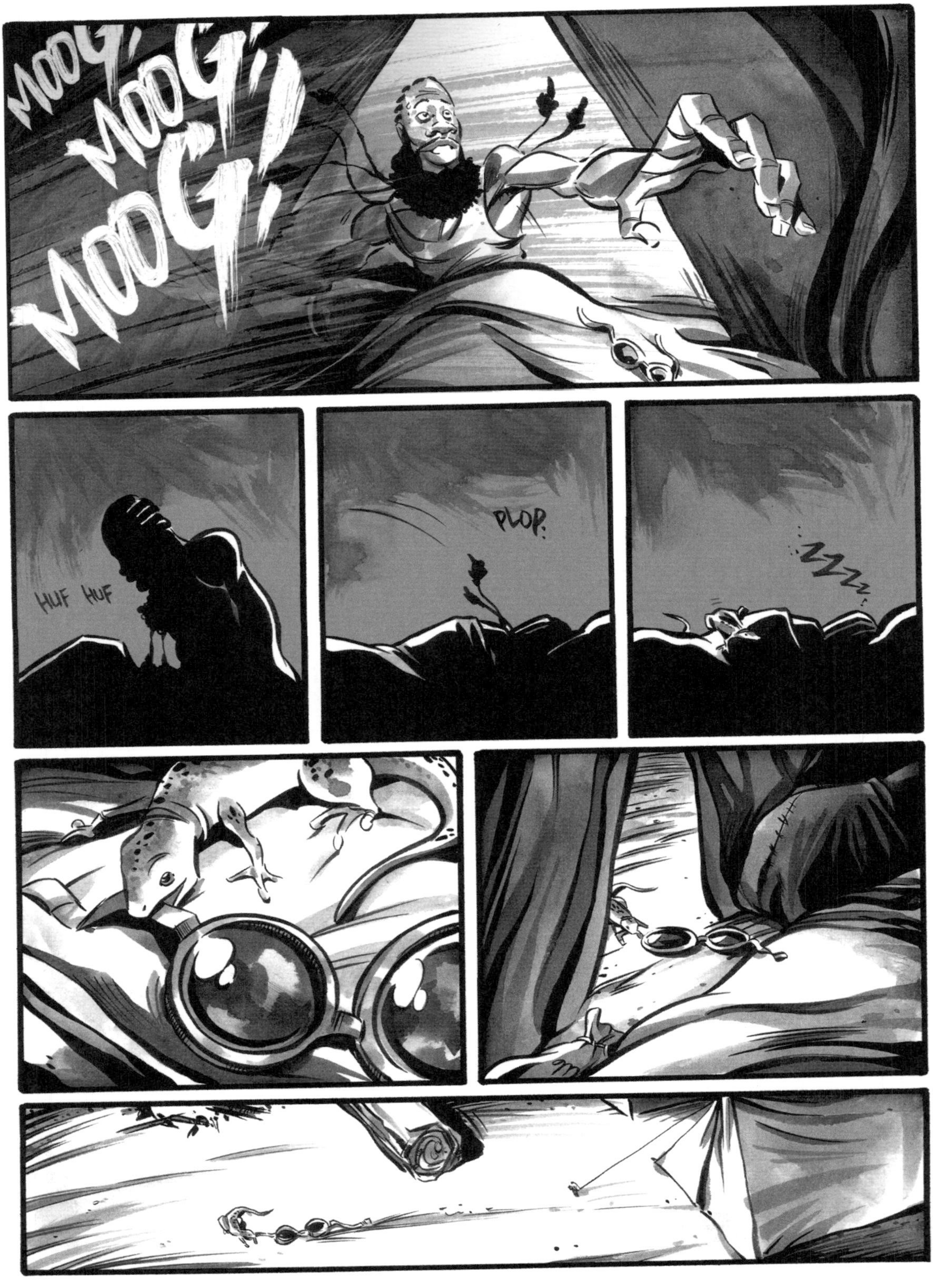
MOOG! MOOG! MOOG!
HUF HUF
PLOP.
ZZZZ

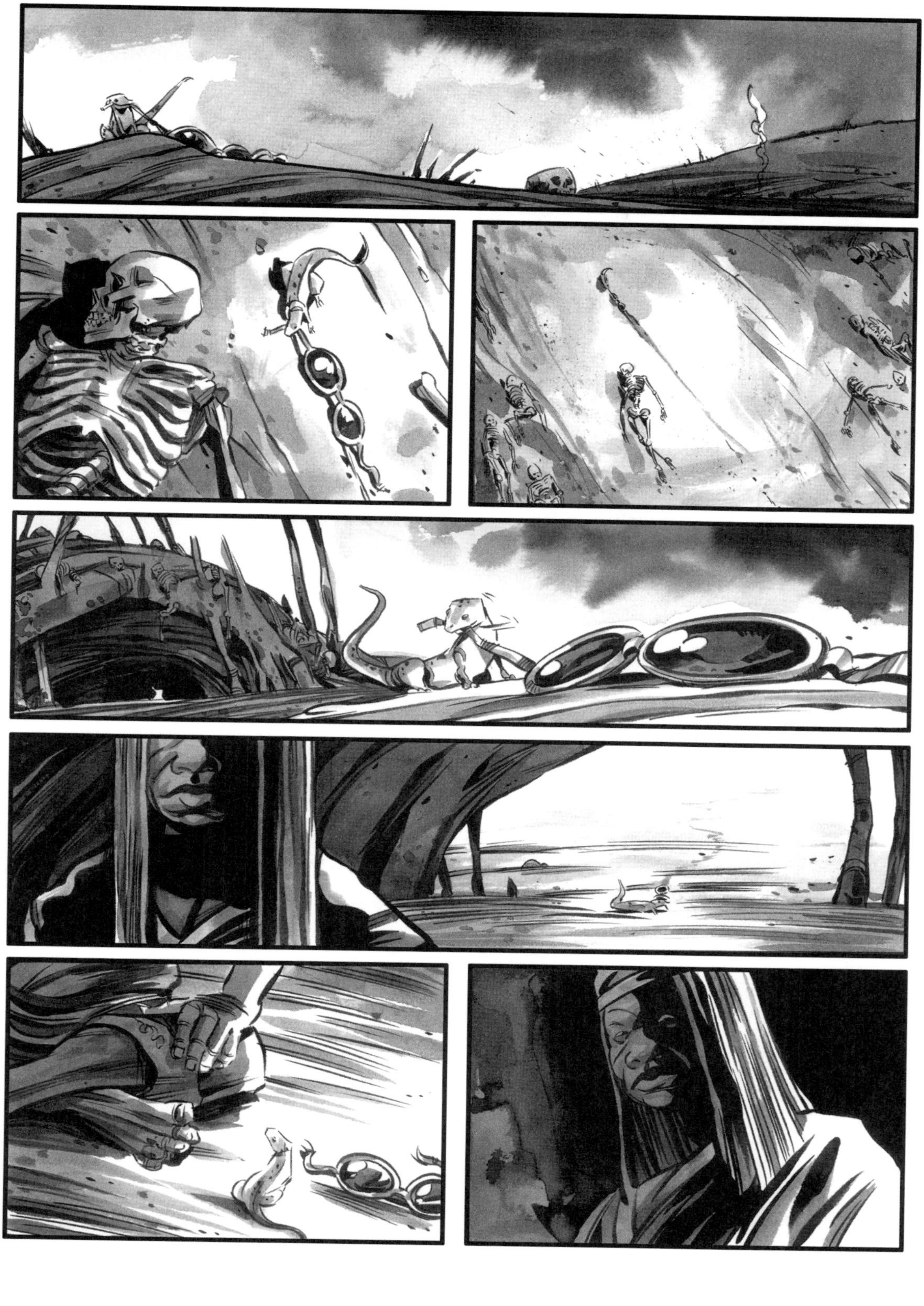

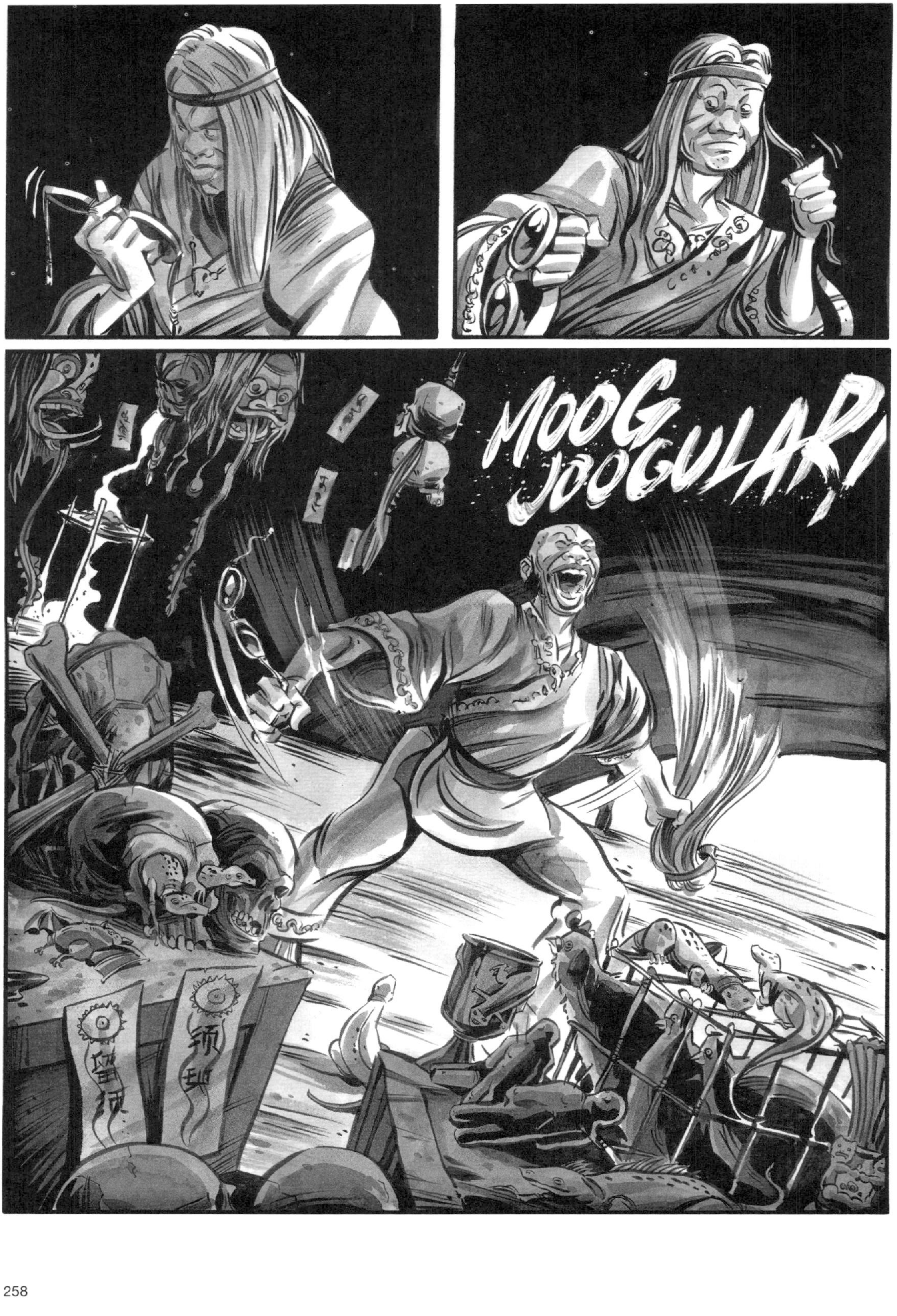
MOOG JOOGULAR!

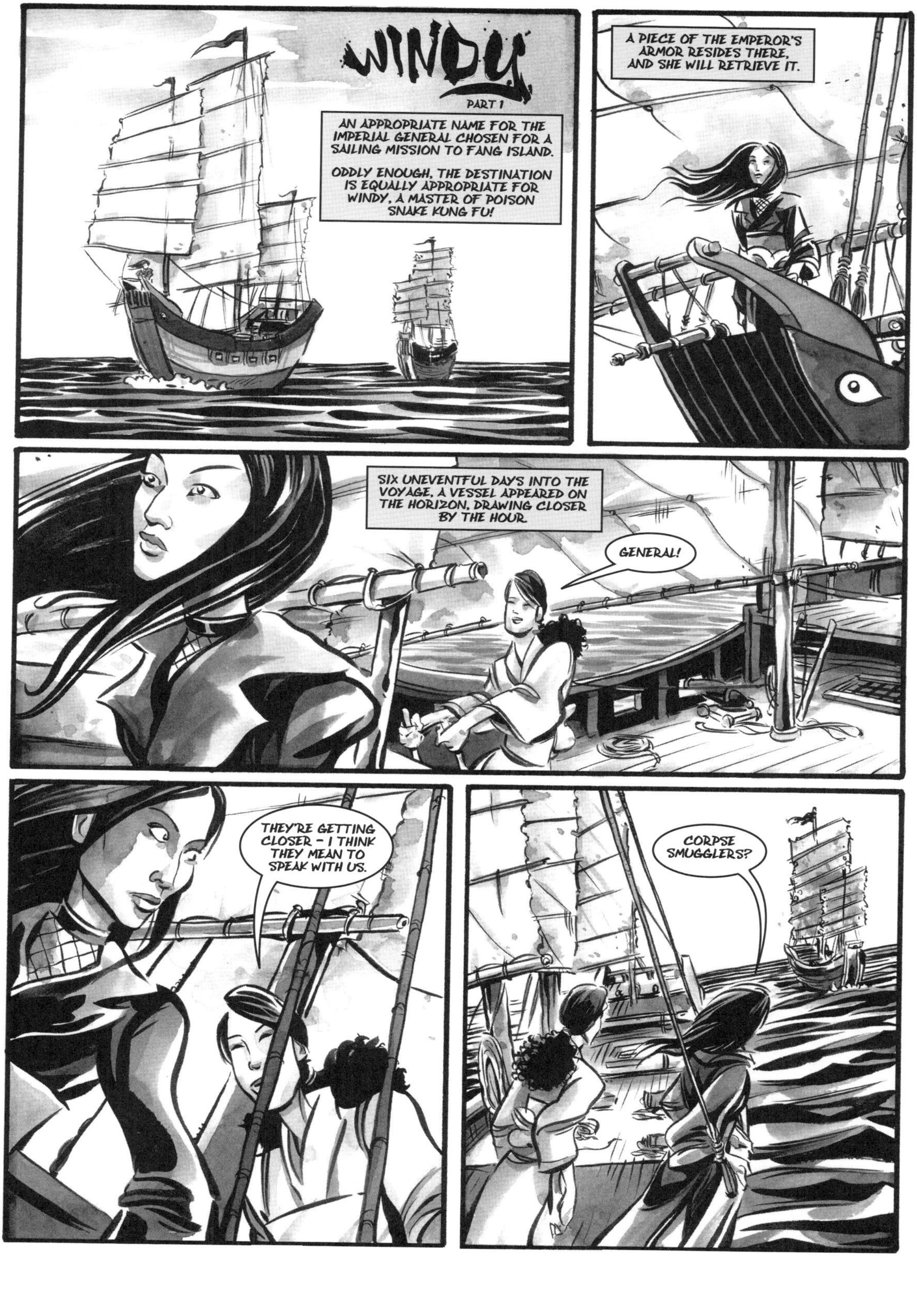
WINDY
PART 1
AN APPROPRIATE NAME FOR THE IMPERIAL GENERAL CHOSEN FOR A SAILING MISSION TO FANG ISLAND.
ODDLY ENOUGH, THE DESTINATION IS EQUALLY APPROPRIATE FOR WINDY, A MASTER OF POISON SNAKE KUNG FU!
A PIECE OF THE EMPEROR'S ARMOR RESIDES THERE, AND SHE WILL RETRIEVE IT.
SIX UNEVENTFUL DAYS INTO THE VOYAGE, A VESSEL APPEARED ON THE HORIZON, DRAWING CLOSER BY THE HOUR.
GENERAL!
THEY'RE GETTING CLOSER - I THINK THEY MEAN TO SPEAK WITH US.
CORPSE SMUGGLERS?

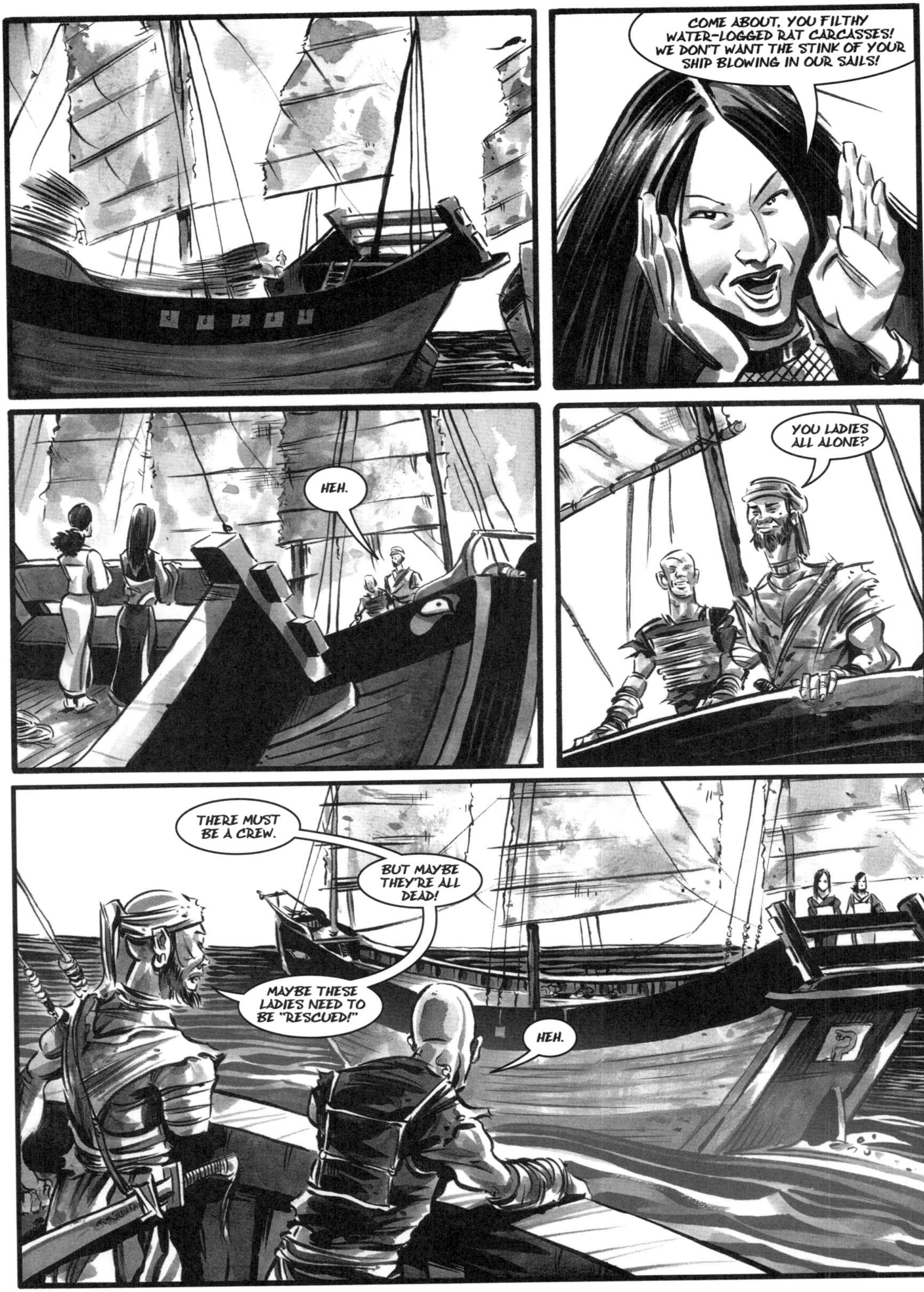
COME ABOUT, YOU FILTHY WATER-LOGGED RAT CARCASSES! WE DON'T WANT THE STINK OF YOUR SHIP BLOWING IN OUR SAILS!
HEH.
YOU LADIES ALL ALONE?
THERE MUST BE A CREW.
BUT MAYBE THEY'RE ALL DEAD!
MAYBE THESE LADIES NEED TO BE "RESCUED!"
HEH.

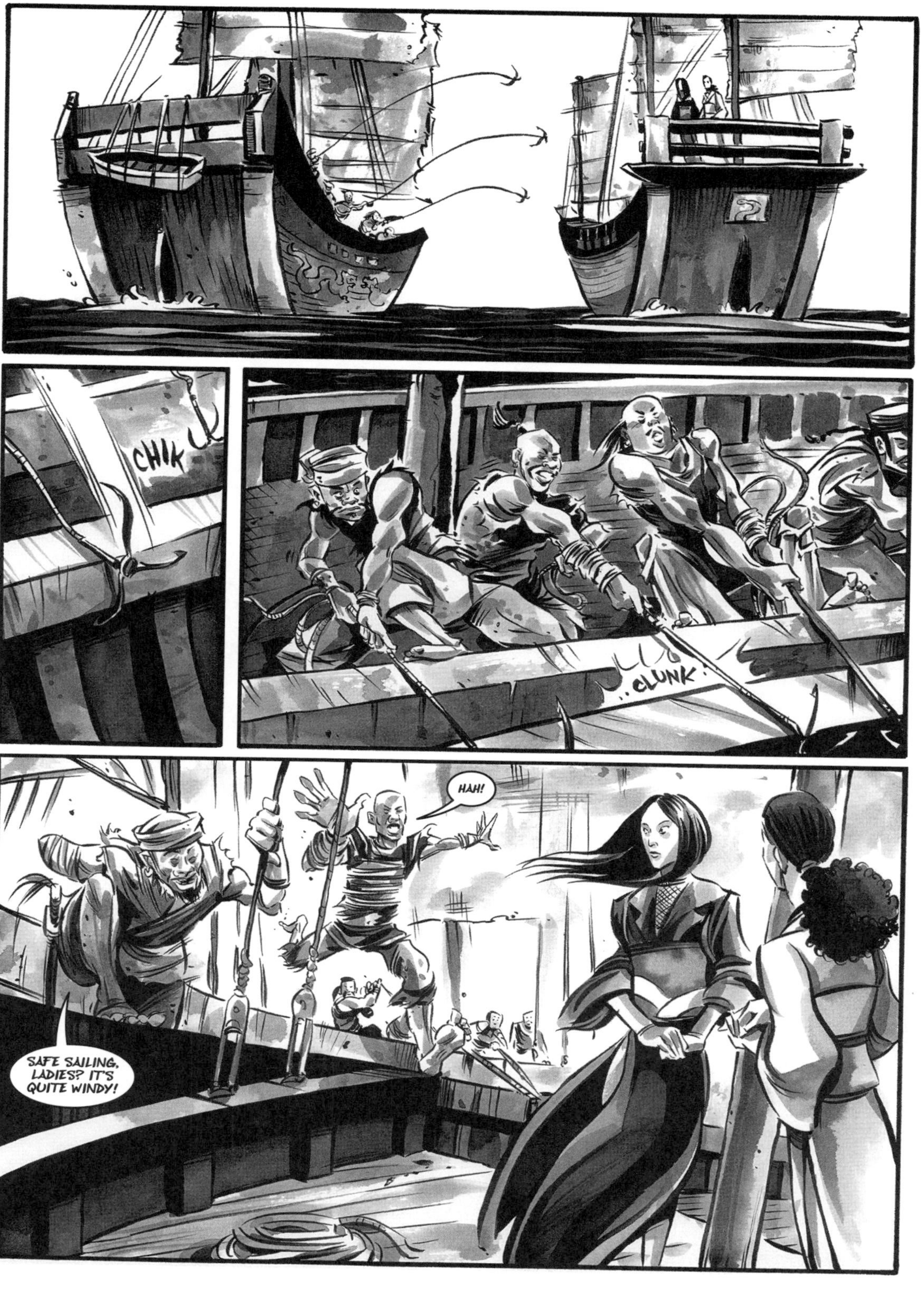
CHIK
CLUNK
HAH!
SAFE SAILING, LADIES? IT'S QUITE WINDY!

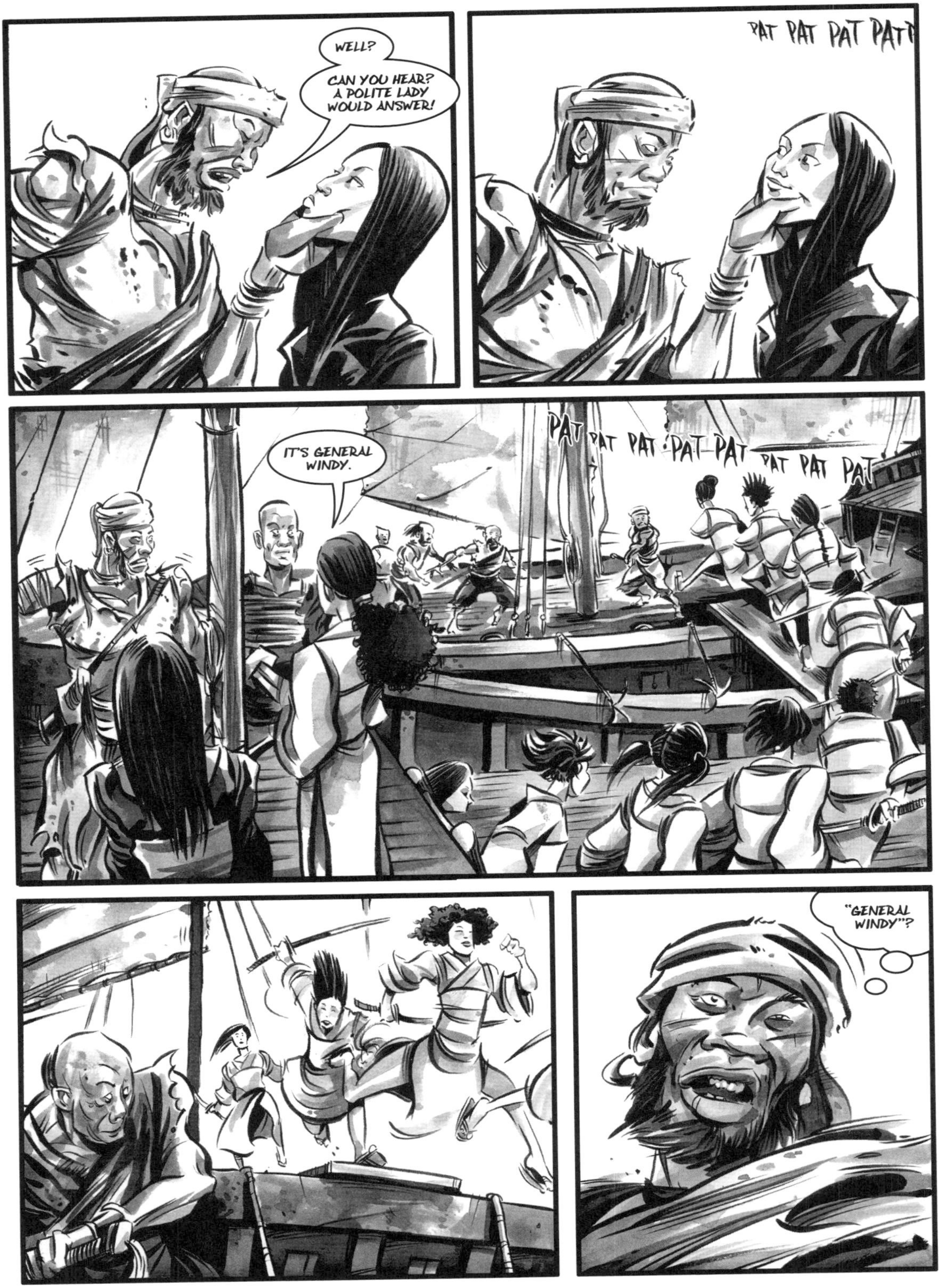
WELL?
CAN YOU HEAR? A POLITE LADY WOULD ANSWER!
PAT PAT PAT PAT
IT'S GENERAL WINDY.
PAT PAT PAT PAT PAT PAT PAT PAT PAT
"GENERAL WINDY"?

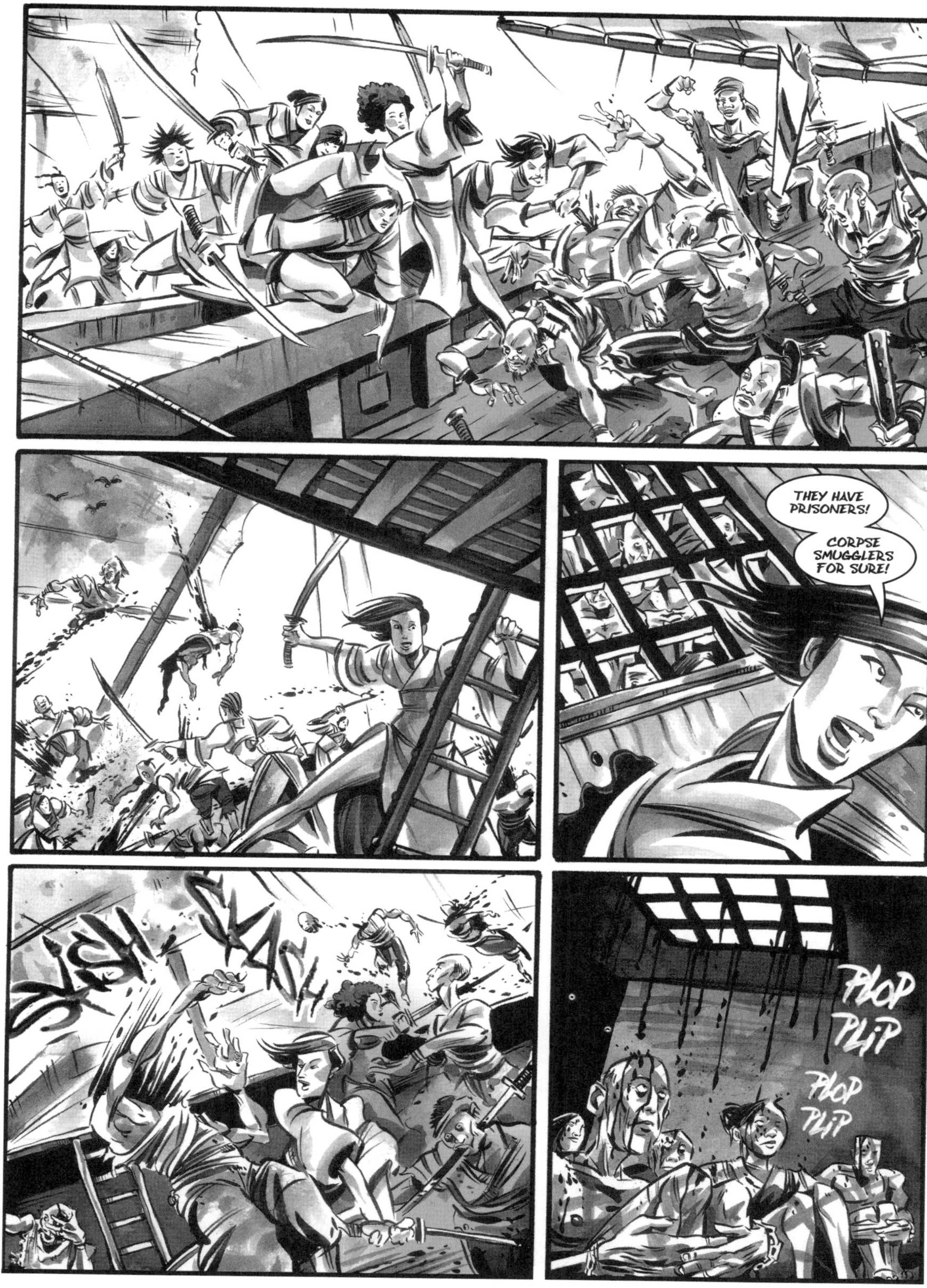
THEY HAVE PRISONERS!
CORPSE SMUGGLERS FOR SURE!
PLOP
PLIP
PLOP
PLIP

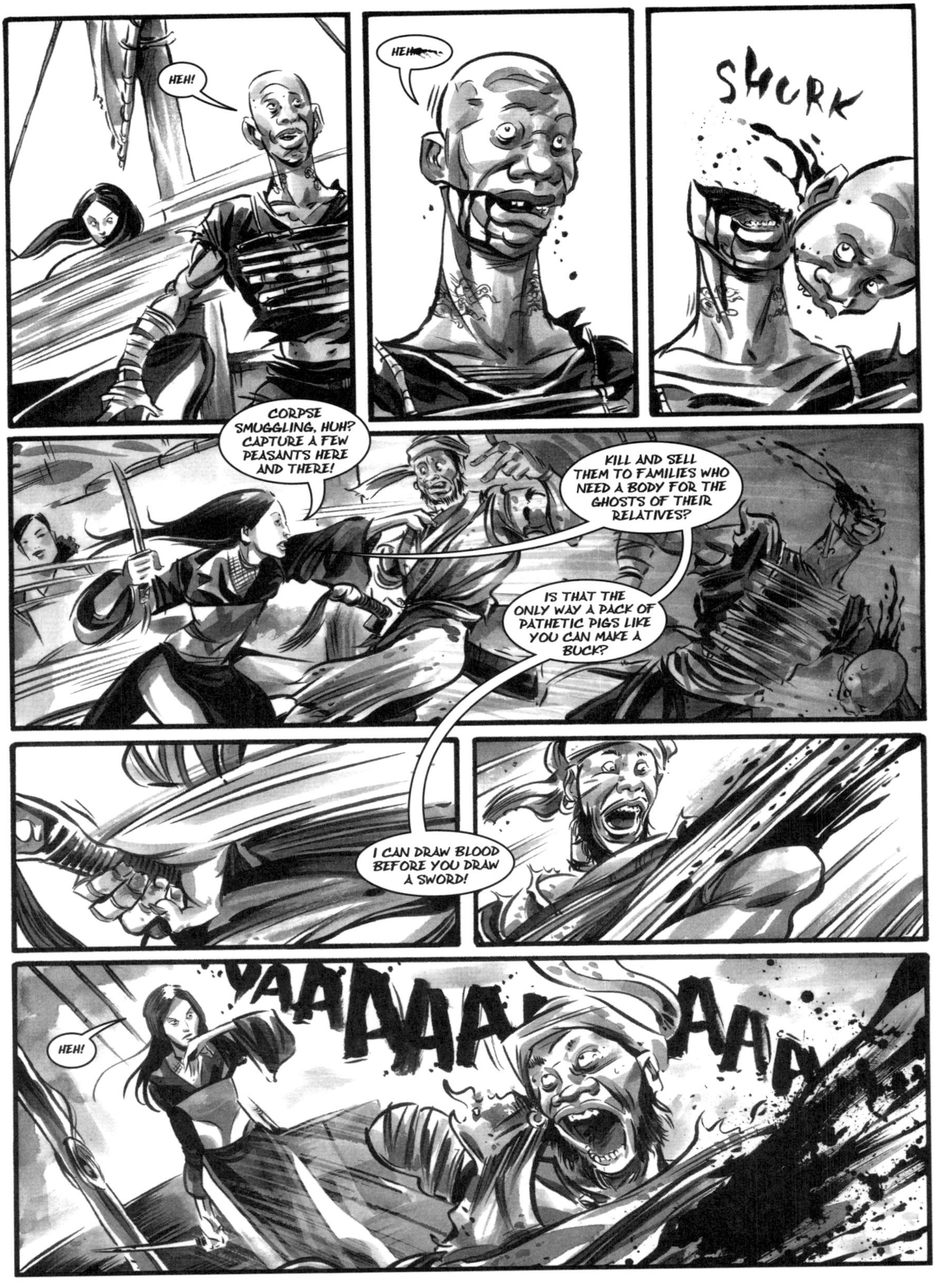
HEH!
HEH—
SHURK
CORPSE SMUGGLING, HUH? CAPTURE A FEW PEASANTS HERE AND THERE!
KILL AND SELL THEM TO FAMILIES WHO NEED A BODY FOR THE GHOSTS OF THEIR RELATIVES?
IS THAT THE ONLY WAY A PACK OF PATHETIC PIGS LIKE YOU CAN MAKE A BUCK?
I CAN DRAW BLOOD BEFORE YOU DRAW A SWORD!
HEH!
AAAAAAAAAA

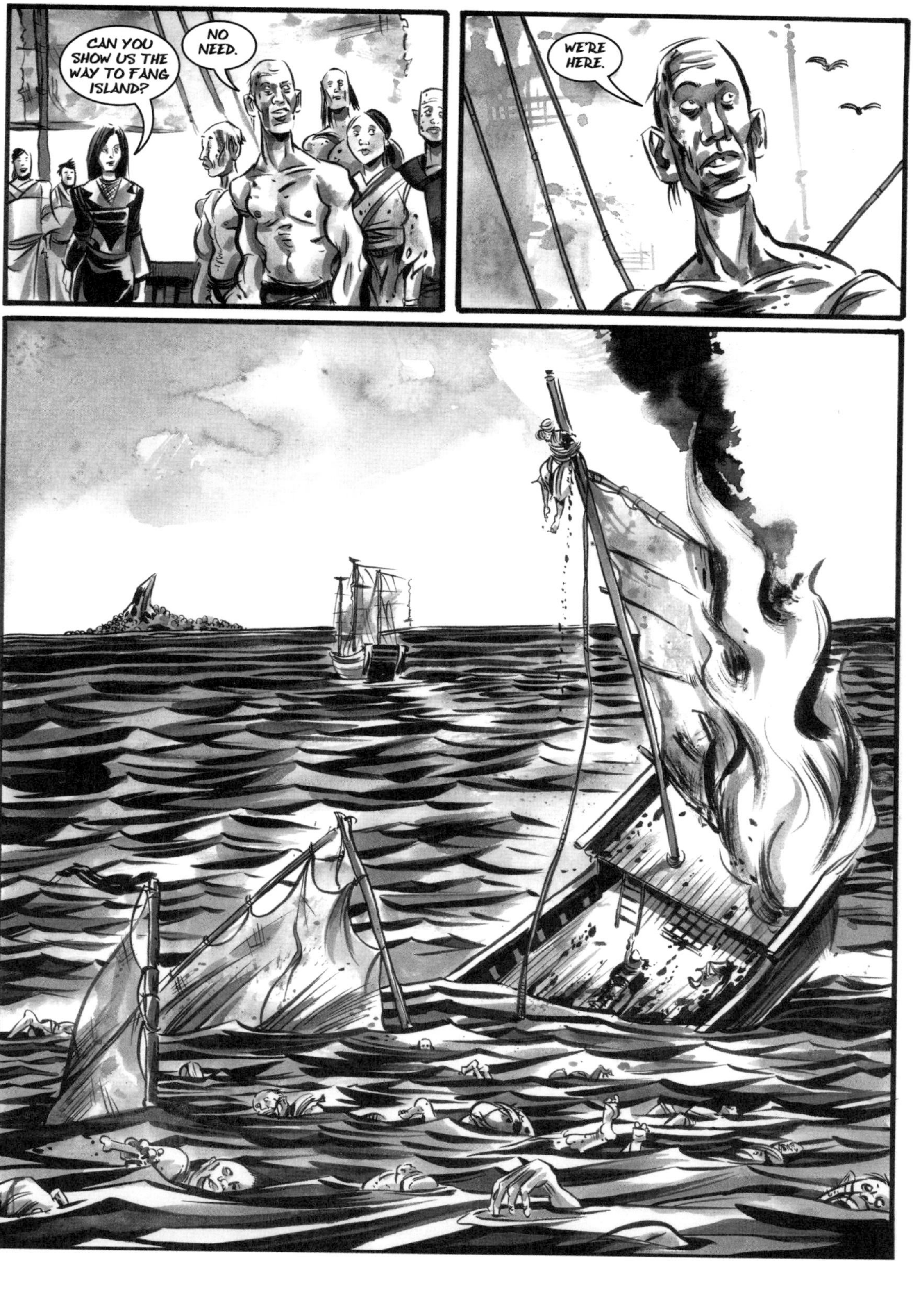
CAN YOU SHOW US THE WAY TO FANG ISLAND?
NO NEED.
WE'RE HERE.

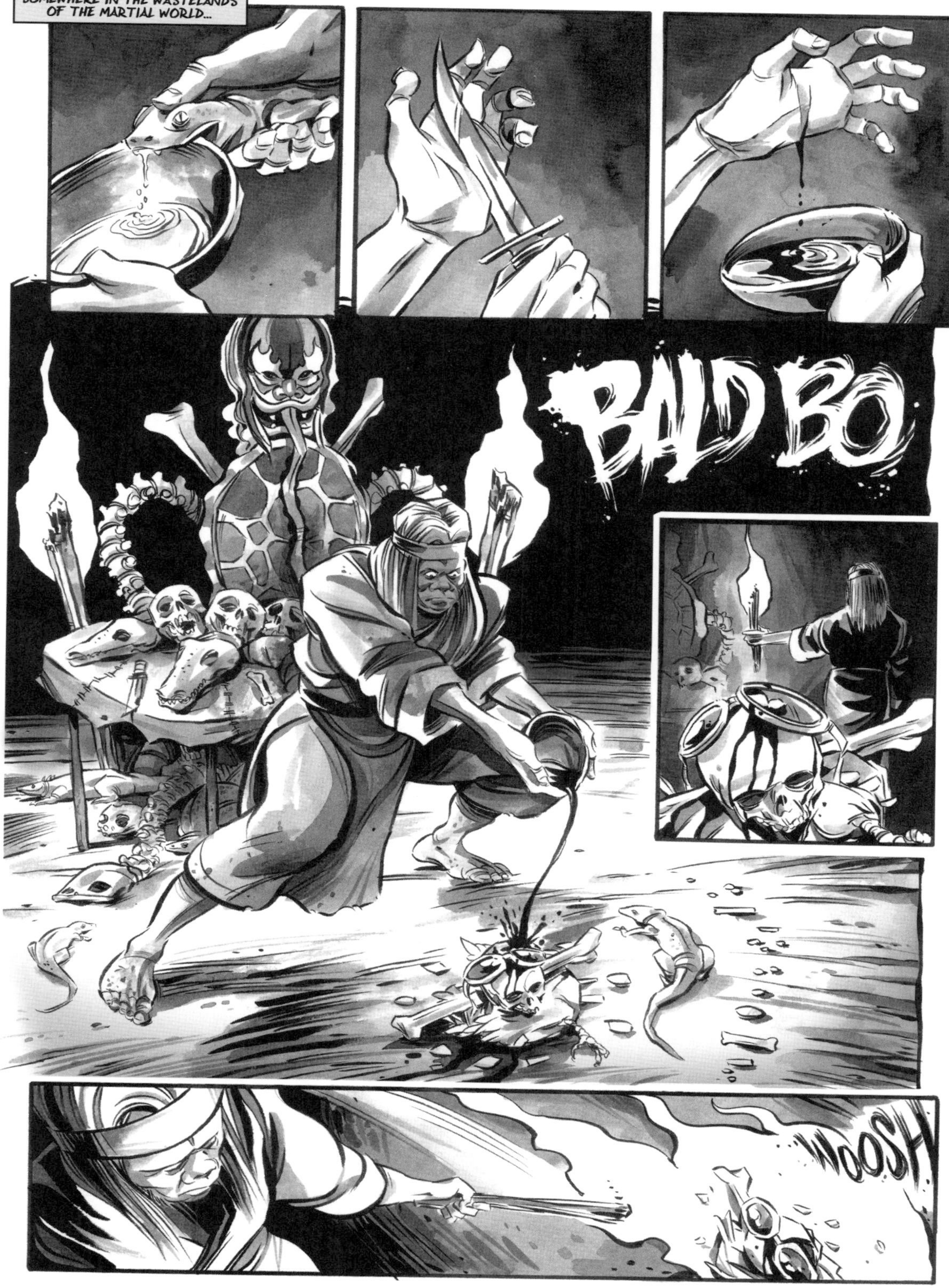
SOMEWHERE IN THE WASTELANDS OF THE MARTIAL WORLD...
BALD BO
WOOSH

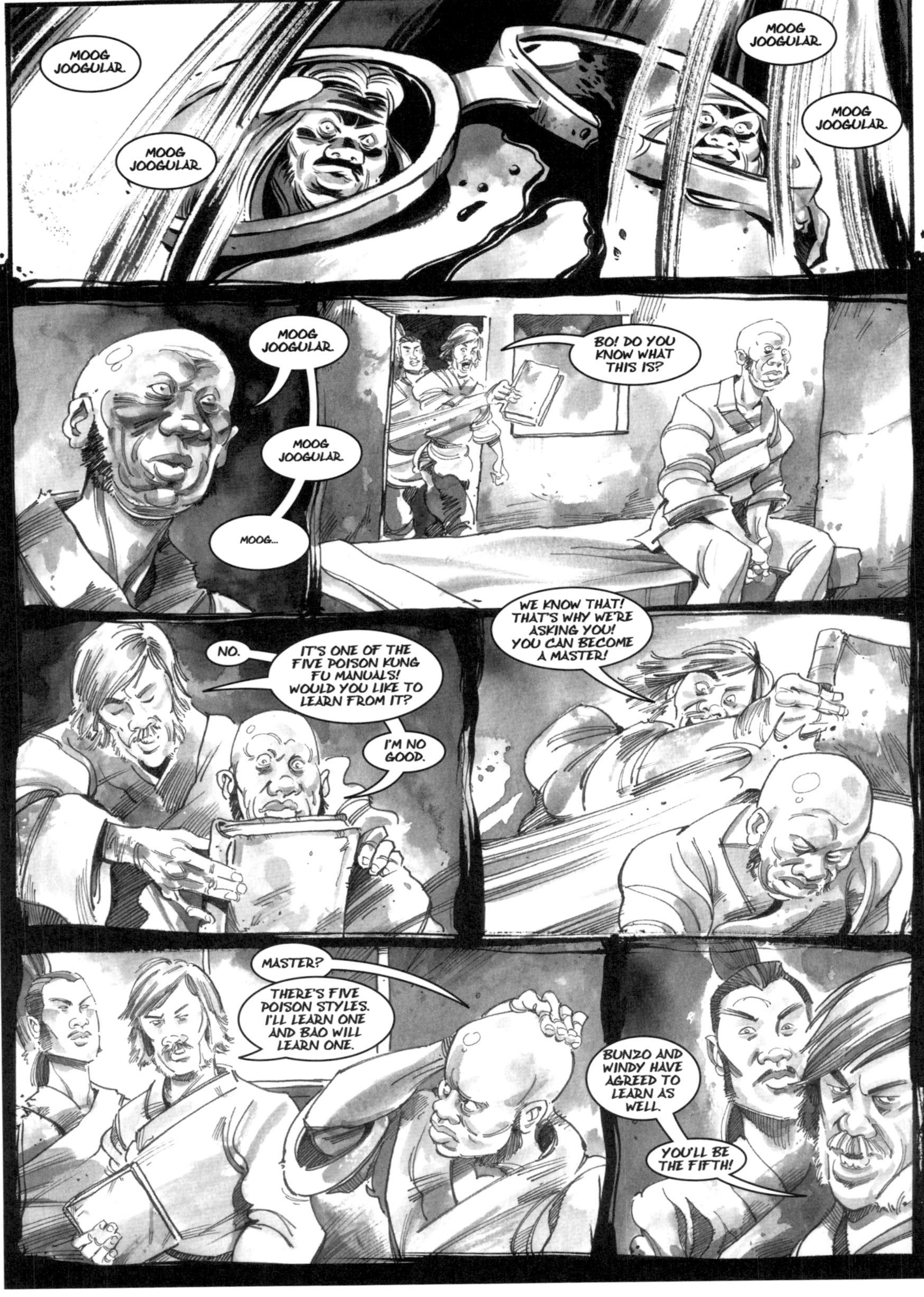
MOOG JOOGULAR.
MOOG JOOGULAR.
MOOG JOOGULAR.
MOOG JOOGULAR.
MOOG JOOGULAR.
MOOG JOOGULAR.
MOOG...
BO! DO YOU KNOW WHAT THIS IS?
NO.
IT'S ONE OF THE FIVE POISON KUNG FU MANUALS! WOULD YOU LIKE TO LEARN FROM IT?
I'M NO GOOD.
WE KNOW THAT! THAT'S WHY WE'RE ASKING YOU! YOU CAN BECOME A MASTER!
MASTER?
THERE'S FIVE POISON STYLES. I'LL LEARN ONE AND BAO WILL LEARN ONE.
BUNZO AND WINDY HAVE AGREED TO LEARN AS WELL.
YOU'LL BE THE FIFTH!

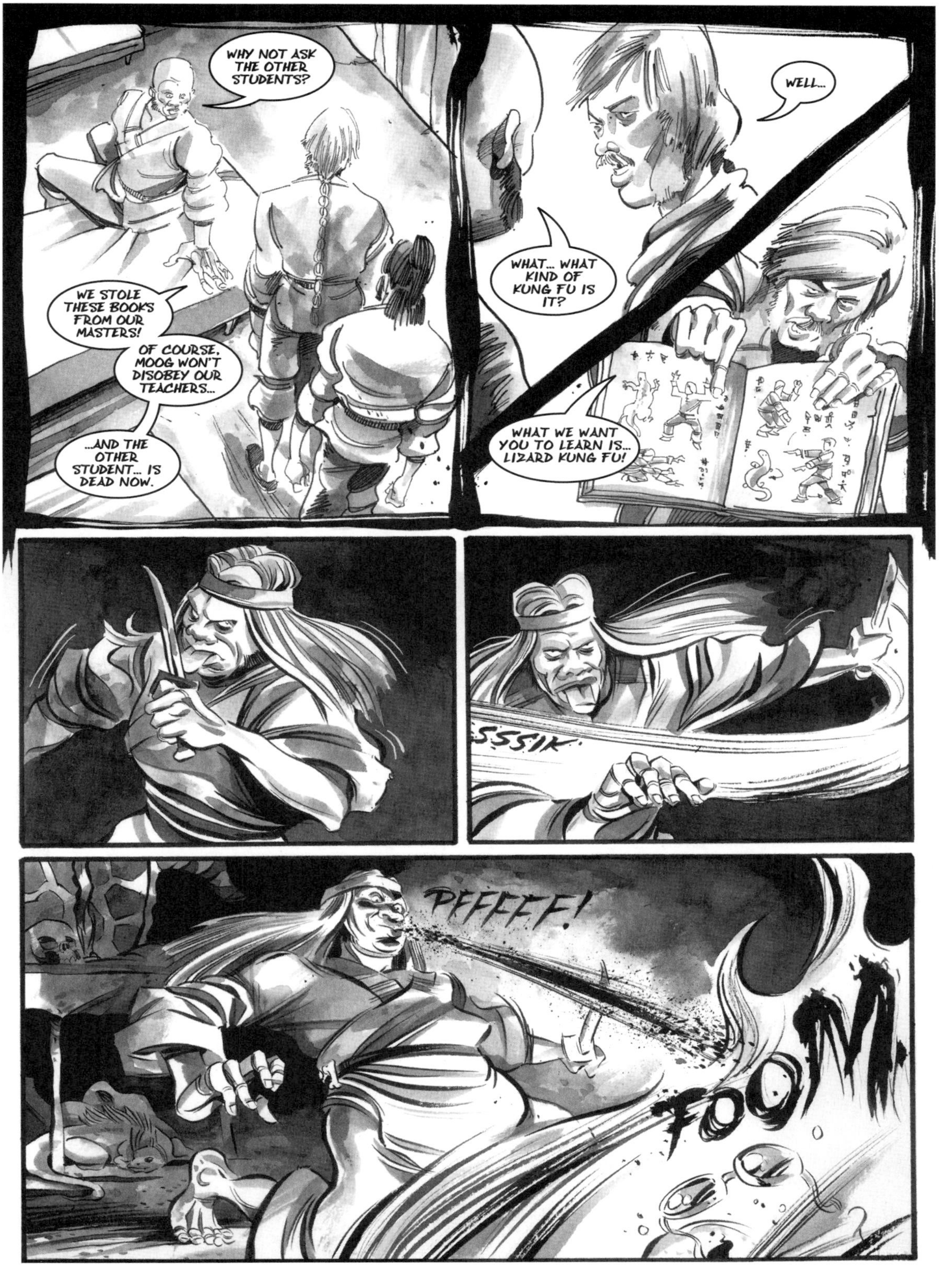

WHY NOT ASK THE OTHER STUDENTS?
WE STOLE THESE BOOKS FROM OUR MASTERS!
OF COURSE, MOOG WON'T DISOBEY OUR TEACHERS...
...AND THE OTHER STUDENT... IS DEAD NOW.
WELL...
WHAT... WHAT KIND OF KUNG FU IS IT?
WHAT WE WANT YOU TO LEARN IS... LIZARD KUNG FU!
SSSIK
PFFFFF!
FOOM!

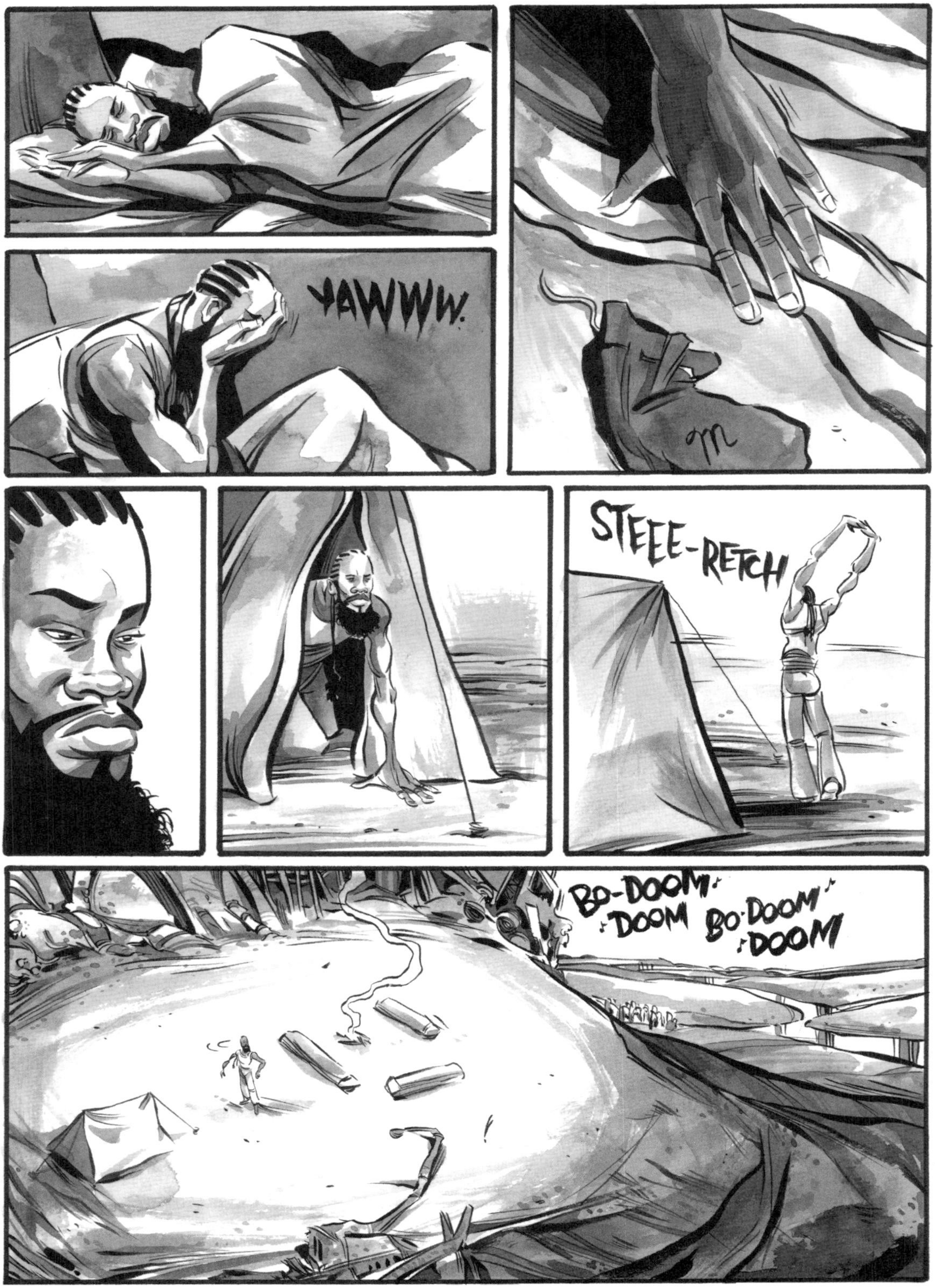
YAWWW.
STEEE-RETCH
BO-DOOM DOOM BO-DOOM DOOM

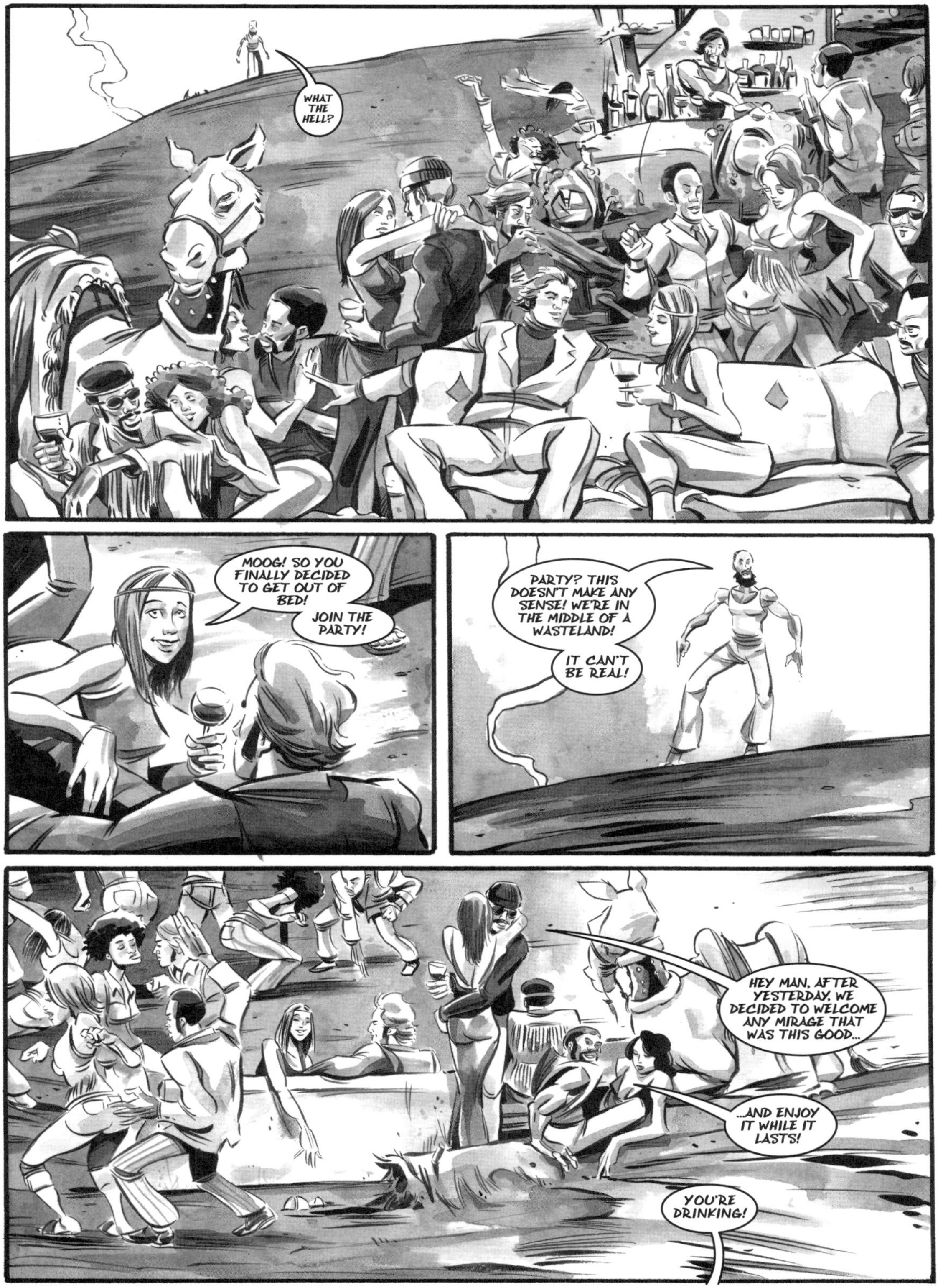
WHAT THE HELL?
MOOG! SO YOU FINALLY DECIDED TO GET OUT OF BED!
JOIN THE PARTY!
PARTY? THIS DOESN'T MAKE ANY SENSE! WE'RE IN THE MIDDLE OF A WASTELAND!
IT CAN'T BE REAL!
HEY MAN, AFTER YESTERDAY, WE DECIDED TO WELCOME ANY MIRAGE THAT WAS THIS GOOD...
...AND ENJOY IT WHILE IT LASTS!
YOU'RE DRINKING!

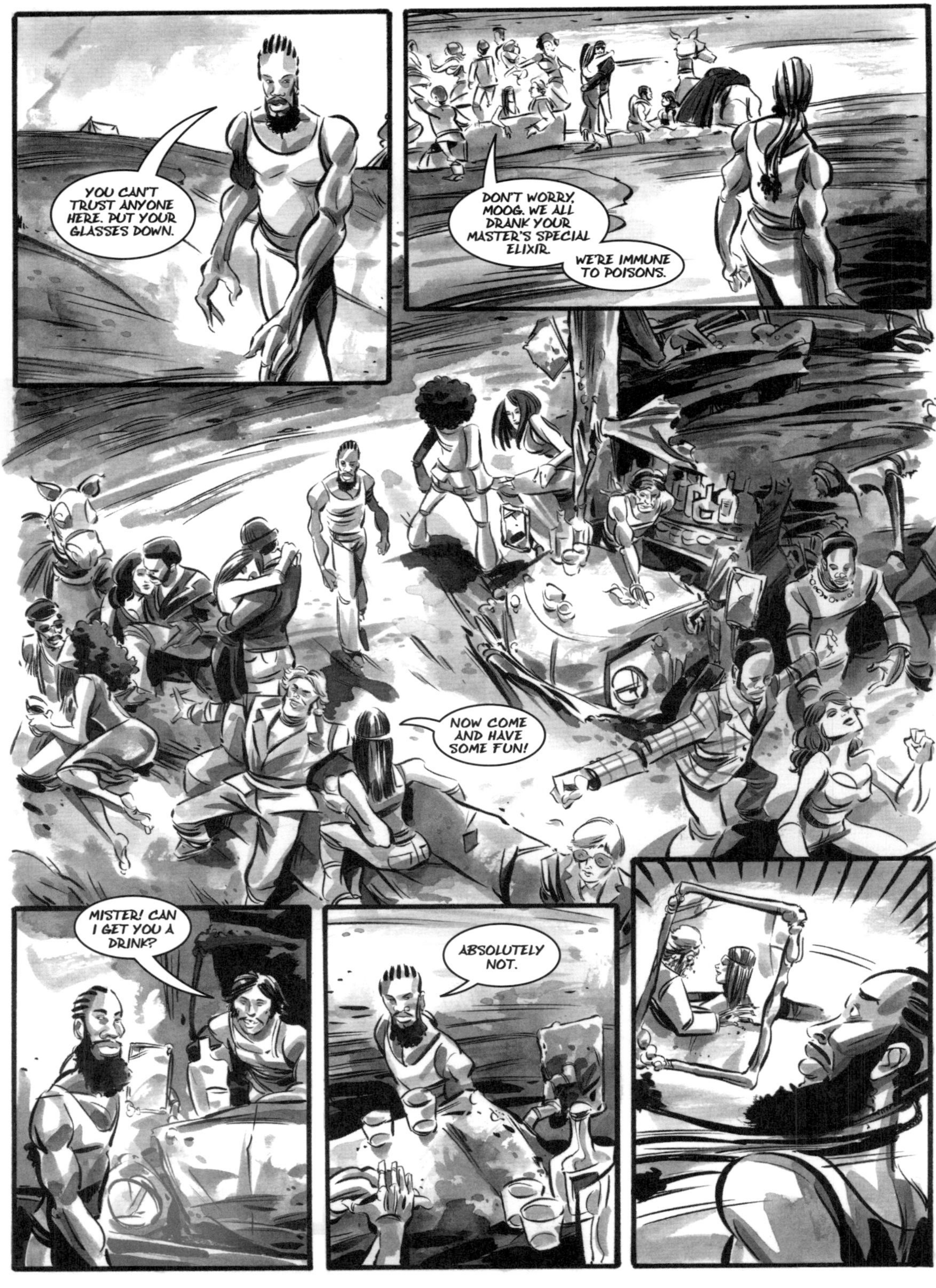
YOU CAN'T TRUST ANYONE HERE. PUT YOUR GLASSES DOWN.
DON'T WORRY, MOOG. WE ALL DRANK YOUR MASTER'S SPECIAL ELIXIR.
WE'RE IMMUNE TO POISONS.
NOW COME AND HAVE SOME FUN!
MISTER! CAN I GET YOU A DRINK?
ABSOLUTELY NOT.

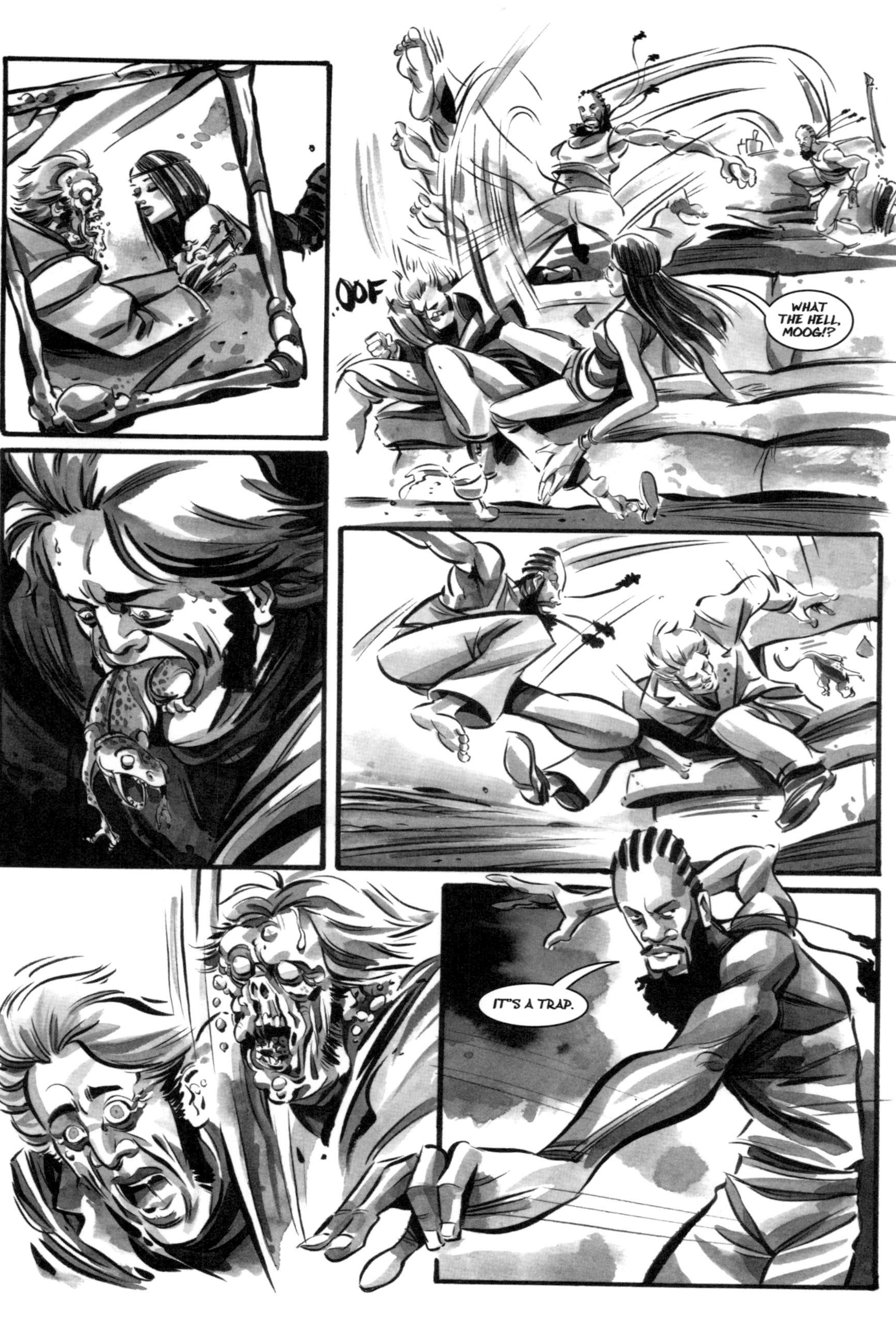
OOF
WHAT THE HELL, MOOG!?
IT'S A TRAP.

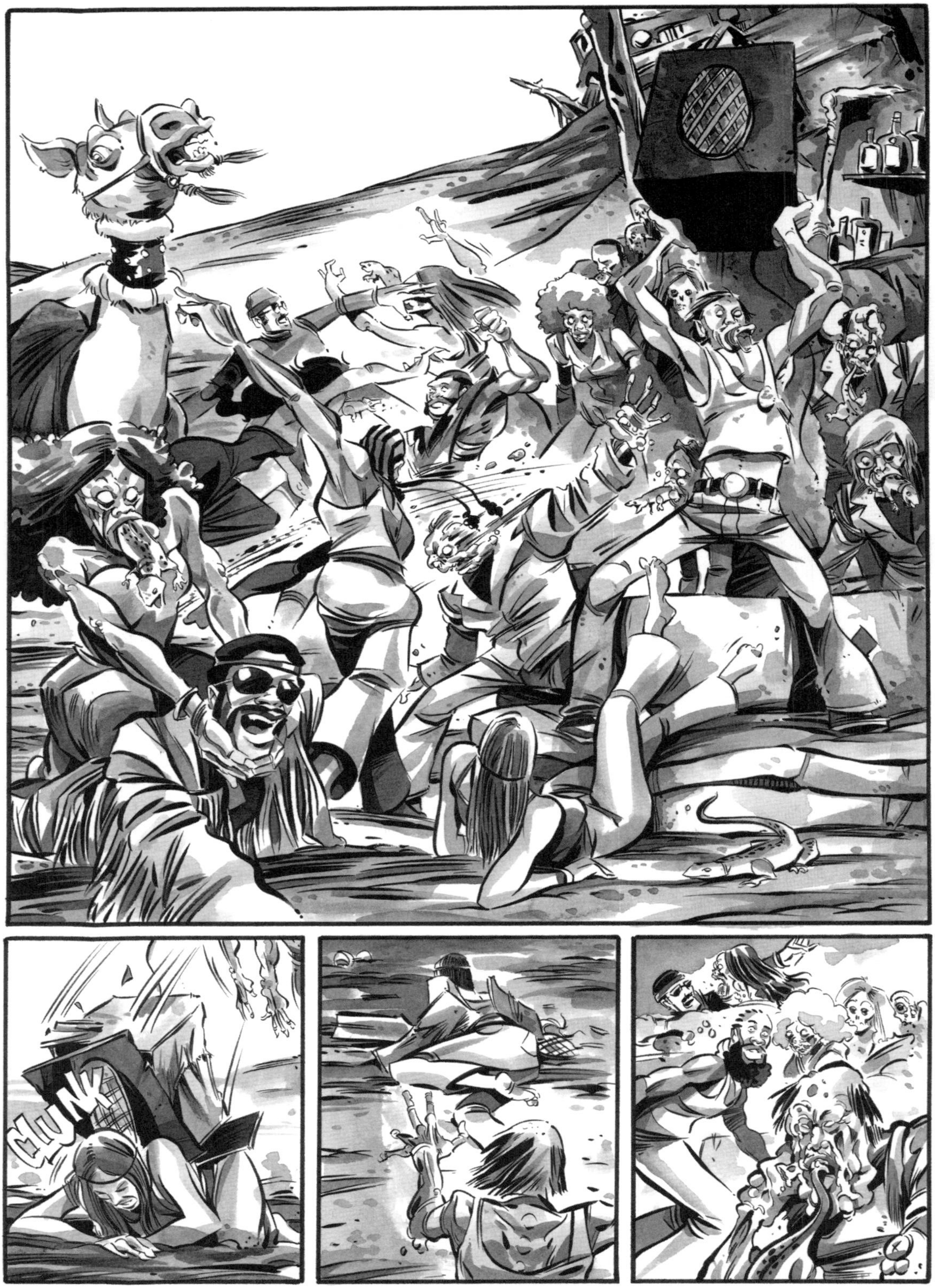
CLUNK

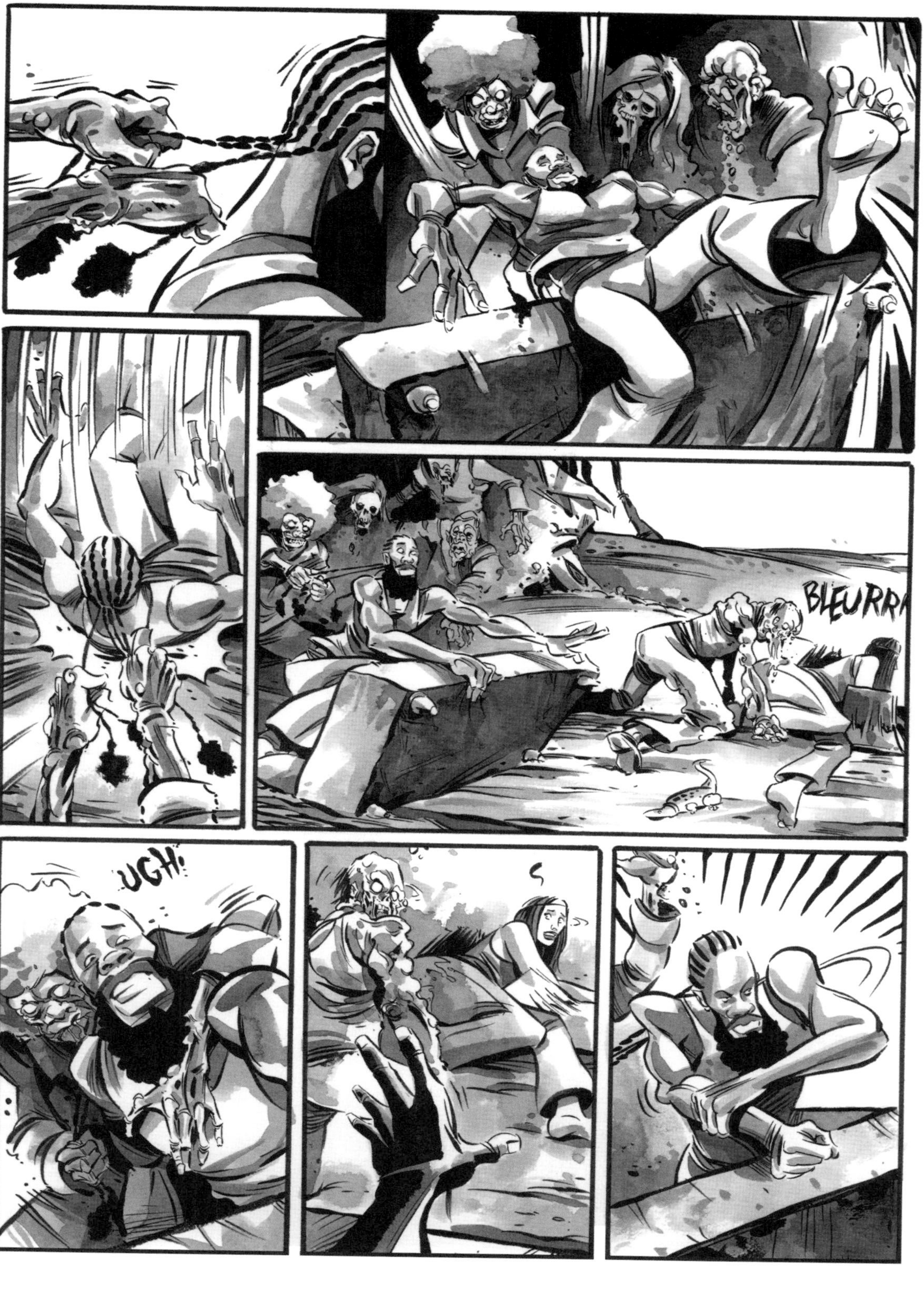
BLEURR
UGH!
?

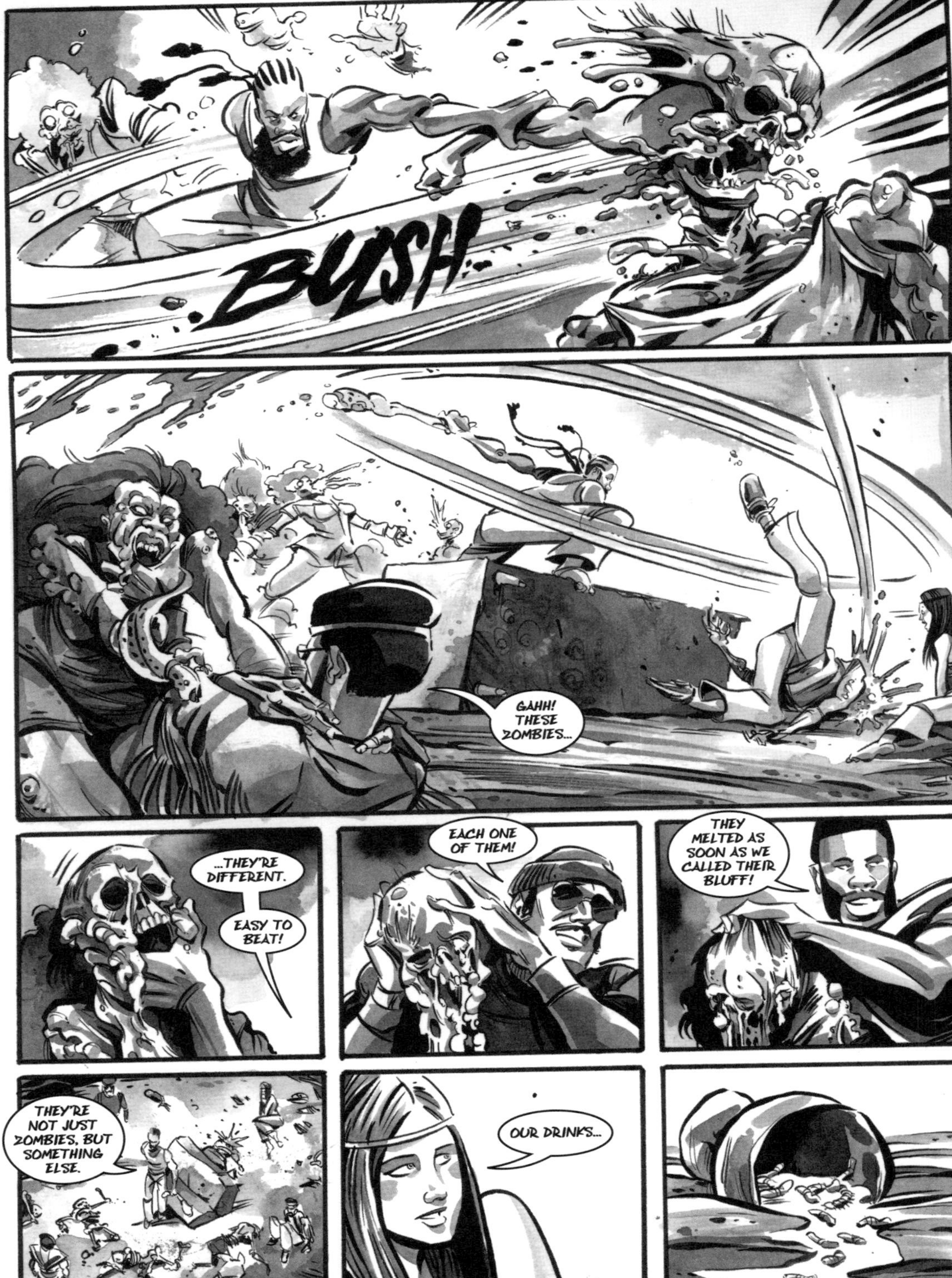
BLUSH
GAHH! THESE ZOMBIES...
...THEY'RE DIFFERENT.
EASY TO BEAT!
EACH ONE OF THEM!
THEY MELTED AS SOON AS WE CALLED THEIR BLUFF!
THEY'RE NOT JUST ZOMBIES, BUT SOMETHING ELSE.
OUR DRINKS...

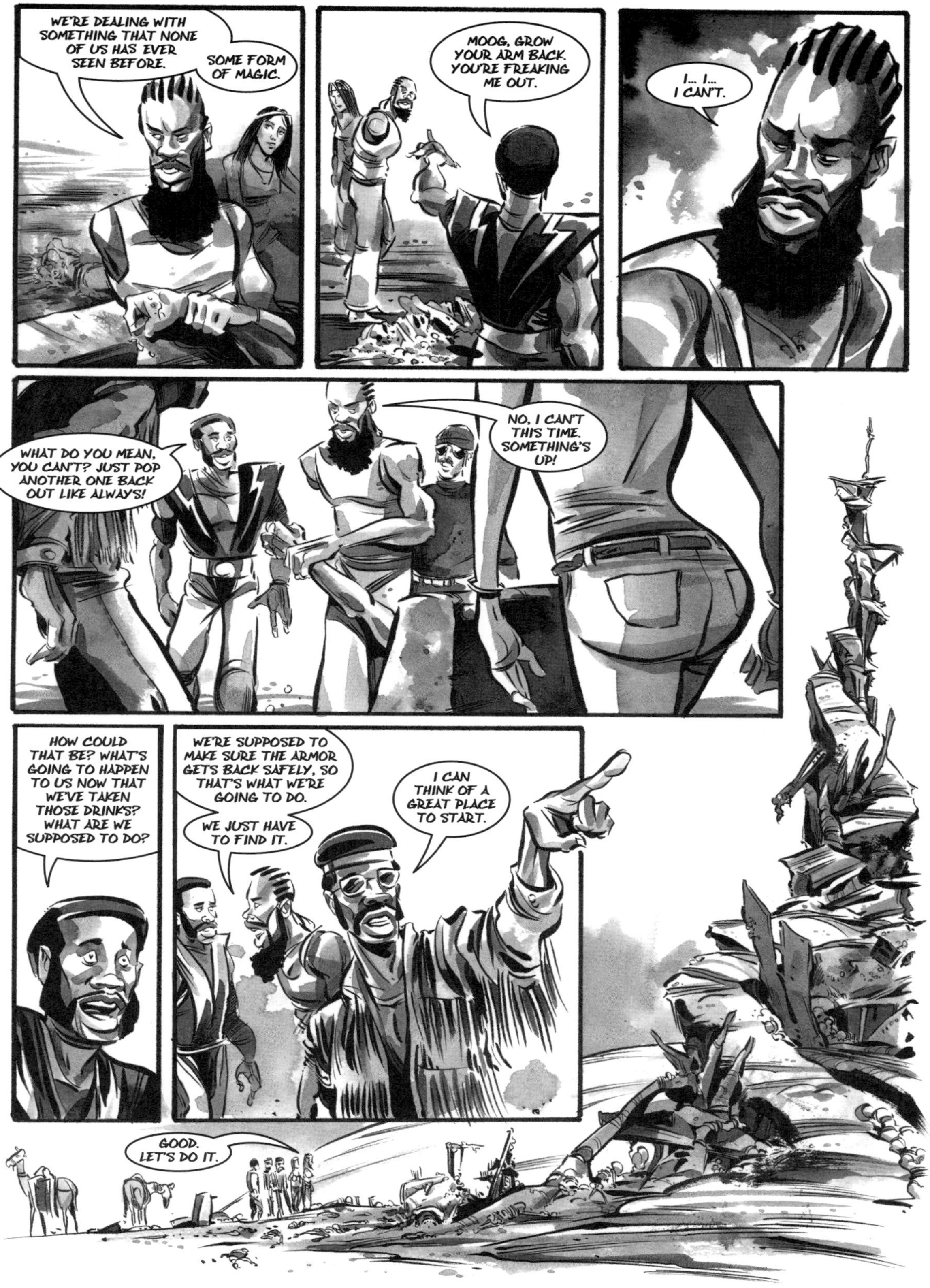
WE'RE DEALING WITH SOMETHING THAT NONE OF US HAS EVER SEEN BEFORE.
SOME FORM OF MAGIC.
MOOG, GROW YOUR ARM BACK. YOU'RE FREAKING ME OUT.
I... I... I CAN'T.
WHAT DO YOU MEAN, YOU CAN'T? JUST POP ANOTHER ONE BACK OUT LIKE ALWAYS!
NO, I CAN'T THIS TIME. SOMETHING'S UP!
HOW COULD THAT BE? WHAT'S GOING TO HAPPEN TO US NOW THAT WE'VE TAKEN THOSE DRINKS? WHAT ARE WE SUPPOSED TO DO?
WE'RE SUPPOSED TO MAKE SURE THE ARMOR GETS BACK SAFELY, SO THAT'S WHAT WE'RE GOING TO DO.
WE JUST HAVE TO FIND IT.
I CAN THINK OF A GREAT PLACE TO START.
GOOD. LET'S DO IT.

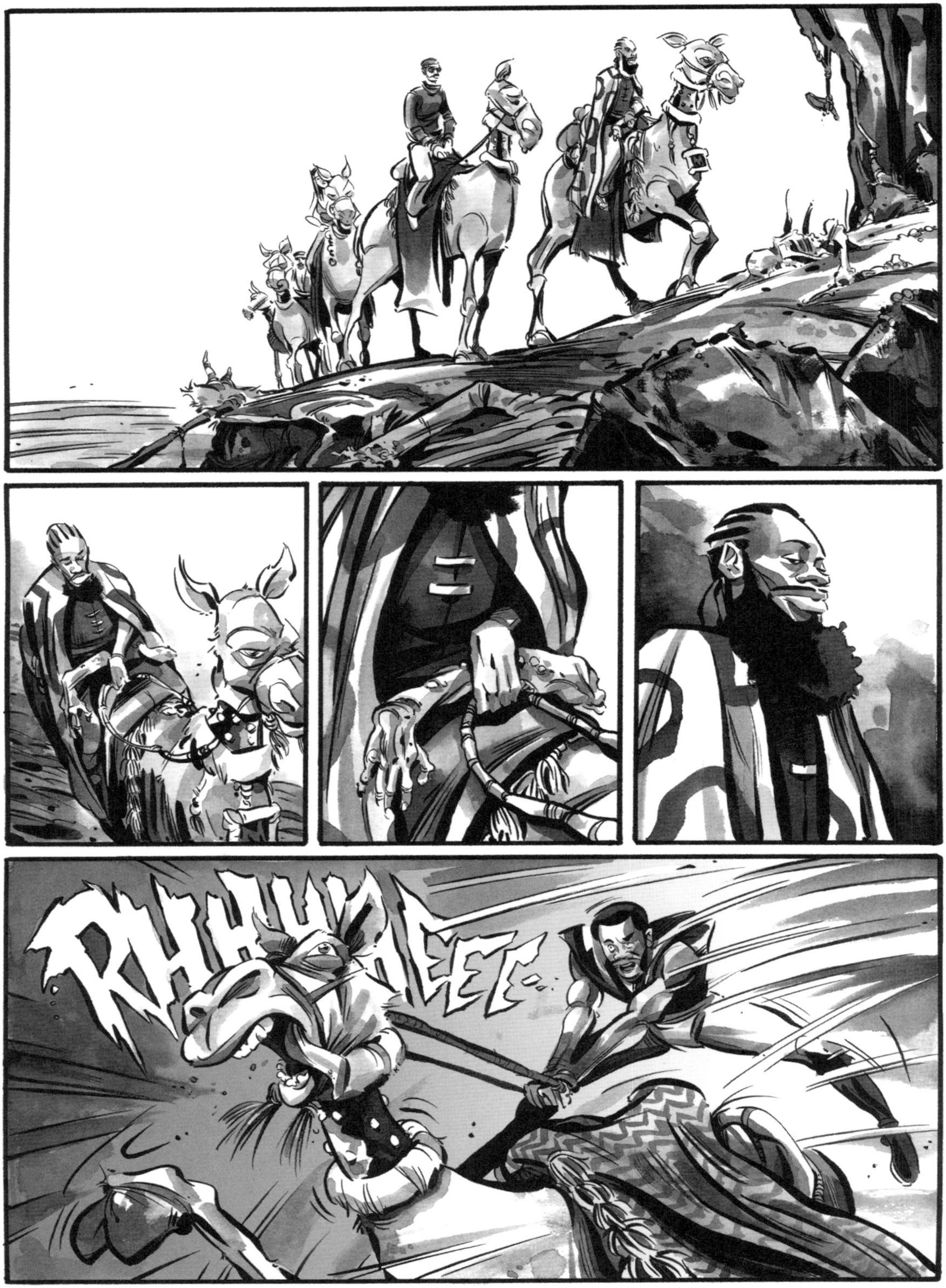

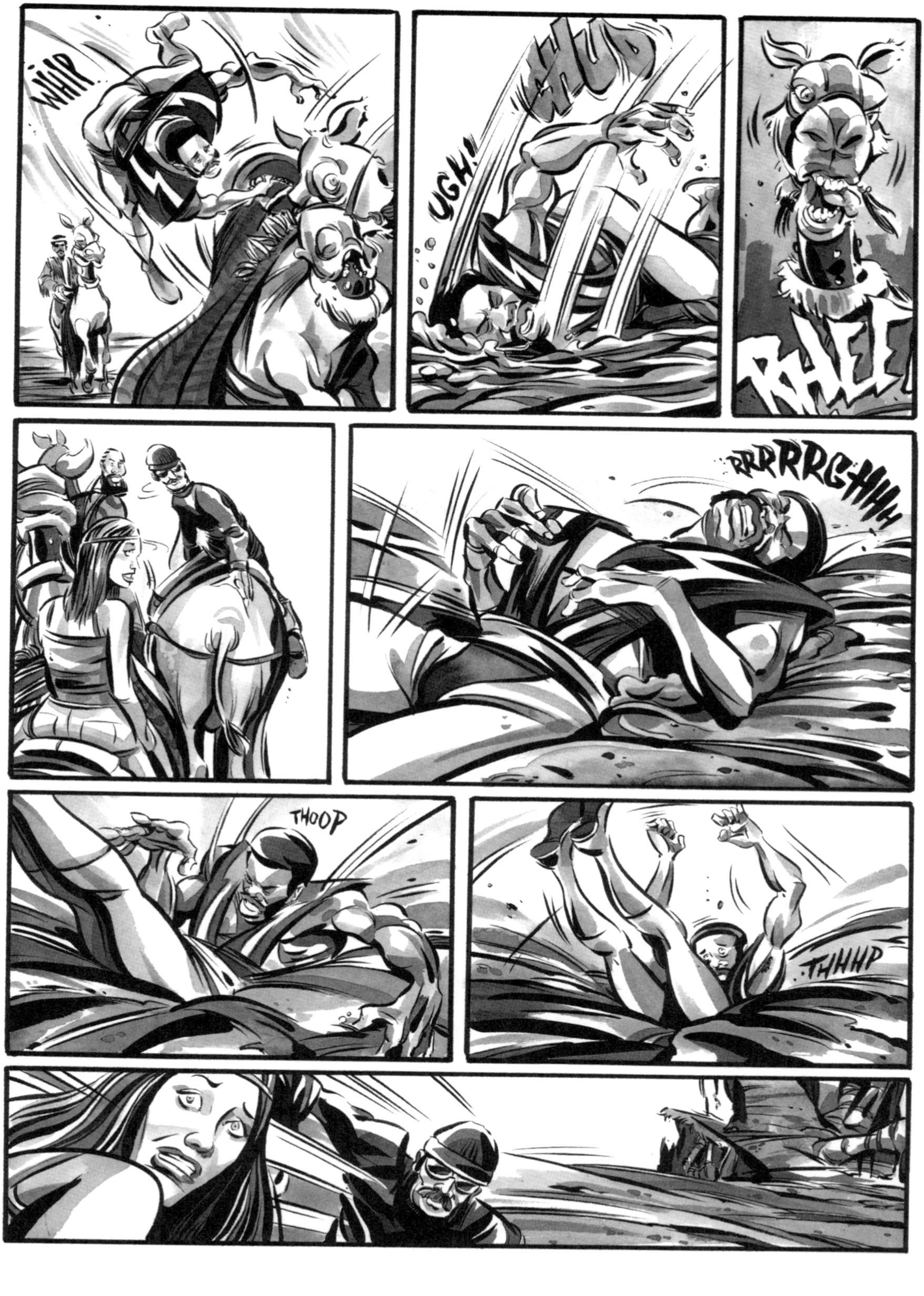
WHIP
UGH!
WHUD
RHEE
RRRRRCHHH
THOOP
THHHP

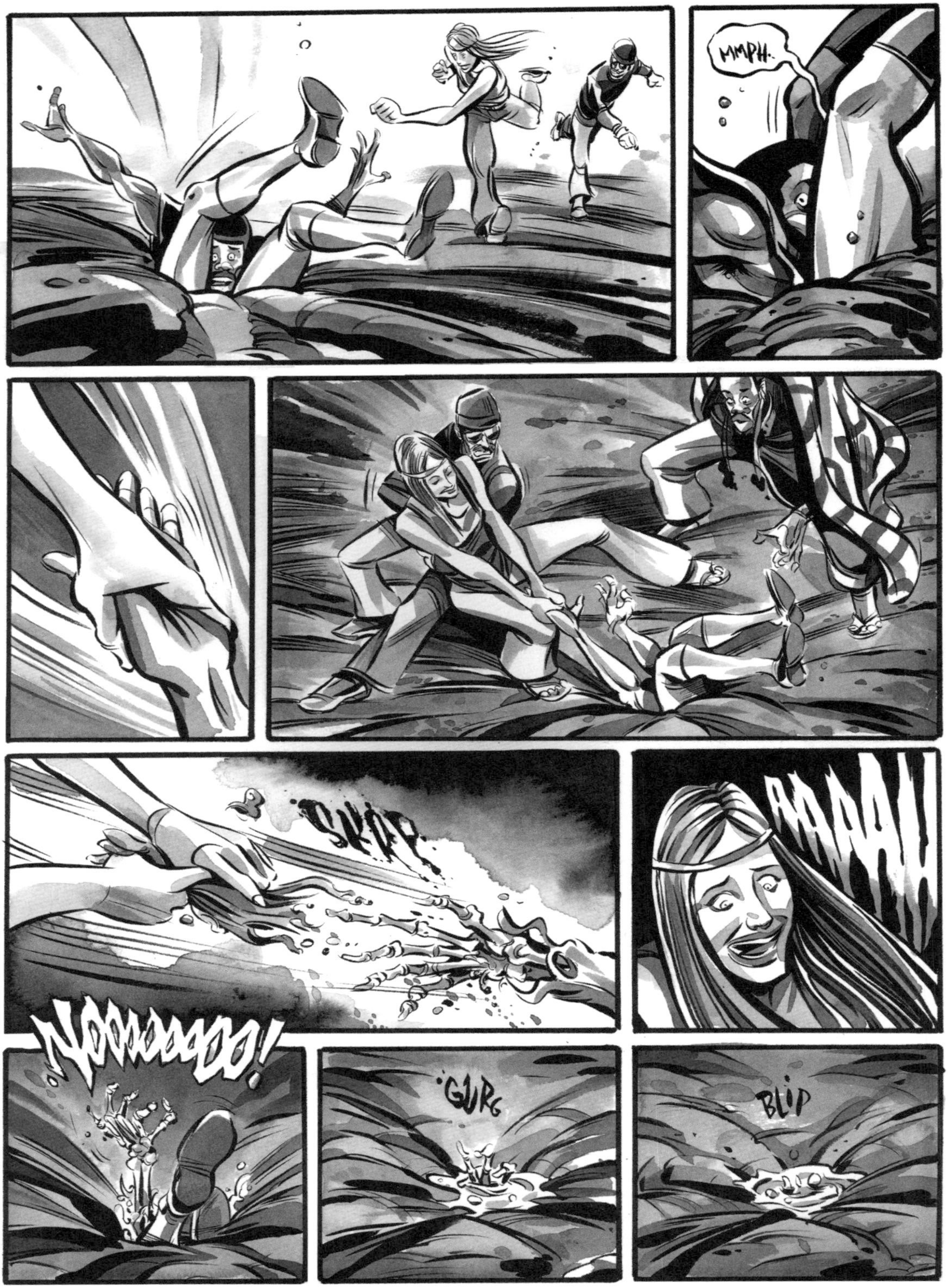
MMPH.
SKRP
AAAAH
NOOOOOOO!
GURG
BLIP

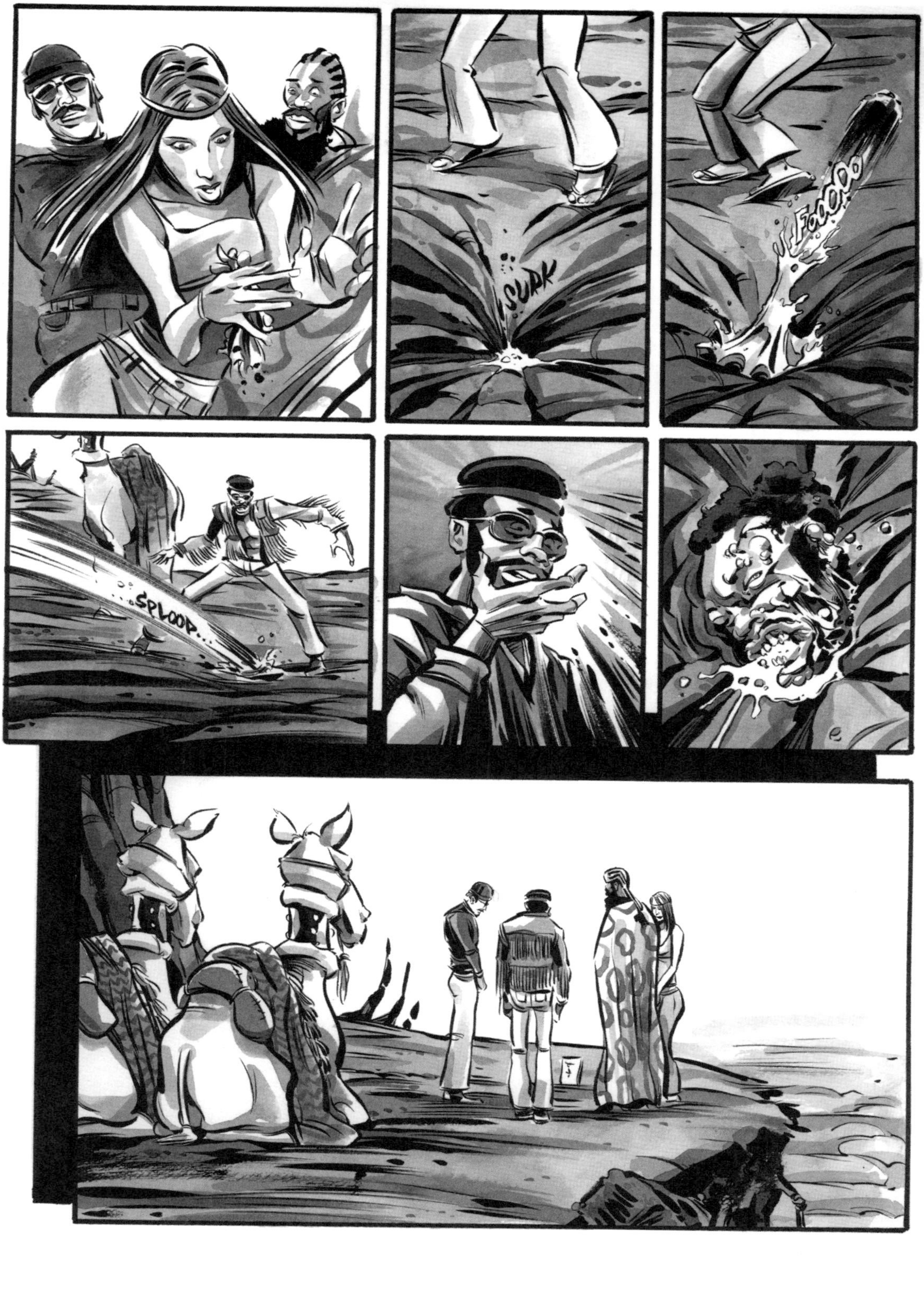
SURK
Fooooo
SPLOOP

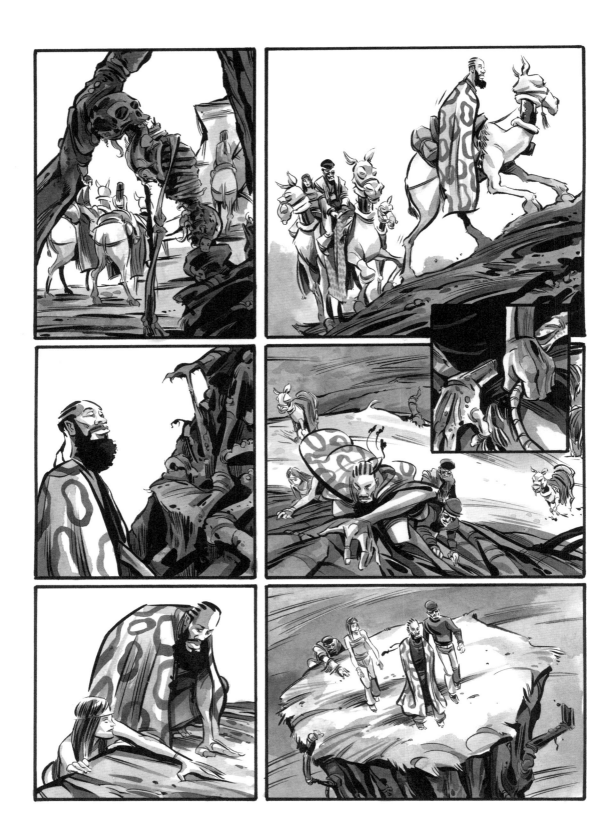

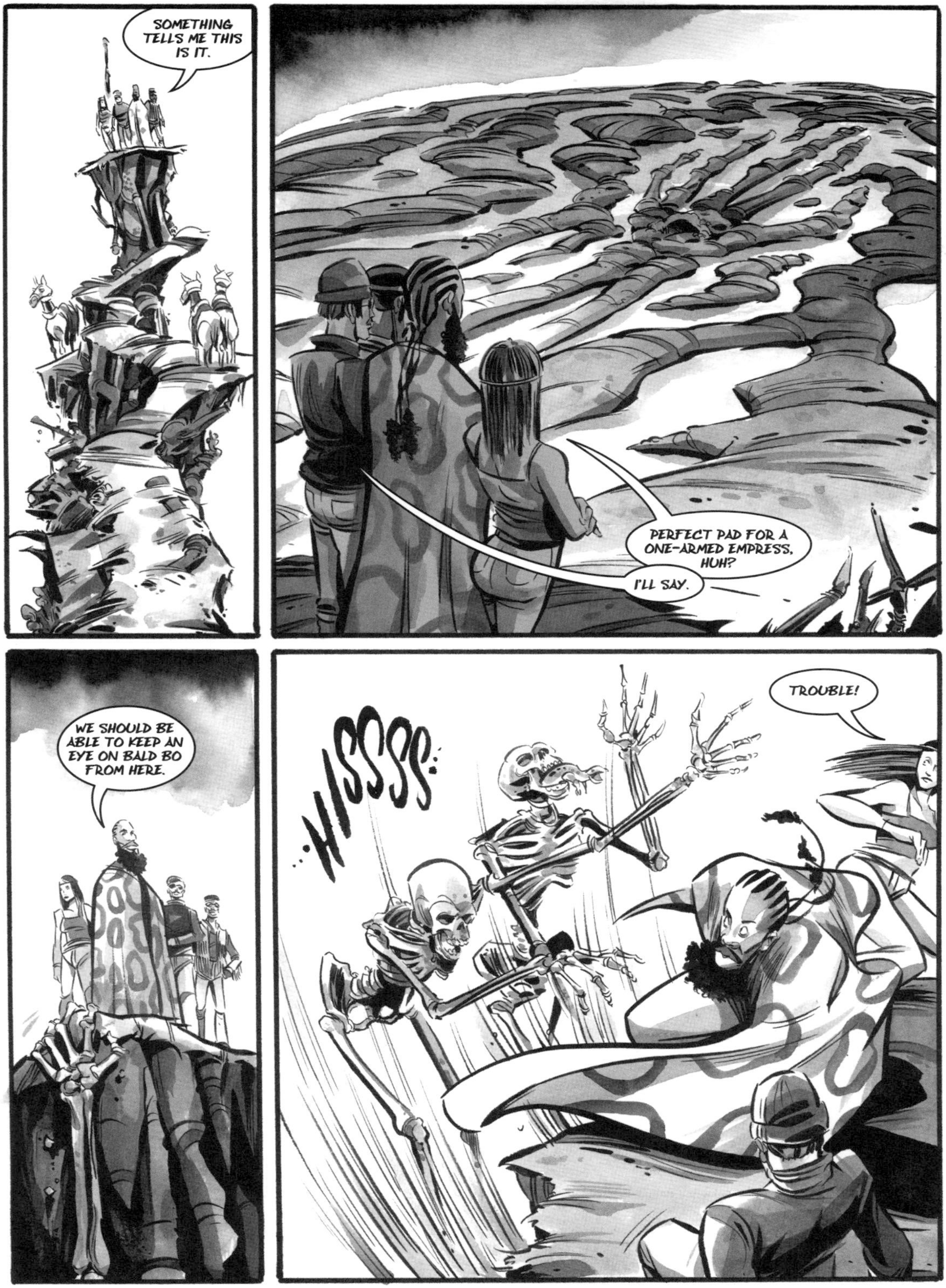
SOMETHING TELLS ME THIS IS IT.
PERFECT PAD FOR A ONE-ARMED EMPRESS, HUH?
I'LL SAY.
WE SHOULD BE ABLE TO KEEP AN EYE ON BALD BO FROM HERE.
HISSSS
TROUBLE!

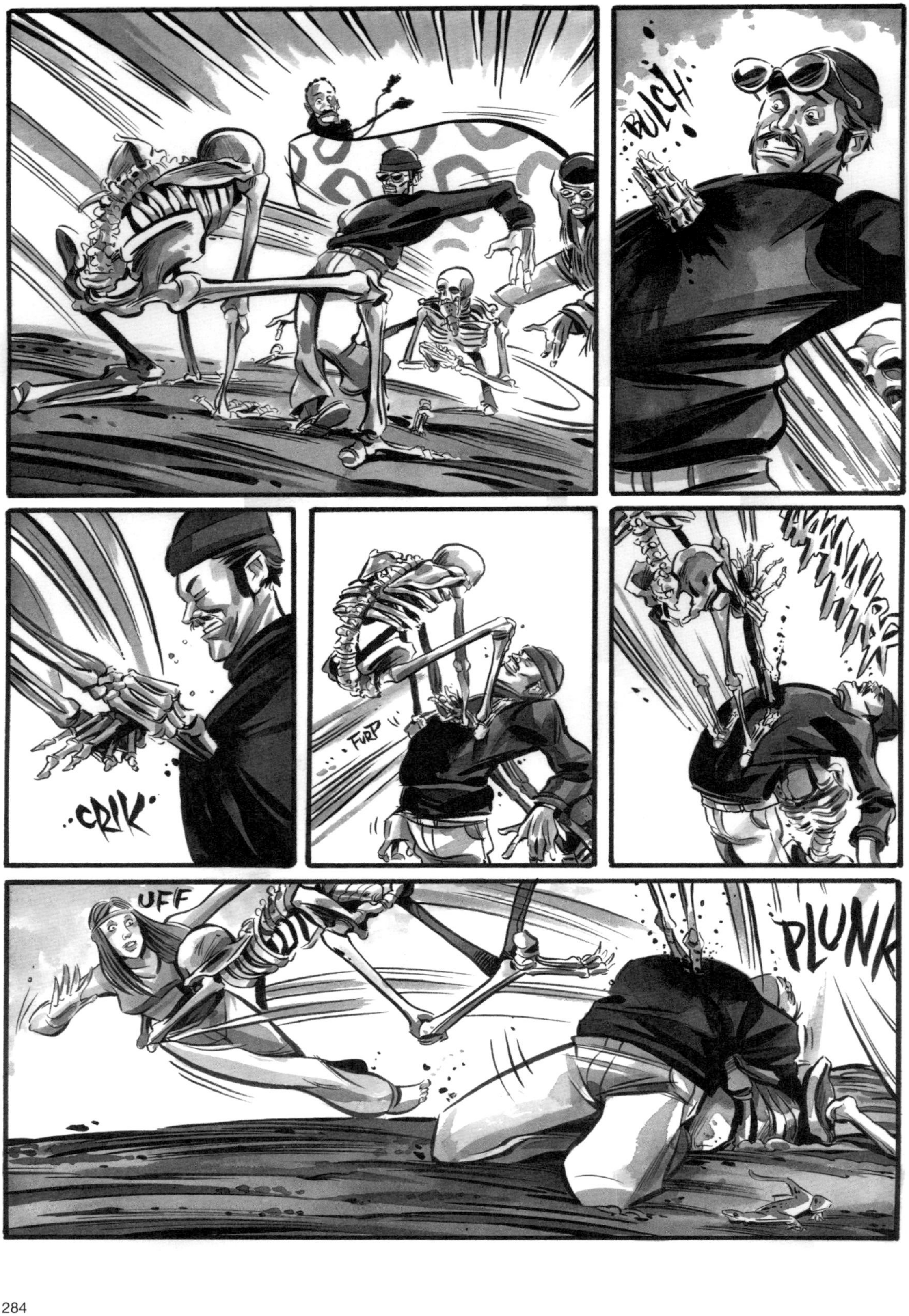
BULCH
CRIK
FURP
UFF
PLUNK

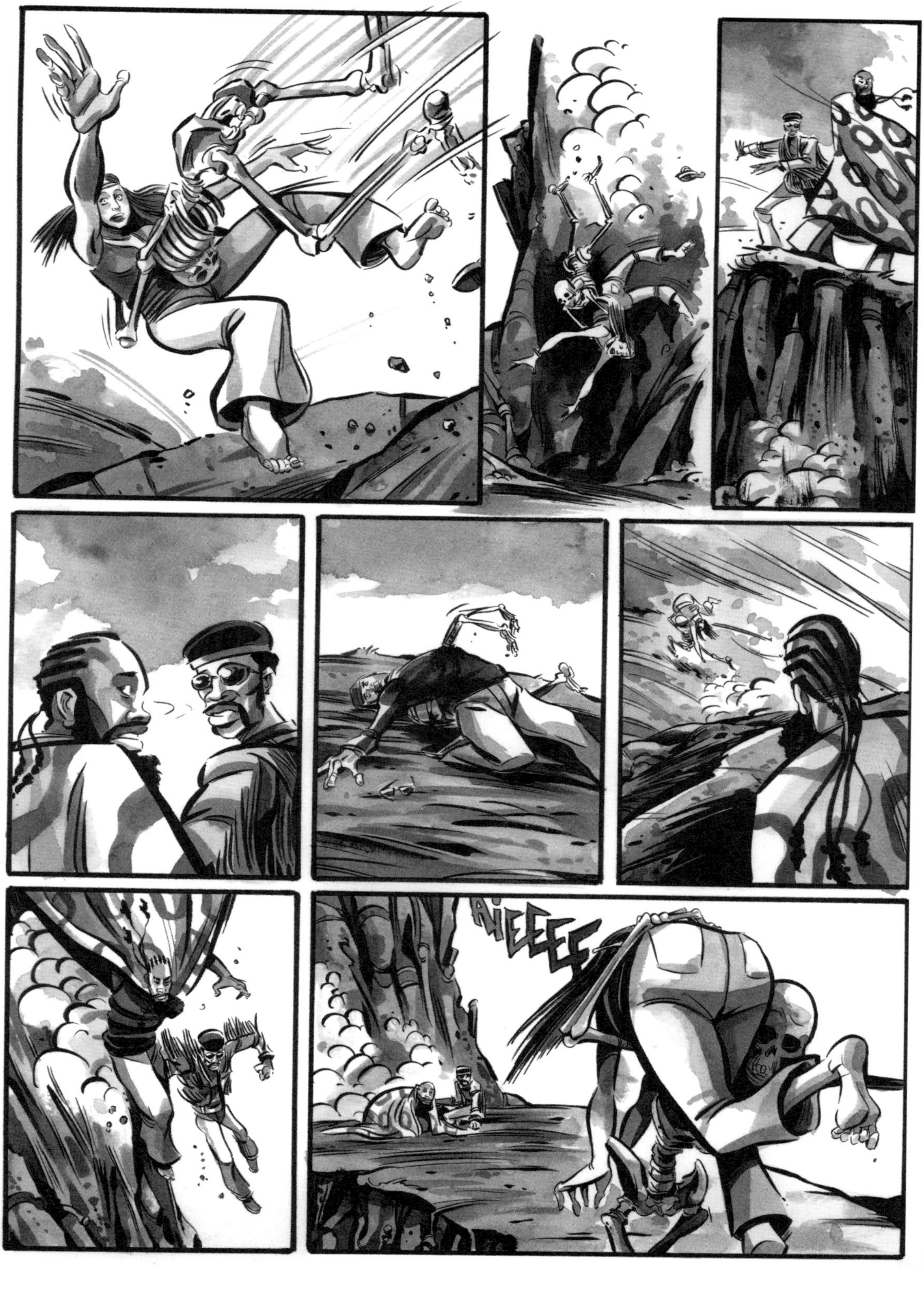
AIEEEE

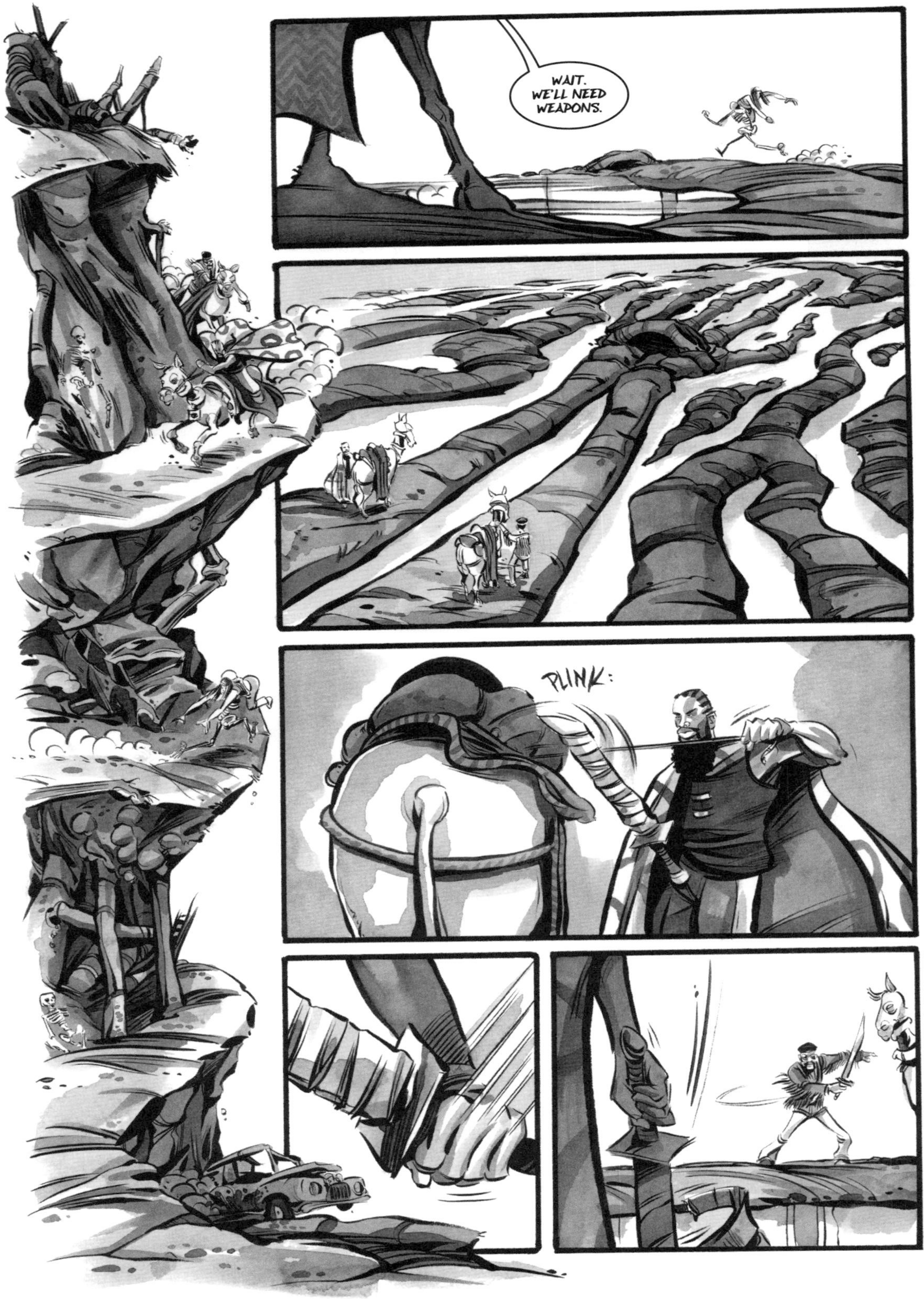
WAIT. WE'LL NEED WEAPONS.
PLINK:

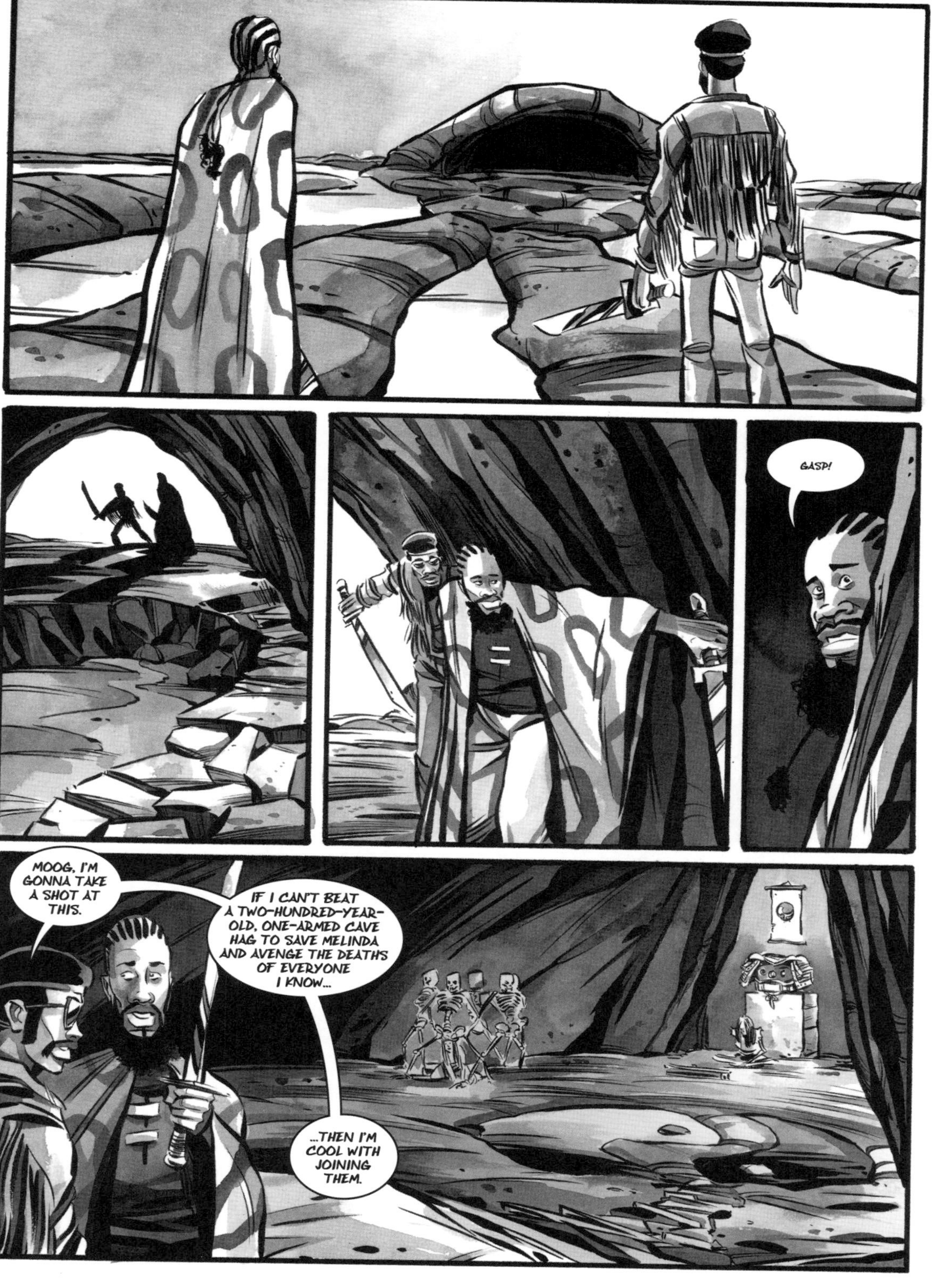
GASP!
MOOG, I'M GONNA TAKE A SHOT AT THIS.
IF I CAN'T BEAT A TWO-HUNDRED-YEAR-OLD, ONE-ARMED CAVE HAG TO SAVE MELINDA AND AVENGE THE DEATHS OF EVERYONE I KNOW...
...THEN I'M COOL WITH JOINING THEM.

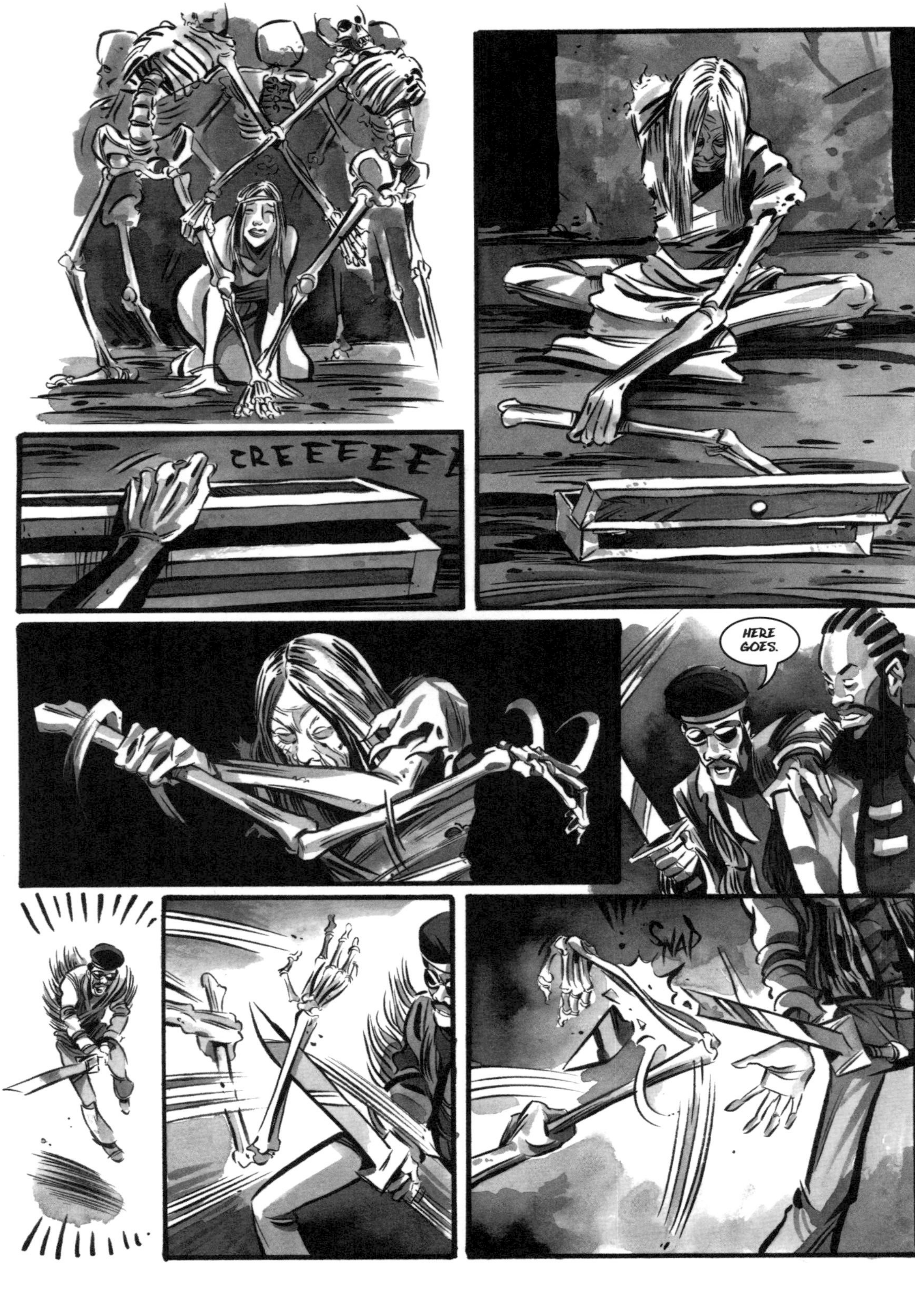
CREEEEEE
HERE GOES.
SNAP

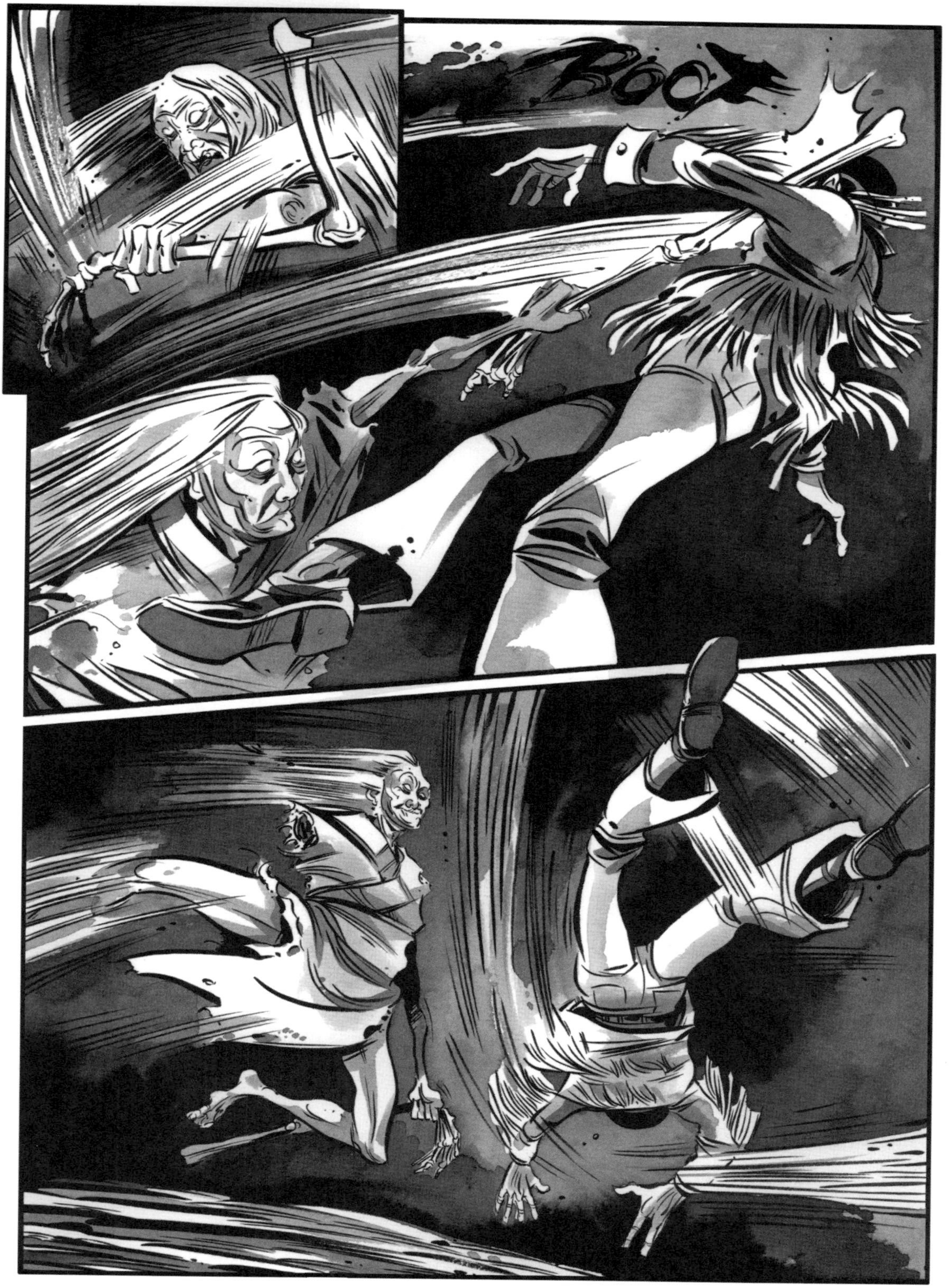

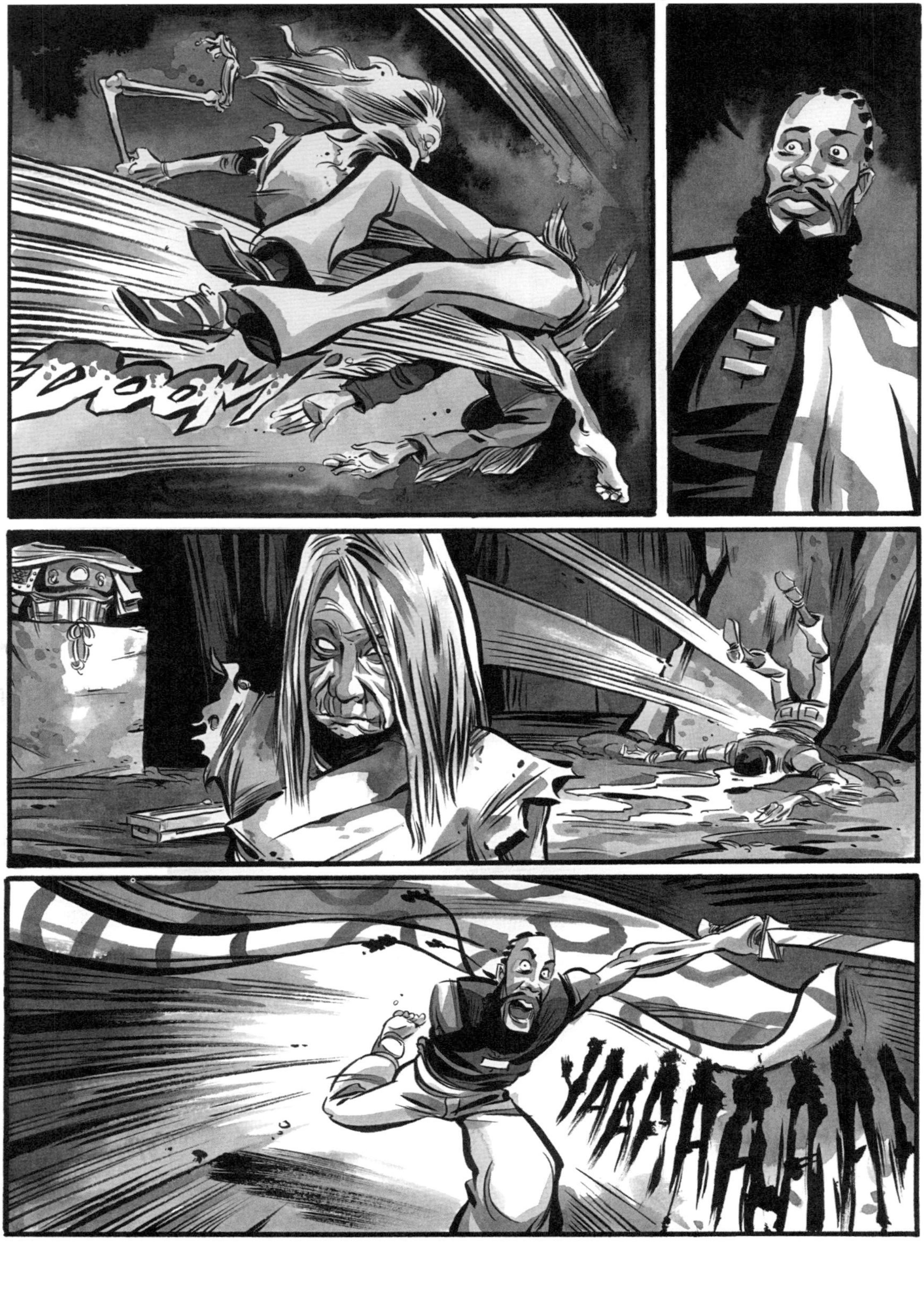
YAAAAAAA

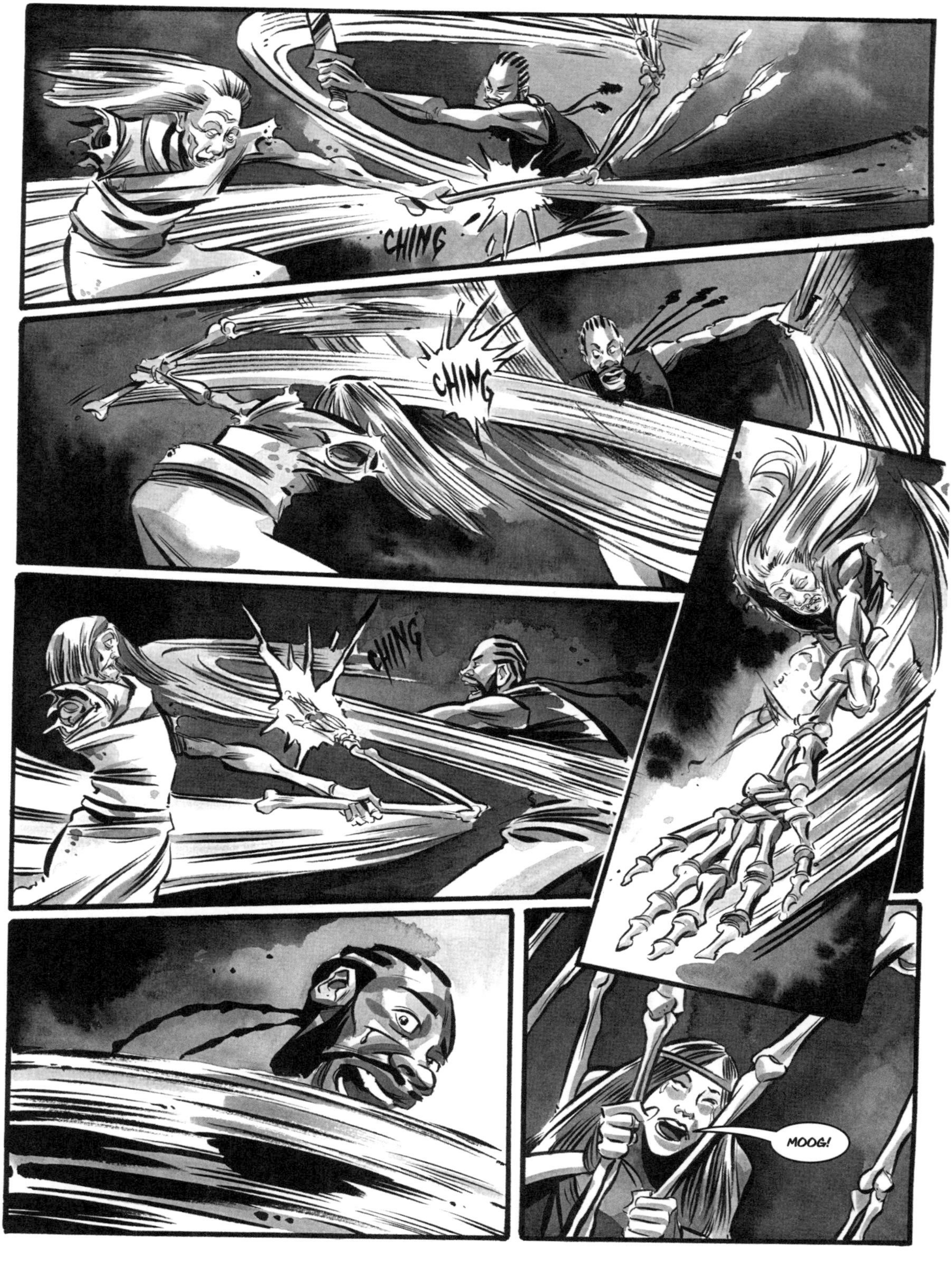
CHING
CHING
CHING
MOOG!

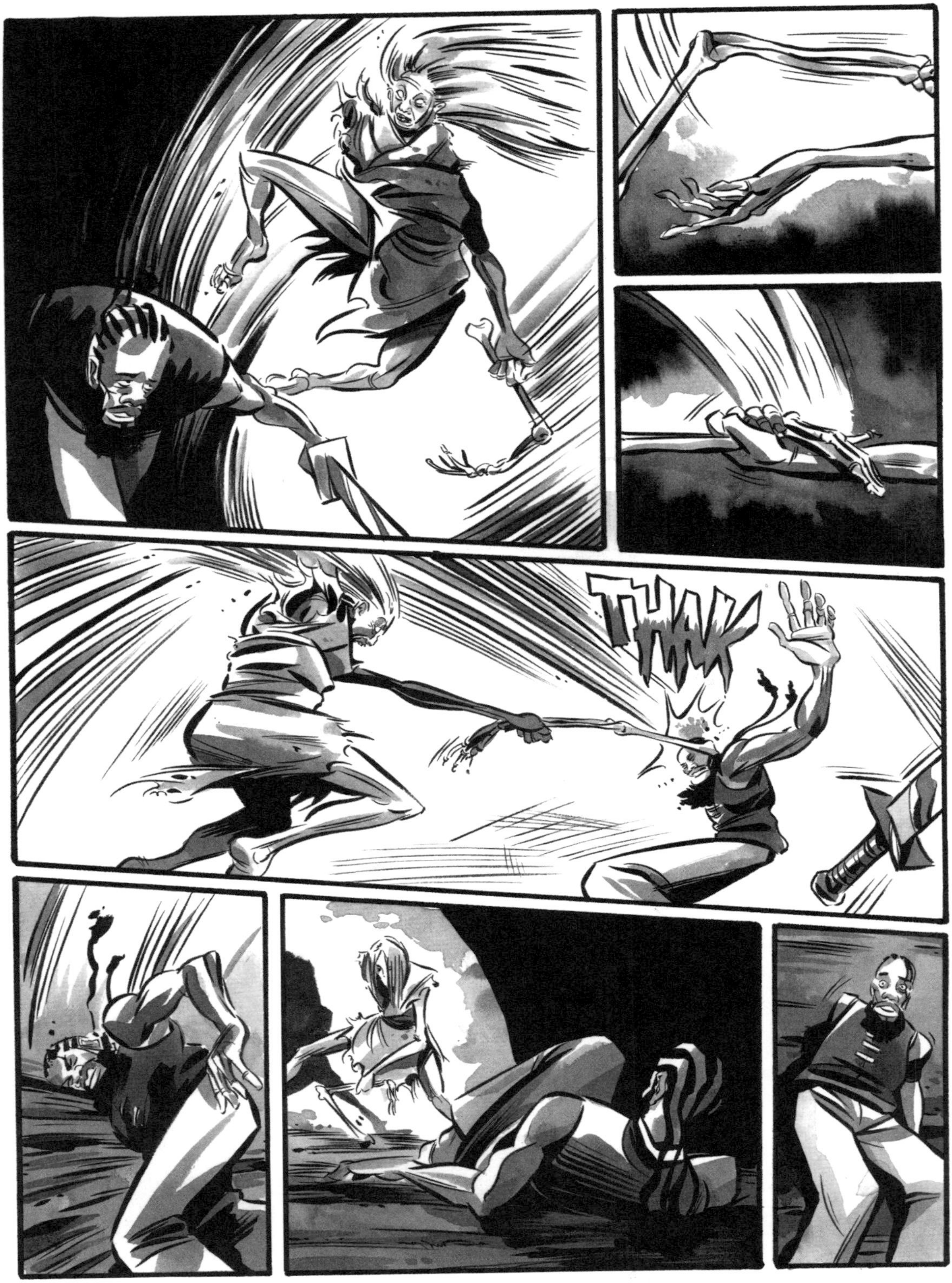
THAK

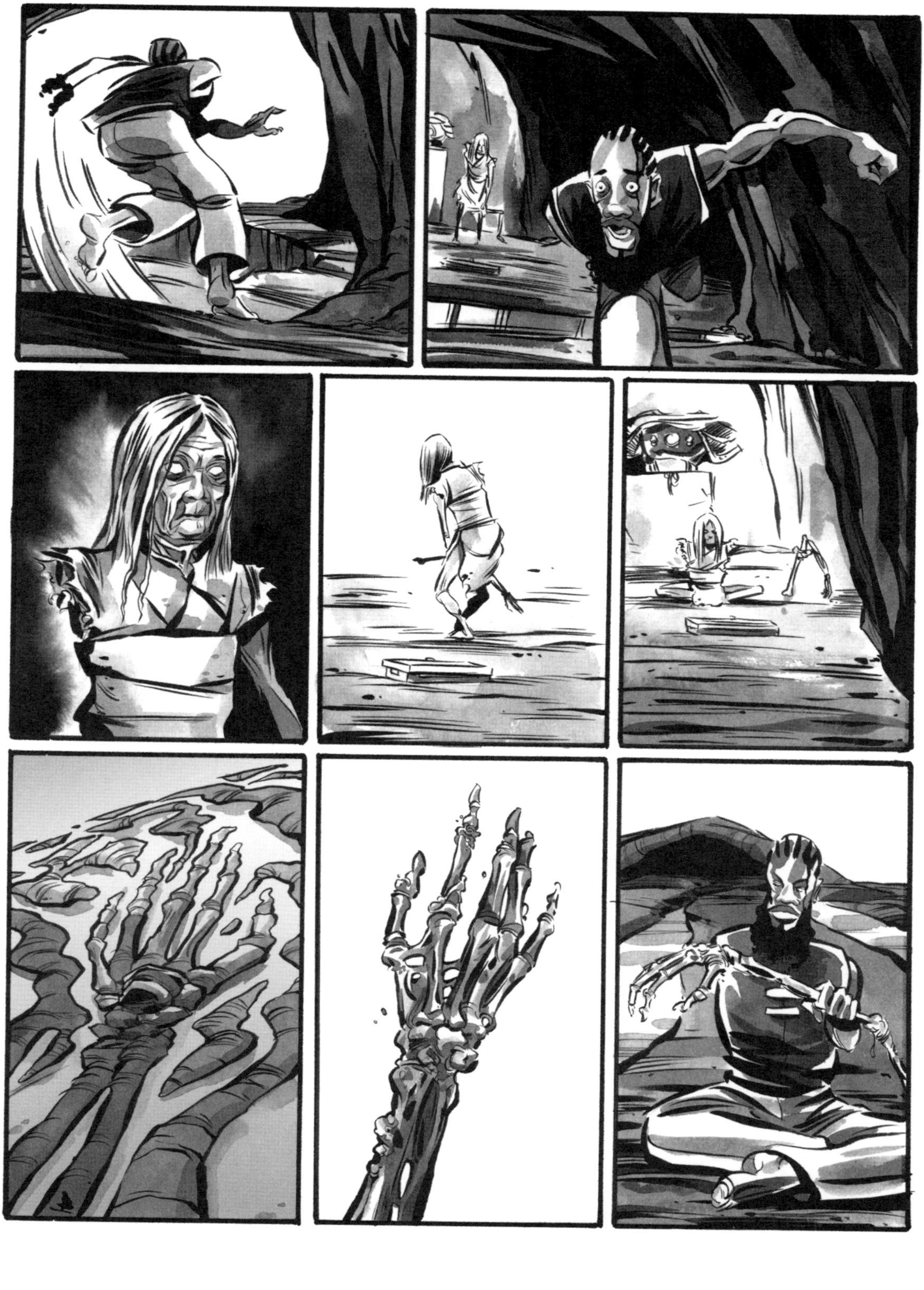

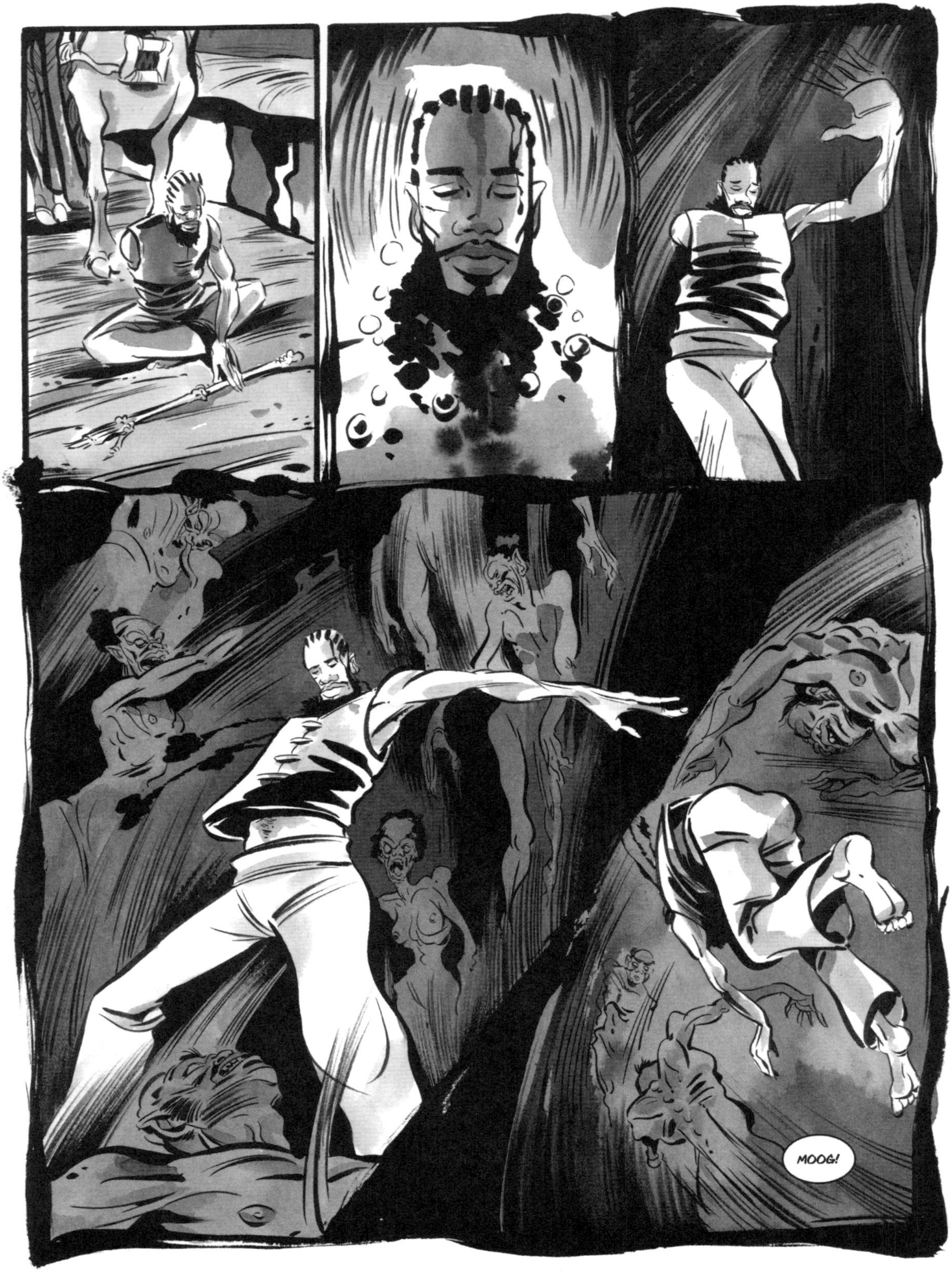
MOOG!

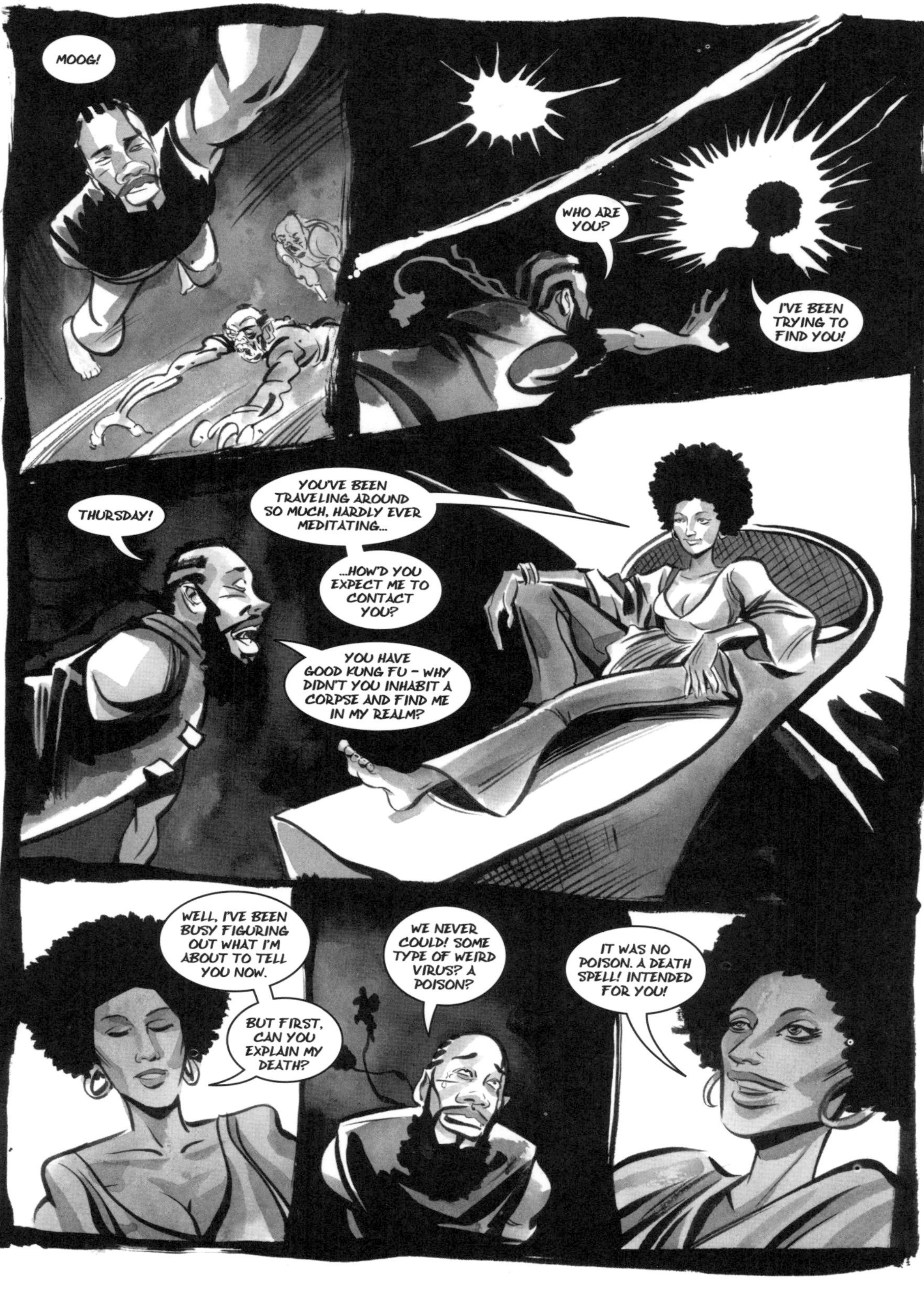
MOOG!
WHO ARE YOU?
I'VE BEEN TRYING TO FIND YOU!
THURSDAY!
YOU'VE BEEN TRAVELING AROUND SO MUCH, HARDLY EVER MEDITATING...
...HOW'D YOU EXPECT ME TO CONTACT YOU?
YOU HAVE GOOD KUNG FU - WHY DIDN'T YOU INHABIT A CORPSE AND FIND ME IN MY REALM?
WELL, I'VE BEEN BUSY FIGURING OUT WHAT I'M ABOUT TO TELL YOU NOW.
BUT FIRST, CAN YOU EXPLAIN MY DEATH?
WE NEVER COULD! SOME TYPE OF WEIRD VIRUS? A POISON?
IT WAS NO POISON. A DEATH SPELL! INTENDED FOR YOU!

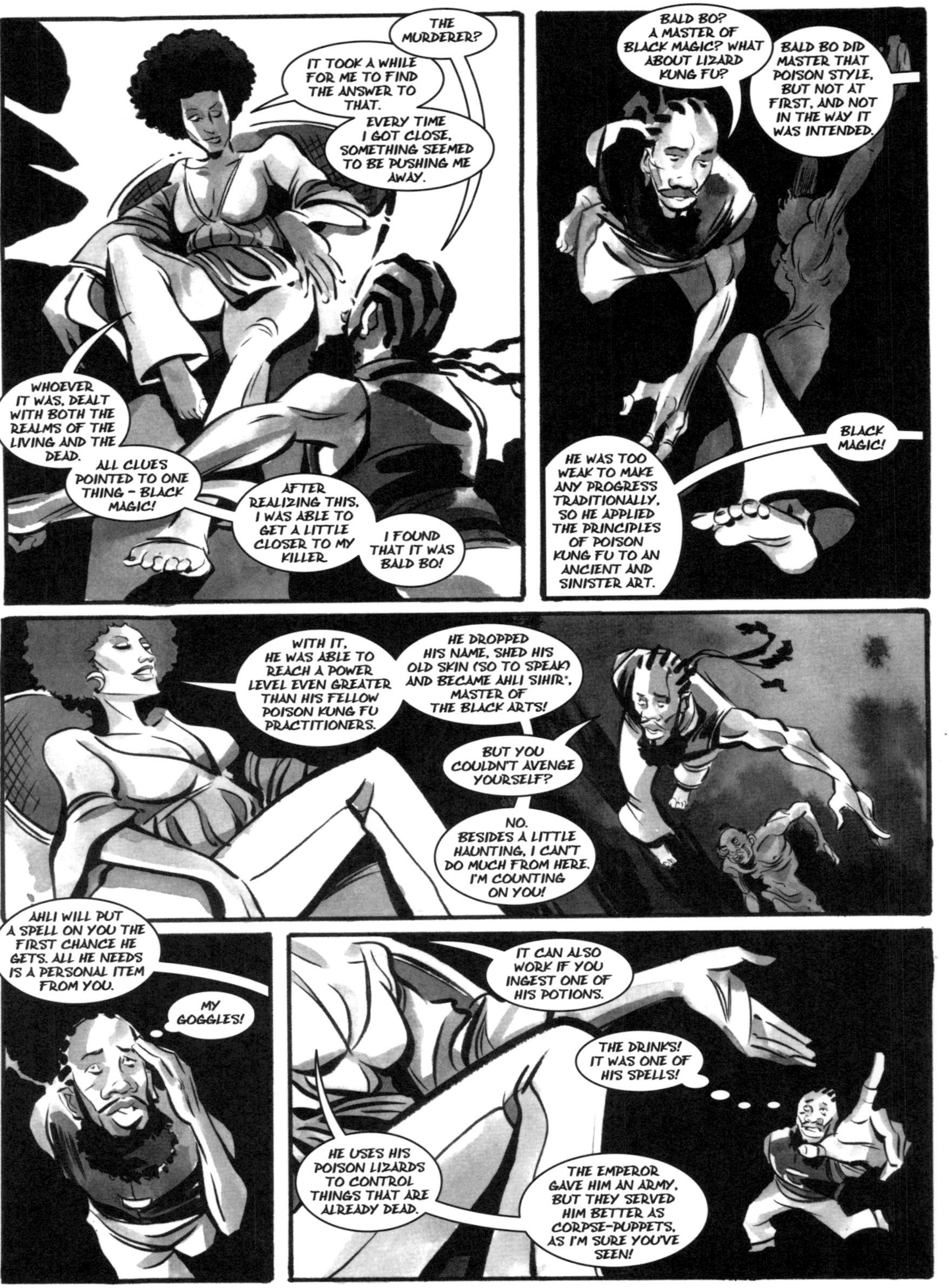
THE MURDERER?
IT TOOK A WHILE FOR ME TO FIND THE ANSWER TO THAT.
EVERY TIME I GOT CLOSE, SOMETHING SEEMED TO BE PUSHING ME AWAY.
WHOEVER IT WAS, DEALT WITH BOTH THE REALMS OF THE LIVING AND THE DEAD.
ALL CLUES POINTED TO ONE THING - BLACK MAGIC!
AFTER REALIZING THIS, I WAS ABLE TO GET A LITTLE CLOSER TO MY KILLER.
I FOUND THAT IT WAS BALD BO!
BALD BO? A MASTER OF BLACK MAGIC? WHAT ABOUT LIZARD KUNG FU?
BALD BO DID MASTER THAT POISON STYLE, BUT NOT AT FIRST, AND NOT IN THE WAY IT WAS INTENDED.
HE WAS TOO WEAK TO MAKE ANY PROGRESS TRADITIONALLY, SO HE APPLIED THE PRINCIPLES OF POISON KUNG FU TO AN ANCIENT AND SINISTER ART.
BLACK MAGIC!
WITH IT, HE WAS ABLE TO REACH A POWER LEVEL EVEN GREATER THAN HIS FELLOW POISON KUNG FU PRACTITIONERS.
HE DROPPED HIS NAME, SHED HIS OLD SKIN (SO TO SPEAK) AND BECAME AHLI SIHIR*, MASTER OF THE BLACK ARTS!
BUT YOU COULDN'T AVENGE YOURSELF?
NO. BESIDES A LITTLE HAUNTING, I CAN'T DO MUCH FROM HERE. I'M COUNTING ON YOU!
AHLI WILL PUT A SPELL ON YOU THE FIRST CHANCE HE GETS. ALL HE NEEDS IS A PERSONAL ITEM FROM YOU.
MY GOGGLES!
IT CAN ALSO WORK IF YOU INGEST ONE OF HIS POTIONS.
THE DRINKS! IT WAS ONE OF HIS SPELLS!
HE USES HIS POISON LIZARDS TO CONTROL THINGS THAT ARE ALREADY DEAD.
THE EMPEROR GAVE HIM AN ARMY, BUT THEY SERVED HIM BETTER AS CORPSE-PUPPETS, AS I'M SURE YOU'VE SEEN!

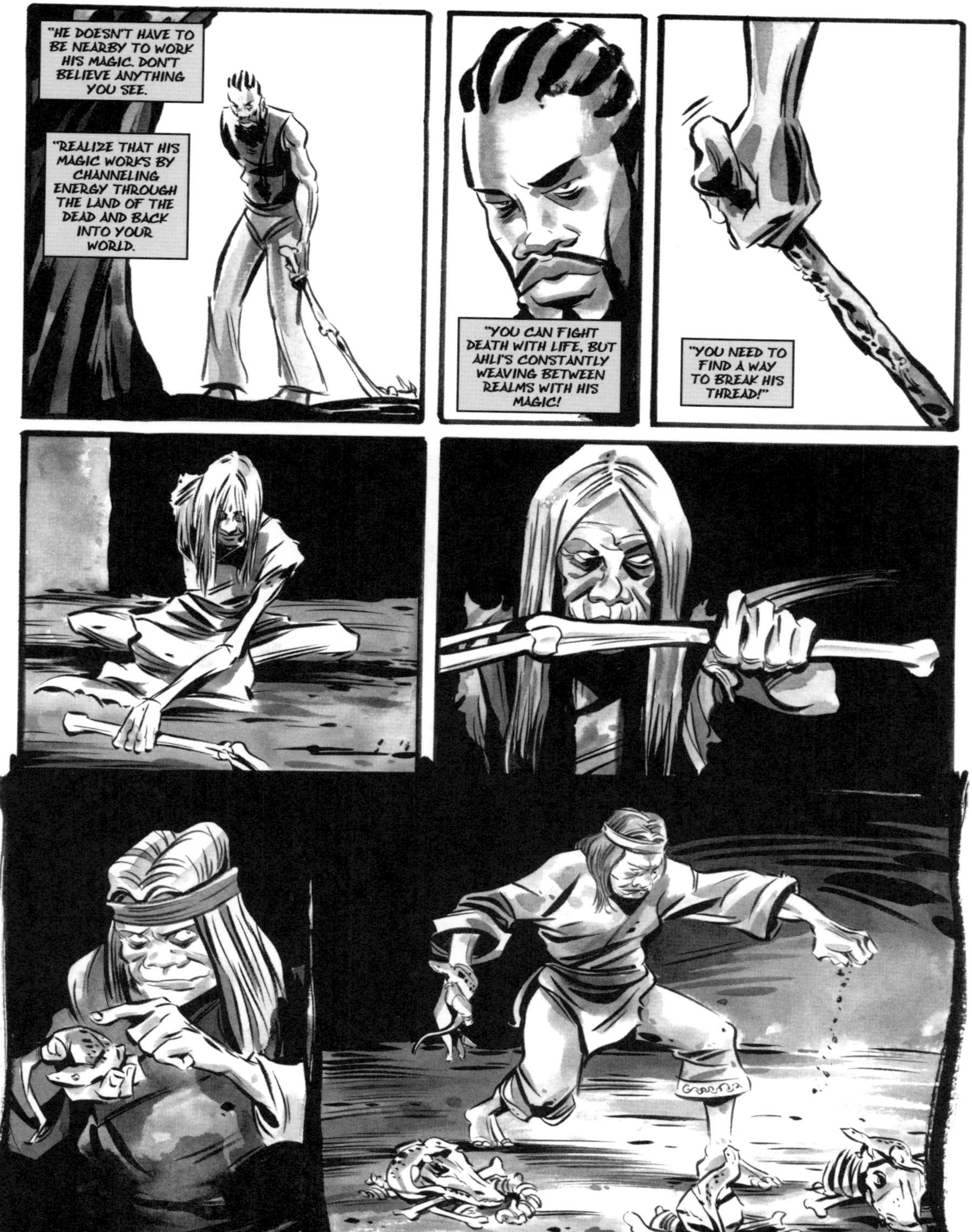
"HE DOESN'T HAVE TO BE NEARBY TO WORK HIS MAGIC. DON'T BELIEVE ANYTHING YOU SEE.
"REALIZE THAT HIS MAGIC WORKS BY CHANNELING ENERGY THROUGH THE LAND OF THE DEAD AND BACK INTO YOUR WORLD.
"YOU CAN FIGHT DEATH WITH LIFE, BUT AHLI'S CONSTANTLY WEAVING BETWEEN REALMS WITH HIS MAGIC!
"YOU NEED TO FIND A WAY TO BREAK HIS THREAD!"

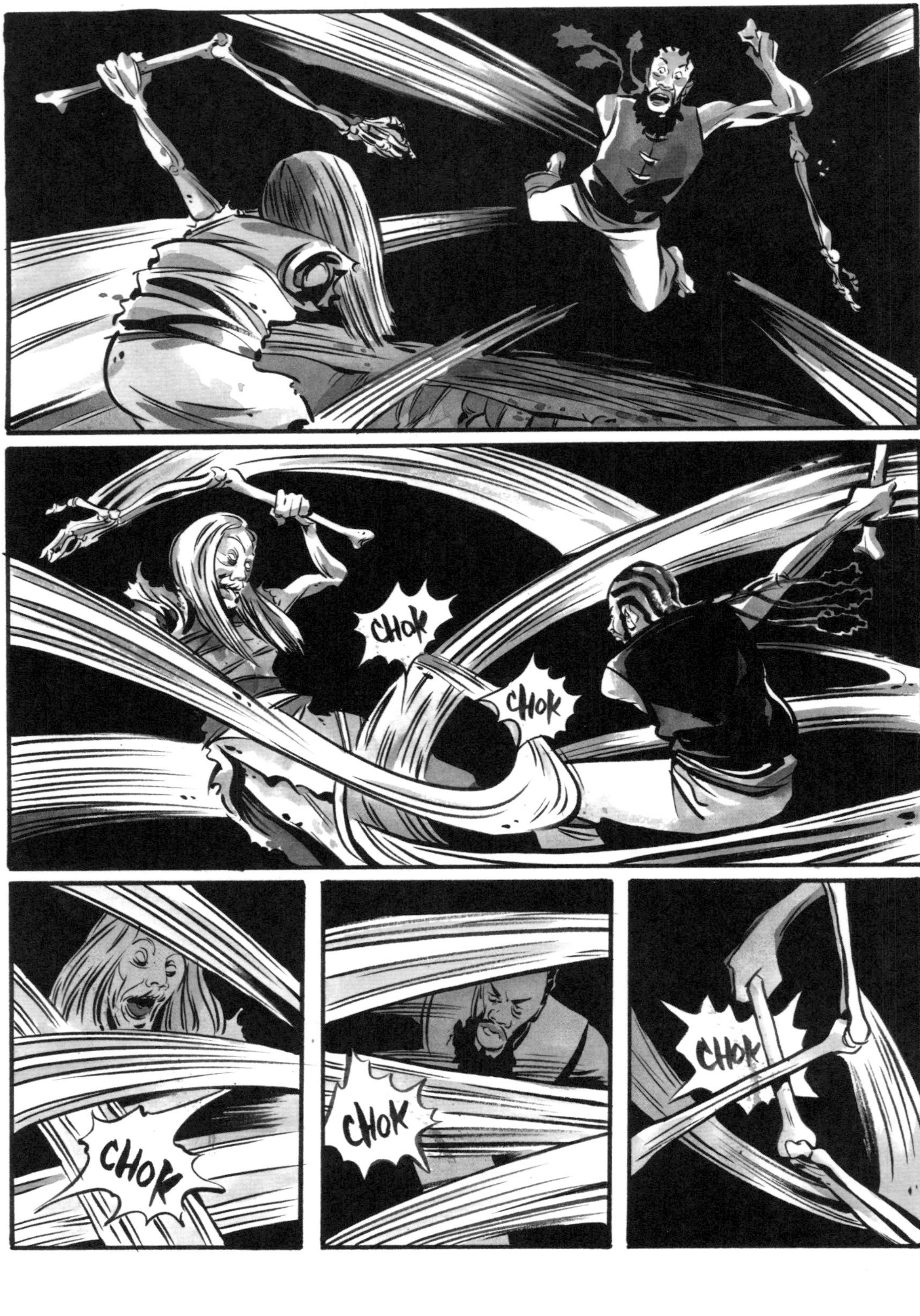
CHOK
CHOK
CHOK
CHOK
CHOK

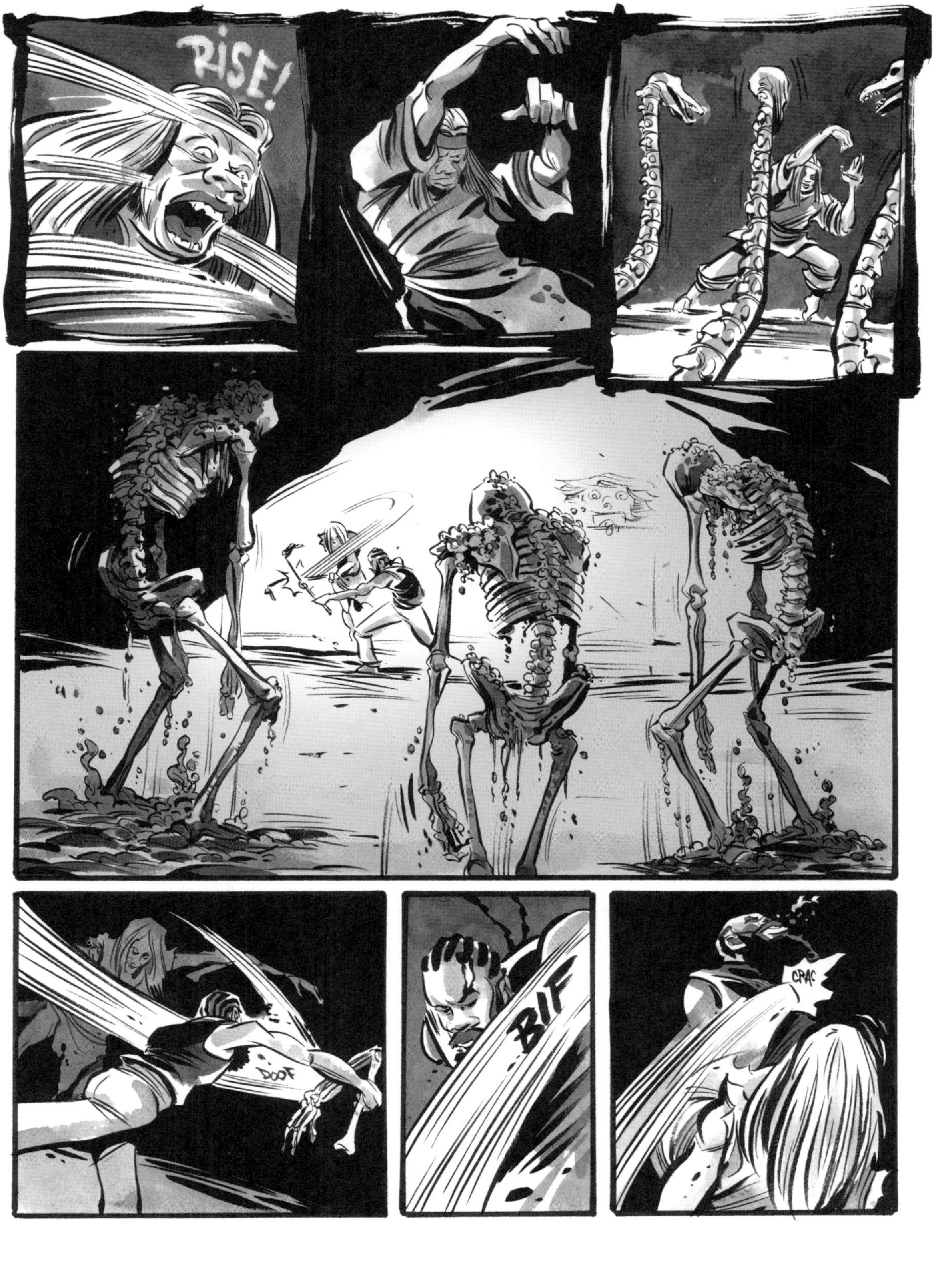
RISE!
DOOF
BIF
CRAC

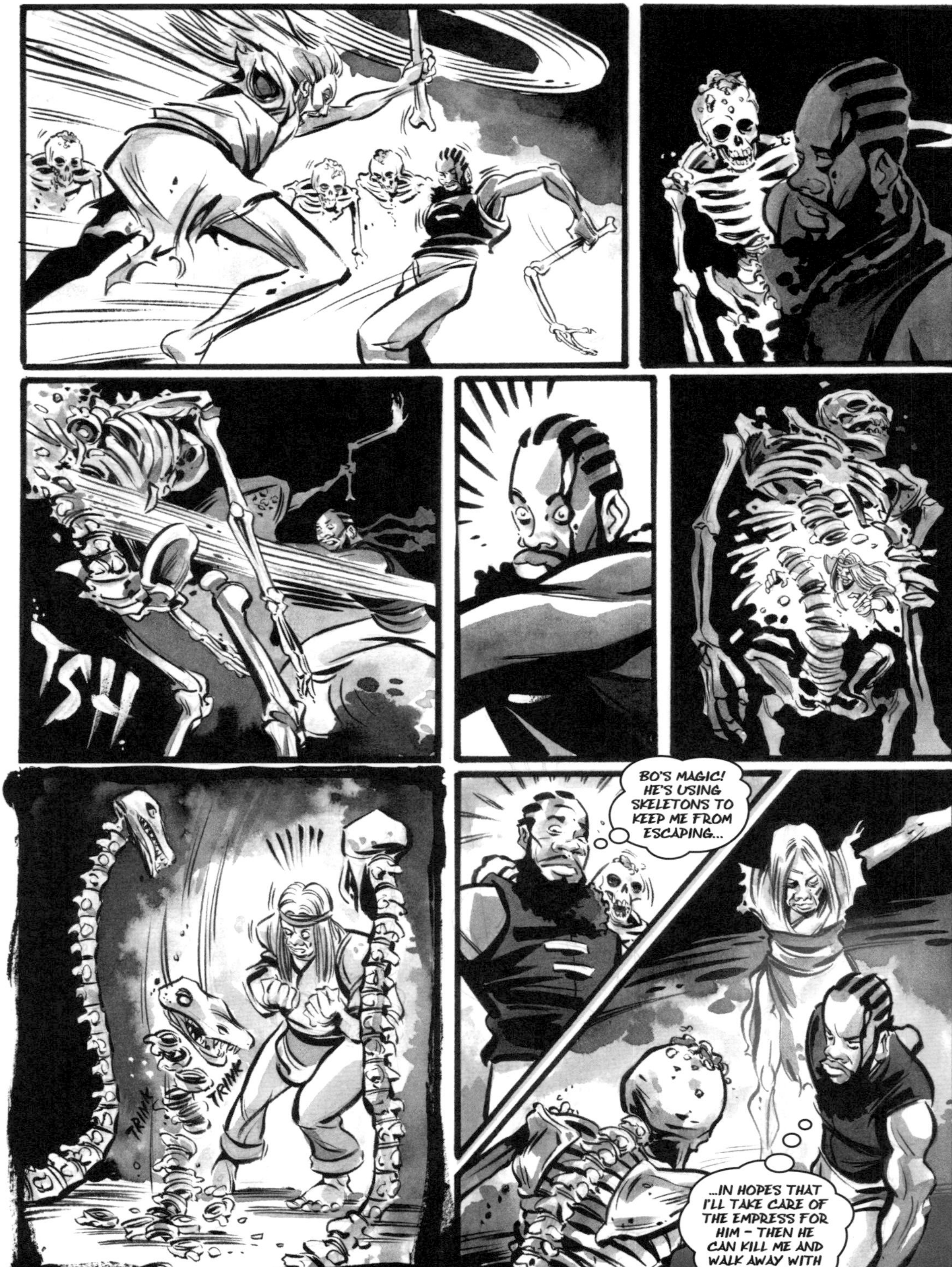
TSH
TRINK
TRINK
BO'S MAGIC! HE'S USING SKELETONS TO KEEP ME FROM ESCAPING...
...IN HOPES THAT I'LL TAKE CARE OF THE EMPRESS FOR HIM - THEN HE CAN KILL ME AND WALK AWAY WITH THE ARMOR!

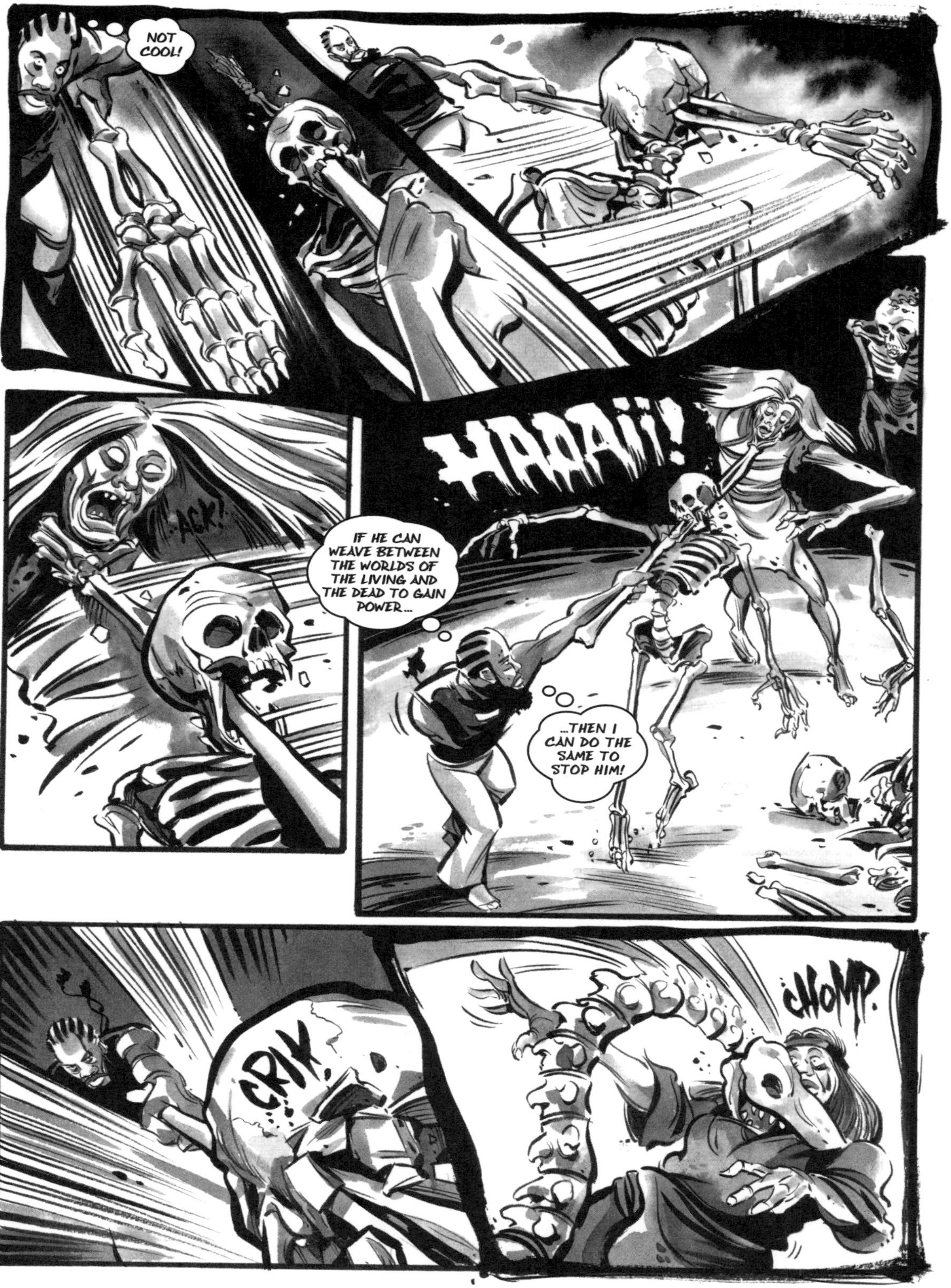

NOT COOL!
HAAAII!
ACK!
IF HE CAN WEAVE BETWEEN THE WORLDS OF THE LIVING AND THE DEAD TO GAIN POWER...
...THEN I CAN DO THE SAME TO STOP HIM!
CRIK
CHOMP

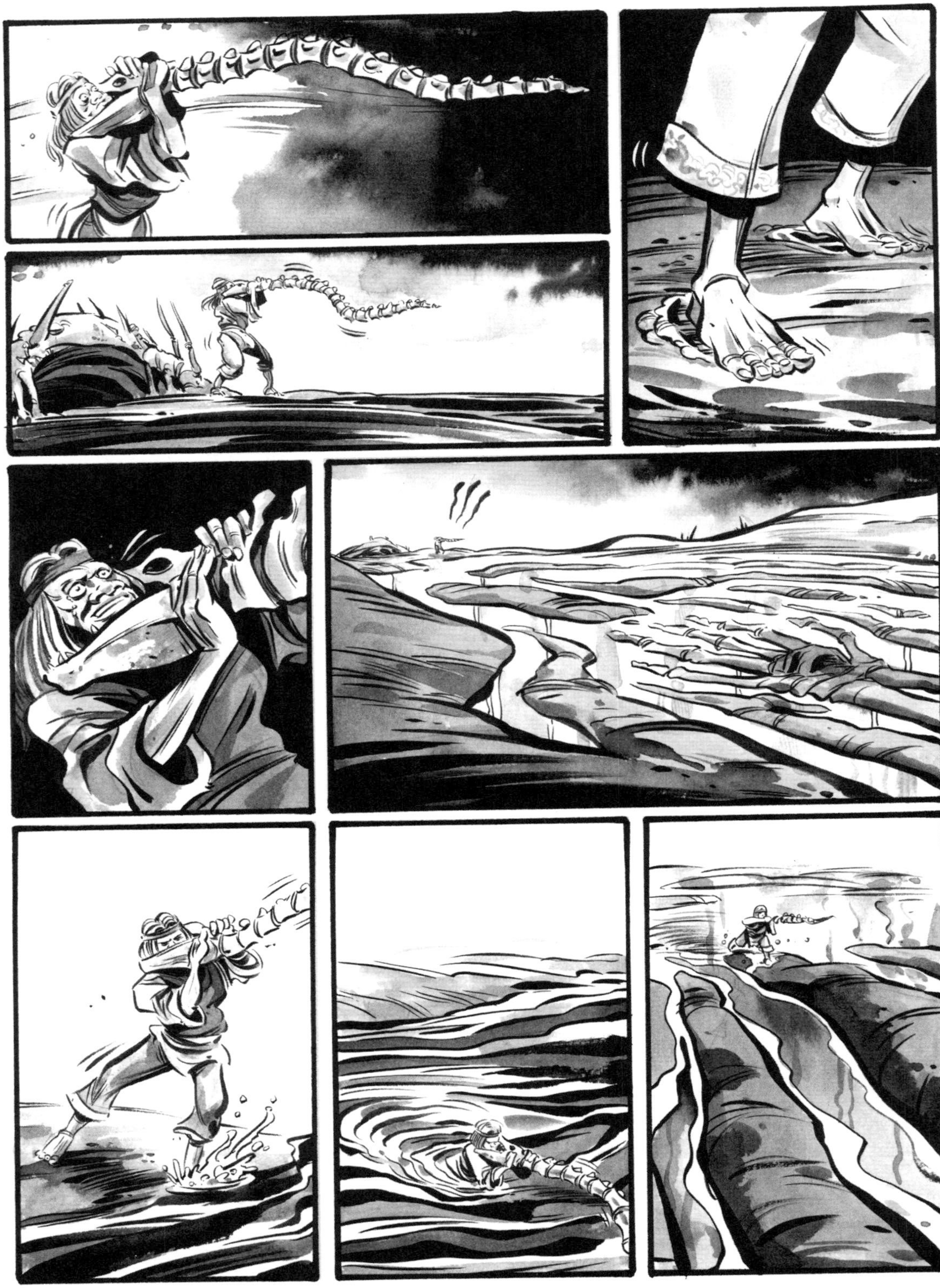

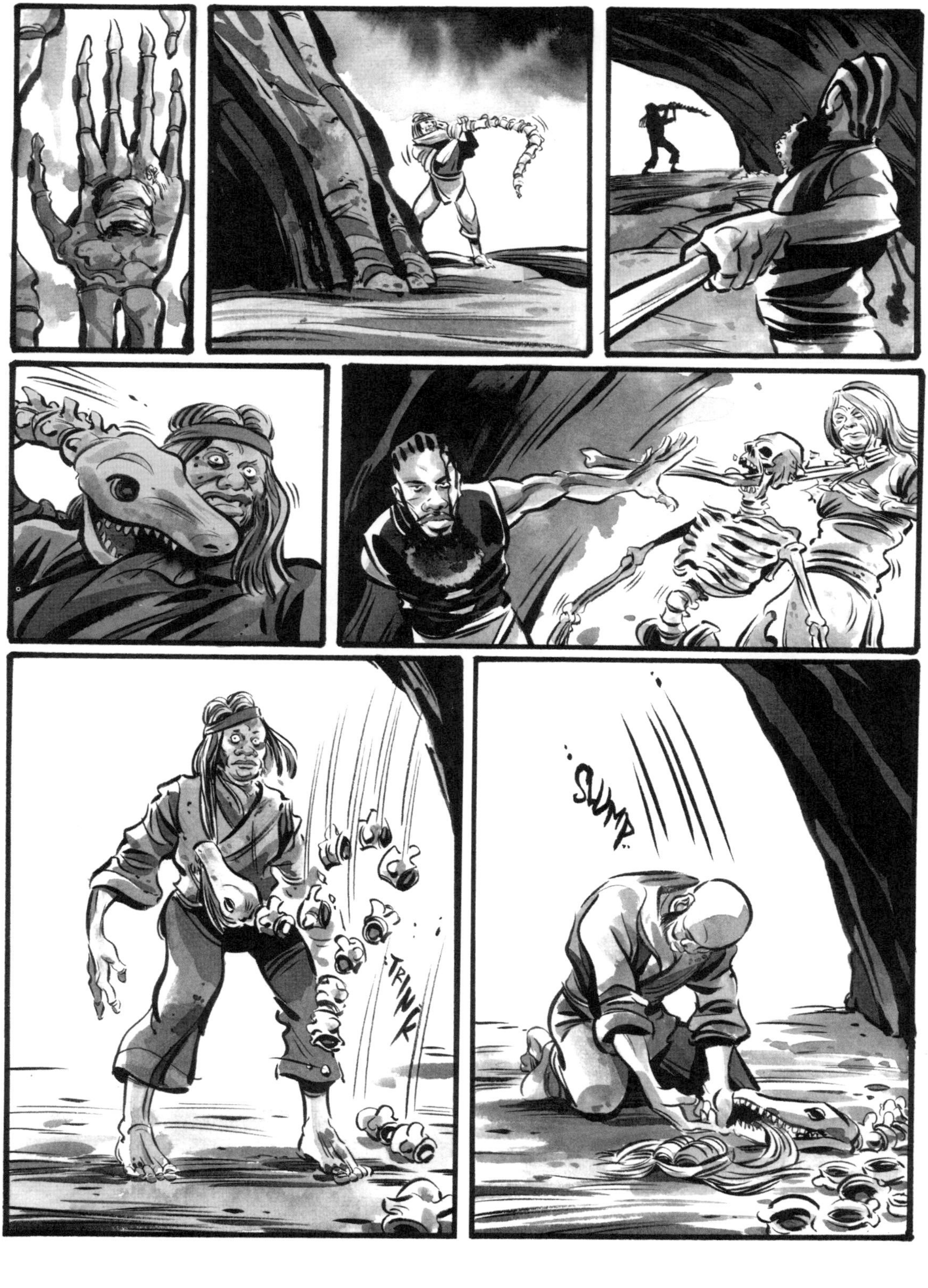
TRINK
SLUMP

MOOG JOOGULAR. YOU'VE WON AGAIN. FINISH ME OFF.

I DON'T WANT TO DO THAT, BO, JUST LIKE I DIDN'T MEAN TO HURT YOUR PETS.

I KNOW IT WAS THE POISON KUNG FU THAT MADE YOU EVIL.

WE CAN HELP YOU LEARN TO BE GOOD AGAIN. YOU CAN USE YOUR MAGIC TO HELP OTHERS!

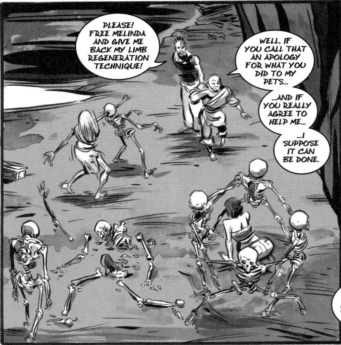

PLEASE! FREE MELINDA AND GIVE ME BACK MY LIMB REGENERATION TECHNIQUE!

WELL, IF YOU CALL THAT AN APOLOGY FOR WHAT YOU DID TO MY PETS...

...AND IF YOU REALLY AGREE TO HELP ME...

...I SUPPOSE IT CAN BE DONE.

YOU'LL HAVE TO SWALLOW THIS CHARM. ONCE YOU INGEST IT, THE CURSE WILL BE BROKEN.

THANK YOU, BO.

GULP

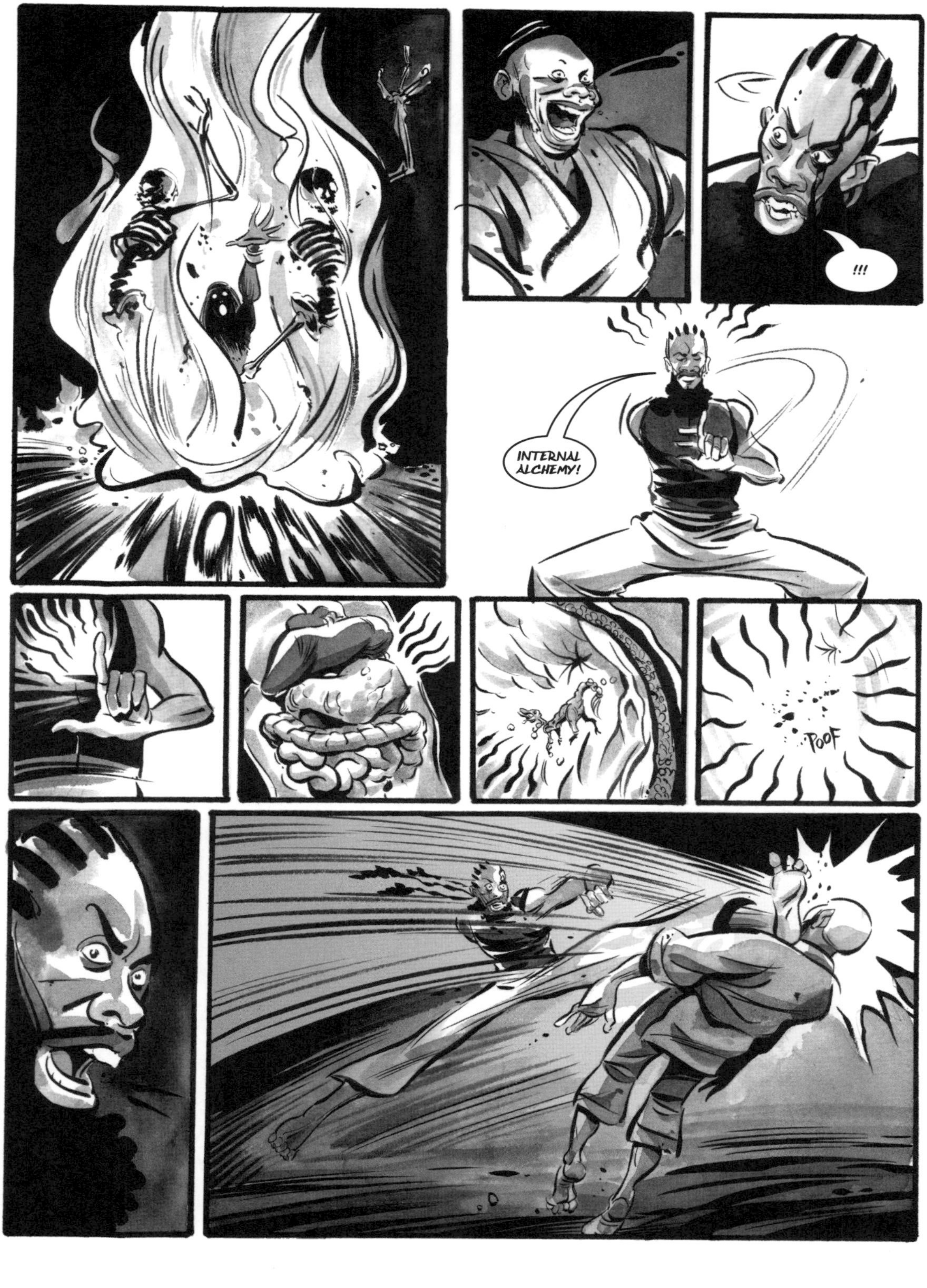

!!!
INTERNAL ALCHEMY!
POOF

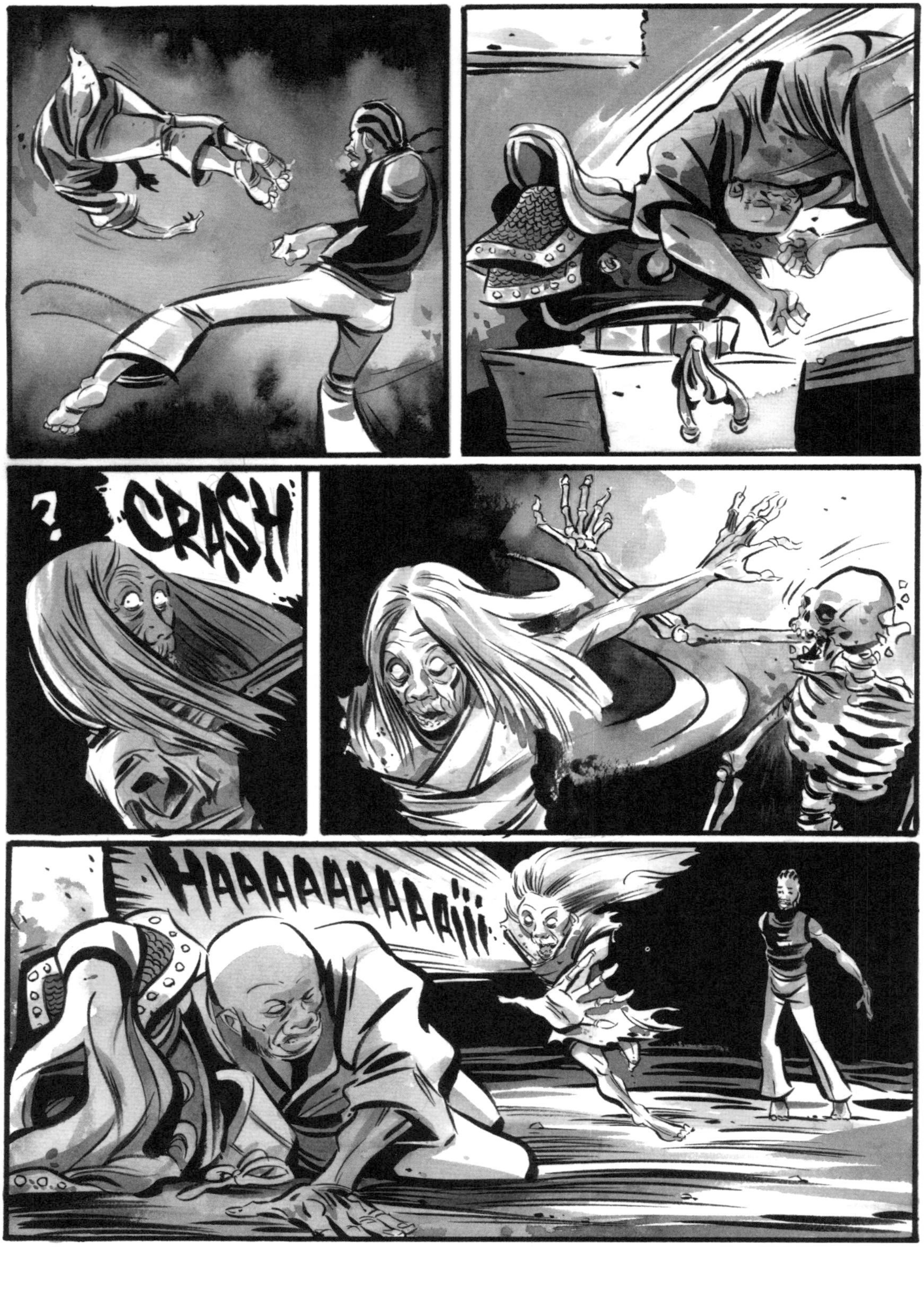
?
CRASH
HAAAAAAAAAiiii

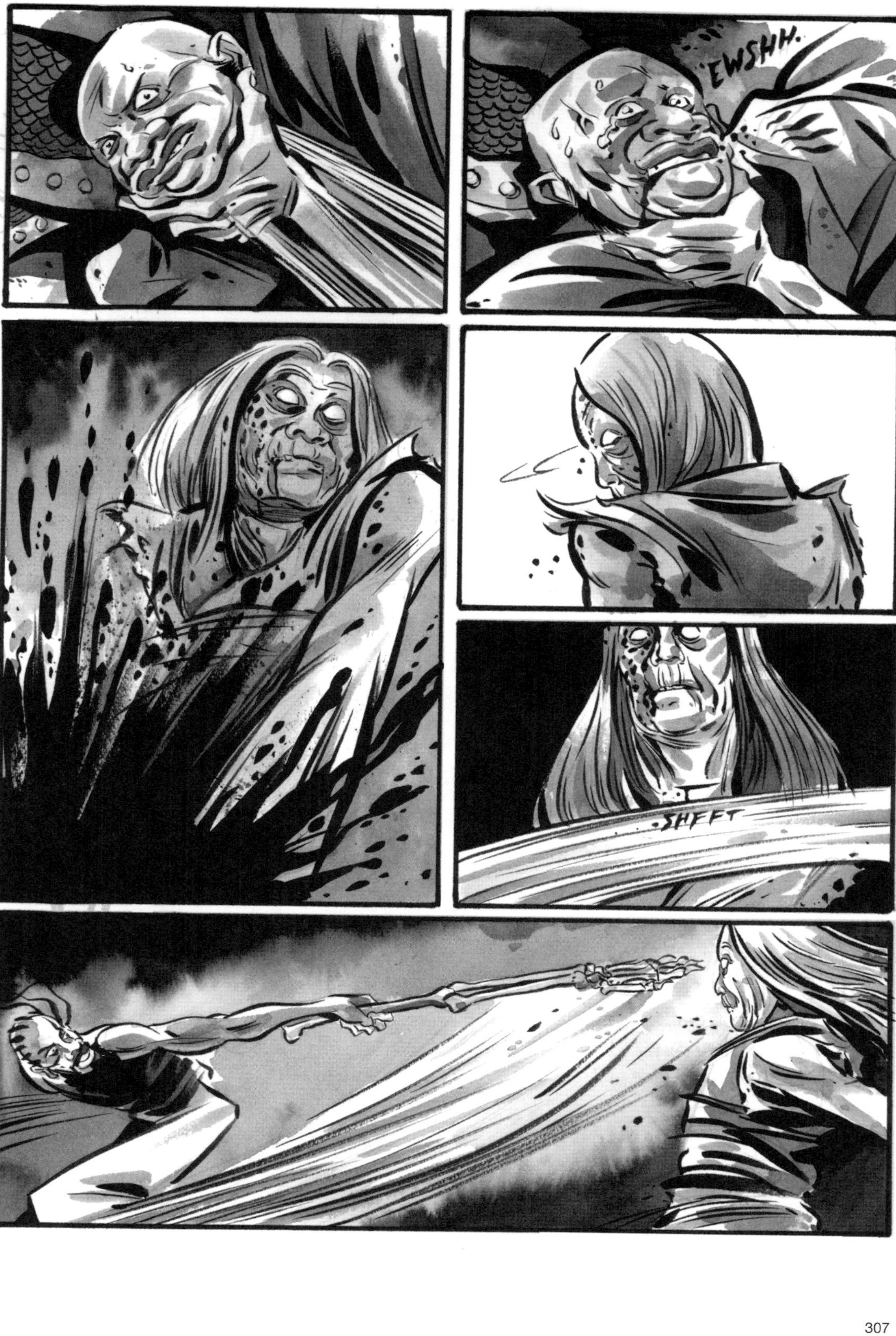
EWSHH.
SHFFT

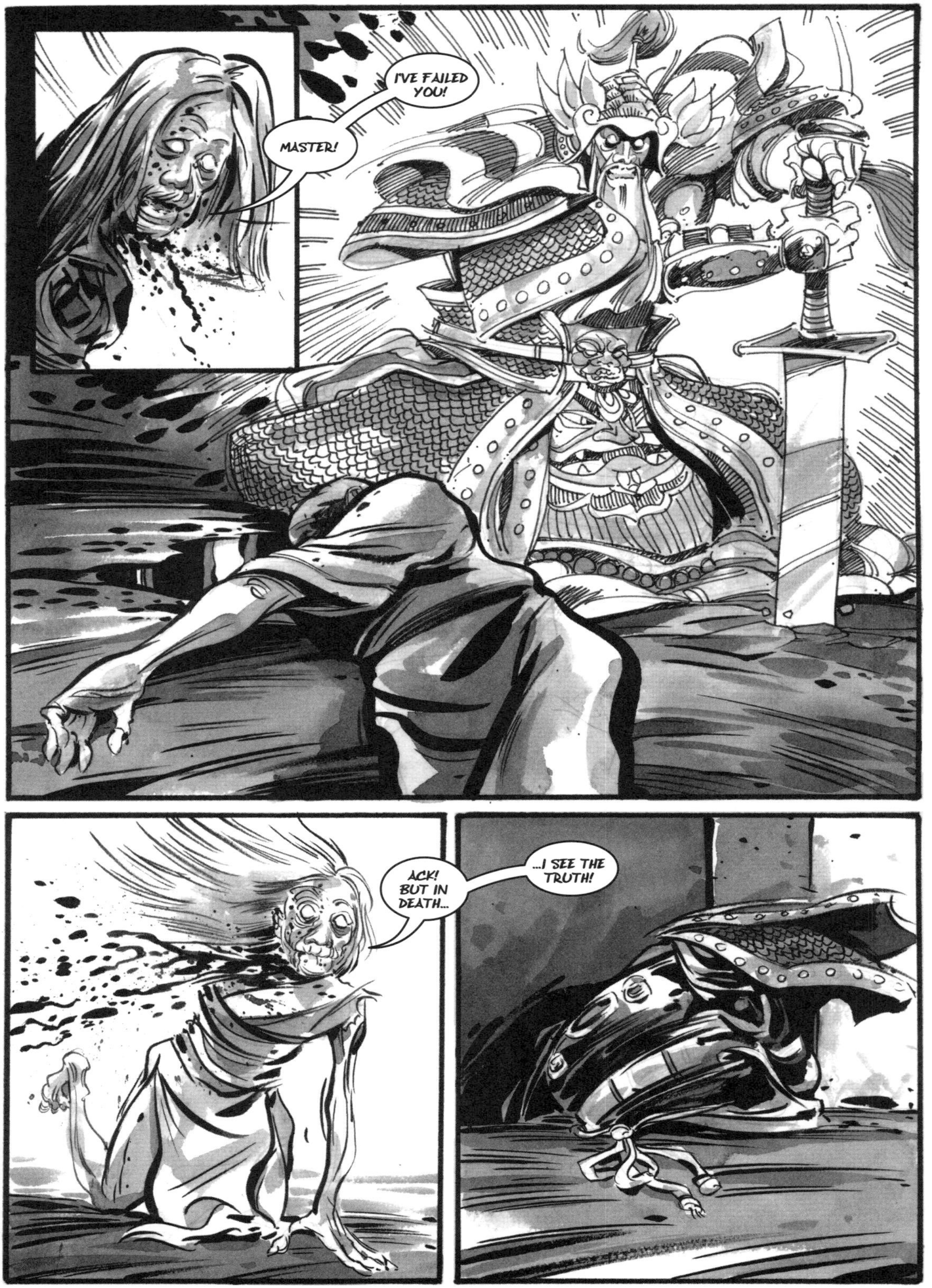
MASTER!
I'VE FAILED YOU!
ACK! BUT IN DEATH...
...I SEE THE TRUTH!

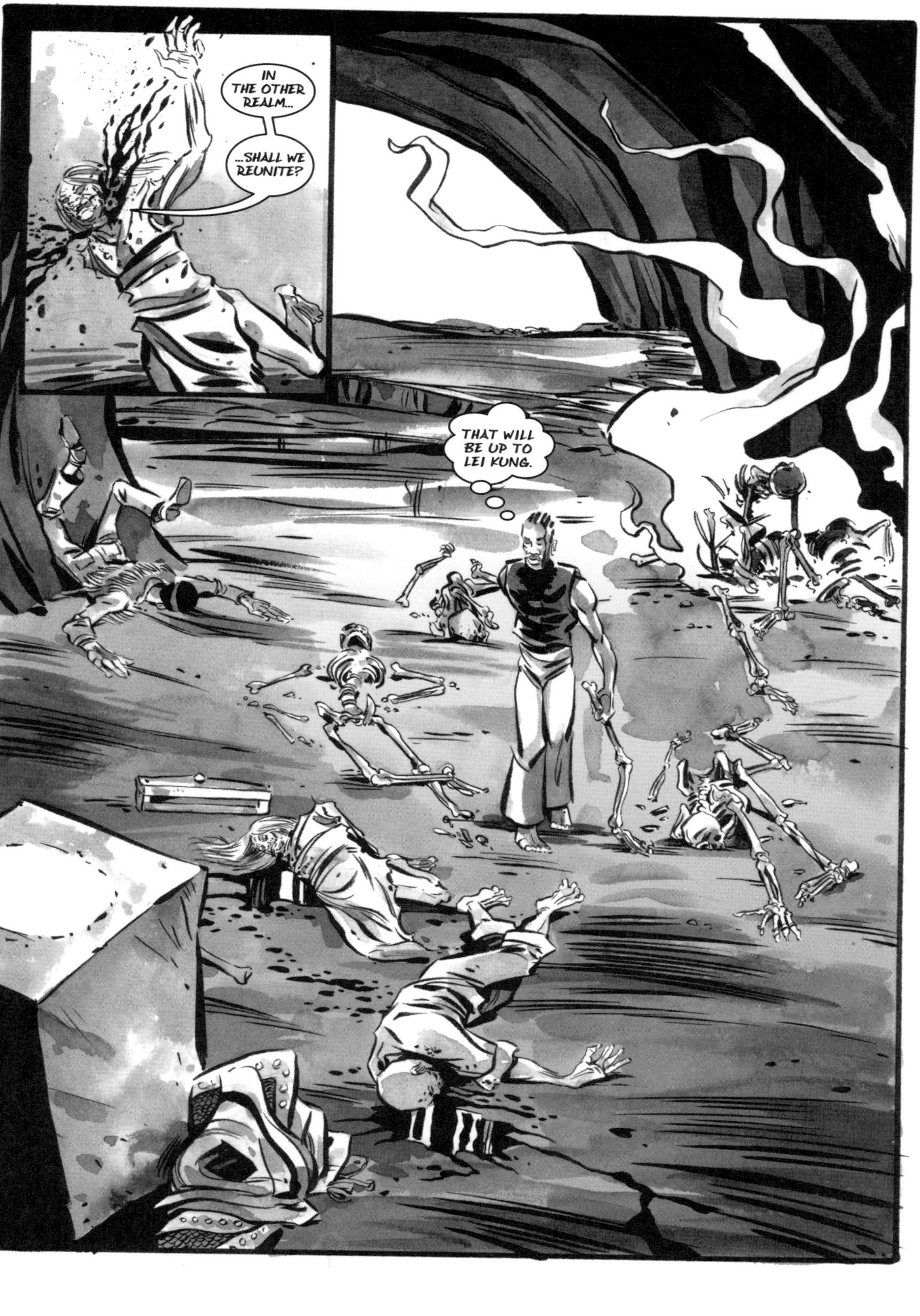
IN THE OTHER REALM...
...SHALL WE REUNITE?
THAT WILL BE UP TO LEI KUNG.

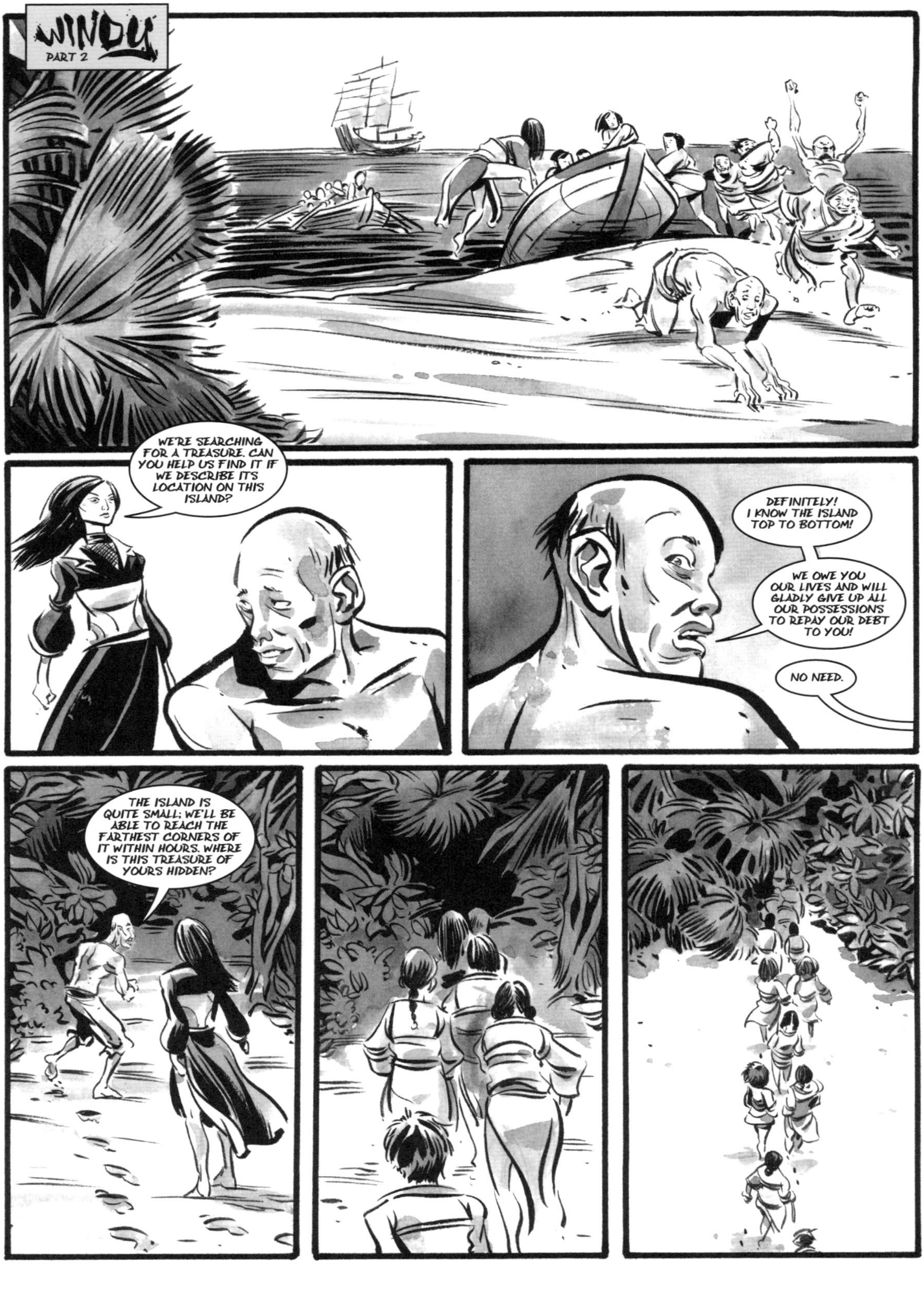
WINDY
PART 2
WE'RE SEARCHING FOR A TREASURE. CAN YOU HELP US FIND IT IF WE DESCRIBE ITS LOCATION ON THIS ISLAND?
DEFINITELY! I KNOW THE ISLAND TOP TO BOTTOM!
WE OWE YOU OUR LIVES AND WILL GLADLY GIVE UP ALL OUR POSSESSIONS TO REPAY OUR DEBT TO YOU!
NO NEED.
THE ISLAND IS QUITE SMALL; WE'LL BE ABLE TO REACH THE FARTHEST CORNERS OF IT WITHIN HOURS. WHERE IS THIS TREASURE OF YOURS HIDDEN?

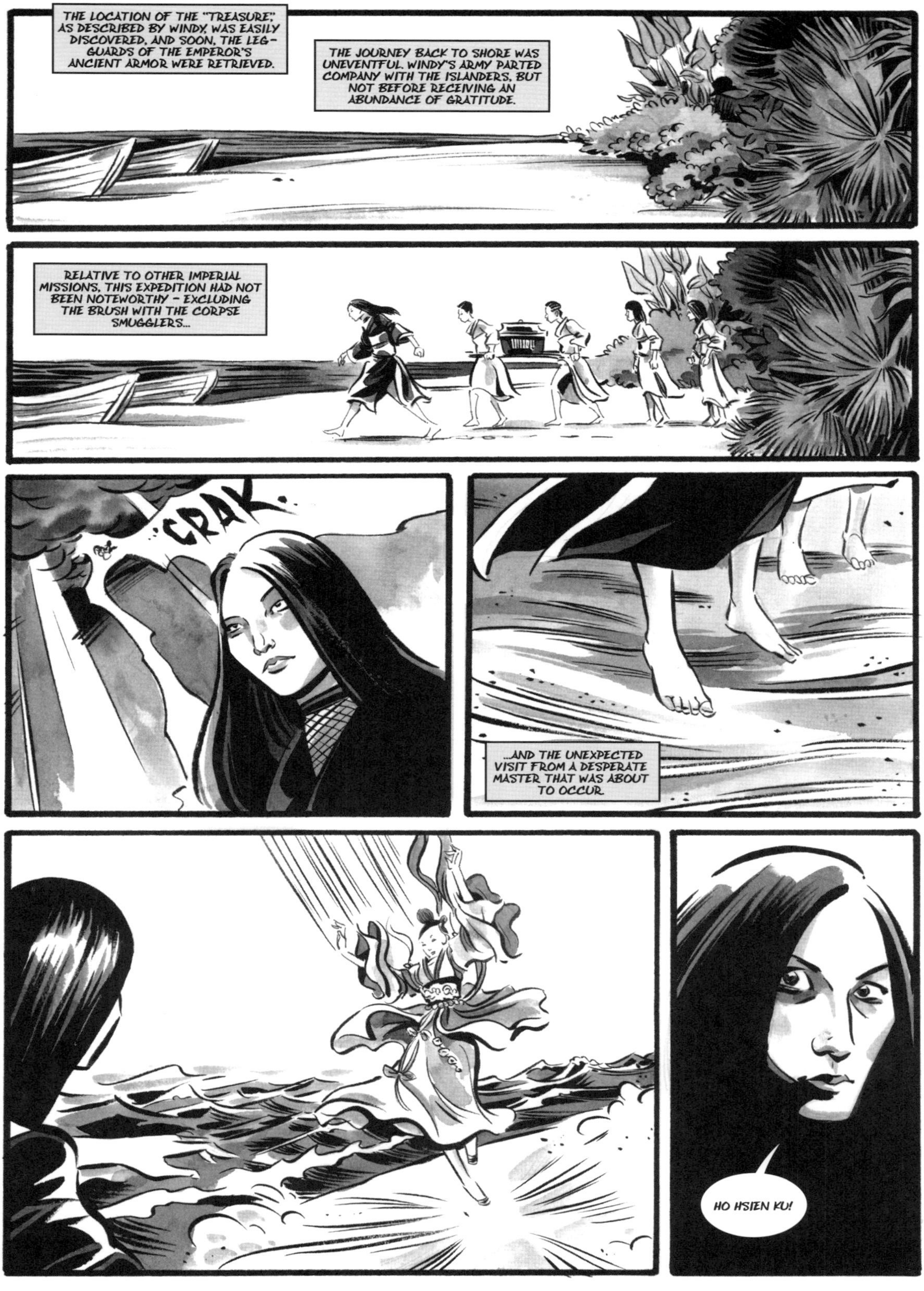

THE LOCATION OF THE "TREASURE," AS DESCRIBED BY WINDY, WAS EASILY DISCOVERED, AND SOON, THE LEG-GUARDS OF THE EMPEROR'S ANCIENT ARMOR WERE RETRIEVED.
THE JOURNEY BACK TO SHORE WAS UNEVENTFUL. WINDY'S ARMY PARTED COMPANY WITH THE ISLANDERS, BUT NOT BEFORE RECEIVING AN ABUNDANCE OF GRATITUDE.
RELATIVE TO OTHER IMPERIAL MISSIONS, THIS EXPEDITION HAD NOT BEEN NOTEWORTHY - EXCLUDING THE BRUSH WITH THE CORPSE SMUGGLERS...
CRAK
...AND THE UNEXPECTED VISIT FROM A DESPERATE MASTER THAT WAS ABOUT TO OCCUR.
HO HSIEN KU!

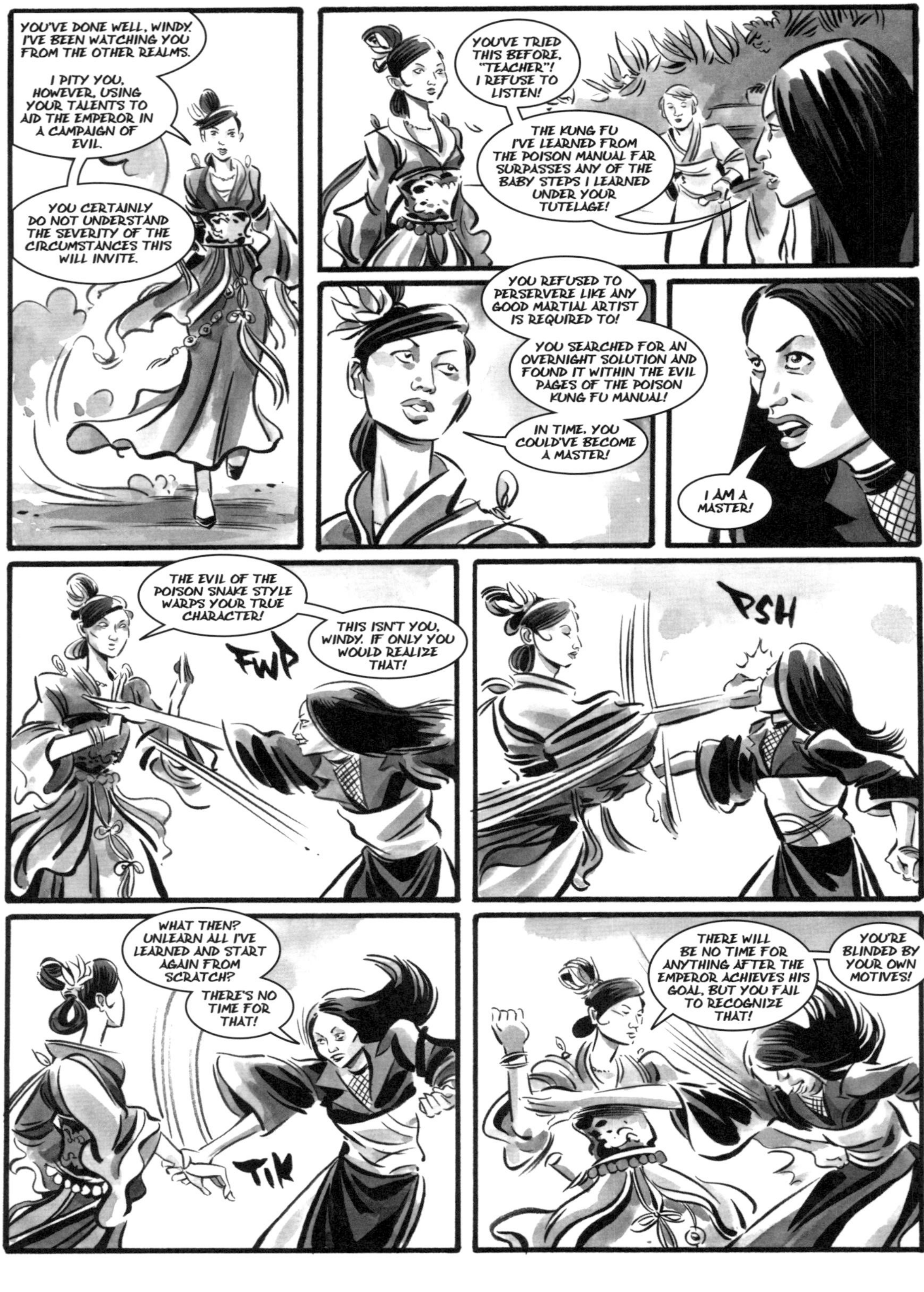
YOU'VE DONE WELL, WINDY. I'VE BEEN WATCHING YOU FROM THE OTHER REALMS.
I PITY YOU, HOWEVER, USING YOUR TALENTS TO AID THE EMPEROR IN A CAMPAIGN OF EVIL.
YOU CERTAINLY DO NOT UNDERSTAND THE SEVERITY OF THE CIRCUMSTANCES THIS WILL INVITE.
YOU'VE TRIED THIS BEFORE, "TEACHER"! I REFUSE TO LISTEN!
THE KUNG FU I'VE LEARNED FROM THE POISON MANUAL FAR SURPASSES ANY OF THE BABY STEPS I LEARNED UNDER YOUR TUTELAGE!
YOU REFUSED TO PERSERVERE LIKE ANY GOOD MARTIAL ARTIST IS REQUIRED TO!
YOU SEARCHED FOR AN OVERNIGHT SOLUTION AND FOUND IT WITHIN THE EVIL PAGES OF THE POISON KUNG FU MANUAL!
IN TIME, YOU COULD'VE BECOME A MASTER!
I AM A MASTER!
THE EVIL OF THE POISON SNAKE STYLE WARPS YOUR TRUE CHARACTER!
THIS ISN'T YOU, WINDY. IF ONLY YOU WOULD REALIZE THAT!
FWP
PSH
WHAT THEN? UNLEARN ALL I'VE LEARNED AND START AGAIN FROM SCRATCH?
THERE'S NO TIME FOR THAT!
TIK
THERE WILL BE NO TIME FOR ANYTHING AFTER THE EMPEROR ACHIEVES HIS GOAL, BUT YOU FAIL TO RECOGNIZE THAT!
YOU'RE BLINDED BY YOUR OWN MOTIVES!

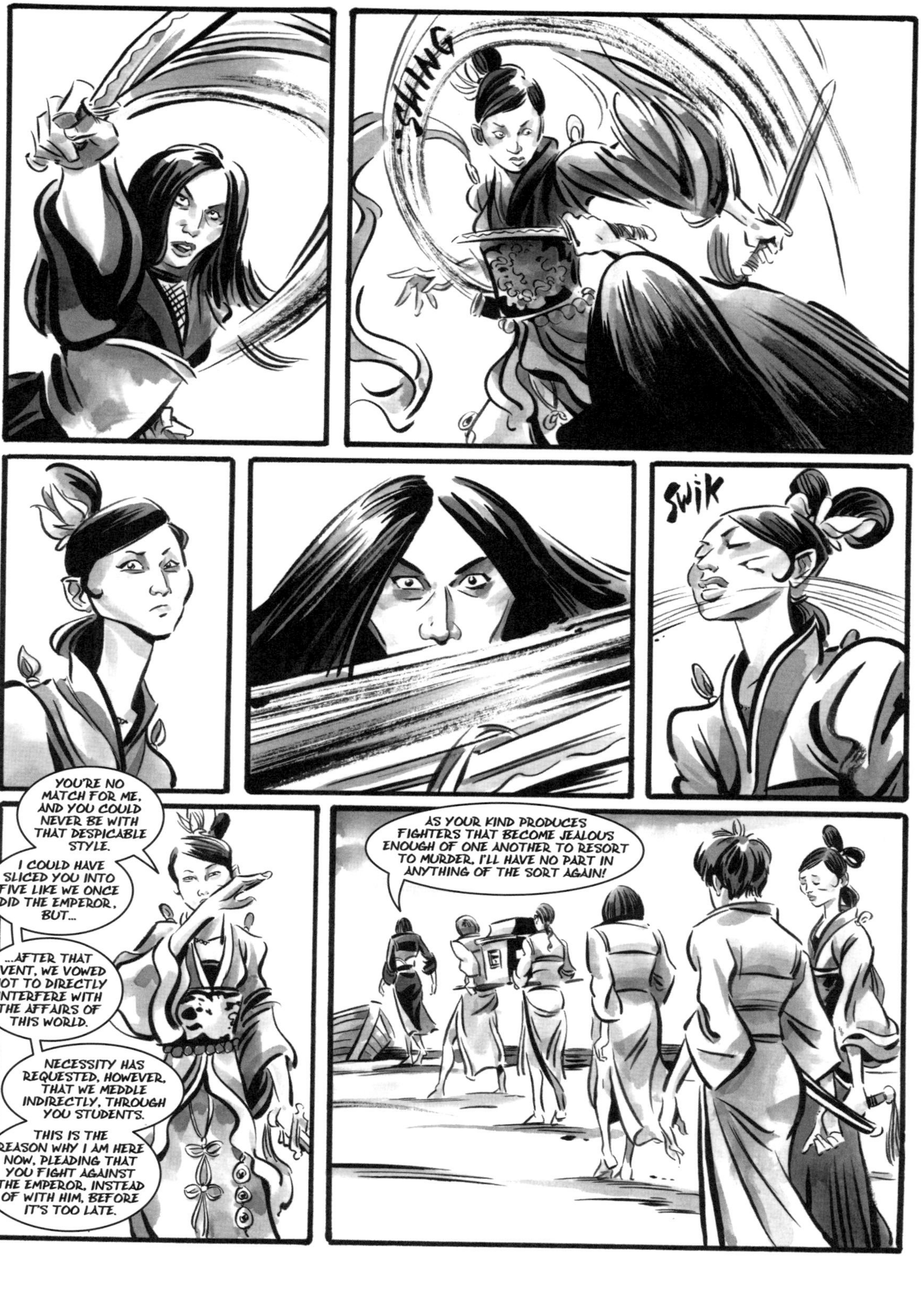
SHING
SWIK
YOU'RE NO MATCH FOR ME, AND YOU COULD NEVER BE WITH THAT DESPICABLE STYLE.
I COULD HAVE SLICED YOU INTO FIVE LIKE WE ONCE DID THE EMPEROR, BUT...
...AFTER THAT EVENT, WE VOWED NOT TO DIRECTLY INTERFERE WITH THE AFFAIRS OF THIS WORLD.
NECESSITY HAS REQUESTED, HOWEVER, THAT WE MEDDLE INDIRECTLY, THROUGH YOU STUDENTS.
THIS IS THE REASON WHY I AM HERE NOW, PLEADING THAT YOU FIGHT AGAINST THE EMPEROR, INSTEAD OF WITH HIM, BEFORE IT'S TOO LATE.
AS YOUR KIND PRODUCES FIGHTERS THAT BECOME JEALOUS ENOUGH OF ONE ANOTHER TO RESORT TO MURDER, I'LL HAVE NO PART IN ANYTHING OF THE SORT AGAIN!

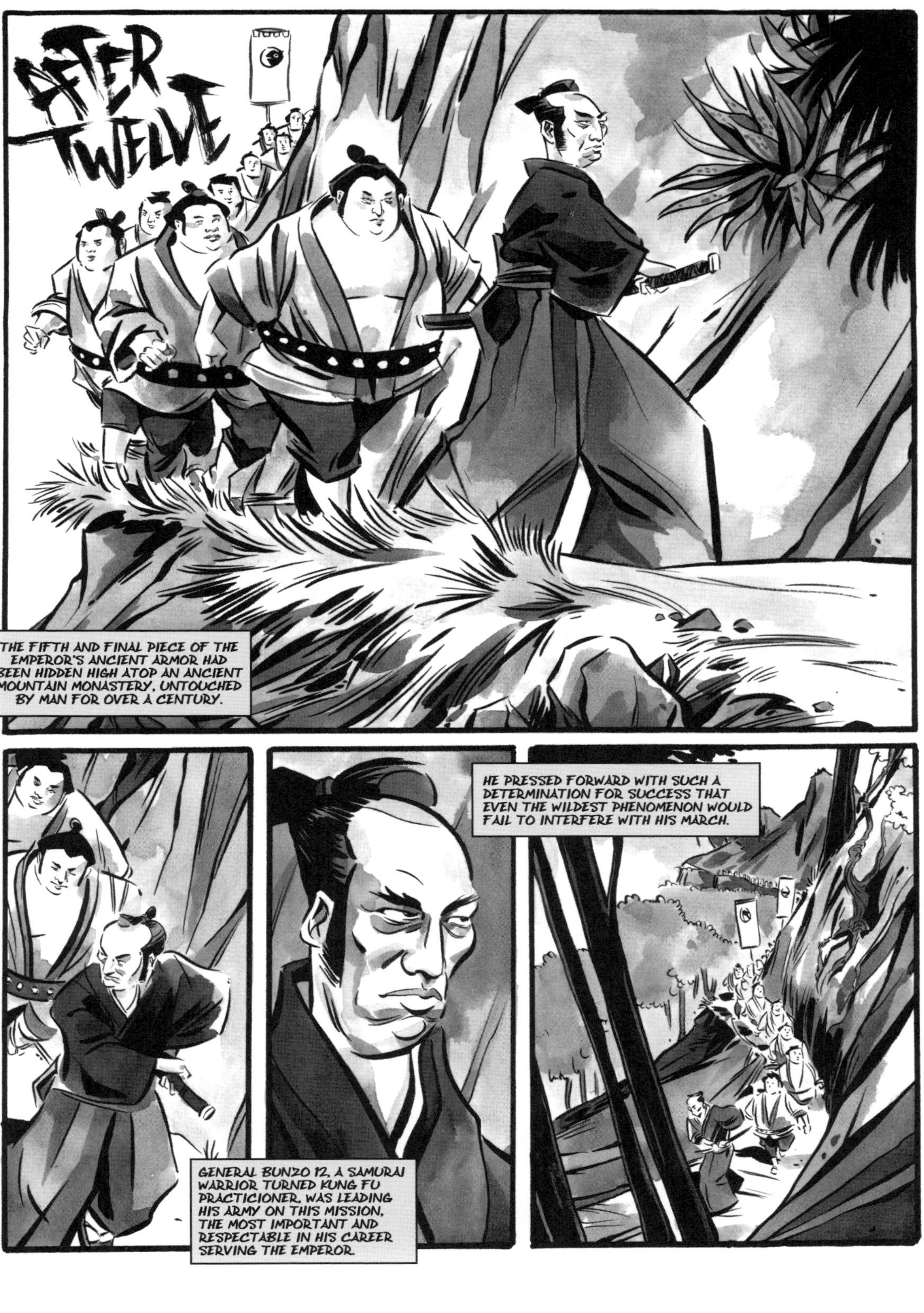
AFTER TWELVE
THE FIFTH AND FINAL PIECE OF THE EMPEROR'S ANCIENT ARMOR HAD BEEN HIDDEN HIGH ATOP AN ANCIENT MOUNTAIN MONASTERY, UNTOUCHED BY MAN FOR OVER A CENTURY.
GENERAL BUNZO 12, A SAMURAI WARRIOR TURNED KUNG FU PRACTICIONER, WAS LEADING HIS ARMY ON THIS MISSION, THE MOST IMPORTANT AND RESPECTABLE IN HIS CAREER SERVING THE EMPEROR.
HE PRESSED FORWARD WITH SUCH A DETERMINATION FOR SUCCESS THAT EVEN THE WILDEST PHENOMENON WOULD FAIL TO INTERFERE WITH HIS MARCH.

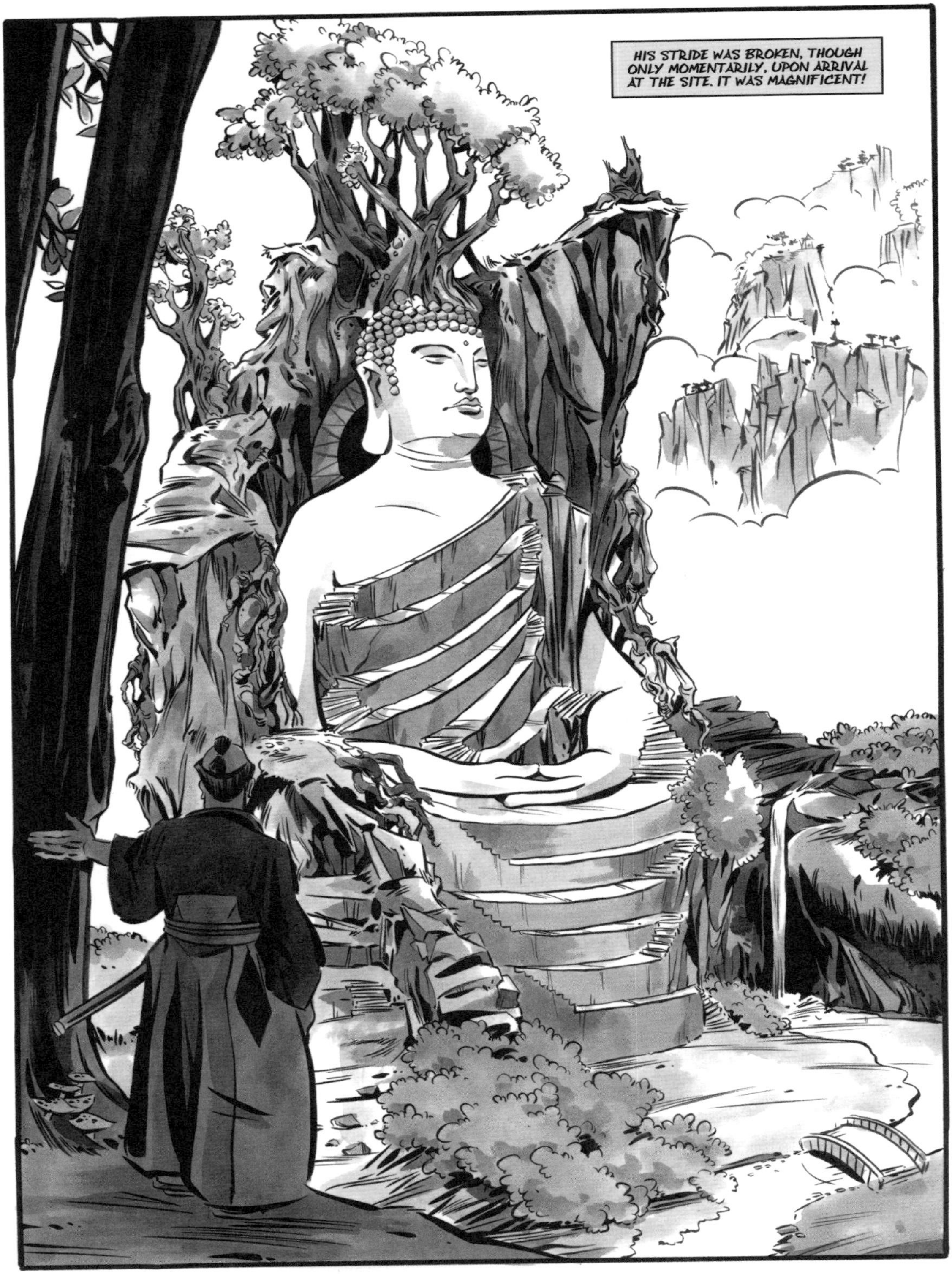
HIS STRIDE WAS BROKEN, THOUGH ONLY MOMENTARILY, UPON ARRIVAL AT THE SITE. IT WAS MAGNIFICENT!

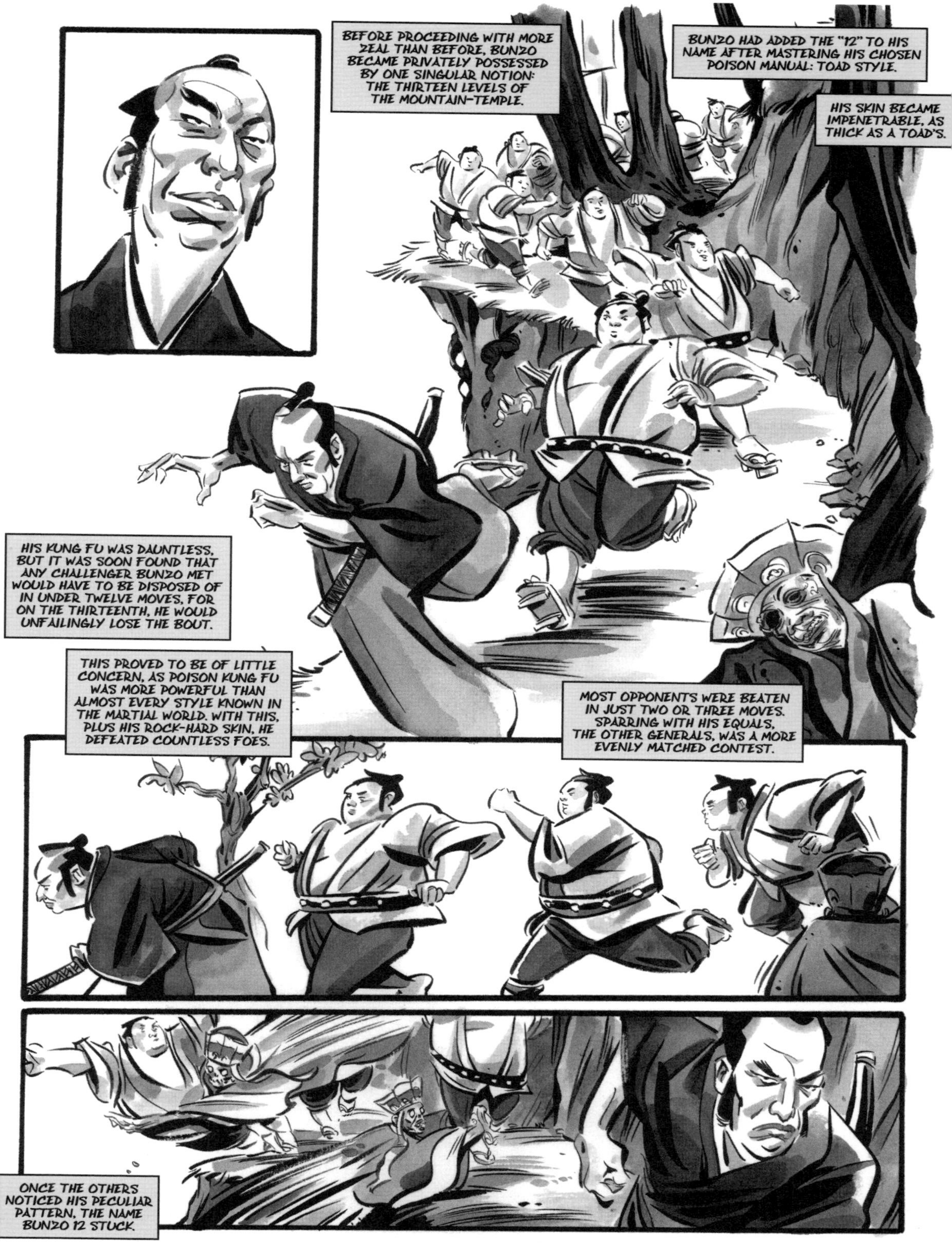

BEFORE PROCEEDING WITH MORE ZEAL THAN BEFORE, BUNZO BECAME PRIVATELY POSSESSED BY ONE SINGULAR NOTION: THE THIRTEEN LEVELS OF THE MOUNTAIN-TEMPLE.
BUNZO HAD ADDED THE "12" TO HIS NAME AFTER MASTERING HIS CHOSEN POISON MANUAL: TOAD STYLE.
HIS SKIN BECAME IMPENETRABLE, AS THICK AS A TOAD'S.
HIS KUNG FU WAS DAUNTLESS, BUT IT WAS SOON FOUND THAT ANY CHALLENGER BUNZO MET WOULD HAVE TO BE DISPOSED OF IN UNDER TWELVE MOVES, FOR ON THE THIRTEENTH, HE WOULD UNFAILINGLY LOSE THE BOUT.
THIS PROVED TO BE OF LITTLE CONCERN, AS POISON KUNG FU WAS MORE POWERFUL THAN ALMOST EVERY STYLE KNOWN IN THE MARTIAL WORLD. WITH THIS, PLUS HIS ROCK-HARD SKIN, HE DEFEATED COUNTLESS FOES.
MOST OPPONENTS WERE BEATEN IN JUST TWO OR THREE MOVES. SPARRING WITH HIS EQUALS, THE OTHER GENERALS, WAS A MORE EVENLY MATCHED CONTEST.
ONCE THE OTHERS NOTICED HIS PECULIAR PATTERN, THE NAME BUNZO 12 STUCK.

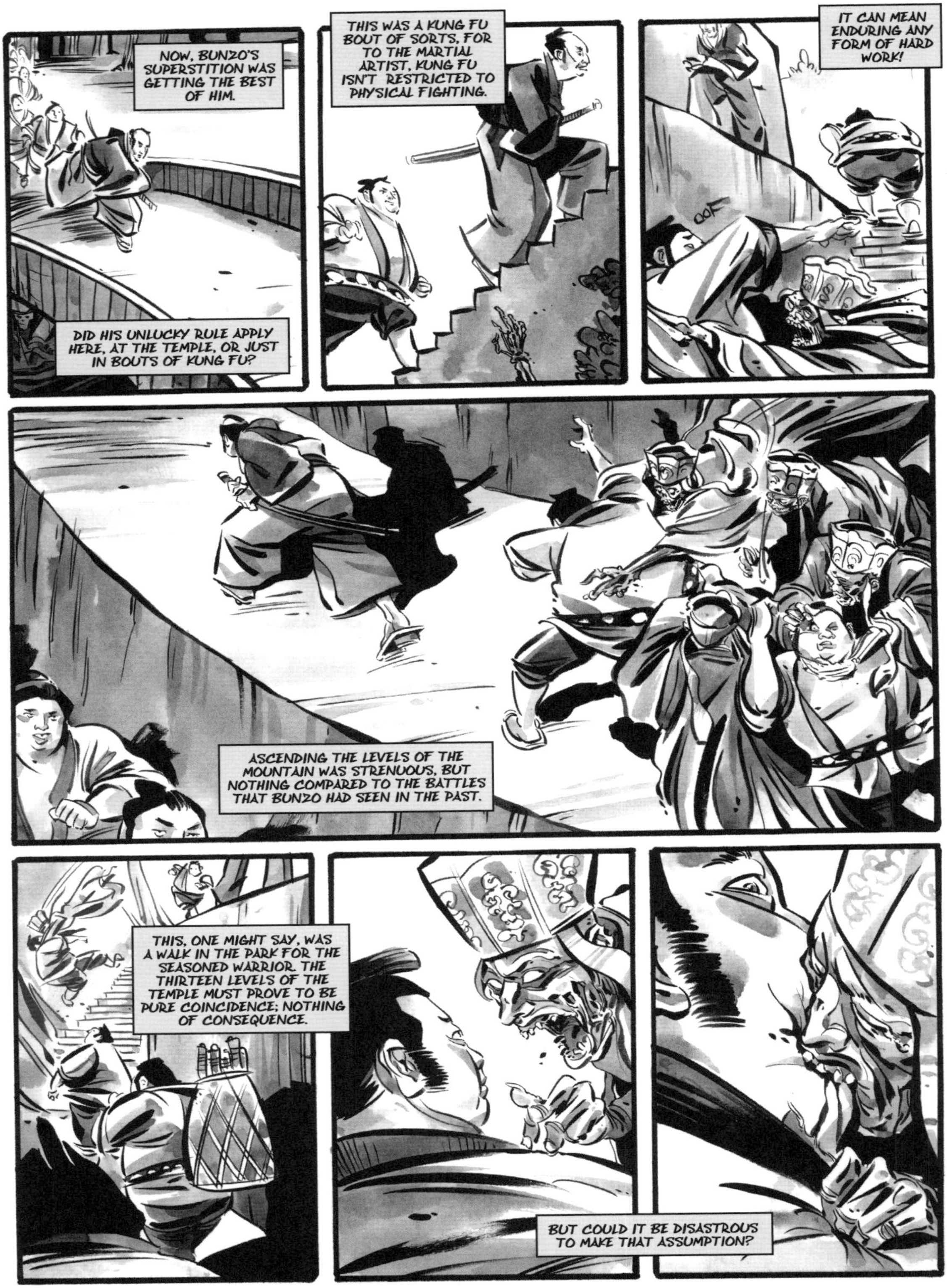
NOW, BUNZO'S SUPERSTITION WAS GETTING THE BEST OF HIM.
DID HIS UNLUCKY RULE APPLY HERE, AT THE TEMPLE, OR JUST IN BOUTS OF KUNG FU?
THIS WAS A KUNG FU BOUT OF SORTS, FOR TO THE MARTIAL ARTIST, KUNG FU ISN'T RESTRICTED TO PHYSICAL FIGHTING.
IT CAN MEAN ENDURING ANY FORM OF HARD WORK!
OOF
ASCENDING THE LEVELS OF THE MOUNTAIN WAS STRENUOUS, BUT NOTHING COMPARED TO THE BATTLES THAT BUNZO HAD SEEN IN THE PAST.
THIS, ONE MIGHT SAY, WAS A WALK IN THE PARK FOR THE SEASONED WARRIOR. THE THIRTEEN LEVELS OF THE TEMPLE MUST PROVE TO BE PURE COINCIDENCE; NOTHING OF CONSEQUENCE.
BUT COULD IT BE DISASTROUS TO MAKE THAT ASSUMPTION?

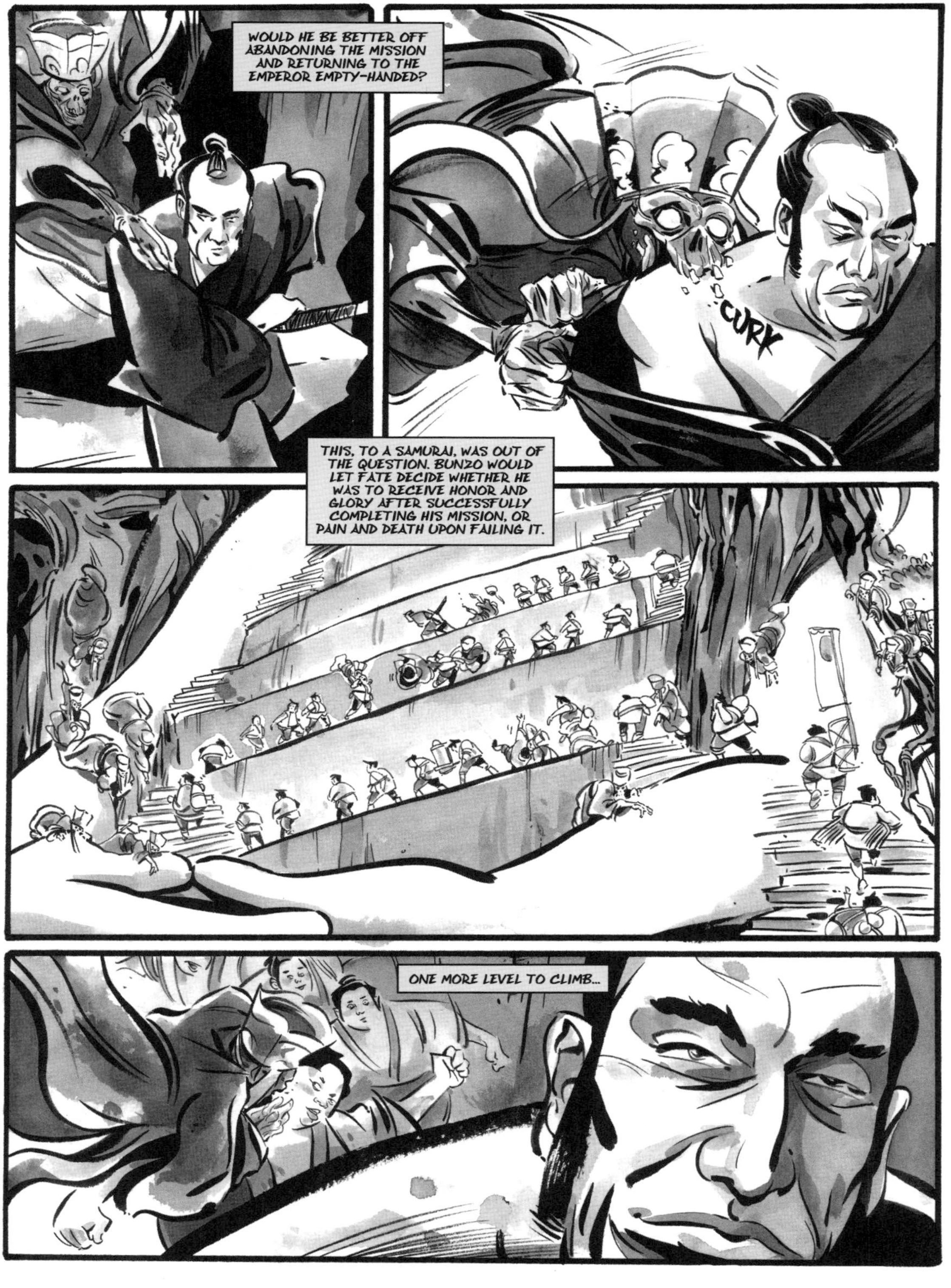
WOULD HE BE BETTER OFF ABANDONING THE MISSION AND RETURNING TO THE EMPEROR EMPTY-HANDED?
CURK
THIS, TO A SAMURAI, WAS OUT OF THE QUESTION. BUNZO WOULD LET FATE DECIDE WHETHER HE WAS TO RECEIVE HONOR AND GLORY AFTER SUCCESSFULLY COMPLETING HIS MISSION, OR PAIN AND DEATH UPON FAILING IT.
ONE MORE LEVEL TO CLIMB...

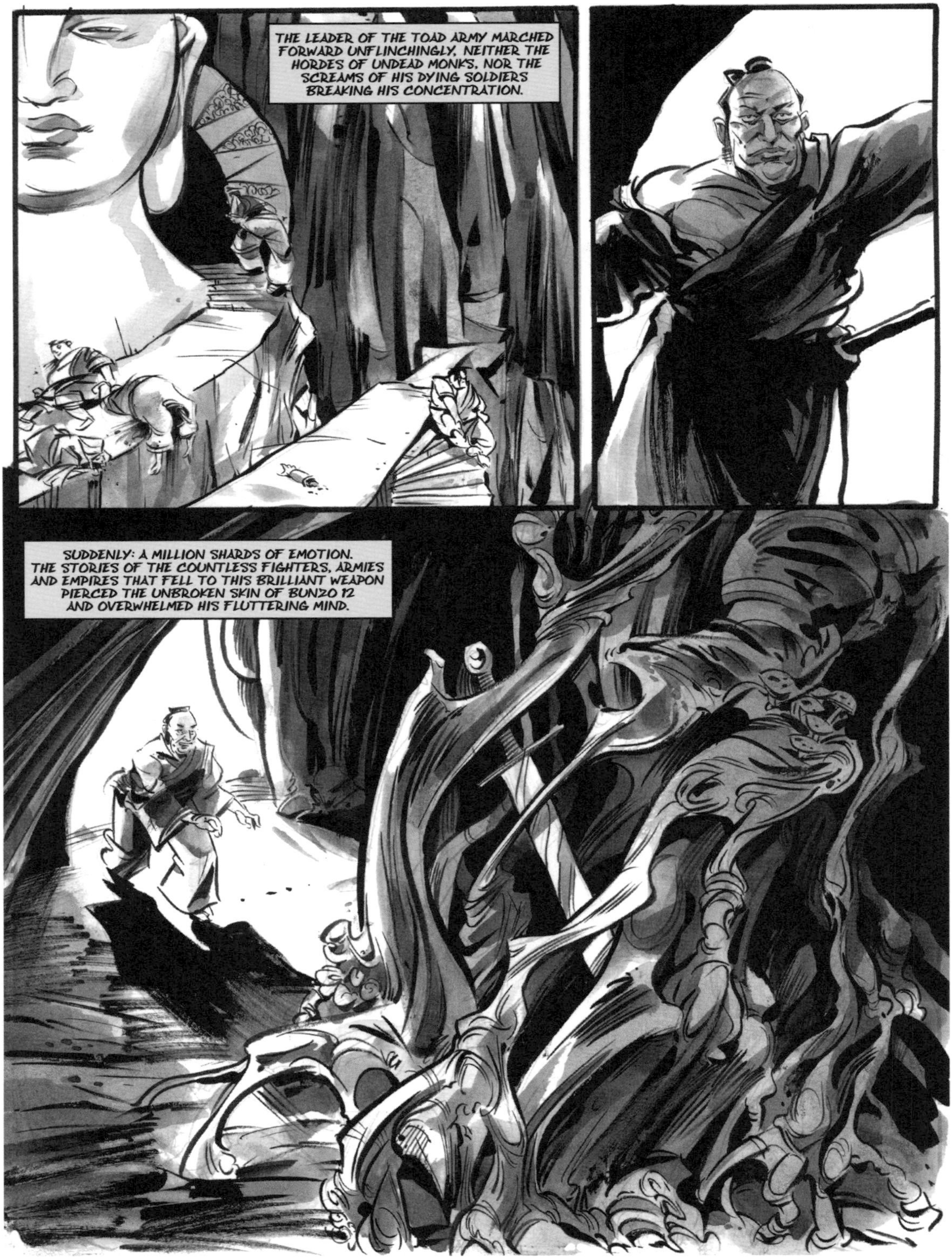
THE LEADER OF THE TOAD ARMY MARCHED FORWARD UNFLINCHINGLY, NEITHER THE HORDES OF UNDEAD MONKS, NOR THE SCREAMS OF HIS DYING SOLDIERS BREAKING HIS CONCENTRATION.
SUDDENLY: A MILLION SHARDS OF EMOTION. THE STORIES OF THE COUNTLESS FIGHTERS, ARMIES AND EMPIRES THAT FELL TO THIS BRILLIANT WEAPON PIERCED THE UNBROKEN SKIN OF BUNZO 12 AND OVERWHELMED HIS FLUTTERING MIND.

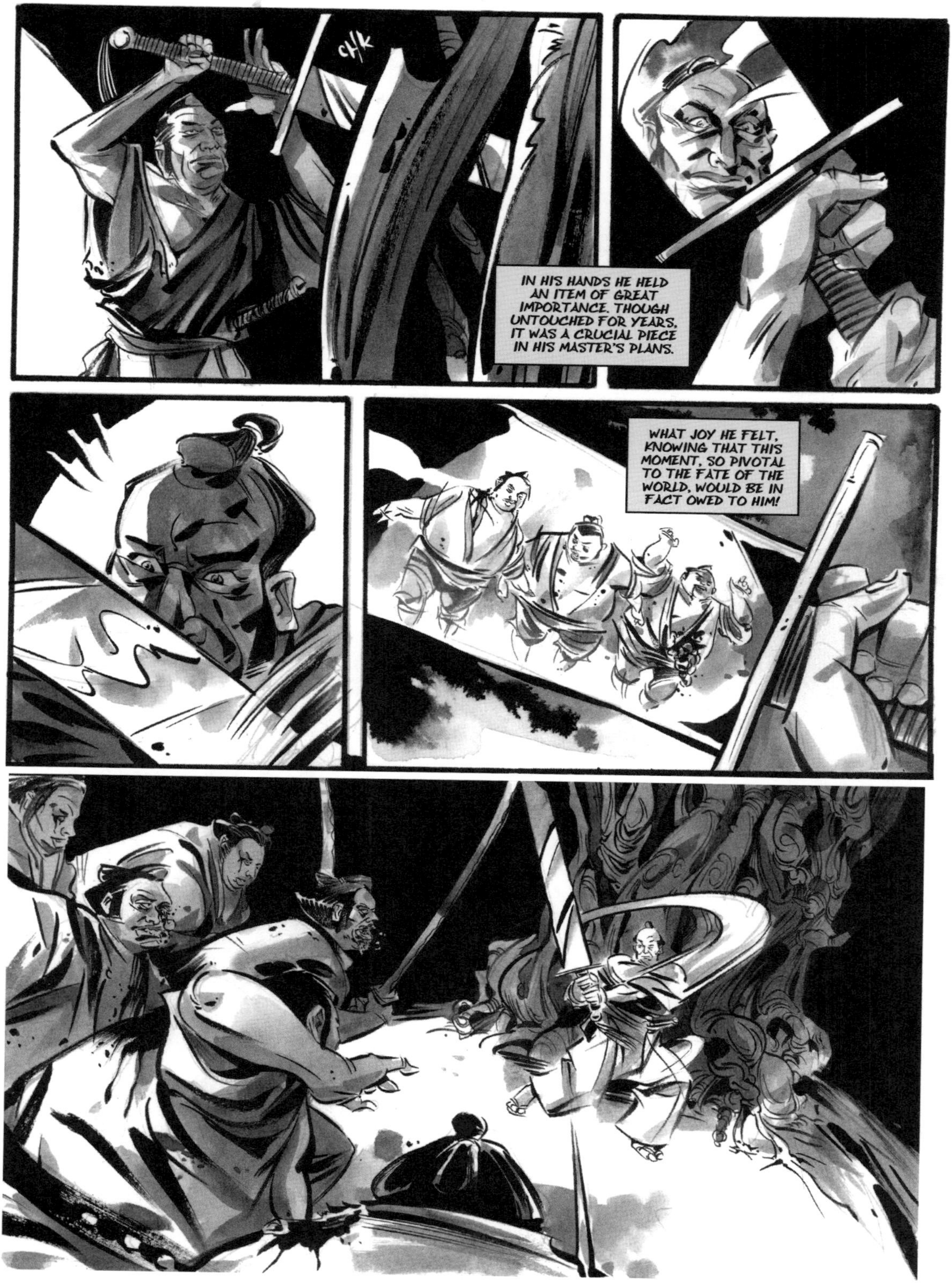
CHK
IN HIS HANDS HE HELD AN ITEM OF GREAT IMPORTANCE. THOUGH UNTOUCHED FOR YEARS, IT WAS A CRUCIAL PIECE IN HIS MASTER'S PLANS.
WHAT JOY HE FELT, KNOWING THAT THIS MOMENT, SO PIVOTAL TO THE FATE OF THE WORLD, WOULD BE IN FACT OWED TO HIM!

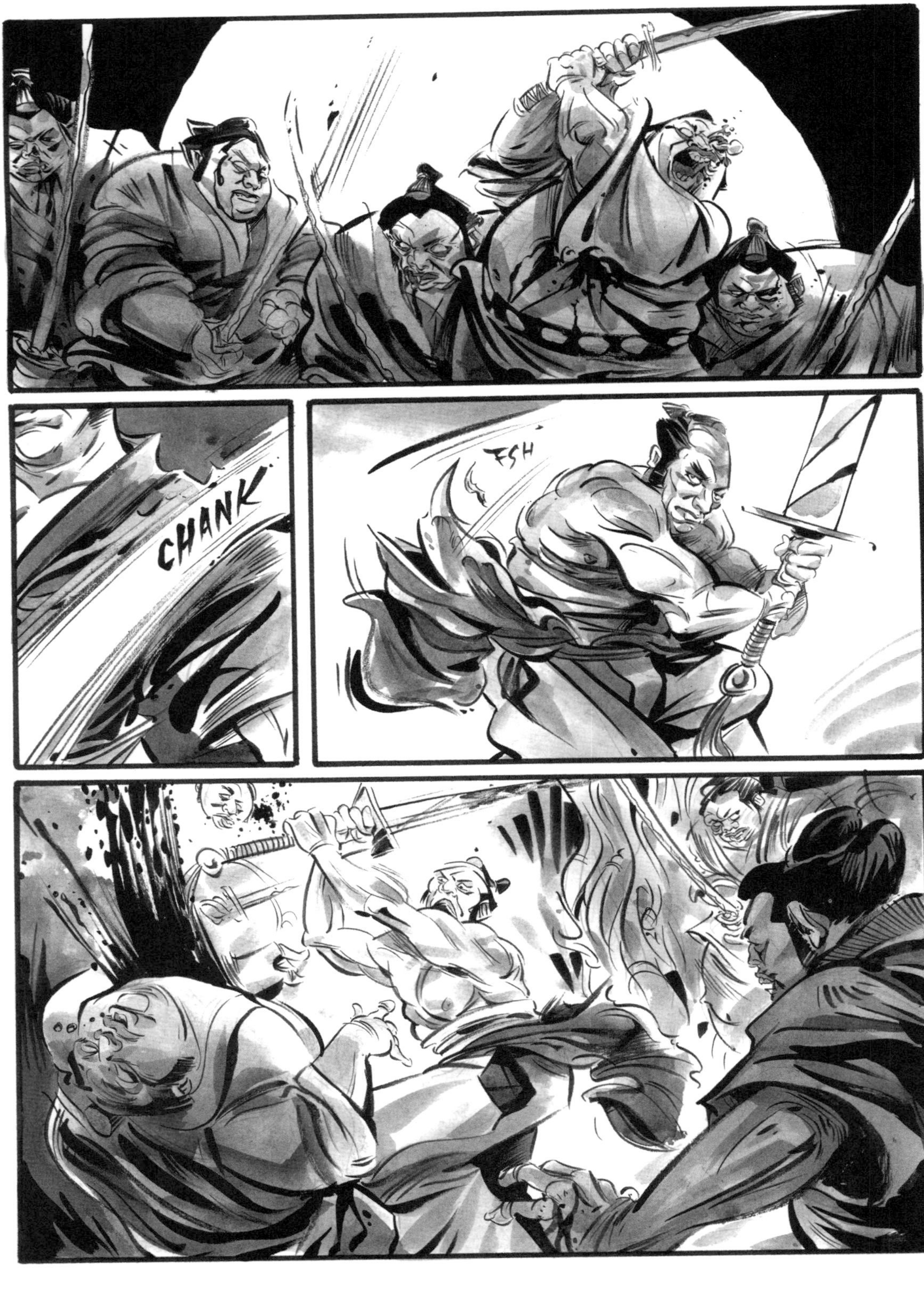
CHANK
FSH

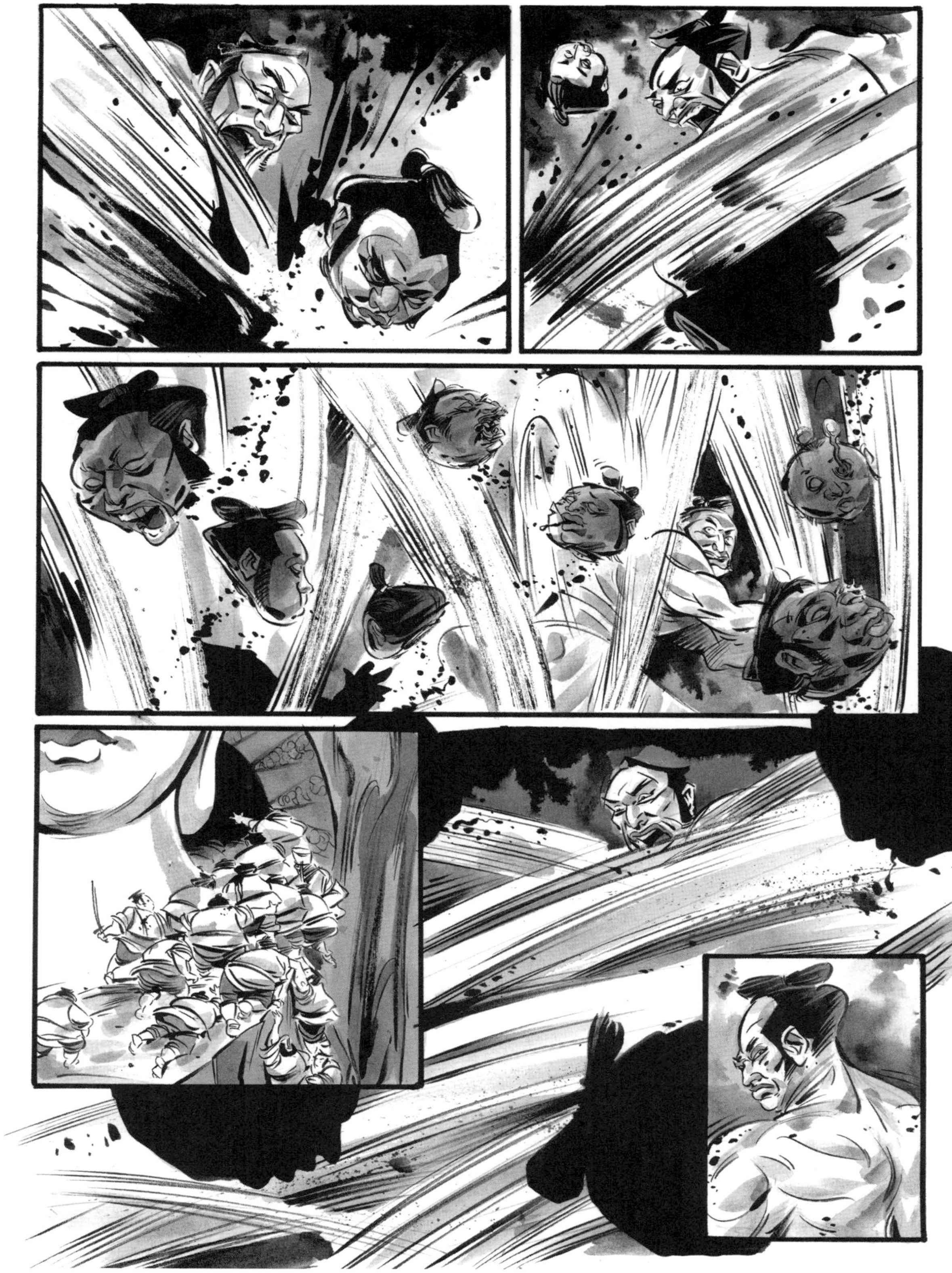

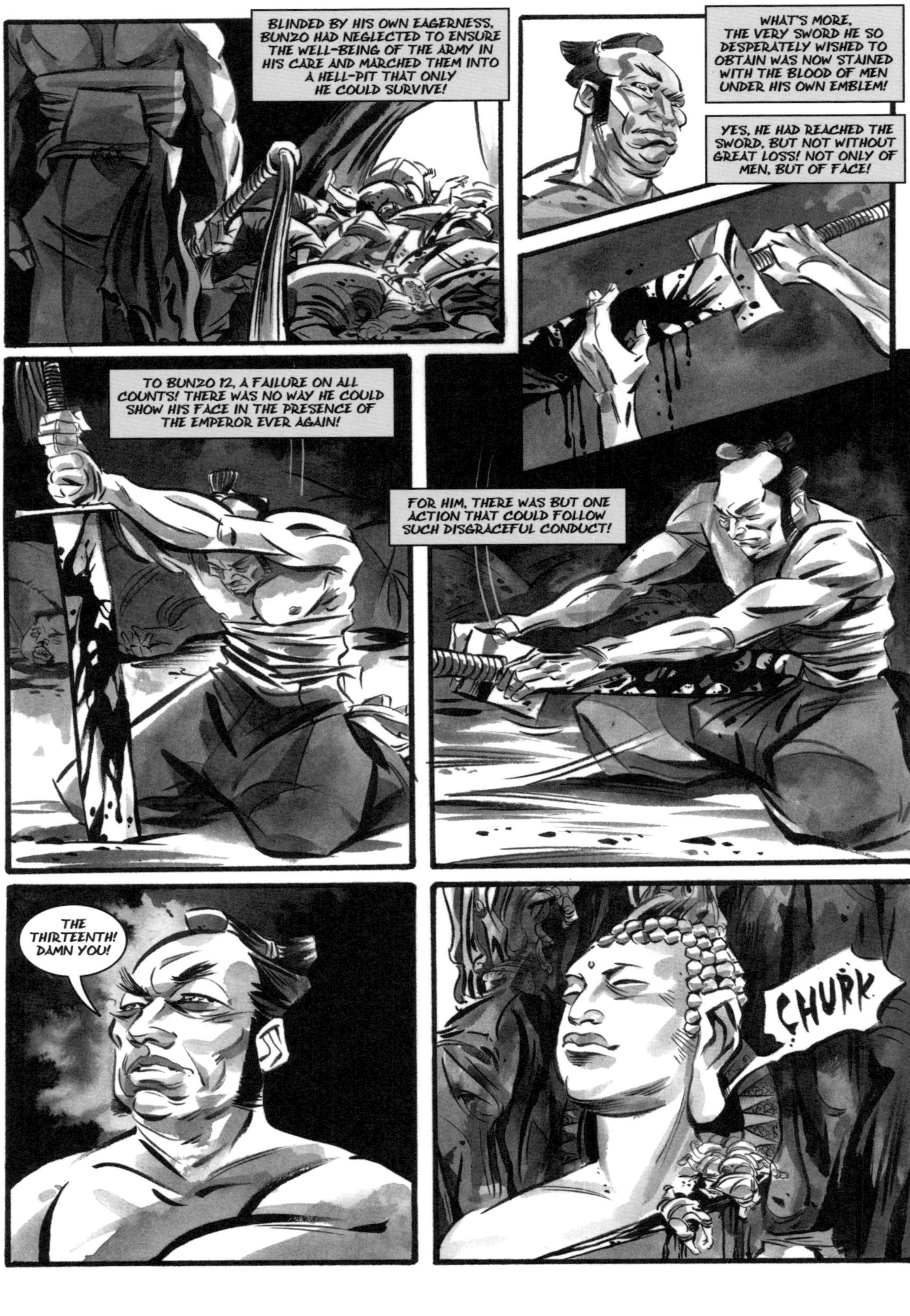
BLINDED BY HIS OWN EAGERNESS, BUNZO HAD NEGLECTED TO ENSURE THE WELL-BEING OF THE ARMY IN HIS CARE AND MARCHED THEM INTO A HELL-PIT THAT ONLY HE COULD SURVIVE!
WHAT'S MORE, THE VERY SWORD HE SO DESPERATELY WISHED TO OBTAIN WAS NOW STAINED WITH THE BLOOD OF MEN UNDER HIS OWN EMBLEM!
YES, HE HAD REACHED THE SWORD, BUT NOT WITHOUT GREAT LOSS! NOT ONLY OF MEN, BUT OF FACE!
TO BUNZO 12, A FAILURE ON ALL COUNTS! THERE WAS NO WAY HE COULD SHOW HIS FACE IN THE PRESENCE OF THE EMPEROR EVER AGAIN!
FOR HIM, THERE WAS BUT ONE ACTION THAT COULD FOLLOW SUCH DISGRACEFUL CONDUCT!
THE THIRTEENTH! DAMN YOU!
CHURK

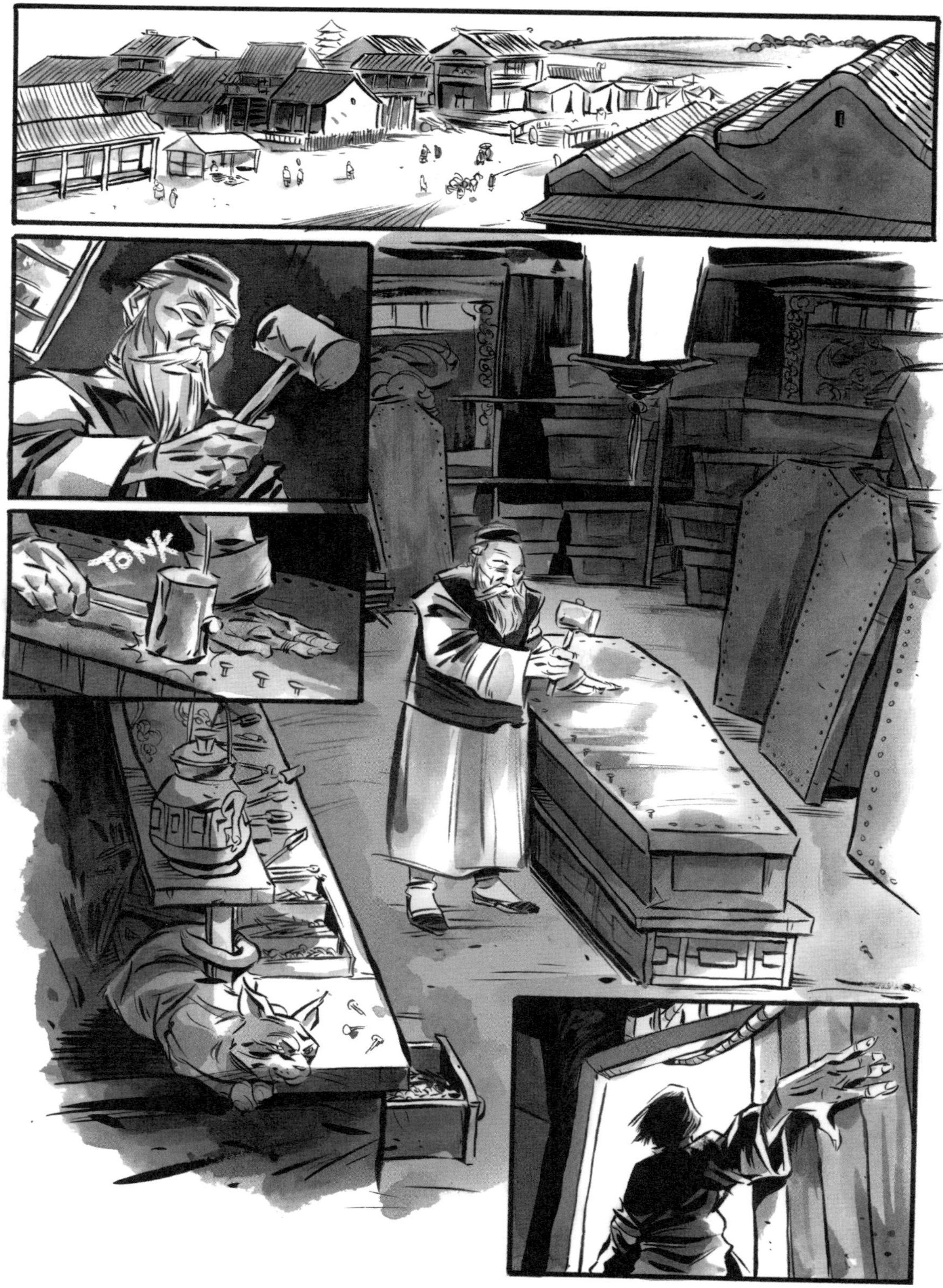
TONK

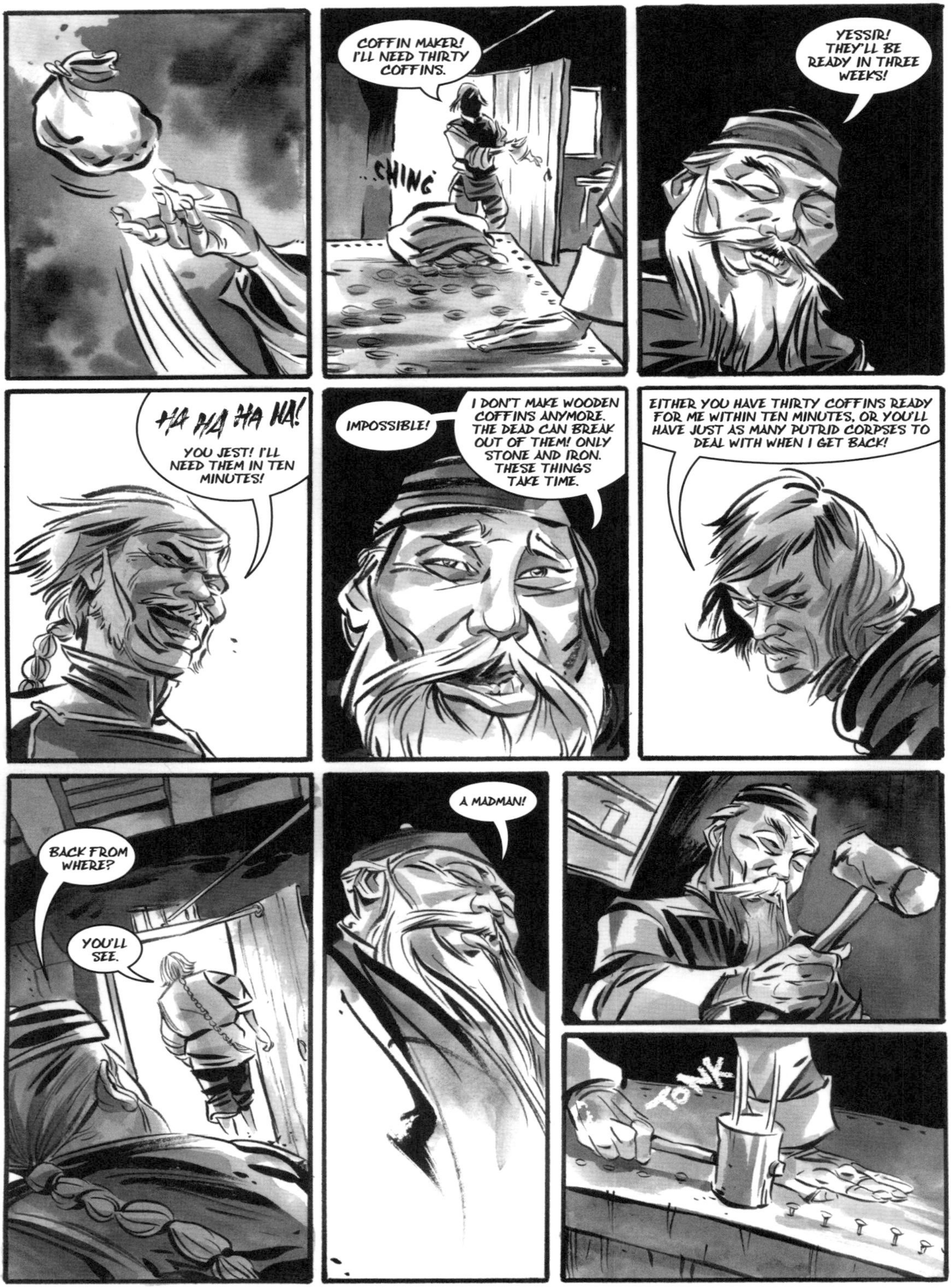
COFFIN MAKER! I'LL NEED THIRTY COFFINS.
...CHING
YESSIR! THEY'LL BE READY IN THREE WEEKS!
HA HA HA HA!
YOU JEST! I'LL NEED THEM IN TEN MINUTES!
IMPOSSIBLE!
I DON'T MAKE WOODEN COFFINS ANYMORE. THE DEAD CAN BREAK OUT OF THEM! ONLY STONE AND IRON. THESE THINGS TAKE TIME.
EITHER YOU HAVE THIRTY COFFINS READY FOR ME WITHIN TEN MINUTES, OR YOU'LL HAVE JUST AS MANY PUTRID CORPSES TO DEAL WITH WHEN I GET BACK!
BACK FROM WHERE?
YOU'LL SEE.
A MADMAN!
TONK

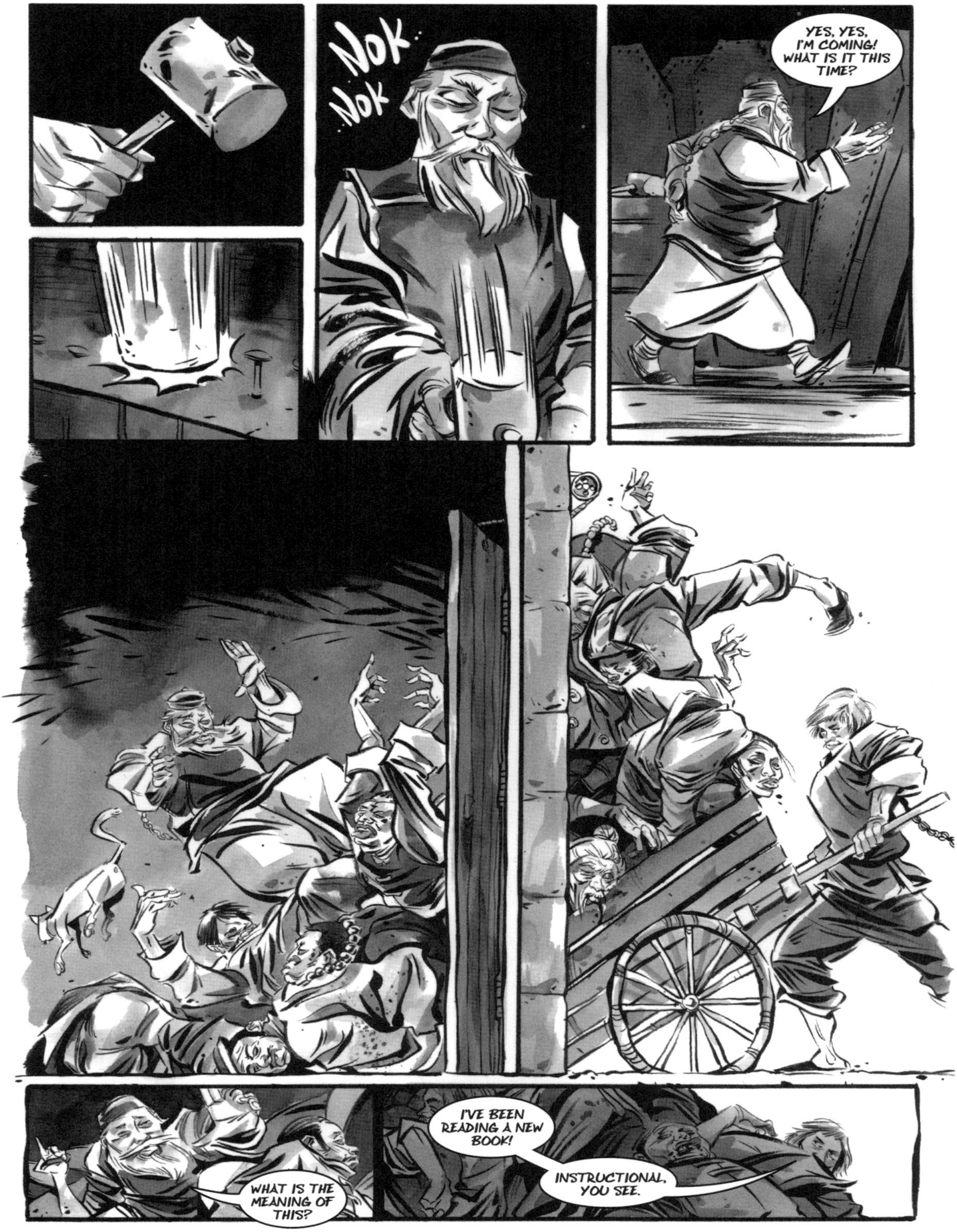

NOK
NOK
YES, YES, I'M COMING! WHAT IS IT THIS TIME?
WHAT IS THE MEANING OF THIS?
I'VE BEEN READING A NEW BOOK!
INSTRUCTIONAL, YOU SEE.

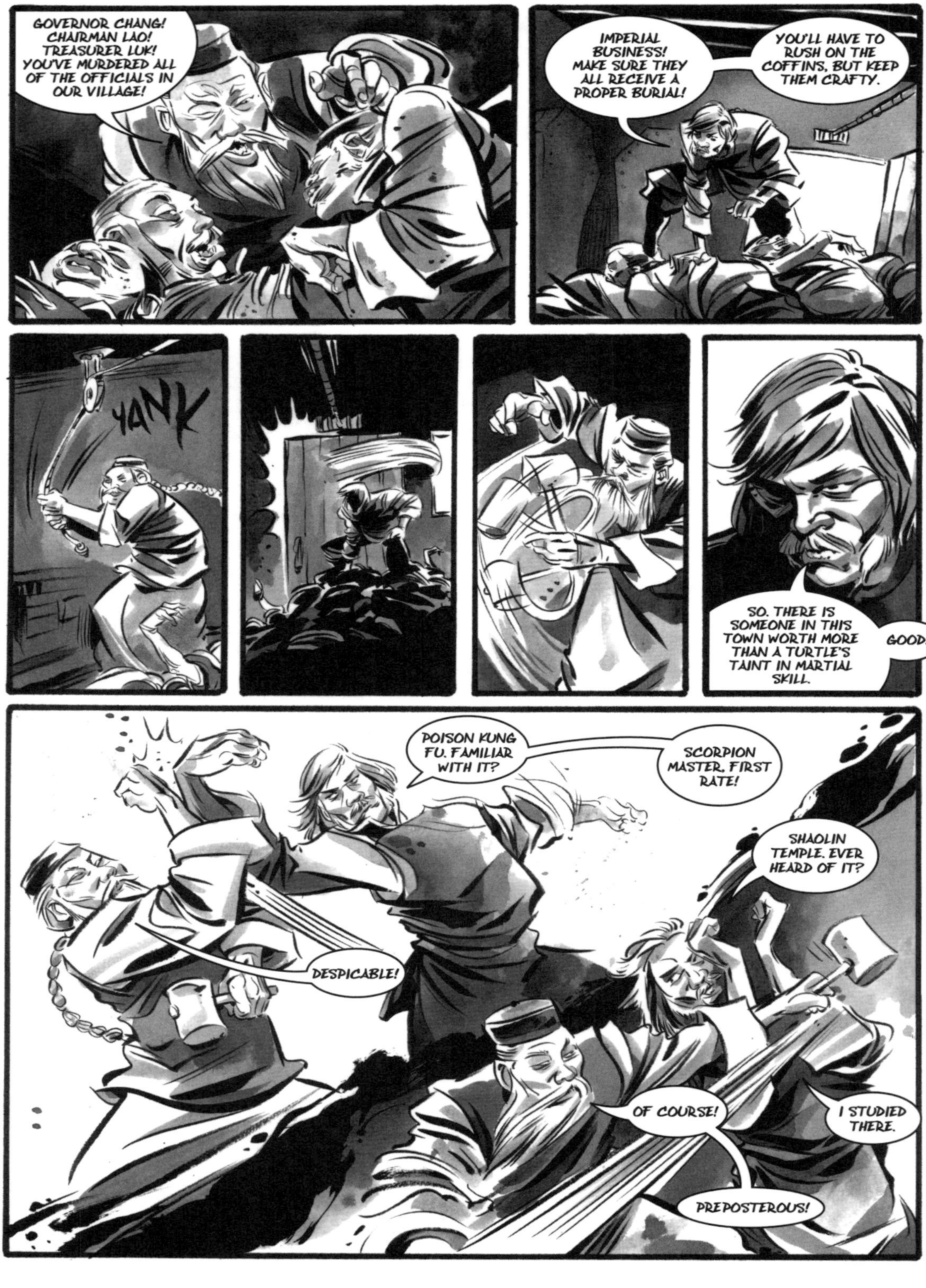
GOVERNOR CHANG! CHAIRMAN LAO! TREASURER LUK! YOU'VE MURDERED ALL OF THE OFFICIALS IN OUR VILLAGE!
IMPERIAL BUSINESS! MAKE SURE THEY ALL RECEIVE A PROPER BURIAL!
YOU'LL HAVE TO RUSH ON THE COFFINS, BUT KEEP THEM CRAFTY.
YANK
SO. THERE IS SOMEONE IN THIS TOWN WORTH MORE THAN A TURTLE'S TAINT IN MARTIAL SKILL.
GOOD.
POISON KUNG FU. FAMILIAR WITH IT?
SCORPION MASTER. FIRST RATE!
DESPICABLE!
SHAOLIN TEMPLE. EVER HEARD OF IT?
OF COURSE!
I STUDIED THERE.
PREPOSTEROUS!

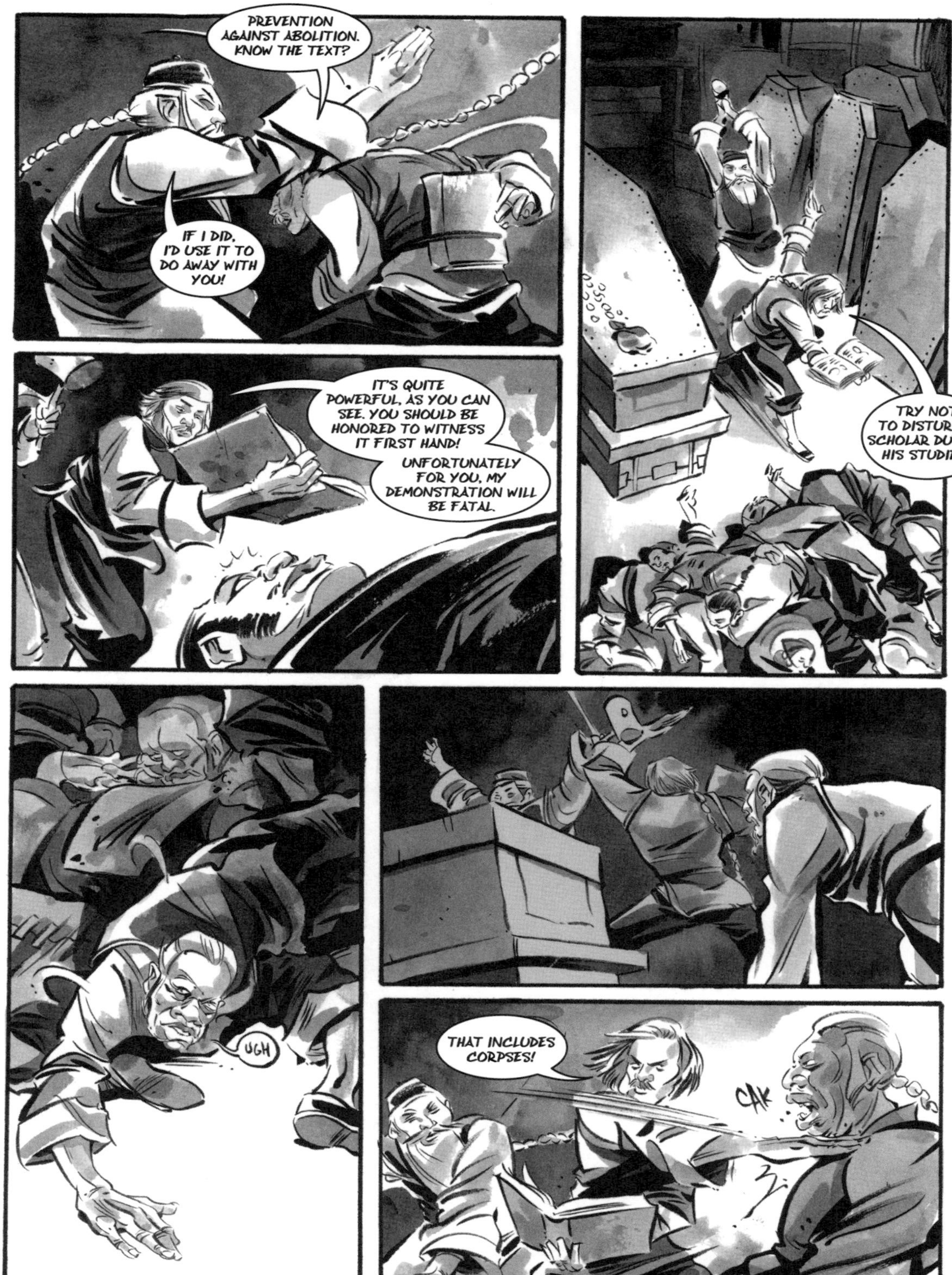
PREVENTION AGAINST ABOLITION. KNOW THE TEXT?
IF I DID, I'D USE IT TO DO AWAY WITH YOU!
IT'S QUITE POWERFUL, AS YOU CAN SEE. YOU SHOULD BE HONORED TO WITNESS IT FIRST HAND!
UNFORTUNATELY FOR YOU, MY DEMONSTRATION WILL BE FATAL.
TRY NOT TO DISTURB A SCHOLAR DURING HIS STUDIES!
UGH
THAT INCLUDES CORPSES!
CAK

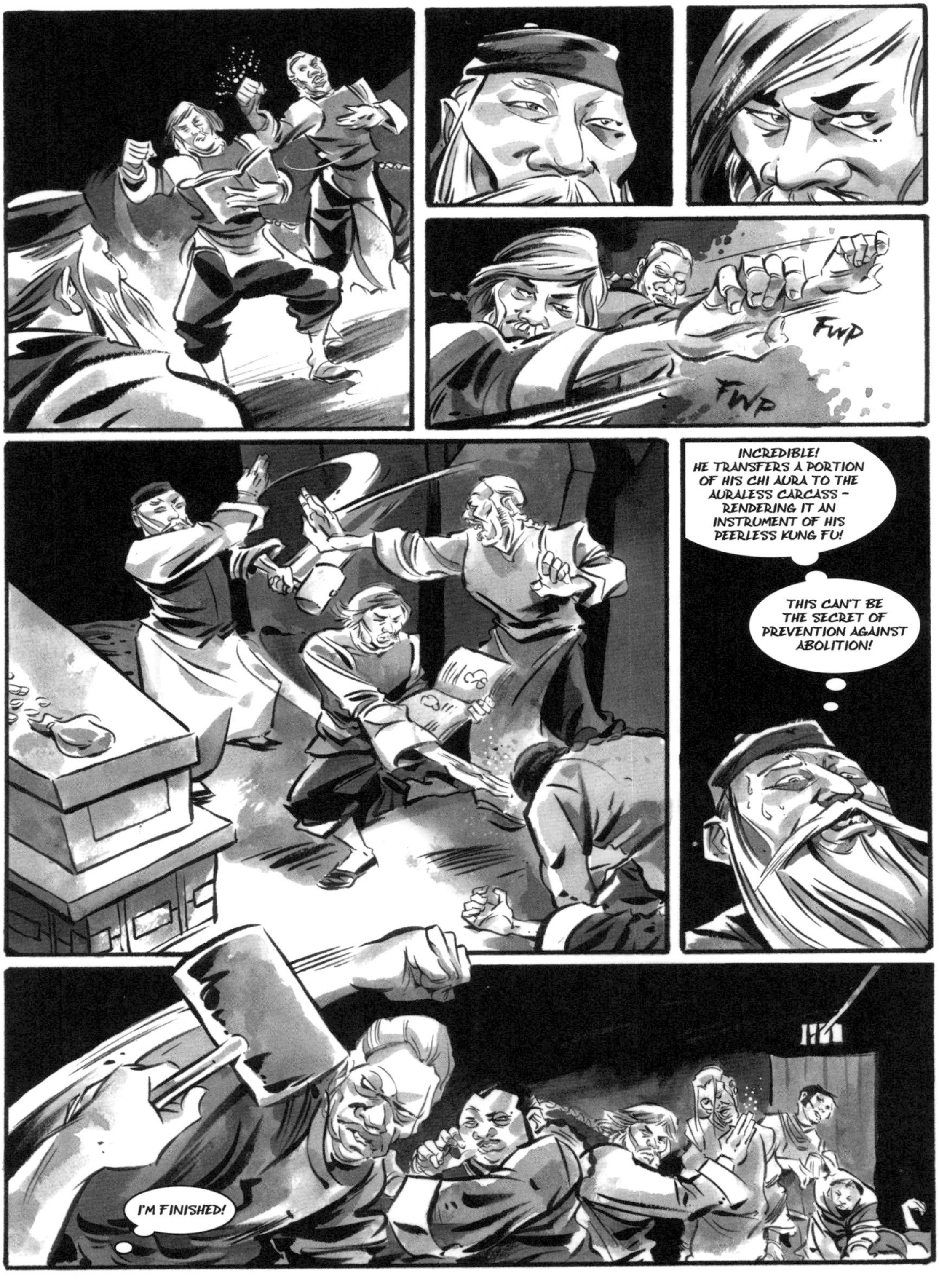
FWP
FWP
INCREDIBLE! HE TRANSFERS A PORTION OF HIS CHI AURA TO THE AURALESS CARCASS – RENDERING IT AN INSTRUMENT OF HIS PEERLESS KUNG FU!
THIS CAN'T BE THE SECRET OF PREVENTION AGAINST ABOLITION!
I'M FINISHED!

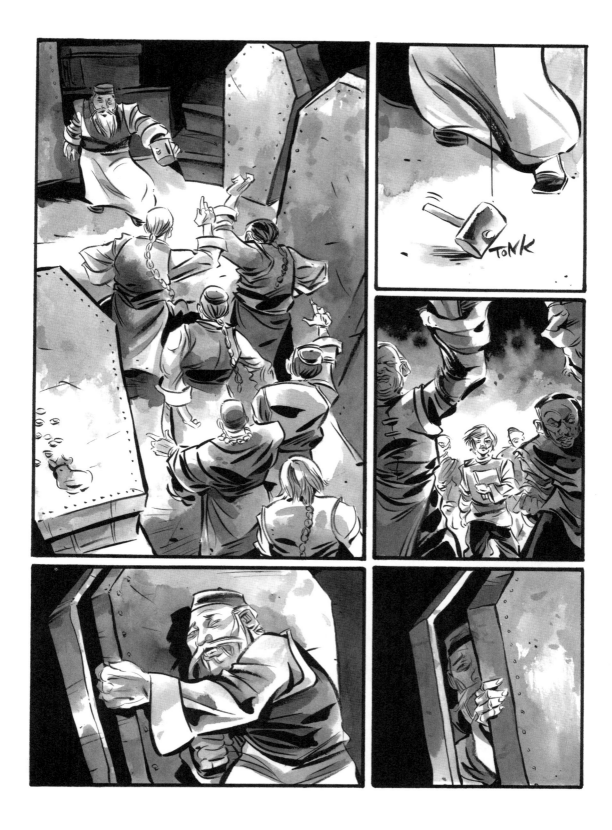

TONK

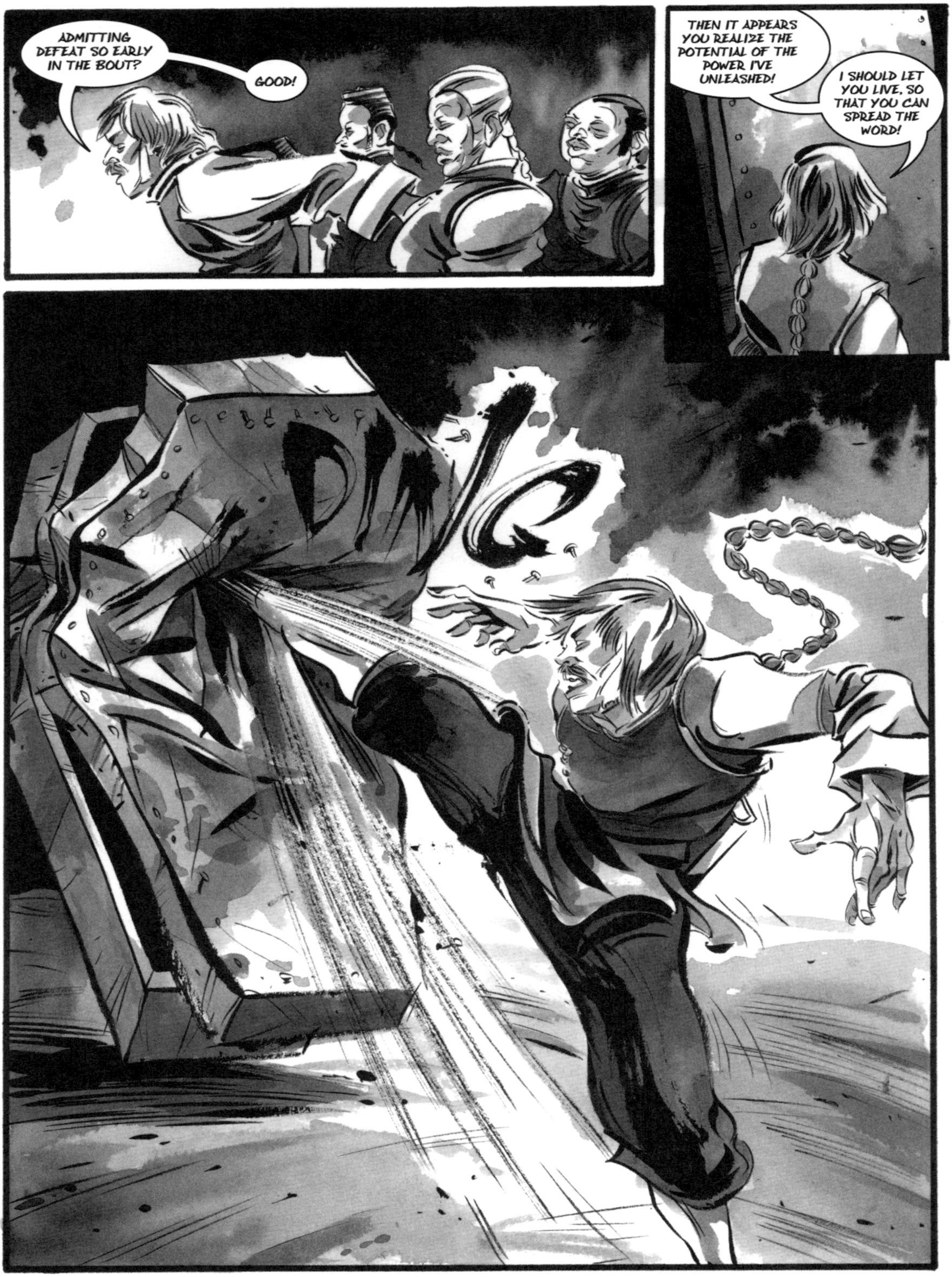

ADMITTING DEFEAT SO EARLY IN THE BOUT?
GOOD!
THEN IT APPEARS YOU REALIZE THE POTENTIAL OF THE POWER I'VE UNLEASHED!
I SHOULD LET YOU LIVE, SO THAT YOU CAN SPREAD THE WORD!
DING

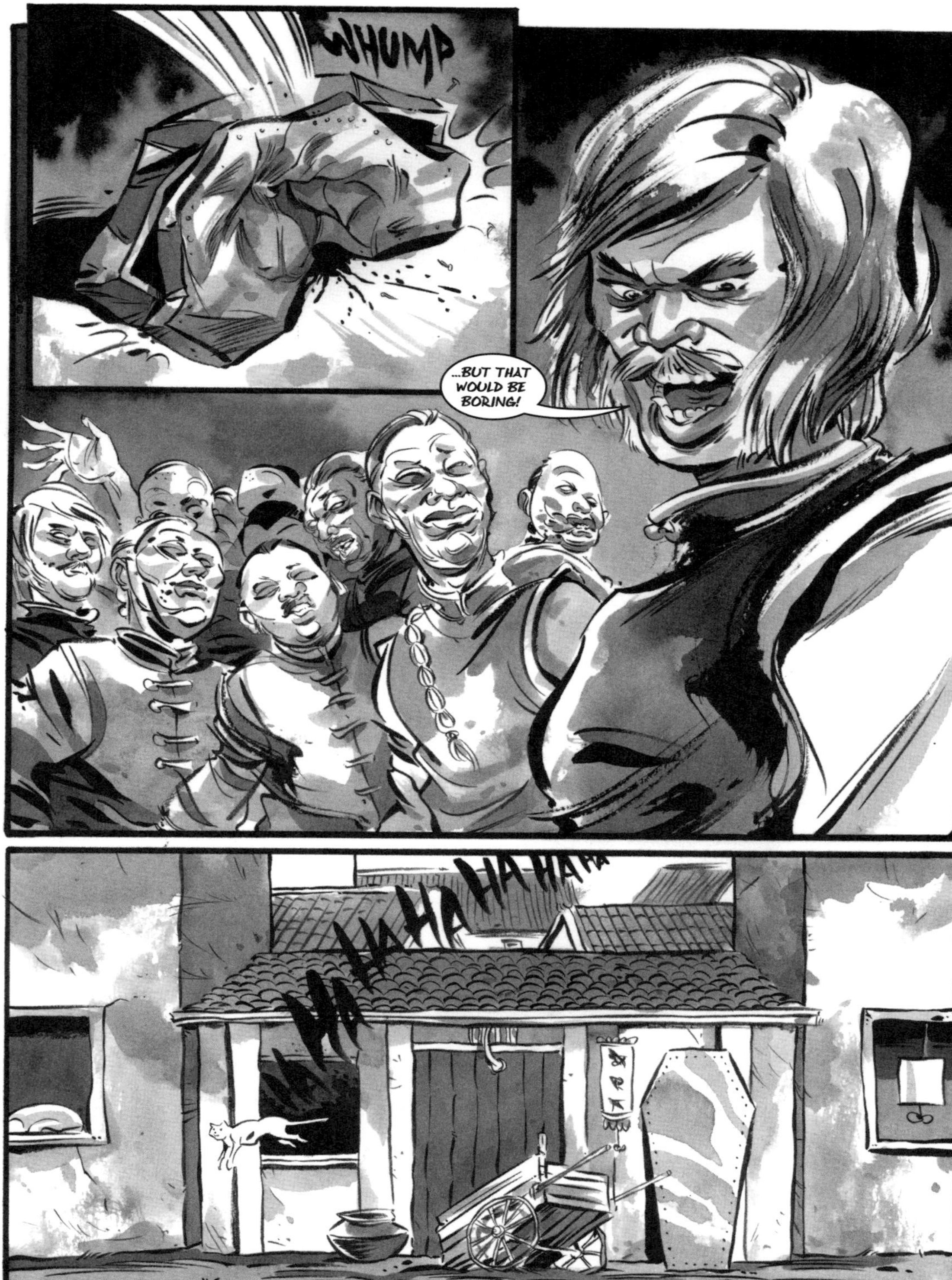
WHUMP
...BUT THAT WOULD BE BORING!
HA HA HA HA HA HA HA

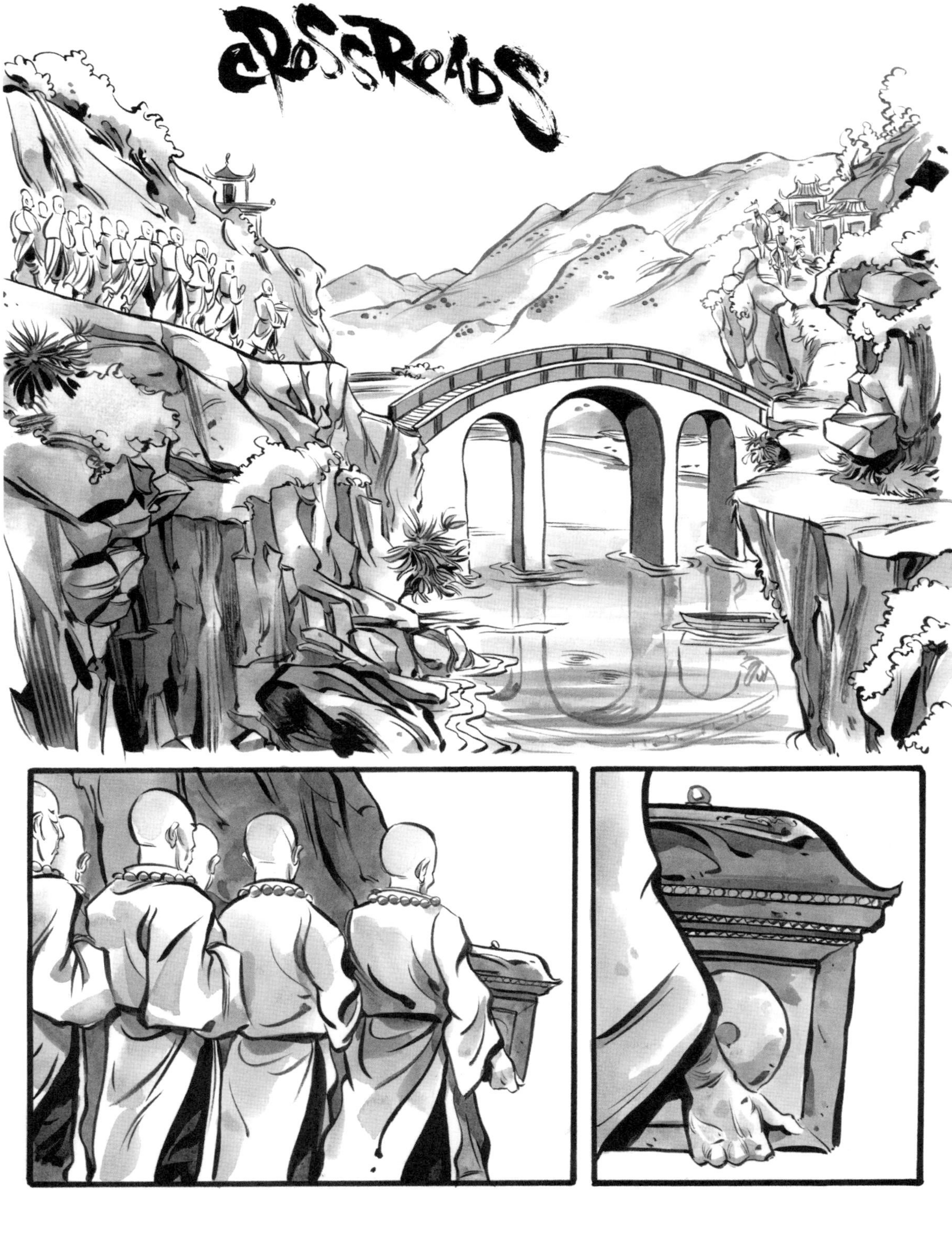
CROSSROADS

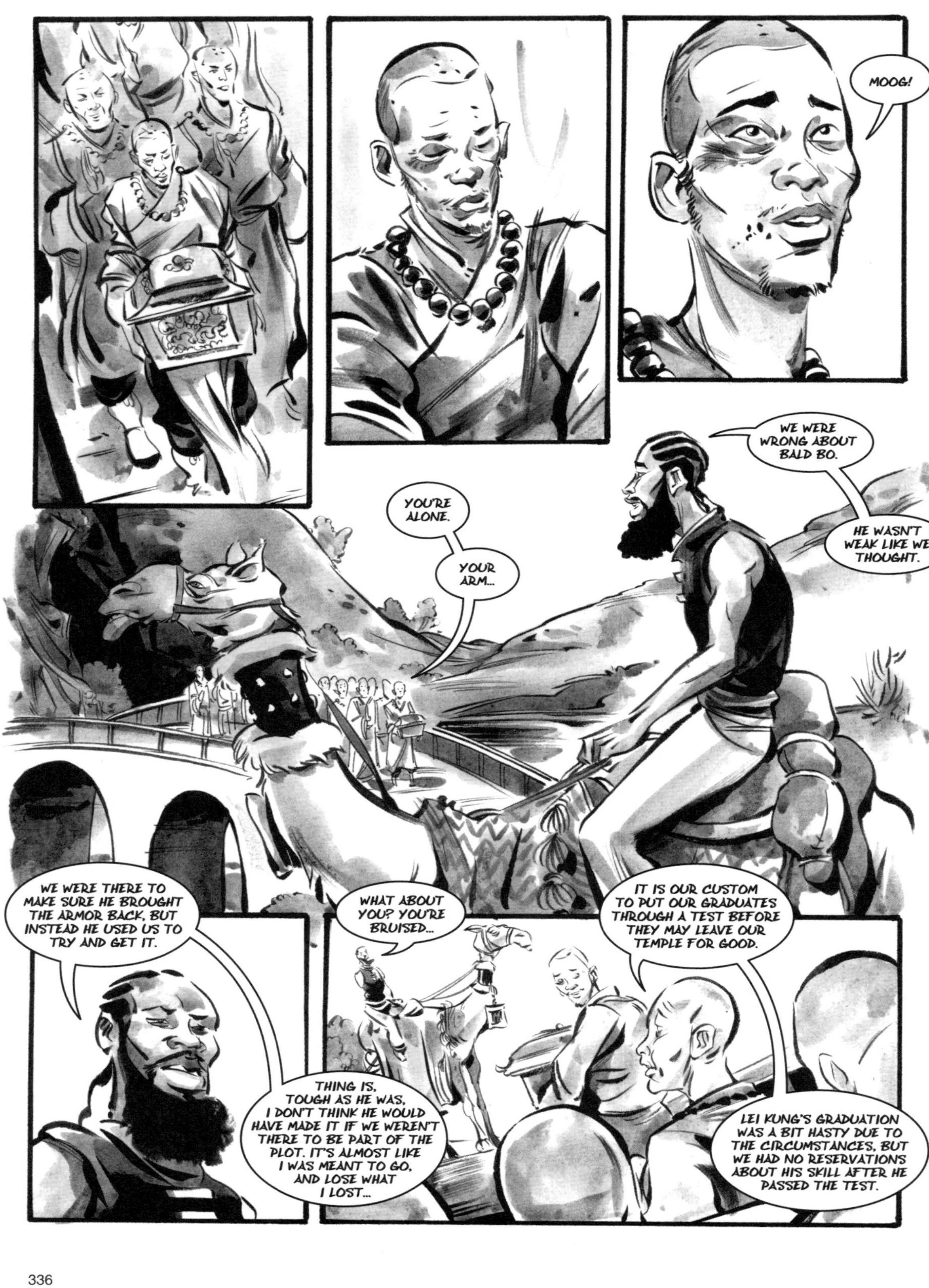
MOOG!
YOU'RE ALONE.
YOUR ARM...
WE WERE WRONG ABOUT BALD BO.
HE WASN'T WEAK LIKE WE THOUGHT.
WE WERE THERE TO MAKE SURE HE BROUGHT THE ARMOR BACK, BUT INSTEAD HE USED US TO TRY AND GET IT.
THING IS, TOUGH AS HE WAS, I DON'T THINK HE WOULD HAVE MADE IT IF WE WEREN'T THERE TO BE PART OF THE PLOT. IT'S ALMOST LIKE I WAS MEANT TO GO, AND LOSE WHAT I LOST...
WHAT ABOUT YOU? YOU'RE BRUISED...
IT IS OUR CUSTOM TO PUT OUR GRADUATES THROUGH A TEST BEFORE THEY MAY LEAVE OUR TEMPLE FOR GOOD.
LEI KUNG'S GRADUATION WAS A BIT HASTY DUE TO THE CIRCUMSTANCES, BUT WE HAD NO RESERVATIONS ABOUT HIS SKILL AFTER HE PASSED THE TEST.

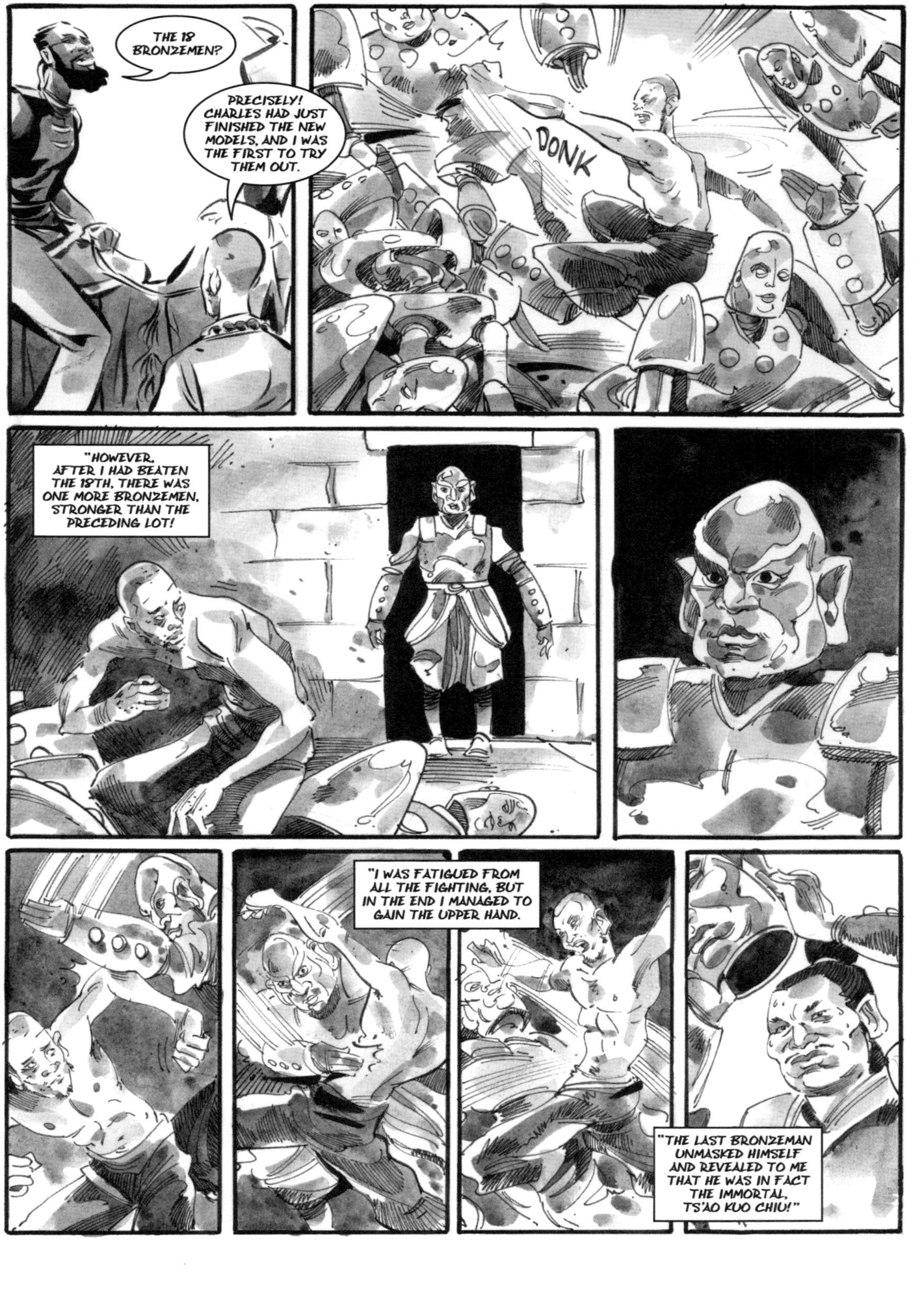
THE 18 BRONZEMEN?
PRECISELY! CHARLES HAD JUST FINISHED THE NEW MODELS, AND I WAS THE FIRST TO TRY THEM OUT.
DONK
"HOWEVER, AFTER I HAD BEATEN THE 18TH, THERE WAS ONE MORE BRONZEMEN, STRONGER THAN THE PRECEDING LOT!
"I WAS FATIGUED FROM ALL THE FIGHTING, BUT IN THE END I MANAGED TO GAIN THE UPPER HAND.
"THE LAST BRONZEMAN UNMASKED HIMSELF AND REVEALED TO ME THAT HE WAS IN FACT THE IMMORTAL, TS'AO KUO CHIU!"

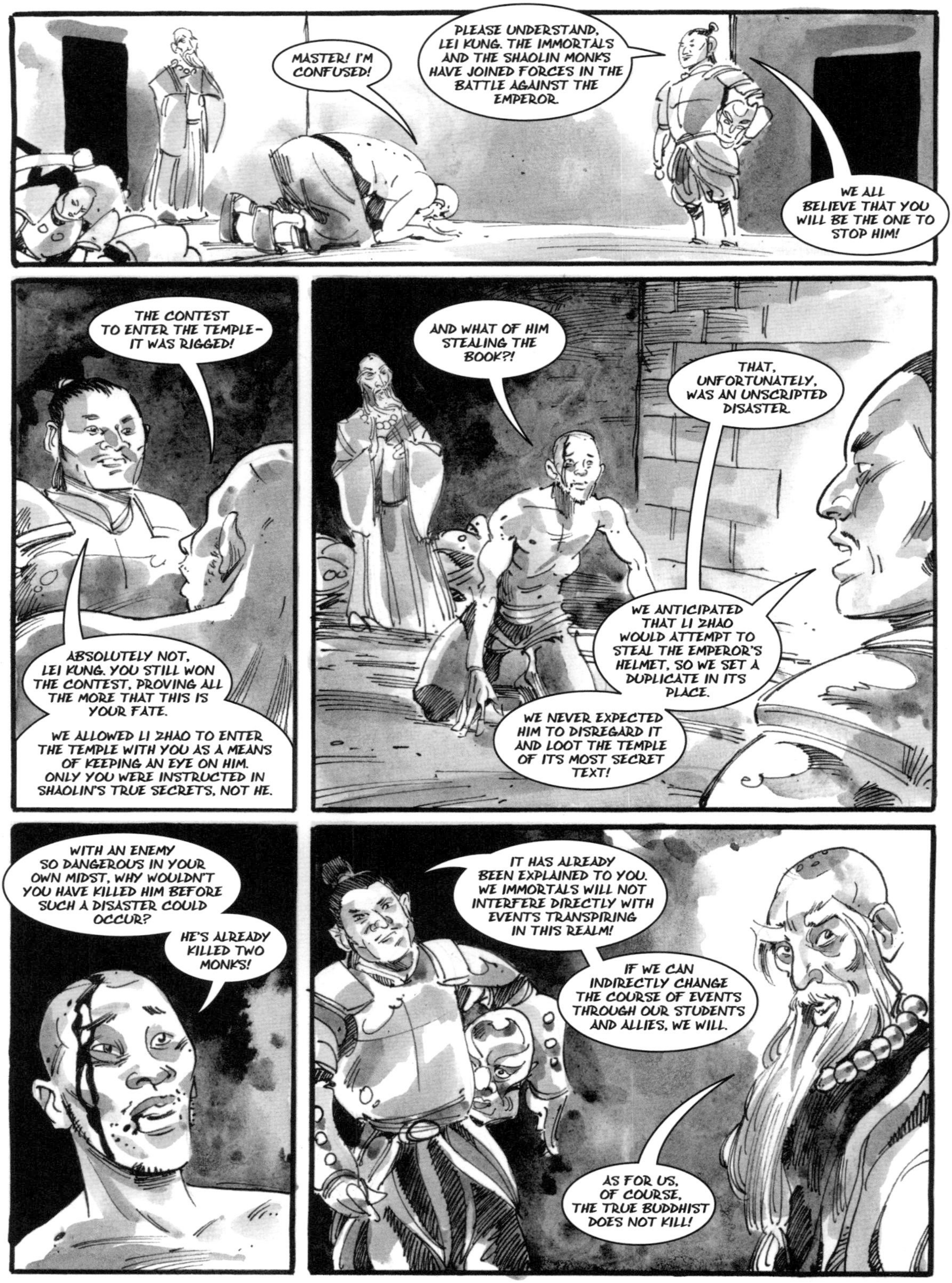
MASTER! I'M CONFUSED!
PLEASE UNDERSTAND, LEI KUNG. THE IMMORTALS AND THE SHAOLIN MONKS HAVE JOINED FORCES IN THE BATTLE AGAINST THE EMPEROR.
WE ALL BELIEVE THAT YOU WILL BE THE ONE TO STOP HIM!
THE CONTEST TO ENTER THE TEMPLE- IT WAS RIGGED!
ABSOLUTELY NOT, LEI KUNG. YOU STILL WON THE CONTEST, PROVING ALL THE MORE THAT THIS IS YOUR FATE.
WE ALLOWED LI ZHAO TO ENTER THE TEMPLE WITH YOU AS A MEANS OF KEEPING AN EYE ON HIM. ONLY YOU WERE INSTRUCTED IN SHAOLIN'S TRUE SECRETS, NOT HE.
AND WHAT OF HIM STEALING THE BOOK?!
THAT, UNFORTUNATELY, WAS AN UNSCRIPTED DISASTER.
WE ANTICIPATED THAT LI ZHAO WOULD ATTEMPT TO STEAL THE EMPEROR'S HELMET, SO WE SET A DUPLICATE IN ITS PLACE.
WE NEVER EXPECTED HIM TO DISREGARD IT AND LOOT THE TEMPLE OF ITS MOST SECRET TEXT!
WITH AN ENEMY SO DANGEROUS IN YOUR OWN MIDST, WHY WOULDN'T YOU HAVE KILLED HIM BEFORE SUCH A DISASTER COULD OCCUR?
HE'S ALREADY KILLED TWO MONKS!
IT HAS ALREADY BEEN EXPLAINED TO YOU. WE IMMORTALS WILL NOT INTERFERE DIRECTLY WITH EVENTS TRANSPIRING IN THIS REALM!
IF WE CAN INDIRECTLY CHANGE THE COURSE OF EVENTS THROUGH OUR STUDENTS AND ALLIES, WE WILL.
AS FOR US, OF COURSE, THE TRUE BUDDHIST DOES NOT KILL!

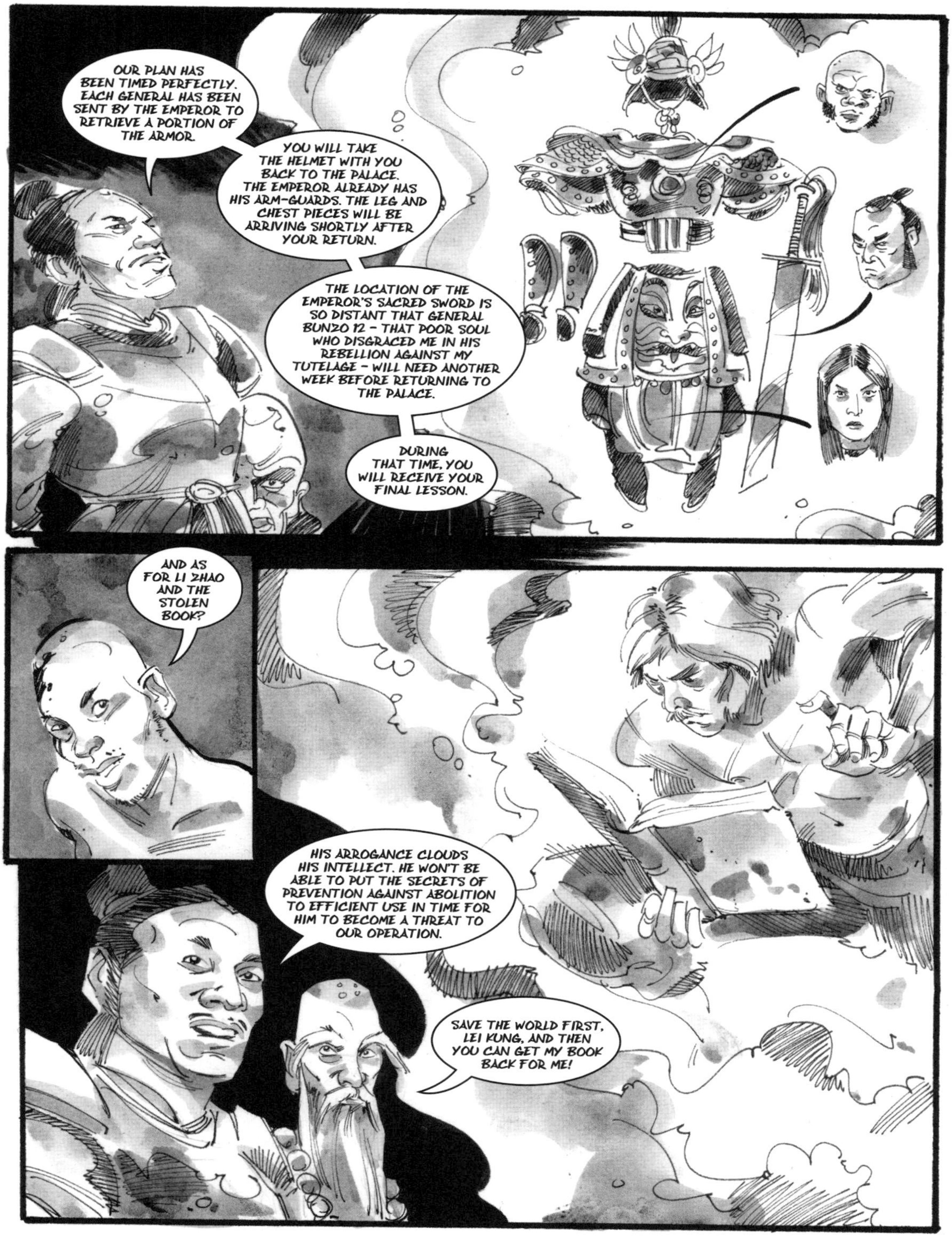
OUR PLAN HAS BEEN TIMED PERFECTLY. EACH GENERAL HAS BEEN SENT BY THE EMPEROR TO RETRIEVE A PORTION OF THE ARMOR.
YOU WILL TAKE THE HELMET WITH YOU BACK TO THE PALACE. THE EMPEROR ALREADY HAS HIS ARM-GUARDS. THE LEG AND CHEST PIECES WILL BE ARRIVING SHORTLY AFTER YOUR RETURN.
THE LOCATION OF THE EMPEROR'S SACRED SWORD IS SO DISTANT THAT GENERAL BUNZO 12 - THAT POOR SOUL WHO DISGRACED ME IN HIS REBELLION AGAINST MY TUTELAGE - WILL NEED ANOTHER WEEK BEFORE RETURNING TO THE PALACE.
DURING THAT TIME, YOU WILL RECEIVE YOUR FINAL LESSON.
AND AS FOR LI ZHAO AND THE STOLEN BOOK?
HIS ARROGANCE CLOUDS HIS INTELLECT. HE WON'T BE ABLE TO PUT THE SECRETS OF PREVENTION AGAINST ABOLITION TO EFFICIENT USE IN TIME FOR HIM TO BECOME A THREAT TO OUR OPERATION.
SAVE THE WORLD FIRST, LEI KUNG, AND THEN YOU CAN GET MY BOOK BACK FOR ME!

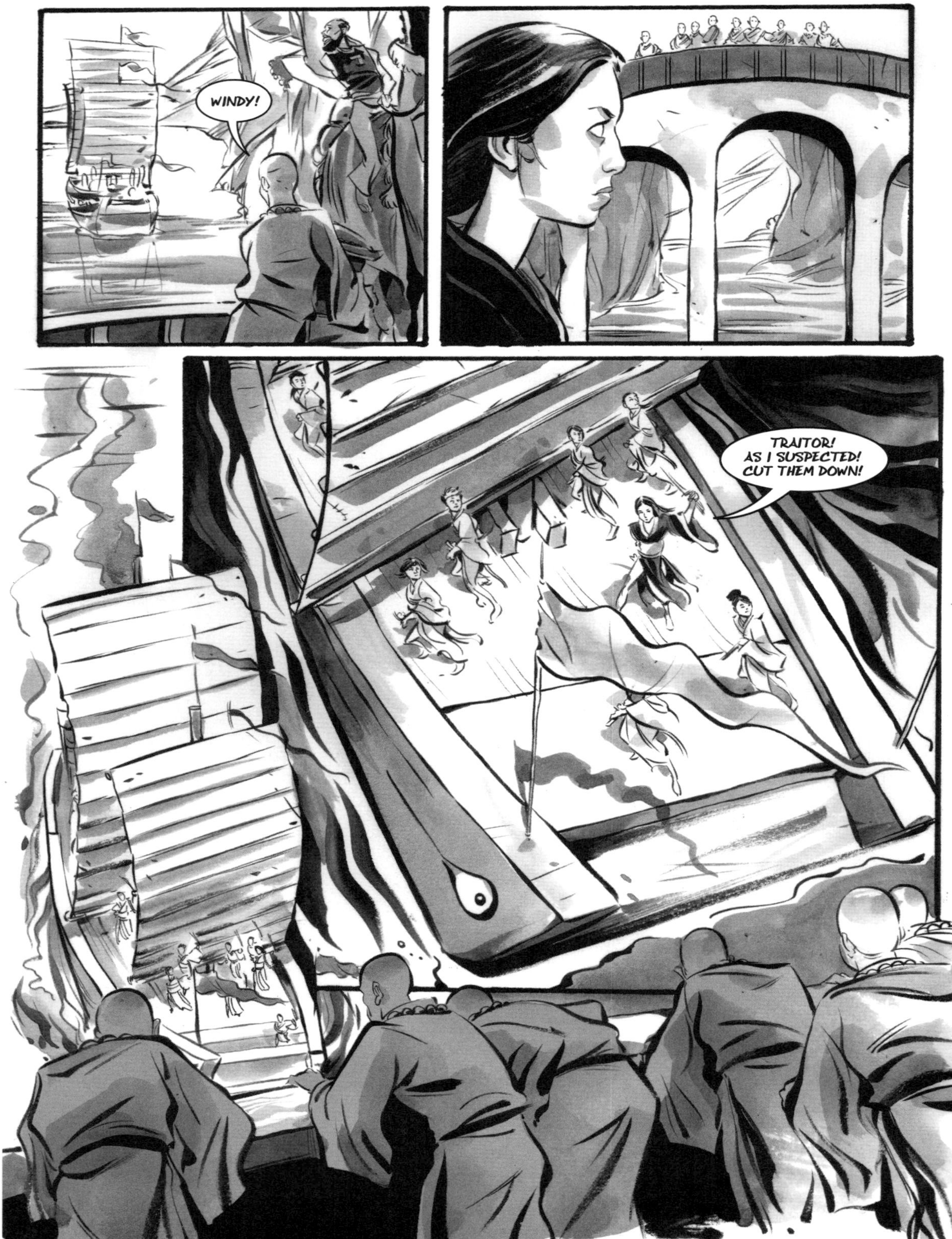
WINDY!
TRAITOR! AS I SUSPECTED! CUT THEM DOWN!

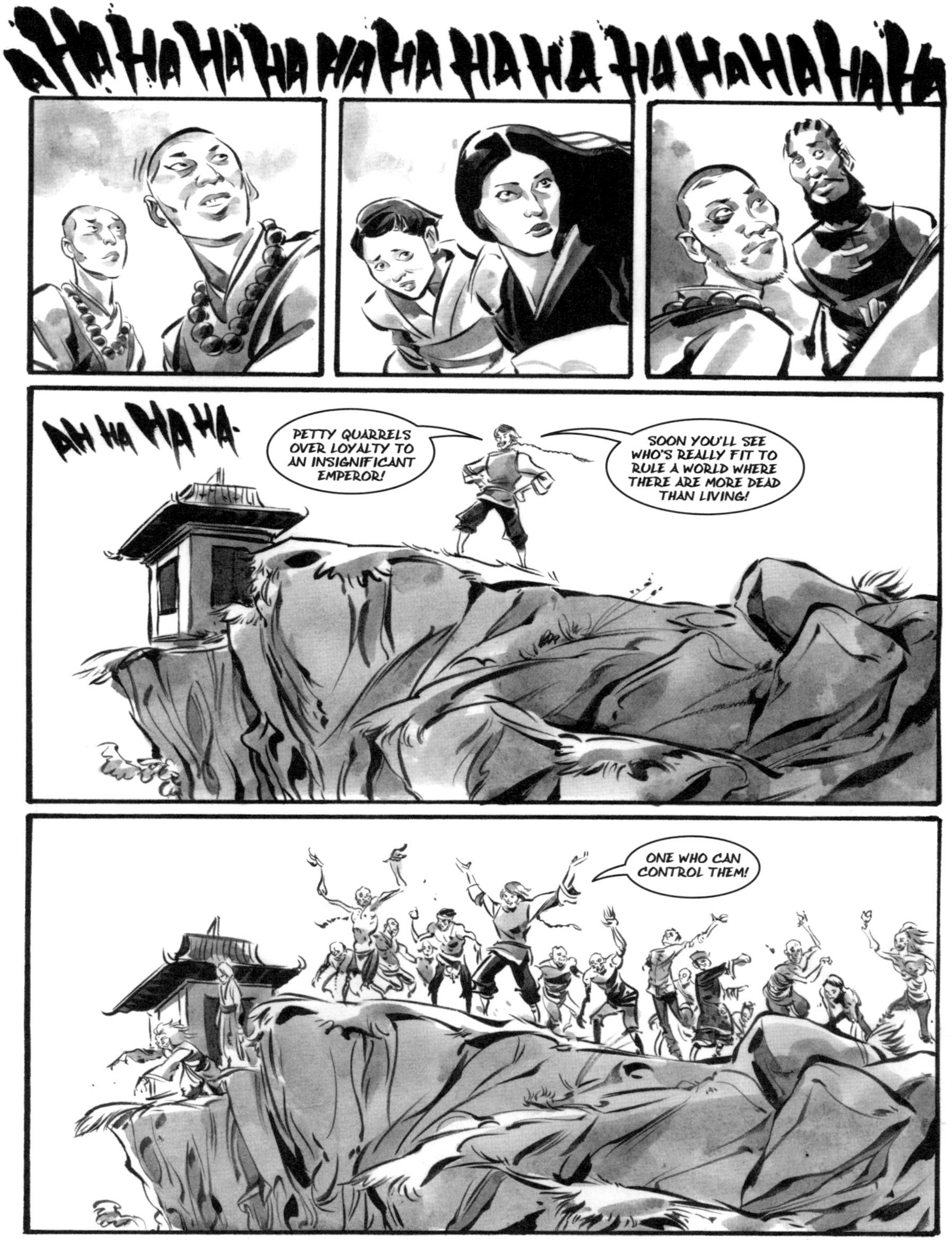

aHA HA HA HA HA HA HA HA HA HA HA HA HA
AH HA HA HA
PETTY QUARRELS OVER LOYALTY TO AN INSIGNIFICANT EMPEROR!
SOON YOU'LL SEE WHO'S REALLY FIT TO RULE A WORLD WHERE THERE ARE MORE DEAD THAN LIVING!
ONE WHO CAN CONTROL THEM!

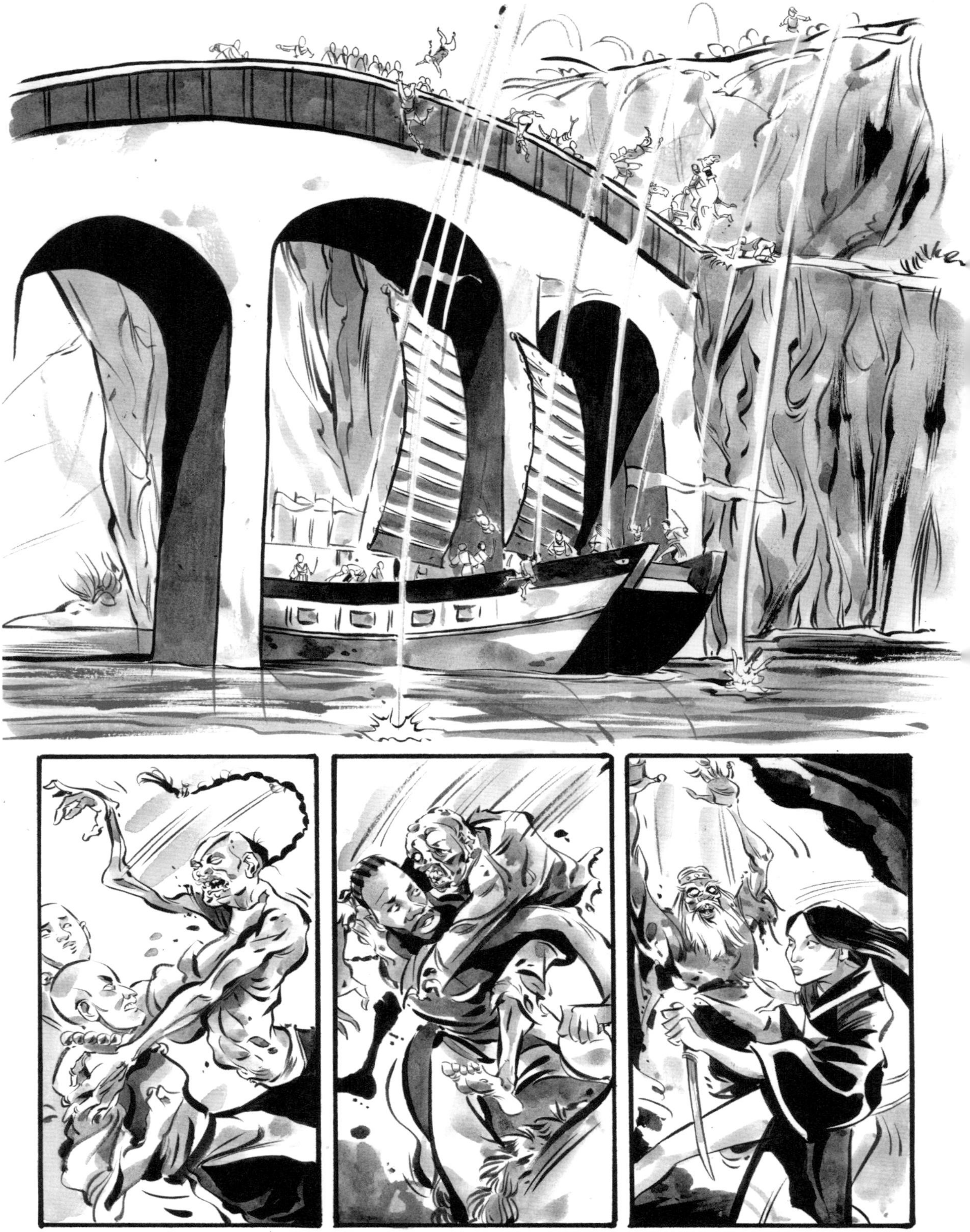

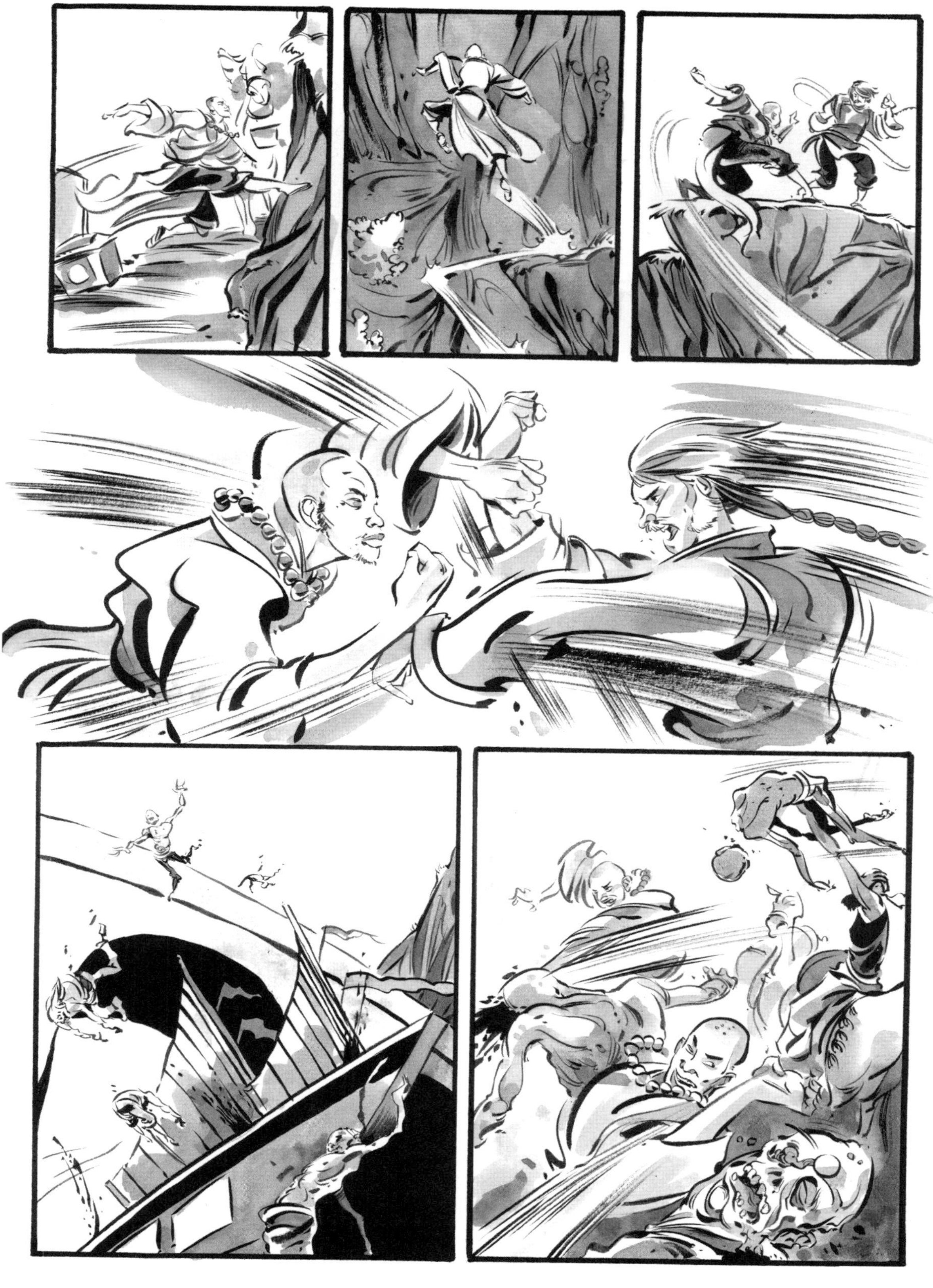

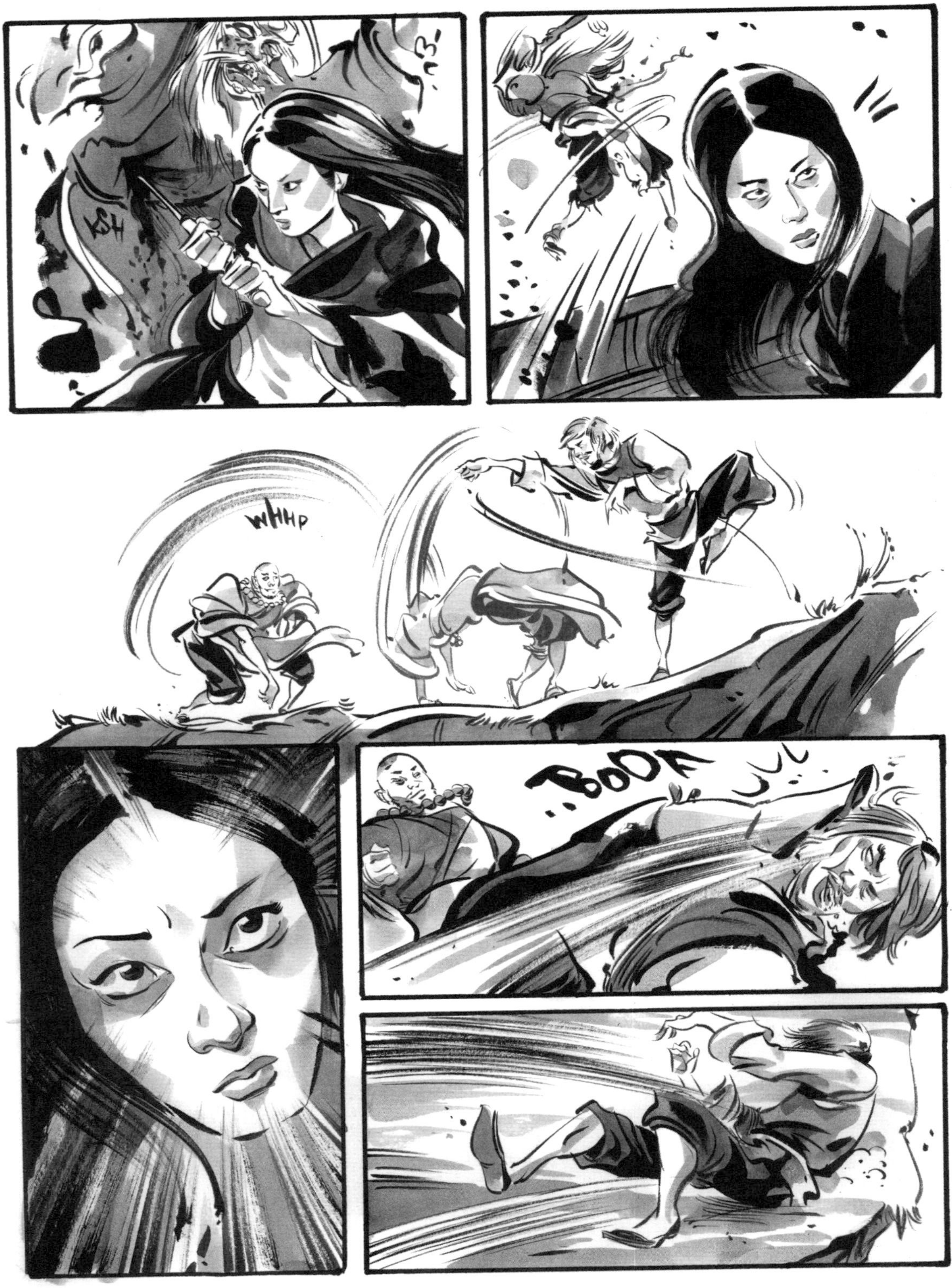
KSH
WHIP
BOOF

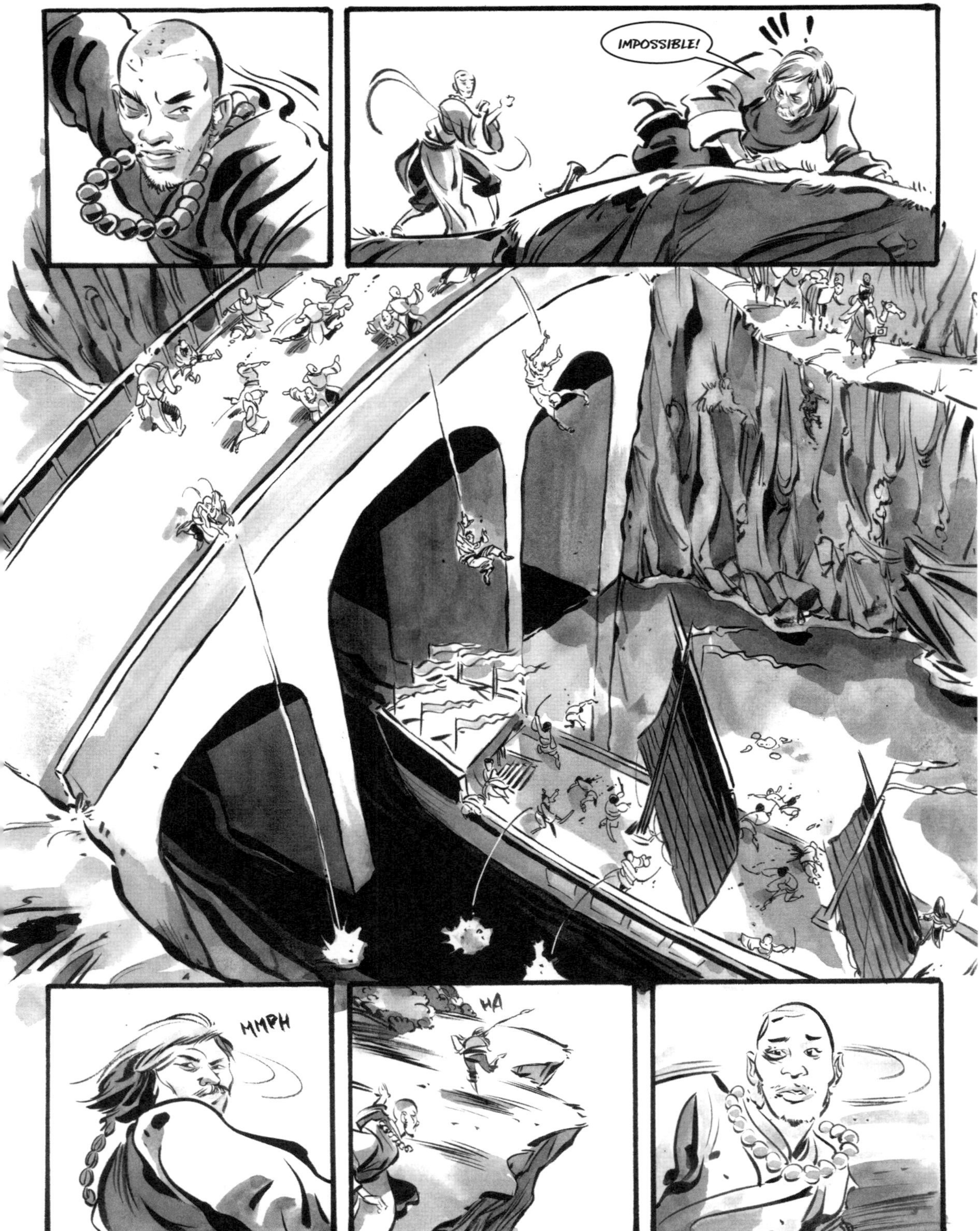
IMPOSSIBLE!
MMPH
HA

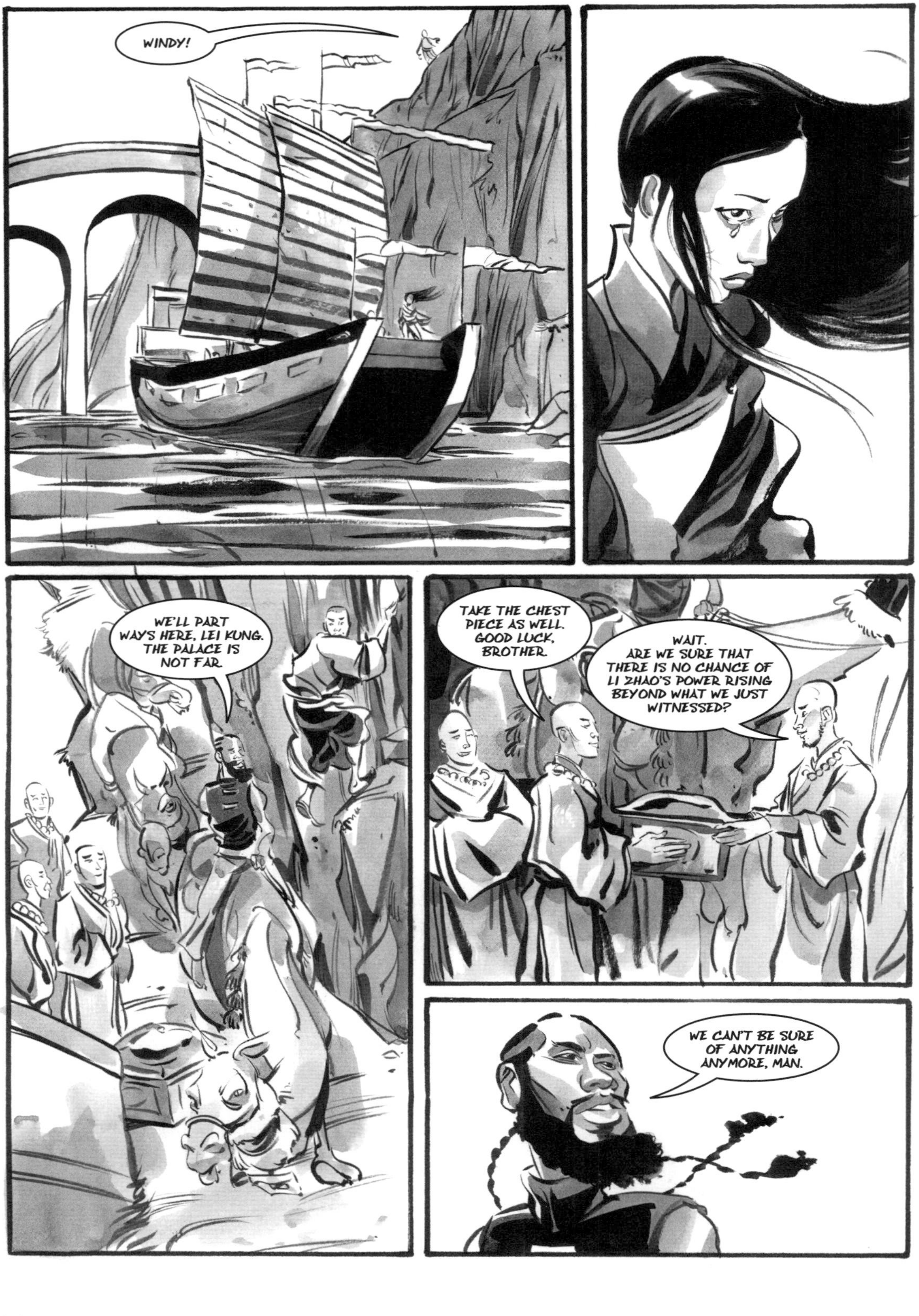
WINDY!
WE'LL PART WAYS HERE, LEI KUNG. THE PALACE IS NOT FAR.
TAKE THE CHEST PIECE AS WELL. GOOD LUCK, BROTHER.
WAIT. ARE WE SURE THAT THERE IS NO CHANCE OF LI ZHAO'S POWER RISING BEYOND WHAT WE JUST WITNESSED?
WE CAN'T BE SURE OF ANYTHING ANYMORE, MAN.

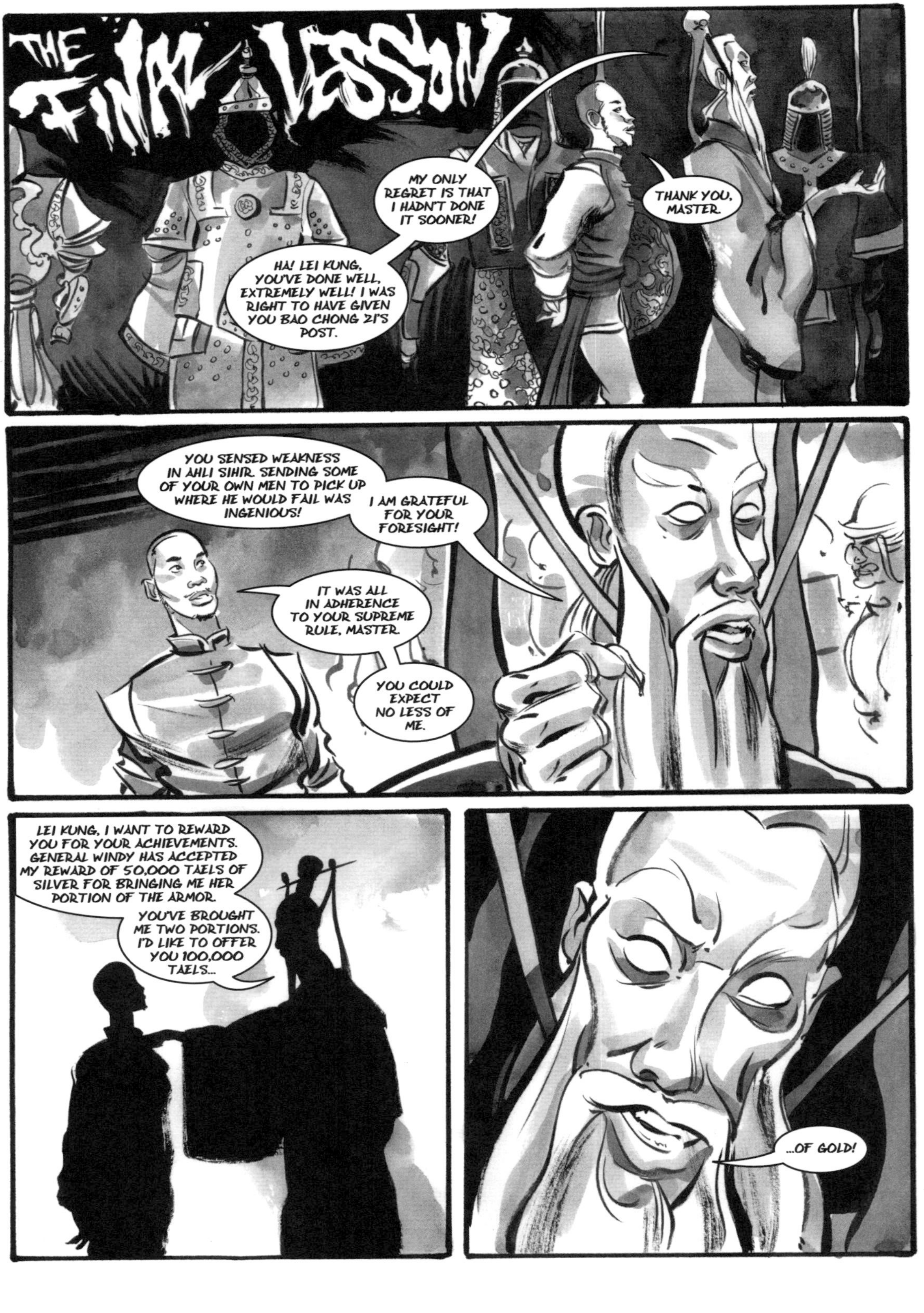
THE FINAL LESSON
HA! LEI KUNG, YOU'VE DONE WELL, EXTREMELY WELL! I WAS RIGHT TO HAVE GIVEN YOU BAO CHONG ZI'S POST.
MY ONLY REGRET IS THAT I HADN'T DONE IT SOONER!
THANK YOU, MASTER.
YOU SENSED WEAKNESS IN AHLI SIHIR. SENDING SOME OF YOUR OWN MEN TO PICK UP WHERE HE WOULD FAIL WAS INGENIOUS!
I AM GRATEFUL FOR YOUR FORESIGHT!
IT WAS ALL IN ADHERENCE TO YOUR SUPREME RULE, MASTER.
YOU COULD EXPECT NO LESS OF ME.
LEI KUNG, I WANT TO REWARD YOU FOR YOUR ACHIEVEMENTS. GENERAL WINDY HAS ACCEPTED MY REWARD OF 50,000 TAELS OF SILVER FOR BRINGING ME HER PORTION OF THE ARMOR.
YOU'VE BROUGHT ME TWO PORTIONS. I'D LIKE TO OFFER YOU 100,000 TAELS...
...OF GOLD!

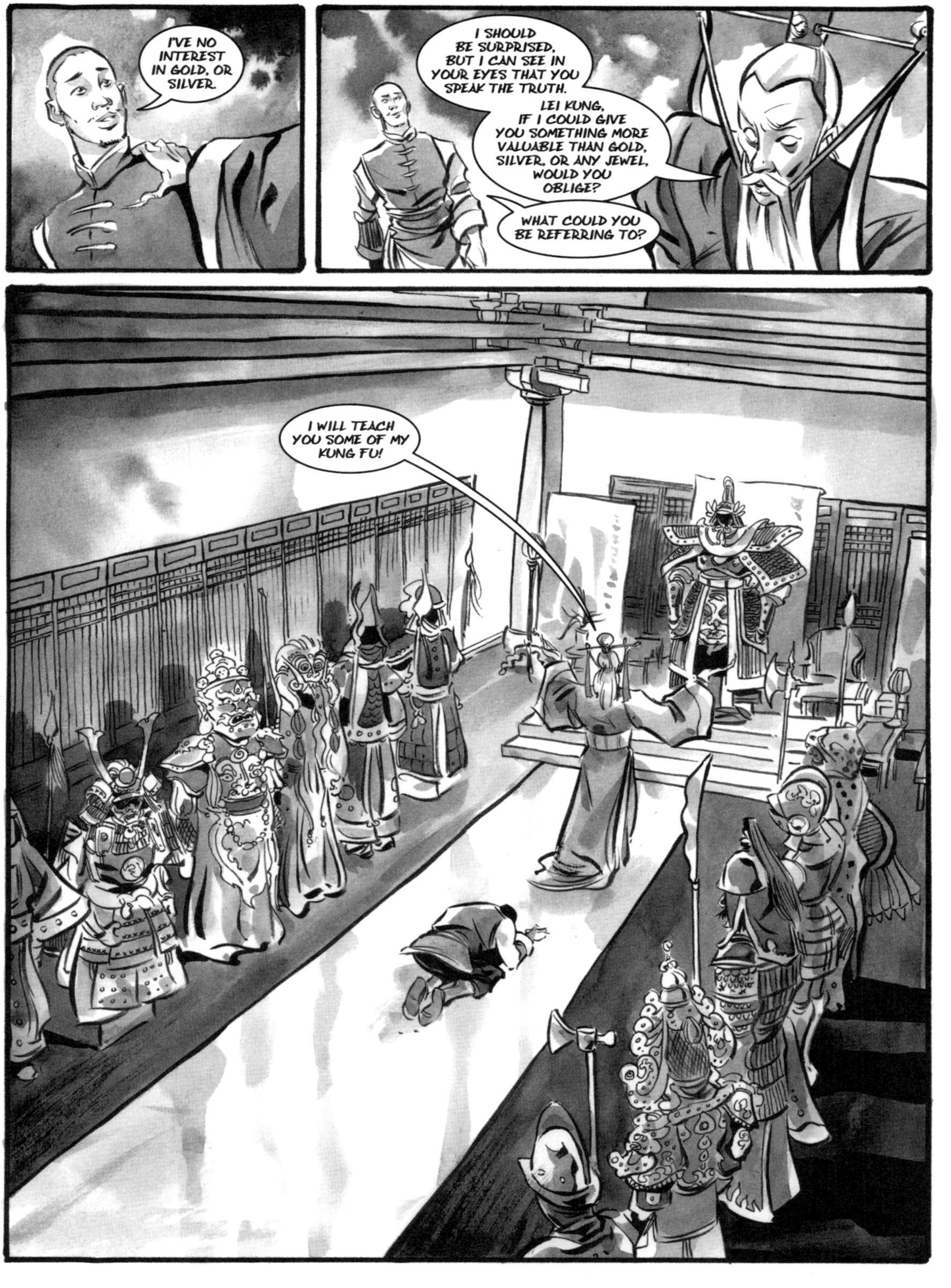
I'VE NO INTEREST IN GOLD, OR SILVER.
I SHOULD BE SURPRISED, BUT I CAN SEE IN YOUR EYES THAT YOU SPEAK THE TRUTH.
LEI KUNG, IF I COULD GIVE YOU SOMETHING MORE VALUABLE THAN GOLD, SILVER, OR ANY JEWEL, WOULD YOU OBLIGE?
WHAT COULD YOU BE REFERRING TO?
I WILL TEACH YOU SOME OF MY KUNG FU!

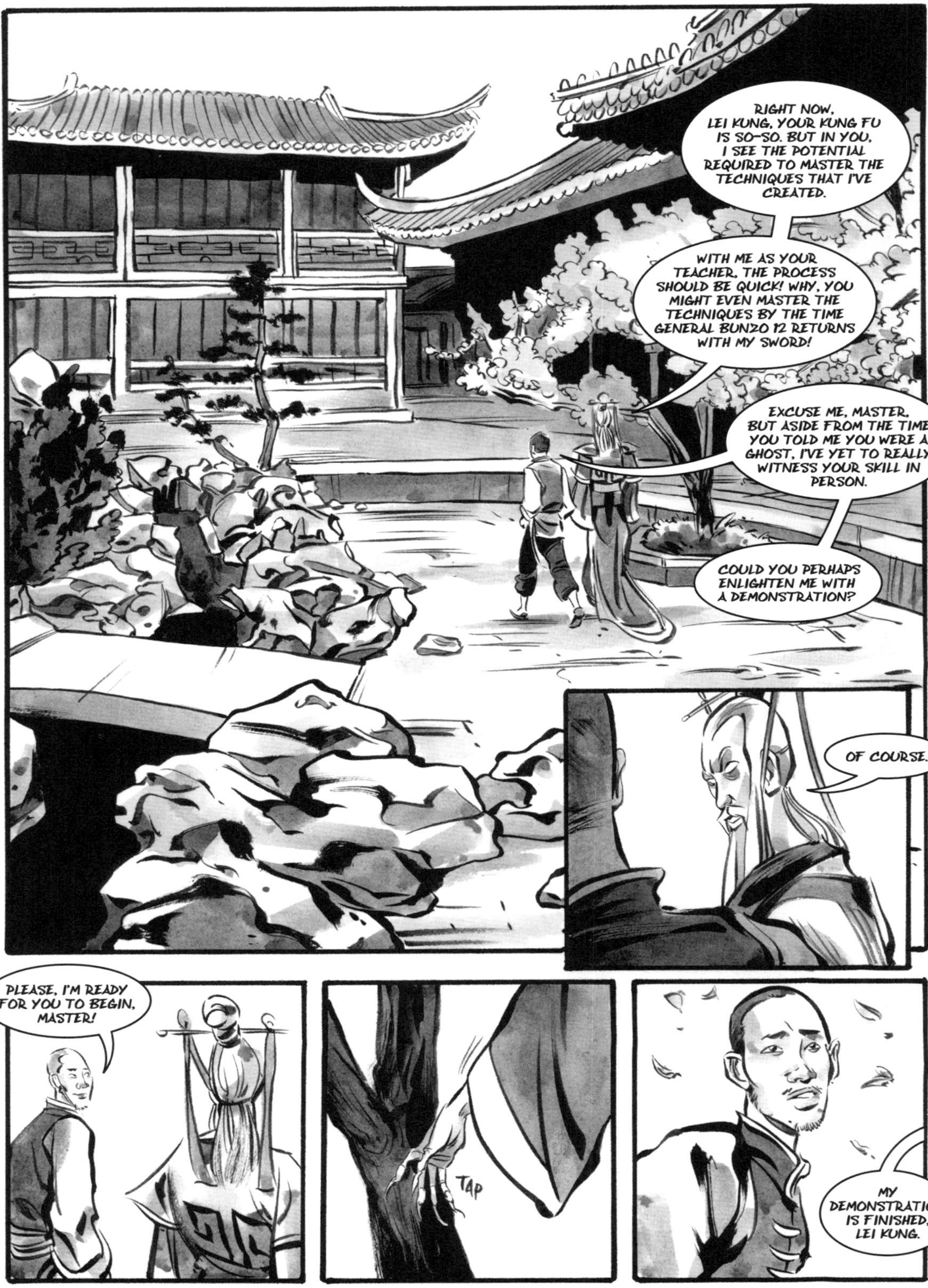
RIGHT NOW, LEI KUNG, YOUR KUNG FU IS SO-SO. BUT IN YOU, I SEE THE POTENTIAL REQUIRED TO MASTER THE TECHNIQUES THAT I'VE CREATED.
WITH ME AS YOUR TEACHER, THE PROCESS SHOULD BE QUICK! WHY, YOU MIGHT EVEN MASTER THE TECHNIQUES BY THE TIME GENERAL BUNZO 12 RETURNS WITH MY SWORD!
EXCUSE ME, MASTER, BUT ASIDE FROM THE TIME YOU TOLD ME YOU WERE A GHOST, I'VE YET TO REALLY WITNESS YOUR SKILL IN PERSON.
COULD YOU PERHAPS ENLIGHTEN ME WITH A DEMONSTRATION?
OF COURSE.
PLEASE, I'M READY FOR YOU TO BEGIN, MASTER!
TAP
MY DEMONSTRATION IS FINISHED, LEI KUNG.

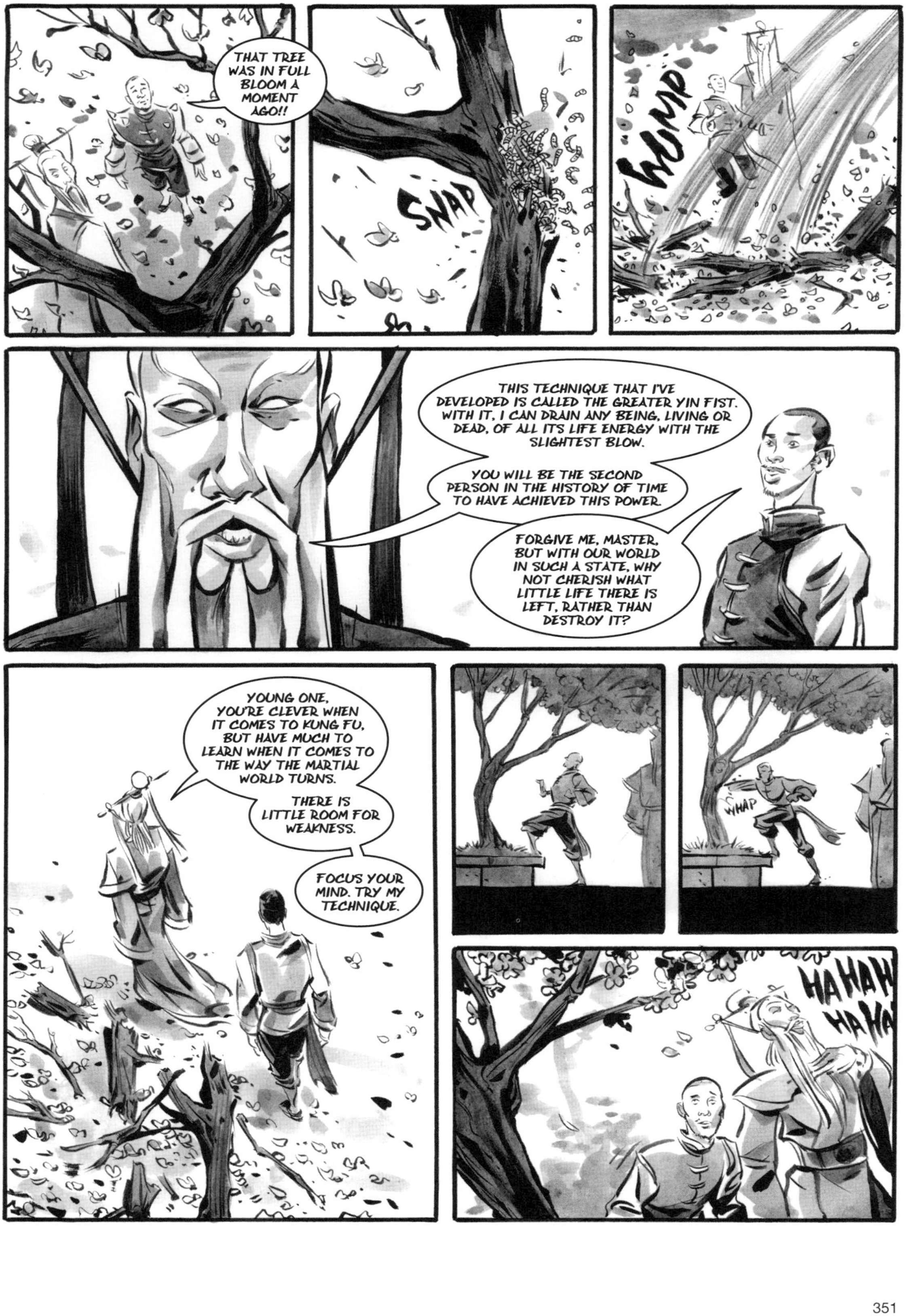
THAT TREE WAS IN FULL BLOOM A MOMENT AGO!!
SNAP
WUMP
THIS TECHNIQUE THAT I'VE DEVELOPED IS CALLED THE GREATER YIN FIST. WITH IT, I CAN DRAIN ANY BEING, LIVING OR DEAD, OF ALL ITS LIFE ENERGY WITH THE SLIGHTEST BLOW.
YOU WILL BE THE SECOND PERSON IN THE HISTORY OF TIME TO HAVE ACHIEVED THIS POWER.
FORGIVE ME, MASTER, BUT WITH OUR WORLD IN SUCH A STATE, WHY NOT CHERISH WHAT LITTLE LIFE THERE IS LEFT, RATHER THAN DESTROY IT?
YOUNG ONE, YOU'RE CLEVER WHEN IT COMES TO KUNG FU, BUT HAVE MUCH TO LEARN WHEN IT COMES TO THE WAY THE MARTIAL WORLD TURNS.
THERE IS LITTLE ROOM FOR WEAKNESS.
FOCUS YOUR MIND. TRY MY TECHNIQUE.
WHAP

WHAP WHAP WHAP.

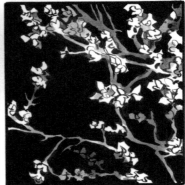

WHAP

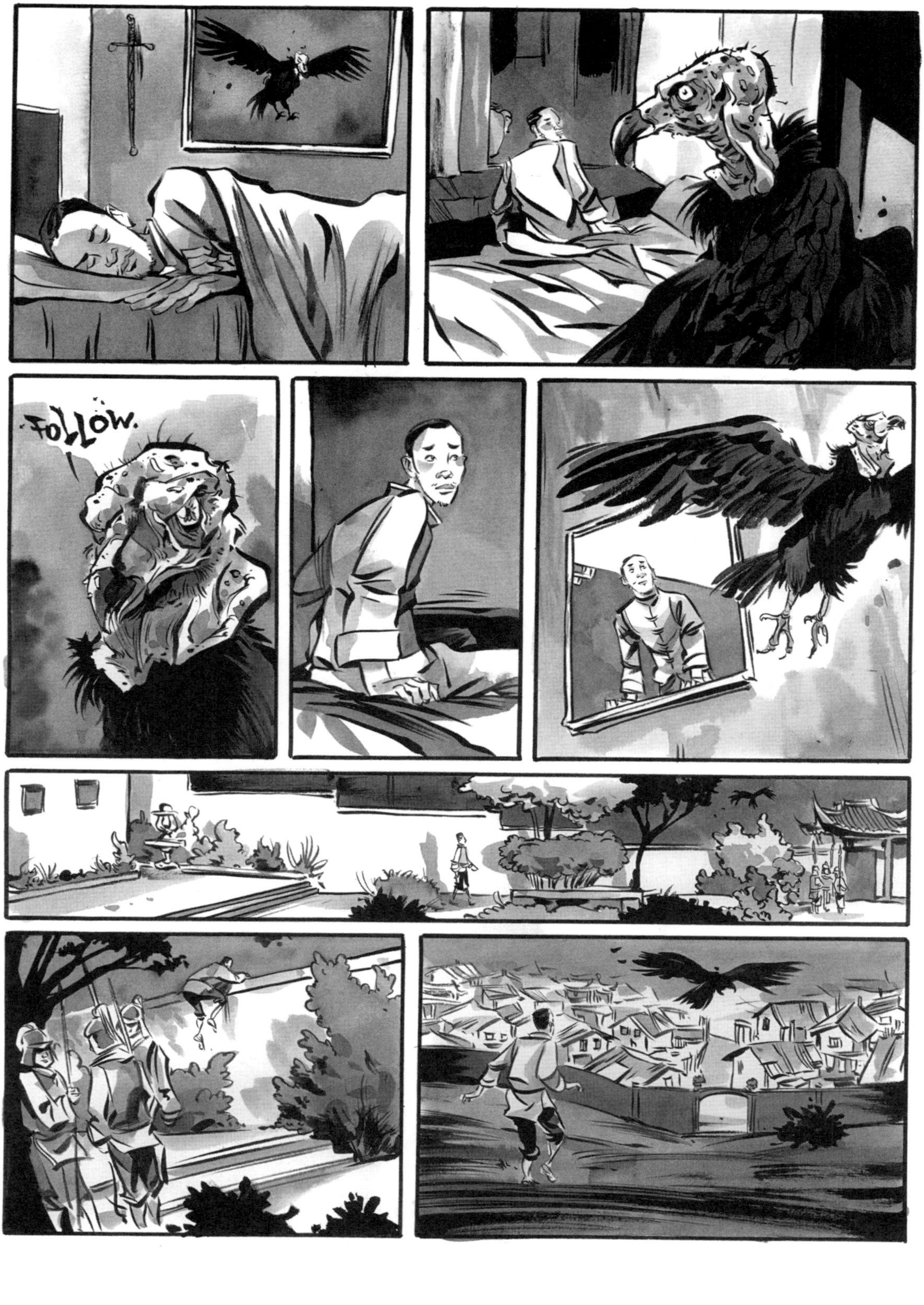
FOLLOW.

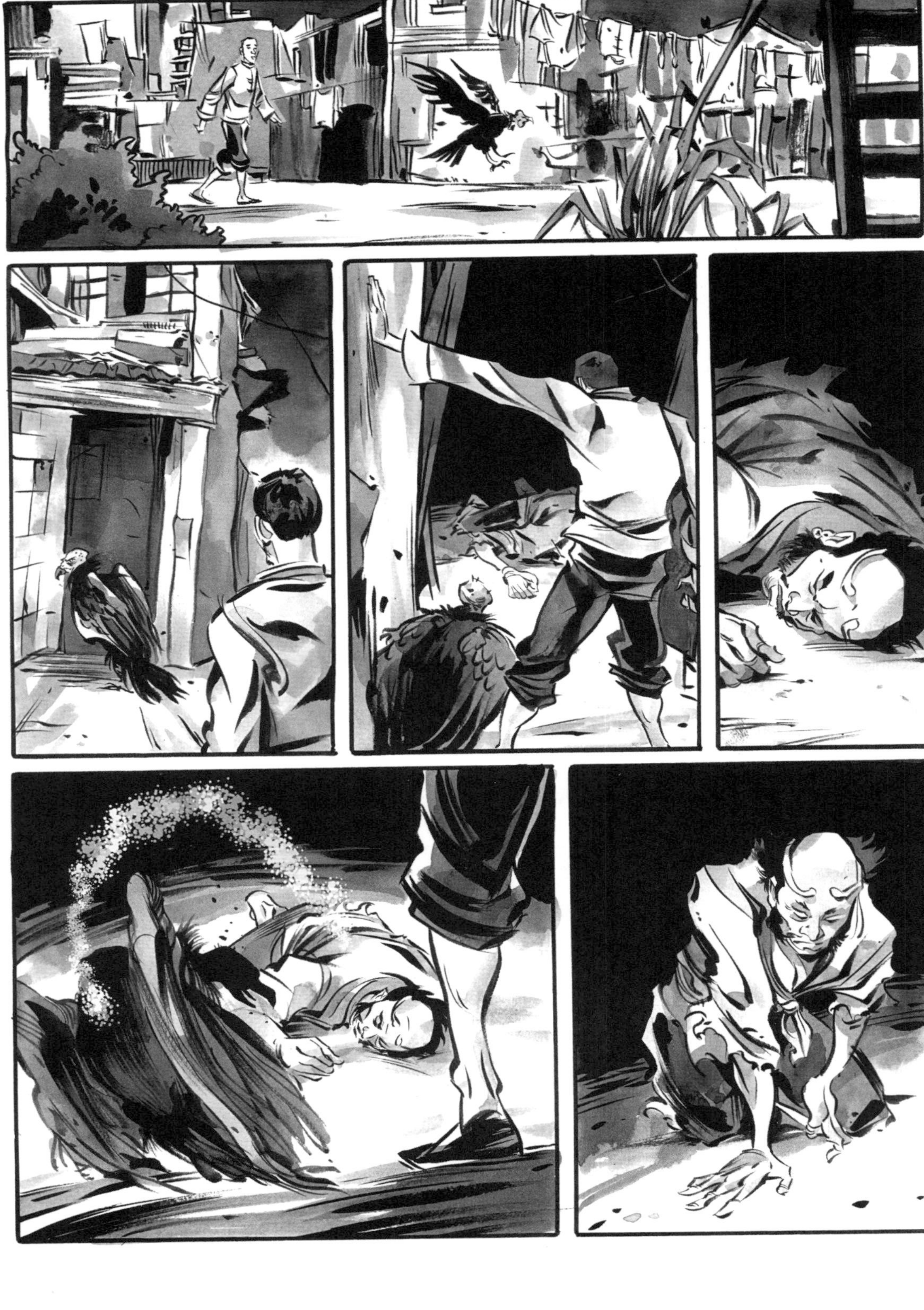

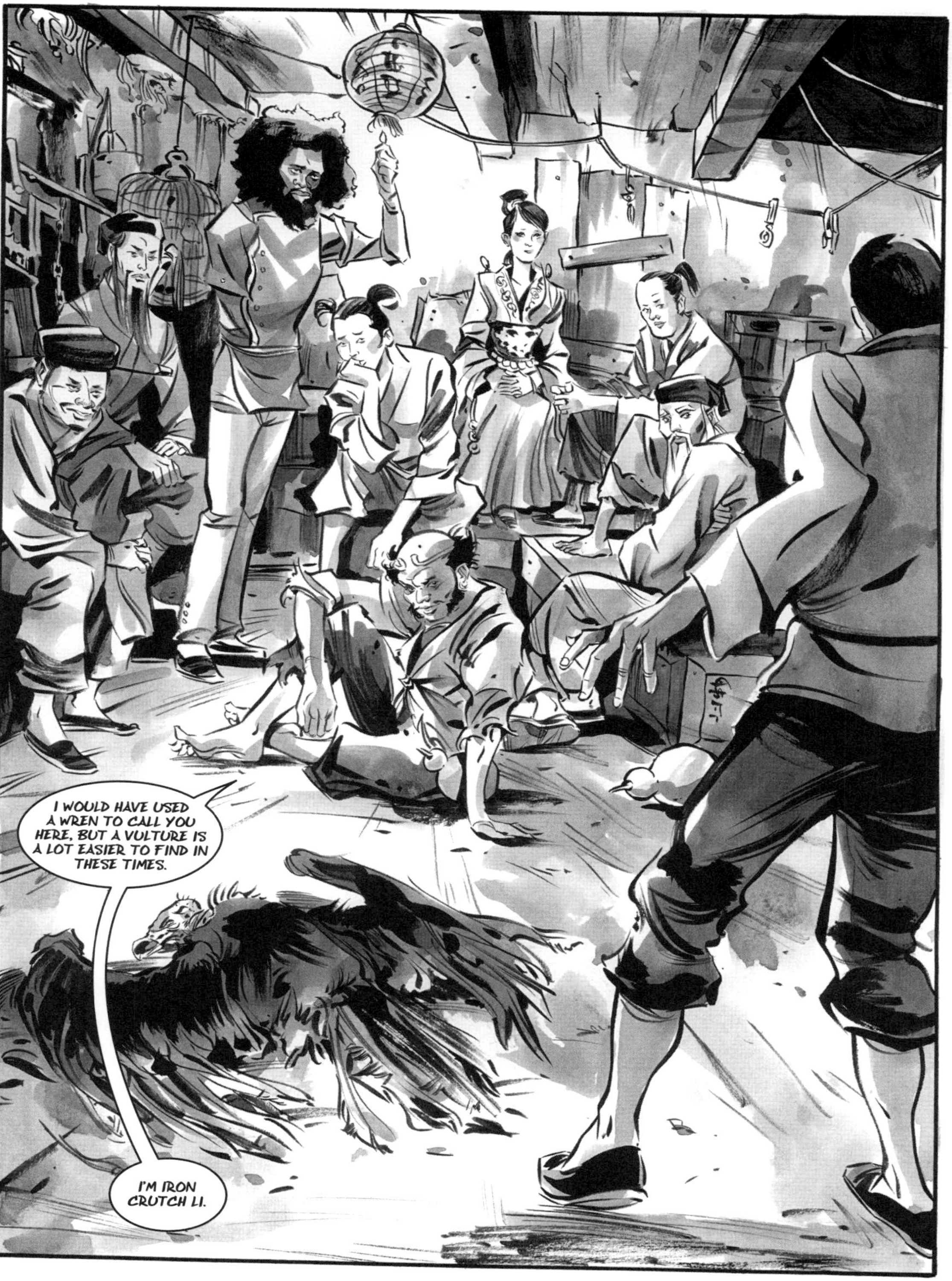
I WOULD HAVE USED A WREN TO CALL YOU HERE, BUT A VULTURE IS A LOT EASIER TO FIND IN THESE TIMES.
I'M IRON CRUTCH LI.

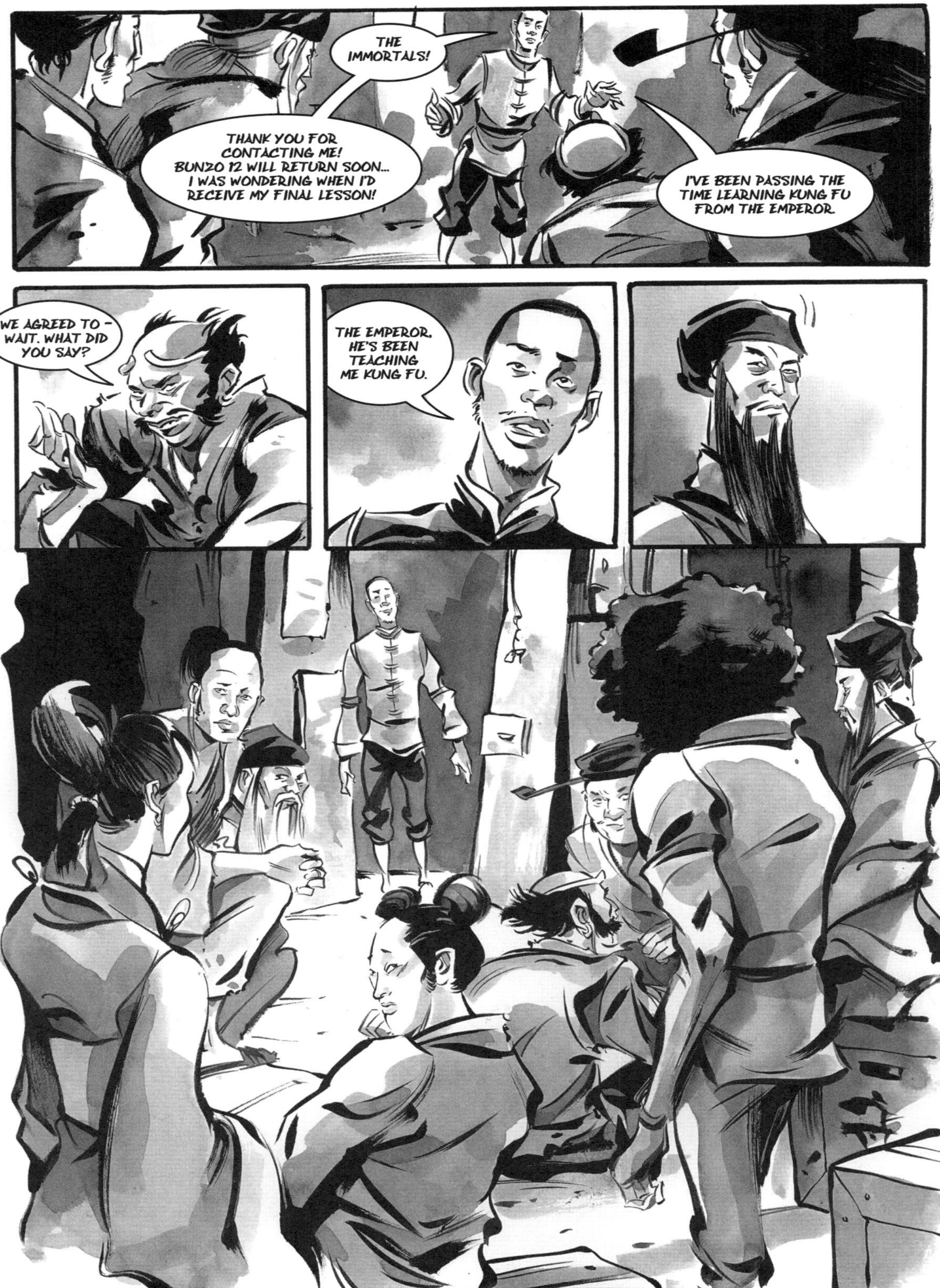
THE IMMORTALS!
THANK YOU FOR CONTACTING ME! BUNZO 12 WILL RETURN SOON... I WAS WONDERING WHEN I'D RECEIVE MY FINAL LESSON!
I'VE BEEN PASSING THE TIME LEARNING KUNG FU FROM THE EMPEROR.
WE AGREED TO - WAIT. WHAT DID YOU SAY?
THE EMPEROR. HE'S BEEN TEACHING ME KUNG FU.

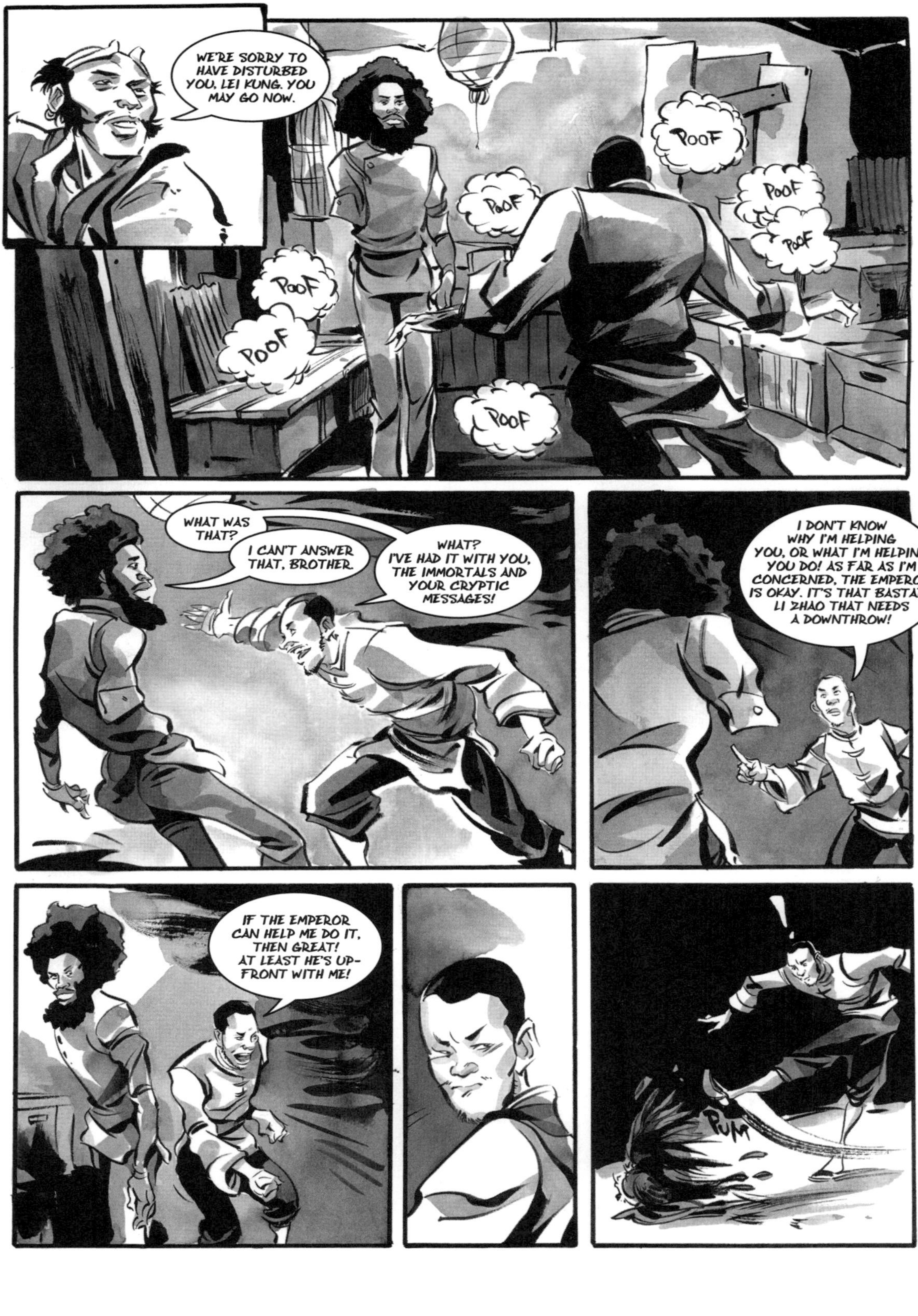
WE'RE SORRY TO HAVE DISTURBED YOU, LEI KUNG. YOU MAY GO NOW.
POOF
POOF
POOF
POOF
POOF
POOF
POOF
WHAT WAS THAT?
I CAN'T ANSWER THAT, BROTHER.
WHAT? I'VE HAD IT WITH YOU, THE IMMORTALS AND YOUR CRYPTIC MESSAGES!
I DON'T KNOW WHY I'M HELPING YOU, OR WHAT I'M HELPING YOU DO! AS FAR AS I'M CONCERNED, THE EMPEROR IS OKAY. IT'S THAT BASTARD LI ZHAO THAT NEEDS A DOWNTHROW!
IF THE EMPEROR CAN HELP ME DO IT, THEN GREAT! AT LEAST HE'S UP-FRONT WITH ME!
!
PUM

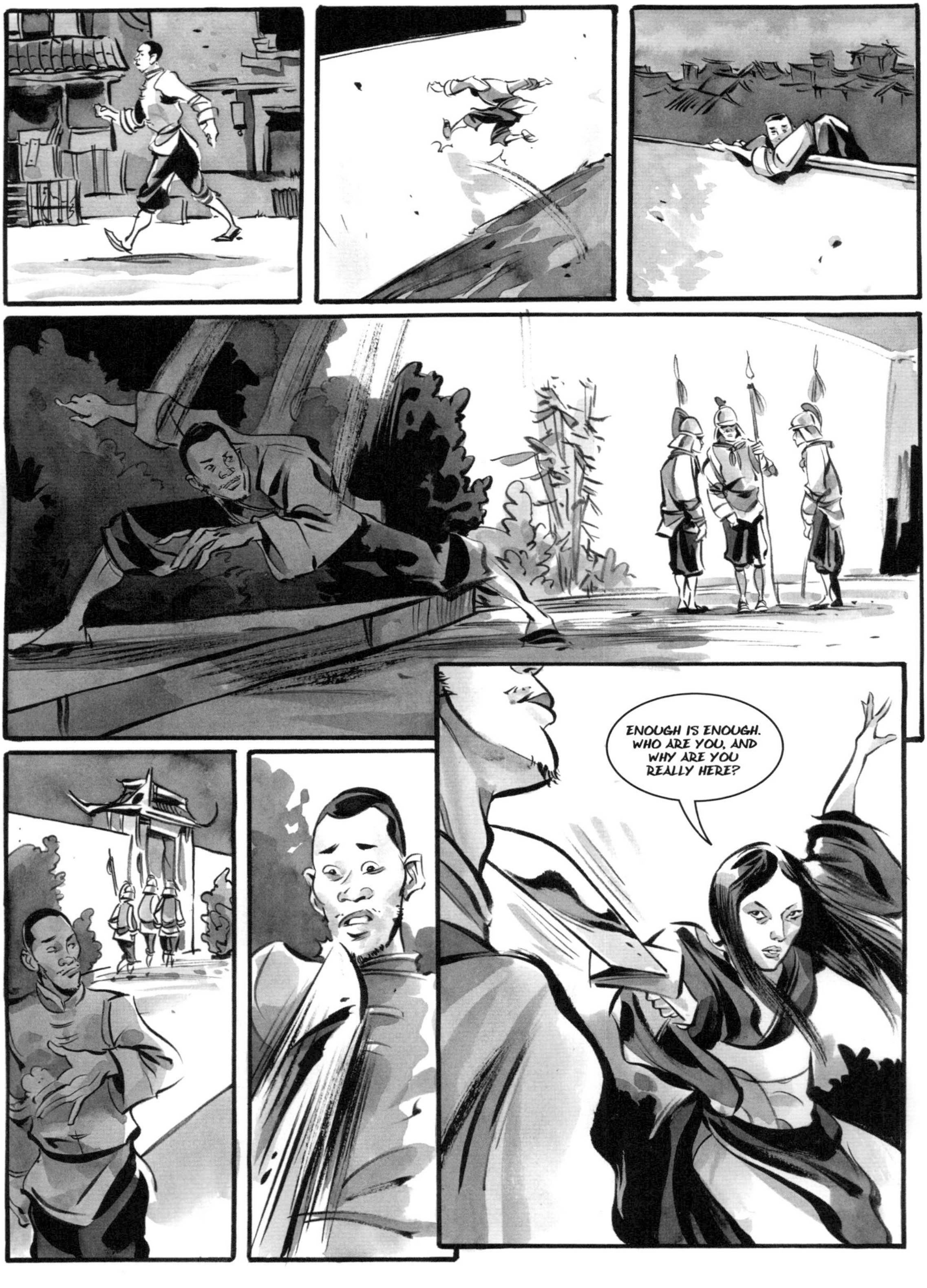
ENOUGH IS ENOUGH. WHO ARE YOU, AND WHY ARE YOU REALLY HERE?

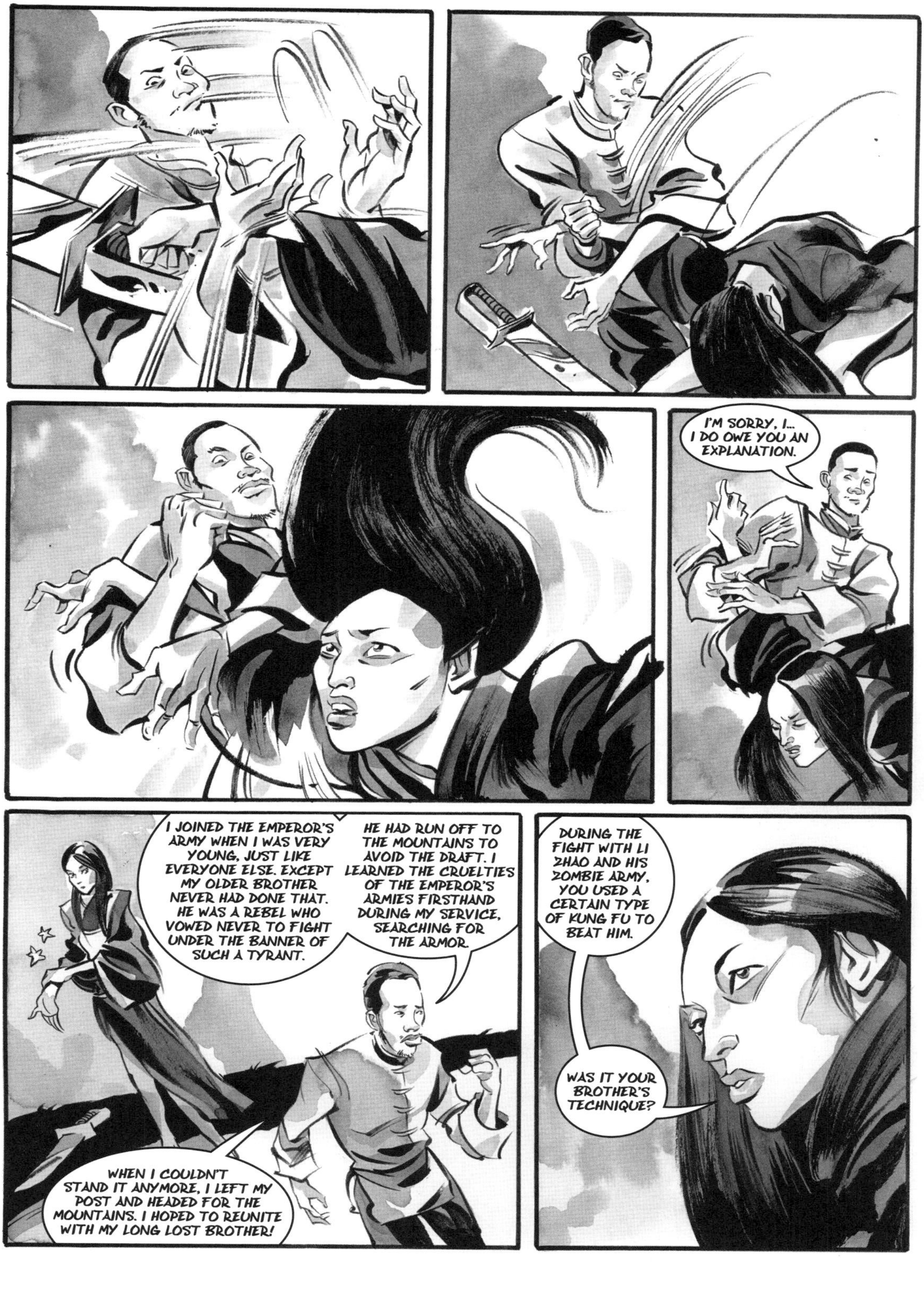
I'M SORRY, I... I DO OWE YOU AN EXPLANATION.
I JOINED THE EMPEROR'S ARMY WHEN I WAS VERY YOUNG, JUST LIKE EVERYONE ELSE. EXCEPT MY OLDER BROTHER NEVER HAD DONE THAT. HE WAS A REBEL WHO VOWED NEVER TO FIGHT UNDER THE BANNER OF SUCH A TYRANT.
HE HAD RUN OFF TO THE MOUNTAINS TO AVOID THE DRAFT. I LEARNED THE CRUELTIES OF THE EMPEROR'S ARMIES FIRSTHAND DURING MY SERVICE, SEARCHING FOR THE ARMOR.
WHEN I COULDN'T STAND IT ANYMORE, I LEFT MY POST AND HEADED FOR THE MOUNTAINS. I HOPED TO REUNITE WITH MY LONG LOST BROTHER!
DURING THE FIGHT WITH LI ZHAO AND HIS ZOMBIE ARMY, YOU USED A CERTAIN TYPE OF KUNG FU TO BEAT HIM.
WAS IT YOUR BROTHER'S TECHNIQUE?

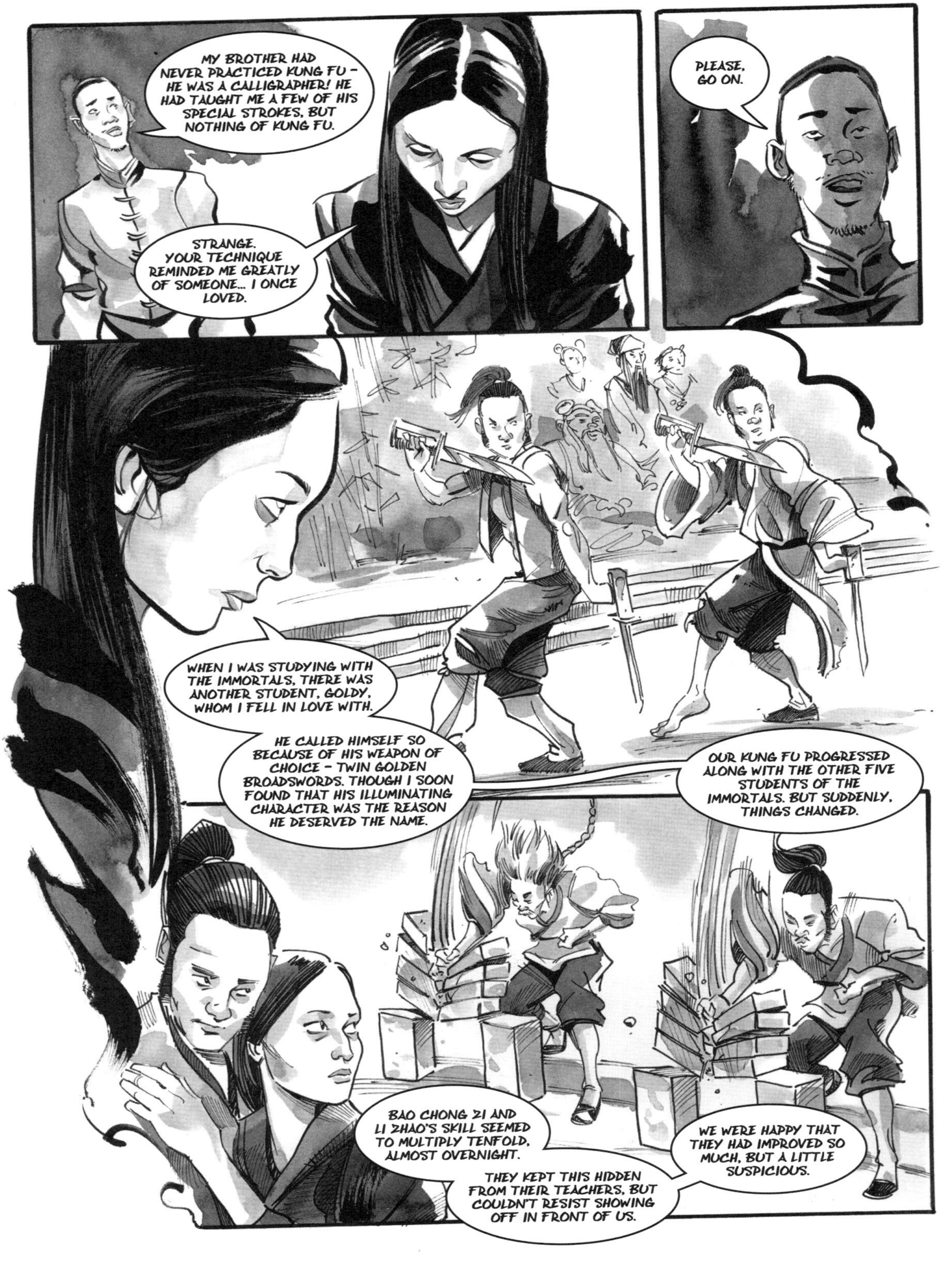
MY BROTHER HAD NEVER PRACTICED KUNG FU - HE WAS A CALLIGRAPHER! HE HAD TAUGHT ME A FEW OF HIS SPECIAL STROKES, BUT NOTHING OF KUNG FU.
STRANGE. YOUR TECHNIQUE REMINDED ME GREATLY OF SOMEONE... I ONCE LOVED.
PLEASE, GO ON.
WHEN I WAS STUDYING WITH THE IMMORTALS, THERE WAS ANOTHER STUDENT, GOLDY, WHOM I FELL IN LOVE WITH.
HE CALLED HIMSELF SO BECAUSE OF HIS WEAPON OF CHOICE - TWIN GOLDEN BROADSWORDS. THOUGH I SOON FOUND THAT HIS ILLUMINATING CHARACTER WAS THE REASON HE DESERVED THE NAME.
OUR KUNG FU PROGRESSED ALONG WITH THE OTHER FIVE STUDENTS OF THE IMMORTALS. BUT SUDDENLY, THINGS CHANGED.
BAO CHONG ZI AND LI ZHAO'S SKILL SEEMED TO MULTIPLY TENFOLD, ALMOST OVERNIGHT.
THEY KEPT THIS HIDDEN FROM THEIR TEACHERS, BUT COULDN'T RESIST SHOWING OFF IN FRONT OF US.
WE WERE HAPPY THAT THEY HAD IMPROVED SO MUCH, BUT A LITTLE SUSPICIOUS.

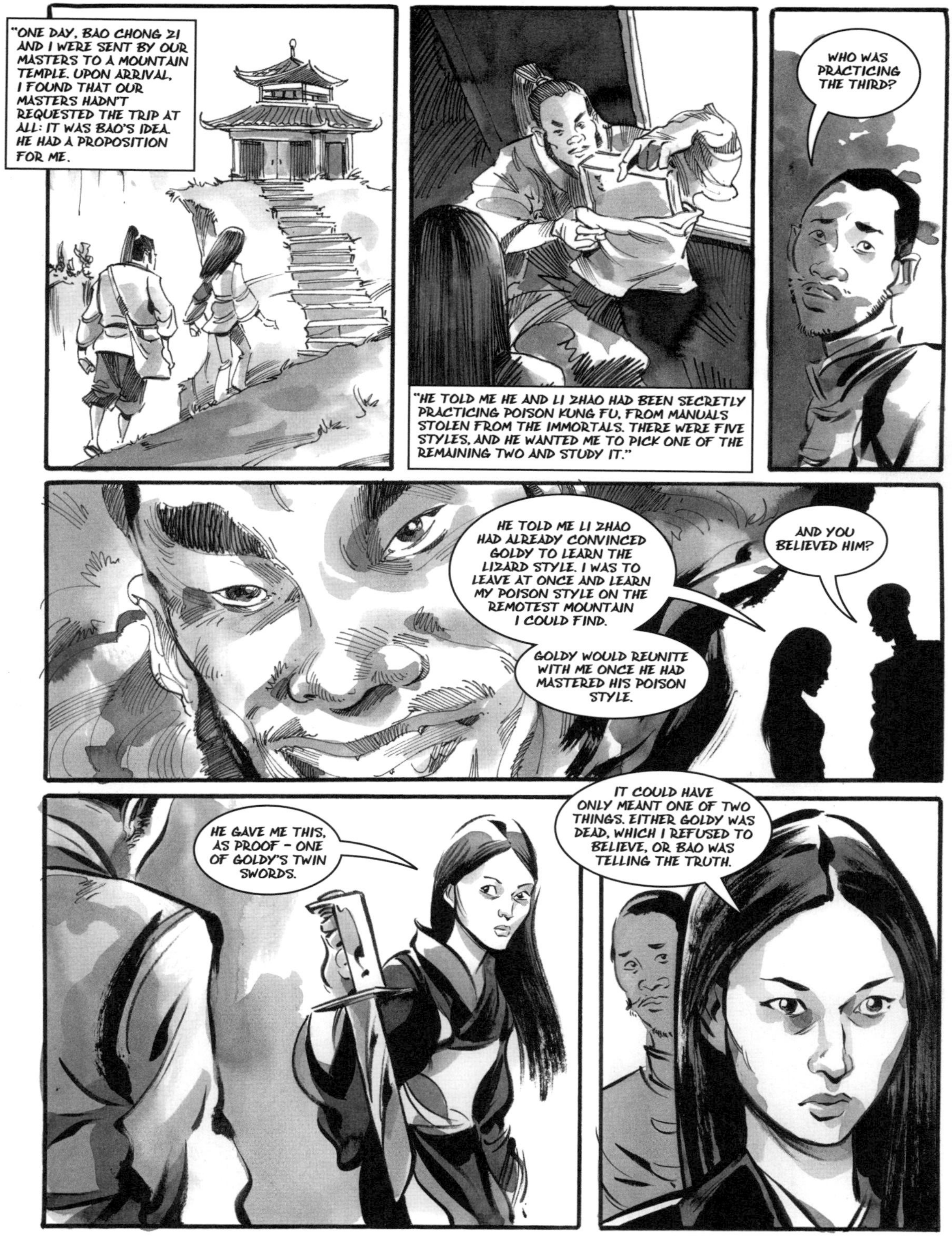
"ONE DAY, BAO CHONG ZI AND I WERE SENT BY OUR MASTERS TO A MOUNTAIN TEMPLE. UPON ARRIVAL, I FOUND THAT OUR MASTERS HADN'T REQUESTED THE TRIP AT ALL: IT WAS BAO'S IDEA. HE HAD A PROPOSITION FOR ME.
"HE TOLD ME HE AND LI ZHAO HAD BEEN SECRETLY PRACTICING POISON KUNG FU, FROM MANUALS STOLEN FROM THE IMMORTALS. THERE WERE FIVE STYLES, AND HE WANTED ME TO PICK ONE OF THE REMAINING TWO AND STUDY IT."
WHO WAS PRACTICING THE THIRD?
HE TOLD ME LI ZHAO HAD ALREADY CONVINCED GOLDY TO LEARN THE LIZARD STYLE. I WAS TO LEAVE AT ONCE AND LEARN MY POISON STYLE ON THE REMOTEST MOUNTAIN I COULD FIND.
GOLDY WOULD REUNITE WITH ME ONCE HE HAD MASTERED HIS POISON STYLE.
AND YOU BELIEVED HIM?
HE GAVE ME THIS, AS PROOF - ONE OF GOLDY'S TWIN SWORDS.
IT COULD HAVE ONLY MEANT ONE OF TWO THINGS. EITHER GOLDY WAS DEAD, WHICH I REFUSED TO BELIEVE, OR BAO WAS TELLING THE TRUTH.

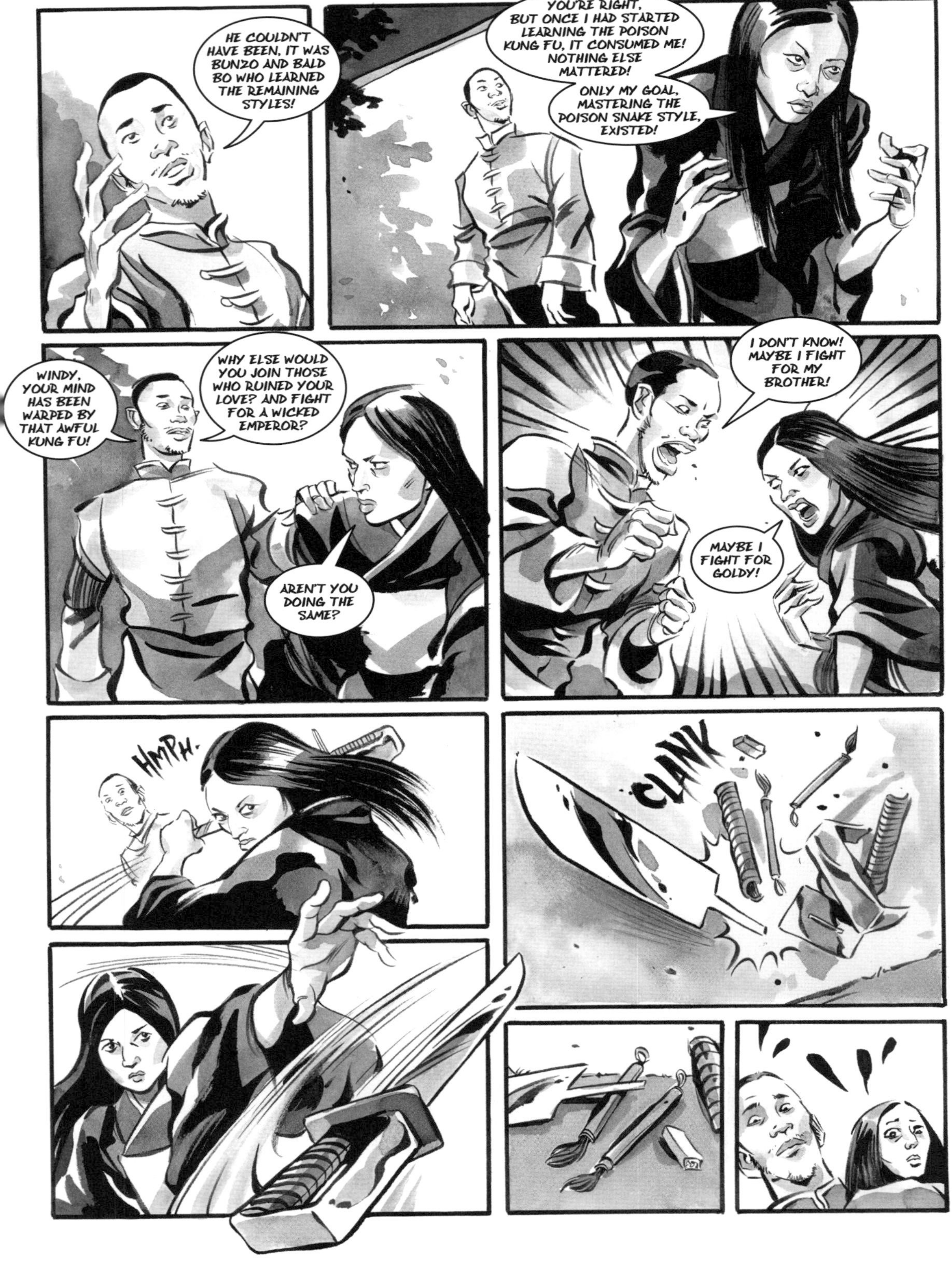
HE COULDN'T HAVE BEEN, IT WAS BUNZO AND BALD BO WHO LEARNED THE REMAINING STYLES!
YOU'RE RIGHT, BUT ONCE I HAD STARTED LEARNING THE POISON KUNG FU, IT CONSUMED ME! NOTHING ELSE MATTERED!
ONLY MY GOAL, MASTERING THE POISON SNAKE STYLE, EXISTED!
WINDY, YOUR MIND HAS BEEN WARPED BY THAT AWFUL KUNG FU!
WHY ELSE WOULD YOU JOIN THOSE WHO RUINED YOUR LOVE? AND FIGHT FOR A WICKED EMPEROR?
AREN'T YOU DOING THE SAME?
I DON'T KNOW! MAYBE I FIGHT FOR MY BROTHER!
MAYBE I FIGHT FOR GOLDY!
HMPH.
CLANK

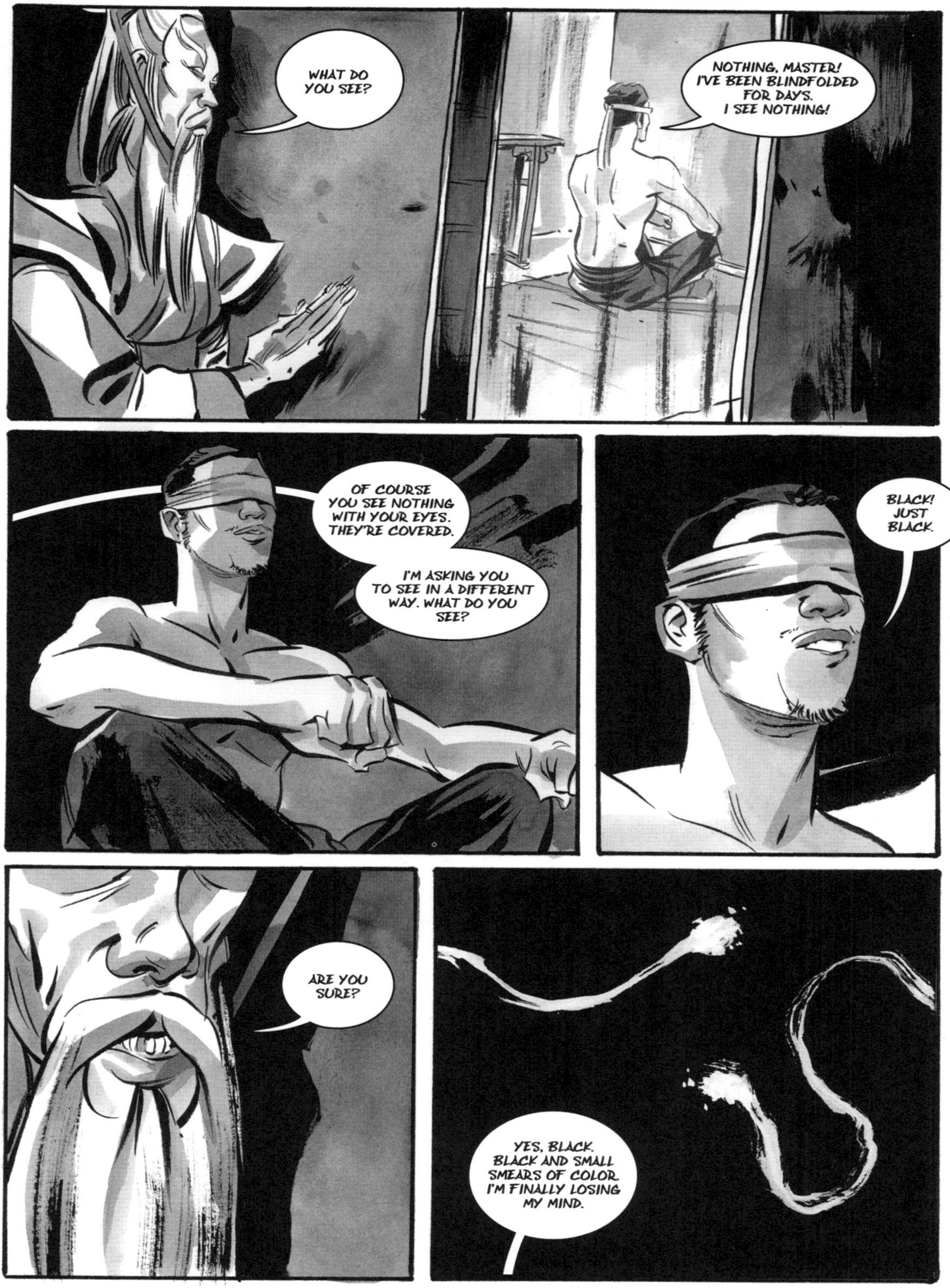
WHAT DO YOU SEE?
NOTHING, MASTER! I'VE BEEN BLINDFOLDED FOR DAYS. I SEE NOTHING!
OF COURSE YOU SEE NOTHING WITH YOUR EYES. THEY'RE COVERED.
I'M ASKING YOU TO SEE IN A DIFFERENT WAY. WHAT DO YOU SEE?
BLACK! JUST BLACK.
ARE YOU SURE?
YES, BLACK. BLACK AND SMALL SMEARS OF COLOR. I'M FINALLY LOSING MY MIND.

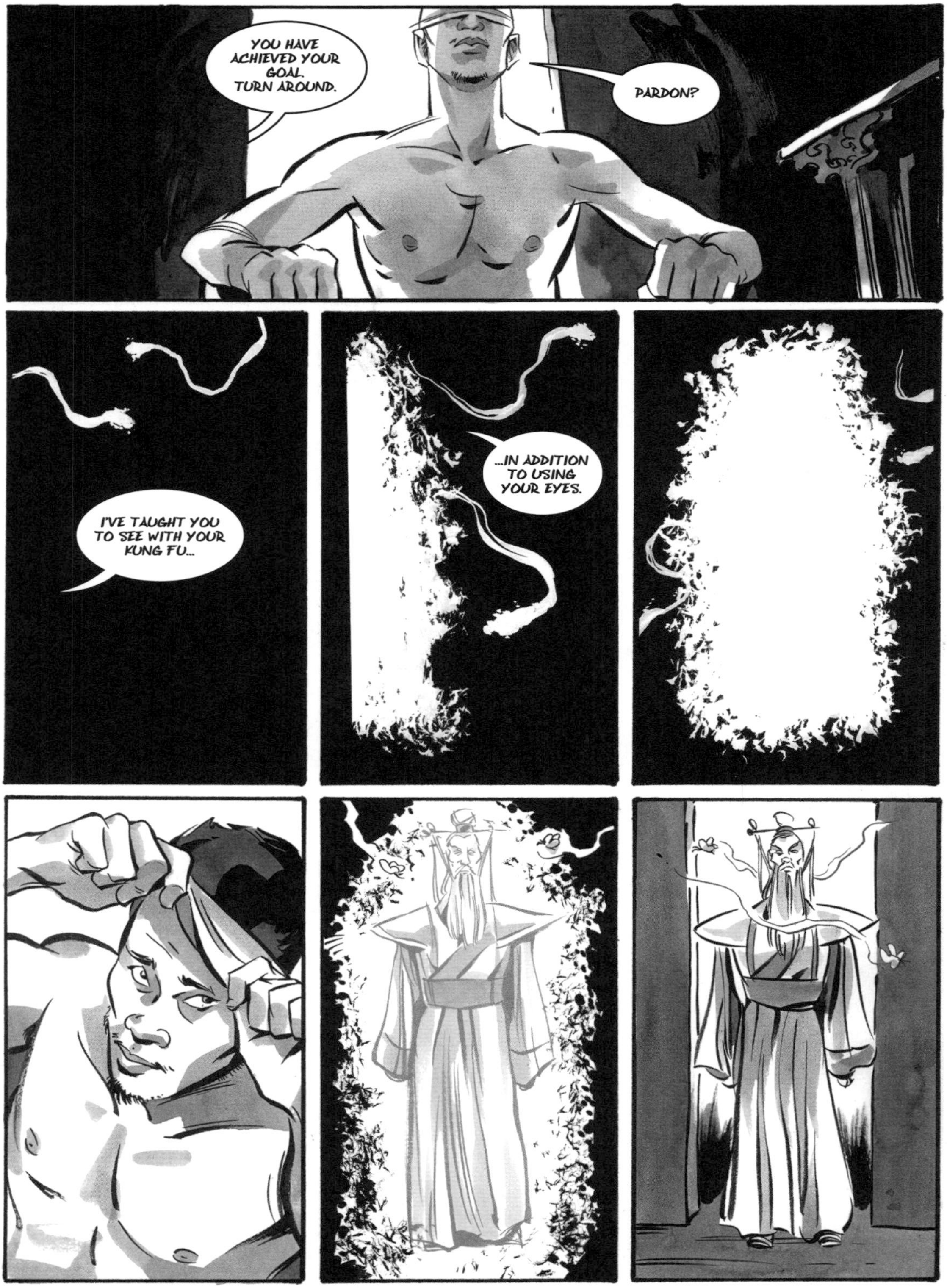
YOU HAVE ACHIEVED YOUR GOAL. TURN AROUND.
PARDON?
I'VE TAUGHT YOU TO SEE WITH YOUR KUNG FU...
...IN ADDITION TO USING YOUR EYES.

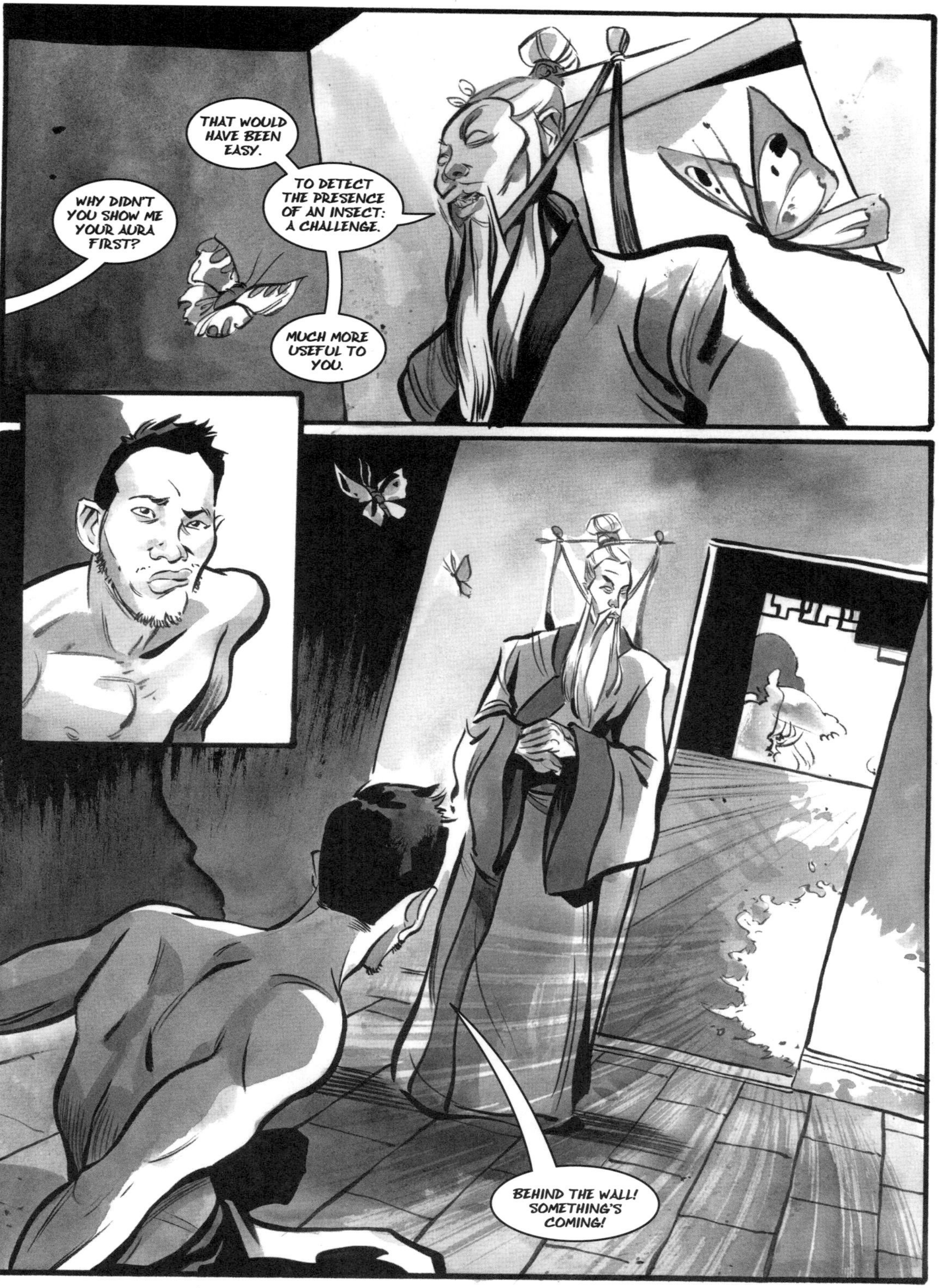
WHY DIDN'T YOU SHOW ME YOUR AURA FIRST?
THAT WOULD HAVE BEEN EASY.
TO DETECT THE PRESENCE OF AN INSECT: A CHALLENGE.
MUCH MORE USEFUL TO YOU.
BEHIND THE WALL! SOMETHING'S COMING!

YOU SEE?
QUITE
USEFUL!

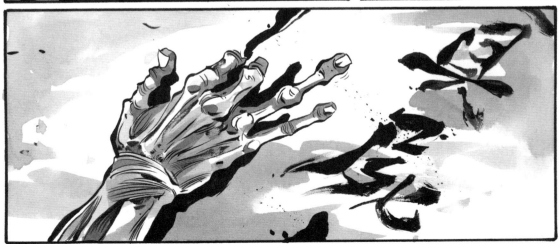

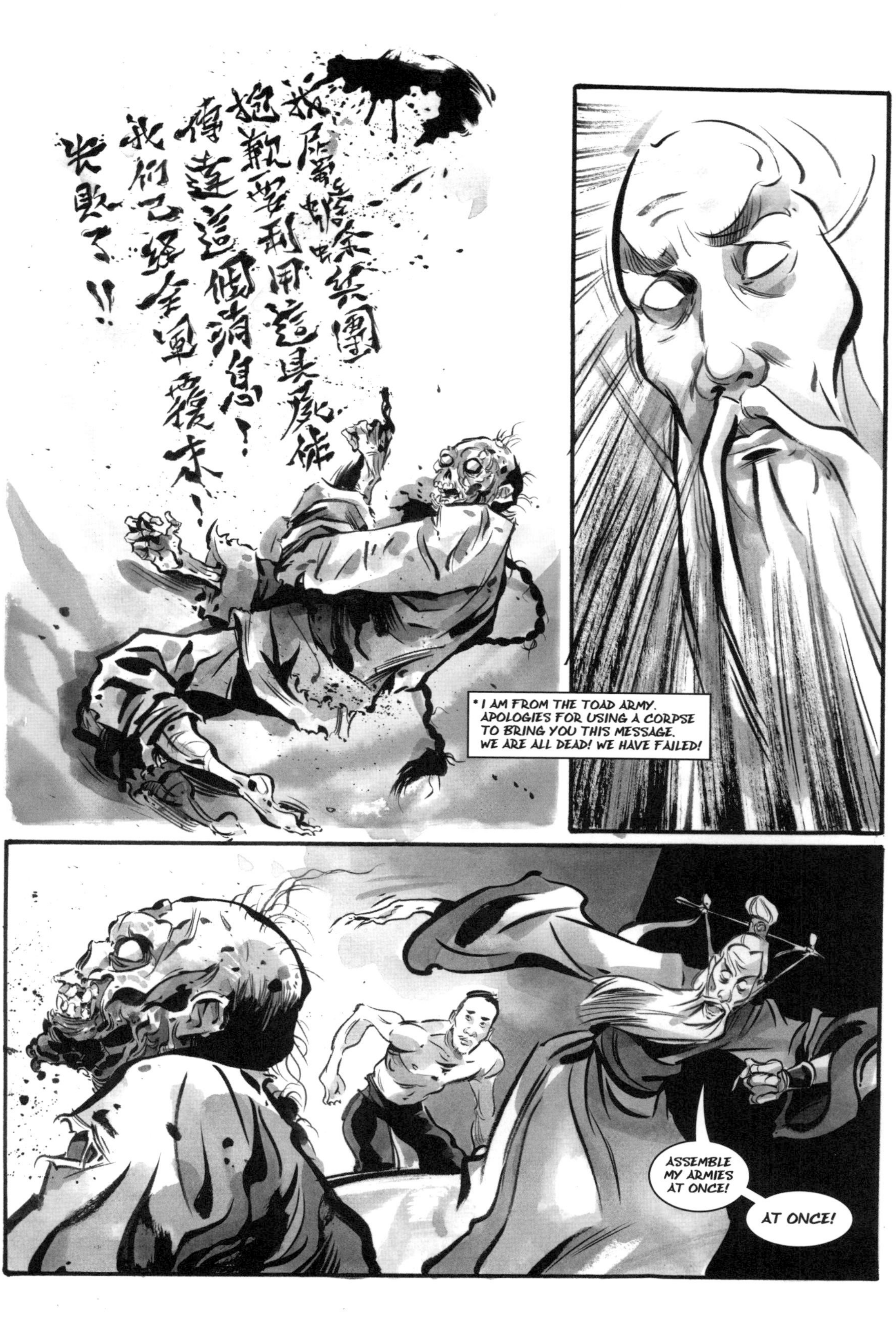
我屬蟾蜍兵團
抱歉要利用這具屍体
傳達這個消息!
我們已經全軍覆沒了!
失敗了!!
* I AM FROM THE TOAD ARMY. APOLOGIES FOR USING A CORPSE TO BRING YOU THIS MESSAGE. WE ARE ALL DEAD! WE HAVE FAILED!
ASSEMBLE MY ARMIES AT ONCE!
AT ONCE!

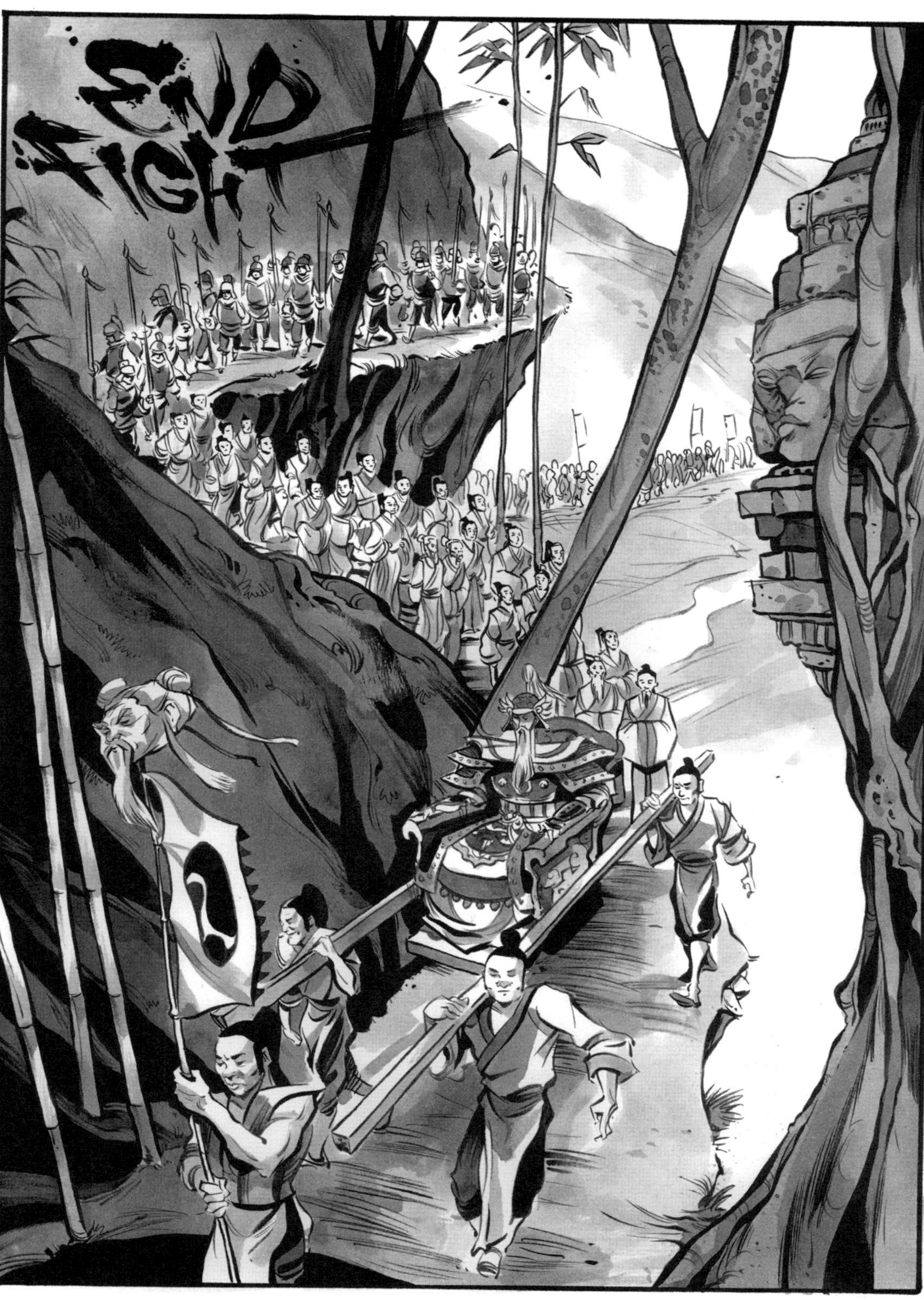
END FIGHT

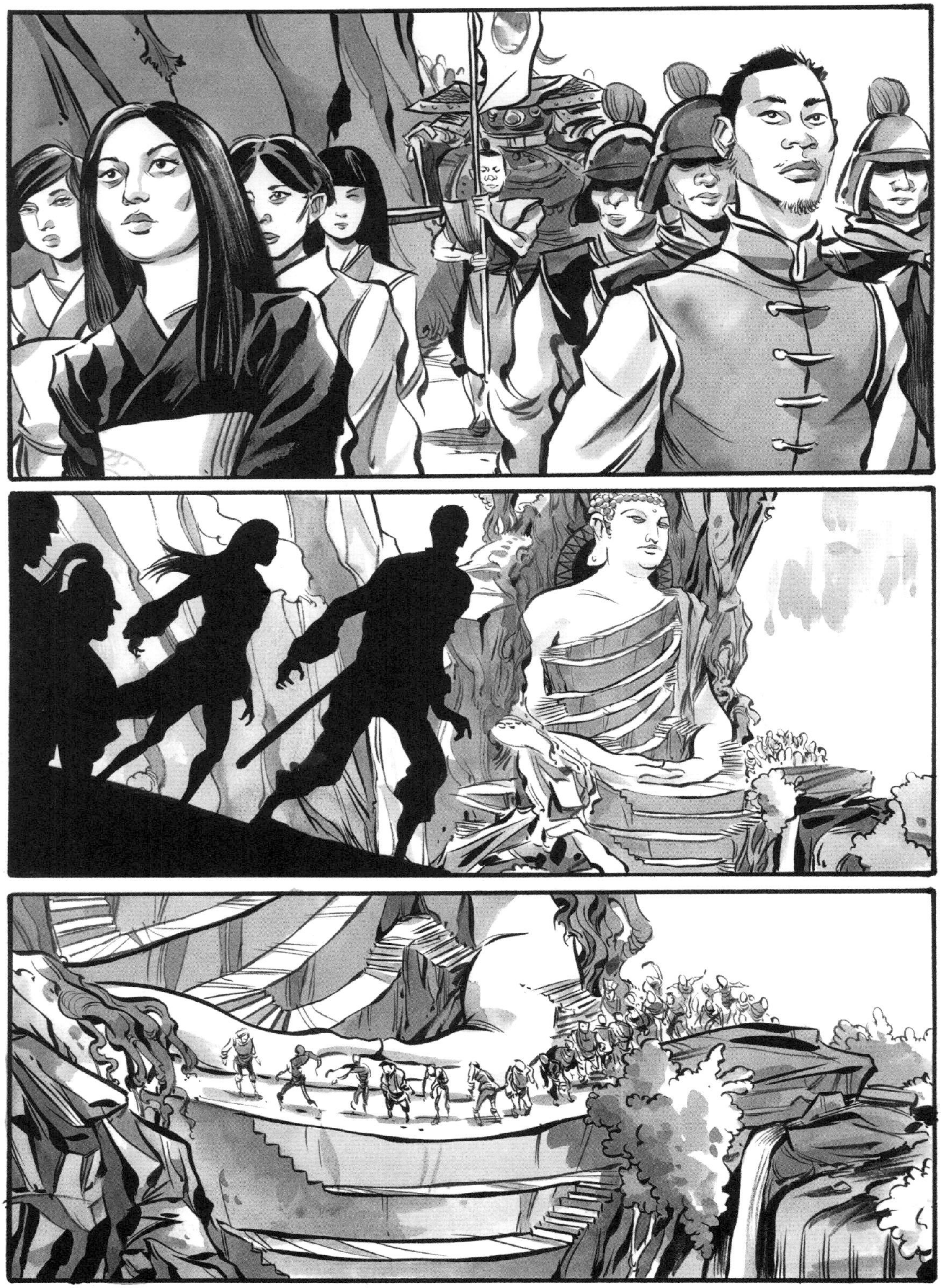

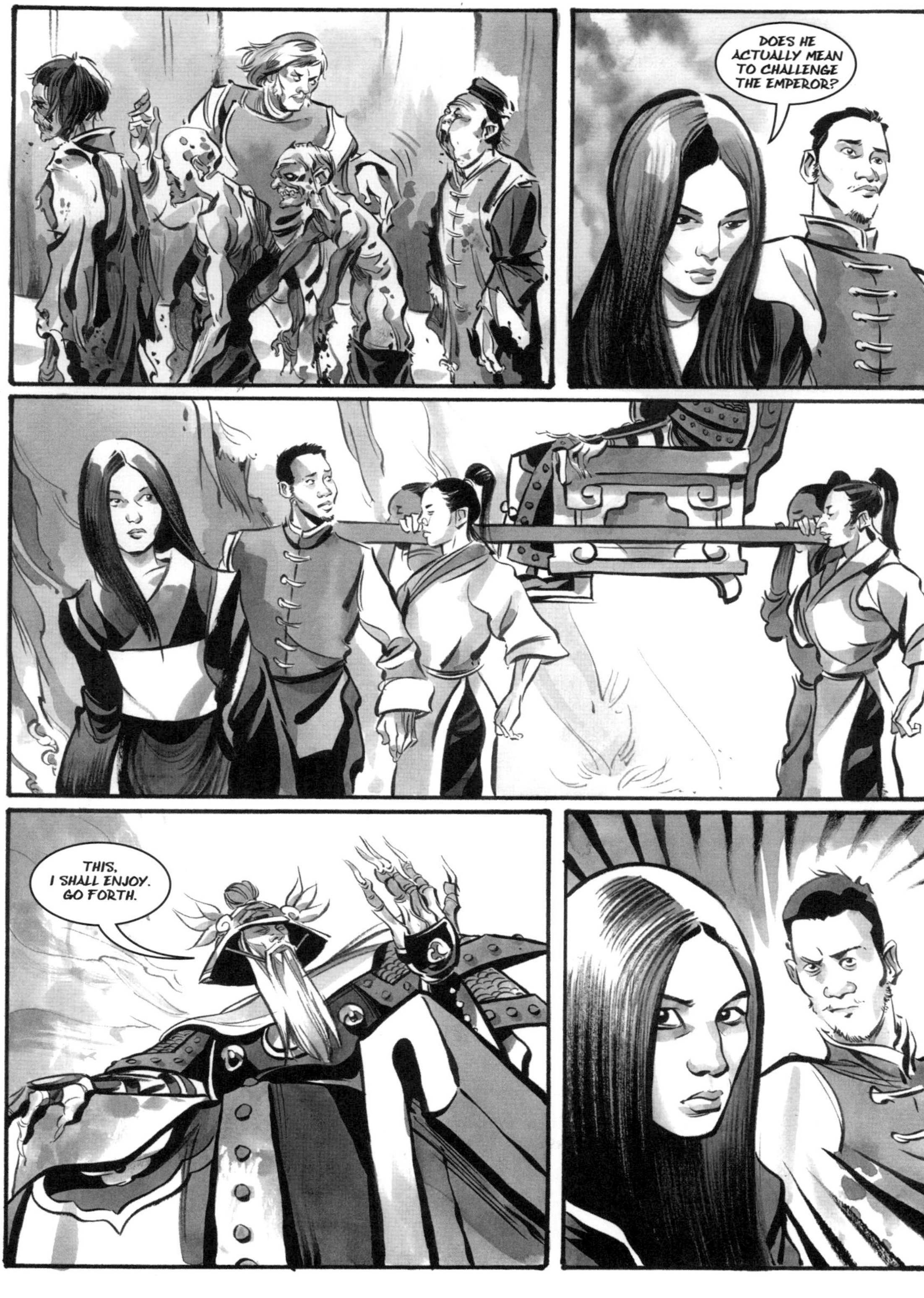
DOES HE ACTUALLY MEAN TO CHALLENGE THE EMPEROR?
THIS, I SHALL ENJOY. GO FORTH.

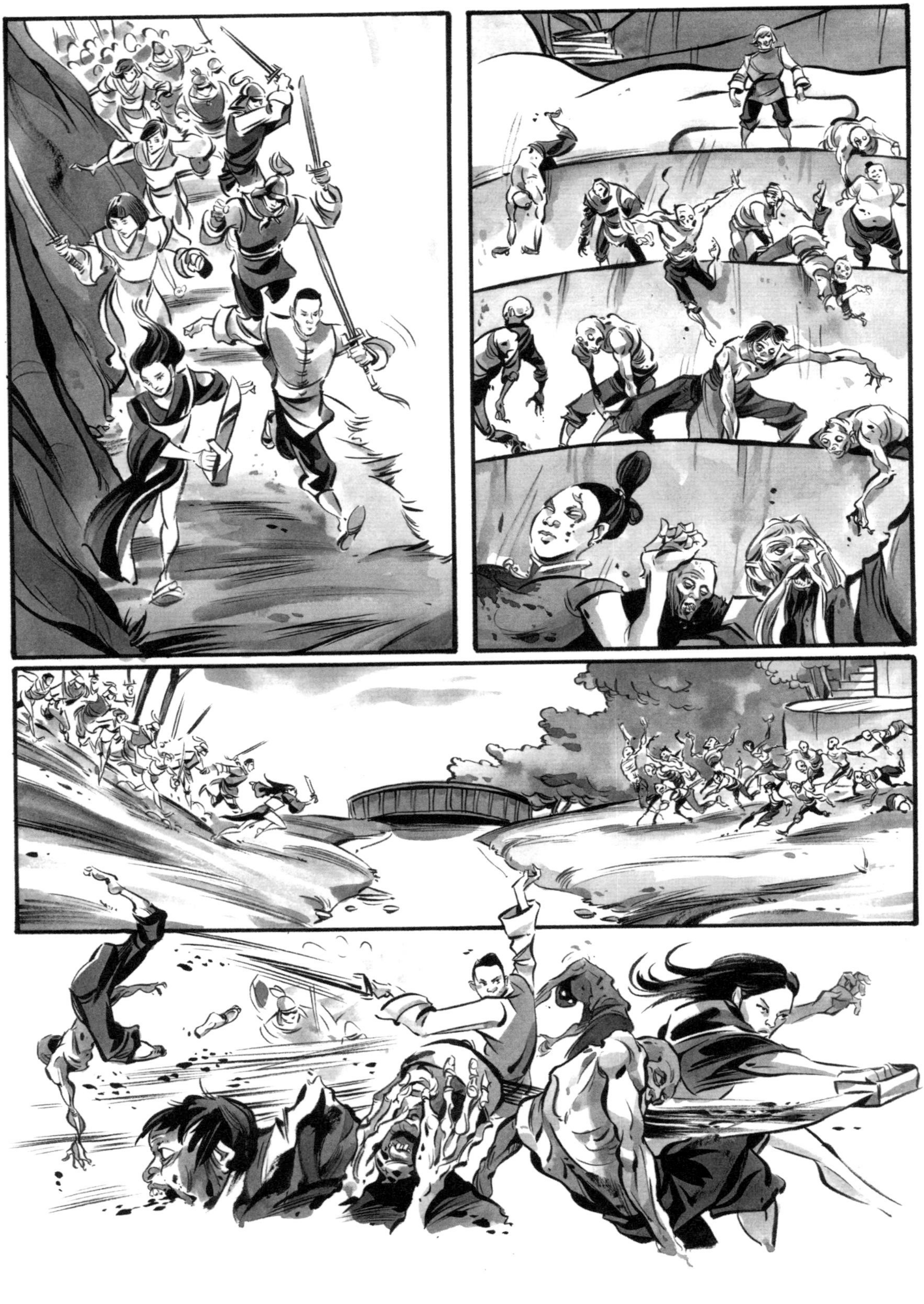

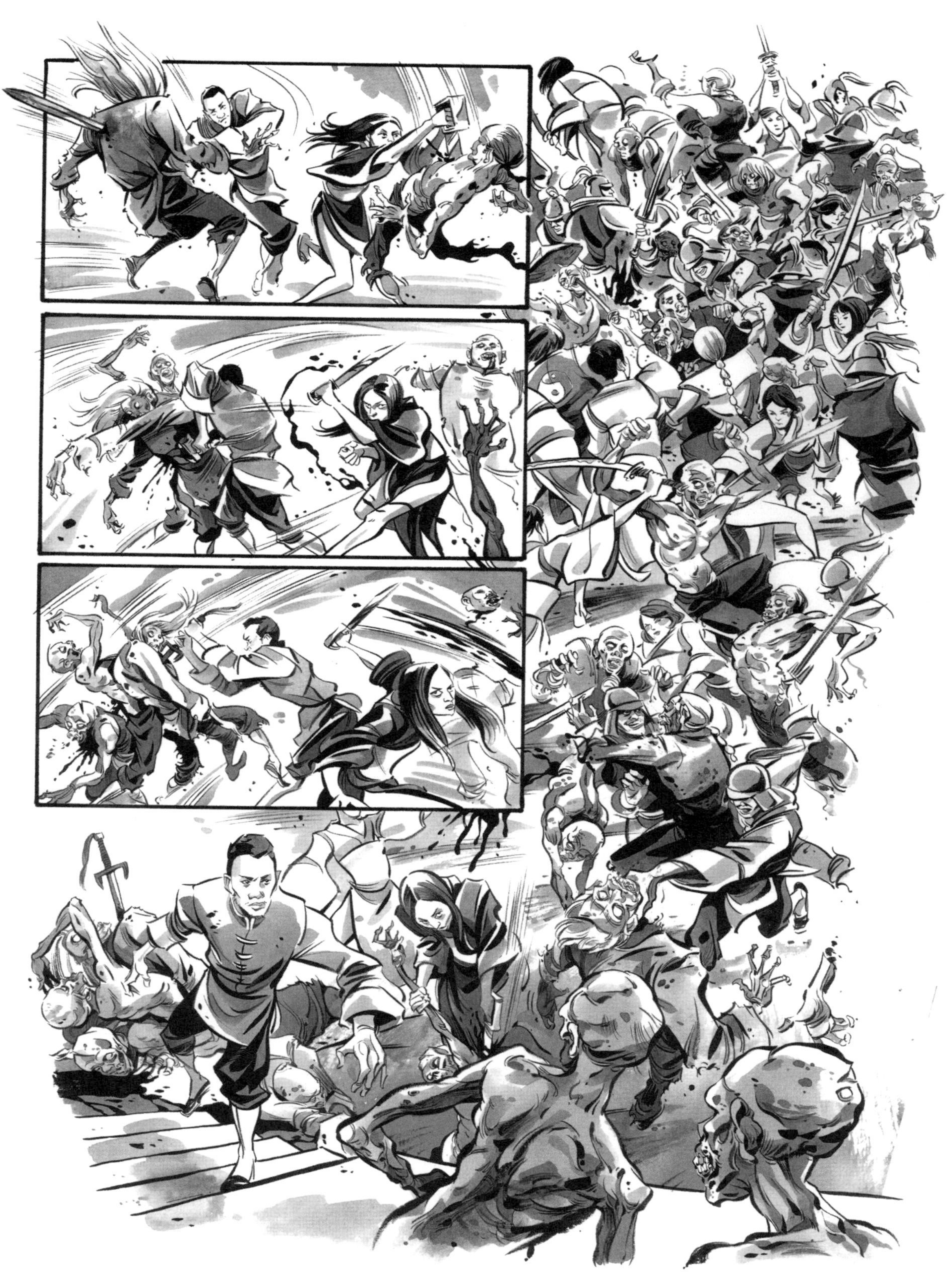

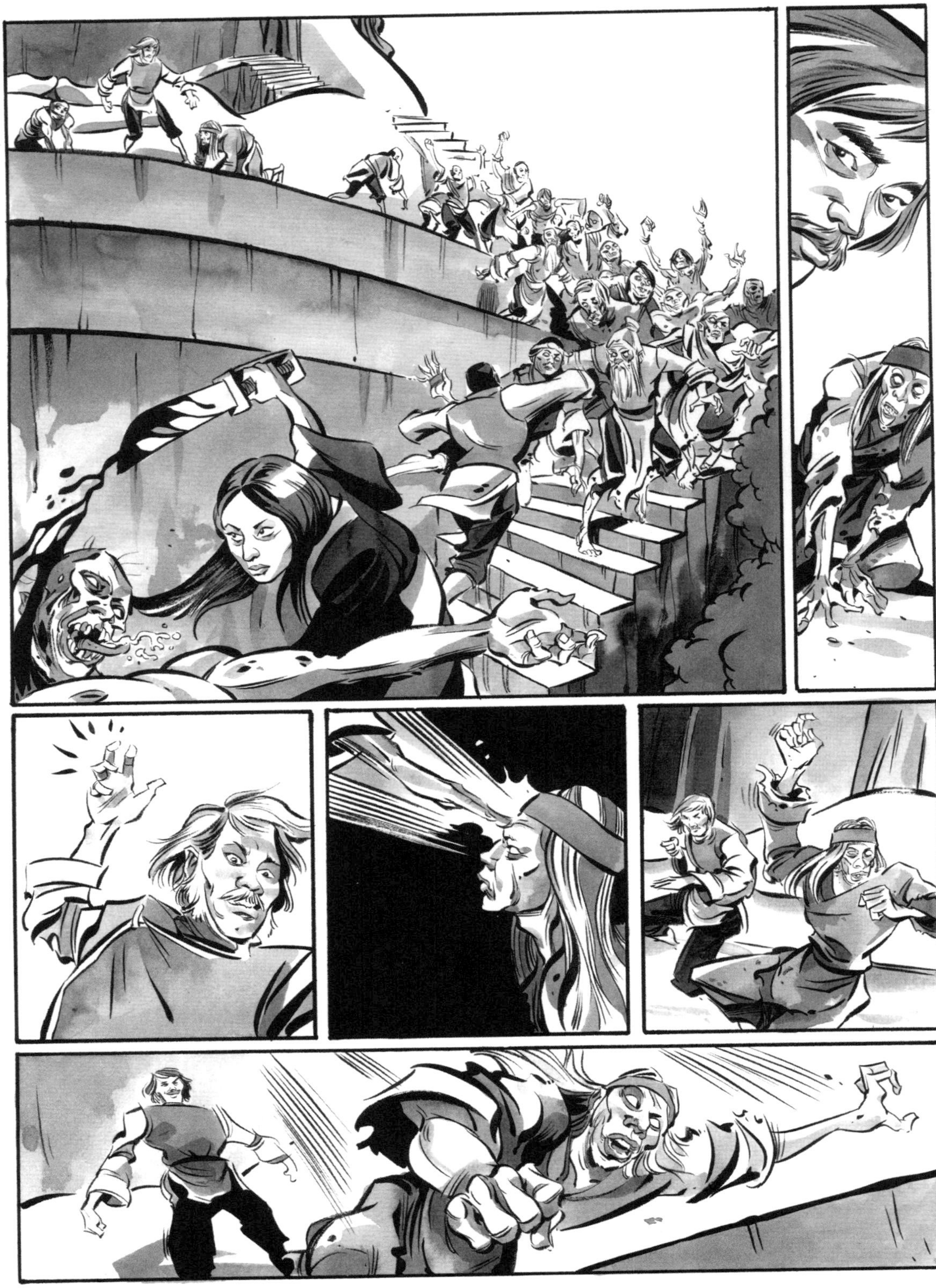

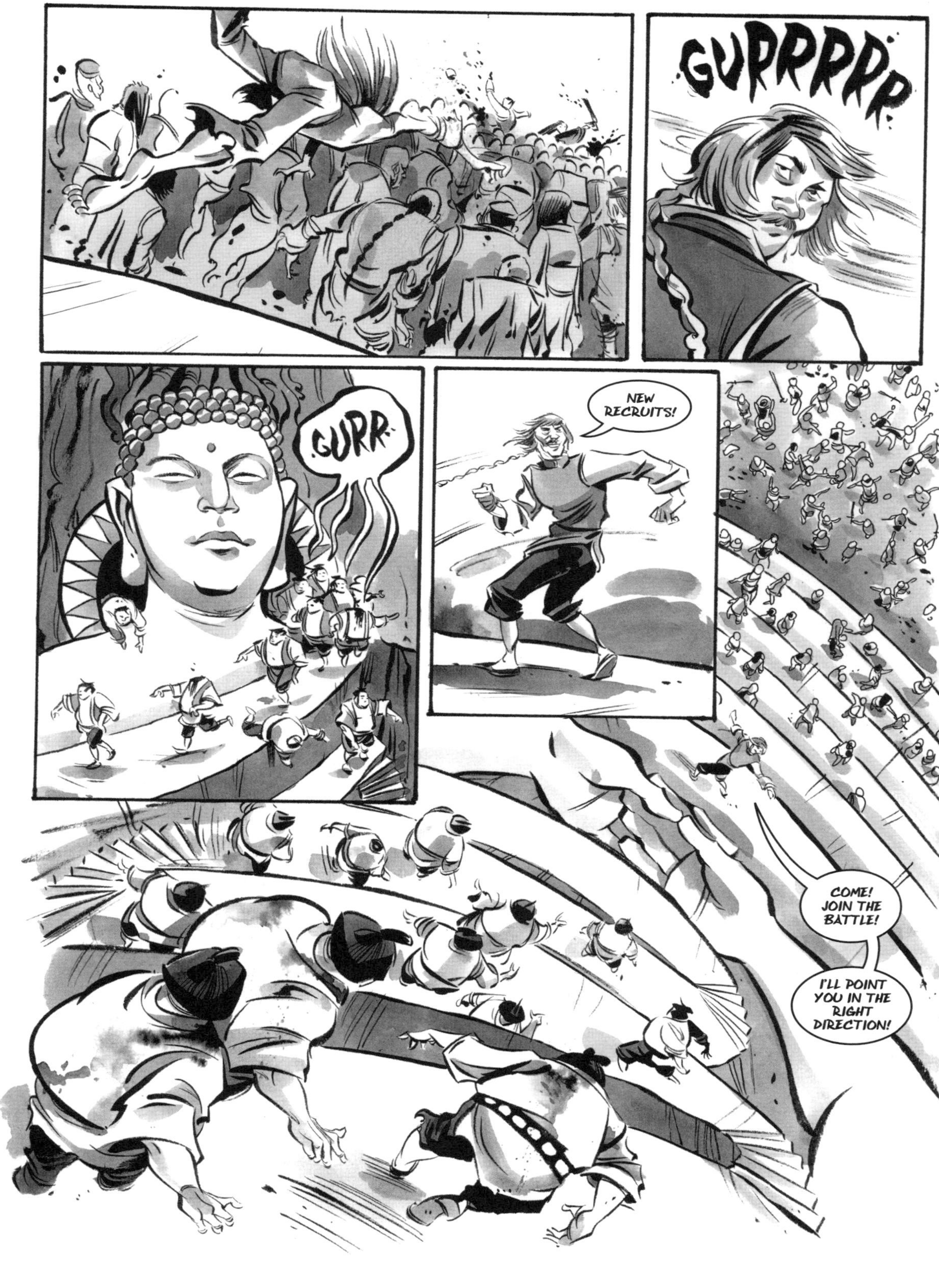
GURRRRR
GURR
NEW RECRUITS!
COME! JOIN THE BATTLE!
I'LL POINT YOU IN THE RIGHT DIRECTION!

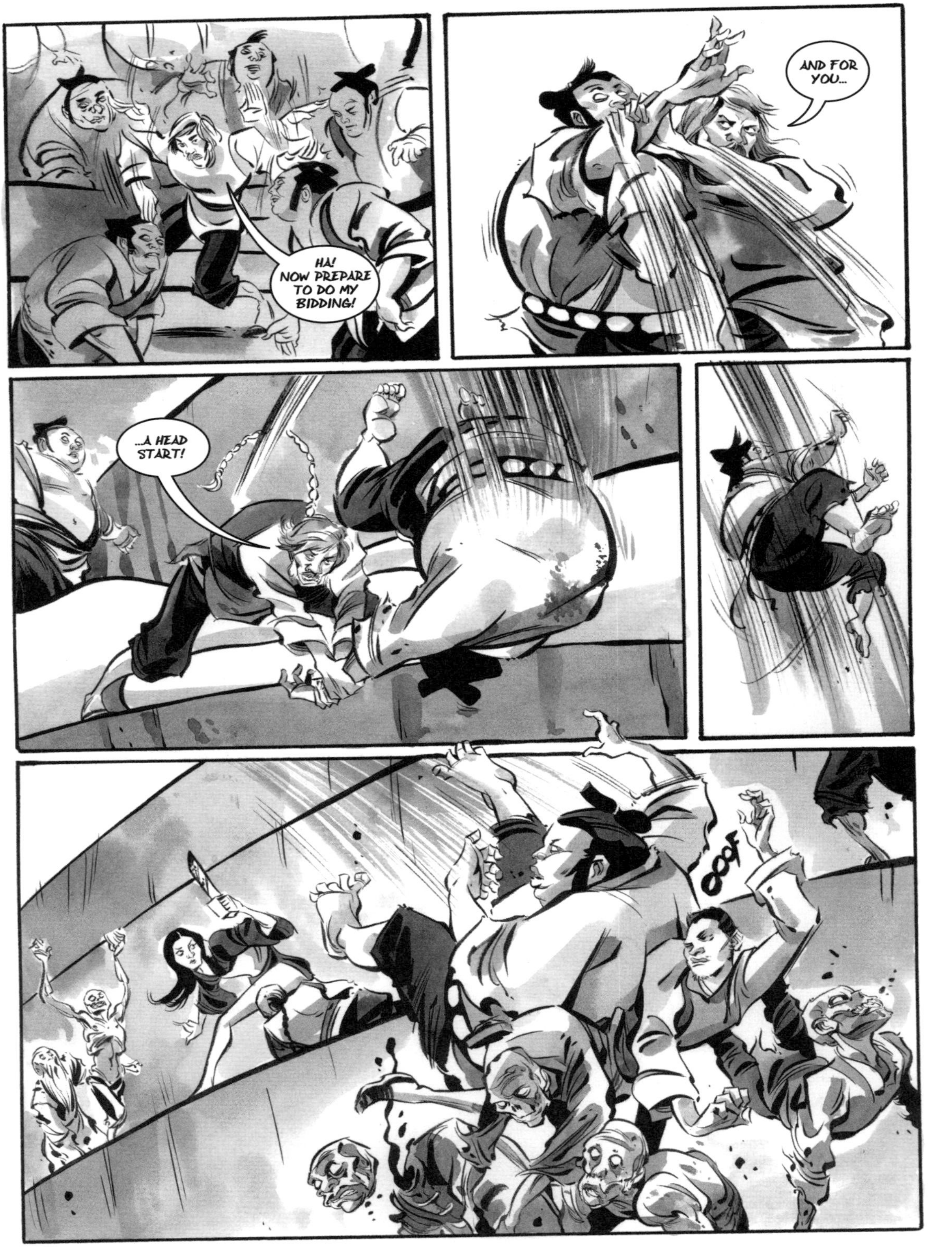
HA! NOW PREPARE TO DO MY BIDDING!
AND FOR YOU...
...A HEAD START!
OOOF

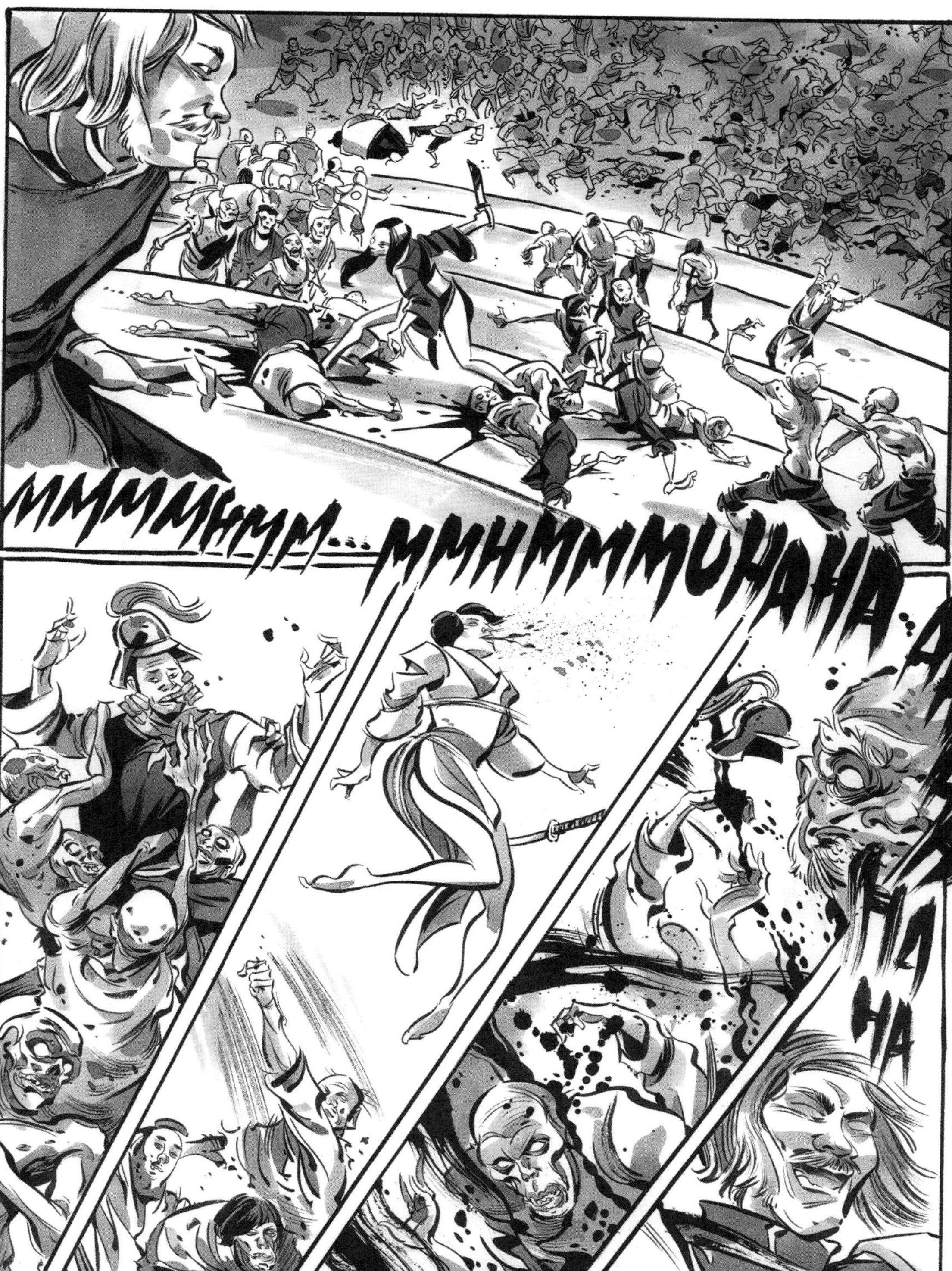
MMMMHMMM...
MMHMMMMUHAHAHA
AHAHAHAHA
HA

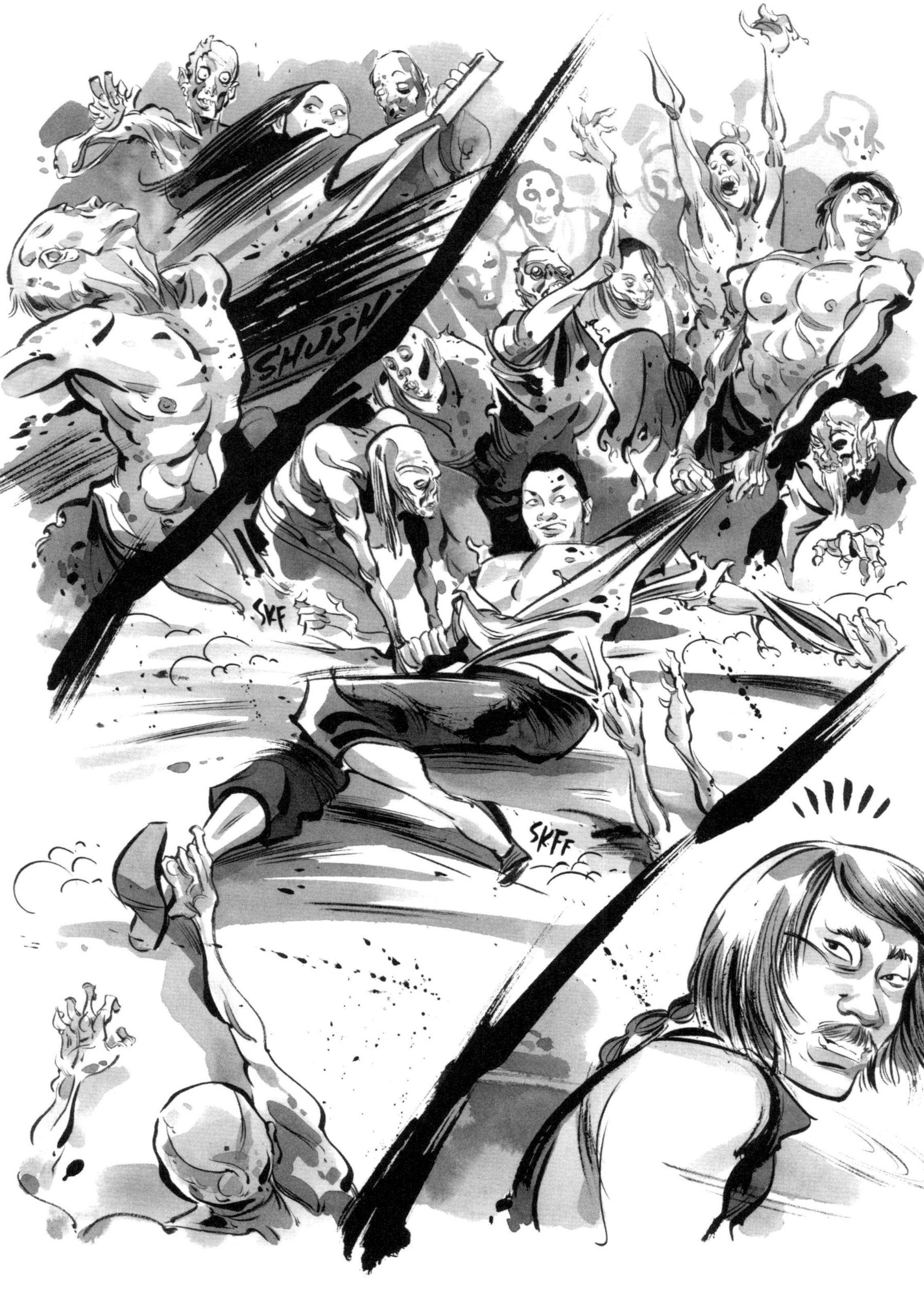
SHUSH
SKF
SKFF

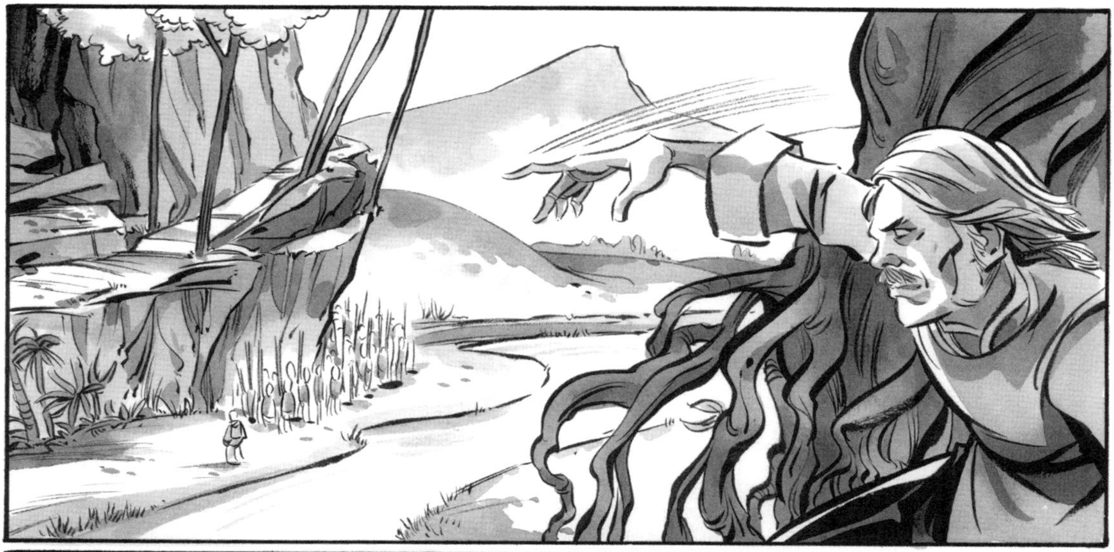

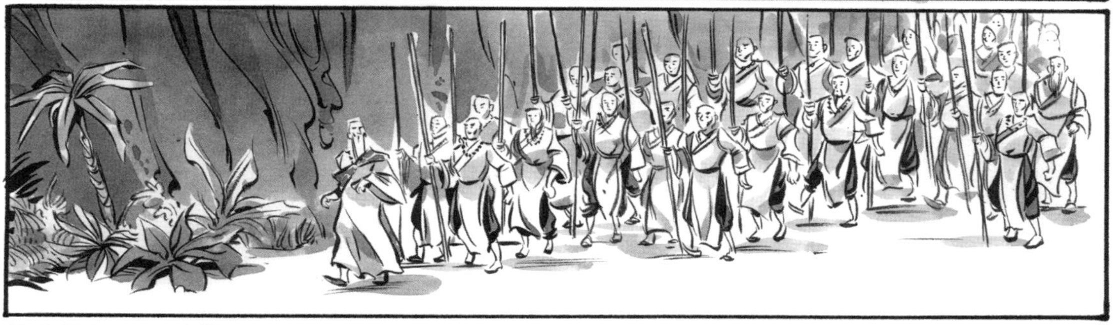

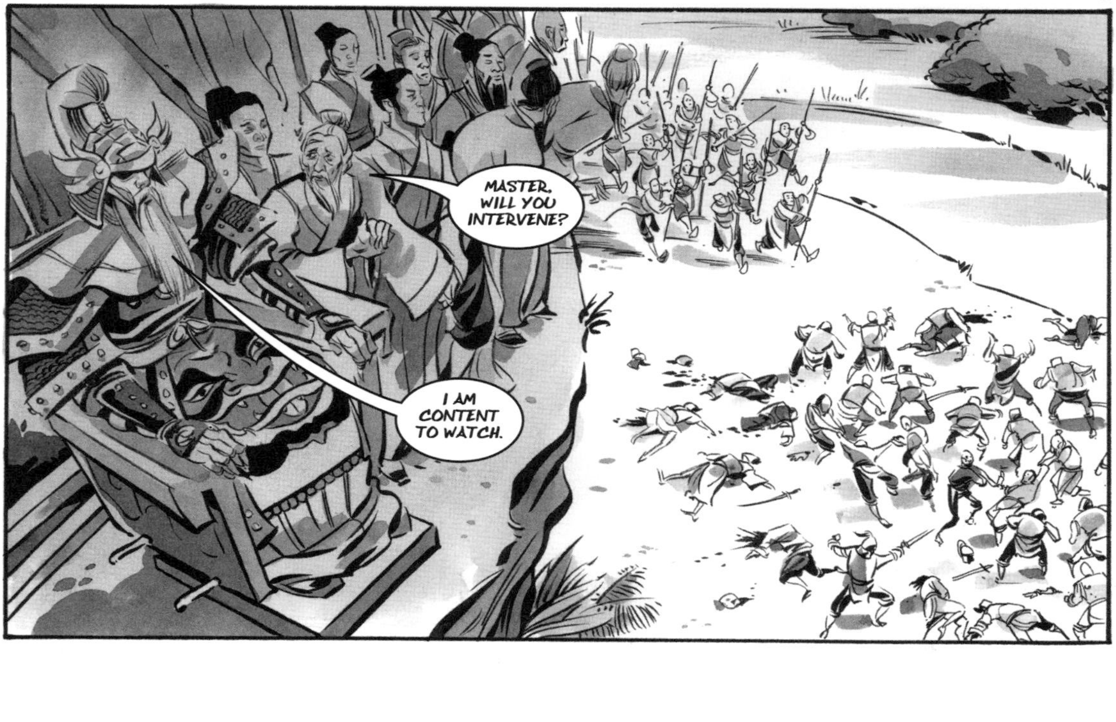
MASTER, WILL YOU INTERVENE?
I AM CONTENT TO WATCH.

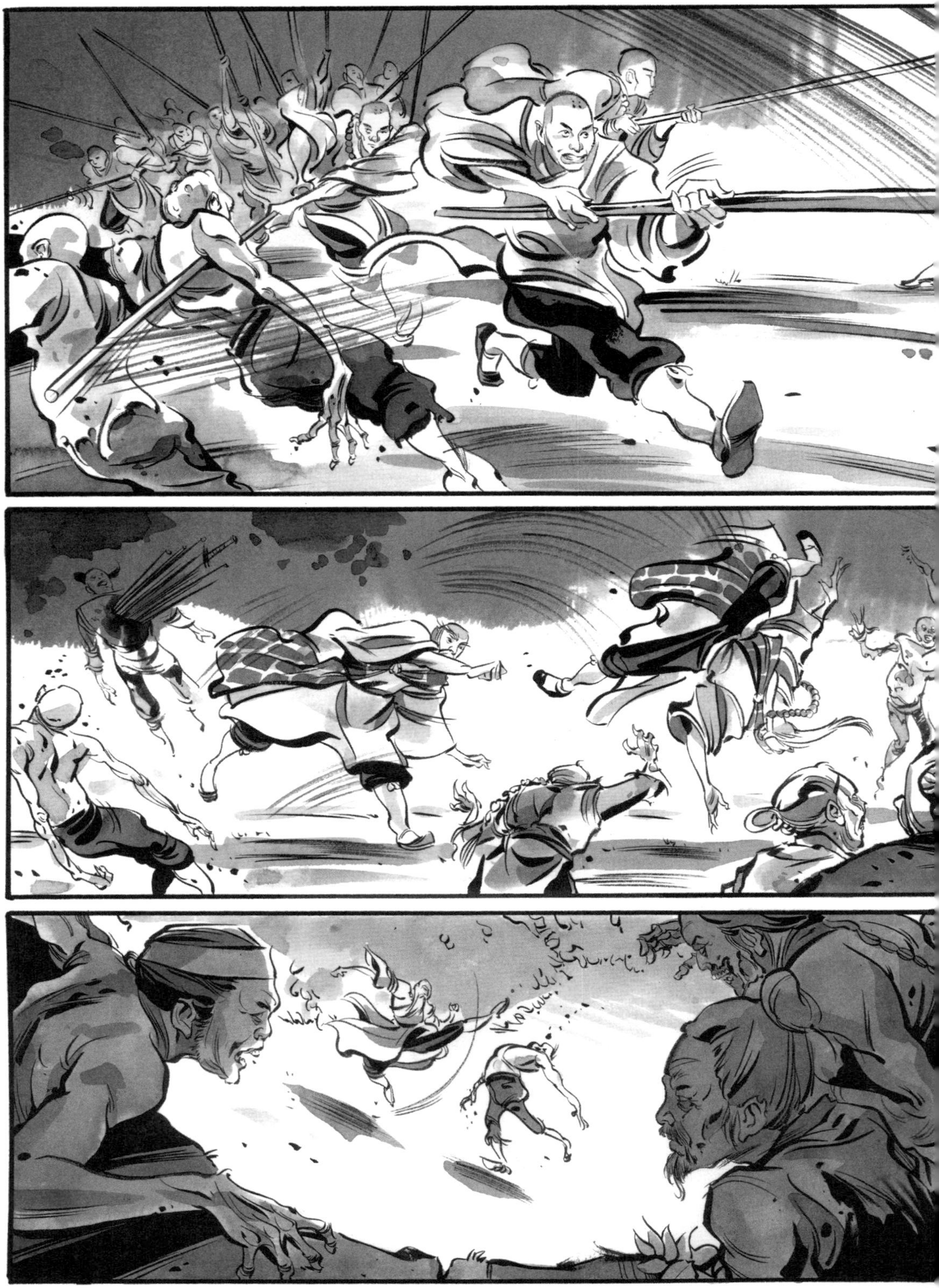

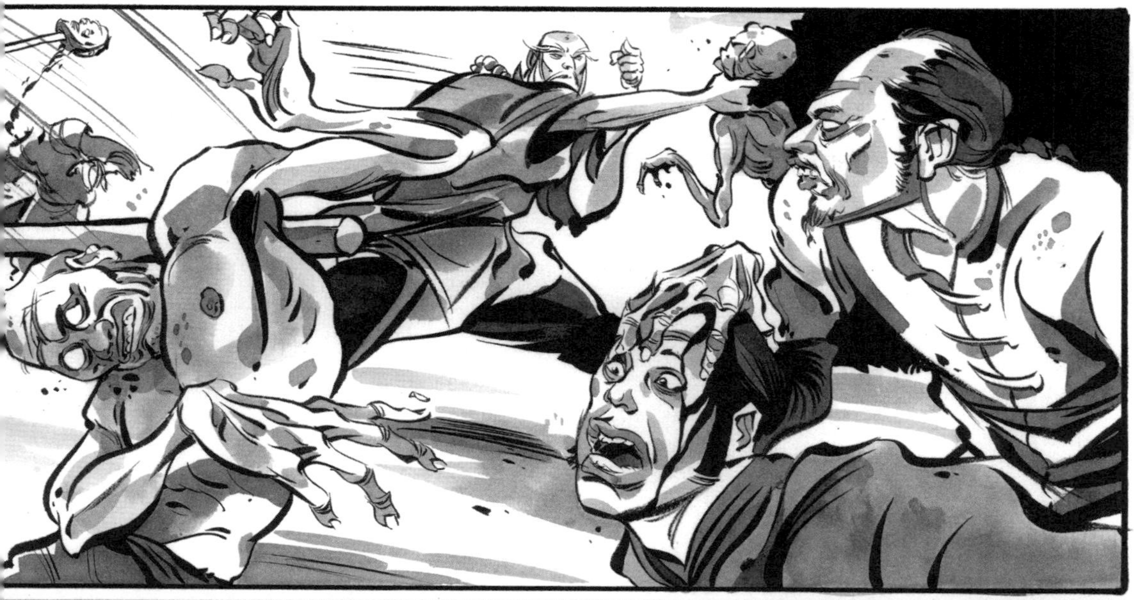
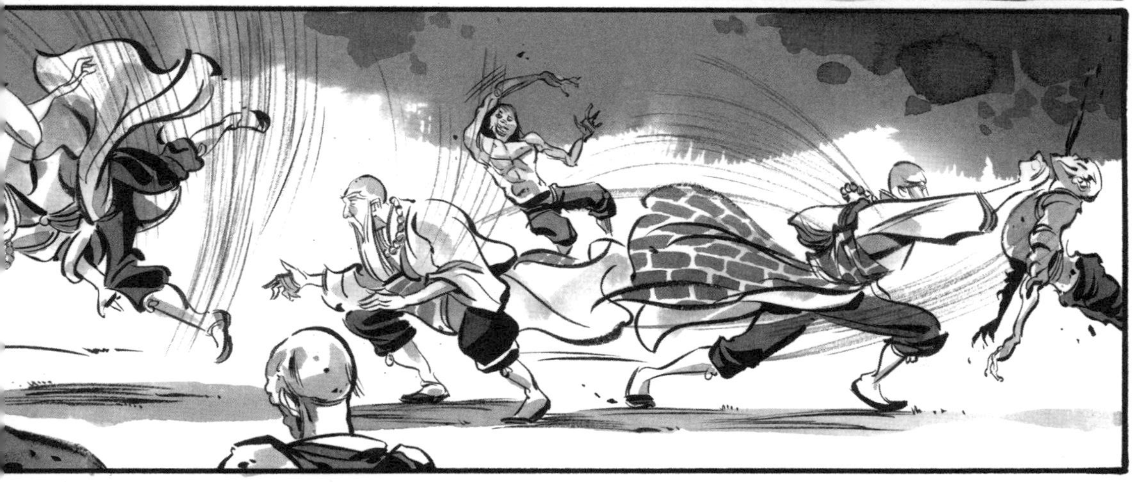
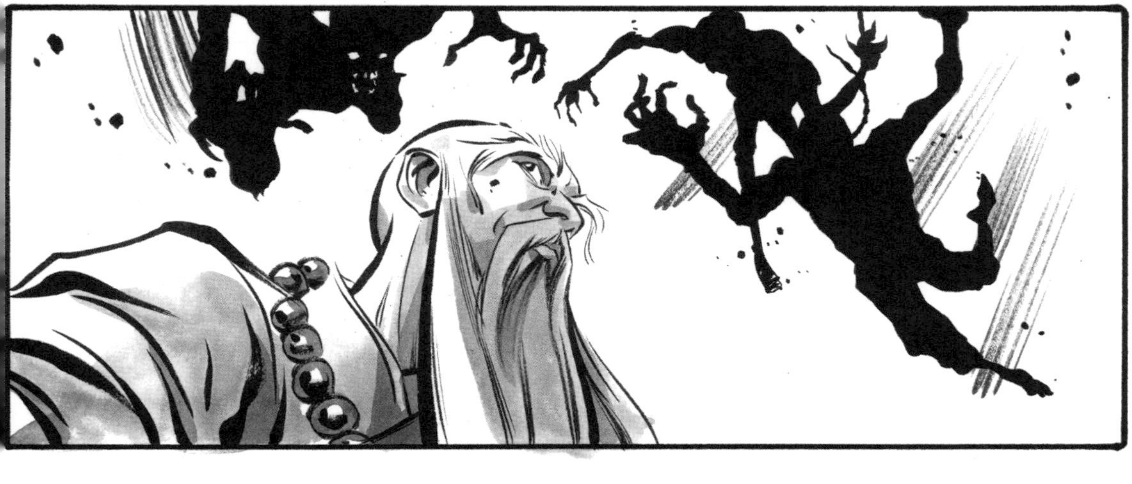

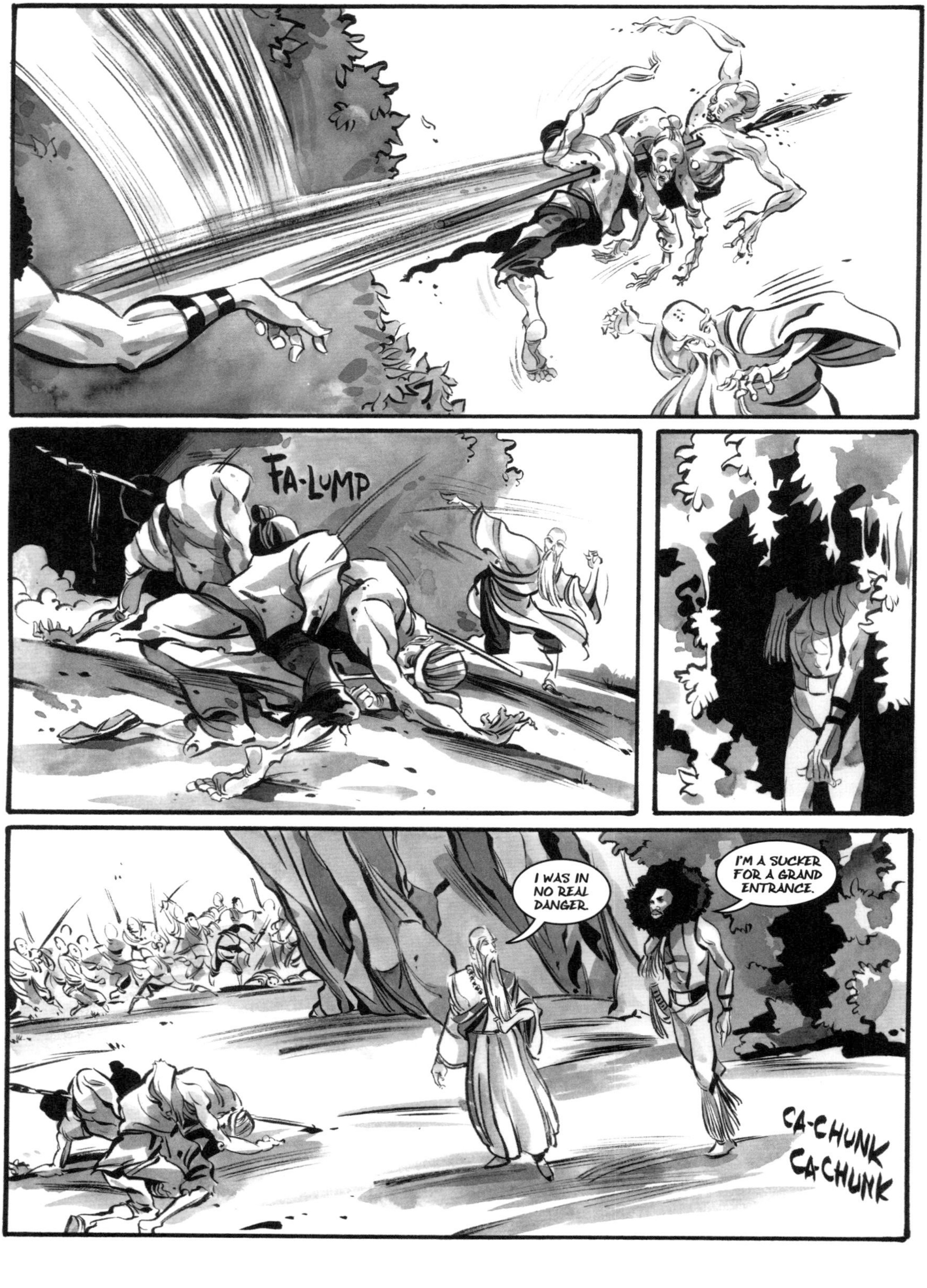
FA-LUMP
I WAS IN NO REAL DANGER.
I'M A SUCKER FOR A GRAND ENTRANCE.
CA-CHUNK CA-CHUNK

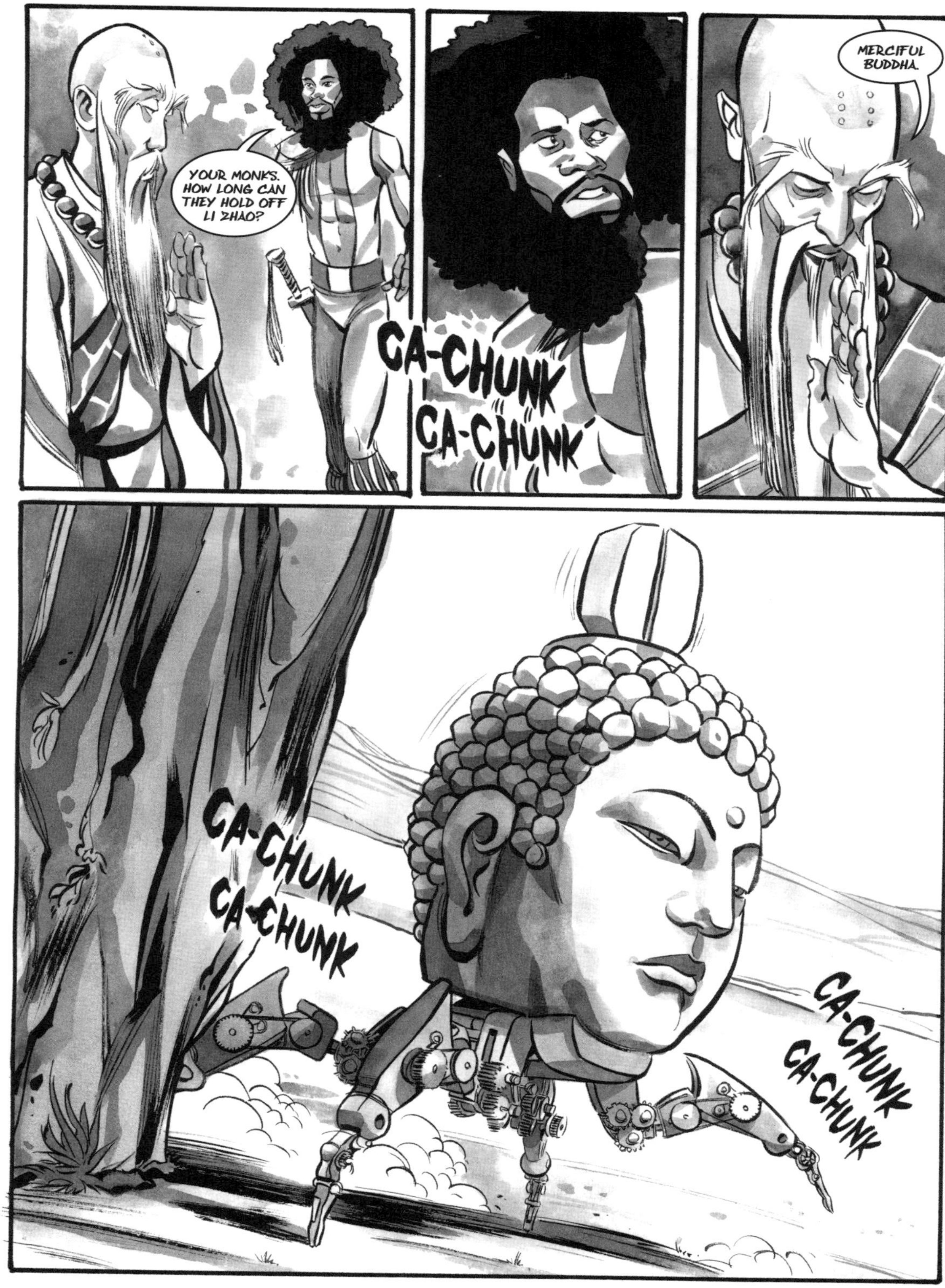
YOUR MONKS. HOW LONG CAN THEY HOLD OFF LI ZHAO?
CA-CHUNK
CA-CHUNK
MERCIFUL BUDDHA.
CA-CHUNK
CA-CHUNK
CA-CHUNK
CA-CHUNK

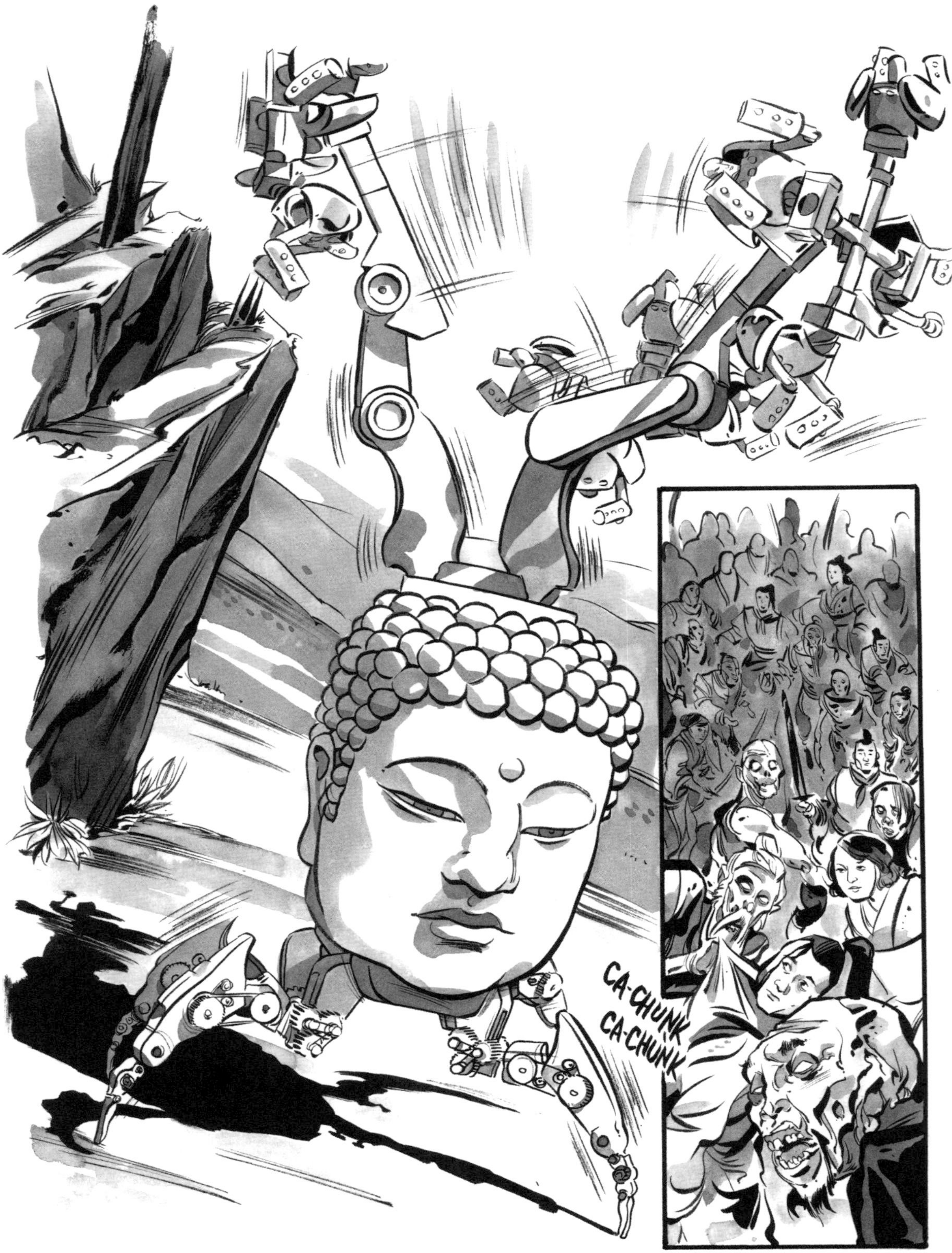
CA-CHUNK
CA-CHUNK

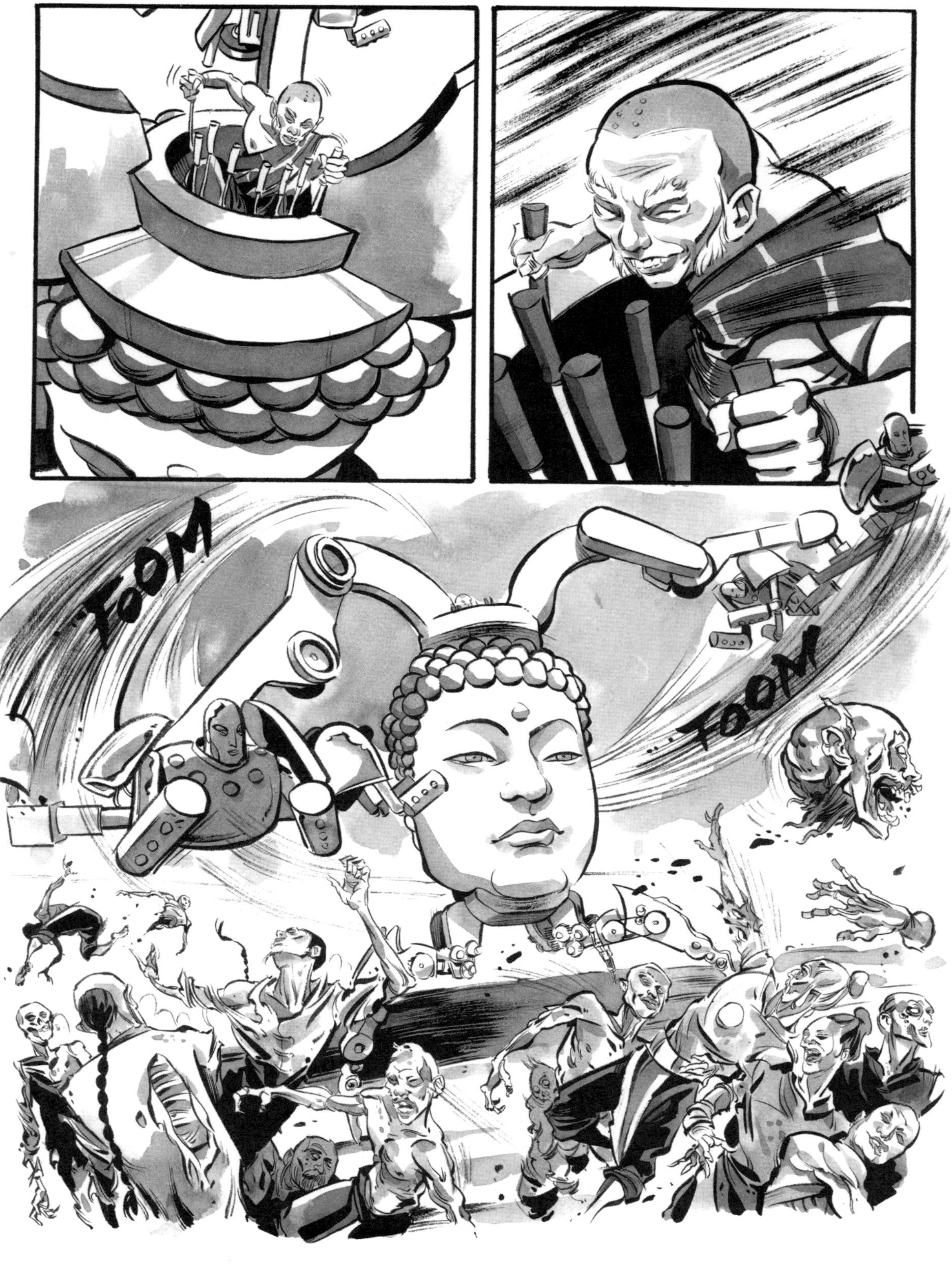
TOOM
TOOM

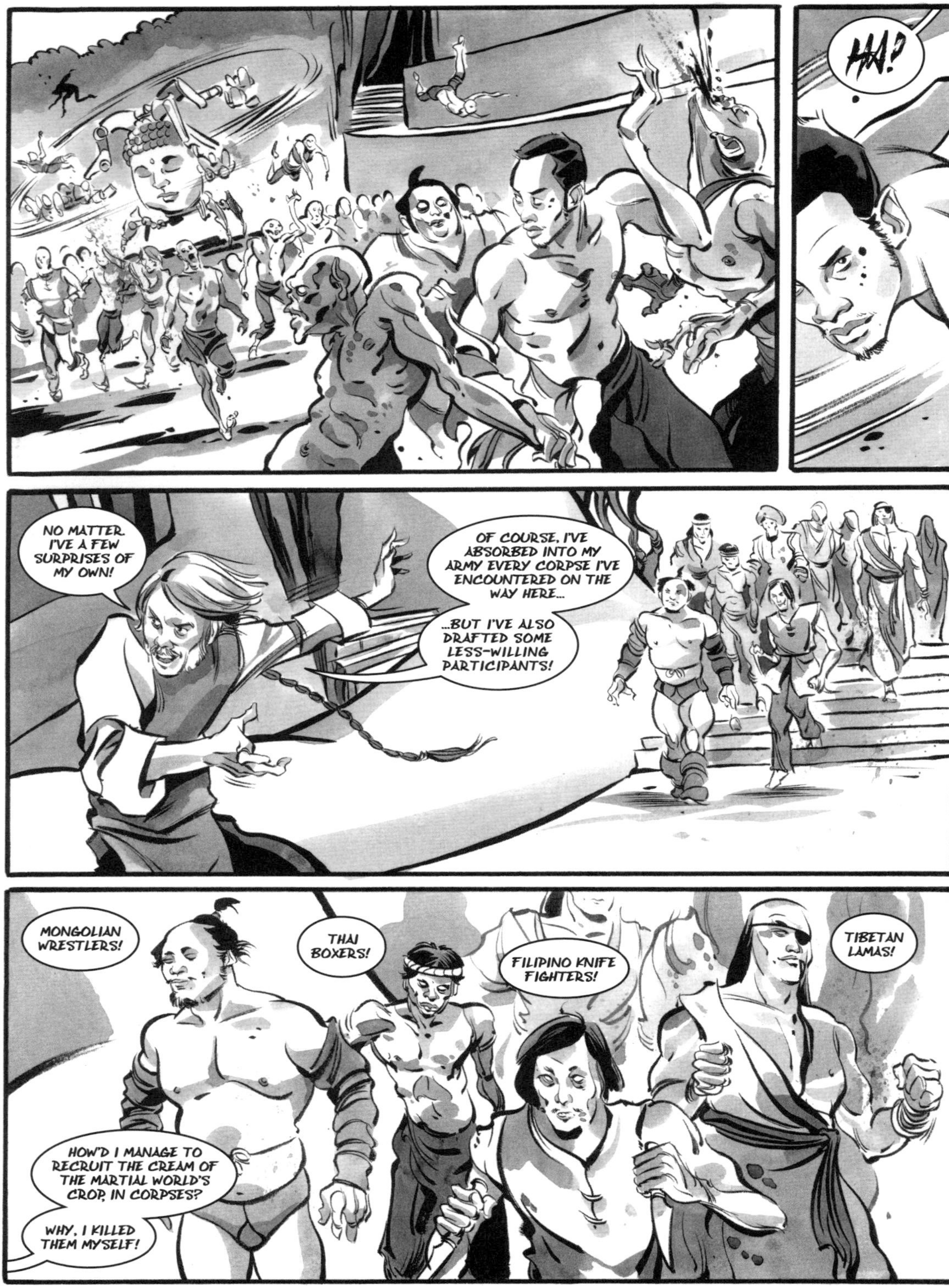
HA?
NO MATTER. I'VE A FEW SURPRISES OF MY OWN!
OF COURSE, I'VE ABSORBED INTO MY ARMY EVERY CORPSE I'VE ENCOUNTERED ON THE WAY HERE...
...BUT I'VE ALSO DRAFTED SOME LESS-WILLING PARTICIPANTS!
MONGOLIAN WRESTLERS!
THAI BOXERS!
FILIPINO KNIFE FIGHTERS!
TIBETAN LAMAS!
HOW'D I MANAGE TO RECRUIT THE CREAM OF THE MARTIAL WORLD'S CROP, IN CORPSES?
WHY, I KILLED THEM MYSELF!

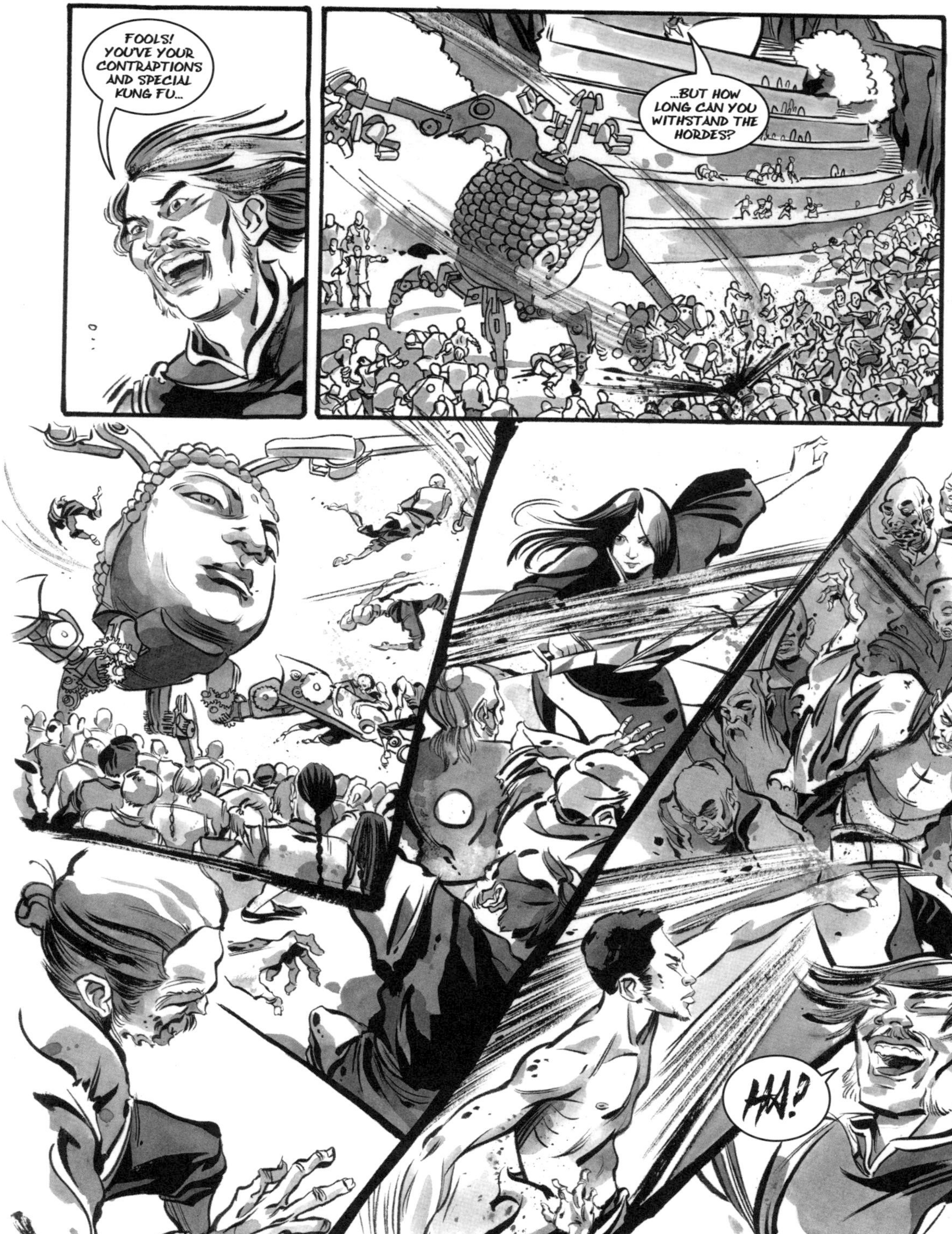
FOOLS! YOU'VE YOUR CONTRAPTIONS AND SPECIAL KUNG FU...
...BUT HOW LONG CAN YOU WITHSTAND THE HORDES?
HA?

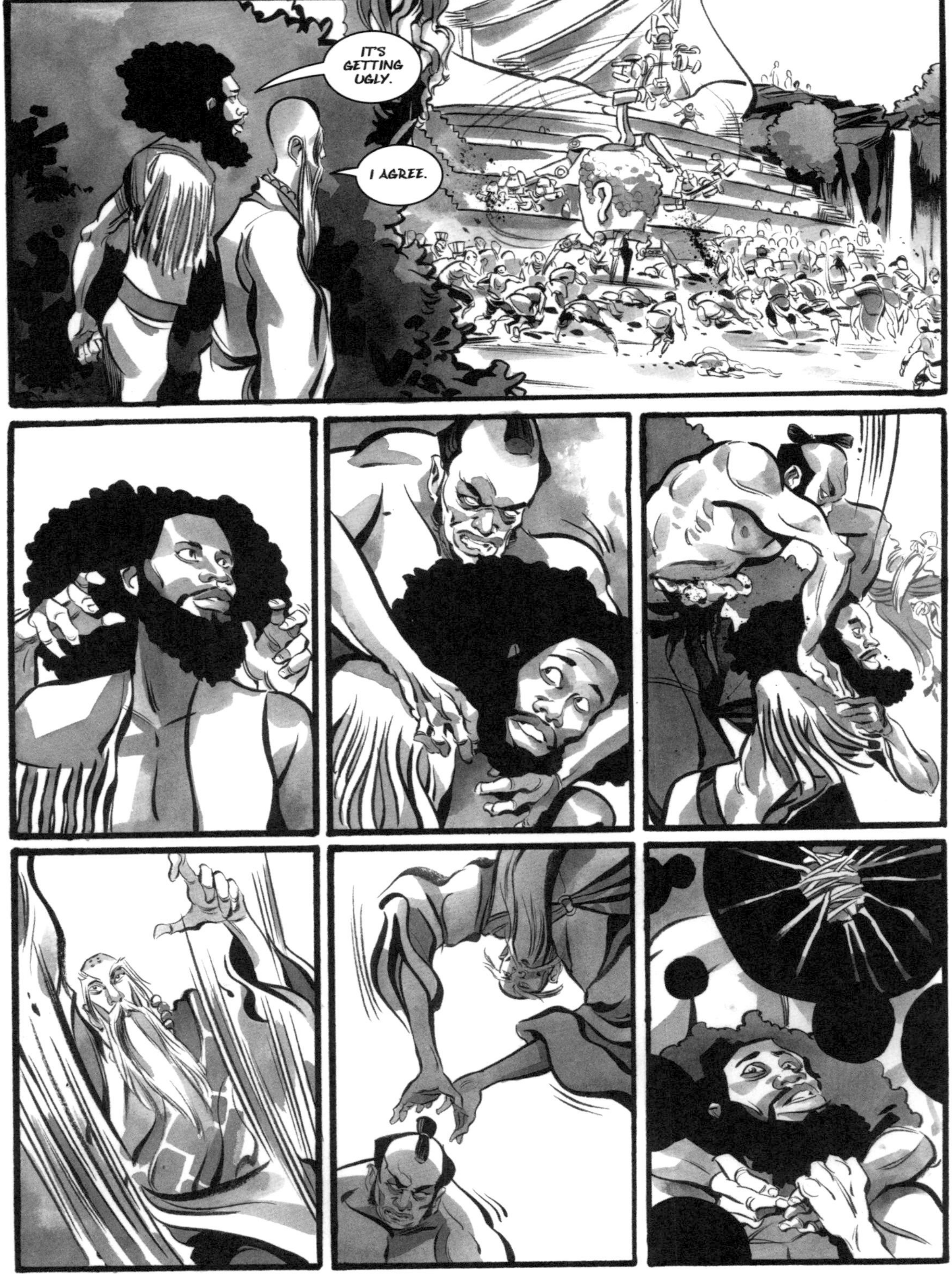
IT'S GETTING UGLY.
I AGREE.

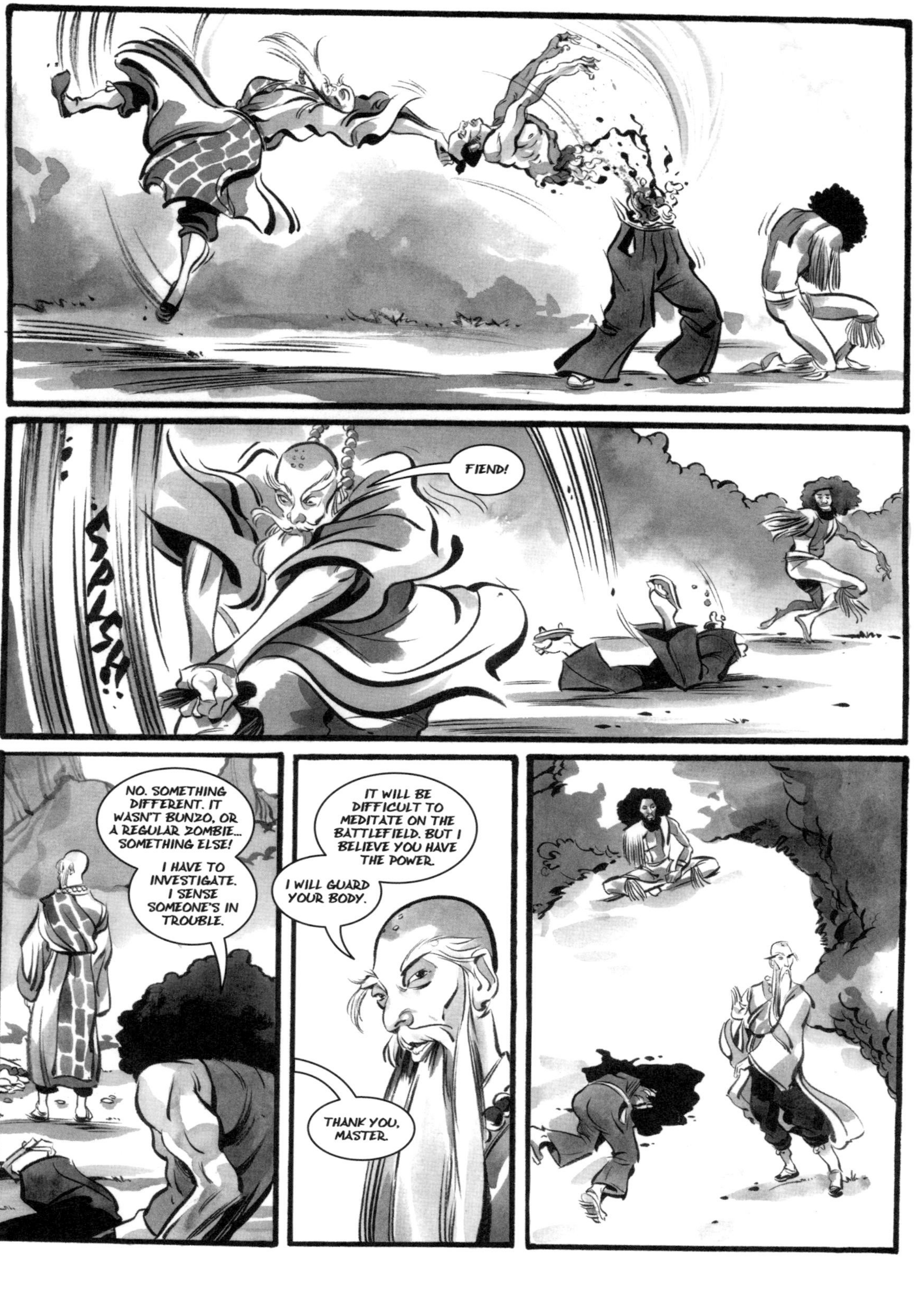
FIEND!
CRNSH
NO. SOMETHING DIFFERENT. IT WASN'T BUNZO, OR A REGULAR ZOMBIE... SOMETHING ELSE!
I HAVE TO INVESTIGATE. I SENSE SOMEONE'S IN TROUBLE.
IT WILL BE DIFFICULT TO MEDITATE ON THE BATTLEFIELD. BUT I BELIEVE YOU HAVE THE POWER.
I WILL GUARD YOUR BODY.
THANK YOU, MASTER.

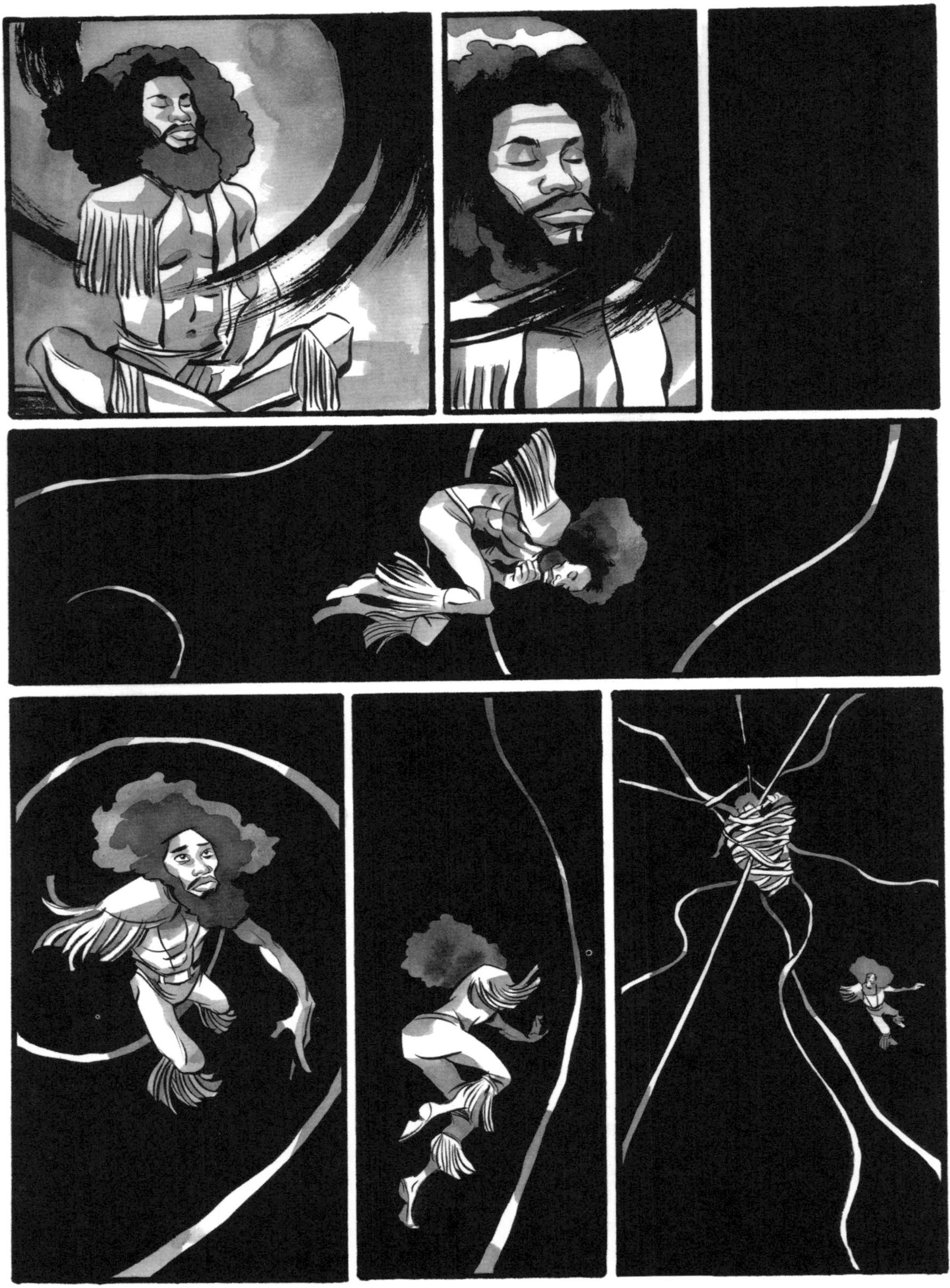

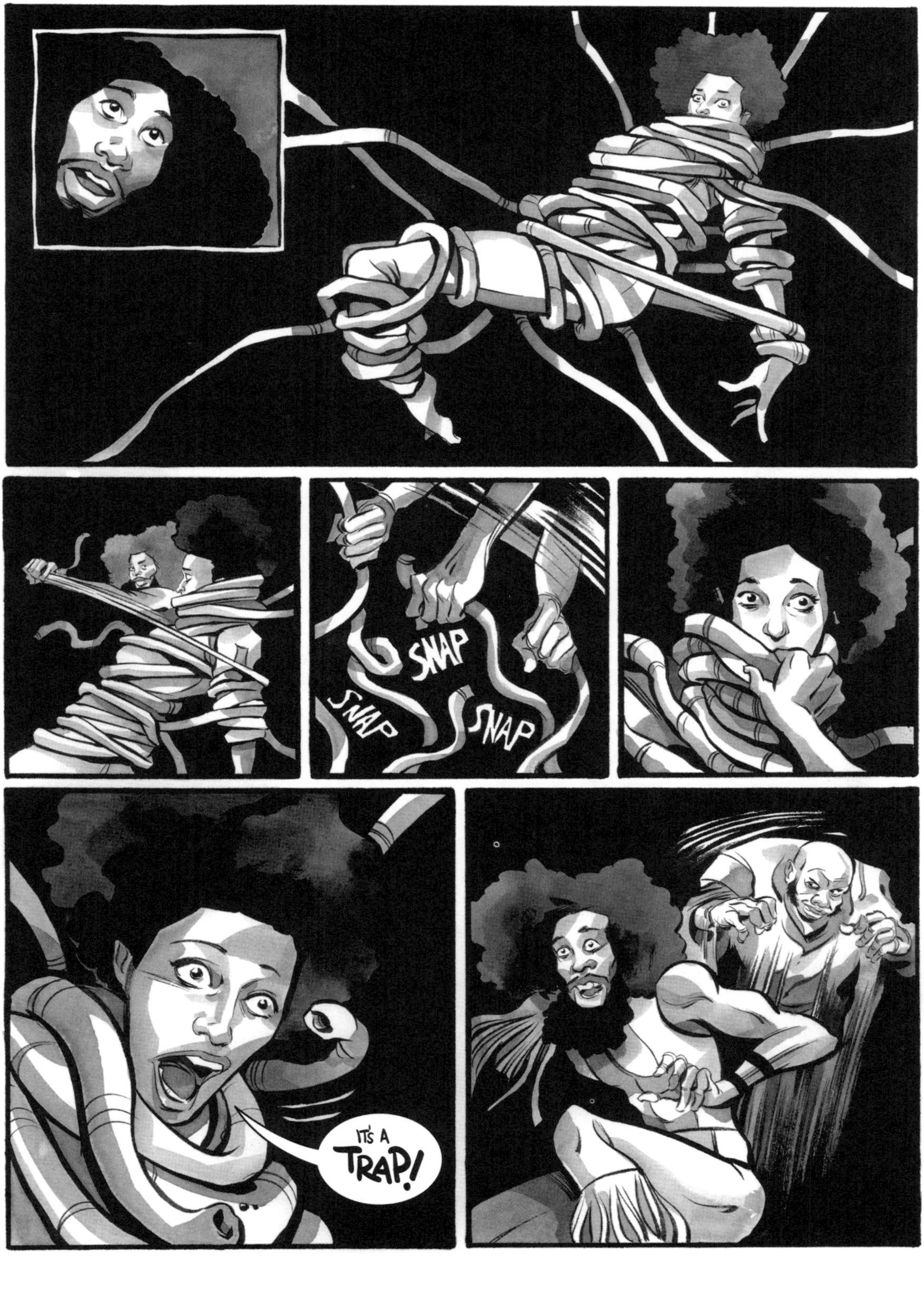
SNAP
SNAP
SNAP
IT'S A TRAP!

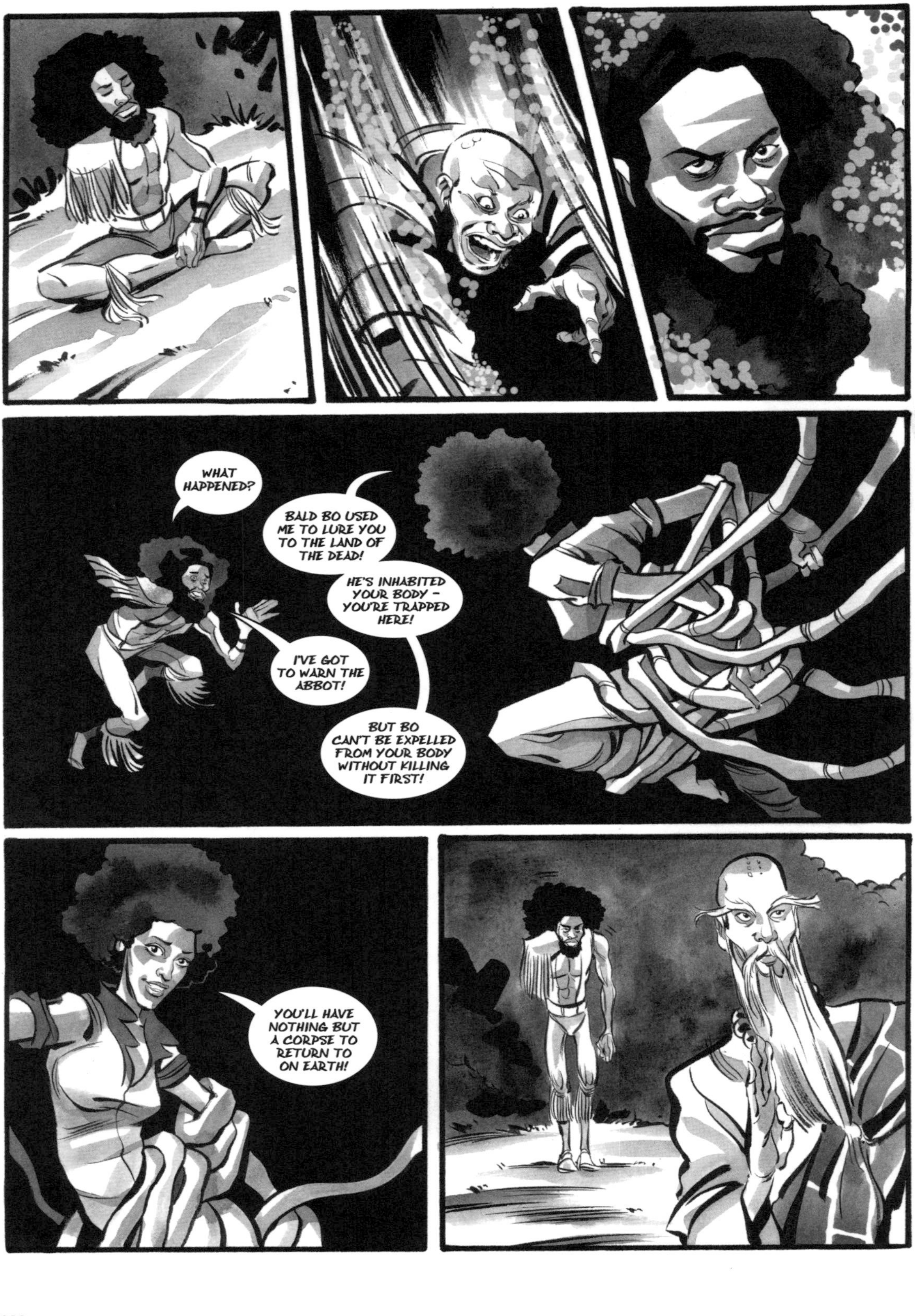
WHAT HAPPENED?
BALD BO USED ME TO LURE YOU TO THE LAND OF THE DEAD!
HE'S INHABITED YOUR BODY - YOU'RE TRAPPED HERE!
I'VE GOT TO WARN THE ABBOT!
BUT BO CAN'T BE EXPELLED FROM YOUR BODY WITHOUT KILLING IT FIRST!
YOU'LL HAVE NOTHING BUT A CORPSE TO RETURN TO ON EARTH!

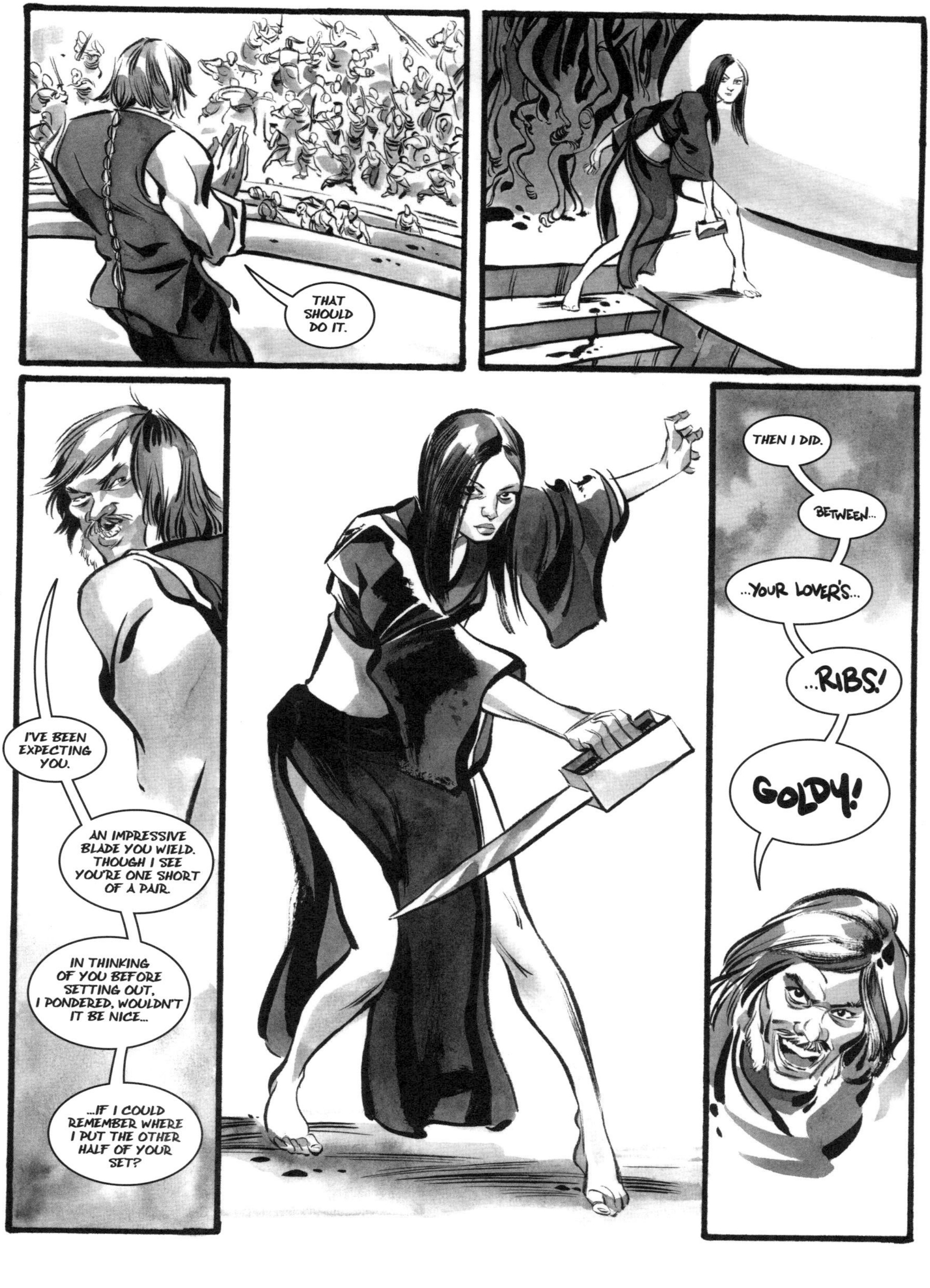
THAT SHOULD DO IT.
I'VE BEEN EXPECTING YOU.
AN IMPRESSIVE BLADE YOU WIELD. THOUGH I SEE YOU'RE ONE SHORT OF A PAIR.
IN THINKING OF YOU BEFORE SETTING OUT, I PONDERED, WOULDN'T IT BE NICE...
...IF I COULD REMEMBER WHERE I PUT THE OTHER HALF OF YOUR SET?
THEN I DID.
BETWEEN...
...YOUR LOVER'S...
...RIBS!
GOLDY!

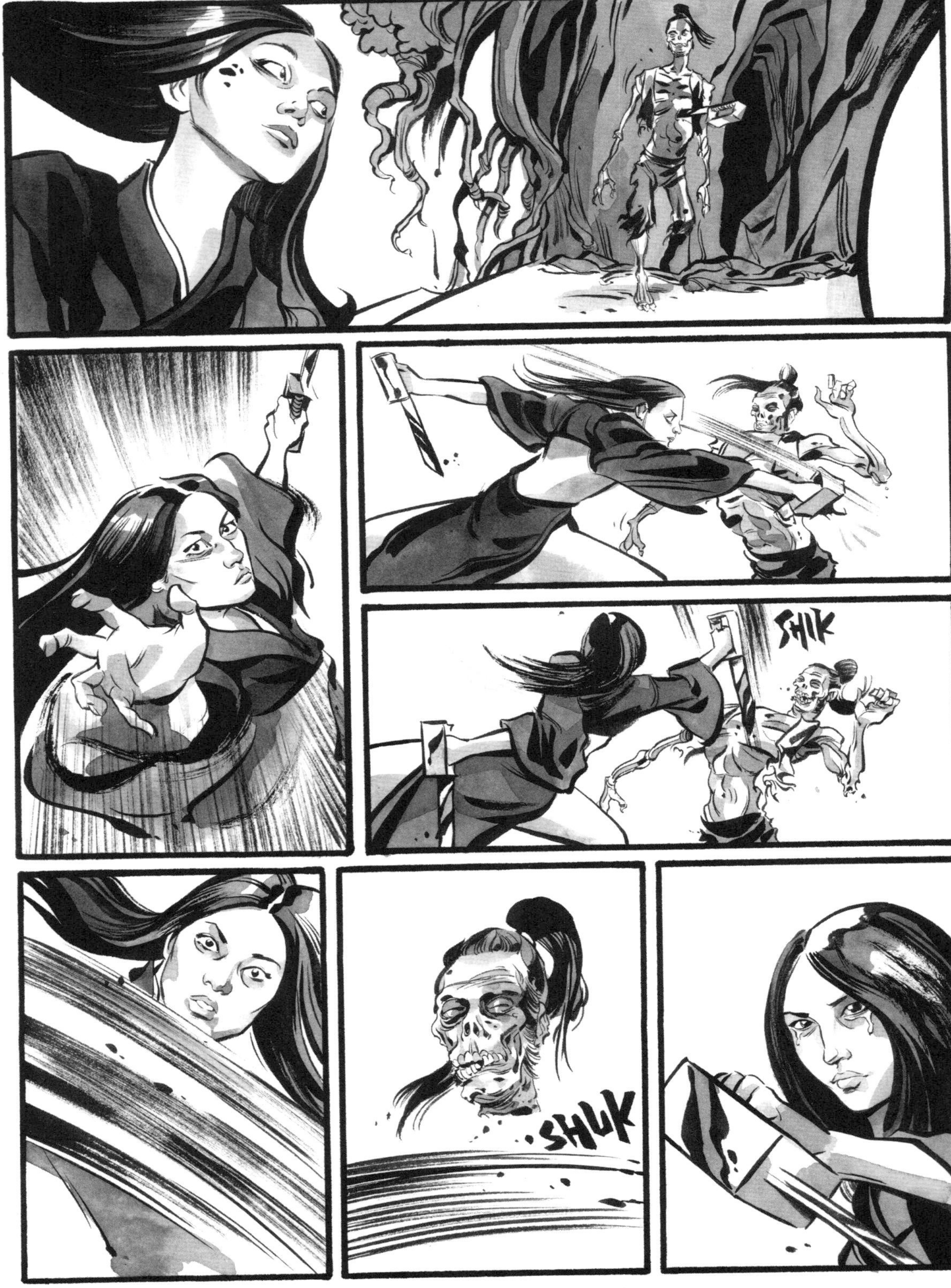
SHIK
SHUK

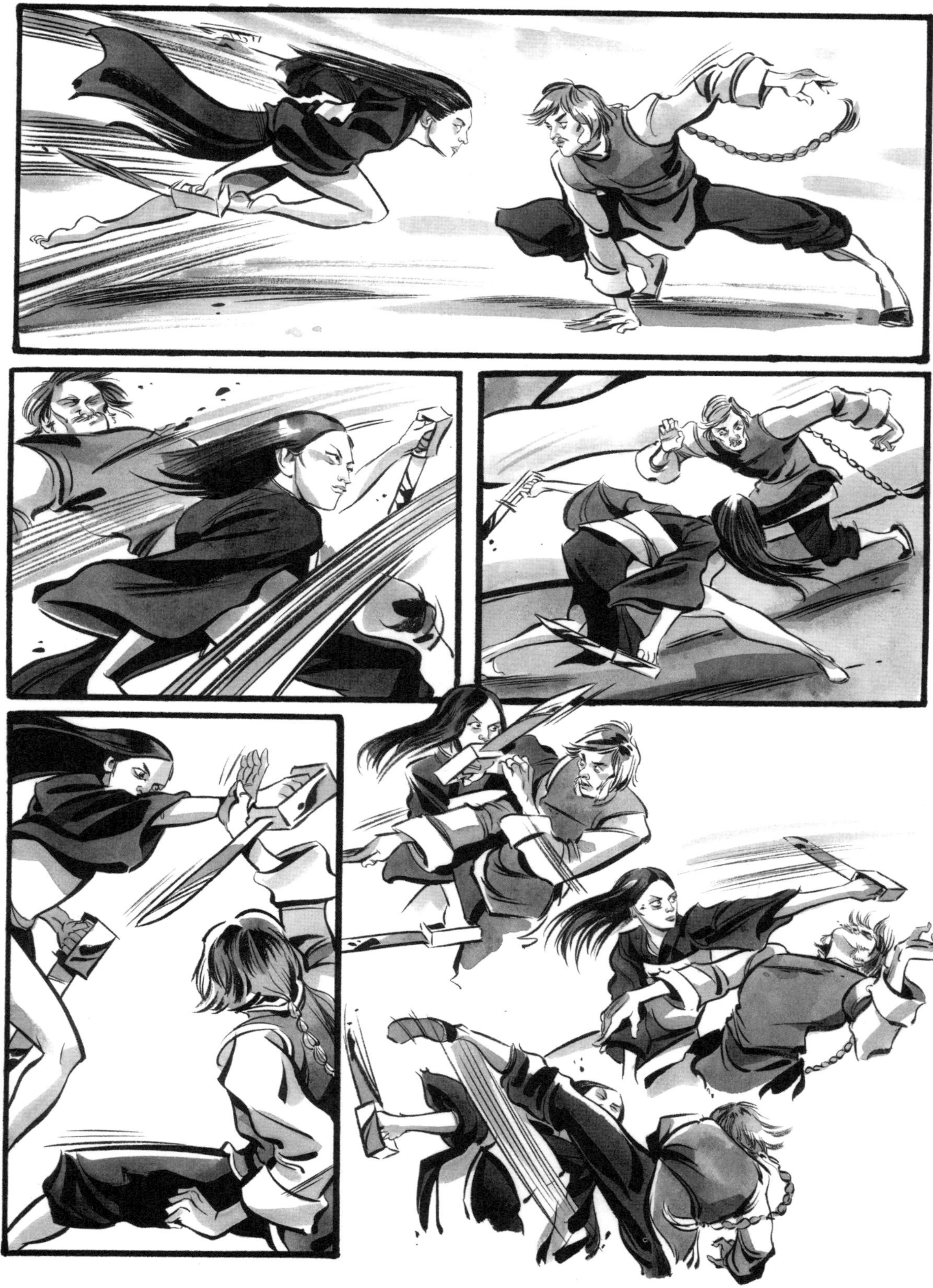

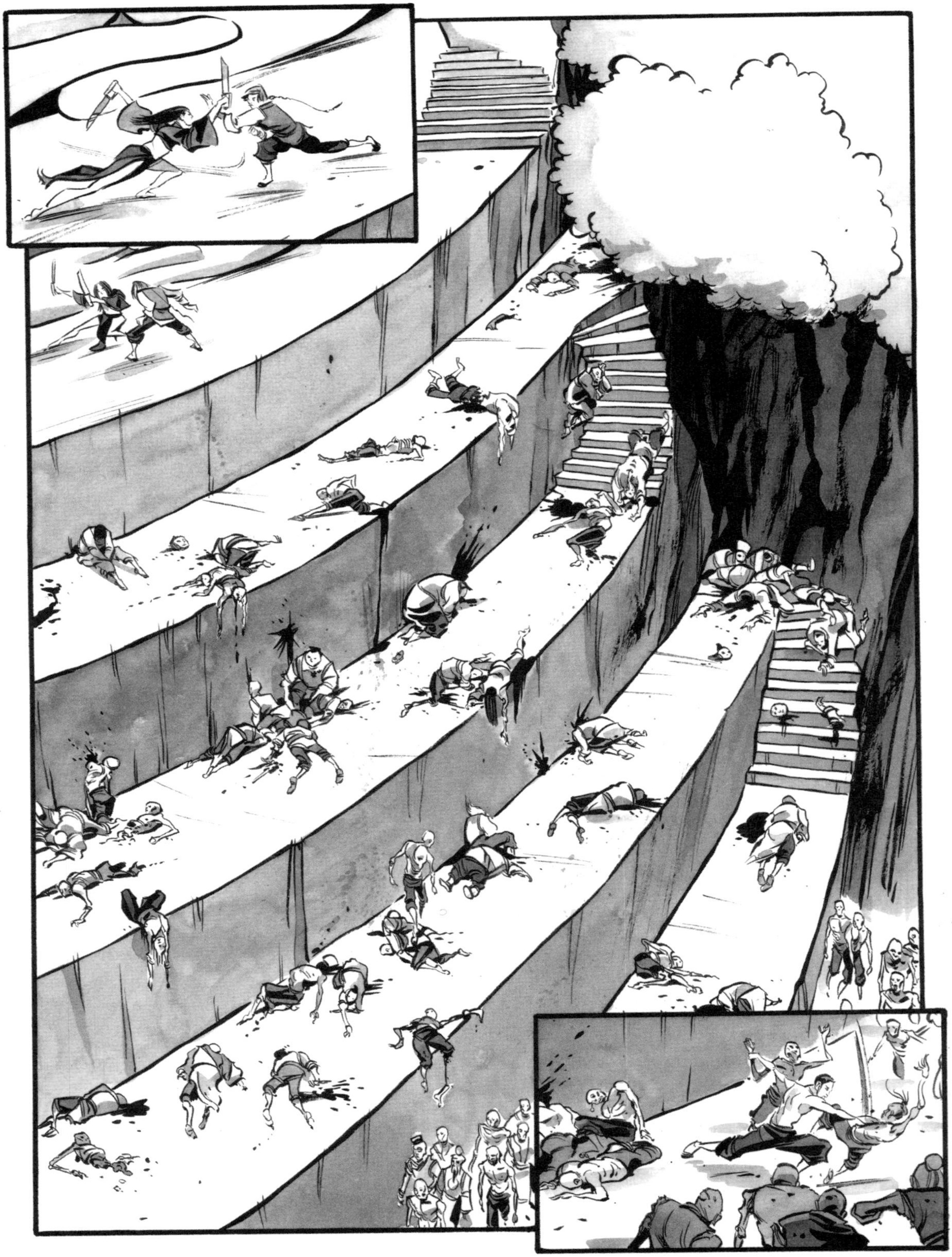

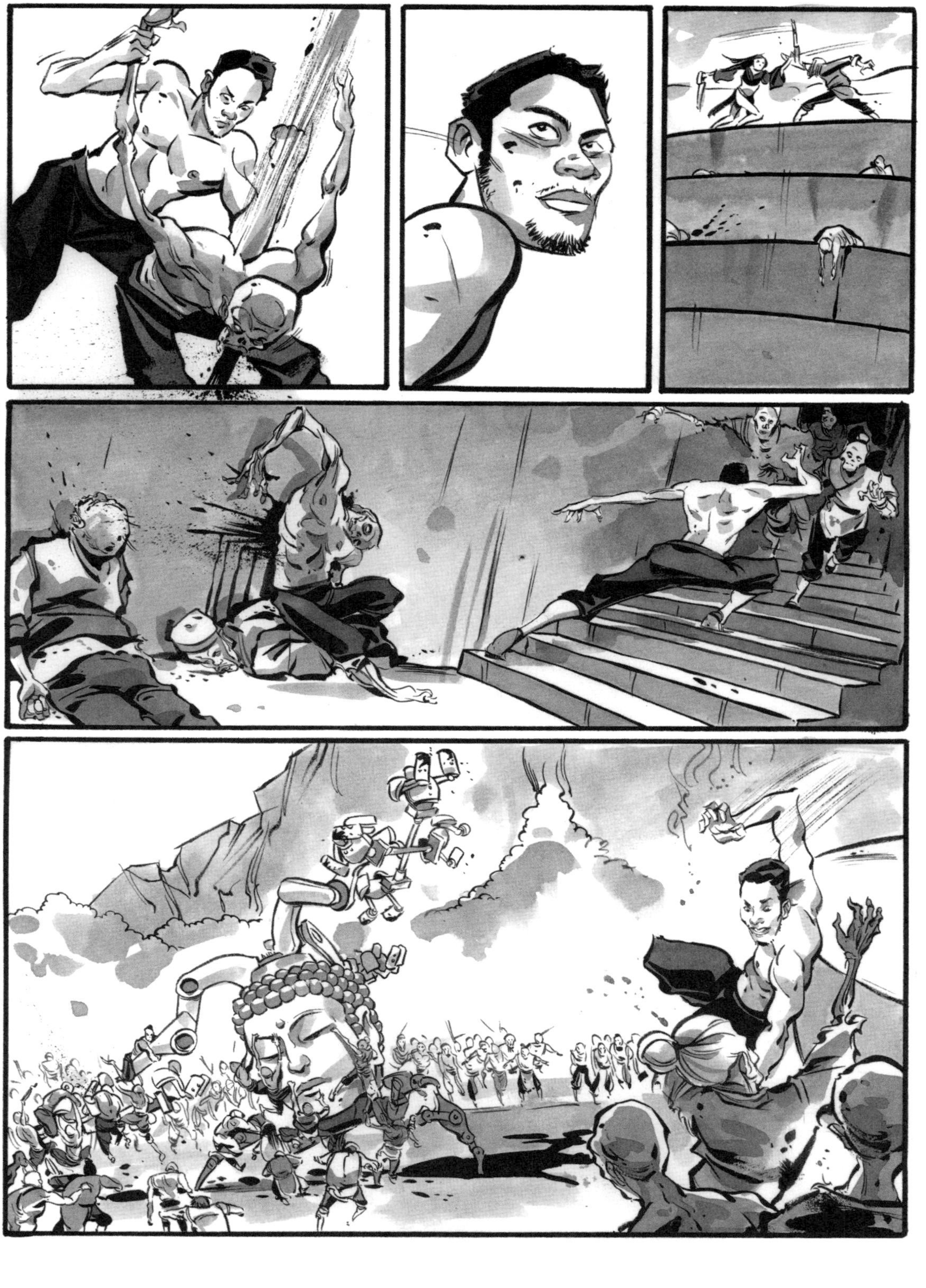

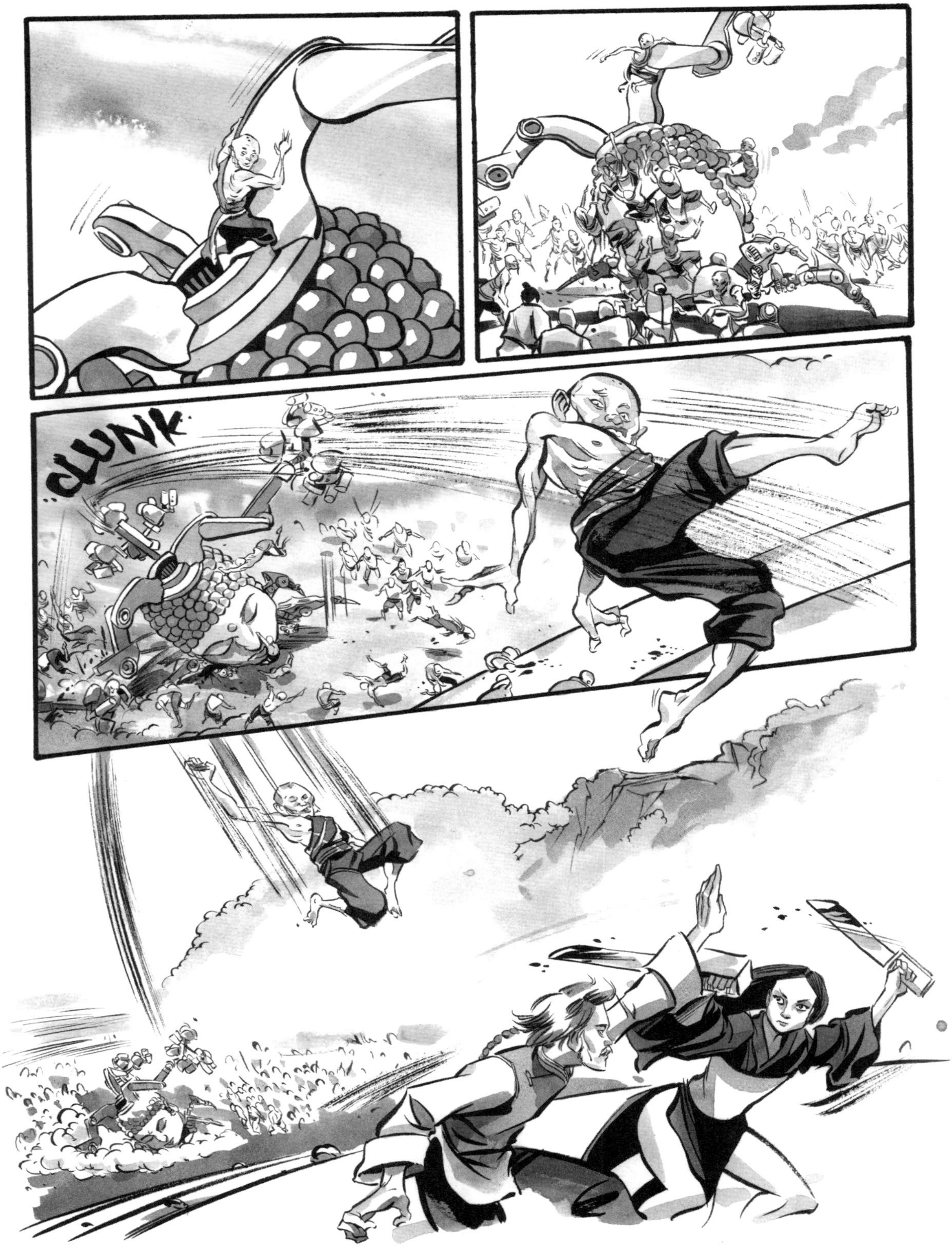
CLUNK

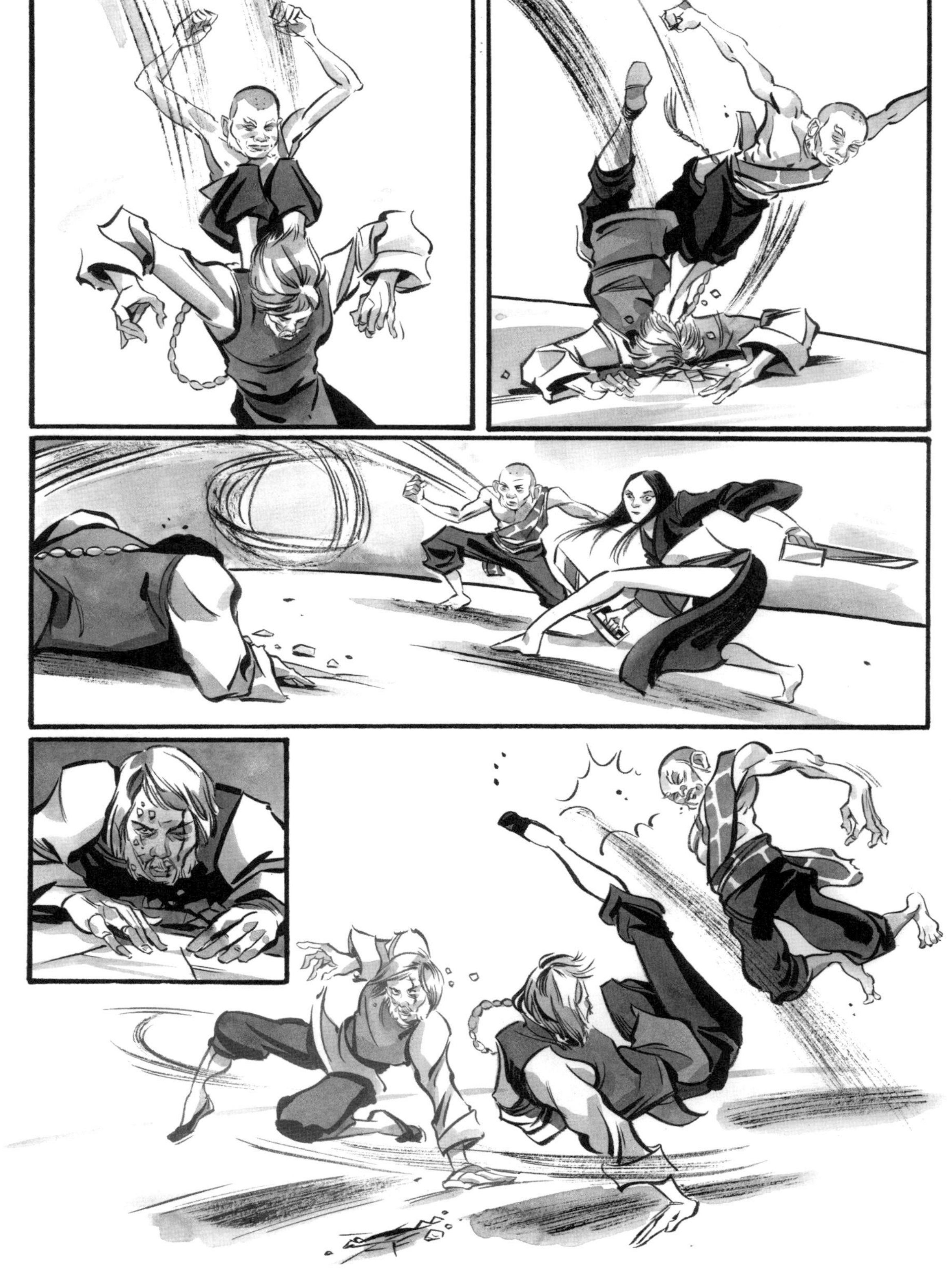

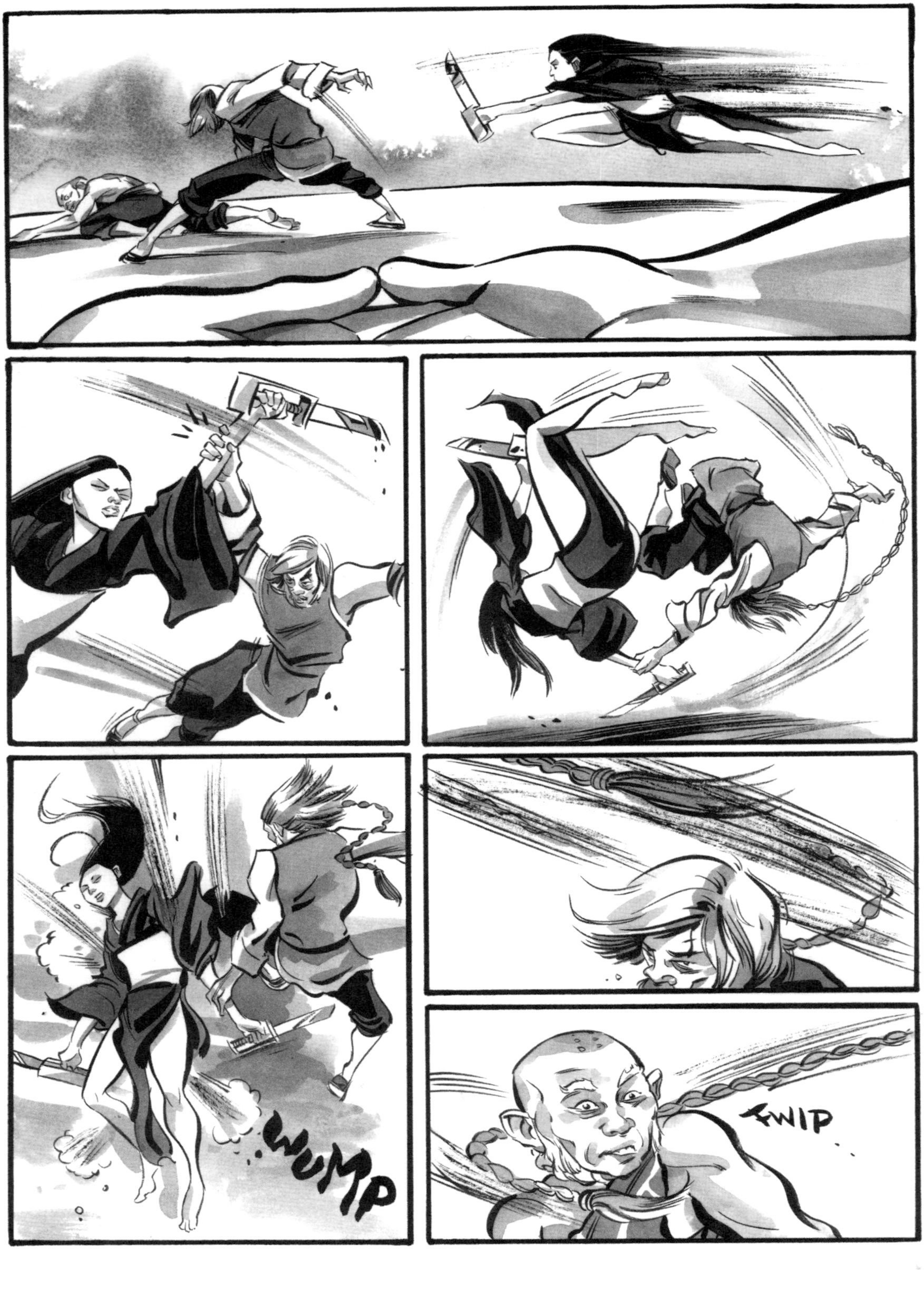
WUMP
FWIP

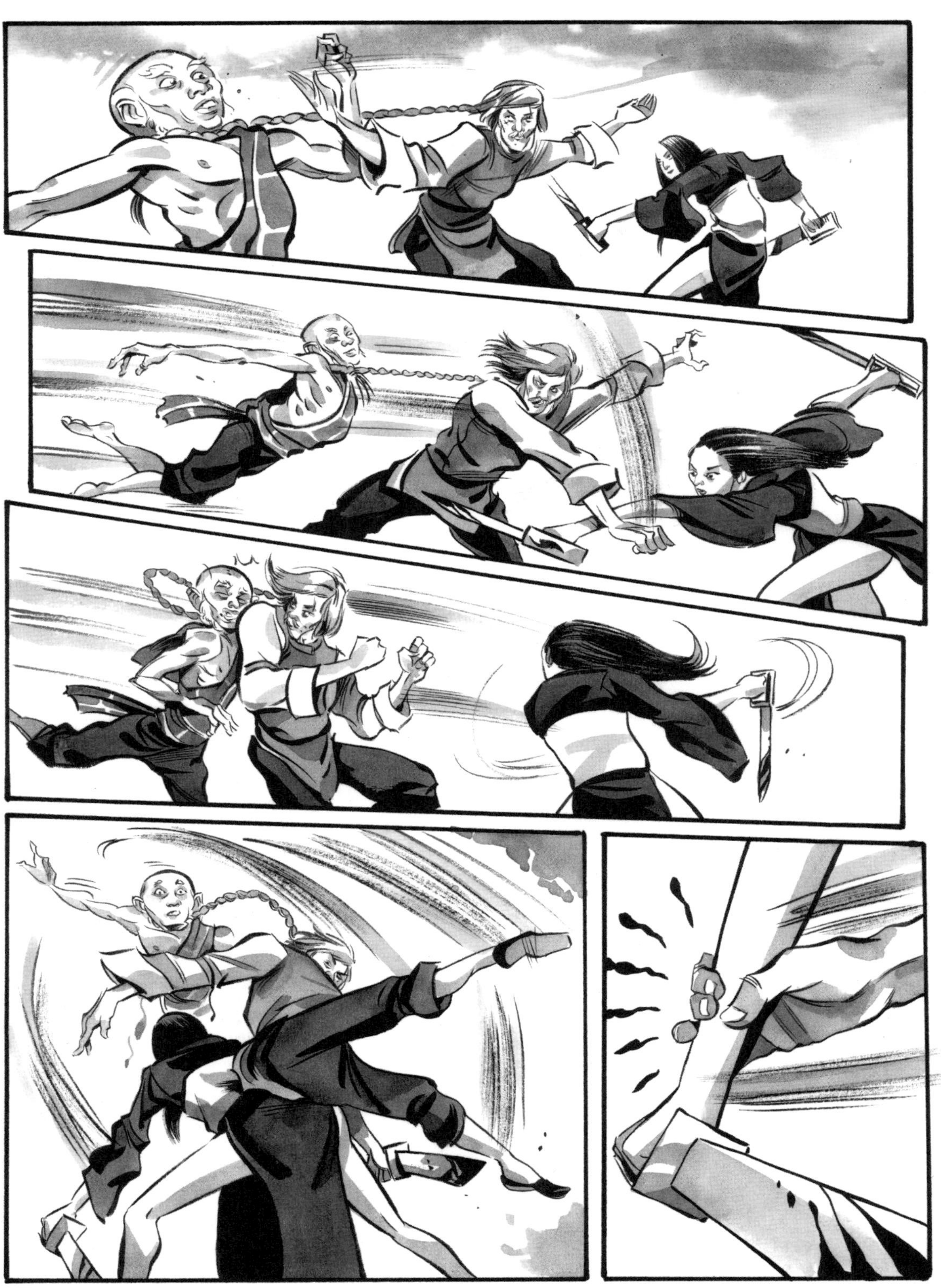

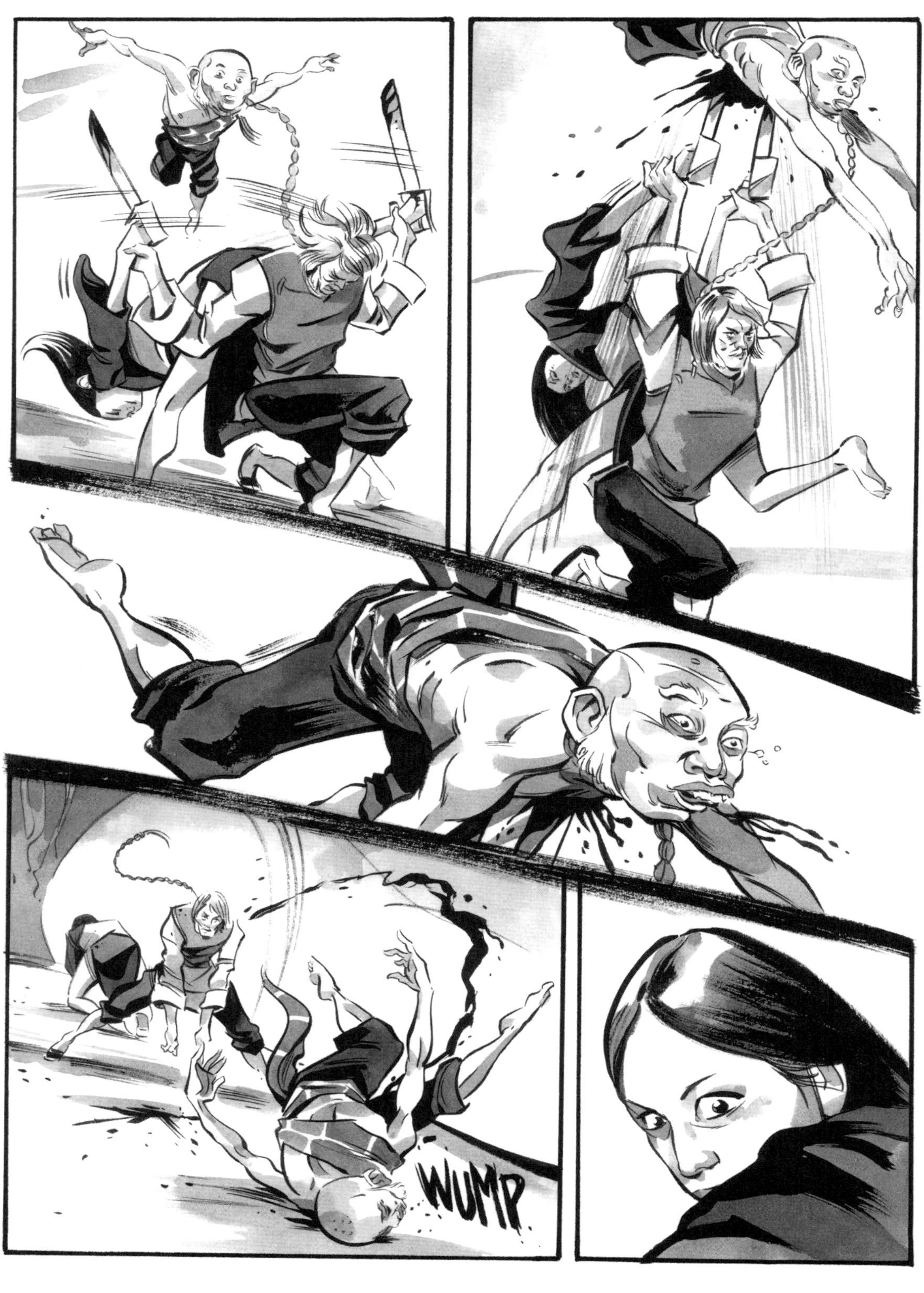
WUMP

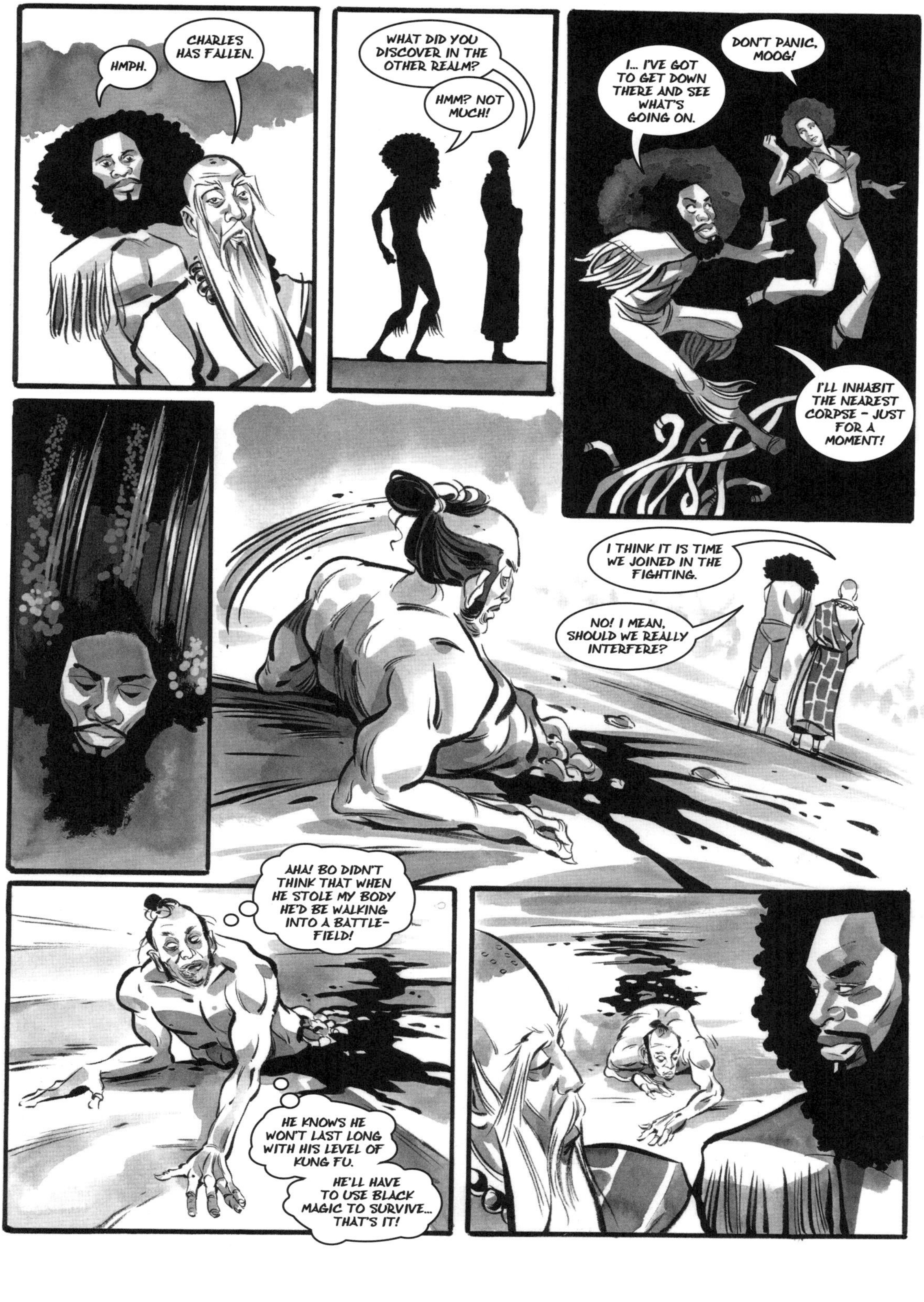
CHARLES HAS FALLEN.
HMPH.
WHAT DID YOU DISCOVER IN THE OTHER REALM?
HMM? NOT MUCH!
DON'T PANIC, MOOG!
I... I'VE GOT TO GET DOWN THERE AND SEE WHAT'S GOING ON.
I'LL INHABIT THE NEAREST CORPSE - JUST FOR A MOMENT!
I THINK IT IS TIME WE JOINED IN THE FIGHTING.
NO! I MEAN, SHOULD WE REALLY INTERFERE?
AHA! BO DIDN'T THINK THAT WHEN HE STOLE MY BODY HE'D BE WALKING INTO A BATTLE-FIELD!
HE KNOWS HE WON'T LAST LONG WITH HIS LEVEL OF KUNG FU.
HE'LL HAVE TO USE BLACK MAGIC TO SURVIVE... THAT'S IT!

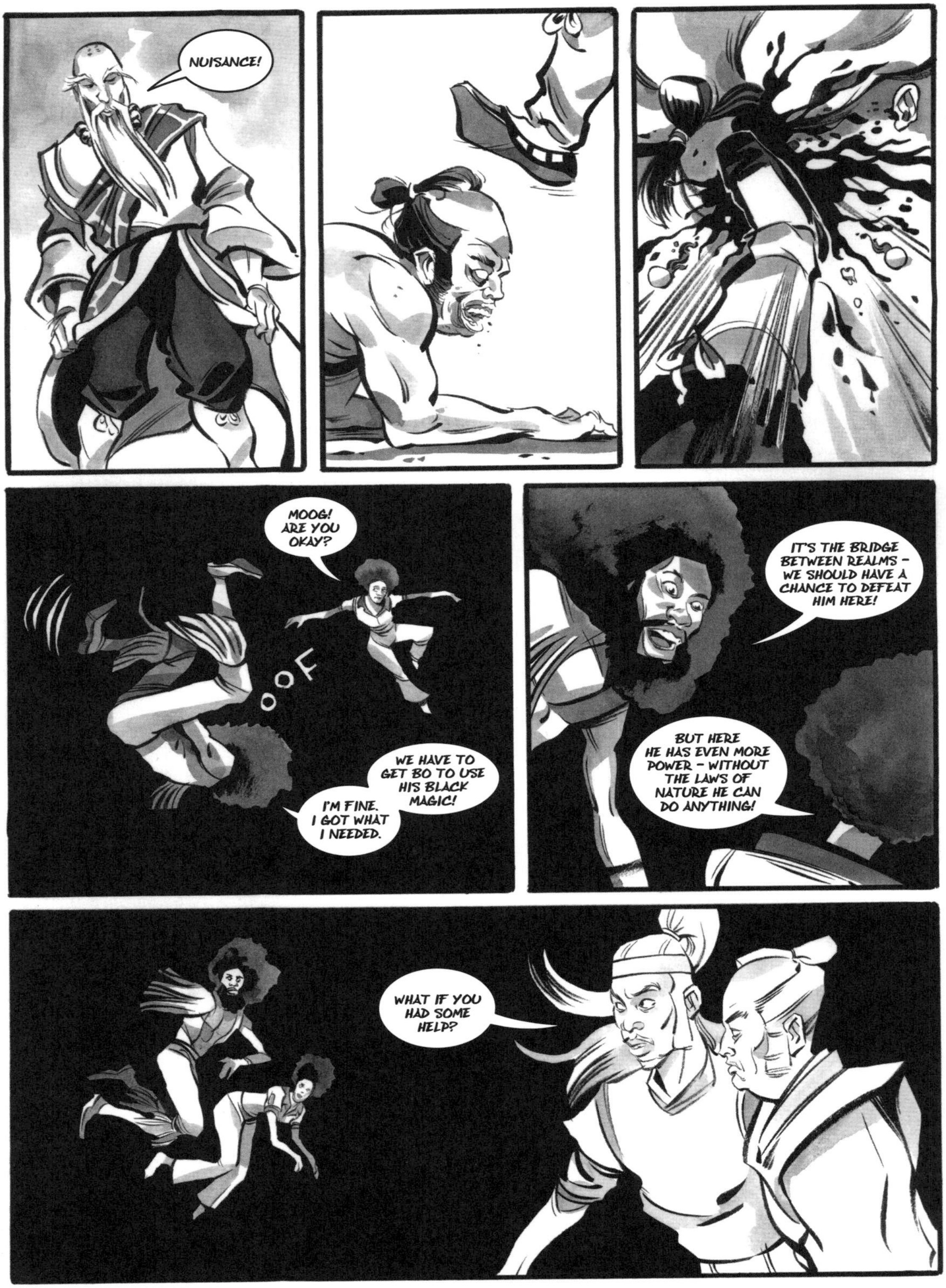
NUISANCE!
MOOG! ARE YOU OKAY?
OOF
WE HAVE TO GET BO TO USE HIS BLACK MAGIC!
I'M FINE. I GOT WHAT I NEEDED.
IT'S THE BRIDGE BETWEEN REALMS - WE SHOULD HAVE A CHANCE TO DEFEAT HIM HERE!
BUT HERE HE HAS EVEN MORE POWER - WITHOUT THE LAWS OF NATURE HE CAN DO ANYTHING!
WHAT IF YOU HAD SOME HELP?

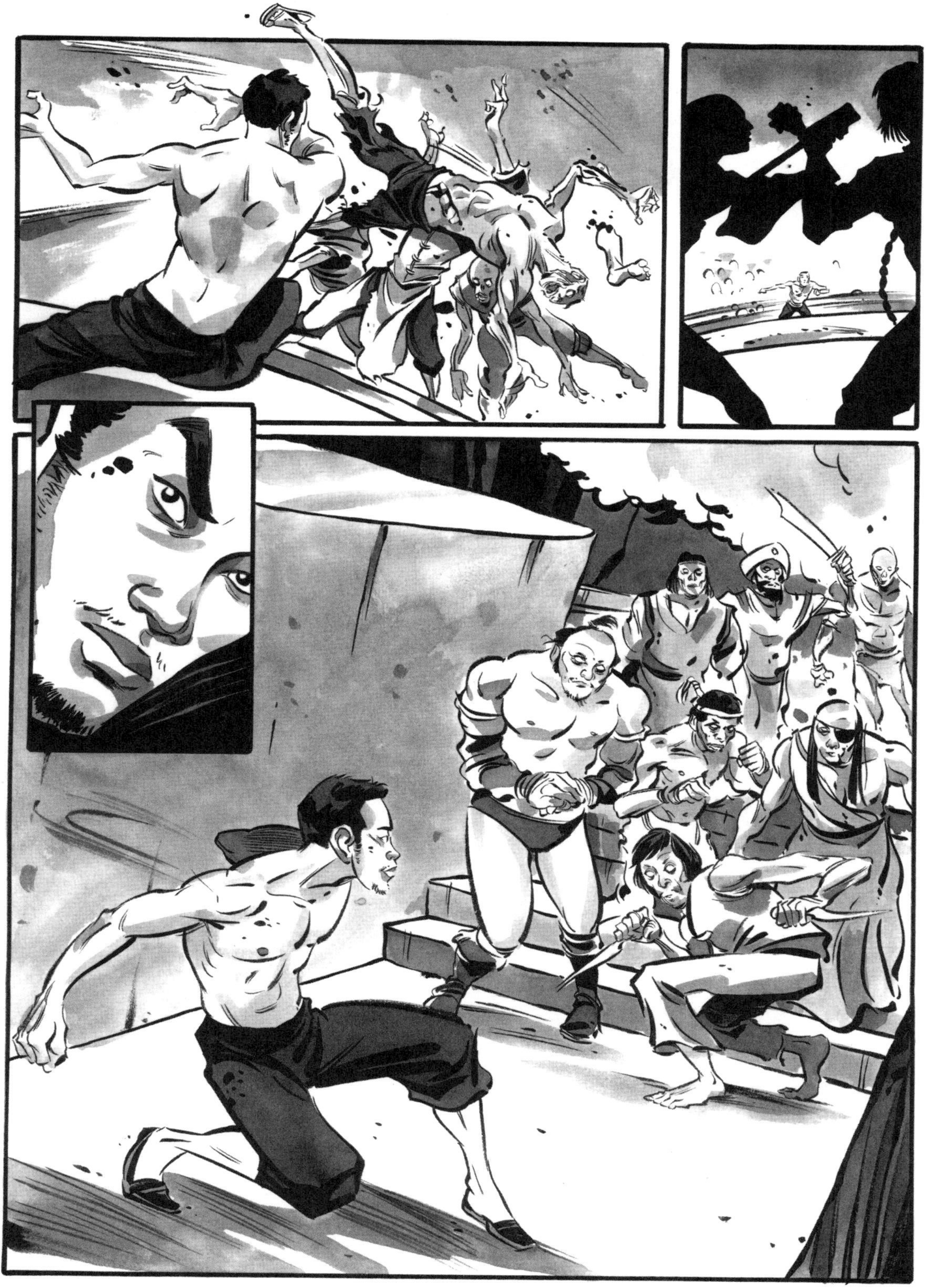

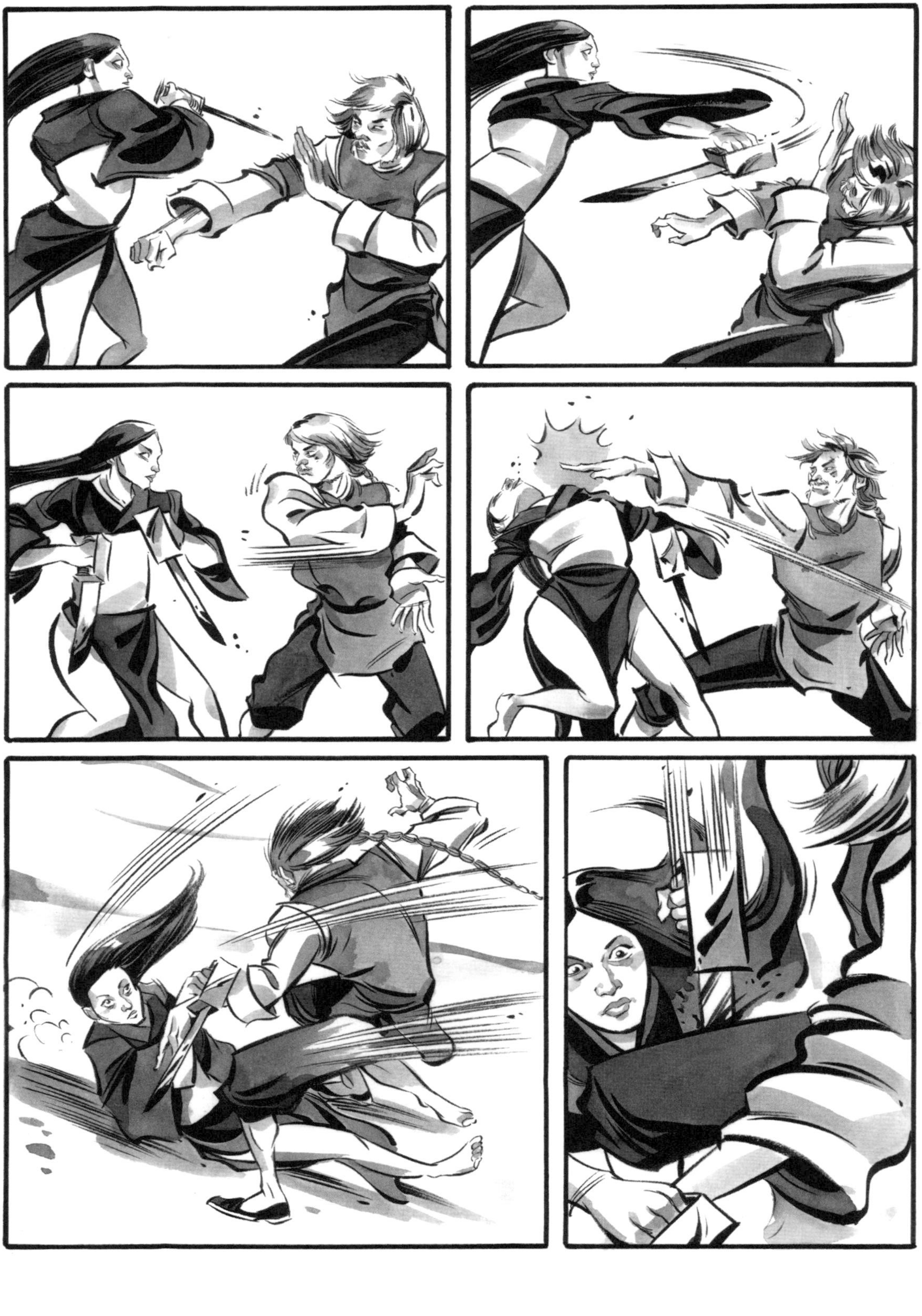

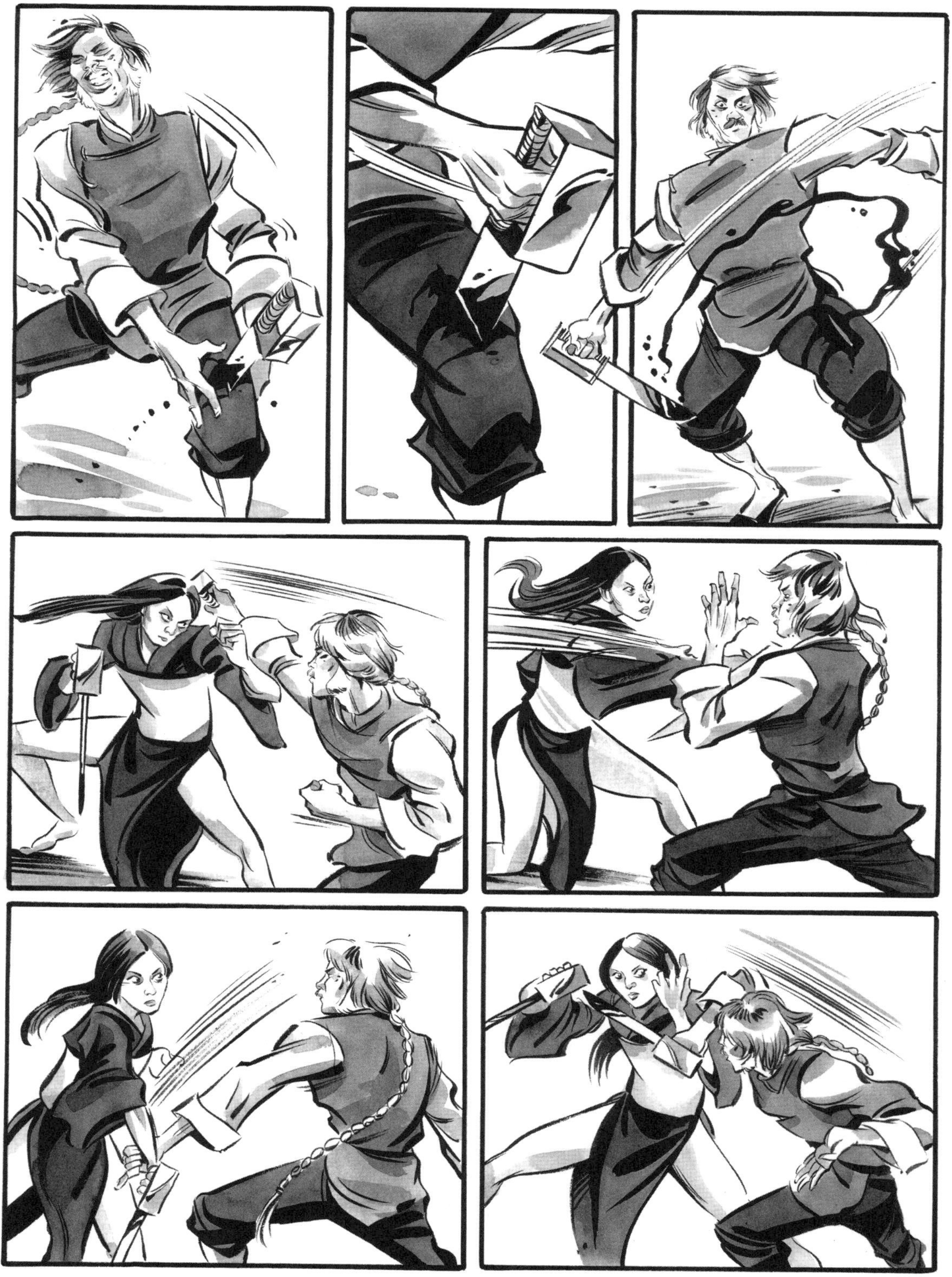

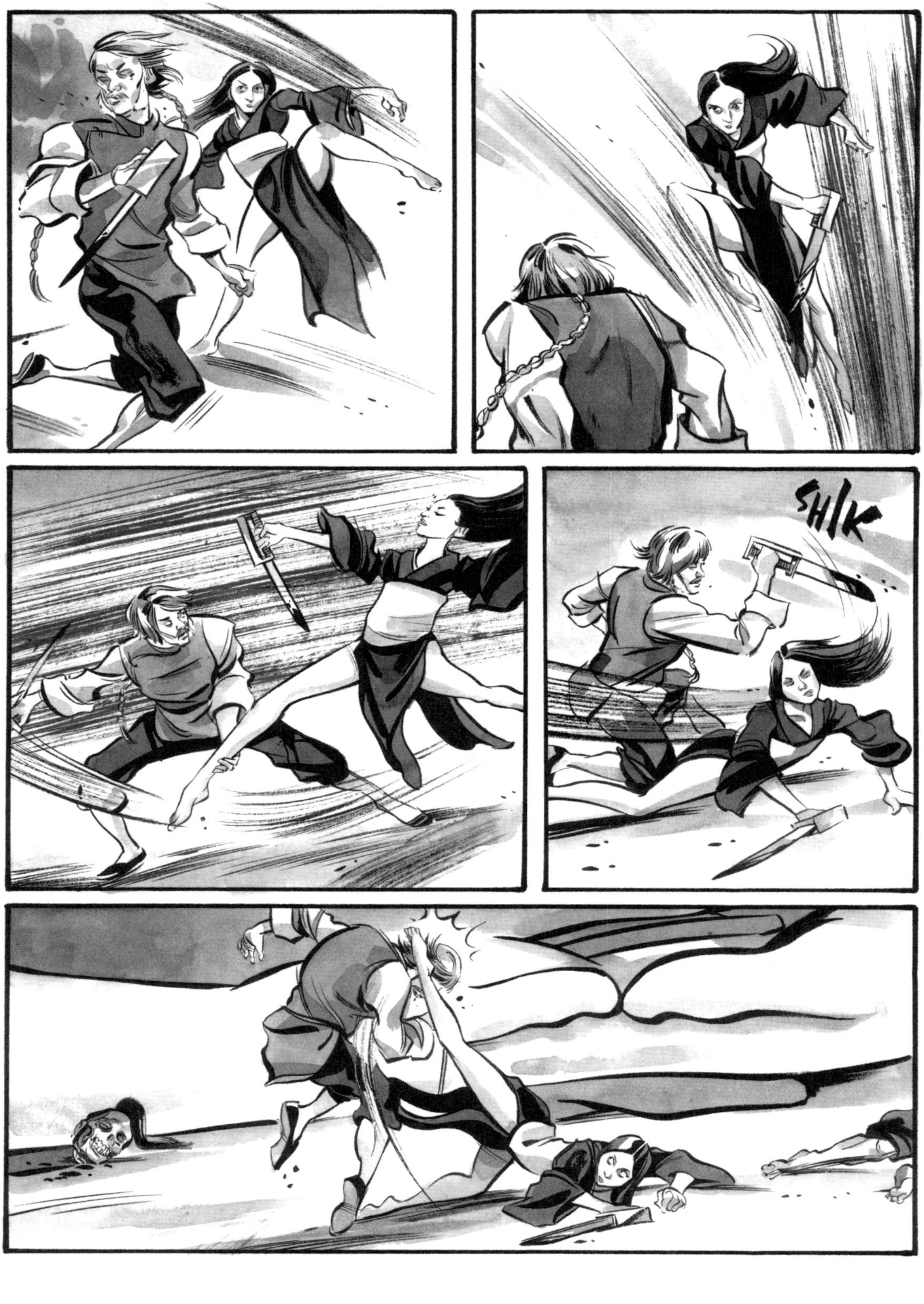
SHIK

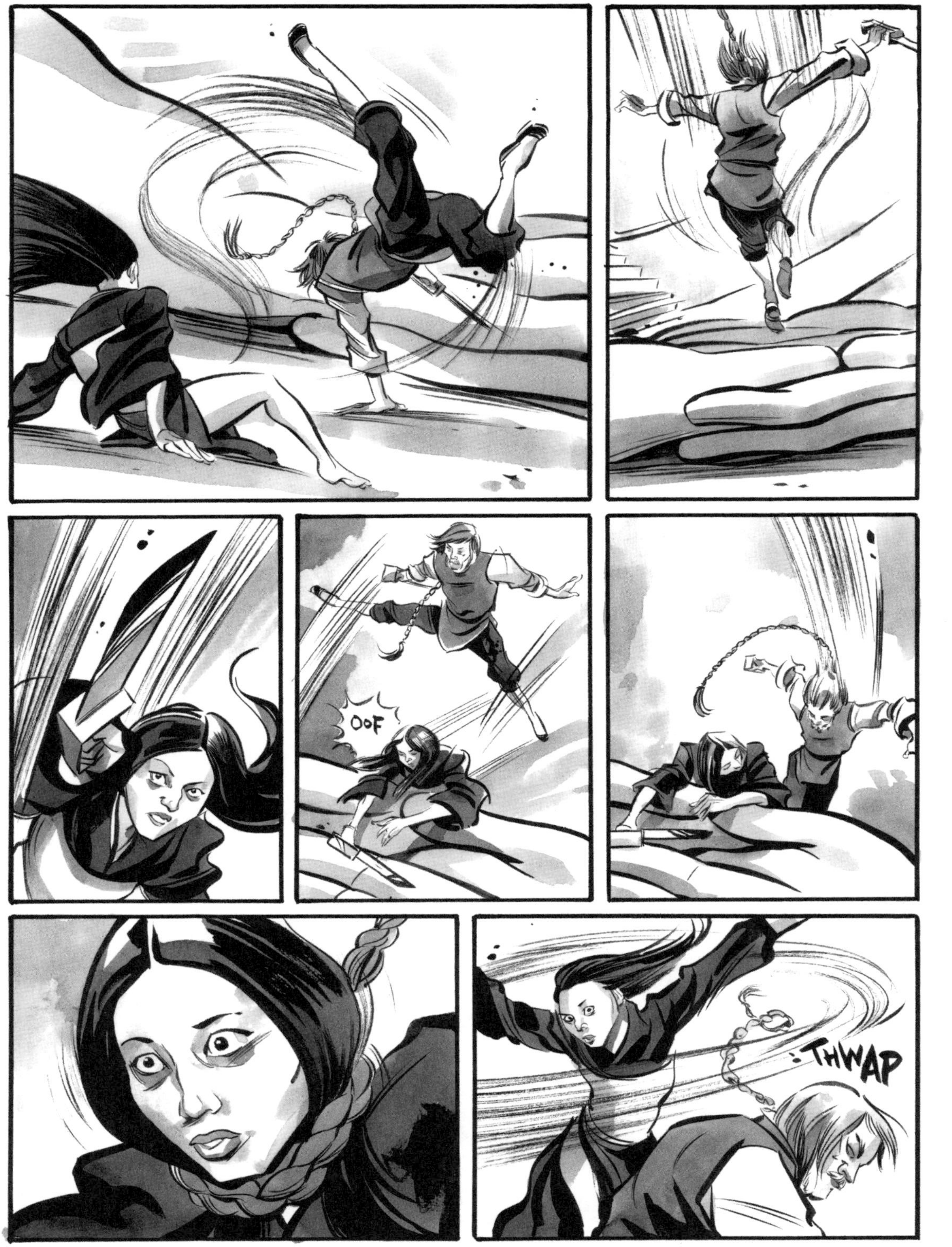
OOF
THWAP

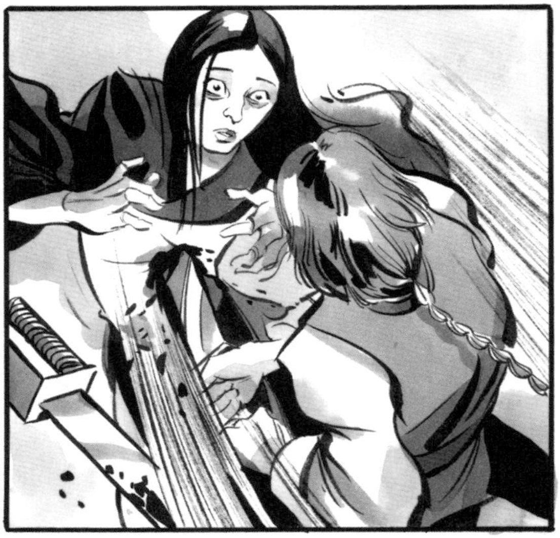

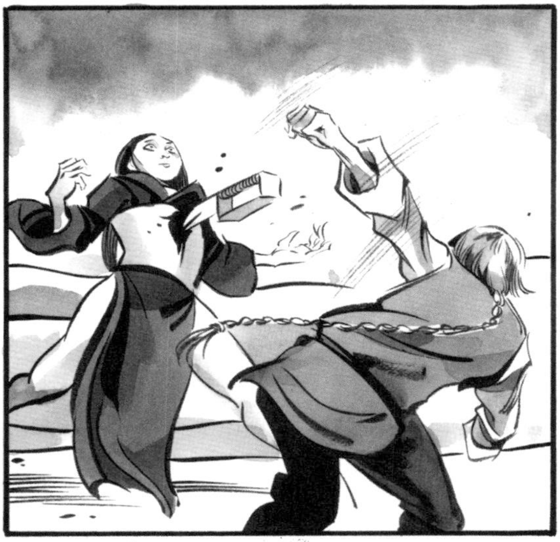

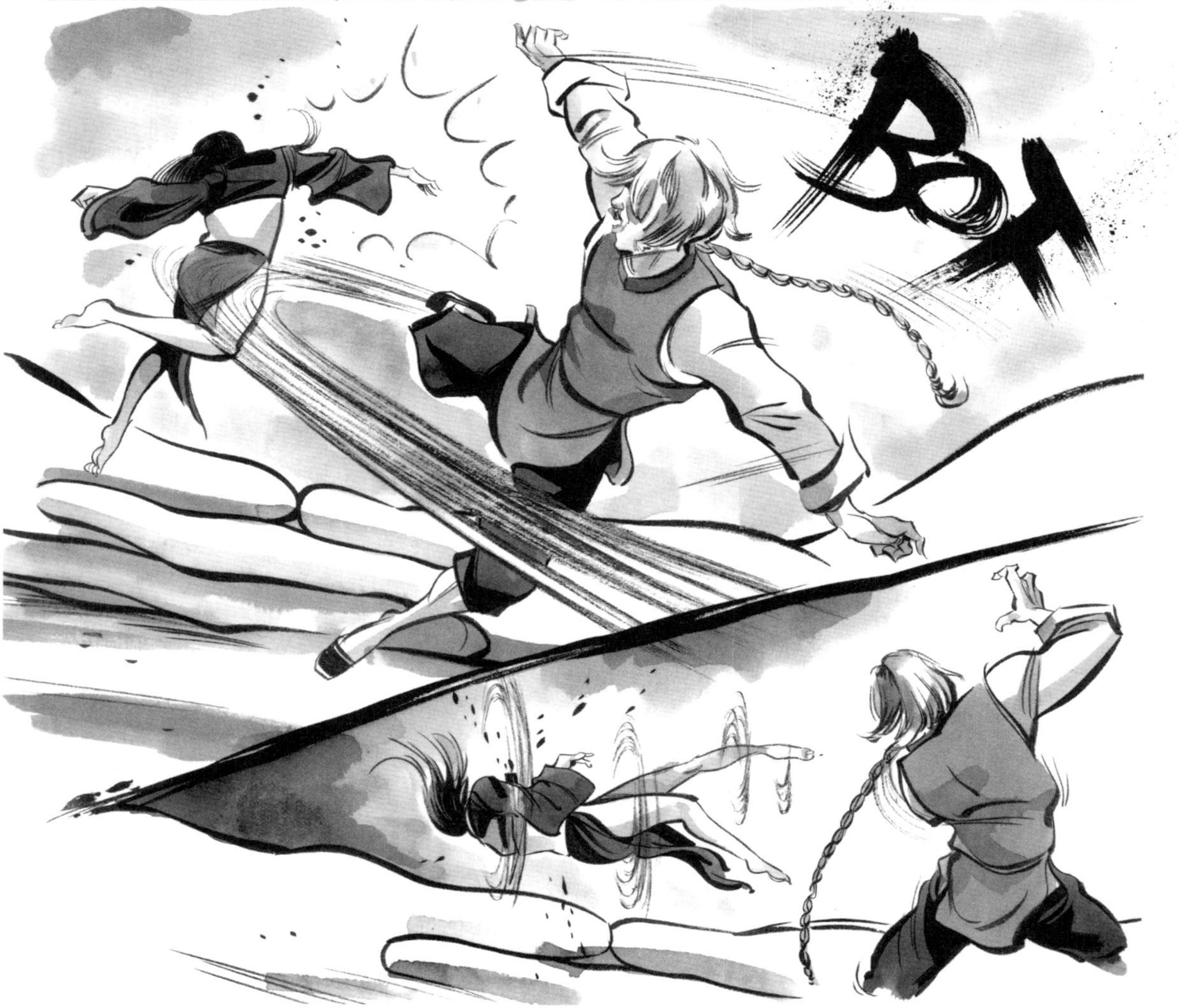

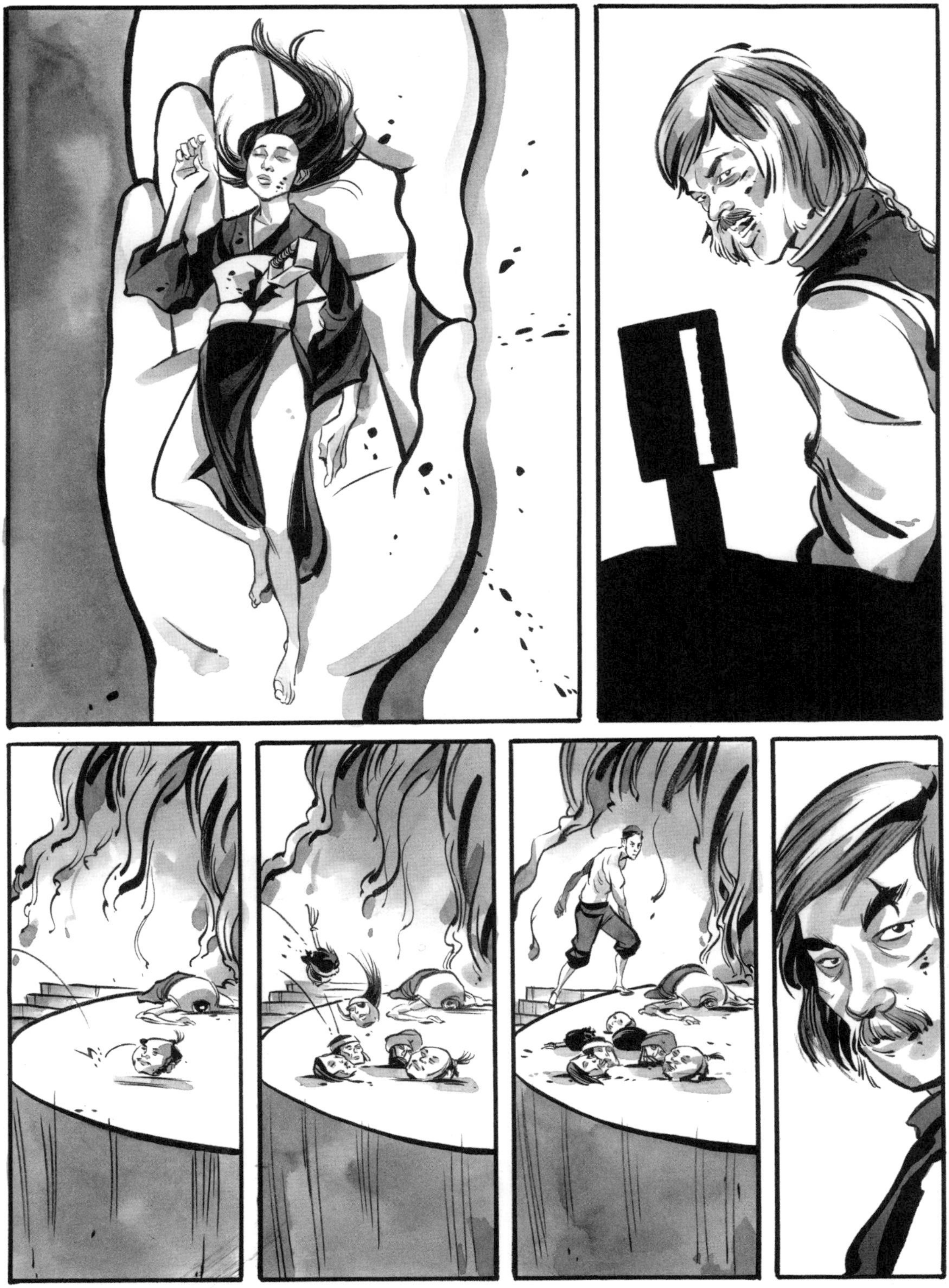

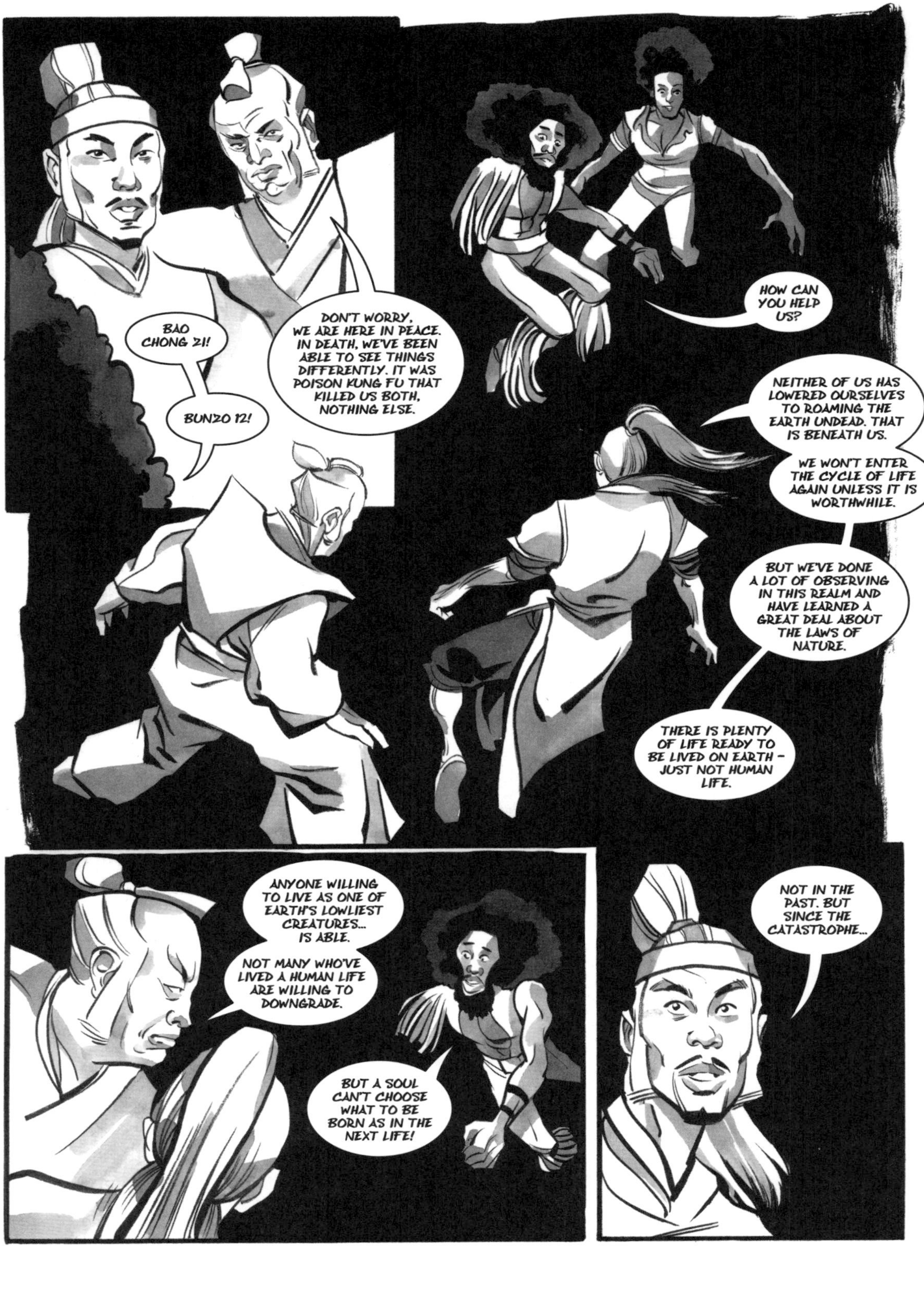
BAO CHONG ZI!
BUNZO 12!
DON'T WORRY, WE ARE HERE IN PEACE. IN DEATH, WE'VE BEEN ABLE TO SEE THINGS DIFFERENTLY. IT WAS POISON KUNG FU THAT KILLED US BOTH, NOTHING ELSE.
HOW CAN YOU HELP US?
NEITHER OF US HAS LOWERED OURSELVES TO ROAMING THE EARTH UNDEAD. THAT IS BENEATH US.
WE WON'T ENTER THE CYCLE OF LIFE AGAIN UNLESS IT IS WORTHWHILE.
BUT WE'VE DONE A LOT OF OBSERVING IN THIS REALM AND HAVE LEARNED A GREAT DEAL ABOUT THE LAWS OF NATURE.
THERE IS PLENTY OF LIFE READY TO BE LIVED ON EARTH - JUST NOT HUMAN LIFE.
ANYONE WILLING TO LIVE AS ONE OF EARTH'S LOWLIEST CREATURES... IS ABLE.
NOT MANY WHO'VE LIVED A HUMAN LIFE ARE WILLING TO DOWNGRADE.
BUT A SOUL CAN'T CHOOSE WHAT TO BE BORN AS IN THE NEXT LIFE!
NOT IN THE PAST. BUT SINCE THE CATASTROPHE...

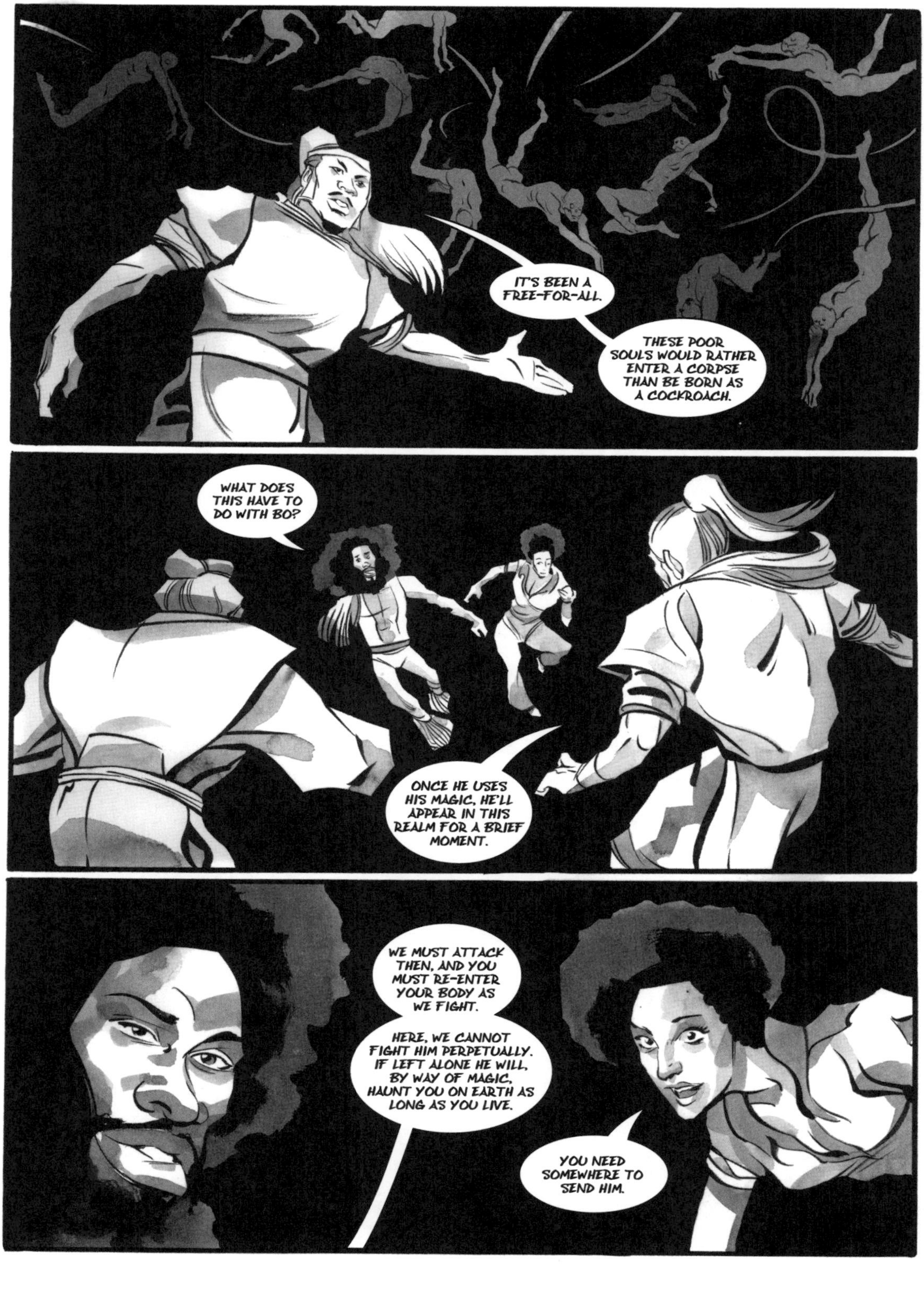
IT'S BEEN A FREE-FOR-ALL.
THESE POOR SOULS WOULD RATHER ENTER A CORPSE THAN BE BORN AS A COCKROACH.
WHAT DOES THIS HAVE TO DO WITH BO?
ONCE HE USES HIS MAGIC, HE'LL APPEAR IN THIS REALM FOR A BRIEF MOMENT.
WE MUST ATTACK THEN, AND YOU MUST RE-ENTER YOUR BODY AS WE FIGHT.
HERE, WE CANNOT FIGHT HIM PERPETUALLY. IF LEFT ALONE HE WILL, BY WAY OF MAGIC, HAUNT YOU ON EARTH AS LONG AS YOU LIVE.
YOU NEED SOMEWHERE TO SEND HIM.

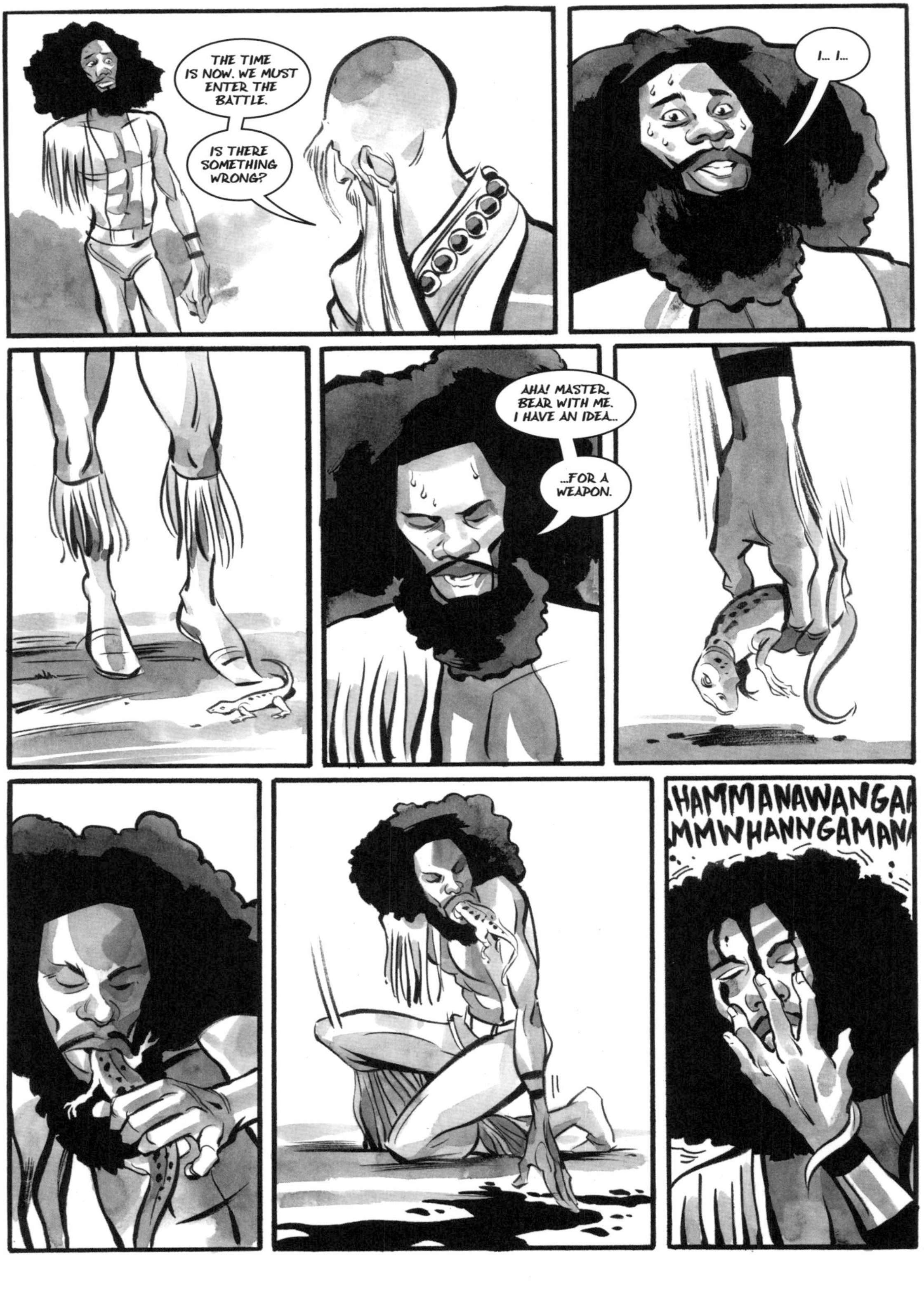
THE TIME IS NOW. WE MUST ENTER THE BATTLE.
IS THERE SOMETHING WRONG?
I... I...
AHA! MASTER. BEAR WITH ME. I HAVE AN IDEA...
...FOR A WEAPON.
HAMMANAWANGA
MMWHANNGAMANA

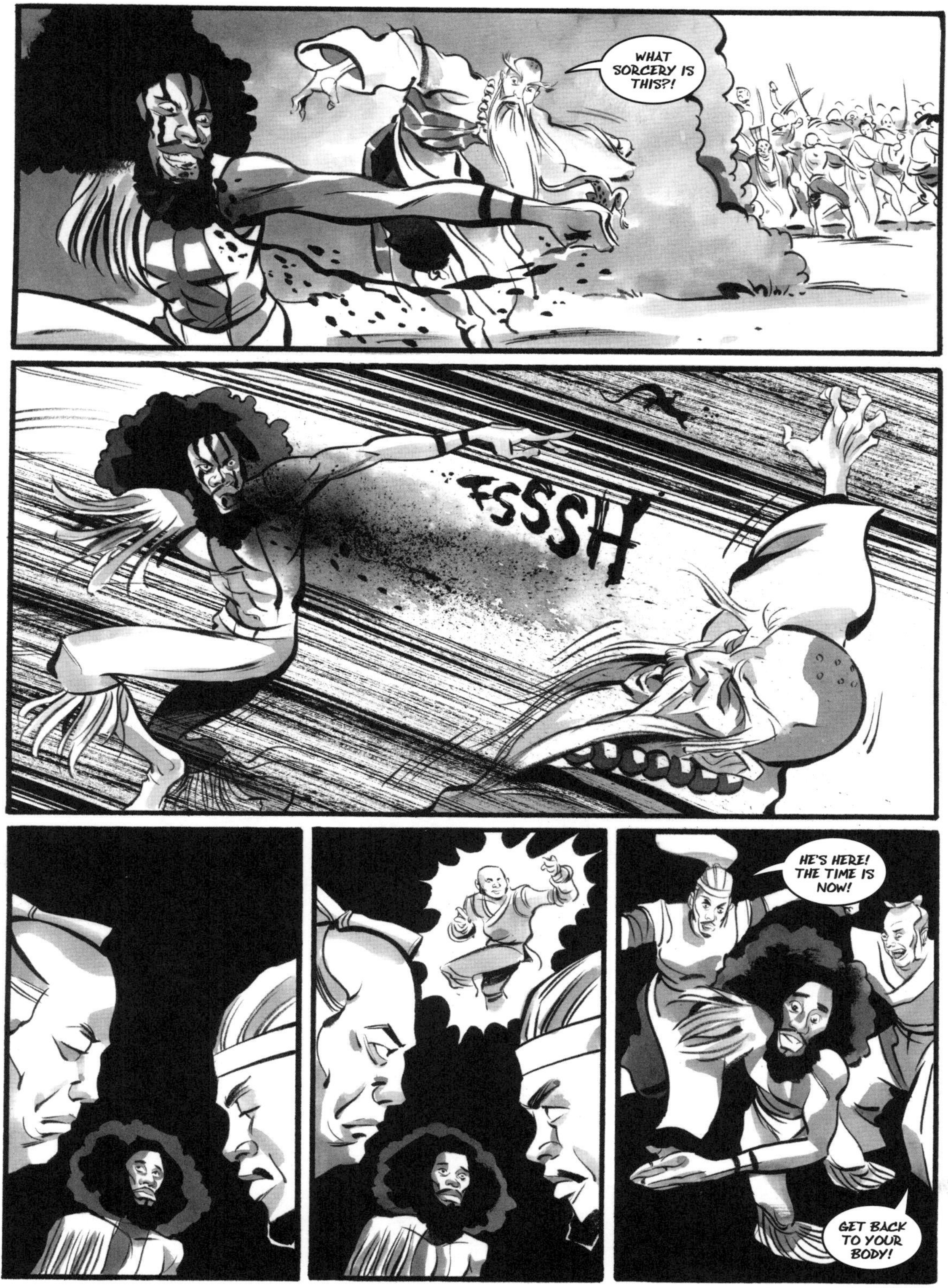
WHAT SORCERY IS THIS?!
FSSSH
HE'S HERE! THE TIME IS NOW!
GET BACK TO YOUR BODY!

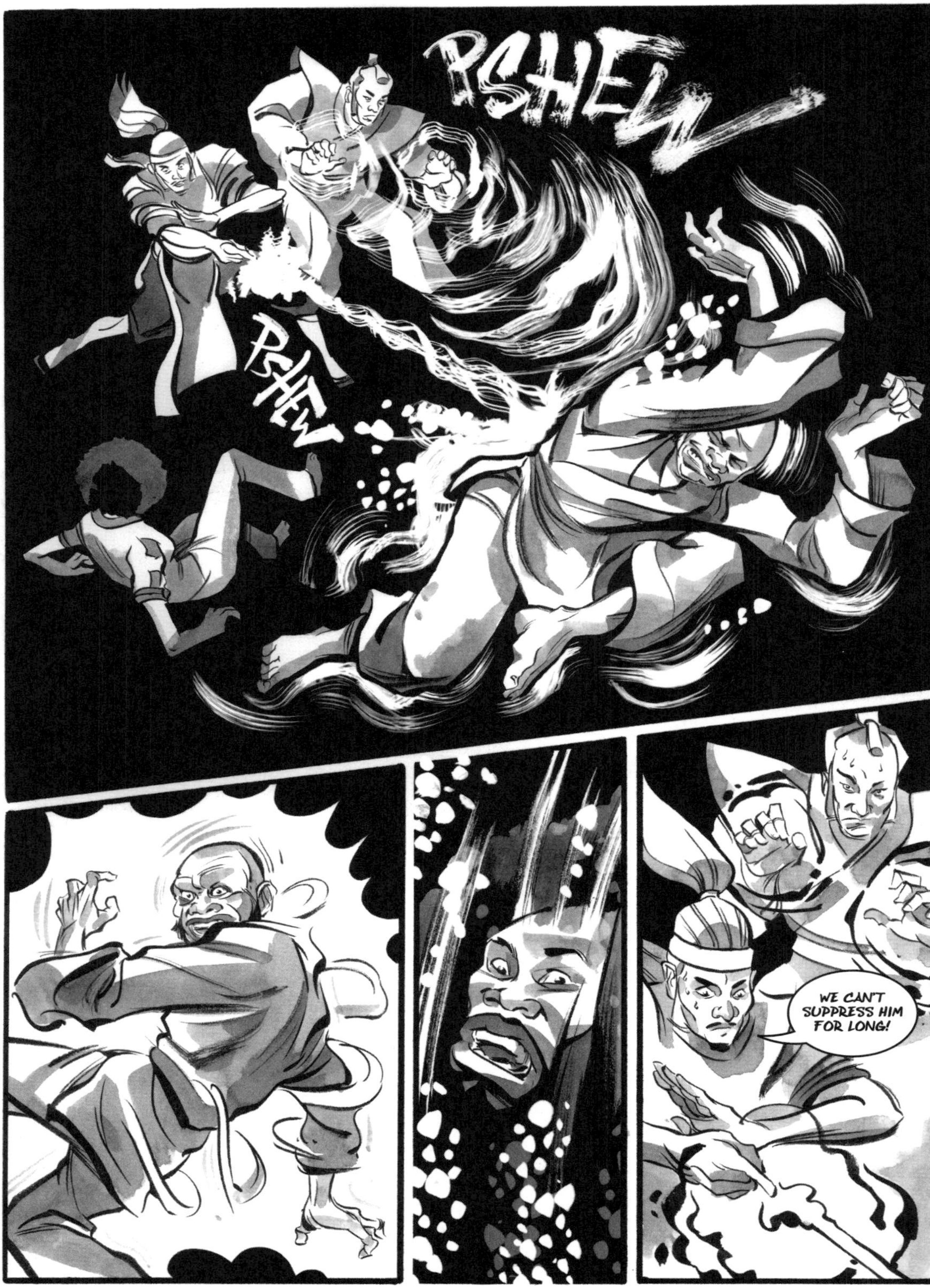
PSHEW
PSHEW
WE CAN'T SUPPRESS HIM FOR LONG!

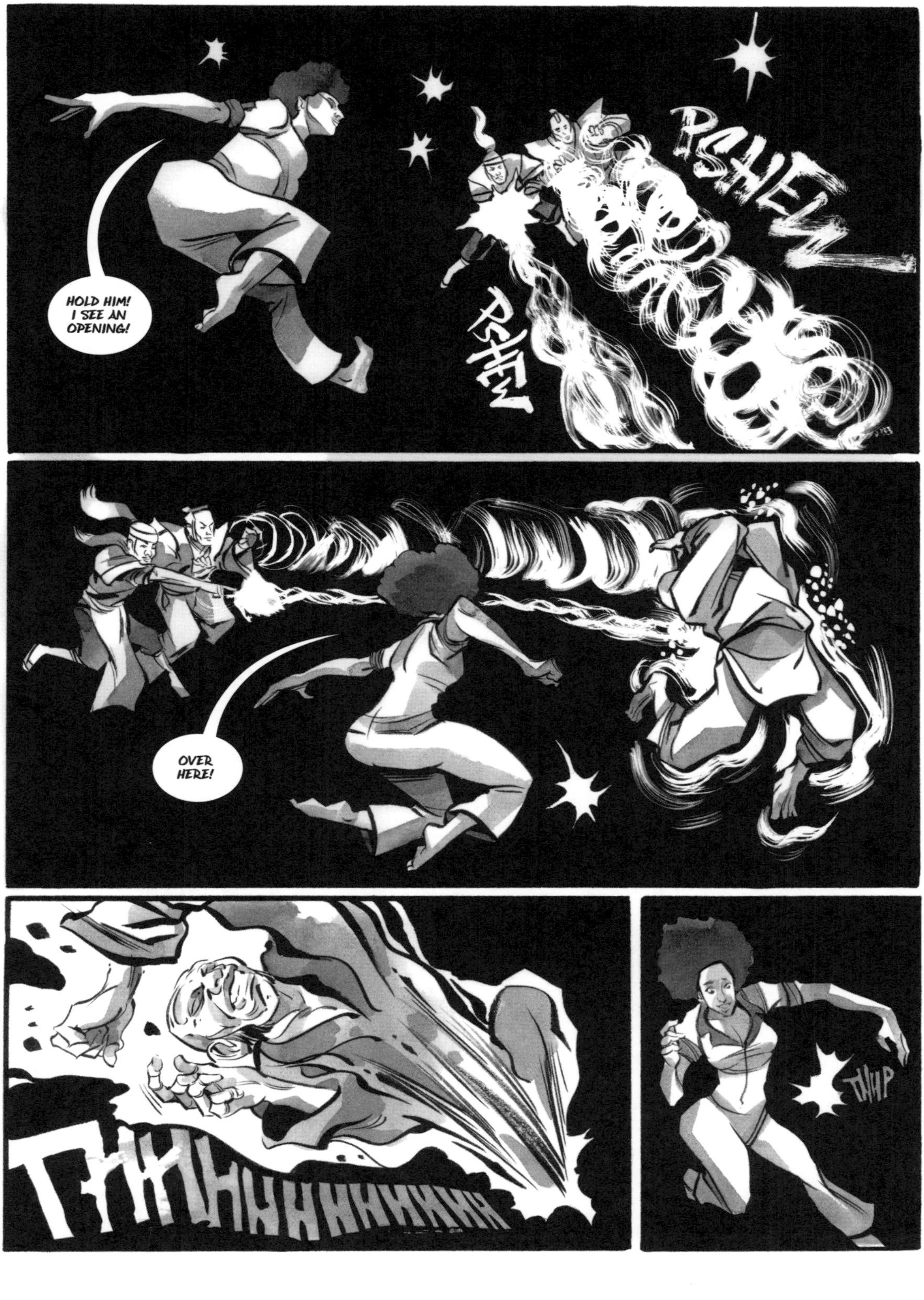
HOLD HIM! I SEE AN OPENING!
PSHEW
PSHEW
OVER HERE!
THHHHHHHHHHHH
THHP

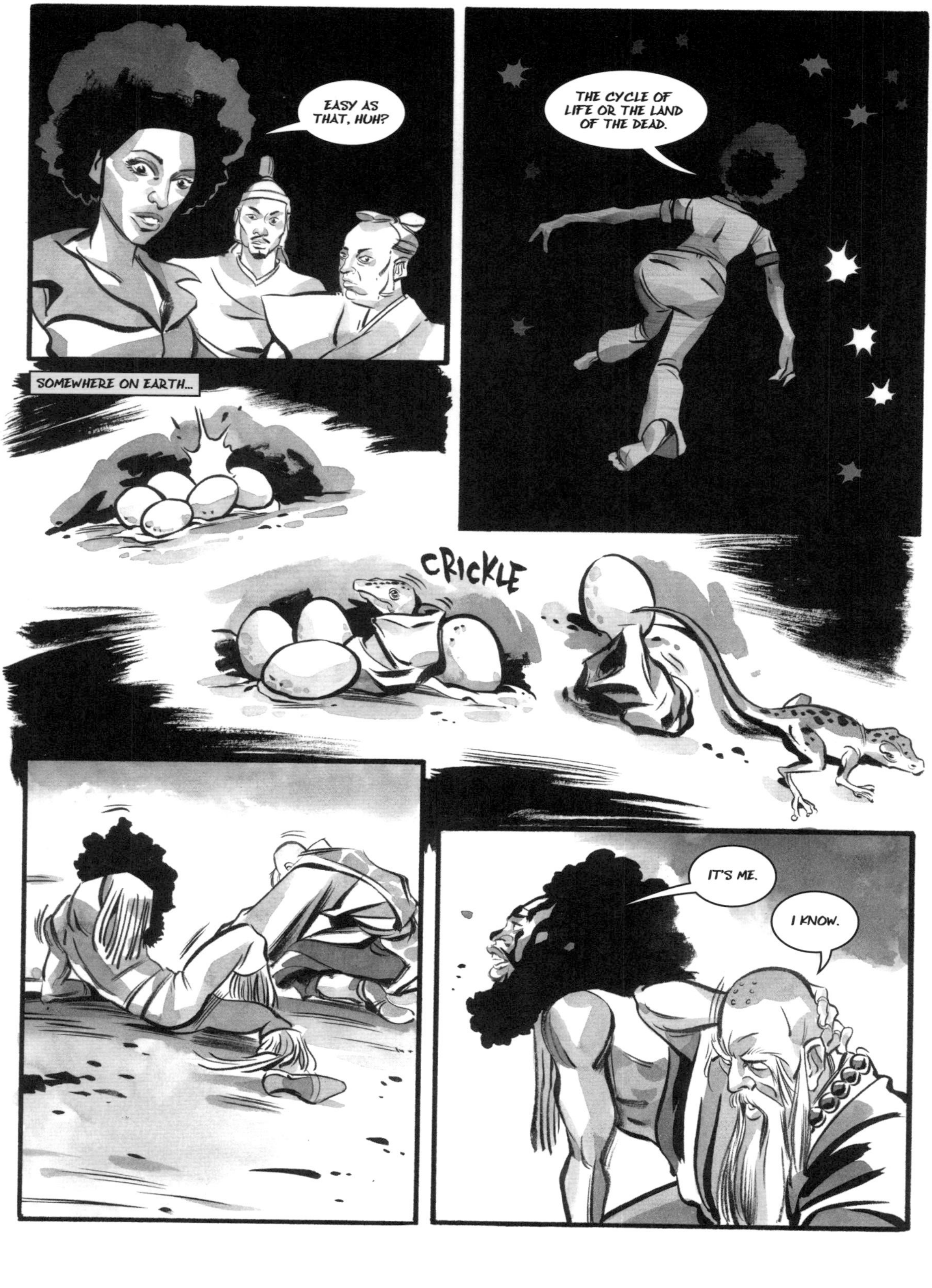
EASY AS THAT, HUH?
THE CYCLE OF LIFE OR THE LAND OF THE DEAD.
SOMEWHERE ON EARTH...
CRICKLE
IT'S ME.
I KNOW.

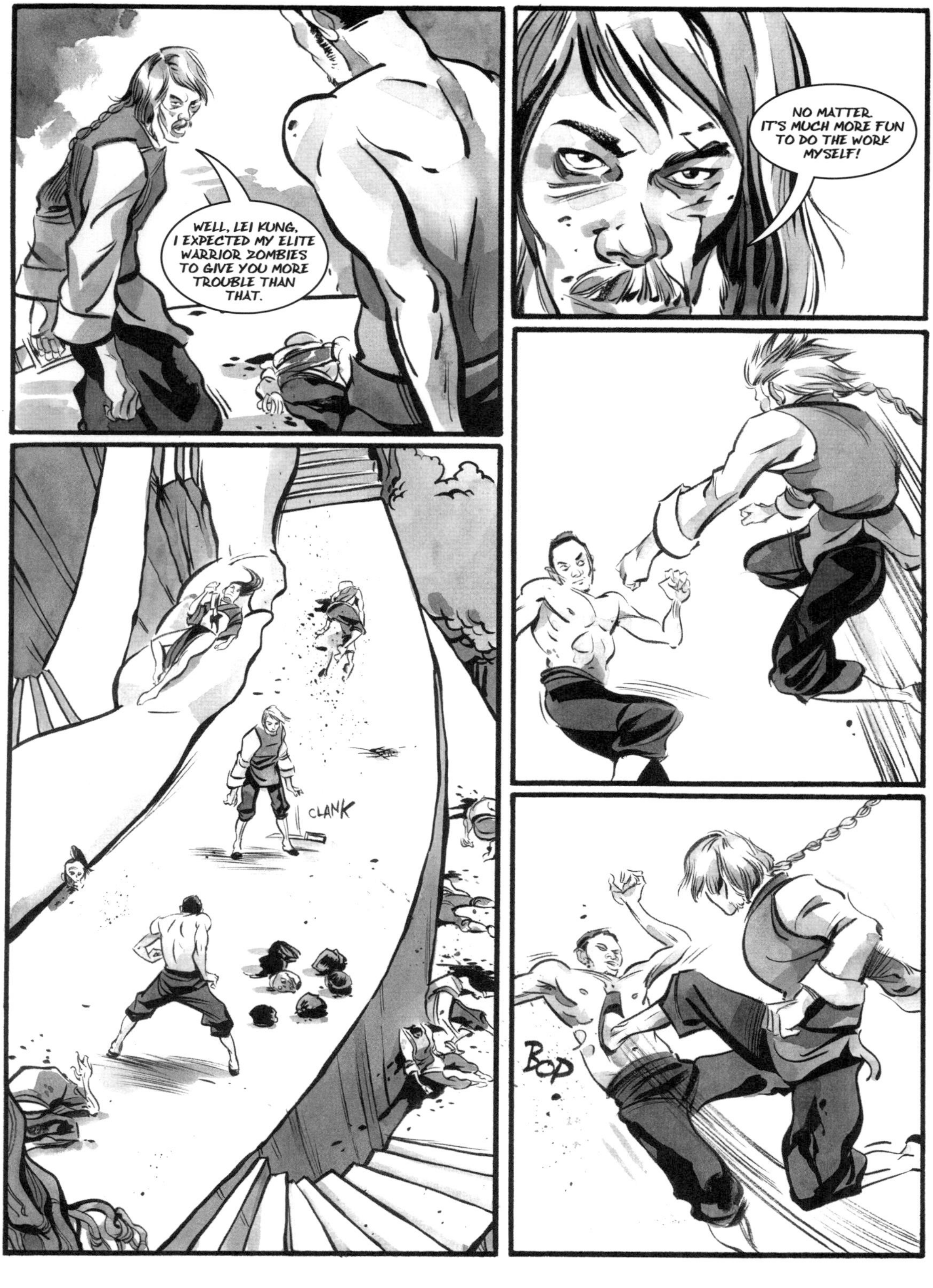
WELL, LEI KUNG, I EXPECTED MY ELITE WARRIOR ZOMBIES TO GIVE YOU MORE TROUBLE THAN THAT.
NO MATTER. IT'S MUCH MORE FUN TO DO THE WORK MYSELF!
CLANK
BOP

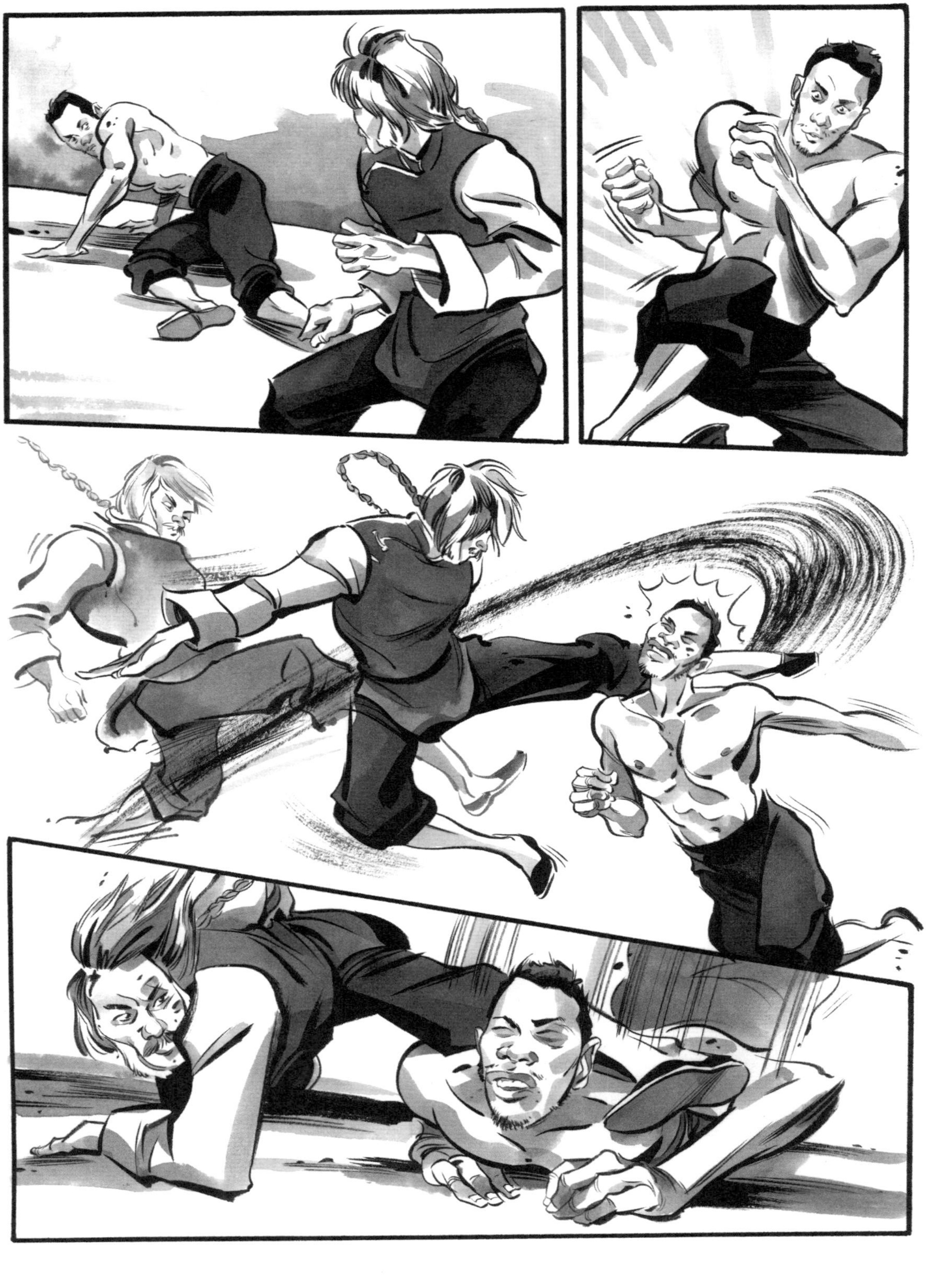

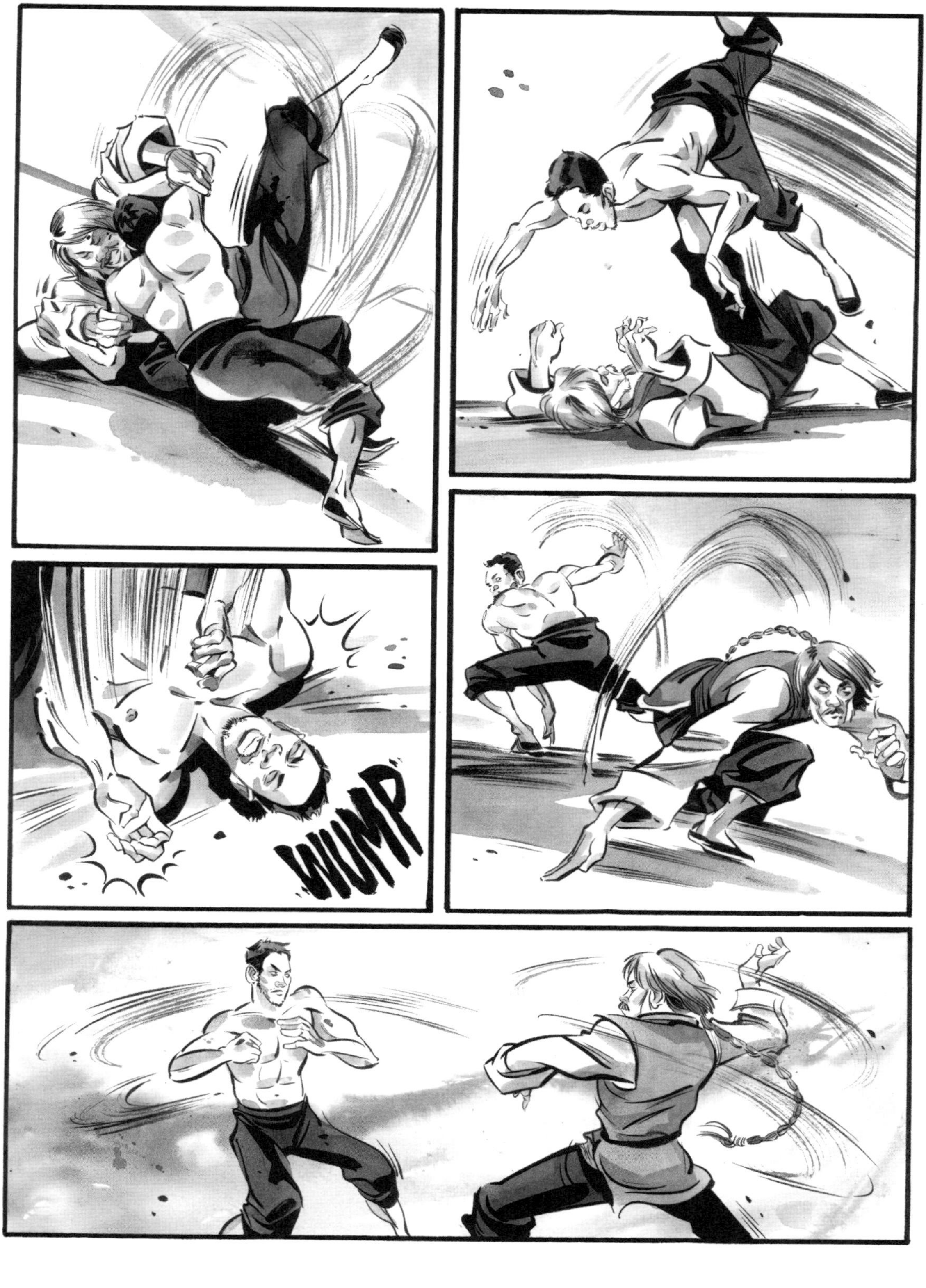
WUMP

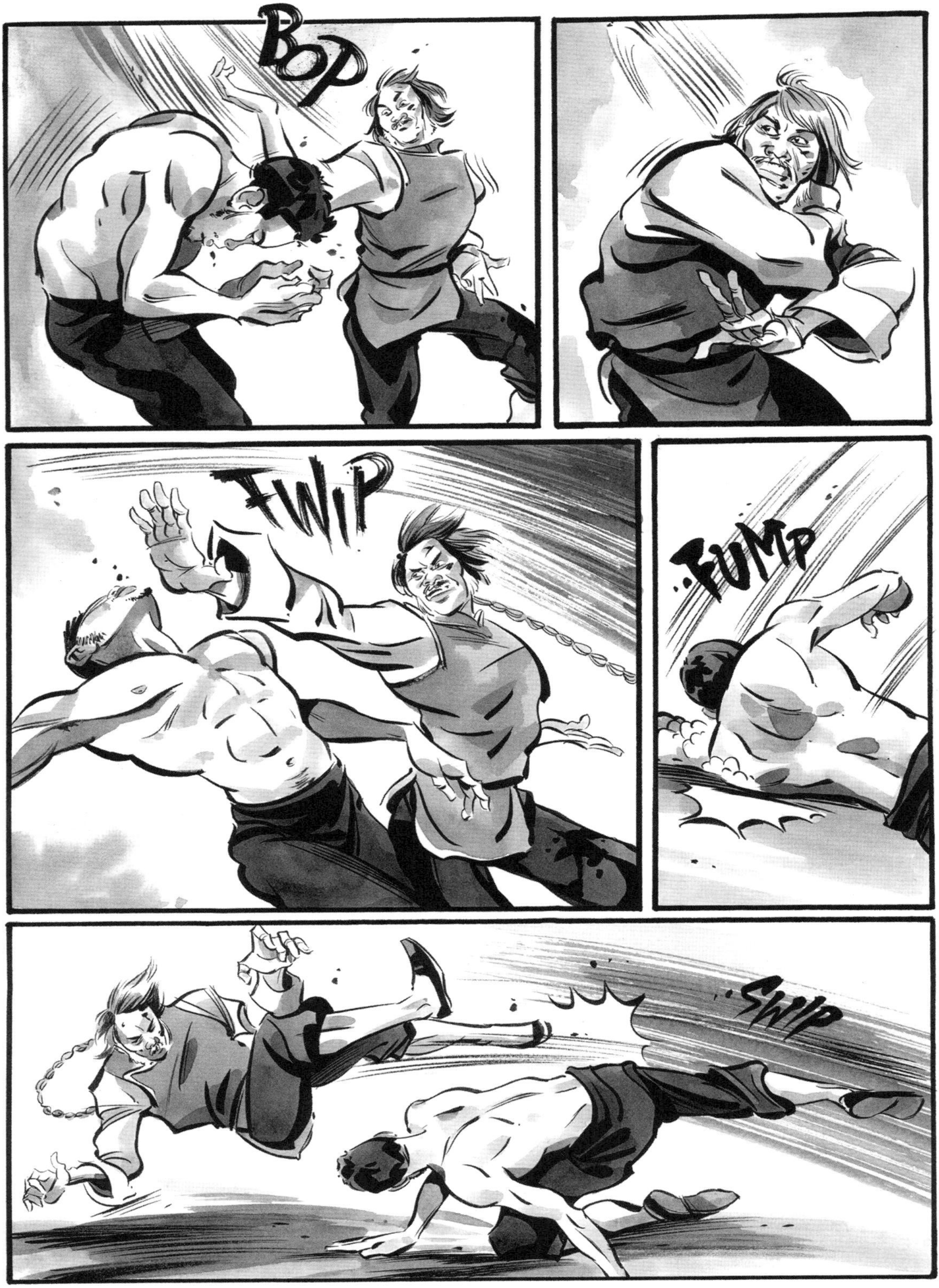
BOP
FWIP
FUMP
SWIP

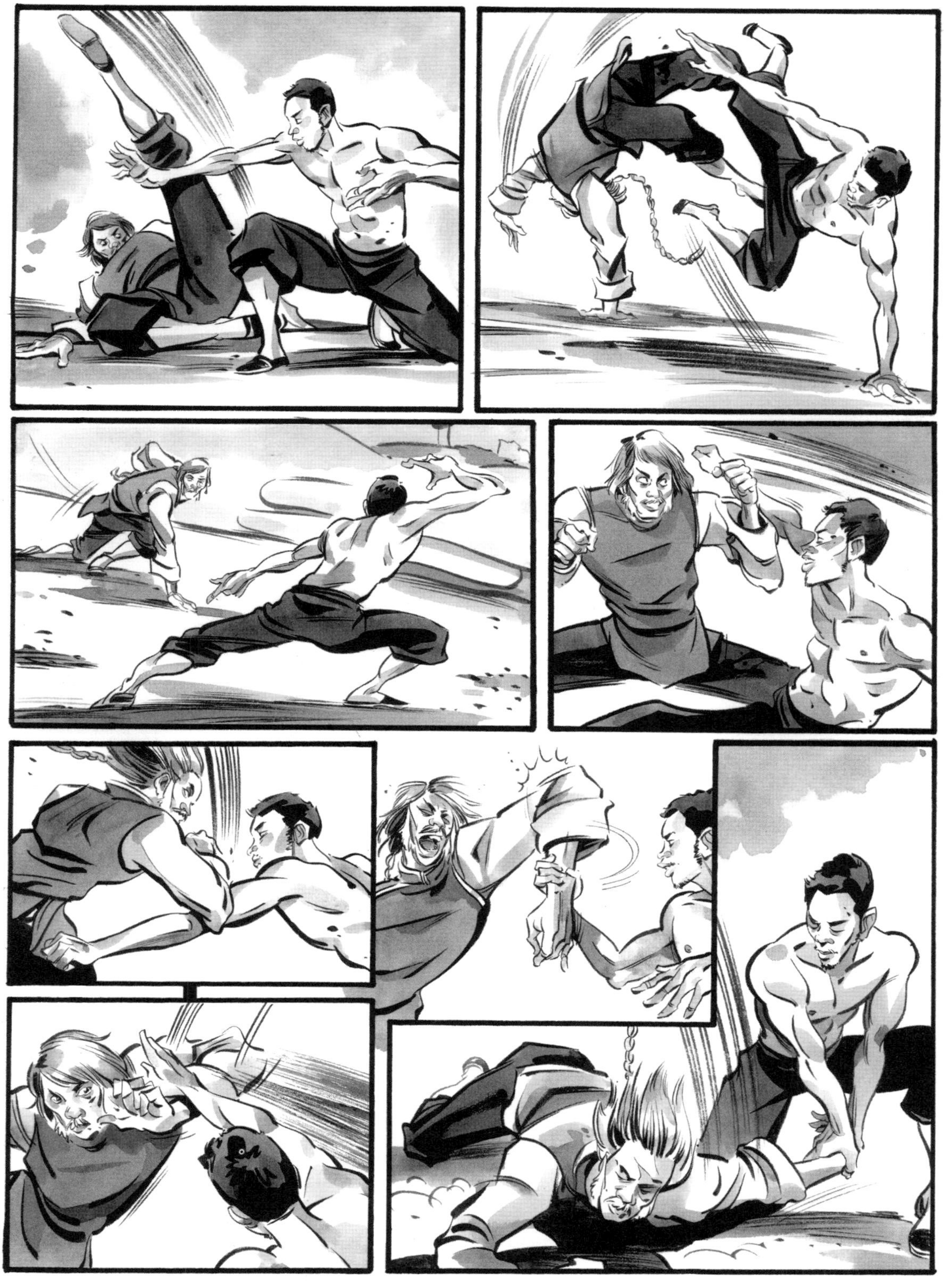

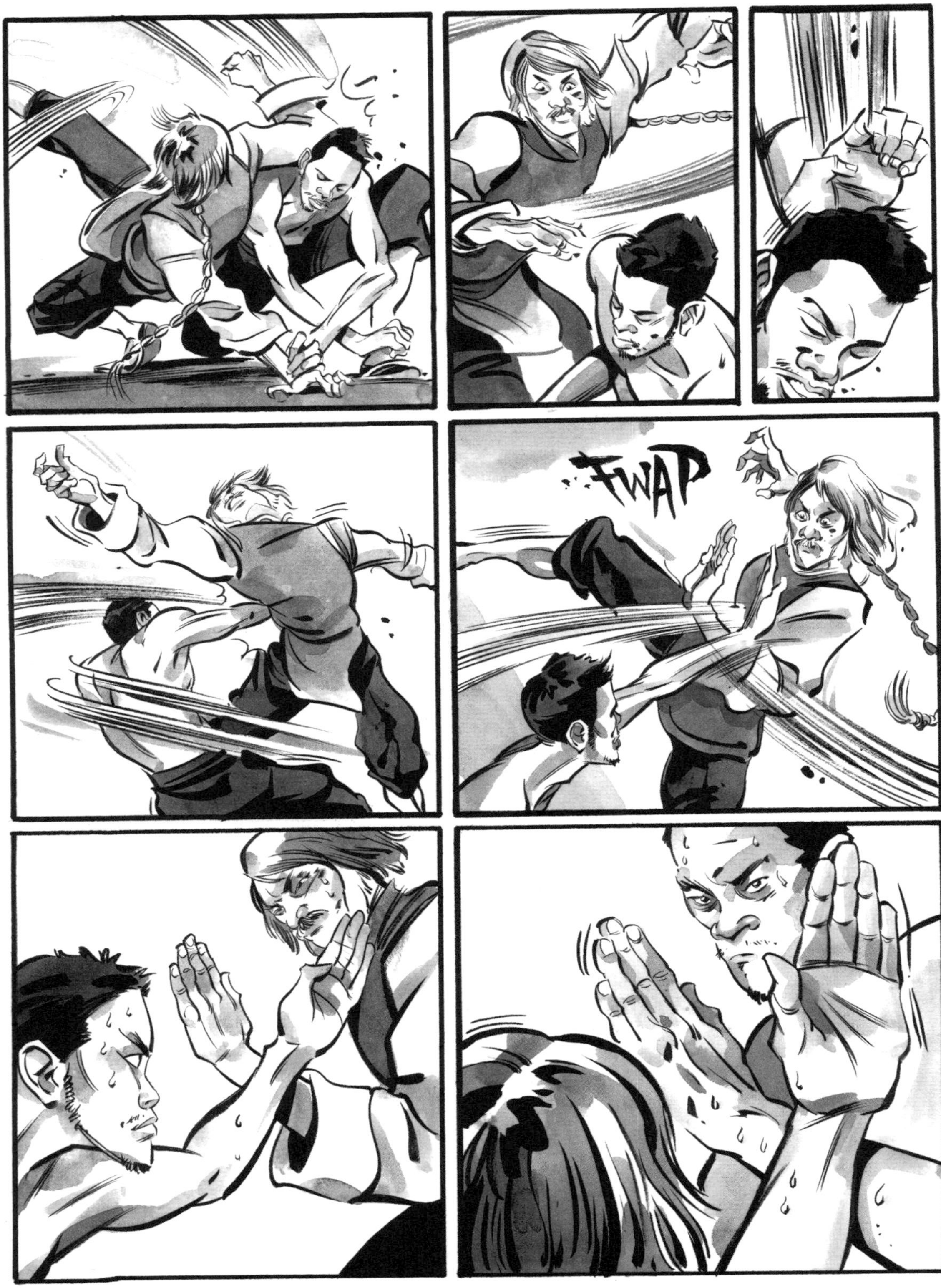
FWAP

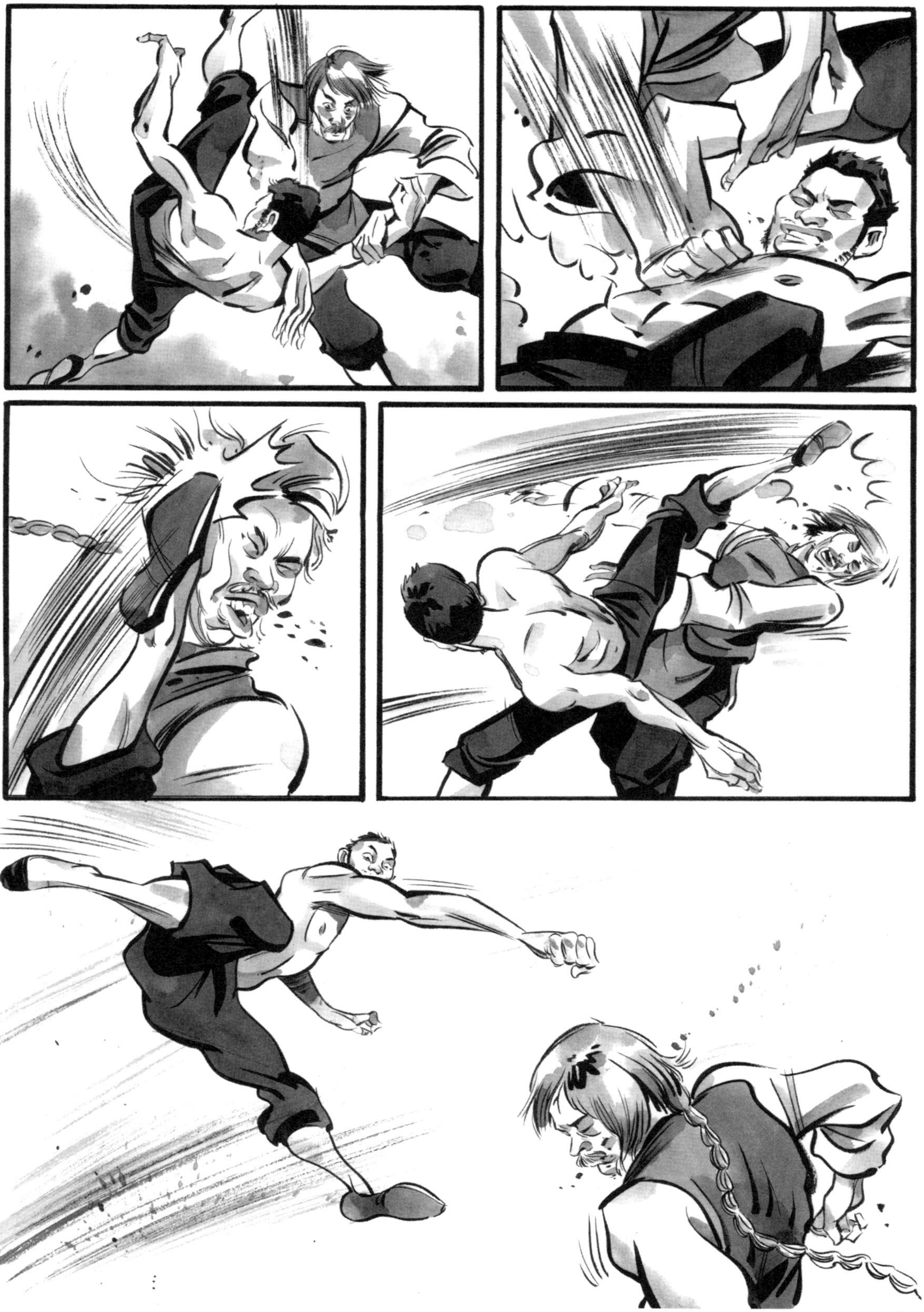

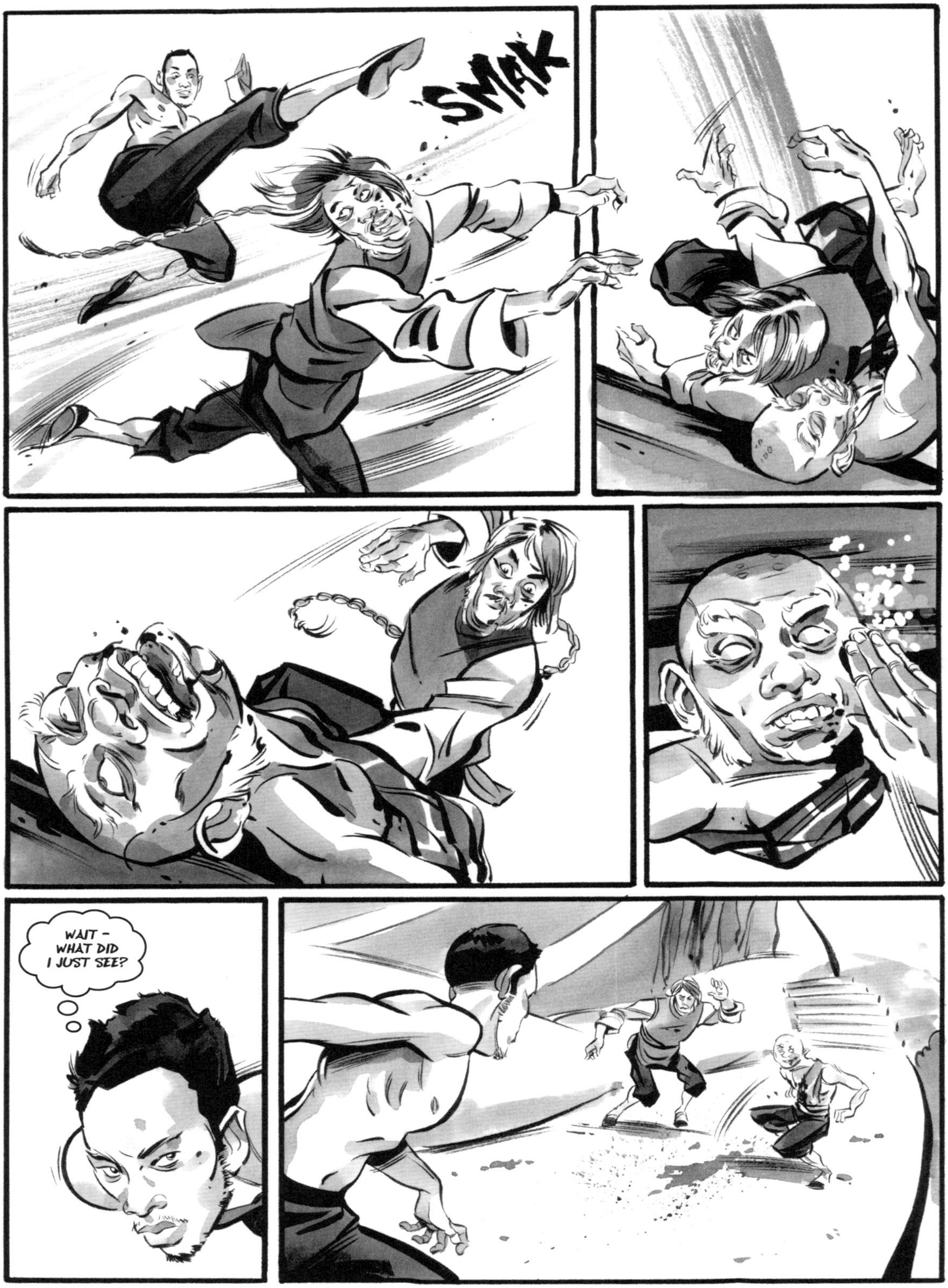
SMAK
WAIT - WHAT DID I JUST SEE?

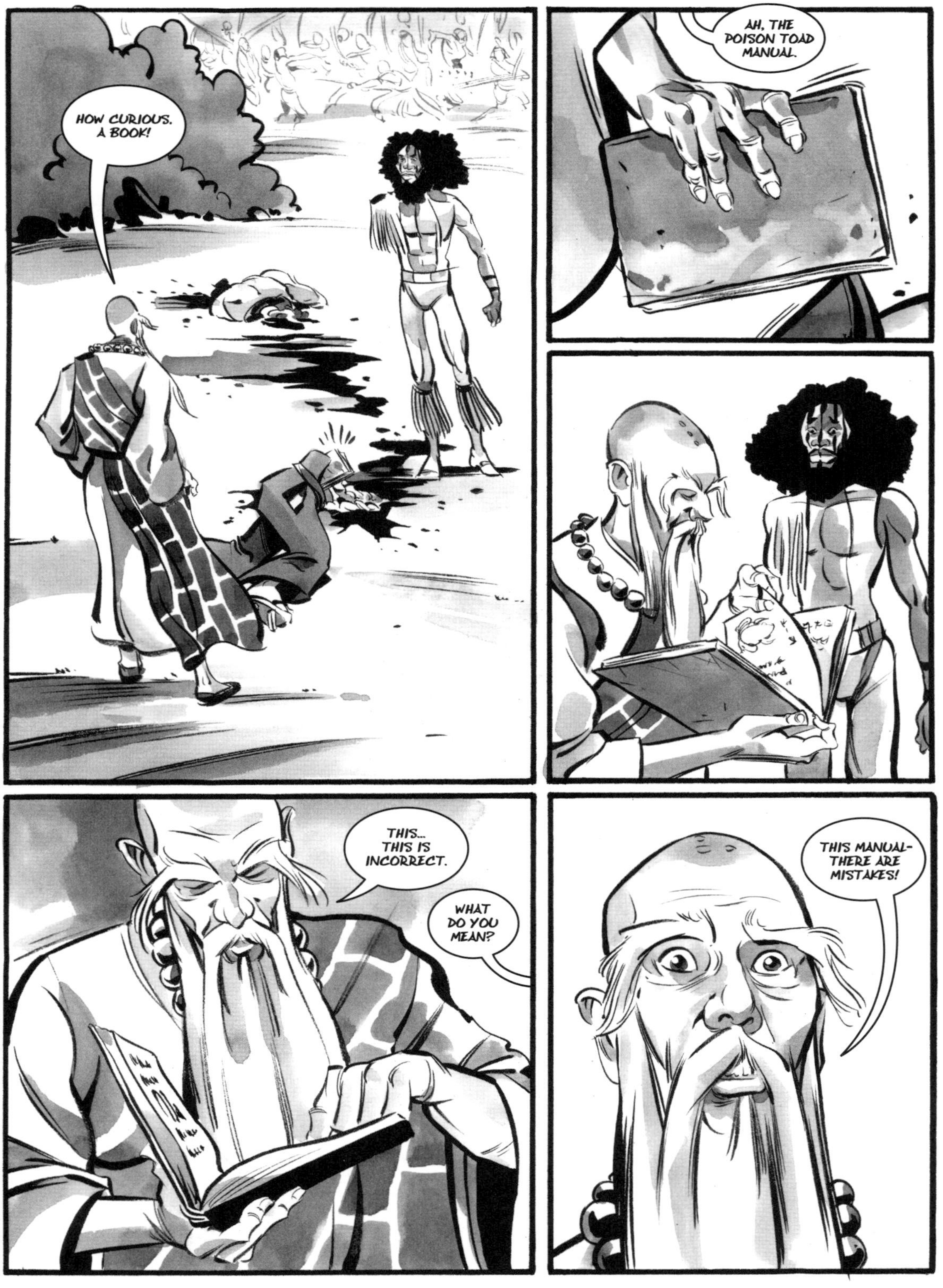
HOW CURIOUS. A BOOK!
AH, THE POISON TOAD MANUAL.
THIS... THIS IS INCORRECT.
WHAT DO YOU MEAN?
THIS MANUAL- THERE ARE MISTAKES!

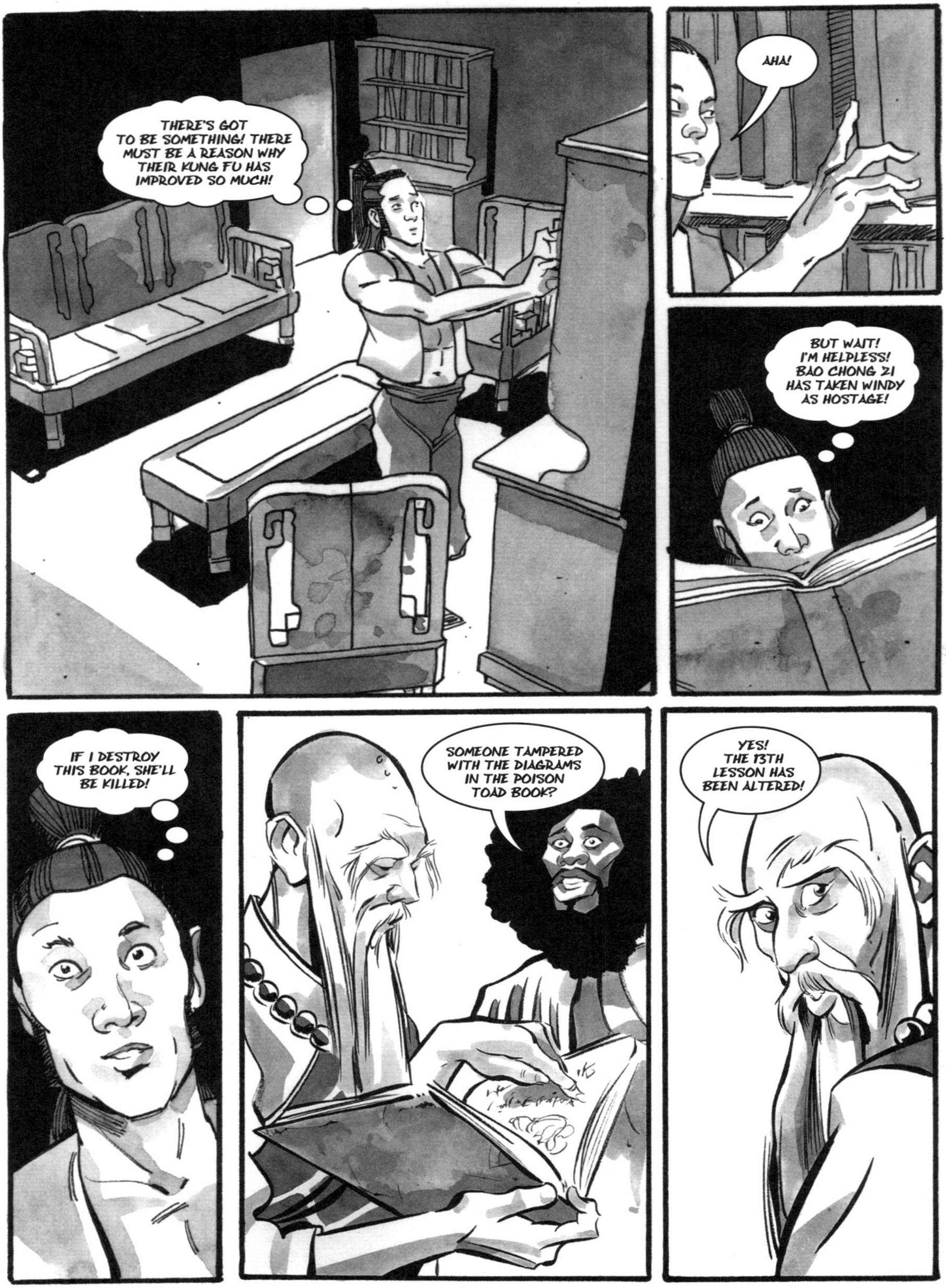
THERE'S GOT TO BE SOMETHING! THERE MUST BE A REASON WHY THEIR KUNG FU HAS IMPROVED SO MUCH!
AHA!
BUT WAIT! I'M HELPLESS! BAO CHONG ZI HAS TAKEN WINDY AS HOSTAGE!
IF I DESTROY THIS BOOK, SHE'LL BE KILLED!
SOMEONE TAMPERED WITH THE DIAGRAMS IN THE POISON TOAD BOOK?
YES! THE 13TH LESSON HAS BEEN ALTERED!

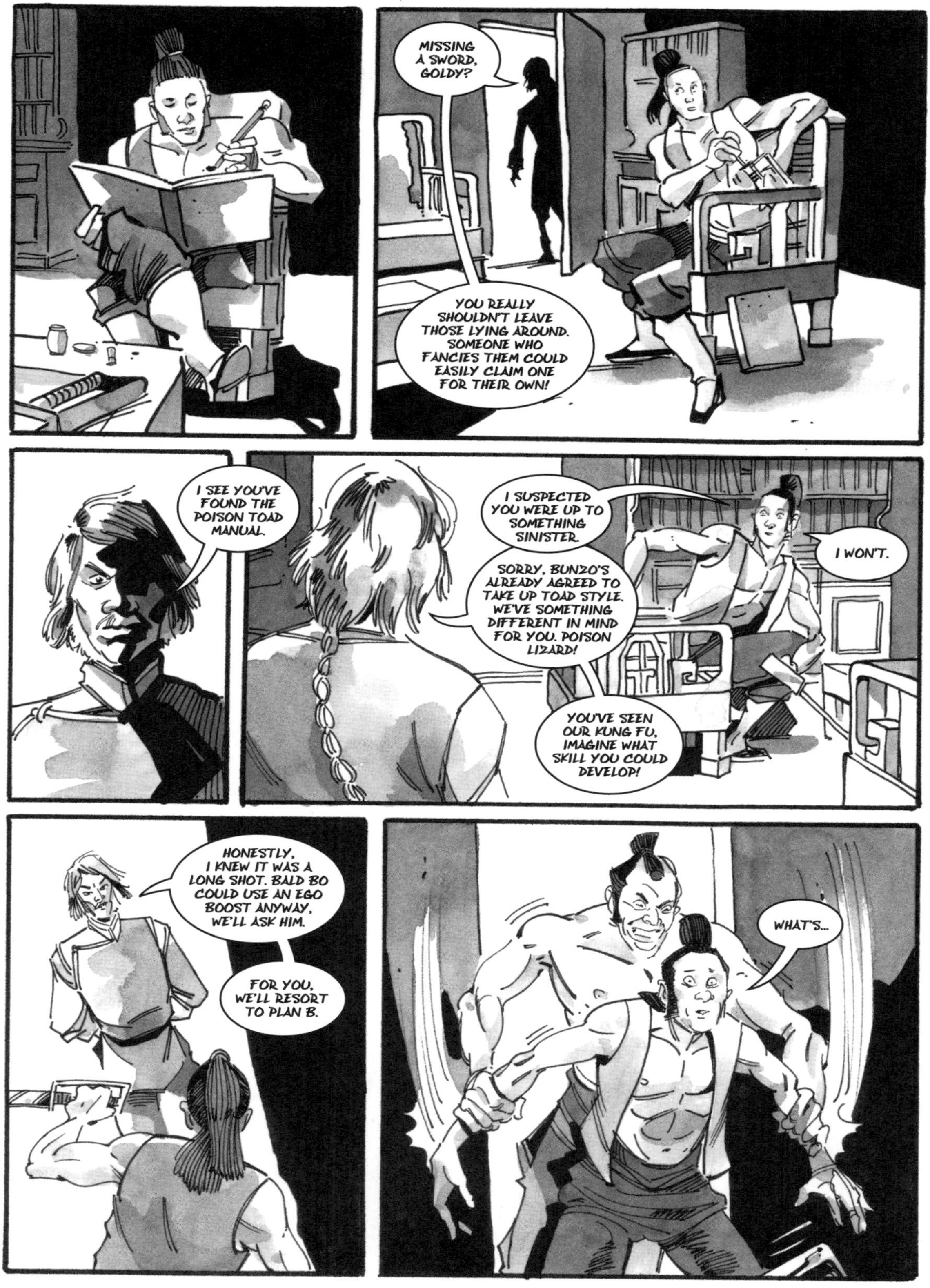
MISSING A SWORD, GOLDY?
YOU REALLY SHOULDN'T LEAVE THOSE LYING AROUND. SOMEONE WHO FANCIES THEM COULD EASILY CLAIM ONE FOR THEIR OWN!
I SEE YOU'VE FOUND THE POISON TOAD MANUAL.
I SUSPECTED YOU WERE UP TO SOMETHING SINISTER.
SORRY, BUNZO'S ALREADY AGREED TO TAKE UP TOAD STYLE. WE'VE SOMETHING DIFFERENT IN MIND FOR YOU. POISON LIZARD!
I WON'T.
YOU'VE SEEN OUR KUNG FU, IMAGINE WHAT SKILL YOU COULD DEVELOP!
HONESTLY, I KNEW IT WAS A LONG SHOT. BALD BO COULD USE AN EGO BOOST ANYWAY, WE'LL ASK HIM.
FOR YOU, WE'LL RESORT TO PLAN B.
WHAT'S...

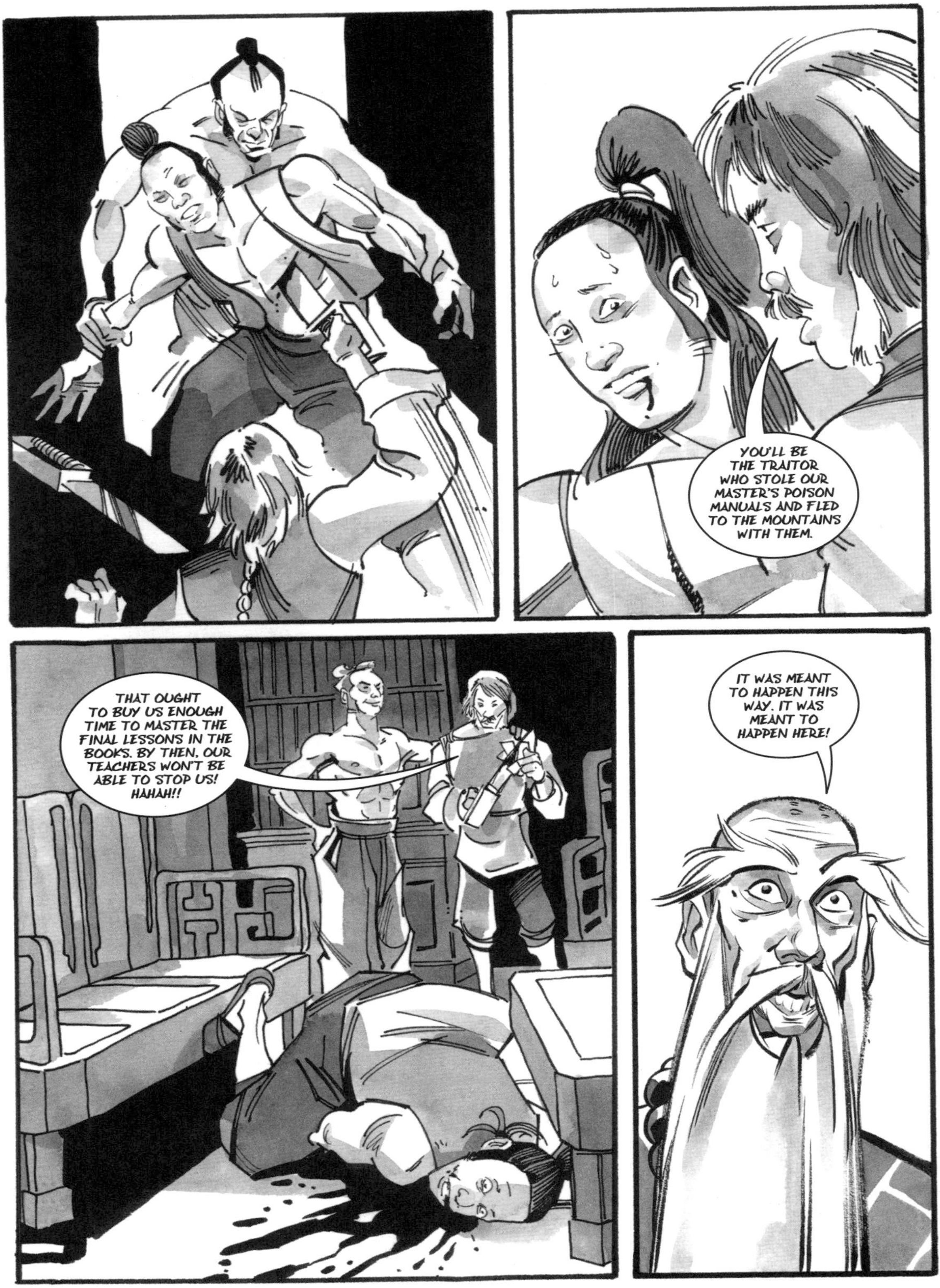
YOU'LL BE THE TRAITOR WHO STOLE OUR MASTER'S POISON MANUALS AND FLED TO THE MOUNTAINS WITH THEM.
THAT OUGHT TO BUY US ENOUGH TIME TO MASTER THE FINAL LESSONS IN THE BOOKS. BY THEN, OUR TEACHERS WON'T BE ABLE TO STOP US! HAHAH!!
IT WAS MEANT TO HAPPEN THIS WAY. IT WAS MEANT TO HAPPEN HERE!

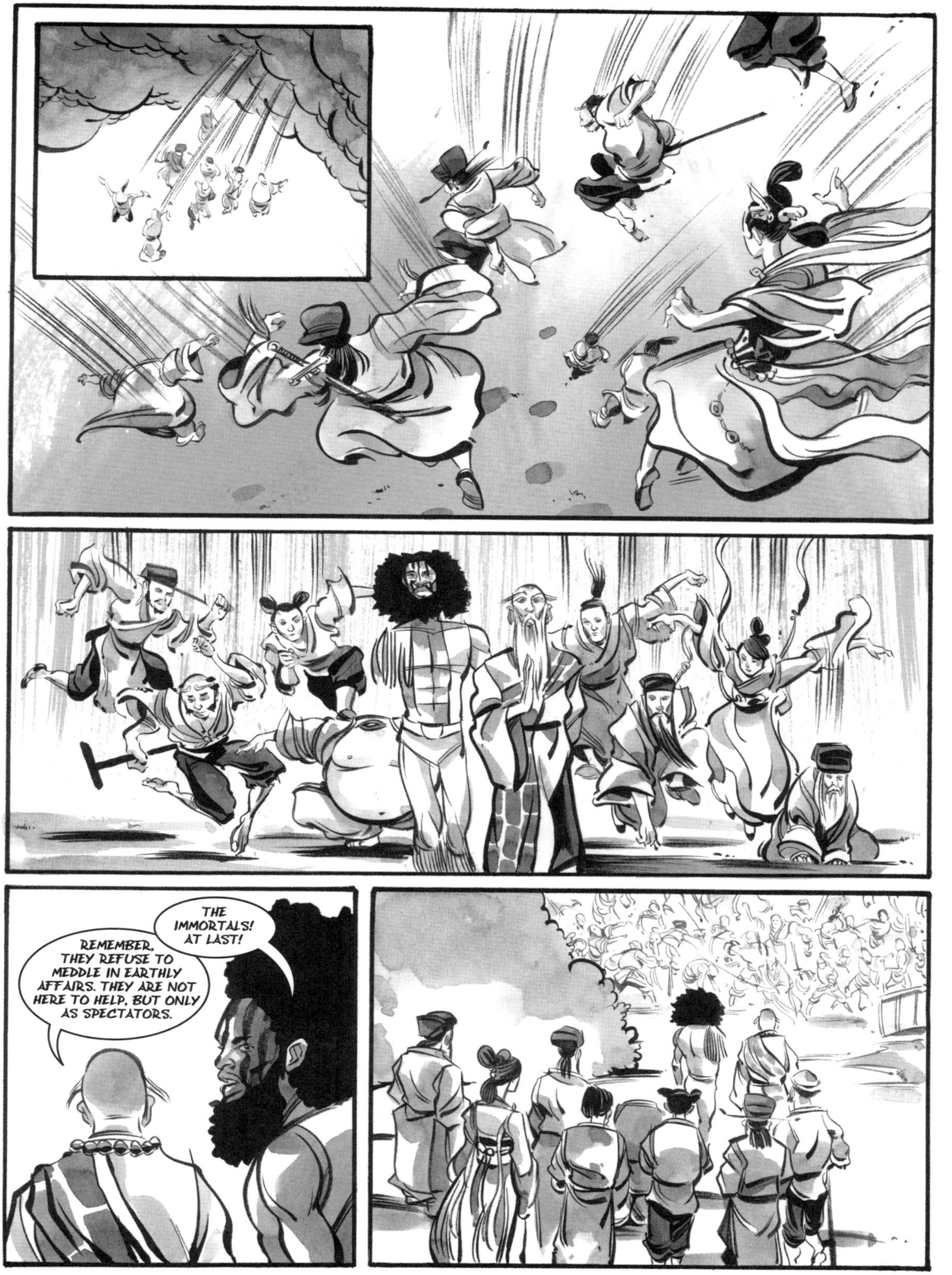
THE IMMORTALS! AT LAST!
REMEMBER. THEY REFUSE TO MEDDLE IN EARTHLY AFFAIRS. THEY ARE NOT HERE TO HELP, BUT ONLY AS SPECTATORS.

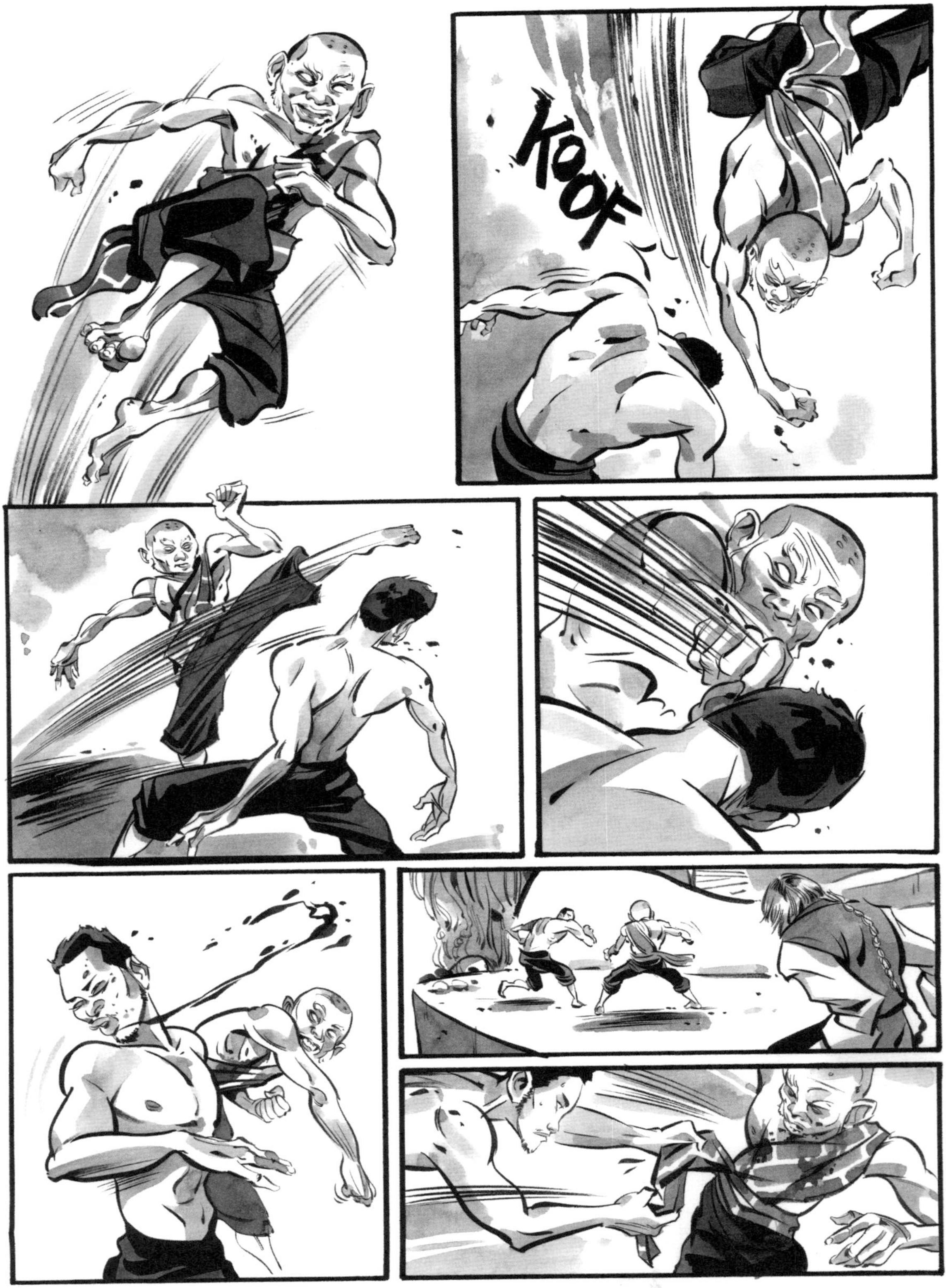
KOOF

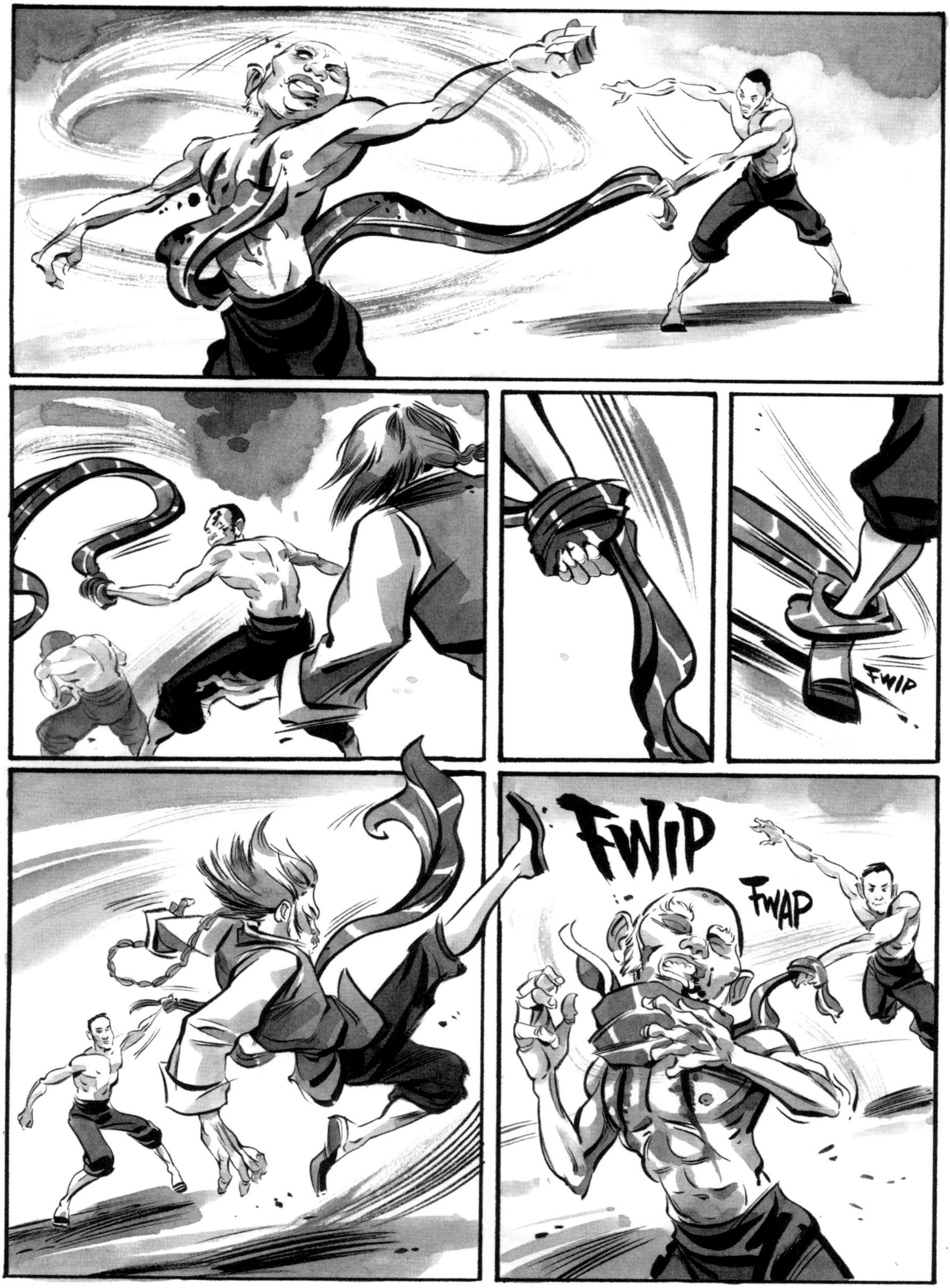
FWIP
FWIP
FWAP

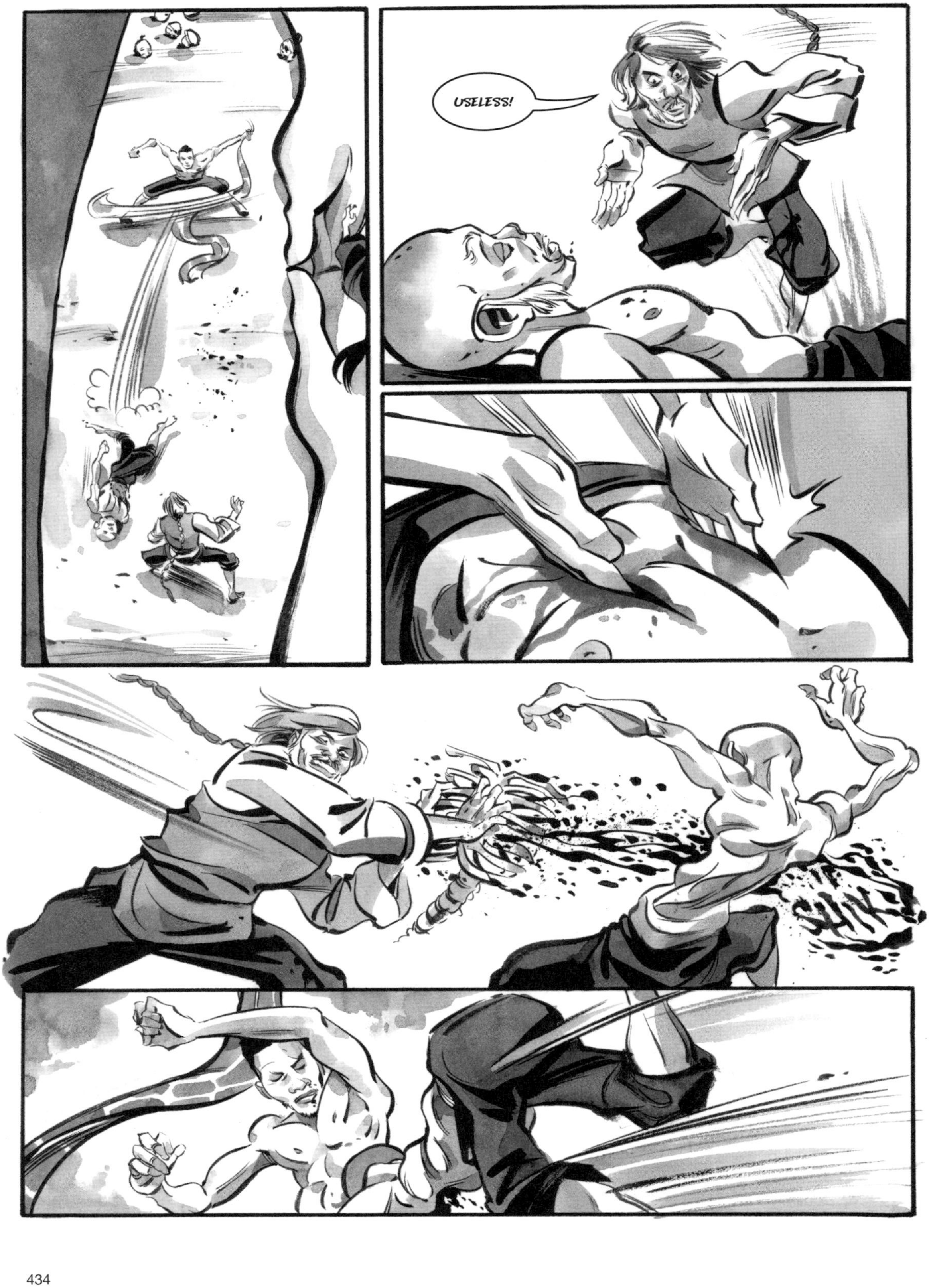
USELESS!
SHK!

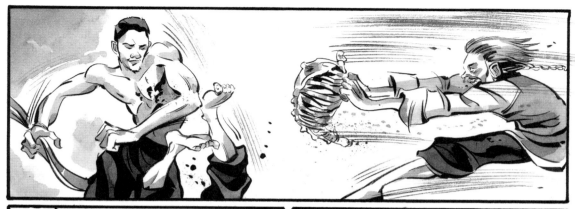

WHAP WHAP WHAP WHAP

HEH. HOW TO FINISH THIS?

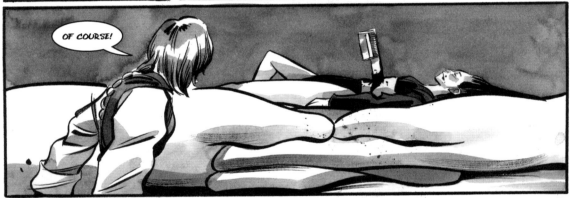

OF COURSE!

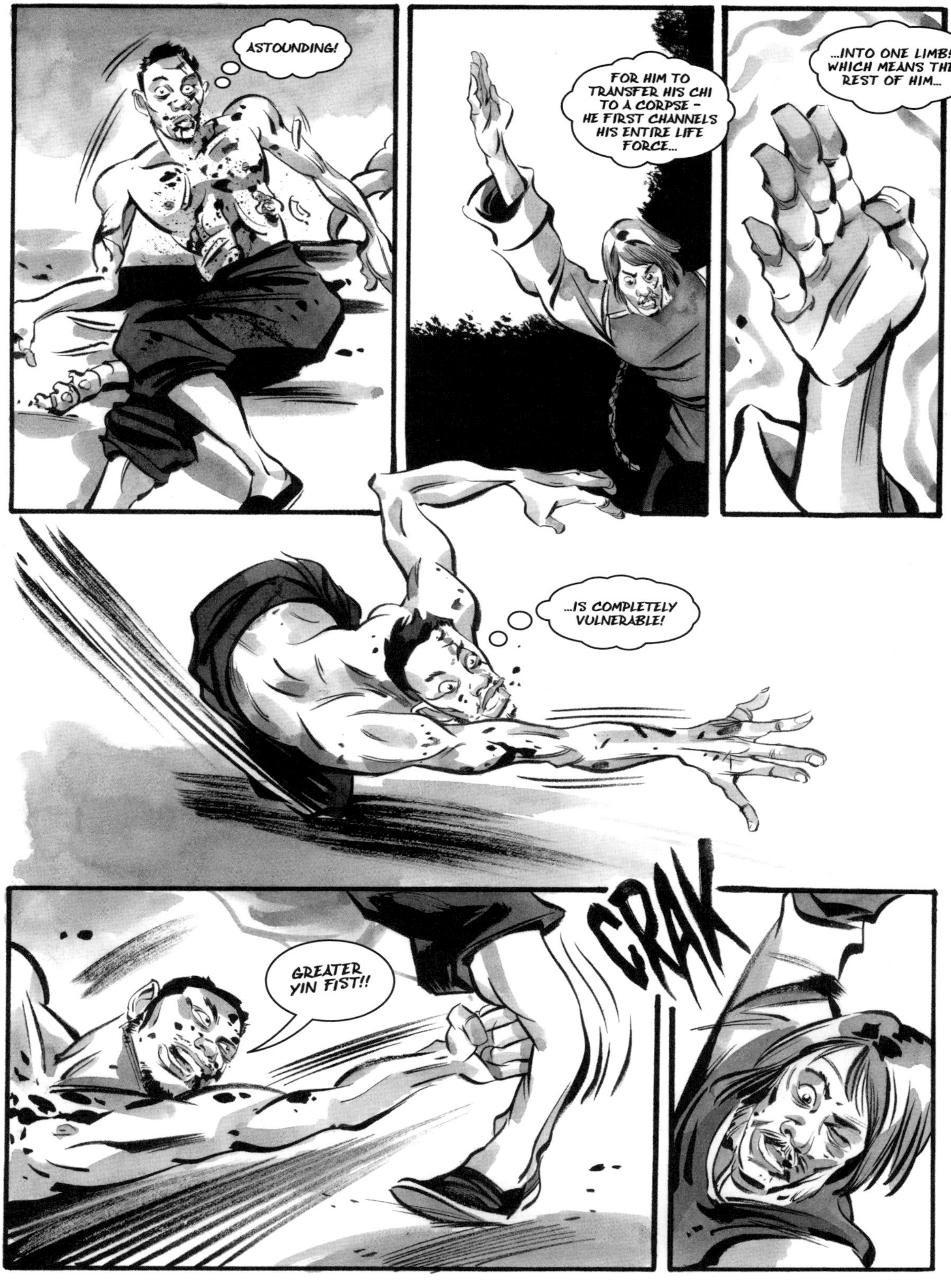
ASTOUNDING!
FOR HIM TO TRANSFER HIS CHI TO A CORPSE - HE FIRST CHANNELS HIS ENTIRE LIFE FORCE...
...INTO ONE LIMB! WHICH MEANS THE REST OF HIM...
...IS COMPLETELY VULNERABLE!
GREATER YIN FIST!!
CRAK

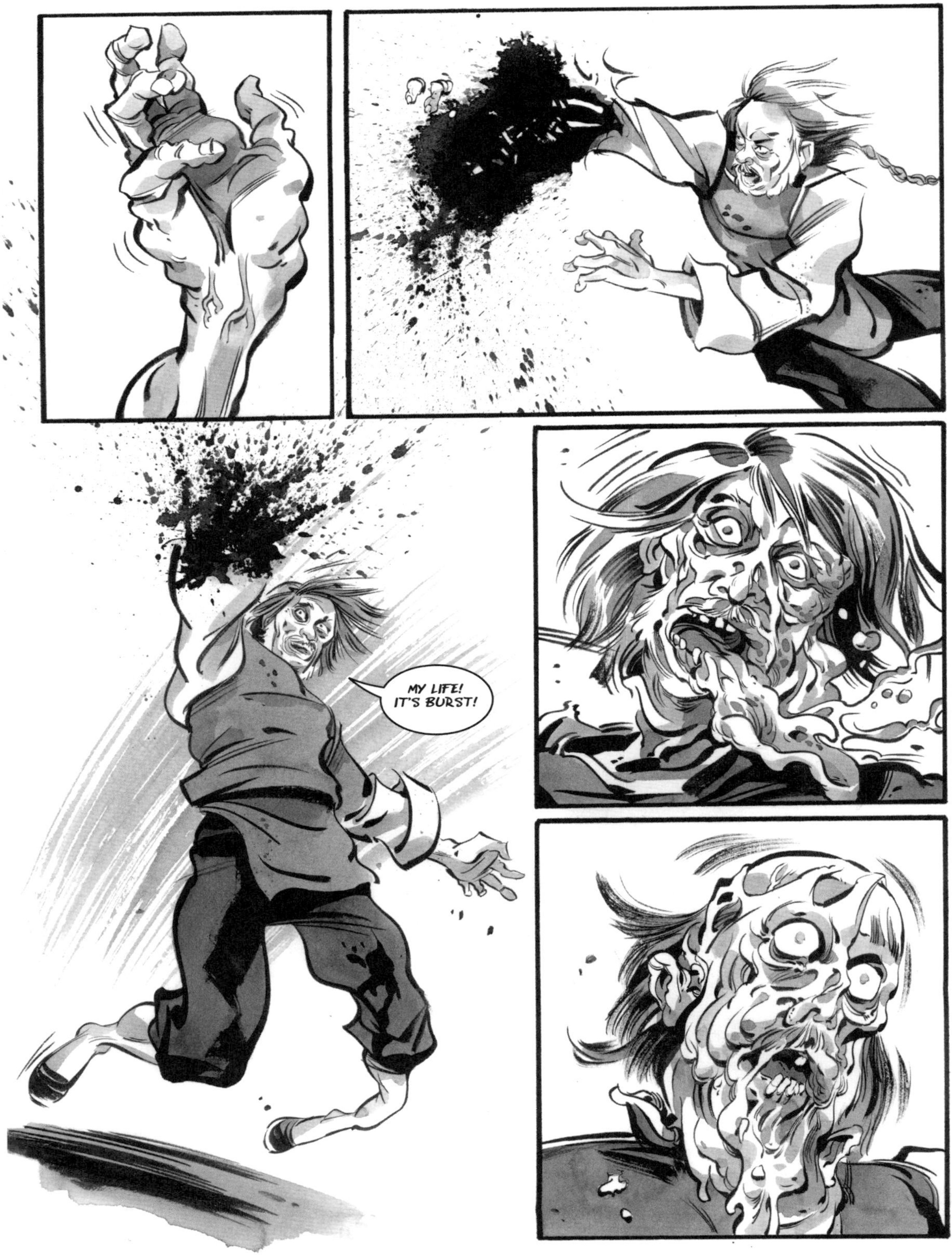
MY LIFE! IT'S BURST!

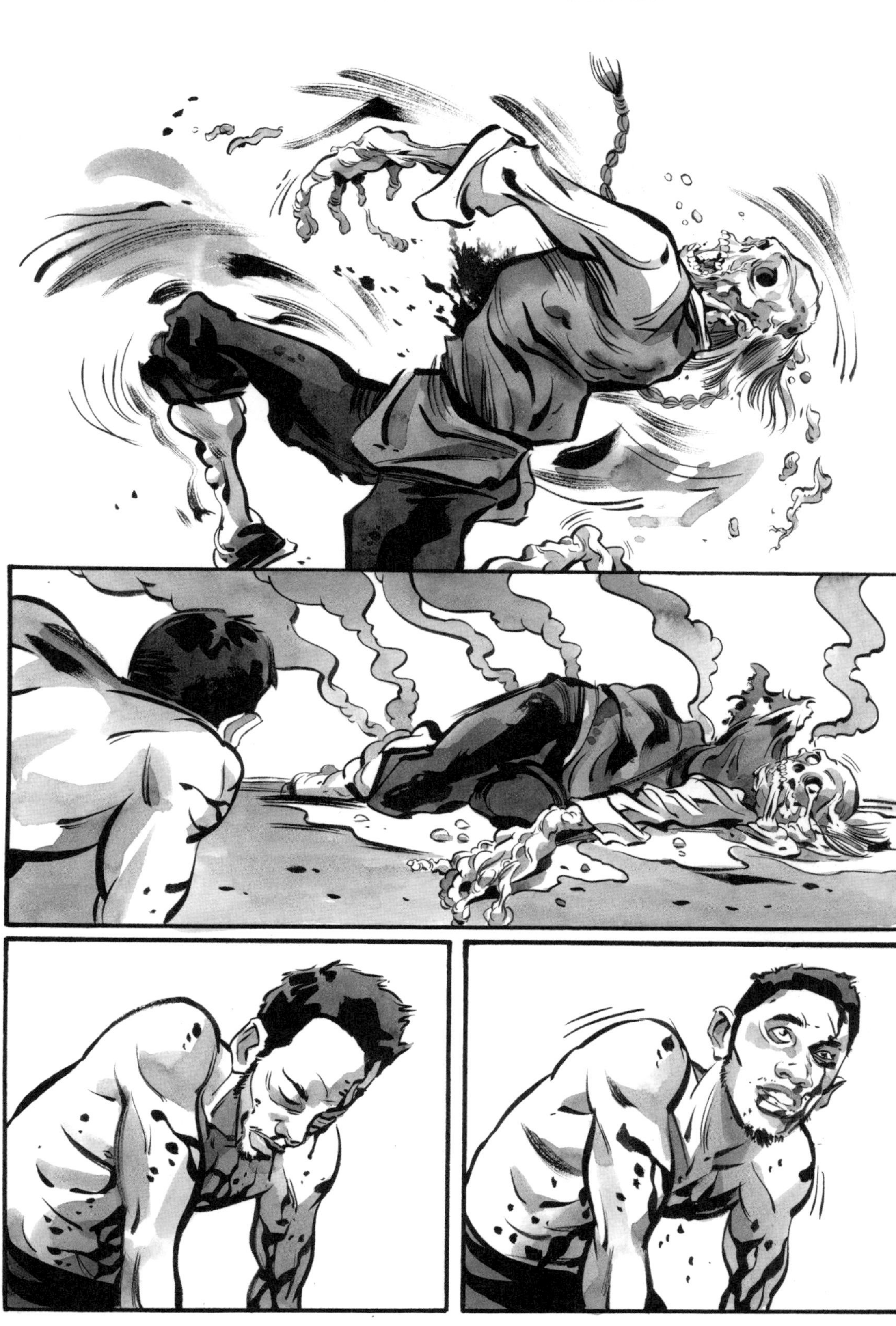

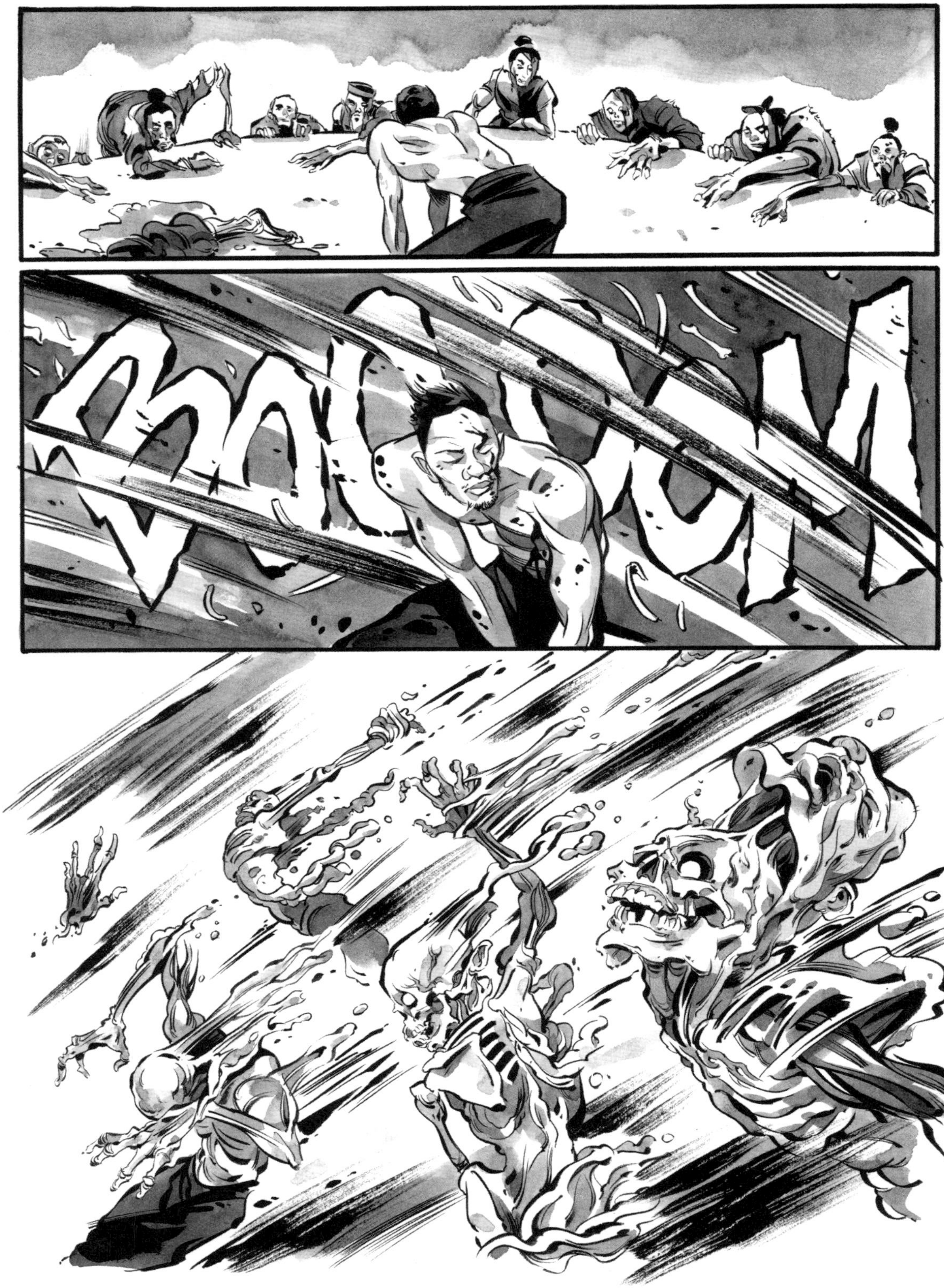

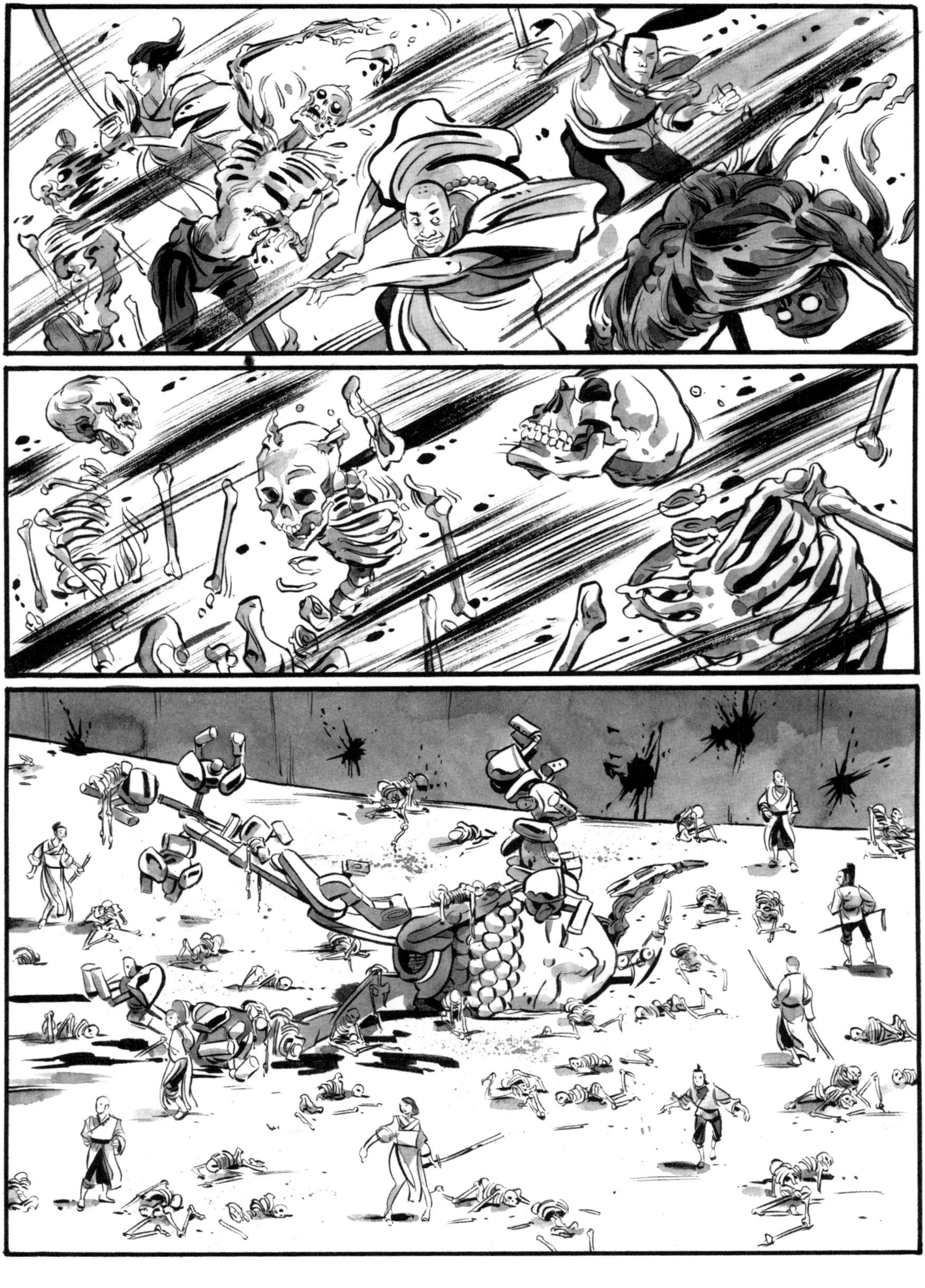

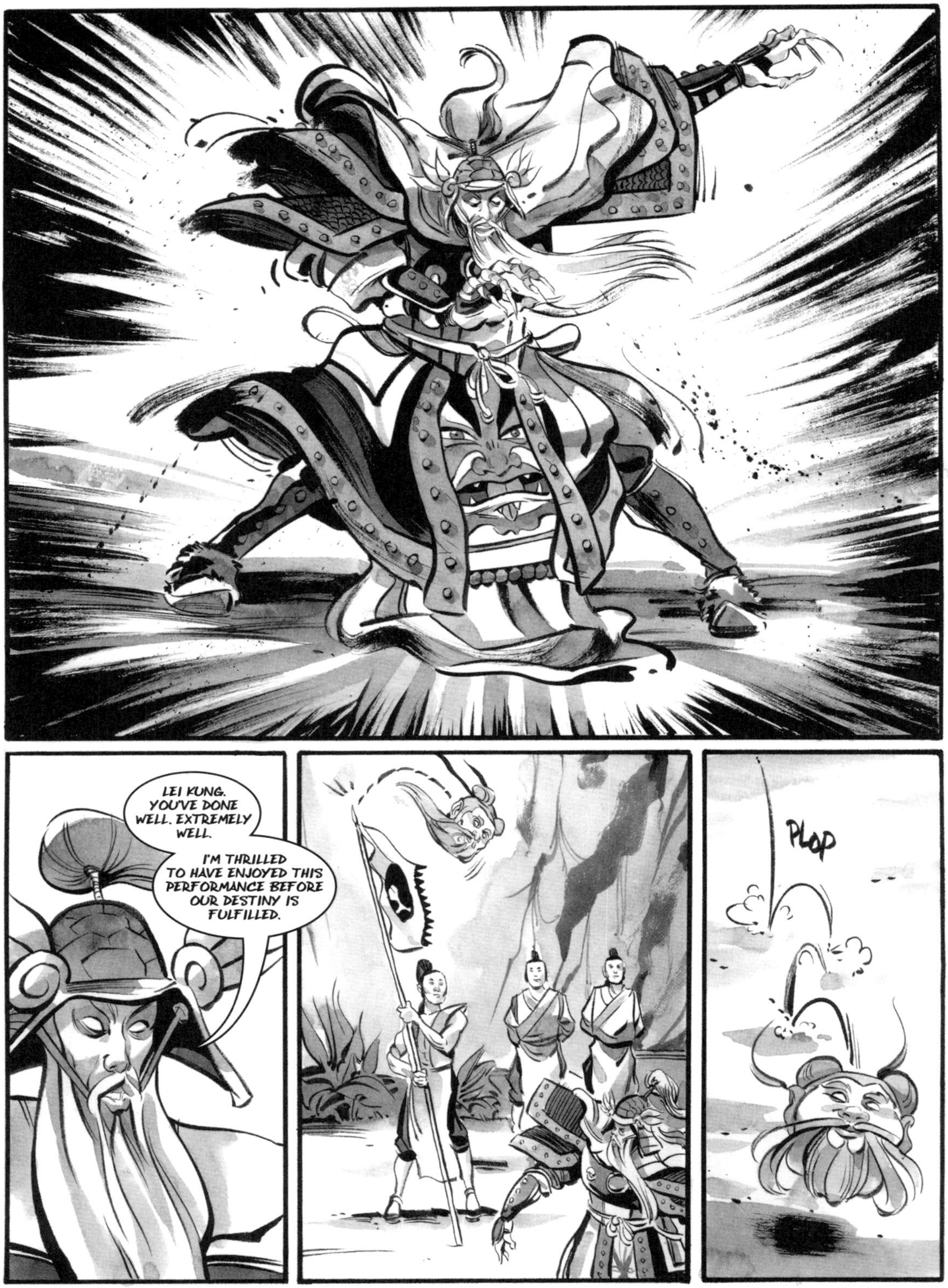
LEI KUNG. YOU'VE DONE WELL. EXTREMELY WELL.
I'M THRILLED TO HAVE ENJOYED THIS PERFORMANCE BEFORE OUR DESTINY IS FULFILLED.
PLOP

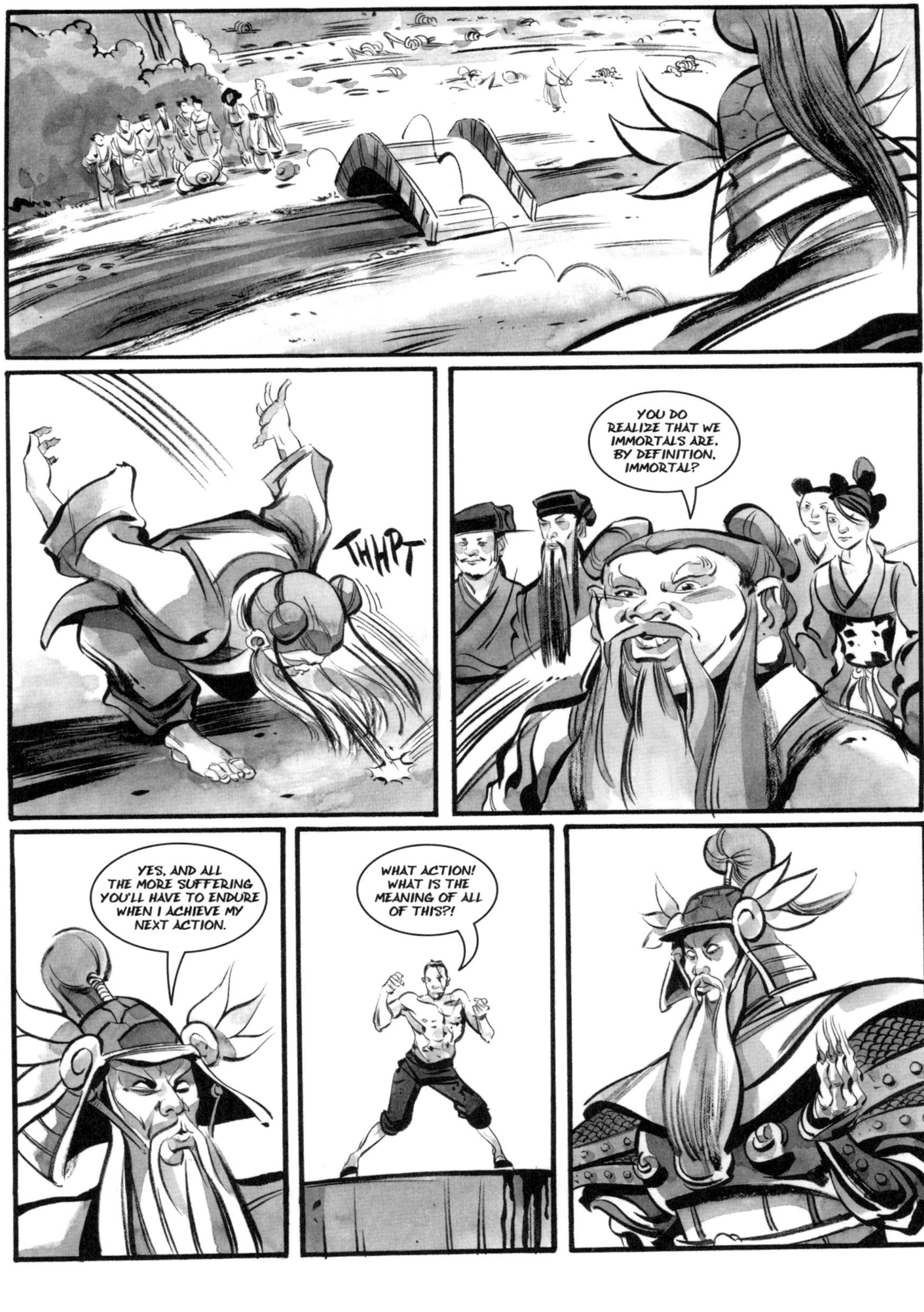
THHPT
YOU DO REALIZE THAT WE IMMORTALS ARE, BY DEFINITION, IMMORTAL?
YES, AND ALL THE MORE SUFFERING YOU'LL HAVE TO ENDURE WHEN I ACHIEVE MY NEXT ACTION.
WHAT ACTION! WHAT IS THE MEANING OF ALL OF THIS?!

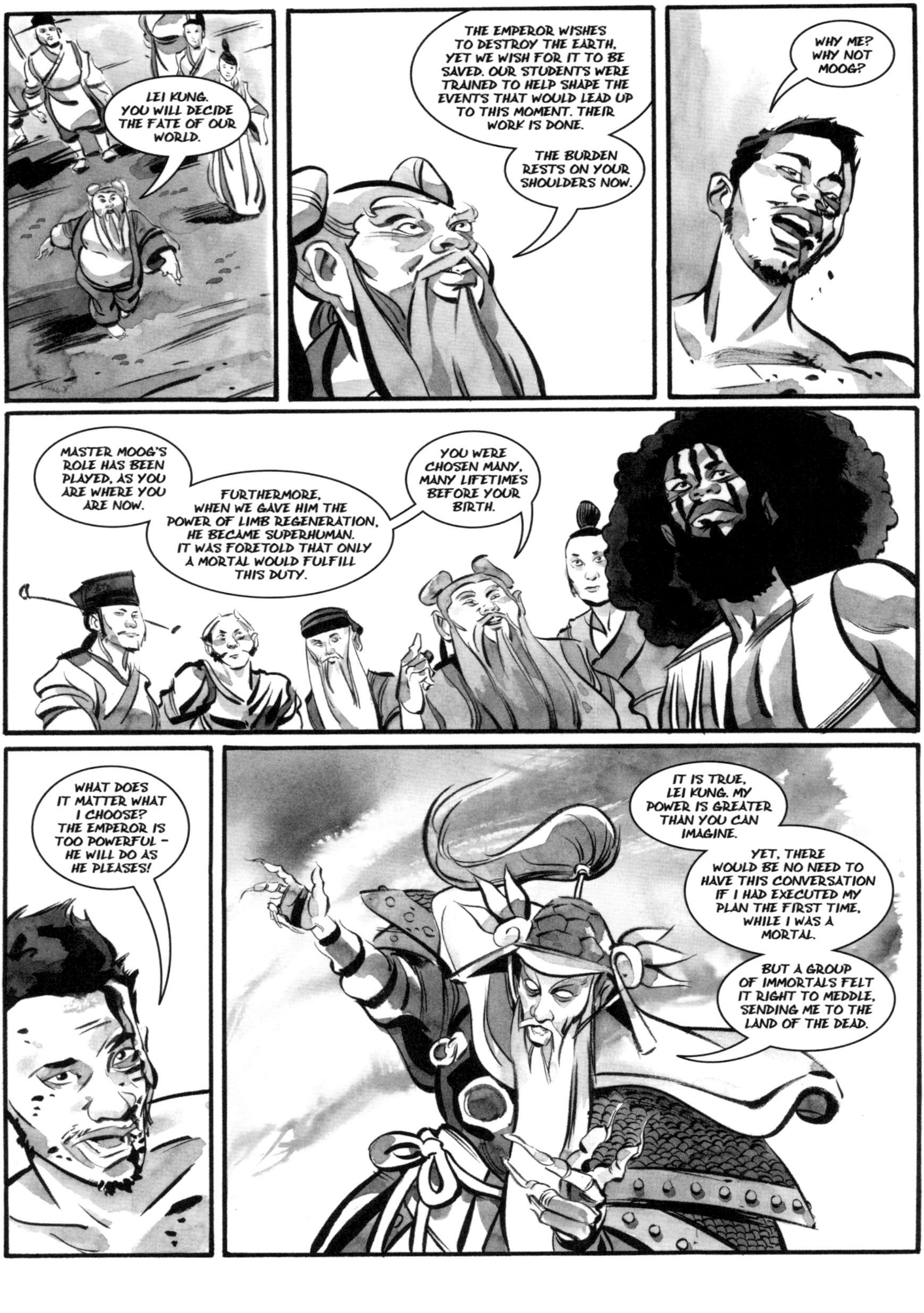
LEI KUNG. YOU WILL DECIDE THE FATE OF OUR WORLD.
THE EMPEROR WISHES TO DESTROY THE EARTH, YET WE WISH FOR IT TO BE SAVED. OUR STUDENTS WERE TRAINED TO HELP SHAPE THE EVENTS THAT WOULD LEAD UP TO THIS MOMENT. THEIR WORK IS DONE.
THE BURDEN RESTS ON YOUR SHOULDERS NOW.
WHY ME? WHY NOT MOOG?
MASTER MOOG'S ROLE HAS BEEN PLAYED, AS YOU ARE WHERE YOU ARE NOW.
FURTHERMORE, WHEN WE GAVE HIM THE POWER OF LIMB REGENERATION, HE BECAME SUPERHUMAN. IT WAS FORETOLD THAT ONLY A MORTAL WOULD FULFILL THIS DUTY.
YOU WERE CHOSEN MANY, MANY LIFETIMES BEFORE YOUR BIRTH.
WHAT DOES IT MATTER WHAT I CHOOSE? THE EMPEROR IS TOO POWERFUL - HE WILL DO AS HE PLEASES!
IT IS TRUE, LEI KUNG. MY POWER IS GREATER THAN YOU CAN IMAGINE.
YET, THERE WOULD BE NO NEED TO HAVE THIS CONVERSATION IF I HAD EXECUTED MY PLAN THE FIRST TIME, WHILE I WAS A MORTAL.
BUT A GROUP OF IMMORTALS FELT IT RIGHT TO MEDDLE, SENDING ME TO THE LAND OF THE DEAD.

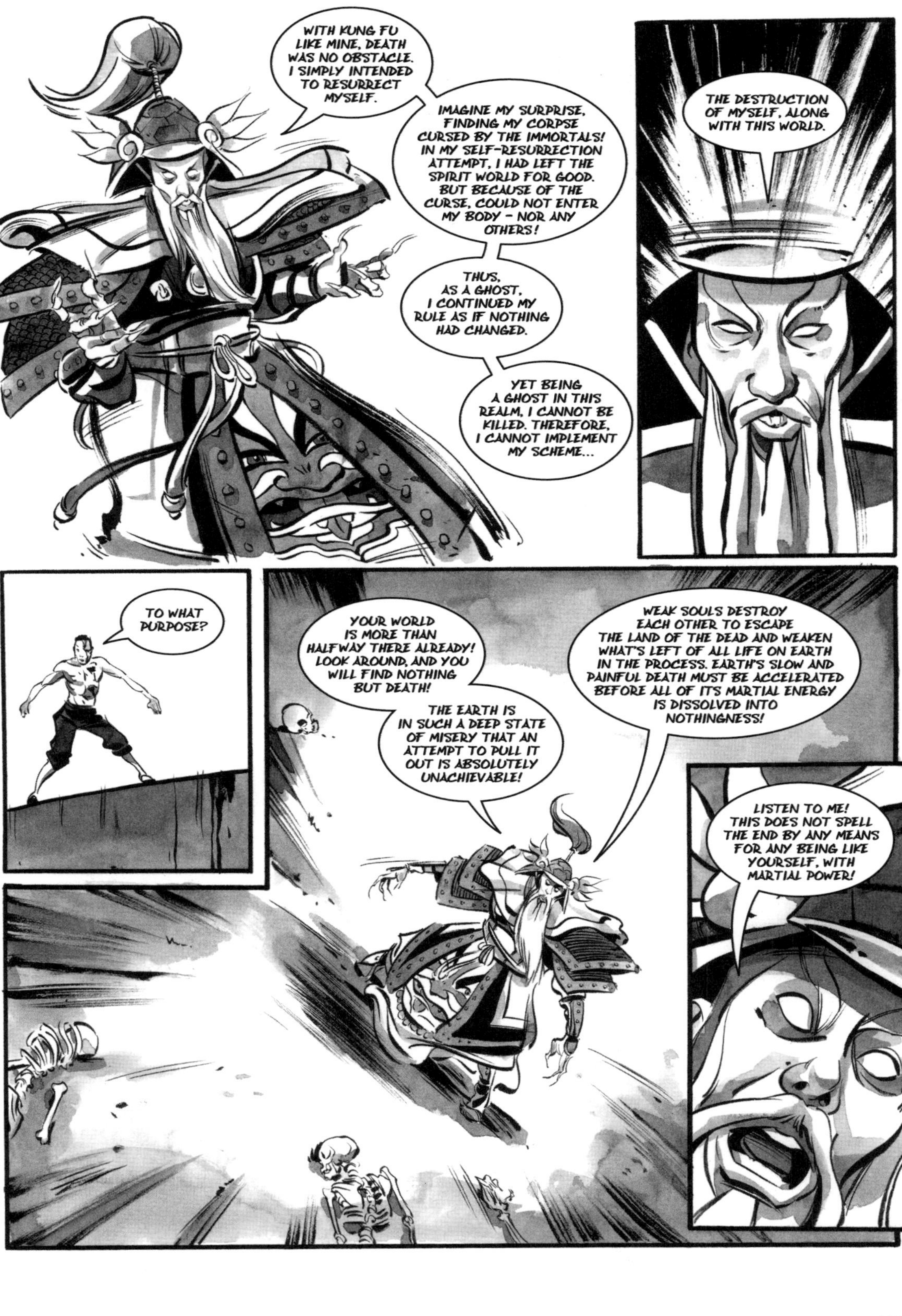
WITH KUNG FU LIKE MINE, DEATH WAS NO OBSTACLE. I SIMPLY INTENDED TO RESURRECT MYSELF.
IMAGINE MY SURPRISE, FINDING MY CORPSE CURSED BY THE IMMORTALS! IN MY SELF-RESURRECTION ATTEMPT, I HAD LEFT THE SPIRIT WORLD FOR GOOD. BUT BECAUSE OF THE CURSE, COULD NOT ENTER MY BODY - NOR ANY OTHERS!
THUS, AS A GHOST, I CONTINUED MY RULE AS IF NOTHING HAD CHANGED.
YET BEING A GHOST IN THIS REALM, I CANNOT BE KILLED. THEREFORE, I CANNOT IMPLEMENT MY SCHEME...
THE DESTRUCTION OF MYSELF, ALONG WITH THIS WORLD.
TO WHAT PURPOSE?
YOUR WORLD IS MORE THAN HALFWAY THERE ALREADY! LOOK AROUND, AND YOU WILL FIND NOTHING BUT DEATH!
THE EARTH IS IN SUCH A DEEP STATE OF MISERY THAT AN ATTEMPT TO PULL IT OUT IS ABSOLUTELY UNACHIEVABLE!
WEAK SOULS DESTROY EACH OTHER TO ESCAPE THE LAND OF THE DEAD AND WEAKEN WHAT'S LEFT OF ALL LIFE ON EARTH IN THE PROCESS. EARTH'S SLOW AND PAINFUL DEATH MUST BE ACCELERATED BEFORE ALL OF ITS MARTIAL ENERGY IS DISSOLVED INTO NOTHINGNESS!
LISTEN TO ME! THIS DOES NOT SPELL THE END BY ANY MEANS FOR ANY BEING LIKE YOURSELF, WITH MARTIAL POWER!

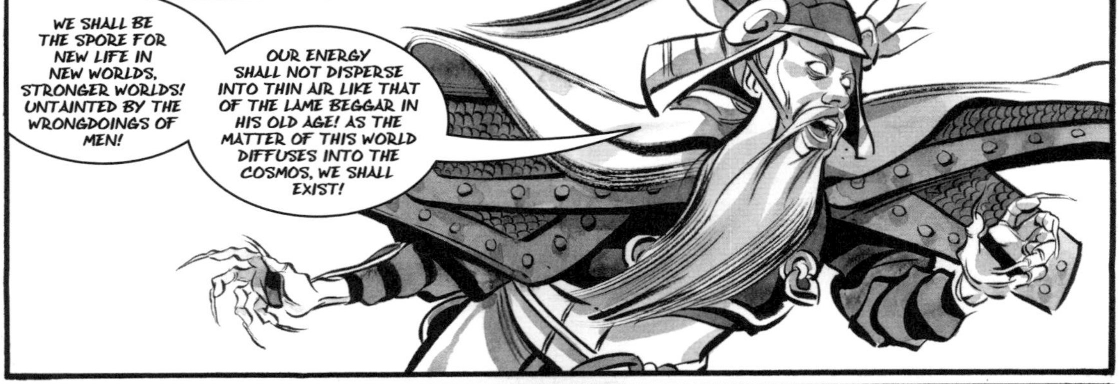
WE SHALL BE THE SPORE FOR NEW LIFE IN NEW WORLDS, STRONGER WORLDS! UNTAINTED BY THE WRONGDOINGS OF MEN!
OUR ENERGY SHALL NOT DISPERSE INTO THIN AIR LIKE THAT OF THE LAME BEGGAR IN HIS OLD AGE! AS THE MATTER OF THIS WORLD DIFFUSES INTO THE COSMOS, WE SHALL EXIST!

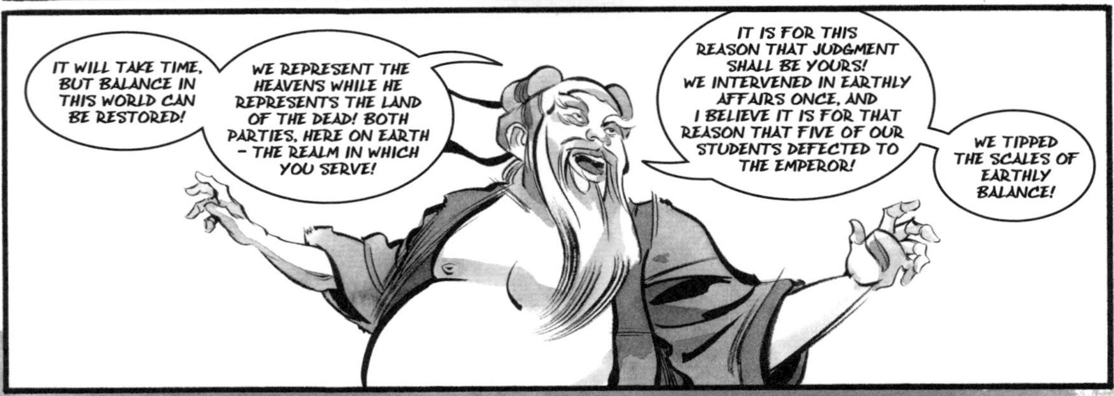
IT WILL TAKE TIME, BUT BALANCE IN THIS WORLD CAN BE RESTORED!
WE REPRESENT THE HEAVENS WHILE HE REPRESENTS THE LAND OF THE DEAD! BOTH PARTIES, HERE ON EARTH - THE REALM IN WHICH YOU SERVE!
IT IS FOR THIS REASON THAT JUDGMENT SHALL BE YOURS! WE INTERVENED IN EARTHLY AFFAIRS ONCE, AND I BELIEVE IT IS FOR THAT REASON THAT FIVE OF OUR STUDENTS DEFECTED TO THE EMPEROR!
WE TIPPED THE SCALES OF EARTHLY BALANCE!

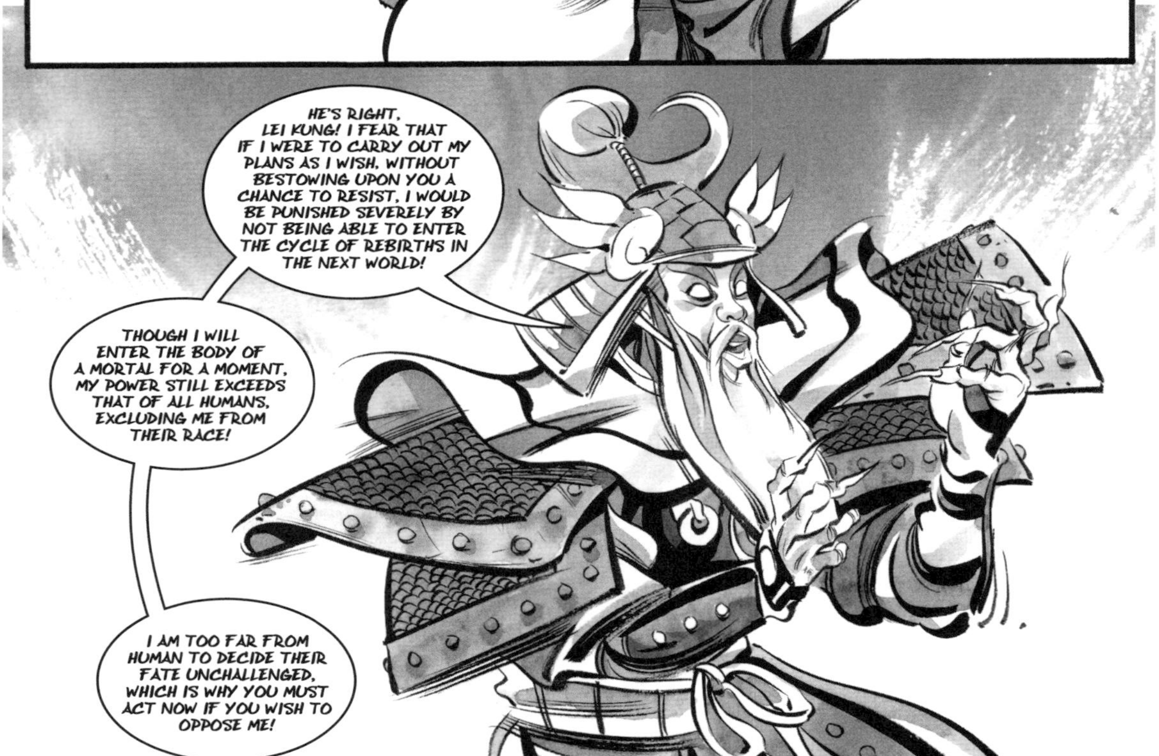
HE'S RIGHT, LEI KUNG! I FEAR THAT IF I WERE TO CARRY OUT MY PLANS AS I WISH, WITHOUT BESTOWING UPON YOU A CHANCE TO RESIST, I WOULD BE PUNISHED SEVERELY BY NOT BEING ABLE TO ENTER THE CYCLE OF REBIRTHS IN THE NEXT WORLD!
THOUGH I WILL ENTER THE BODY OF A MORTAL FOR A MOMENT, MY POWER STILL EXCEEDS THAT OF ALL HUMANS, EXCLUDING ME FROM THEIR RACE!
I AM TOO FAR FROM HUMAN TO DECIDE THEIR FATE UNCHALLENGED, WHICH IS WHY YOU MUST ACT NOW IF YOU WISH TO OPPOSE ME!

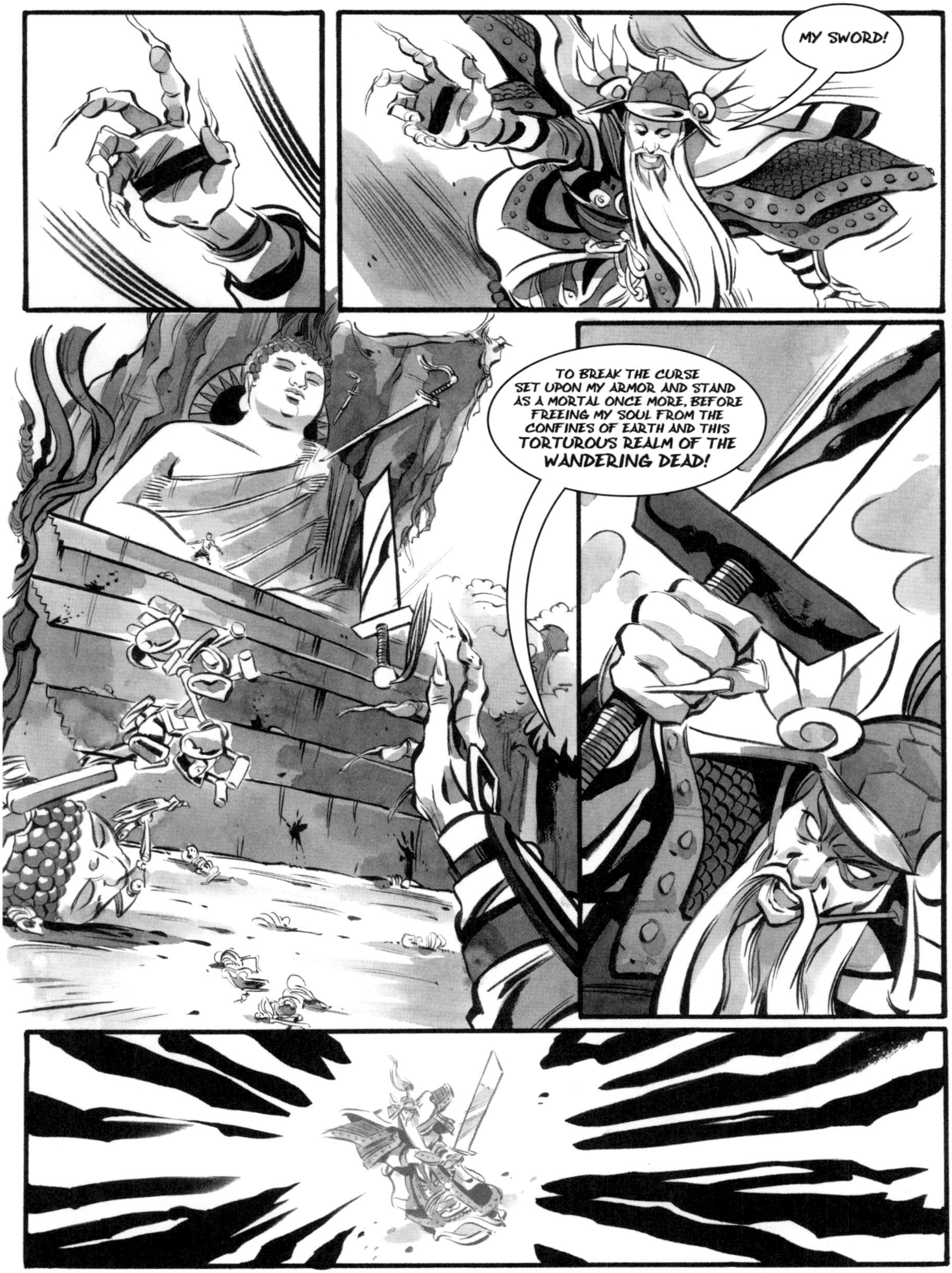
MY SWORD!
TO BREAK THE CURSE SET UPON MY ARMOR AND STAND AS A MORTAL ONCE MORE, BEFORE FREEING MY SOUL FROM THE CONFINES OF EARTH AND THIS TORTUROUS REALM OF THE WANDERING DEAD!

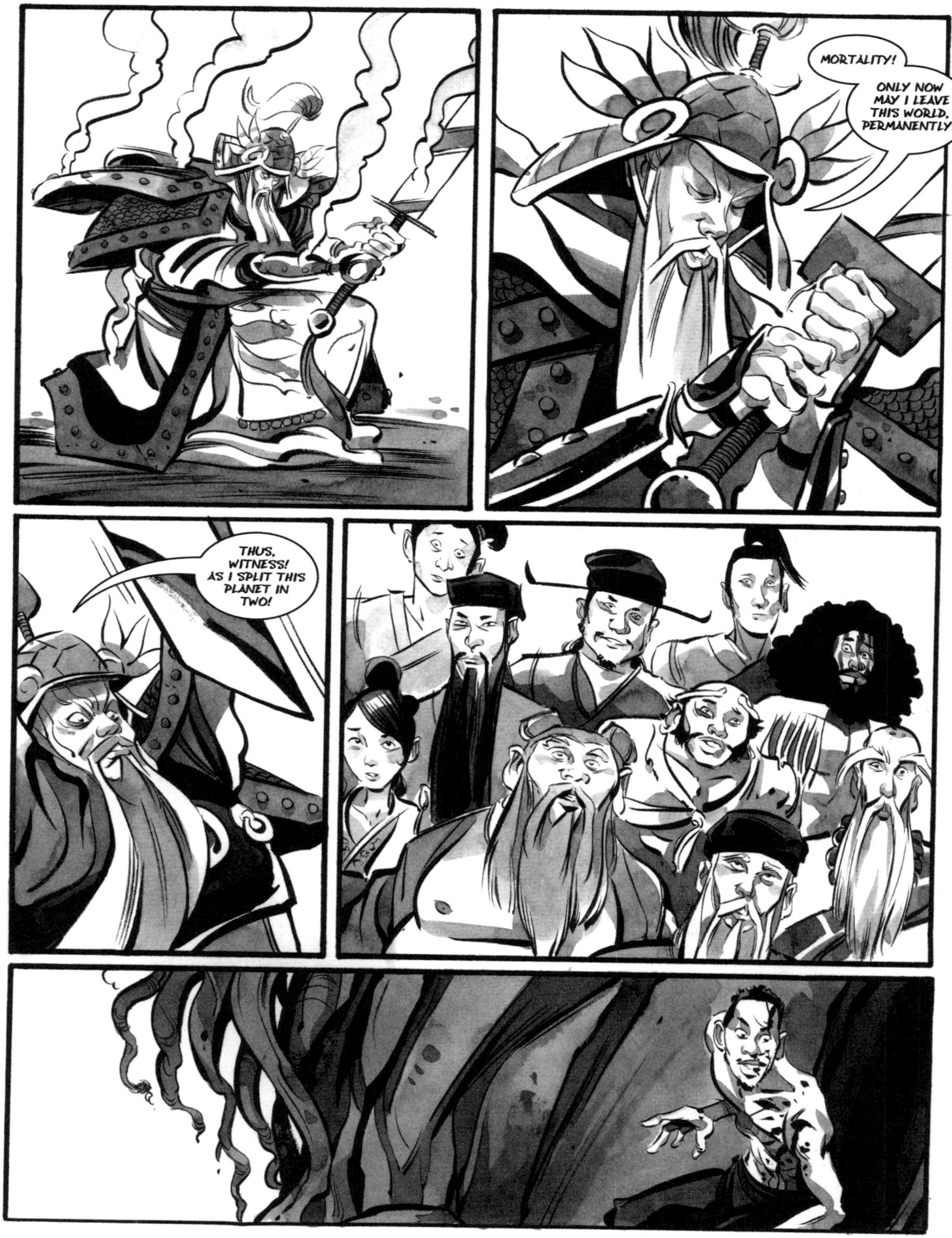
MORTALITY!
ONLY NOW MAY I LEAVE THIS WORLD, PERMANENTLY!
THUS, WITNESS! AS I SPLIT THIS PLANET IN TWO!

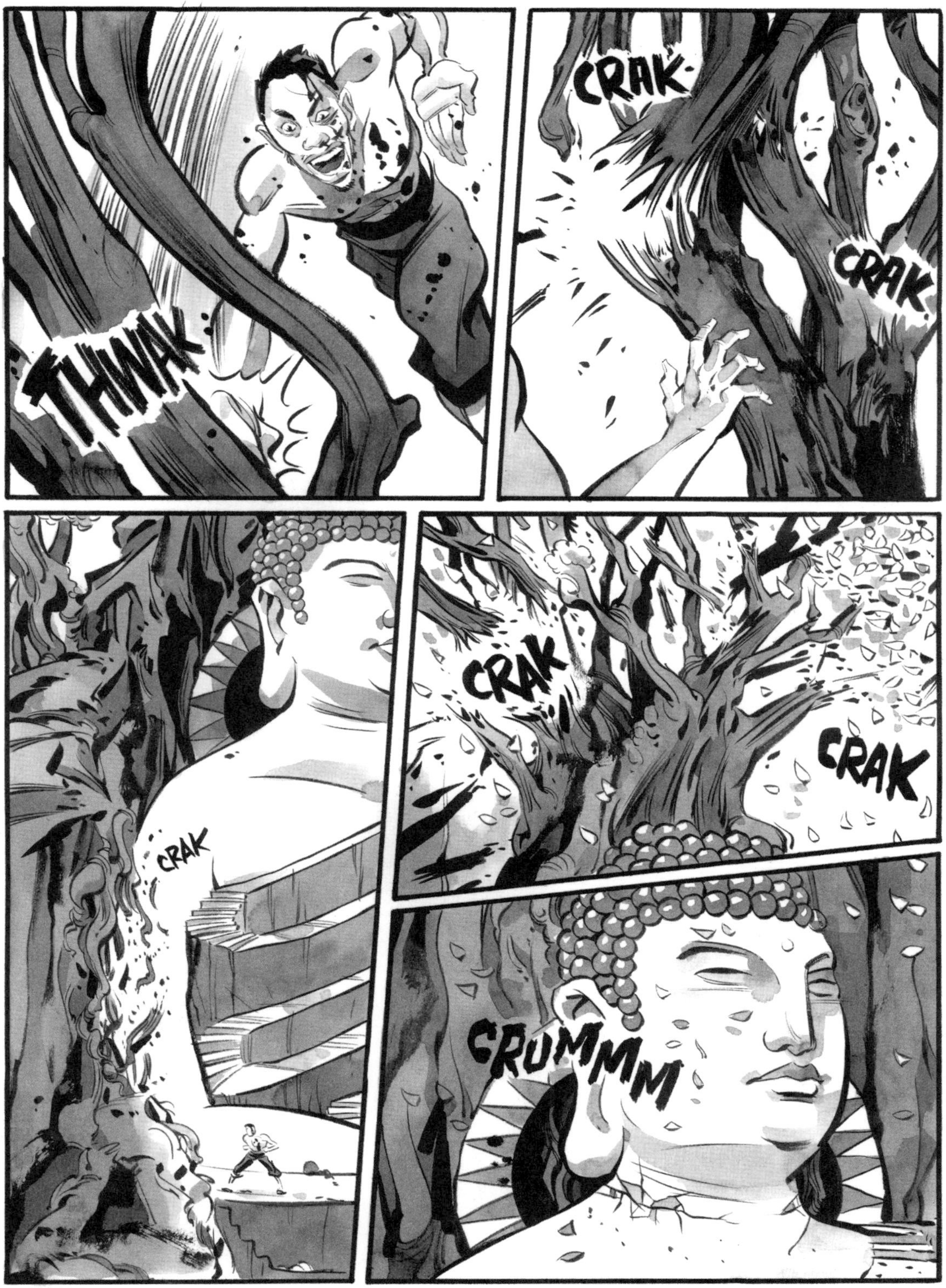
THWAK
CRAK
CRAK
CRAK
CRAK
CRAK
CRUMMM

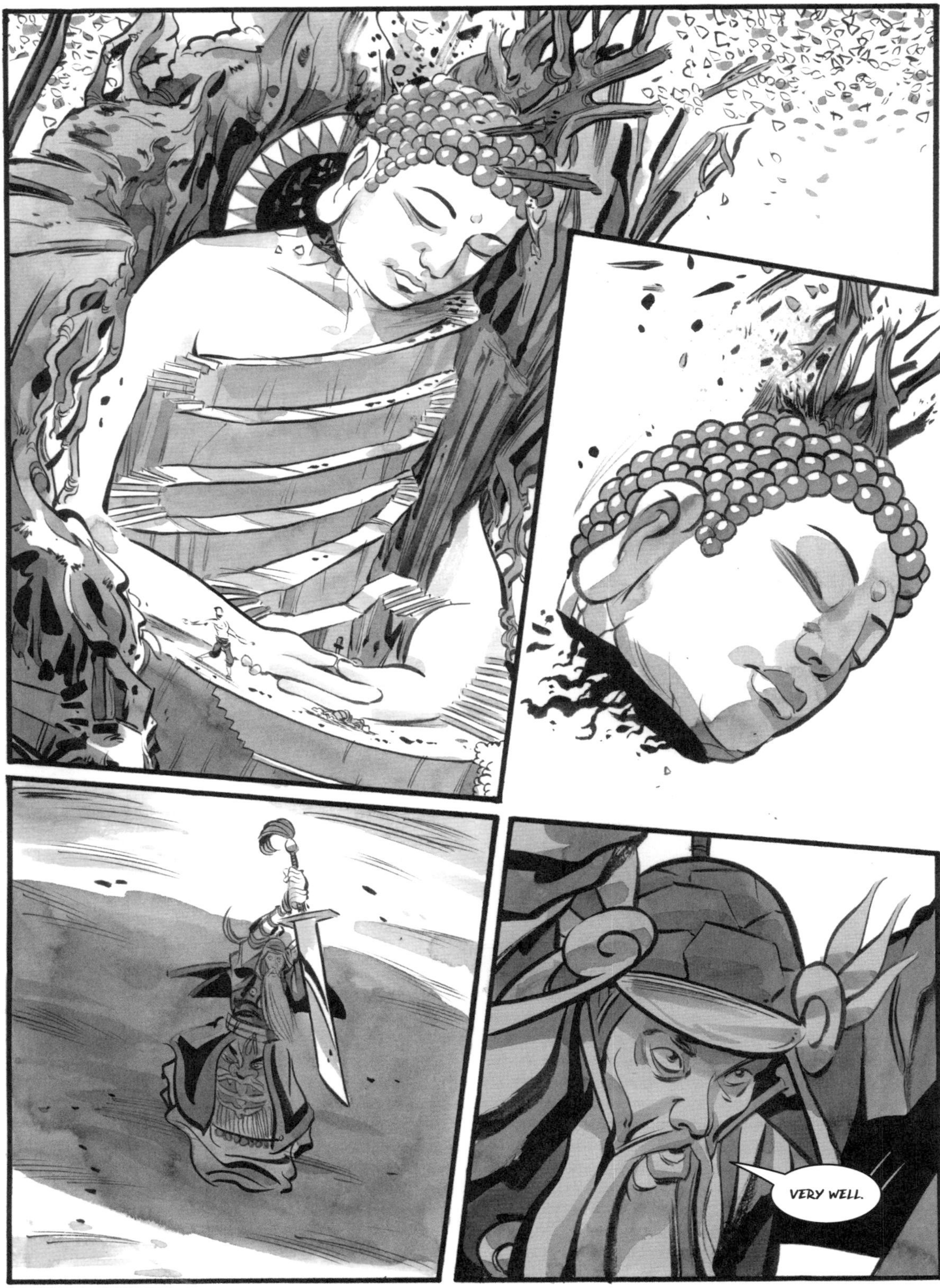
VERY WELL.

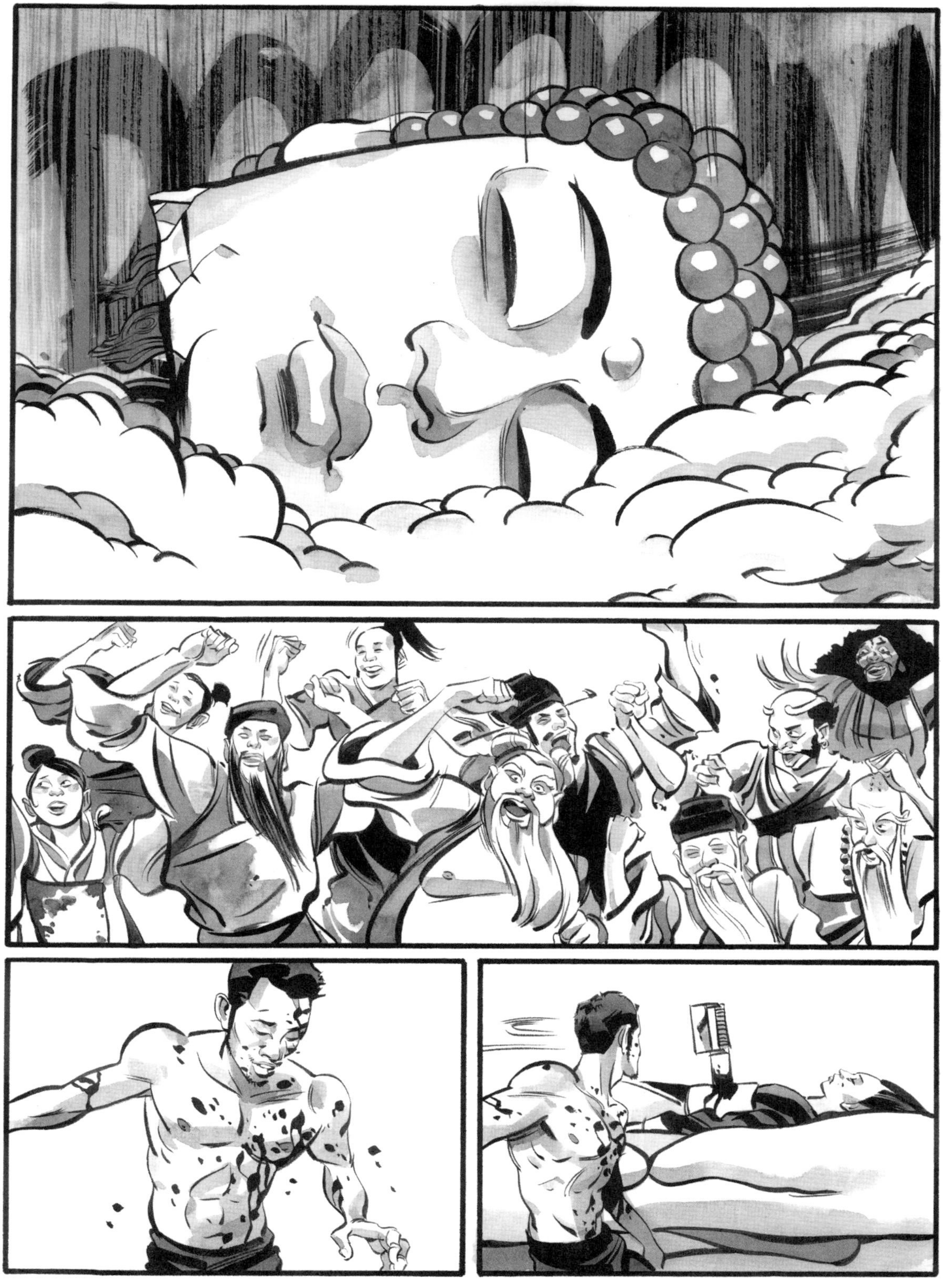

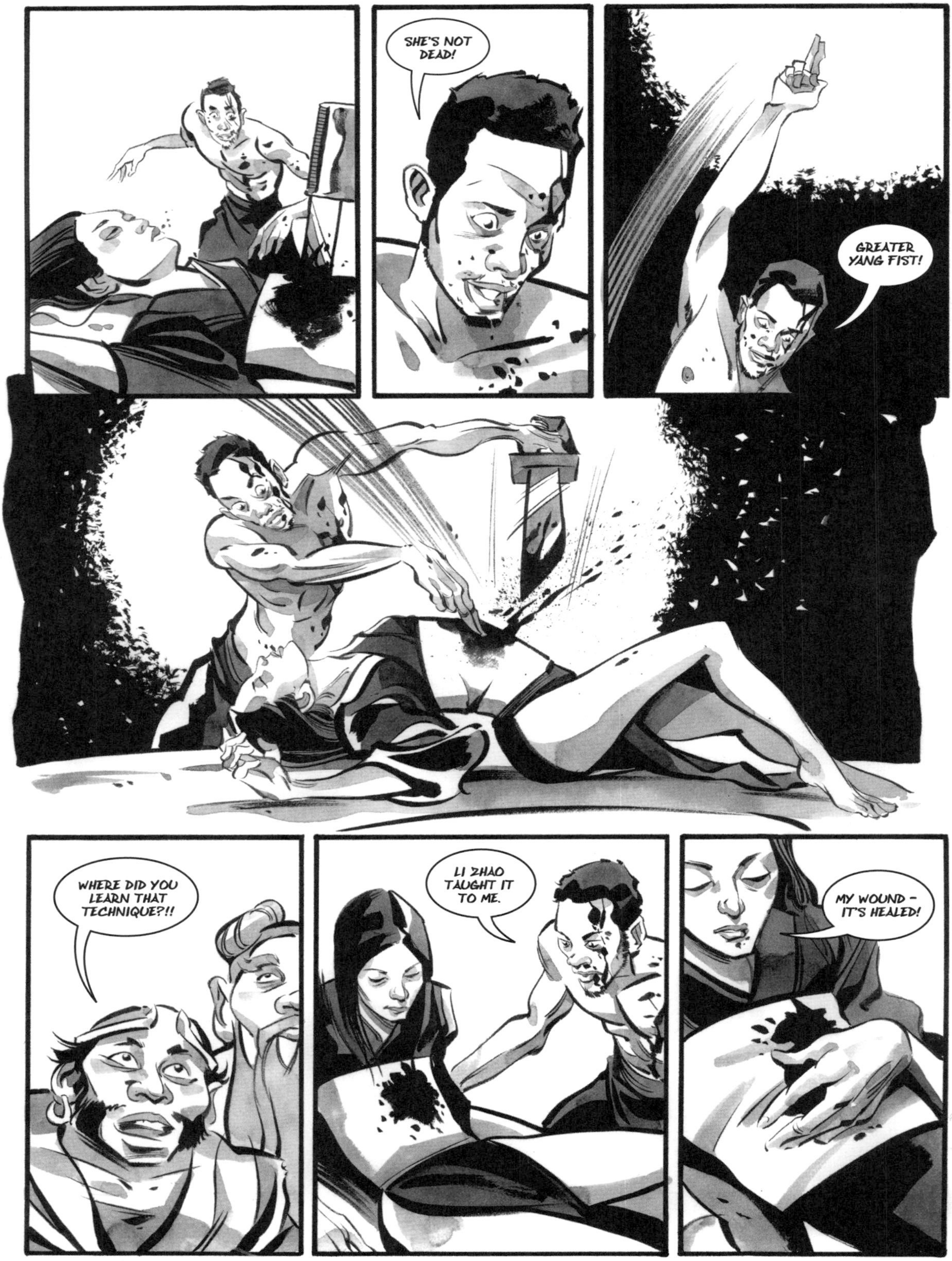
SHE'S NOT DEAD!
GREATER YANG FIST!
WHERE DID YOU LEARN THAT TECHNIQUE?!!
LI ZHAO TAUGHT IT TO ME.
MY WOUND - IT'S HEALED!

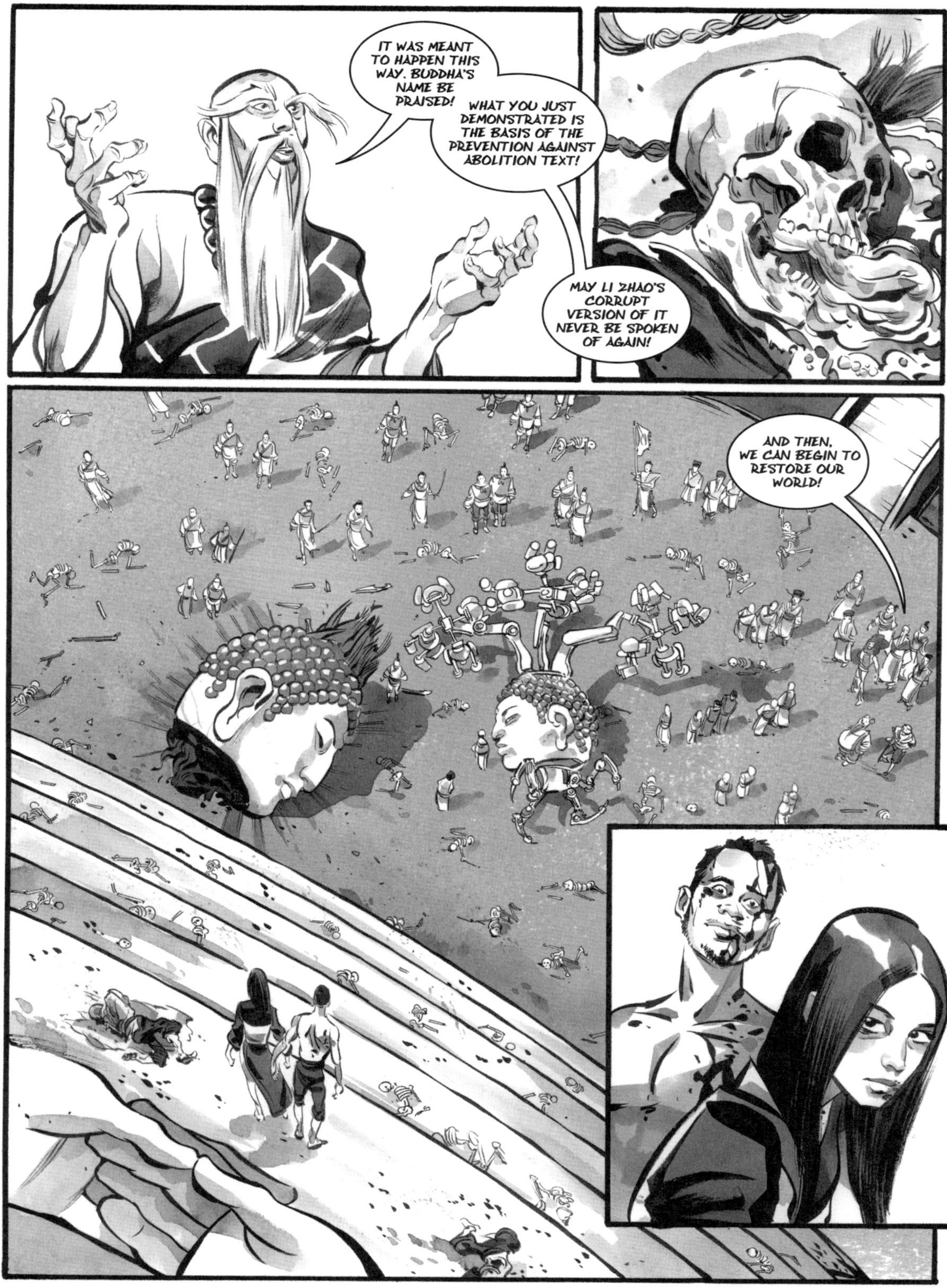
IT WAS MEANT TO HAPPEN THIS WAY. BUDDHA'S NAME BE PRAISED!
WHAT YOU JUST DEMONSTRATED IS THE BASIS OF THE PREVENTION AGAINST ABOLITION TEXT!
MAY LI ZHAO'S CORRUPT VERSION OF IT NEVER BE SPOKEN OF AGAIN!
AND THEN, WE CAN BEGIN TO RESTORE OUR WORLD!

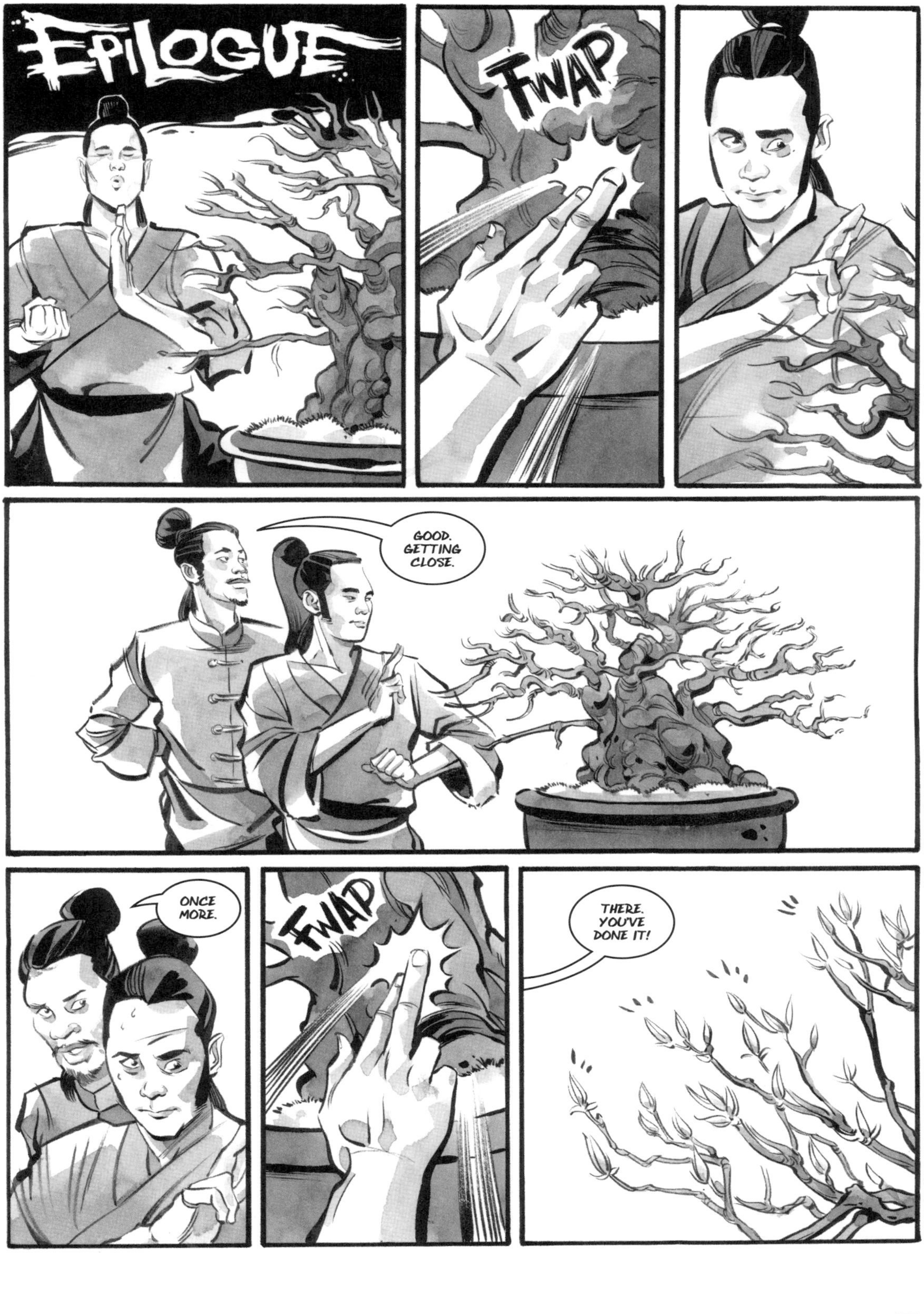
EPILOGUE
FWAP
GOOD. GETTING CLOSE.
ONCE MORE.
FWAP
THERE. YOU'VE DONE IT!

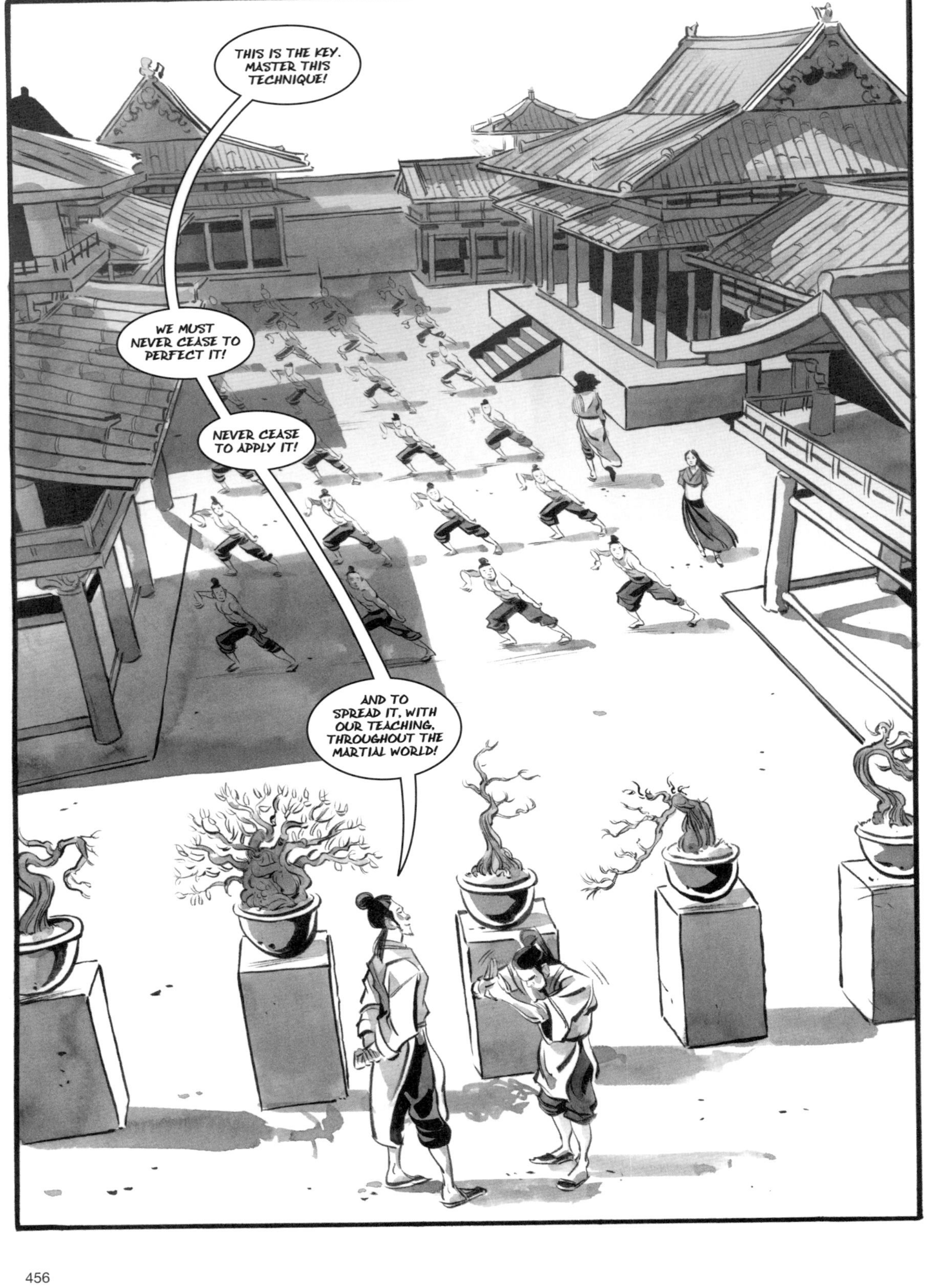
THIS IS THE KEY. MASTER THIS TECHNIQUE!
WE MUST NEVER CEASE TO PERFECT IT!
NEVER CEASE TO APPLY IT!
AND TO SPREAD IT, WITH OUR TEACHING, THROUGHOUT THE MARTIAL WORLD!

# INFINITE KUNG FU

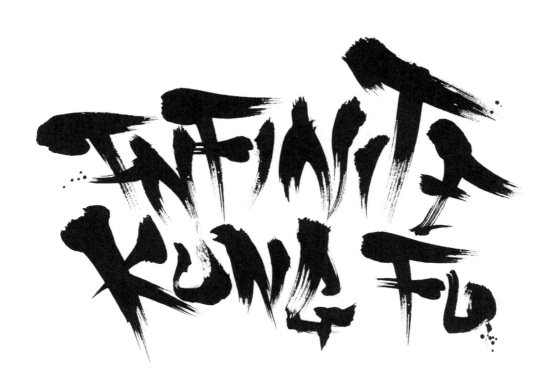

# KUNGFUSCHOOL

**T**wo unarmed men engaged in a rhythmic fight, advancing up the steps of a great temple. One combatant grabbed the other's wispy grey beard and, with a quick tug, shockingly ripped it out.

"What's that?" I asked my mom, eyes fixed to the TV set.

"That's kung fu!" her answer.

I was only 4 or 5 years old in the early 1980s, when I first learned the term. By then, the kung fu craze of the 1970s had waned, and it wouldn't be until my teenage years that I truly discovered the film genre for myself, and devoured it.

To a non-Chinese, comic book-loving nerd looking for his next hobby, it was like opening a portal to an alternate universe. One with fresh heroes and villains with new powers and schemes, and weird laws of ethics and physics to govern them both. As I dove deeper into the genre, I honed a greater understanding of its subtleties, though losing bits in translation was also part of the fun. Inspiration for the work you now hold in your hands had set in.

Martial arts films have had an undeniable influence on Western pop culture, though most Western audiences' experiences with the roots of the genre have been minimal. My first hope is that *Infinite Kung Fu* entertains, but second, that it provokes one to open (or reopen) that portal to the universe that inspired it — the martial world!

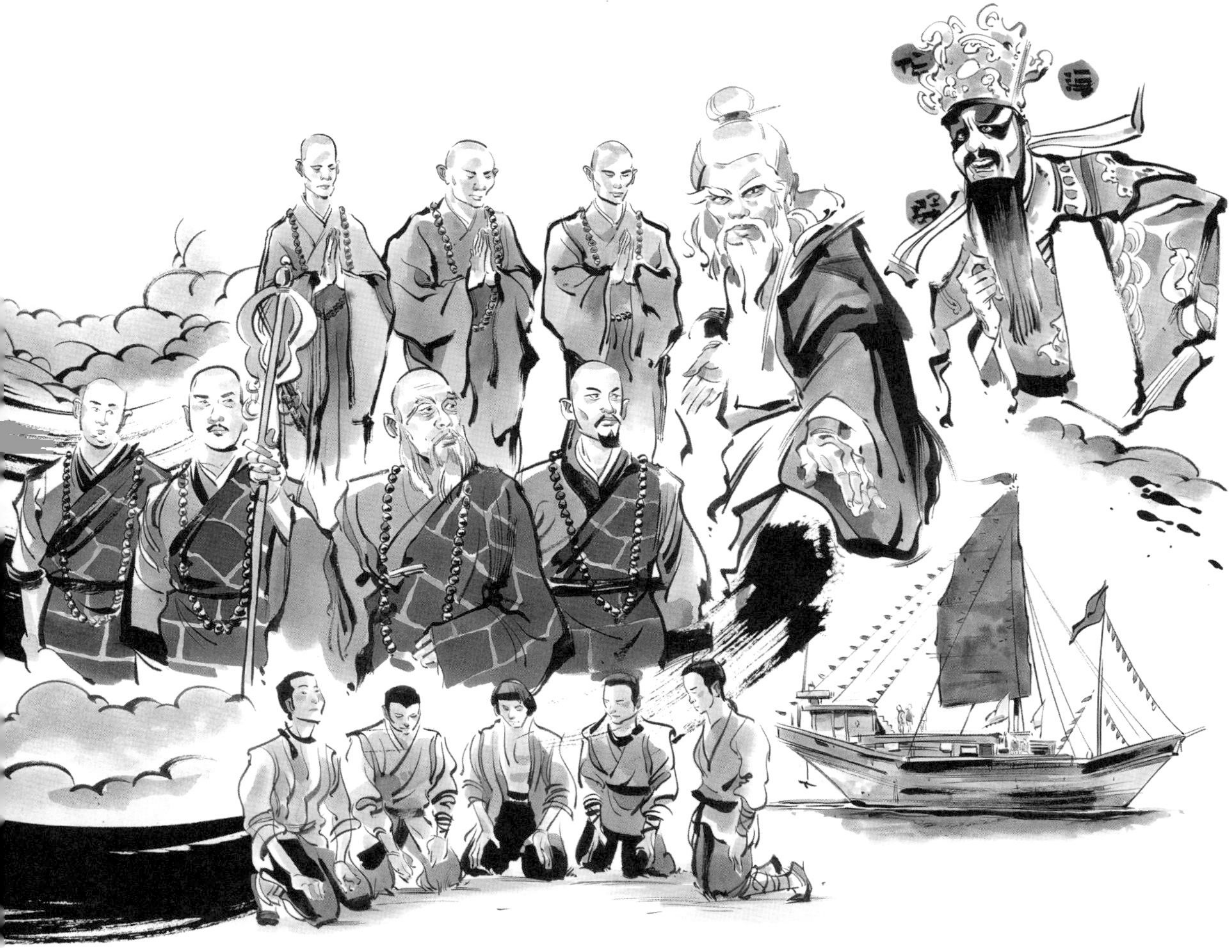

To help with that, I've attempted to present here a very brief, sweeping history of martial arts in film.

All Chinese martial arts ultimately derive from the Shaolin temple. It was founded by the Indian Buddhist Bodhidharma around A.D. 520, who quickly noticed that many monks didn't have the stamina to remain awake during the meditative practices he introduced. His solution was to instruct the monks in proper breathing techniques using postures based on yoga.

Years later, in response to the violence of bandits and passing gangs, the monks developed new fighting skills inspired by local wildlife. Sister temples popped up over the next few centuries, including the Wu Tang temple in A.D. 980, established jointly with Taoist sects.

Imperial leaders who feared the martial powers of the monks attacked repeatedly, sacking the temple and burning it on many occasions. Events from this period up until around 1900, along with the *wuxia* (martial chivalry) novels of the past, provide much of the fodder for storylines in martial arts films.

By 1700, individual animal styles became the norm, and the Shaolin order had split into Northern and Southern schools. Shaolin kung fu was outlawed by the ruling Manchus in 1727. With the help of a traitorous ex-Shaolin priest named Pai Mei, the Manchus attacked the temple once again. Only five monks are said to have survived. They practiced in secret and began teaching common people their kung fu. Tai Chi was created by slowing down the moves — to disguise the fact that they were part of a fighting art.

One of the five survivors, Jee Shin, joined the Peking Opera and began to teach martial arts to its actors. By the 1860s, the actors

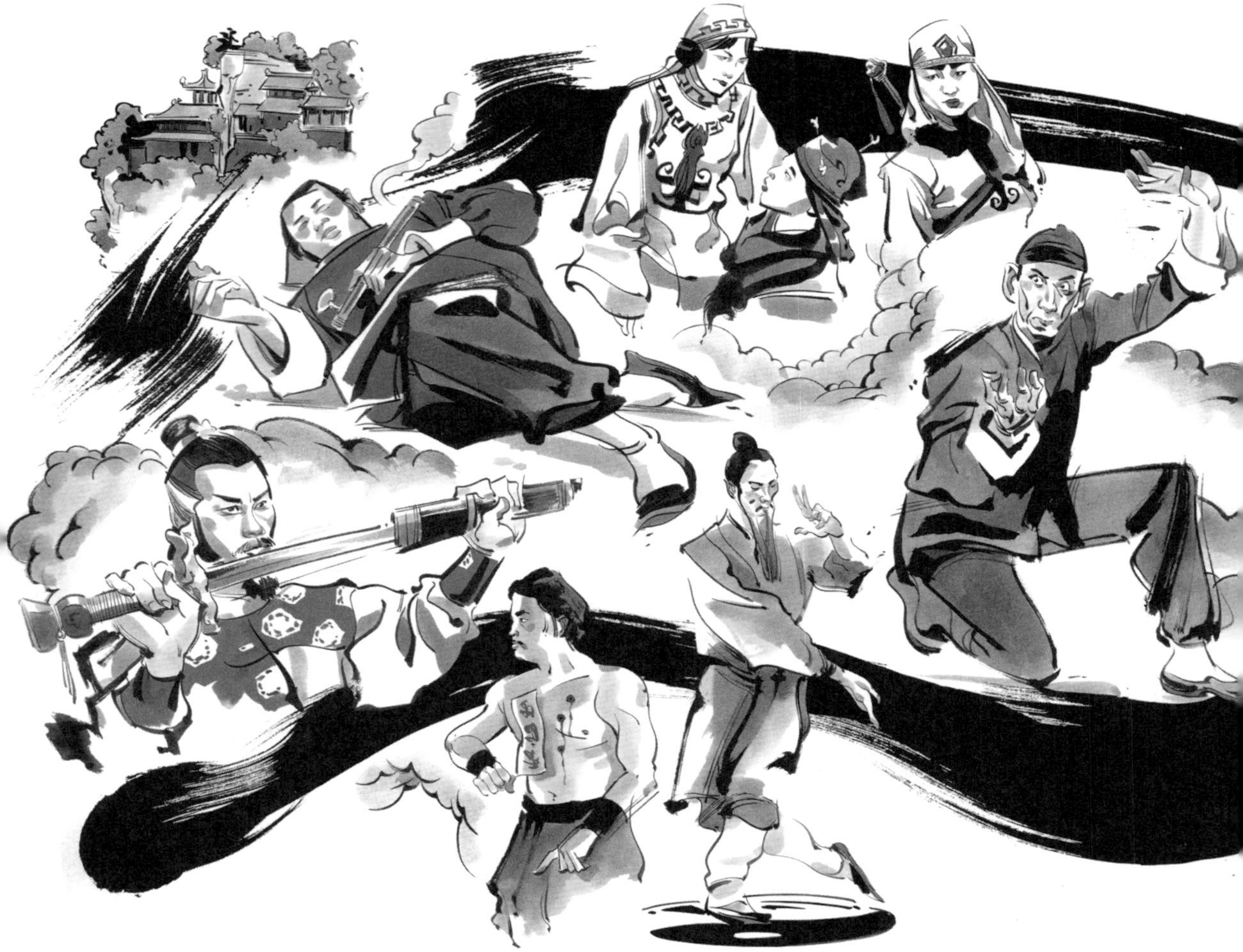

themselves attempted a rebellion and failed. Acting was banned and they began to train in secret.

Pai Mei, or in English, "White Eyebrow," was associated with the dark aspects of Taoism and the Wu Tang branch of Shaolin. This branch became increasingly active in attempts to overthrow the imperial government in the late 1800s. As political interference was taboo for the Shaolin order, Wu Tang lost its affiliation in 1878. Pai Mei's style became forbidden at Shaolin; no one could speak his name, nor his history.

By 1901, the British had turned the imperial family into a puppet regime through their import and sale of opium. Legendary martial artists lead the Boxer Rebellion, where war was declared on all foreigners. The Boxers believed in kung fu spells that could make them impervious to bullets, and were eventually overthrown.

Animosity between Shaolin and Wu Tang grew during these years. At Wu Tang temple, internal, soft and flowing martial methods with Taoist principles were largely promoted, whereas Shaolin was Buddhist, with hard, external techniques. Wu Tang saw no problem in staging a rebellion, and hated Shaolin for their lack of involvement.

Films arrived in the early 20th century. The Peking opera actors (all male, even for female roles) refused to lower themselves to be seen on film. Only women ended up acting in movies, playing the parts of men. *The Burning of Red Lotus Monastery* (1928) is considered by many the first martial arts film. In the 1930s, the film industry began booming in Hong Kong. The fantasy-based subgenre, *wuxia*, was dominant.

By the 1950s, male actors were accepted, although females continued to play male leads well into the

1960s. Actor Kwan Tak Hing portrayed Chinese folk hero Wong Fei Hung in a film using realistic martial arts and not fantasy-based kung fu. It was an instant hit, and dozens more in the series were produced.

Soon there were two major film companies, Cathay and the Shaw Brothers. The Shaw studios were a self-contained city where the cast and crew lived and worked.

Shaw director King Hu,

influenced by Japanese samurai films, made martial arts films with more realism and less fantasy. His 1966 film starring Chang Pei Pei, *Come Drink With Me*, showcased sophisticated choreography, changing the modern martial arts film. *Dragon Inn* (1966) and *A Touch of Zen* (1969) are also King Hu classics.

The prolific director Chang Cheh is known as the Godfather of Hong Kong cinema. His film *One-Armed*

*Swordsman* (1967) paved the way for new trends in the genre, featuring tortured anti-heroes and buckets of blood. Typical Chang Cheh films focused on male brotherhood and a thirst for revenge.

Cathay Film's *From the Highway* and Shaw Brothers' *The Chinese Boxer* (both 1970) focused on un-armed combat and spawned a wave of imitations. Kung fu replaced swordplay for the next decade.

Shaw Brothers production chief Raymond Chow left the company in 1970. He formed his own company, Golden Harvest, and discovered an actor named Bruce Lee. Lee had already played the role of Kato on the American show *The Green Hornet*, but was rejected for the role of Kane on the TV series *Kung Fu*. He moved back to Hong Kong and made *The Big Boss* in 1971 with Golden Harvest. He quickly became an

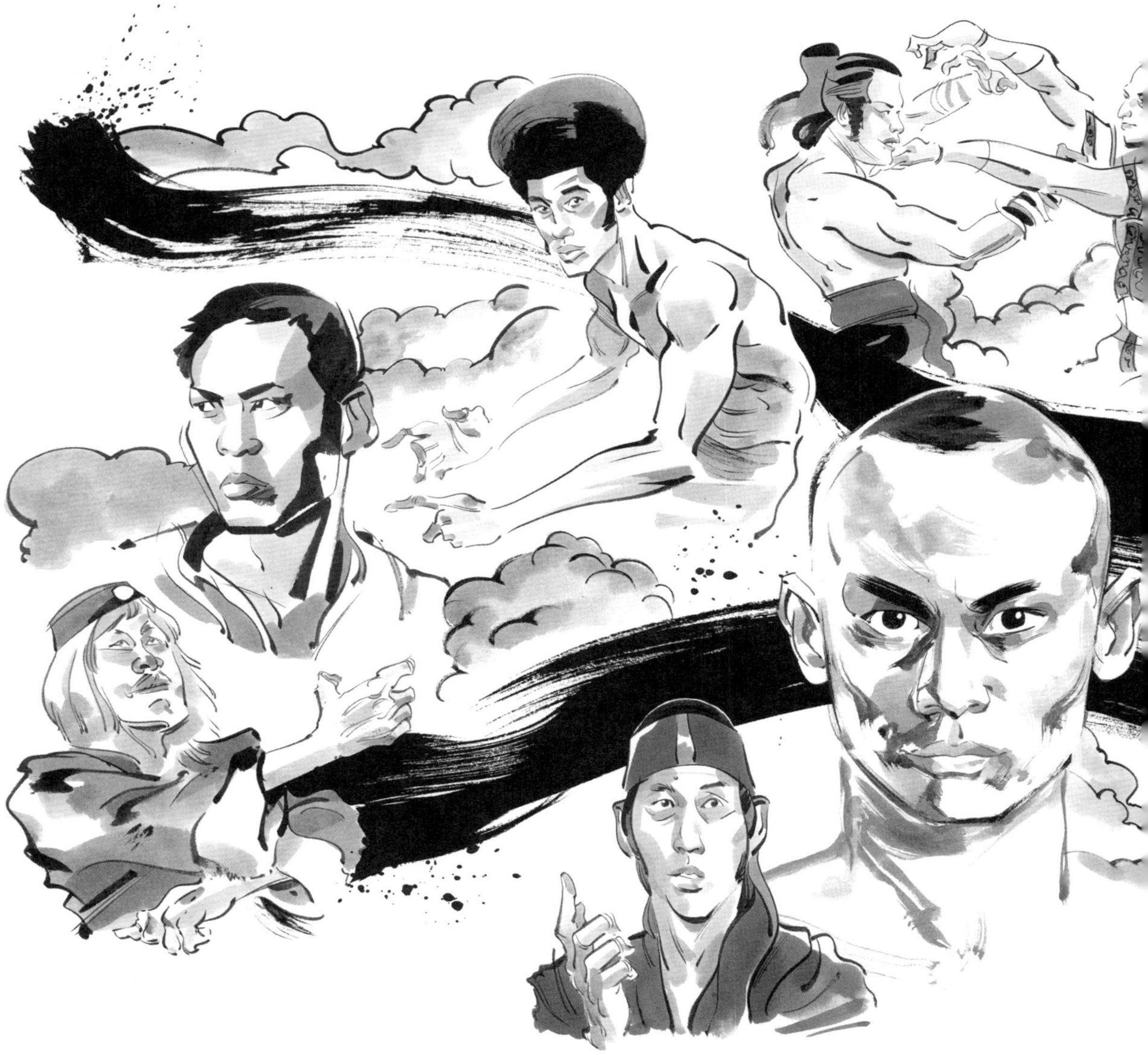

international hero, but died in 1972 after completing only four films.

Countless knockoffs and Bruce Lee clones filled the genre, accounting for much of its laughability. Kung fu movies dubbed in English were exported in droves to the West (*King Boxer*, retitled as *Five Fingers of Death,* was the first). African-American audiences were drawn to theatres in support of non-white, underdog heroes, and elements of kung fu bled into the blaxploitation genre.

Director and martial arts instructor Lau Kar Leung (a.k.a. Liu Chia Liang) is remembered largely for his films featuring monks, a difficult sell with the absence of love interests. His 1978 classic, *The 36th Chamber of Shaolin (Master Killer* in the U.S.) focused on the monk's rigorous training. It starred Leung's adopted brother (and writer of the intrduction to this book), Gordon Liu, who played the historic monk, San Te.

Leung, a kung fu master himself, has a martial lineage that traces back to the real life Wong Fei Hung, and back to Jee Shin, one of the five original Shaolin survivors.

The late 1970s were led by a new wave of action heroes — Sammo Hung, Yuen Biao and Jackie Chan — all brothers in the Peking Opera. Producers wanted Jackie to become the next Bruce Lee, but his unique brand of kung fu comedy made him famous. Things took off for Chan after the release of *Drunken Master* in 1978.

Teenage wushu champion Jet Li starred in his first film, *Shaolin Temple*, in 1983 and quickly became a martial arts star.

In the 1980s and '90s,

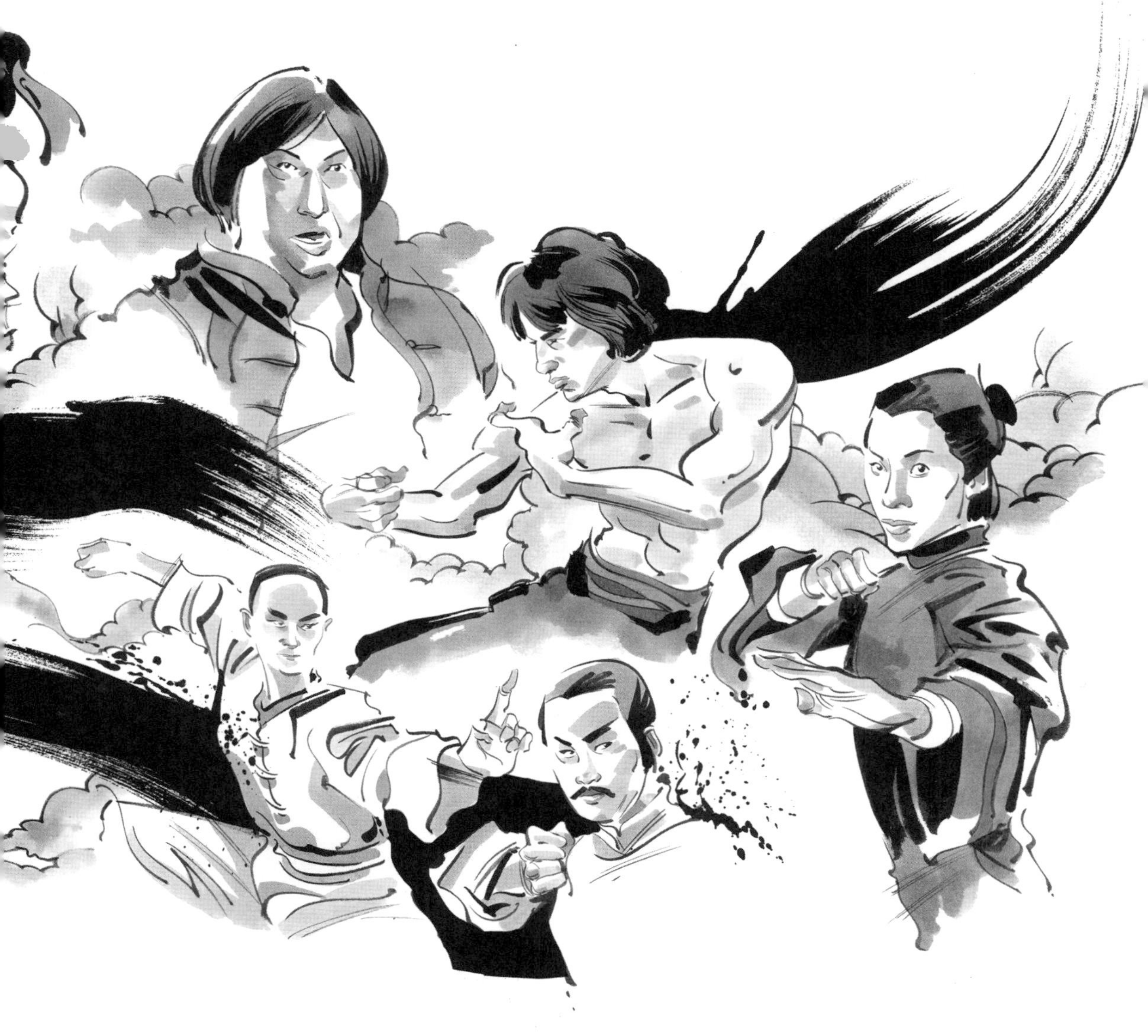

special effects ruled as a sword and sorcery revival replaced unarmed combat as the popular trend. Director's like Tsui Hark lead this new direction with films like *Zu Warriors of Magic Mountain* (1983) and *A Chinese Ghost Story* (1987).

John Woo gained international attention with *The Killer* (1989), a crime film with a contemporary setting. His unique brand of action was soon dubbed "gun fu."

Director and choreographer Yuen Woo Ping, son of veteran kung fu actor Simon Yuen (or Sam Seed), began working with Jackie Chan in 1978 and more recently on Hollywood blockbusters *The Matrix (*1999) *Crouching Tiger, Hidden Dragon (*2000) *Kill Bill (*2003) and *Kung Fu Hustle (*2004). His choreography continues to define the genre today.

— Kagan McLeod

*Toronto-based illustrator* **Kagan McLeod** *has had work published in a wide variety of magazines, including Entertainment Weekly, Glamour, GQ, Mad, Newsweek, The New York Times, People, Sports Illustrated and Time. He has been included in Lürzer Archive's 200 Best Illustrators Worldwide and recognized by the Society of News Design for his work in Canada's National Post. Infinite Kung Fu is his first major work in comics.*


**SOURCES:**

*A Study of the Hong Kong Martial Arts Film*, The Urban Council, 1980

*Martial Arts Movies* by Richard Meyers, Citadel Press, 1985

*Heroic Grace: The Chinese Martial Arts Film*, UCLA Television and Film Archive, 2003

*The Shaolin Grandmasters' Text*, Order of the Shaolin Ch'an, 2004